Instructor's Manual to Accompany

THE MANAGEM
AND CONTR
OF QUALITY

THIRD EDITION

JAMES R. EVANS
UNIVERSITY OF CINCINNATI
WILLIAM M. LINDSAY
NORTHERN KENTUCKY UNIVERSITY

WEST PUBLISHING COMPANY
MINNEAPOLIS/ST. PAUL   NEW YORK   LOS ANGELES   SAN FRANCISCO

WEST'S COMMITMENT TO THE ENVIRONMENT

In 1906, West Publishing Company began recycling materials left over from the production of books. This began a tradition of efficient and responsible use of resources. Today, up to 95% of our legal books and 70% of our college texts and school texts are printed on recycled, acid-free stock. West also recycles nearly 22 million pounds of scrap paper annually—the equivalent of 181,717 trees. Since the 1960s, West has devised ways to capture and recycle waste inks, solvents, oils, and vapors created in the printing process. We also recycle plastics of all kinds, wood, glass, corrugated cardboard, and batteries, and have eliminated the use of Styrofoam book packaging. We at West are proud of the longevity and the scope of our commitment to the environment.

Production, Prepress, Printing and Binding by West Publishing Company.

 TEXT IS PRINTED ON 10% POST CONSUMER RECYCLED PAPER    PRINTED WITH SOY INK

Contents

PART 3 - TECHNICAL ISSUES IN QUALITY MANAGEMENT AND CONTROL

Preface

In this instructors' manual, we have once again made a conscious effort to "continuously improve" and "build quality" into our supporting materials. This manual provides updated and new chapter teaching notes for instructors that highlight the important topics and objectives, detailed answers to all Quality in Practice questions, answers to end-of-chapter Questions for Review and selected Questions for Discussion, solutions to end of chapter problems, and notes and/or answers to questions for the many new and updated end-of-chapter cases.

Additional features in the manual are the 1995 Malcolm Baldrige National Quality Award Training Case and Evaluation Report and the 1995 Malcolm Baldrige National Quality Award Criteria. They are an excellent resource for use in MBA classes. Upon request to a West Publishing representative, instructors who adopt the textbook may obtain in a separate package the microcomputer software and user's manual for The Quality Management Analyst and the SPC Simulation designed to accompany the text, as well as notes for use with the *Quality Gamebox*™ referenced in the text, which is also on the computer disk.

We are especially grateful for the work of Robert Lindsay, son of one of the authors, who assisted in preparing answers to many of the Review Questions and the Discussion Questions. You will occasionally notice his flashes of off-beat humor in some of the answers. Thanks go to our students who contributed to the cases, answered questions, and solved problems from several chapters. Even though we have made every effort to ensure error-free work, even multiple inspections are no guarantee of perfection. Any unidentified errors remain our responsibility. We plan to continuously improve our text in anticipation of a fourth edition.

If you have any suggestions for improvement, or run across case materials that may be used for this course, let us know. To report any errors or omissions, please contact either of us at:

Northern Kentucky University   OR   University of Cincinnati
College of Business   P.O. Box 210130
Department of Mgt./Mkt.   Department of QAOM
Highland Heights, KY 41099-0506   Cincinnati, OH 45221
(606) 572-5157   (513) 556-7152
e-mail: LINDSAY @ NKU.EDU   e-mail: EVANS @ UC.EDU

William M. Lindsay
James R. Evans

Cincinnati, Ohio
June, 1995

The Management and Control of Quality, 3rd Edition
USER SURVEY

We would appreciate knowing how you use this book. Please copy this page and mail or fax to the address below. Thank you!

Name_____

School_____

Address_____

_____

_____

Phone/fax/e-mail_____

Course Title and Level_____

Semester or Quarter_____

CHAPTER	Full	Partial	None
1. Introduction to Quality	____	____	____
2. Quality in Production and Service Systems	____	____	____
3. Quality Management Philosophies	____	____	____
4. Principles of Total Quality Management	____	____	____
5. Focusing on Customers	____	____	____
6. Leadership and Strategic Planning	____	____	____
7. Quality in Product and Process Design	____	____	____
8. Measurement and Strategic Information Management	____	____	____
9. Process Management and Continuous Improvement	____	____	____
10. Human Resource Management for Quality	____	____	____
11. Employee Involvement and Participative Management	____	____	____
12. Quality Management Evaluation and Assessment	____	____	____
13. Organizing and Implementing TQM	____	____	____
14. Quality Assurance and Control	____	____	____
15. Fundamentals of Statistical Process Control	____	____	____
16. Additional Topics in Statistical Process Control	____	____	____
17. Reliability	____	____	____

Extent of coverage: Full / Partial / None

Suggestions for Improvement:

Professor James R. Evans   (FAX: 513 556-5499)
University of Cincinnati
P.O. Box 210130
Department of QAOM   (E-MAIL: evans@uc.edu)
Cincinnati, OH 45221

CHAPTER 1

Introduction to Quality

Teaching Notes

The first chapter provides an overview of the importance of quality in a rapidly changing business environment. Students at both the undergraduate and graduate level are likely to be taking this course as an elective, so you may have a tendency to assume that they are "self-motivated" by simply being there. This is not necessarily the case. You should try to "hook" them on the excitement of quality by using a variety of teaching methods and media. Key objectives should include:

• To provide a variety of definitions, including those for: relative quality, product-based quality, fitness for use, and conformance to specifications. The official definition of quality is "the totality of features and characteristics of a product or service that bears on its ability to satisfy given needs." Most businesses today define quality as "meeting or exceeding customer expectations."

• To introduce the key dimensions of quality as: performance, features, reliability, conformance, durability, serviceability, and aesthetics. All these play an important role in how customers perceive quality.

• To point out that Total Quality is vital to <u>every</u> organization at every level, not just to manufacturing firms in their production areas.

• To instill in every student the idea that quality is a <u>managerial</u> concept first, and a technical concept, second.

• To introduce the concept of competitive advantage that denotes a firm's ability to achieve market superiority over its competitors. Quality is a key source of national and international competitive advantage, and studies have shown that quality is positively related to increased market share and profitability.

• To provide examples that show how successful companies are developing and using total quality in their day-to-day operations.

In the first class session we provide a few introductory remarks about the importance of quality (see overhead transparency masters for use in your lectures) and then often show a videotape. A three-part video series entitled "Quality -- or Else," by Lloyd Dobyns, producer of "If Japan Can, Why Can't We?," is the available from CC-M Productions, 7755 16th St. N.W., Washington, DC, 20012, (301) 588-4095. This series of tapes provides a number of good case studies of manufacturing and service companies that are competing internationally, such as Motorola, Nucor, Saachi & Saachi, etc., as well as the struggles of U.S. automotive manufacturers to recapture market share and international quality reputations that they have lost. Another favorite tape is Peters and Waterman's first video, "In Search of Excellence," especially the first two segments on Disneyworld and Stew Leonard's Dairy. (Contact Films Incorporated, 5547 N. Ravenswood Ave., Chicago, IL 60640-1199 for purchase information). These segments are especially good, because they tend to dispel the notion that quality management "only applies to manufacturing." Also, associations such as the Association for Quality and Participation, the American Society for Quality Control, Society for Manufacturing Engineers, and the Institute of Industrial Engineers are excellent sources for quality films and materials.

Another video is the NBC White Paper, "If Japan Can, Why Can't We?" Part I explains how and why the quality revolution got started and was a "call to arms" for American managers in the early 1980's. It is more manufacturing oriented and may be considered to be "dated," by some students. Never-the-less, it provides valuable insights into the importance of quality and of knowing something about Japanese management practices and their quality focus.

Note on QIP's and Cases

Quality in Practice (QIP) case situations in every chapter are brief quality incidents designed to give students the opportunity to see how quality theories and concepts are being applied in real organizations. The questions at the end of the QIP's are meant to focus attention on the critical concepts of quality and serve as a springboard for discussion. Students should be encouraged to "go beyond" merely answering the questions to take a broader perspective on the QIP's.

In addition, in the 3rd Edition, we have included a number of **new**, more comprehensive cases at the end of all chapters to give students additional opportunities to analyze quality practices and deal with substantive quality issues of real or fictional organizations.

The cases may be used in a number of different ways for a variety of purposes, such as:

- As a basis for class discussion. Students can be asked to answer the QIP questions as preparation for case discussion.

- As a vehicle for team presentations. Students may be divided into teams and asked to present the case situation to the class, with accompanying theory and analysis of quality practices. To enrich their perspective, the teams may be asked to "update" the case from outside sources, such as corporate annual reports, interviews with corporate managers (locally or at the company's headquarters), and recent articles from business periodicals.

- As a model for developing their own cases. Students could be asked to prepare their own cases, similar to QIP's and cases, within their own, or an assigned manufacturing, service, or non-profit organization.

A Note on Answers to End-of-Chapter Questions

Most chapters in the text have both Questions for Review and Questions for Discussion at the end. In this manual, all the Questions for Review have definitive answers that have been drawn directly from the body of the chapter. Since the Questions for Discussion are designed to give the students practice in dealing with process issues (as opposed to just recalling or locating factual "content"), all of these questions are not answered in this manual. At times, where a "mini-case" is the subject of the question that is posed, or some data can be analyzed, an answer is provided in this manual. It should be recognized that alternative solutions may be equally correct, so the answers here should be considered to be "suggestive" of the solution, rather than a definitive solution to the question or case situation.

ANSWERS TO QUALITY IN PRACTICE KEY ISSUES

The Xerox Transformation

1. After stumbling badly, Xerox made a remarkable turn-around in quality by developing principles that were very similar to the core principles in this chapter. They incorporated the core principles of: 1) a focus on customer satisfaction; 2) striving for continuous improvement; and 3) encouraging the full involvement of the workforce by their three objectives of *Leadership Through Quality* These could be summarized as:

    · Quality improvement is everyone's job.
    · Meeting the needs of internal and external customers is essential.
    · Management and work processes that focus on continuous improvement and customer requirements become a way of life.

2. In saying that *Quality is a race without a finish line* Xerox management has focused on two things: a) quality is not just a "program" that will fade out in a year or two; and b) to embrace the idea of continuous improvement, people must assume that there will always be better ways found to do things. Procter and Gamble developed a continuous methods change approach many years earlier in which it was pointed out that: "Perfection [in a process] should be no barrier to improvement." In other words, employees should be encouraged to "tinker" with a process that is running well in order to make it work

even better! The significance to Xerox or any organization is that if you continue to do things the same way, you will soon be behind the competition, if they are making continuous improvements.

The Cadillac Quality Story

1.   The Cadillac quality story is a familiar one -- a company that has a reputation for quality becomes complacent and only realizes that quality has "slipped" when a minor, or major competitive crisis arises. Quality was defined when Cadillac chose the slogan "the standard of the world." When Cadillac could not simultaneously meet customer requirements for emissions, fuel economy, and product design features in the mid 1980's, they became aware of the quality "gap". Instead of being an afterthought, Cadillac set about making "focus on the customer" the center of their quality strategy. This entailed some major changes in planning and in the culture of their organization.

2.   The three strategies that Cadillac used to bring about the quality transformation included:

- a cultural change
- a constant focus on customers
- a disciplined approach to planning

These were all of equal importance. If there had not been a cultural change, employees would have seen productivity and "business as usual" in the way that things were done. Customers had not been the focus in the old culture. Planning had apparently been haphazard and objectives had not been clearly defined in the past. Previously, customer satisfaction, based on limited feedback from internal customers (the "voice of the assembler") and external customers (dealers), as well as final consumers, had been ignored in the planning process. It is apparent that if all three strategies had not been implemented in an integrated fashion, then teamwork, employee involvement, customer focus, and continuous improvement would not have occurred. It is also **extremely** unlikely that Cadillac would have won the Baldrige Award in 1990.

ANSWERS TO REVIEW QUESTIONS

1.   Evidence of the search for quality dates back to ancient Egypt, as indicated in the precision and uniformity of methods used in the construction of the pyramids. The craftsperson of the Middle Ages took special care to ensure quality in his/her product, a necessary step since he/she dealt directly with the customer. In the late 18th Century, Eli Whitney helped trigger the Industrial Revolution with his development of interchangeable machine parts. The Industrial Revolution itself was a key turning point, since it made quality assurance a critical component of the production process. However, quality was determined only <u>after</u> the products were finished, rather than during the manufacturing process, so as volume increased and costs decreased, craftsmanship decreased.

Quality control techniques were further developed in the early 20th Century, when methods of inspection to improve and maintain quality were gradually separated from production techniques.

2.   The factors contributing to increased awareness of quality include the realization of the superior quality of Japanese products, extensive product recalls by the Consumer Product Safety Commission in the early 1980's, and the Challenger disaster in 1986. Improvements in technology, inadequate managerial philosophies, and the economic impact of international competitiveness have also been important factors.

3.   Quality has been a topic of national interest since the discovery that many foreign goods and services have higher quality standards in production and better track records with consumers. In the past, American negligence of quality resulted in a preference for foreign-made products. This preference has increased business for foreign competitors, allowing them to buy into American business, and decreasing sales of American-made products, domestically, as well as internationally. Thus, the economic health of the nation suffers. However, more and more U.S. businesses have recognized that they are vulnerable to both foreign and domestic competition if they don't have competitive quality, so they are taking steps to counter the competitive threat.

4.   Webster's definition of quality is vague and simplistic. "(Quality is) that which makes something what it is; characteristic element." The ANSI/ASQC definition states quality is "the totality of features and characteristics of a product or service that bears on its ability to satisfy given needs."

Garvin, however, identifies eight separate definitions of quality. Five of his list cover most of the scope of the broad field of quality. Garvin's transcendent definition is the layperson's definition, defining quality in terms of a study of the comparative of strengths and weaknesses of a product. The product-based definition says quality is based on quantity--the more or less a product has of a certain attribute, the better. The user-based definition is based on consumer reports of how well the product performs its intended function. The value-based definition states that quality in a single operation can, and needs to, be viewed from several different perspectives. Finally, the manufacturing-based definition recognizes quality as an outcome of engineering and manufacturing practice, or *conformance to specifications*.

One definition does not fit all situations. Perspectives change at different points in an organization. Reliance on a single definition of quality is a frequent source of problems.

5.   Consumers are the final purchasers of a product or service. In the case of fast-food restaurants, they are the everyday people who buy and literally consume the restaurant's ready-made burgers, pizzas, tacos, etc. External customers are companies within a "chain of customers," a chain of many firms who work together to produce the final consumer product. A firm which relies on the product or service of another company to produce

its own product or service is an external customer. For example, most hamburger-based fast food restaurants use a special device, known among employees as "The-Little-Metal-Canister-Thing-That-Shoots-Shredded-Onions-Down-On-Top-Of-The-Hamburger-Patty." The fast food restaurant is therefore an external customer of the separate manufacturing company that makes this device. Internal customers are people or divisions within the company who receive products or services from suppliers within the company. In the fast food restaurant, the employee who operates The-Little-Metal-Canister-Thing-That-Shoots-Shredded-Onions-Down-On-Top-Of-The-Hamburger-Patty is an internal customer to the employee who slices onions.

6. Total quality refers to the involvement of all employees in achievement of customer satisfaction through continuous improvement activities, while at the same time continually decreasing real cost. Total quality is a total system approach involving all employees and departments of a corporation, and extending to include supply and customer chains.

7. The core principles of TQM include: **a.** focusing on achieving customer satisfaction; **b.** striving for continuous improvement, and **c.** encouraging the involvement of the entire work force. These principles are departures from traditional management practices in that they seek to identify the needs of both external and internal customers, they attempt to build quality into the work process (as opposed to attempting to control it through post-production inspections), and they seek to continuously evaluate and improve all work functions, rather than solving problems as they occur.

8. In his classic book, *In Search of Excellence*, Peters said that the new quality dynamic requires excellent companies to "provide unparalleled quality, service, and reliability -- things that work and last." He expanded on that idea by describe how business functions, processes, and concepts must continually change to meet the needs of a dynamic environment.

In the <u>manufacturing</u> area, Peters identified the old focus on volume, low cost, and efficiency to the detriment of quality, responsiveness, and people. The new mindset shifts to flexibility in "focussed factories." Quality, responsiveness, and people have become more important than capital, per se.

In the <u>people</u> area, the old approach focusses on capital rather than people, tight control, close supervision, adversarial union relations, money as the sole motivator, and minimum training. The new focus on quality emphasizes the importance of people to an organization's success.

The old approach to <u>leadership</u> used the detached, analytic "manager as leader," with centralized strategic planning, and decision-making dominated by central corporate and group staffs. The new approach is decentralized, with top managers and lean staff in touch with customers and field operations.

9.   A firm's competitive advantage is its ability to achieve market superiority. The incorporation of quality enhances a firm's competitive advantage by producing a more efficient use of resources and production methods within the company, thus producing products or services superior to those of competitors.

10.   A product's value in the marketplace is influenced by the quality of its design. Improvements in performance, features, and reliability within the product will differentiate it from its competitors, improving the firm's quality reputation and the perceived value of the product, and allowing the company to command higher prices and achieve a greater market share. This in turn leads to increased revenues, which offset the costs of improving the design. Improved conformance to quality standards in production also saves rework, scrap, and warranty expenses, thus decreasing manufacturing and service costs.

11.   Both Xerox and Cadillac have developed specific quality objectives and management practices to suit their respective companies. Both companies have taken steps to see that all company employees understand and adopt these objectives and practices, and both have collaborated closely with workers' unions to achieve mutual problem-solving approaches. Also, both companies have used surveys of their customers to determine consumer needs, complaints, and satisfaction with the product sold. While Xerox has taken to reducing the number of suppliers it deals with, and introducing TQM to the remaining suppliers, Cadillac has gone one step further and asked suppliers to take on additional product-development responsibilities, leading to reductions in the supplier base, and a closer, more-focused relationship.

There appear to be some significant differences between Cadillac's and Xerox's approach, however. Cadillac appears to be taking a structured "strategic planning" approach and relying on their own resources and internal capabilities to "flesh out" their quality "journey." Xerox seems to have heeded the warning that the "not invented here" attitude can be dangerous in the long run. Therefore, Xerox is trying to decentralize strategic quality planning and relies heavily on benchmarking to determine their best practices. Xerox does not appear afraid to say that they don't know everything about quality and excellence, so they try to learn from other divisions of Xerox (such as Fuji Xerox) and from companies outside the industry (such as L.L. Bean).

ANSWERS TO DISCUSSION QUESTIONS

1.   Students will have varied opinions on the "Japanese revolution." Some may see the realization of Japan's superior quality in production as a turning point, since the consumer's recognition of this factor led to increased sales of Japanese products. This increase in sales has made the Japanese rich enough to infiltrate America's business community. Also, the impact of the realization may have prompted American companies to act in order to bring their quality standards up to par with their Japanese competitors.

Other students may see it differently. They may consider the differences between U.S. and Japanese quality as being insignificant. Also, depending on future developments in the Japanese labor community (a workers' rebellion, on the part of the younger workers, has been predicted), the relative economic strength of the country, and the presence or absence of U.S. and other nations trade sanctions against Japan, the emphasis on the superior Japanese quality may be seen as a passing trend.

2. Using Garvin's transcendent definition, one could compare a product to others versions of itself, produced by other manufacturers, rating according to an overall scale of superiority. At the same time, a comparison of products by different manufacturers may show this particular product having more or less quantity of some product attribute; in this we use the product-based definition. In applying the user-based definition, one would use consumer feedback to find out how well the product performs its intended function. The manufacturing-based definition measures quality by the product's "conformance to specifications;" in other words, how much does the product resemble the perfected prototype when it rolls off the assembly line. The final definition is value-based, defining a quality product as one that provides performance at an acceptable price or conformance at an acceptable cost.

3. Student answers will vary here, according to their own experience.

4. In answering this question, students should pick a specific product (e.g., The Impact Home Tooth-Extraction Kit), and apply Garvin's definitions to it. Students should answer questions such as: Does the product conform to the perfected prototype? Is the product user-friendly, and affordable for both consumers AND the manufacturer? How does the product stack up against other home tooth-extraction kits, which may use lasers or a drill and tongs? Does it matter if another kit provides 200 C.C.s of novocaine, as opposed to Impact's 125 C.C.s?

    In applying these definitions to a service (i.e. Bob's Anti-Roach Heat-Seeking-Missile Extermination Service), students should ask questions such as: Is the service affordable? Cost-efficient? Are employees sensitive to customer needs? Does the way it's run resemble the working model of an efficient organization? How does this service compare with, say, government air strikes against cockroaches? How often do the exterminators hit the intended targets with their missiles? Are the missile launchers leftovers from the contractors' scrap heaps, or are they the modern XL-236A "Fire-And-Forget" model? Are the launchers equipped with laser-guided target sites? Are quality assurances offered, say, guarantees that the exterminator won't aim for a roach and accidentally disintegrate the family dog?
    (Answer by Rob Lindsay, irrepressible son of one of the authors and substantial contributor to other answers throughout this manual).

5. For this question, students will need to determine the targets and tolerances for their individual service activities that permit "conformance-to-specifications" to be measured.

Targets will be the specific services that employees should provide, and the specific values that employees will demonstrate. Tolerances will be the standards set up to determine what is necessary when employees miss the mark; in other words, what is acceptable (i.e. an employee being five minutes late 5 times) and what is unforgivable (an employee being two hours late three times)?

6. Customers of a college or university might include students, the board of regents, employers, and families of students. Questions which might be asked concerning quality in an institution might include: Does the college provide and/or require a variety of core and specific courses for each student? Are the courses of study offered in each major sufficient to train the student to work well in his or her field after college? Are the courses sufficiently thorough to "add value" to students knowledge and skills, well-planned, and well-taught so that the student and/or the student's parents would come away with not only a degree, but also a feeling that he/she is properly prepared to work in that field? To what extent are TQM approaches used by faculty, administration, and support functions to "build in" quality into educational processes?

7. In applying Garvin's quality dimensions to manufactured goods, students should demonstrate what the product does (performance), what sets this product apart from others, and what makes it so special? They should examine reliability: how much use can you get out of it before it breaks down? Durability: will it last for many years, or self-destruct three days after the warranty expires? And serviceability: When it breaks, who will fix it? Who CAN fix it? The product's conformance to requirements should be determined, as well as its aesthetics and perceived quality, or how the customer perceives it in use and on the open market.

    In applying this to a customer service, students should measure what the service provides, what sets it apart from other such services, how reliable is the service; to what extent do they do what you ask? How durable are the firms; if you need them a year from now will they still be there? How fast or slow is their service? Is the organization efficient? Finally, how does the service look, sound, feel, in its appeal to you, in its image, its advertisements, etc.?

8. Student answers will vary here, according to their own experience.

9. Student answers will vary here, according to their own experience.

10. This is a research assignment which students should complete on their own time. Again, answers will vary.

ANSWERS TO CASE QUESTIONS

I. Chrysler's Transmission Headache

Students should be encouraged to find "outside" evidence as to what the current perceived and actual quality level of Chrysler's minivan transmission now is. Obviously, this is a "moving target" and Chrysler must "catch up" or leap-frog the competition.

1. In the past, Chrysler has had a reputation for high-quality engineering, which may have made it complacent. In addition, of course, it was the pioneer and market leader in the minivan segment, so perhaps the feeling was that the overall reputation of the product would insulate the product line from serious competition. Overconfidence, historic dominance, and failure to heed the "voice of the customer" are all factors that may contribute to a firm losing its market leadership.

2. Chrysler could have done things differently by monitoring frequency of repairs, seeking customer input, and using systematic problem-solving techniques to isolate and correct the problems before they became critical.

3. A stronger focus on quality principles would have mandated a customer focus. Customers should include dealers, suppliers and line workers, as well as the ultimate customer, the buyer. In additional, "management by fact" and continuous improvement might have helped to stop the erosion in quality reputation and market share.

II. Deere & Company

There is no "correct" solution to this case problem, but a number of useful teaching points can be brought out after students have done their analyses. Specifically:

• In the 1984 annual report, the company referred to increasing competitive pressures and the need to provide for more value per dollar to the customer. The ways that the company proposed to achieve this seemed to revolve around the "technological fix" with references to use of robotics and increased efficiency in operations. Quality was beginning to be recognized as important in design, manufacturing, and in meeting customer needs for reliability in the forestry equipment line.

• In 1986 report the theme was still focussed on value to the customer. A major market "niche" was identified as OEM (original equipment manufacturers), who were recognizing Deere's ability to supply parts and components. It was implied that their leveraged engineering (perhaps a form of concurrent engineering?) gave them a competitive advantage in time-to-market for high-quality components that were produced to meet customer needs in a cost-effective manner.

• In the 1987 report, a major emphasis on <u>quality</u> seemed to develop, even though cost-reduction and value to the customer continued as an underlying theme. The "total value" concept of quality, reliability, dealer support, finance plans and resale value was defined.

• The 1988 report again highlighted productivity improvement across the areas of production, sales and net income per employee. It did give credit for their successful year to excellence of products, manufacturing facilities, R&D to provide excellent new products, and technological advances that allowed lower costs and improved value to customers.

• In 1989, corporate values such as integrity, quality and value of products and services, and corporate image in the marketplace were featured. Value-added features and an independent dealer network were mentioned, as was employee participation in improvement of manufacturing efficiencies.

These summaries definitely show a gradually increasing commitment to TQM concepts. However, nowhere was it stated in the quoted passages that Deere had committed itself to the TQM concept. Management continually emphasizes productivity and cost reduction as the key to excellence. In the mature and very competitive heavy equipment industry, cost reduction and "value to the customer" may be seen as the language that will convey a quality image to the average customer.

III. Is Quality Good Marketing or Is Good Marketing Quality?

The value in this case study is to show students that quality concepts can be applied in retail service operations, and thus is not limited only to the production of tangible goods.

1.   The actions taken by the company to please the customer address points 7 and 8 of Garvin's quality dimensions -- aesthetics and perceived quality. Store appearance, warehousing policies, delivery standards, and customer relations all reinforce the visual (aesthetic) dimension of quality and add to the "image" (perceived quality) of the store(s). One area that was not addressed was that of support functions, such as accounting and purchasing, who may interact with customers and/or suppliers. Have they been trained to use TQM concepts to improve product quality and excellent service, as well? For example, are accounting and purchasing processes being continually improved? Are suppliers (including company and non-company manufacturers) aware of the quality specifications and goals of the retailer? Are they working together to reduce time-to-market and to design products that will keep the customers coming back, based on quality of design as well as service excellence?

2.   The franchiser's statement that: "The best way to assure quality is through product inspection and market research," could be open to some debate. If market research is not closely linked to product design, then customers may not be offered the product that they want or need. If continuous improvement and teamwork is not part of the process for

delivering the desired product or service, then product inspection may come too late to be advantageous.

3.   To answer the question: "Is quality good marketing, or is good marketing quality?" one must realize that the field of marketing grew up as a result of a "backlash" against "salesmanship" in the 1950's. At that time, the purpose of a "salesperson" was to sell whatever products could be produced by the factory, whether the customer wanted to buy them or not. Marketing suggested the radical concept of trying to find out what the needs of the customer were and then providing a product to fill those needs. As the PIMS studies have shown, quality is directly related to market share and to profitability. Other studies have shown that people are willing to pay more for products that they perceive as having high quality. Thus, without high quality, good marketing of products and services would appear to be impossible, since salespeople would have little to sell that would meet the needs of their customer. However, without good marketing, where salespeople listen and respond to the needs of customers, even the best-designed products will remain unsold.

CHAPTER 2

Quality in Production and Service Systems

Teaching Notes

This chapter introduces the concept of production and service systems and develops the idea that quality is central to effective operation of these systems. Students should become aware of the fact that quality is not an "add-on" to organizational processes, but that it is "a way of doing business." Key objectives should include:

• To reinforce the importance of a total quality focus for effective operation of manufacturing and service systems, including support systems. In particular, to examine Deming's view of a production system that focuses on lateral relationships, as opposed to the traditional hierarchical view of organizations.

• To point out that businesses should view quality at three levels: the organizational level, the process level and the performer level, which cuts across traditional boundaries and provides better information for achieving customer satisfaction.

• To differentiate between production and service organizations and to highlight the differences in service organizations that must be addressed when designing and implementing quality assurance systems.

• To show that quality in manufacturing and quality in services must be approached differently in terms of employees' responsibilities and type and use of technology.

• To link the concepts of quality and productivity and to show that quality improvements generally lead to productivity improvements.

• To introduce the term *total quality management* and its forerunners and to explain how the concept works in practice.

ANSWERS TO QUALITY IN PRACTICE KEY ISSUES

The Spare Parts Quality System at DEC

1.   Management responsibilities at DEC seem to mirror the requirements for quality in production systems discussed in the chapter. Product development responsibilities are carried out by engineering, possibly with some assistance from field service managers. The production process, and associated logistics activities deal with product and process quality, testing, defective product removal, and protecting the product. Product use is defined by marketing as an input to product design and by field service as they handle customer enquiries, service, and adjustments.

2.   The Field Service Organization at DEC has many of the characteristics that are typical of a service organization. They deal with tangible items (computer parts), but must respond as a service organization to customer needs. They are competing with IBM along the dimensions of speed and quality of customer service in maintenance and consulting service. They are called upon to handle thousands of transactions per day, interact with customers on identifying and solving problems, product specifications are sometimes difficult to define, etc. The eight important dimensions of service quality listed in the body of the chapter certainly apply to DEC.

Service Quality at the Ritz-Carlton Hotel Company

1.   The character-trait recruiting instrument is used in an attempt to match the right person to the right job within the hotel. The benefits are that it sends a message to employees that the company is serious about choosing high quality personnel to fill each position. Also, assuming that the instrument is well-designed, the employees will tend to be more satisfied, more likely to be productive and enhance the quality image of the company.

While the approach of filling the right job with the right person is an admirable objective, there are numerous possible pitfalls that must not be overlooked. For example, people who may not have the "right" traits could be denied the opportunity to move to a job that they could easily learn and contribute to. Also, such instruments are often easy to "fake." For example a candidate who was eager to be chosen a front desk position could respond positively to questions about politeness, ability to listen, etc., even if he/she did not actually exhibit these traits. Also, the instrument would need to be monitored over time to determine if it was actually predicting success on the job for the people who scored high.

2.   The company uses information technology to both monitor standards and also to enhance the quality of services. Every employee is involved with these systems. By gathering data on quality performance, Ritz-Carlton can see where the improvements are paying off and where more improvement is needed. By profiling guests, employees can provide service that is "tailored" to the needs of individual customers.

3.   Productivity improvements were evident in reducing the number of employees per guest room during pre-opening by 12%, labor hours per guest room by 8%, and average time to clean a room from 30 to 28.5 minutes. Indirect indications of productivity improvement may be inferred from the fact that turnover was reduced to the 48% level. More experienced employees are often more productive. Also, elevator waiting time and housekeeping cost reductions could indicate that the productivity improvements were resulting in lower housekeeping costs and higher utilization of elevators, although other factors could enter into these changes, such as materials costs or technological improvements (new sweepers or faster elevator motors).

ANSWERS TO REVIEW QUESTIONS

1.   The three major components of a production system include: **a.** *Inputs*--physical facilities, materials, capital, equipment, people, and energy; **b.** *Outputs*--the products and services produced by the system; **c.** *Processes*--activities (i.e. machining) that transform inputs into outputs. Deming's production system model departed from the traditional model in that it went beyond the simple production process to include considerations of customers and suppliers, as part of an interdependent organizational process.

2.   The three levels of quality include: **a.** *Organizational level*--Here, quality concerns center on meeting external customer requirements. An organization must seek customer input on a regular basis. Customer-driven performance standards should be used as bases for goal-setting, problem solving, performance appraisal, incentive compensation, nonfinancial rewards, and resource allocation. **b.** *Process level*--Here, organizational units are classified as functions or departments (i.e. marketing, design, finance, purchasing, etc.). Process managers must select processes so as to produce quality products while most effectively meeting the needs of internal customers. **c.** *Performer level*--Sometimes called the job level or task level design. Output standards (i.e. requirements for accuracy, completeness, cost, etc.) should be based on quality and customer-service requirements originating at the organizational and process levels. Employees should have input on quality standards and ways of improving their own work processes in order to produce high quality intermediate, as well as finished products.

3.   Quality concerns within a manufacturing system vary, as follows:

Marketing and Sales - Effective market research and solicitation of customer feedback are necessary for developing quality products.

Product Design and Process Engineering - Here technicians must make sure products are not over- or under-engineered. Over-engineering results in ineffective use of a firms resources and lower products. Under-engineered products' poor process designs result in lower quality as well.

Purchasing and Receiving - The purchasing department must ensure that purchased parts meet the quality requirements specified by product design and engineering. Receiving must ensure that the purchased items that are delivered are of the quality that was contracted for by purchasing and that defective parts are not received.

Production Planning and Scheduling - The correct material, tools, and equipment must be available at the proper time and in the proper places to maintain a smooth flow of production.

Manufacturing and Assembly - Quality must be built into a product; it cannot be inspected into it. Proper control of labor, materials, and equipment is necessary to achieve high quality.

Tool Engineering--Tools used in manufacturing and inspection must be designed and maintained for continual production of a quality product. Tool performance should be consistently monitored so that worn or defective tools can be identified and replaced.

Industrial Engineering and Process Design - Must work with product design engineers to develop realistic specifications of quality. In addition, they must select appropriate technology, equipment, and work method that will produce quality products.

Finished Goods Inspection and Tests - If quality is built into the product properly, inspection should be unnecessary. However, some inspection based on random sampling, or 100 percent inspection of critical components, may still be necessary to ensure that no defective items reach the customer.

Packaging, Shipping, and Warehousing - Logistic activities that protect quality after goods are produced.

Installation and Service - Users must understand the product and have adequate instructions for proper installation and operation.

4.   Business support systems must aid in quality production in their own separate ways:

General Management--Top managers must provide leadership that motivates the entire organization, develop strategic quality plans, and ensure that quality initiatives are present in every process and involve very individual in the organization.

Finance and Accounting--Finance must authorize sufficient budgeting for equipment, training, and other means of assuring quality. Financial studies can help expose the costs of poor quality and ways of reducing it. Accounting data are useful for identifying areas for quality improvement and tracking the progress of quality improvement. Financial and accounting personnel can also apply quality improvement techniques to improve their own operations.

Human Resource Management--Human resource managers must ensure that employees have the proper skills, training, and motivation to do quality work, and that they are recognized and rewarded for such. They must also be given the authority and responsibility to make critical quality decisions when necessary.

Quality Assurance--Because managers may lack the technical expertise necessary for performing needed statistical tests or data analyses, a separate quality assurance department may be essential, consisting of quality specialists to perform these studies on a regular basis.

Legal Services--The legal department must ensure that the firm follows all laws concerning product labeling, packaging, safety, and transportation, that all warranties are properly constructed and written, that the firm satisfies its contractual requirements, and has proper procedures and documentation in place in case of liability claims against it.

5.   A *core* service is the initial service or services of an industry. For example, in the case of a bank, a checking account or savings account service is a core service. A *facilitating* service is a service that enhances the value of a core service to a customer. With the bank, automatic teller service would be an example of a facilitating service, allowing bank customers easier access to the core services.

6.   Quality in services is important because poor service often leads to lost customers and therefore lost income. Retaining customers can mean a profit increase because it is more cost effective to retain them than to acquire new customers. Companies with long-time customers can financially outperform competitors with higher customer turnover even when their unit costs are higher and their market share is smaller.

7.   The output of service systems is generally intangible, while manufacturing systems produce tangible and visible products; therefore, the behavioral aspects of management, such as motivation, are critical to quality control and enhancement in the service sector. Service organizations handle a large volume of transactions, which increases the opportunity for error. Inspection cannot be used as a means of quality control in services, since they are consumed as they are created and cannot be inventoried as can manufactured goods. Manufacturing is more capital intensive, whereas services are generally more labor intensive; hence, quality can frequently be automated into the manufacturing process. The service delivery system is often very time sensitive, and customers and service workers must often interact for delivery of quality service.

8.   Research has repeatedly shown that when service employee job satisfaction is high, customer satisfaction is high, and that when job satisfaction is low, customer satisfaction is low. Regretfully, in many companies, the front-line employees--those who have the most contact with customers--are the recipients of low pay, minimal training, and minimal authority or responsibility, and are therefore most likely to be dissatisfied with their jobs. High-quality service organizations have taken to training front-line employees in the

interaction skills necessary for effective handling of customer accounts, inquiries, complaints, etc. on a personal level. They have also initiated rewards for increased customer satisfaction.

Information technology is essential in modern service organizations because of the high volumes of information they must process and because customers demand service at ever-increasing speeds. Intelligent use of information technology improves quality and productivity, and also leads to competitive advantage, especially when technology is used to better serve the customer.

Avis's motto, "We try harder," reflects the company's desire to satisfy the customer, and also its recognition that this begins with satisfied employees. Avis has therefore made a "pro-people" practice of retaining employees, continually improving the workplace environment, and maintaining employee-management communications through its Employee Participation Group program. It has worked to maintain good employee-customer communications, by training employees to continually keep pace with changes in customer needs and the workforce. Avis has also created the nationwide "Wizard" computer system, enabling employees to handle customer reservations, rental concerns and credit-card payments with speed and accuracy.

9.   Productivity is defined as a measure of how well resources are being used in a firm. In its general form (productivity = output/input), productivity increases as output increases for a constant level of input, or as input decreases for a constant level of output.

10.   The *hidden factory* is the portion of plant capacity that exists to rework unsatisfactory parts, to replace products recalled from the field, or to retest and reinspect rejected units.

11.   Traditionally, quality and productivity have been seen as conflicting, since product efficiency has been a major force driving manufacturing decisions. Many managers will state that quality cannot be improved without significant losses in production and increased costs. But the modern view is that improved quality leads to improved productivity and vice versa.

If we look at productivity as an equation, being output over input (input consists of capital, labor, material, and energy, or some subset of these), we find productivity increases as output increases for a constant level of input, or input decreases for a constant level of output.

Clearly, there is something to be said for getting a product right the first time. This eliminates the increase in input (labor, material, energy, etc.) necessary to correct the problem. It also eliminates the decrease in output that would result from simply giving up the defective material for scrap.

ANSWERS TO DISCUSSION QUESTIONS

1.   Students should use Deming's view of a production system (see Review Question 1, above) as a "springboard" for discussion of this question.

2.   This question may be related to Review Question 2, above.

3.   This exercise is designed to get the student out into the business community to see how processes work (or don't work) there.

4.   This should be an easy topic for most students to discuss. Try to find a balance between "horror stories" and exceptionally good quality examples. You may have to probe student's memories to have them relate some "good quality" stories.

5.   This question may be related to Review Question 7, above, as well as the dimensions, stated in the chapter, that differentiate service quality from manufacturing quality.

6.   Student answers will vary, depending on their experiences.

7.   Student answers will vary, depending on their experiences.

8.   See Review Question 10 for a definition that can be used to help structure this answer.

9.   These three scenarios show that traditional approaches to productivity improvement first, and quality improvement second, leave a "gap" that must be filled. In none of the scenarios is quality or productivity likely to be considerably improved by the measures that are in place.

In part a, the implication is that the organization is trying to "inspect in" quality, rather than deal with the root causes of quality problems. This is resulting in rejected parts, rework, and time wasted on review boards to dispose of the poor quality product. A better approach would be to certify vendor quality, work to bring internal quality under control, and seek to obtain more output from the labor hours and material cost than is now apparent.

In part b, quality standards need to be explained to the operators in a training program that would emphasize the importance of quality and how the operators' jobs fit into the overall production process. To make the inspectors more productive, the number of inspectors possibly needs to be reduced, and they need to have their roles redefined to assist operators in preventing quality problems, rather than catching them and screening them out.

In part c, the emphasis, again, seems to be on "inspecting in" quality, rather than improving it. 100% inspection is rarely effective or efficient in removing all the defects from a bad production process, and it can give operators a false sense of security about the fact that their mistakes will all be caught by the inspectors. Therefore, they feel no responsibility for monitoring and improving their own quality.

ANSWERS TO CASE QUESTIONS

I. Shiny Hills Farms

1.   The case describes the quality assurance (QA) function of Shiny Hills Farms, which seems to take a very traditional approach to "inspecting quality into" the product. The activities include controlling product weight, appearance and shelf life of the product. The emphasis is on QA specifications, monitoring procedures and temperatures, weights, USDA standards, and charting performance. Other departments do seem to have a concept of modern quality methods that could contribute to TQM. For example, R&D uses focus groups to help design products that meet customer needs. Engineering personnel are replacing lines with ergonomically correct designs, although this may be pointed toward productivity improvement, as opposed to quality improvement.

2.   The QA department sees quality as a "control" function as indicated by the case narrative and the answer to Question 1. The concept of total quality, with a high level of employee involvement and commitment, QA personnel serving as trainers and technical support people and the concept of internal customers seem to have little place at Shiny Hill.

3.   Shiny Hill could improve its quality by focusing on both internal and external customer needs, reducing reliance on inspection, implementing continuous improvement concepts, promoting employee involvement. The culture of inspecting quality into the product and preventing defective products from reaching the customer should be replaced by the concept of process control and self-monitoring to prevent any defective product from reaching the *next operation*, rather than the final consumer. At the same time, the use of appropriate quality standards, sampling inspection, new product development with customer input and continued progress toward ergonomic equipment design should not be discarded.

II. Mercantile Stores

1.   Mercantile views quality as part of their mission. Two aspects of this are to provide the highest level of customer service and a broad assortment of fashionable high-quality, high-value products. Information technology (*Quick Response*) was implemented to improve point-of-sale information needed by salespeople and inventory planning and control. This technology allows higher efficiency in "back-room" operations and also serves the customer better by ensuring that the right amount and type of inventory will be on the shelves when needed. Through the University Business School, everyone from sales associates to managers are trained and empowered to take responsibility for their jobs and to make customer satisfaction a priority.

2.   The emphasis in this case appears to be on internal quality, although a customer focus is evident. Components of *time, timeliness, consistency and accuracy* are certainly addressed by the new information system. However, *completeness, courtesy, accessibility and convenience, and responsiveness* are the responsibilities of people, more than technology. Thus internal quality is a necessary, but never a "sufficient" condition for excellent external quality. One must complement the other, based on a consistent mission and a customer focus.

CHAPTER 3

Quality Management
Philosophies

Teaching Notes

This chapter focuses on the "founding fathers" of total quality management -- Deming, Juran, Crosby, Feigenbaum, and Ishikawa. The chapter does not give in-depth biographical sketches of the quality "gurus," but summarizes their philosophies and principles on which they believe that quality rests. Key objectives should be:

• To develop an appreciation for the insight, wisdom, contributions, and forward thinking of Deming, Juran, Crosby, Feigenbaum, and Ishikawa -- the pioneering "gurus" of quality.

• To study Deming's 14 points, his "chain reaction," and the resulting radical changes in organizations.

• To survey Deming's concept of "profound knowledge," including components of systems thinking, statistical understanding of variation, the theory of knowledge and psychology.

• To see how the Red Bead and Funnel Experiments illustrate the dangers of misunderstanding variation and poor decisions that may result.

• To investigate how Juran's approach to change and improvement within the American management system, through the use of his "quality trilogy," differs from Deming's.

• To appreciate how Crosby's "Absolutes of Quality Management" emphasize behavioral change rather than improvements through the use of statistical techniques.

• To explore the impacts of A.V. Feigenbaum and Kaoru Ishikawa on the quality movement through the development of the concepts of "total quality control" and the Japanese concept of "companywide quality control," respectively.

ANSWERS TO QUALITY IN PRACTICE KEY ISSUES

Ford Becomes a "Deming Company"

1.   It is evident that the Deming philosophy has been incorporated in Ford's mission, values and guiding principles. The creation and publication of these statements shows that Ford is serious about quality, and accepts Deming's first point. Other themes include learning the new philosophy throughout the organization, continuous improvement, teamwork, teaching and instituting leadership, striving for excellence (Deming's "pride of workmanship"), trust and respect (driving out fear), and supplier partnerships (end the practice of awarding business on price tag alone). Other Deming themes will undoubtedly be uncovered by students as they study Ford's public statements about quality.

2.   Ford has apparently adopted the *user-based definition of quality*, as discussed in Chapter 1, since it emphasizes customer satisfaction and <u>fitness for use</u>. Garvin's dimensions of performance, reliability, conformance, durability and serviceability seem to be emphasized in the copy from Ford's 1985 annual report. Of course, Ford is using this quality strategy in an effort to develop "perceived quality" in the mind of customers and potential customers.

3.   The answers to this will vary, depending on the year(s) reviewed.

Zytec Corporation

1.   Zytec has adopted Deming's view of a production system by concentrating on four primary areas: 1) suppliers of materials and equipment, 2) testing of processes, machines, methods and costs, 3) customers and 4) product design. The results have been impressive: 99.7% product quality level, major reliability improvements (10 X in 5 years), cuts in warranty costs, scrap rate and cycle time and almost flawless customer performance and acceptance rates.

2.   From the information given in the QIP, it seems obvious that Zytec has implemented many of the 14 Points in their daily operations. Specifically, these include:

      o Point 1 - Create and publish the aims and purposes - Zytec has an operational mission statement.

      o Point 2 - Management has "learned the new philosophy" and is teaching it to all employees.

      o Points 3 & 4 - little was said about inspection, but the data that were given and their supplier support (along with expected quality standards) indicate that their quality control system is working.

o Points 5, 6, 7 and 9 are exemplified in Zytec's emphasis on continuous improvement, 72 hours per year of quality-related training, and movement to self-managed teams, with managers as "coaches."

o Points 8, 10, and 11 were not specifically addressed, but it was implied that trust had been created and exhortations and numerical quotas were not needed, because employees had "adopted the new philosophy"

o Zytec is busy removing barriers (Point 12), encouraging education and self-improvement (Point 13) and continuing their actions in the short and long-term to accomplish the transformation (Point 14).

ANSWERS TO REVIEW QUESTIONS

1.   The Deming "chain reaction" theory states that by (a) improving quality, a firm can (b) decrease costs because of less rework, fewer mistakes, delays, and snags, and better use of time and materials, thus (c) improving productivity. The firm will therefore be able to (d) capture the market with better quality and lower prices, and thus, not only (e) stay in business, but also (f) provide and create more jobs. Student answers to the second part of the question will vary, based on their readings.

2.   Deming's System of Profound Knowledge consists of four interrelated parts: (1) appreciation for a system; (2) understanding of variation; (3) theory of knowledge; and (4) psychology. Appreciating a system involves understanding how each component of the system works to produce the end product or service, and understanding how the system may be optimized for better or smoother performance. Understanding of variation involves knowing and anticipating factors (i.e. increasing personnel, the wearing out of tools) which may cause the system to change, for better or worse. Theory of knowledge involves understanding the system and current and possible variations within to the point where past and present events and performance can suggest possible outcomes of future courses of action within the system.

3.   Common causes of variation occur as a natural part of the process and are difficult to change without making a major change in the system of which they are a part. Special causes of variation arise from sources outside the system and can generally be traced back to a specific change that has occurred and needs correction. For example, a process may be stable and running well until the supplier of a critical material is changed. The new vendor's material causes the process to go out of control (becomes unstable), so the "solution" to the special cause is to have the vendor correct the deficiency, or return to the previous supplier for materials.

4.   The two fundamental mistakes which managers can make in attempting to improve a process are: (1) To treat as a special (or outside) cause any fault, complaint, mistake, breakdown, accident, or shortage which is actually due to common causes, and (2) to

attribute to common causes any fault, complaint, mistake, breakdown, accident, or shortage which is actually due to a special cause. In the first case, tampering with a stable system can increase the variation in the system. In the second case, the opportunity to reduce variation is missed because the amount of variation is mistakenly assumed to be uncontrollable.

5.   Taguchi measured quality as the variation from the target value of a design specification, and then translated that variation into an economic "loss function" that expresses the cost of variation in monetary terms. In doing this, Taguchi offered a method of measuring the monetary loss resulting from creation of products or services that do not conform to quality standards. This method has been used by Deming to compare the decreased costs of producing products or services with quality values closer to those of standard quality specifications.

6.   Theory of knowledge is the branch of philosophy concerned with the nature and scope of knowledge, its presuppositions and basis, and its general reliability of claims to knowledge. In Deming's system, this involves understanding the complete system and current and possible variations within it to the point where past and present events and performance can suggest possible outcomes of future courses of action within the system.

For the Wall Street analyst, the theory of knowledge raises severe questions as to whether the Stock Market is a stable system whose operations are subject to "knowledge" about what makes prices rise and fall. If the complete system and what drives it cannot be known with a fairly high degree of certainty, then it is foolish to try to predict earnings of a company or group of companies on a quarterly basis.

7.   The Red Bead experiment emphasizes that little, if anything, can improve quality in a poorly-managed production system. In the experiment, managers control incoming material (white and red beads) and work procedures so rigidly that there is little room for change. It is their mistake that there is an input of red bead production material the workers cannot stop the red beads from coming. Management inspects the beads only *after* they (and the mistakes involved) have been made. No amount of encouragement, threats, or promises of rewards will improve quality production when it is inevitable, by the nature of the process, that red beads will be produced. Furthermore, the managers have mistakenly believed that the variables in the process *are* controllable, and therefore that the workers are simply not trying hard enough in their labors. The final point of the Red Bead experiment is that *all factors* of a process must be examined to locate and correct negative variations.

The Funnel experiment is designed to show how people can and do affect the outcome of a process and create unwanted variation by "tampering" with the process, or indiscriminately trying to remove common causes of variation. The system of dropping the ball through the funnel towards the target is damaged by the variation of each participant moving the funnel around to "get a better aim" at the target. The lesson is that once a plan or process is determined to be correct and is set in motion, no components of the process should be tampered with. The process should be adjusted only if the entire process has been thoroughly examined and found to be in need of change in some way.

8.   Deming feels that a company - the whole company - must commit to quality as a total effort, as published in their aims and purposes. This means that all 14 points must be adopted as a package. You can't embrace the quality philosophy in one area of work and ignore it in another. If each person is responsible for their own quality, then you don't need many of the rules, regulations, and external controls that have been the "norm" in many organizations for decades. This suggests that management must take on a new leadership role to foster innovation, change, improvement and high quality at every level in the organization.

9.   Deming's 14 points may be put into the six categories listed, but it should be realized that some of his 14 points apply to more than one category.

a. Organizational purpose and mission: Points 1, 7, 9, 14. These relate the need to develop a mission statement (aims and purposes), publish the statement, develop leadership to carry out the purpose, focus the efforts of <u>everyone</u> on the mission, and <u>act</u> to ensure that the transformation happens.

b. Quantitative goals: Points 3, 4, 8, 10, 11.a. & 11.b. These points may not be chosen by everyone, but several have "hidden agendas" that relate to quantitative goals. Inspection (point 3) is frequently used to develop quantitative goals and to "catch" problems (and the people who supposedly caused them) after they have occurred. Price tags (point 3), rather than overall quality levels, are the quantitative goal used to measure the <u>efficiency</u>, rather than effectiveness of the purchasing function. Fear (point 8) has been heightened, as workers are exhorted (point 10) to "do better" and meet their quotas and goals (points 11a. and b.).

c. The revolution in management philosophy: Points 2, 7, and 14. These points are keys to the change in management philosophy, but all 14 points really are needed to encompass the philosophy.

Deming said that leadership, training, appropriate uses of inspection, purchasing based on quality (instead of cost, alone), self-development, and continuous improvement go hand-in-hand.

d. Elimination of seat-of-the-pants decisions. Points 3, 4, 5, and perhaps 11. Seat-of-the-pants decisions seem to flow from faulty logic and the short-term pressure to meet goals in order to make the "bottom line" look good. The best decisions seem to be made when the system is thoroughly understood, workers are taught personal responsibility and problem-solving skills, and the focus is on long-term objectives and <u>constant</u> long-term commitment to quality.

e. Build cooperation. Points 1, 2, and 6-13. All of the development of a common philosophy, leadership, training, and casting out fear is aimed toward improving cooperation.

f. Improve manager-worker relations. Points 7, 8, 9, 12, and 13. These points cover management-worker relations in more detail, but building cooperation, as covered by the points in part (e), above, also contributes to improved worker-manager relations.

10.   Deming's "Deadly Diseases" include:

1.   *Lack of constancy of purpose*--This goes against Deming's point that the road to quality must begin with a clear statement of purpose and an ironclad commitment. Short-term quality programs will not hold out in the long run.

2.   *Emphasis on short-term profits*--Firms seeking only to increase the quarterly dividend undermine quality in favor of the "quick fix." This goes against Deming's philosophy that firms must stop measuring everything by what it will cost (or how much money they will lose), that they must eliminate standards and quotas ("we want to reach this level of profits by March"), and that they must eliminate fear, which may cause them to go for the "quick fix" in a jittery marketplace.

3.   *Evaluation of performance, merit rating, or annual review of performance*--Again, Deming advocates the elimination of quotas and standards, and the elimination of rewards based on quotas and standards.

4.   *Mobility of management*--Managers must stay in one place long enough to understand the products or services the company produces, and long enough to implement long-term changes necessary for quality improvement.

5.   *Running a company on visible figures alone*--The most important figures, such as the effect of a satisfied customer, are unknown and often unknowable.

6.   *Excessive medical costs for employee health care that increase the final costs of goods and services.*

7.   *Excessive costs of warranty, fueled by lawyers who work on the basis of contingency fees.*

11.   Juran's "Quality Trilogy," like a great many trilogies these days, consists of three parts: Quality planning--the process for preparing to meet quality goals; quality control--the process for meeting quality goals during operations; and quality improvement--the process for breaking through to unprecedented levels of performance.

Quality planning begins with identifying customers, both external and internal, determining their needs, and developing product features that respond to customer needs. Quality goals are then established that meet the needs of customers and suppliers alike, and do so at a minimum combined cost.

Quality control involves determining what to control, establishing units of measurement so that data may be objectively evaluated, establishing standards of performance, measuring actual performance, interpreting the difference between actual performance and the standard, and taking action on the difference.

Juran specifies a program for quality improvement which involves proving the need for improvement, identifying specific projects for improvement, organizing guidance for the projects, diagnosing the causes, providing remedies for the causes, proving that the remedies are effective under operating conditions, and providing control to maintain improvements.

12.   Like Deming, Juran advocated company-wide quality management, with a never-ending process of quality improvement, involving such activities as market research, product development, production process control, inspection and testing, and customer feedback. He emphasized the need for management commitment to quality improvement, and the need for training of all employees in quality techniques. Juran also asked workers to know their external and internal customers, and to identify and reduce causes of variation by determining the difference between standard and actual performance and taking action on the difference.

Unlike Deming, Juran did not propose major cultural changes in the organization, but sought to improve quality within the system familiar to U.S. managers. His detailed plan was based on identifying areas for improvement and acting accordingly. Juran also recognized the different "languages," or trains of thought, which occupy different levels of an organization, and advocated communication between these "languages," where Deming proposed that statistics be shared as a common language.

13.   Crosby's Absolutes of Quality Management are:

(1) Quality means conformance to requirements, not elegance. Crosby sees requirements as being ironclad; they are communication devices which must be clearly stated so that they cannot be misunderstood. Once this is done, a company can take measurements to determine conformance to those requirements.
(2) Crosby maintains there is no such thing as a quality problem. Problems must be identified by those individuals or departments that cause them, so there are accounting problems, manufacturing problems, logic problems, algebra problems, etc. (3) There is no such thing as the economics of quality; it is always cheaper to do the job right the first time. Most of us will remember this one as a frequent and rather annoying axiom, used by our mothers every time we had to perform some complicated chore, such as changing a light bulb or filling an ice tray. Crosby supports the premise that "economics of quality"

has no meaning. Quality is free. What costs money are all actions that involve not doing jobs right the first time.

(4) The only performance measurement is the cost of quality. The cost of quality is the expense of nonconformance. Crosby's program calls for measuring and publicizing the cost of poor quality.

(5) The only performance standard is "Zero Defects." Zero Defects is a performance standard, NOT a motivational program. The idea behind ZD is to do it right the first time, to concentrate on preventing defects rather than just finding and fixing them.

(6) People are conditioned to believe that error is inevitable; thus they not only accept error, they anticipate it. Each of us have limits to which we can accept errors. Eventually we reach a point where the errors tick us off. This usually occurs when the errors affect us personally, such as when you discover your VCR will make toast, coffee, and Eggs Benedict, but won't play your VHS tapes.

According to Crosby, most human error is caused by lack of attention rather than lack of knowledge. Lack of attention is created when we assume that error is inevitable.

Crosby's Basic Elements of Improvement include determination, education, and implementation. By determination, Crosby means that top management must be serious about quality improvement. The Absolutes must be understood by everyone; this can be accomplished only through education. Finally, every member of the management team must understand the implementation process.

Like Deming, Crosby advocated interior searches by individual departments (i.e. manufacturing, accounting) within a firm for sources of negative variation and acting to reduce these. He also advocated the policy of doing the job right the first time. Unlike Deming, Crosby's plan focuses on managerial thinking, calling for change within the current system, not a complete organizational overhaul.

14. A.V. Feigenbaum is primarily known for three contributions to quality -- his international promotion of the quality ethic, his development of the concept of total quality control, and his development of the quality cost classification. Kaoru Ishikawa was instrumental in the development of the broad outlines of Japanese quality strategy, the concept of CWQC, the audit process used for determining whether a company will be selected to receive the Deming award, the quality control circle, and cause-and-effect diagrams--a principle tool for quality management.

Today, firms must be aware of, and conform to the international challenges on the quality front. Quality is a competitive weapon for developing countries who are trying to bring their standards of living up to those of the developed nations. If domestic manufacturing and service firms ignore these international challenges, they are inviting their world-wide competitors to steal their markets from them.

ANSWERS TO DISCUSSION QUESTIONS

1.   Deming never actually gave a definition of quality. However, if he had explicitly defined quality, he might have said:

   Quality is the result of action taken by management, acting as leaders, with the willing cooperation of knowledgeable workers, to constantly and forever improve products and services by reducing variability and uncertainty in processes, thereby remaining competitive and providing profits and enough jobs for everyone.

2.   Answers will vary, depending on the experience and interests of the students.

3.   Answers will vary, depending on the experience and interests of the students.

4.   See Review Question 7, above, for a definition from which to begin discussion.

5.   See Review Question 7, above, for a definition from which to begin discussion.

6.   Answers will vary, depending on the experience and interests of the students.

7.   Although opinions may vary, Points 11.a and 11.b are perhaps the most controversial of all. Eliminating numerical quotas, MBO goals and programs, and substituting process capability analysis and improvement methods is difficult for managers to understand. Organizations have legitimate objectives to attain, but goals are frequently set without knowledge of the capabilities of processes or people who are to accomplish them. The focus tends to be on short-term profits and goals. The "fad of the month" proposes short-term solutions to long-term problems. Loyalty of firms toward their workers and workers toward their firms has almost vanished. Deming believes that we **must** take a long-term view of the objectives of the organization.

8.   Deming's philosophy can be applied to an academic environment, but only with concerted efforts on the part of faculty, administrators, and students. Professors obviously serve in a key role in transforming the classroom to a "total quality" environment. Unless they "adopt the new philosophy," change will never come about. Many classes operate on a "control" model and the professor must work hard to "cast out fear." Administrators have a long way to go in learning how to "Improve constantly and forever the system of production and service." Students must learn to work together in teams to "Optimize toward the aims and purposes of the [organization]..." Still, there are a number of departments, colleges of business and engineering, and even universities that are trying and succeeding in applying the Deming principles to improve classroom performance.

9.   See Review Question 2, above, for a definition from which to begin discussion. Understanding the system should be emphasized.

10.   The answers will vary here, depending on students' perspectives.

11.   Answers to this question will possibly vary by how aware students are of international competitiveness issues.

12.   This project can expand awareness of the breadth of the "quality movement" and how the theory of quality is being applied in practical settings in business and industry.

13.   The answers will vary here, depending on students' perspectives.

ANSWERS TO CASE QUESTIONS

I. The Disciplinary Citation

1.   This case study shows Deming's "Red Bead" Experiment in action. Drivers are being blamed for conditions that are not under their control. The problem could be addressed by process measurement, eliminating "special causes" and working to reduce common causes of variation.

2.   A run chart would appear to be a way to begin to understand the process and to determine if it is in control or not. Based on the available data, we have:

Center Line (average) for the chart = 240/40 = 6.0 mistakes

By inspecting the data, one sees that 12 drivers have exceeded the average. Also, 6 drivers had "no defects". The characteristics of drivers who are having difficulty should be examined to explain their higher error rates. Are their errors far above normal, or just a little above? Are they well trained? Are they overworked, with more than the average number of difficult orders? Do they have poor equipment? A useful control chart cannot be established, unless "special causes" are dealt with.

Once the information is clarified, a new chart (called a "c-chart" and discussed in Chapter 16) on the stable process can be set up. Then steps can be taken to reward those who consistently do well and to seek to improve the performance of those who have an unsatisfactory level of errors.

Case II. Value Pricing at Procter & Gamble

1.   Under the previous system, retail customers learned of promotions, "stocked up" on goods at "low" sale prices, creating huge demand for P&G's factories, which then "ramped up" production by using overtime and placing similar large demands on suppliers for materials. As the plant got into full swing on production, the retailers were notified that the price of the product was being increased (back to its "normal" level). They stopped ordering until their excess inventory was worked off. The P&G plant had to "gear down,"

cut overtime, and cutting back on orders of materials. This problem was called the "Accidental Adversaries" situation by Jennifer Kemeny in Peter M. Senge, et al. *The Fifth Discipline Field Book*. (New York: Currency-Doubleday, 1994), pp. 145-148. A systems model is shown in that reference.

2.   Deming (and Peter Senge) would explain this problem as a failure to understand the entire system. Both P&G's customers and the company were acting perfectly rationally when looking at it from a "local" level. P&G's customers wanted to "buy low and sell high," while P&G wanted to boost market share and cut costs by producing at a higher volume. Unfortunately, large, unpredictable variations in volume create chronic out-of-control processes. Simply understanding the **fundamentals** of TQM is sometimes inadequate. Deming's term **profound knowledge** means that even well-informed managers still have things to learn about TQM!

Case III. The Reservation Clerk

1.   Mary's job is to *satisfy customers* who are trying to obtain information or make reservations, while she simultaneously attempts to satisfy her internal customers, the supervisor and the account manager.

2.   Using Deming's principles, her supervisor (and the supervisor's customer, the account manager) need to "adopt the new philosophy" of quality, to remove the barriers in the system that are preventing Mary from satisfying her customers and to provide the encouragement and support that she needs so that she can take pride in her work. These include analyzing the problems with the slow computer; the missing information in the system; the quota that often prevents her from giving adequate customer service; and the fact that she may need training on use of printed directories and guides (if they must be used), as well as how to courteously handle customers.

CHAPTER 4

Principles of Total Quality Management

Teaching Notes

This chapter centers on the integrative nature of total quality management. It also provides an overview of the foundations concepts of TQM. Key objectives for this chapter should include:

- To learn the core concepts of TQM: customer focus; participation and teamwork; continuous improvement; infrastructure, practice and tools; and corporate culture as applied to both goods and service producing organizations.

- To examine the benefits of successful implementation of TQM in organizations.

- To present the new role of managers and leaders and the changes needed in organizations for TQM to succeed.

- To understand how the TQM movement has grown and been adopted in manufacturing, service, government, school systems and universities.

ANSWERS TO QUALITY IN PRACTICE KEY ISSUES

Total Quality Management at AT&T

1.   AT&T's quality principles of customers, people, work processes, supplier integration, prevention through planning and never-ending improvement incorporate and expand upon the three core principles of: 1) customer focus, 2) participation and teamwork and 3) continuous improvement that are developed in the chapter. These principles are actively practiced by AT&T employees as show in the examples in the case of the AT&T employee who helped locate the woman who was afflicted with Alzheimer's disease (customer focus and beyond); the cross functional team of engineers and production

people who came up with a superior method for calibrating test and measurement equipment; and the revision of the access billing process that cut the time required for the validation process from three months to 24 hours.

2.   TQM infrastructure requires:

- leadership
- strategic quality planning
- data and information management
- process management
- supplier management
- human resources management

AT&T and its leadership made the commitment to align their overall corporate strategy with their quality goals and objectives. This required "turning the organization upside down" and articulating and living by the values of: respect for people, customer focus, integrity, innovation and teamwork. Quality is structured around supplier partnerships and process management, performed by people through leadership and involvement, and focused on the customer. There are now a quality council, steering committee, and a variety of involvement processes in place such as quality improvement in daily work teams, cross-functional process teams, quality of worklife teams, and suggestion systems. Suppliers are viewed as an integral part of the business. Data and information management, although not specifically mentioned, empowers employees to service customers' needs in a timely fashion.

Saturn Corporation is Built on Quality

1.   Saturn's infrastructure is focused on workers, work teams, customers, and continuous improvement. As stated in the case, *partnership* is a key value at Saturn. Exceptional leadership and management foresight was required to visualize the Saturn project.

Work processes at Saturn are designed with workers in mind. For example, the cars move down the production line on wood pallets, and the workers move with them, which is easier than standing on concrete floors. Workers are involved in quality councils at every level from the production floor to the division's president. Workers even engaged in a production slowdown to emphasize to top management their commitment to quality. Workers are given extensive training in many facets of strategic, tactical, and operational decision-making.

Strategic quality vision has been translated into effective administrative processes and systems. Administrative procedures enhance quality through timely payment of vendors (as the automobile unit moves off the assembly line, payment is "triggered" for parts and components) and an integrated financial database that simplifies the financial processes.

Suppliers are seen as *partners*, and the company seeks to establish long-term relationships built on trust, high quality standards, just-in-time delivery, and continuous improvement.

To meet customers' needs, dealers have a protected territory, and a "no-dicker" price policy on all Saturn models that are sold. Customer feedback from the field is received within 24 hours, and analysis and timely corrective action is taken.

Quality control and improvement is accomplished through daily monitoring of quality, use of statistical methods, adherance to Saturn's quality systems and procedures, use of quality tools for problem-solving, team-related quality training, and building on team motivation and enthusiasm.

2.   The "clean sheet" approach that was used to develop Saturn's unique organization has proven to be very effective when innovation must be the key objective. To develop a total quality focused organization, the corporate culture must fully support and people must "buy into" the philosophy. The "clean sheet" approach virtually eliminates a major barrier to the TQM philosophy that exists in an established culture -- the attitude that says: "We've tried that before, and it didn't work."

Other advantages of the "clean sheet" approach are that the organization can be designed based on the "best practices" and technology that is available at that point in time. Mistakes of the past are not as much of a barrier at "green field" sites as they are in established facilities. Also, there is a major advantage to selecting workers based heavily on their interpersonal skills, as Saturn and most Japanese firms that produce in the U.S. have done. They can be taught from the beginning to work together in teams, made to feel important, and given responsibility far beyond those who came from a traditional, highly structured form of organization.

ANSWERS TO REVIEW QUESTIONS

1.   TQM is a term that conveys the total companywide effort -- through full involvement of the entire workforce and a focus on continuous improvement -- that companies use to achieve customer satisfaction. TQM is both a comprehensive management philosophy and a collection of tools and approaches for its implementation. It is useful in improving customer satisfaction, enhancing the quality of goods and services, and reducing waste, inventory, costs, cycle time of operations, work in process, and delivery times. It also allows increased flexibility in marketing products and enhances the use of human resources.

2.   The four characteristics of the "engineered total quality system," as defined by Feigenbaum, are:

a. It represents a point of view for thinking about the way quality really works in a modern business or governmental agency and how quality decisions can best be made.

b. It represents the basis for the deeply-thought-through documentation...of key, enduring quality activities and integrated, people-machine-information relationships which make a particular activity viable and communicable throughout the firm.

c. It is the foundation for making the broader scope quality activities of the company manageable because it permits the management and employees of the plant and company to get their arms firmly around their customer-requirements-to-customer-satisfaction quality activities.

d. It is the basis for systematic engineering of order-of-magnitude improvements throughout the major quality activities of the company.

There has been surprisingly little change in the need for these "engineered" quality systems principles to apply to today's businesses in the same way as they did in the 1950's. The only difference is, that the U.S. was a manufacturing economy in those days, and today it is a service economy.

3.   Companywide quality control is the Japanese version of Feigenbaum's concept of total quality control. It was successful in Japan because it was initiated by upper managers as a never-ending process of improving quality, involving and training all company employees to this end. Quality became a managerial issue, not a technical issue, and the TQM concept was born, based on this standpoint.

4.   The three core principles of Total Quality Management are:

a. A focus on the customer--A consistent effort to meet or exceed customer expectations, according to the *customer's* definition of quality.

b. Participation and teamwork--Given the right tools and the chance to participate, employees can implement significant quality contributions.

c. Continuous improvement--The quality improvement job is never-ending.

Two other concepts of great significance are: infrastructure, practice and tools; and corporate culture.

5.   The elements of the TQM infrastructure include:

■ leadership--Managers must create clear quality values and high expectations, and build these into the company's operations.

■ strategic quality planning--Planning long-range and short-range strategies for quality improvement based on the company mission and principles, and the wants and needs of customers.

■ data and information management--Collecting data on the on the quality of products, internal processes, and customer satisfaction, in order to understand variations and identify causes of quality problems

■ process management--Focusing on the design of an internal process and possible ways to improve it.

■ supplier management--Companies must accurately communicate their principle requirements and expectations to suppliers.

■ human resources management--The company work force must be fully committed to quality, and well-trained in handling the needs of external and internal customers. They must be full participants in the quality process.

6.   The *principles* of TQM are the concepts and objectives which must be enacted in order to successfully implement a TQM system--that is, firms wishing to incorporate TQM must focus on the customer's wants and needs, must work toward participation and teamwork for all company employees, and must work for continuous quality improvement. The *infrastructure* of TQM includes the basic management systems (i.e. strategic quality planning, process management) which enable a firm to realize the core principles of TQM. The *practices* and *tools* (described in other chapters) are the methods used to incorporate the infrastructure into a company.

7.   The types of facts and data needed for an accurate assessment of quality and of quality improvement prospects include information on:

• customer needs
• product and service performance
• operations performance
• market assessments
• competitive comparisons
• supplier performance
• employee performance
• cost and financial performance

8.   Continuous improvement takes place within many companies, today. For example, companies such as Intel in the computer industry are constantly striving to make their own products obsolete and to bring out better, faster, cheaper units to meet the needs of increasingly demanding customers.

9.   The corporate culture is simply "the way things are done" at a company. Peters and Waterman have noted several strong characteristics which effective corporate cultures share with TQM. These include:

a. An employee bias for action, that is, a desire to "get out there and get it done"
b. Effective and perpetual contact with the customer
c. Autonomy and entrepreneurship within the company
d. Productivity through people
e. Hands-on, value-driven operations
f. Sticking to knitting (that is, focusing on doing what you do best)
g. Simple form, lean staff
h. Simultaneous loose-tight controls

10.   P&G's policy of "really knowing our customers and consumers" relates to the TQM concept of knowing quality by the customers' definitions. Their commitments to "do right things right" and to "concentrate on improving systems" reflects the TQM concept of continuously maintaining and improving quality. Their practice of "empowering people" reflects TQM's requirement for participation and teamwork from all employees within an organization.

11.   A study of 20 companies which were finalists for the Malcolm Baldridge award found that, in nearly all cases, companies that used TQM achieved better employee relations, higher productivity, greater customer satisfaction, increased market share, and improved profitability.

12.   Refer to section under "TQM and Traditional Management Practices."

13.   TQM requires managers to develop new skills and new styles of management including:

- Thinking in terms of systems.
- Defining customer requirements, planning for quality improvement with each customer, and dealing with customer satisfaction.
- Ensuring ongoing quality efforts, and developing a life-long quality improvement style.
- Teambuilding
- Encouraging openness, creating climates of trust and eliminating fear, listening and providing feedback
- Leading and participating in group meetings
- Solving problems with data
- Clarifying goals and resolving conflicts, delegating and coaching, implementing change
- Making continuous improvement a way of life.

TQM has also required managers to learn "new languages." These are, in many cases, the old languages of management and business put to a new use. The basis for the new language is statistics, with its bell curves, probabilities and standard deviations expressed in units of sigma. In addition, the dialects of marketing, customer service, organization behavior, industrial and mechanical engineers, cost accountants and employee involvement team coordinators have been added. These languages and dialects are important because they must be understood in order to converse and communicate about total quality concepts, quality issues, and problems.

14.   TQM requires a long-term commitment. Companies that incorporate it into their management practice should not expect instant miracles; it takes time to fully incorporate the system into company management (A study found it takes a minimum of four years to persuade employees to buy in to the TQM philosophy, and eight to ten years to establish a TQM culture).

ANSWERS TO DISCUSSION QUESTIONS

1.   Polaroid found many issues about customer needs, suppliers, training, and quality that had existed for years were not recognized until a survey was done. Obviously, someone became concerned about quality and suggested to management that a problem existed. Students can give many examples of how lack of awareness has led to deteriorating quality, poor customer response and competitiveness.

2.   Answers will vary, depending on the experience and availability of information to the students.

3.   Key success factors required for TQM include:

- A long-term perspective
- A customer focus
- Top management commitment
- Systems thinking
- Training and tools
- Participation
- Measurement and reporting systems
- Communication
- Strong leadership

All of the above are inter-related, helping to make total quality management an organization-wide concept, whether the organization is a fraternity, student organization, etc. If applied with patience, they can help to turn theory into practice when implemented as part of an on-going TQM process.

4.   Teamwork and participation can be promoted by taking a process approach, focusing on customers, providing needed leadership, empowering employees to participate, giving them the training and tools to solve problems, and implementing their solutions to problems that they have analyzed and brought forth solutions for.

5.   The answers will vary here, depending on students' perspectives.

6.   This is a "hands on" library exercise for the student.

7.   See Review Question 12, above, for a definition from which to begin discussion.

8.   A variety of ideas are now being presented at conferences and seminars around the country. Some that the authors use include having students to do a "personal TQM" project (see Case II in Chapter 11), where they learn to apply quality tools for personal improvement; using a student advisory board in the classroom to give feedback on areas that are going well and those needing improvement; having students to do exercises where

they consider themselves as customers and other students as suppliers and vice-versa; and using "fast feedback" questionnaires at the end of class periods to determine areas of confusion in lectures and assignments.

9.   This is a "hands on" field exercise for the student.

10.   The editor of *Quality Digest* was implying by his statement that good managers must and do find ways to make TQM work. They know that an organization can no longer consider that quality is optional. Survival and growth depend on TQM becoming part of good management practice.

ANSWERS TO CASE QUESTIONS

I. Hillshire Farm/Kahn's

An assessment of the quality function and activities at Hillshire Farms/Kahn's (HF-K) shows a number of strengths and weaknesses under the administrations of two CEO's: Milton Schloss and Bill Geoppinger. Since two different management philosophies and styles seemed to be practiced, it might prove useful to compare and contrast the strengths and weaknesses of each.

Milton Schloss took a "hands-on" management approach and thus modelled quality leadership and a customer focus. Under his management, various quality measures were defined (fact-based management). Employees were encouraged to develop a quality attitude (appearance standards for the plant and grounds); to exhibit quality in their daily work (standards for number of telephone rings and promptness and accuracy in accounting function); and to participate in continuous improvement of their work processes. Despite his strengths, he was still a traditional manager and was accustomed to the "command-and-control" style where employees were <u>required</u> to obey the commands of the CEO and not ask too many (if any) questions.

Under Bill Geoppinger, the CEO who succeeded Schloss, a new corporate culture was required. Geoppinger's philosophy was based on openness, employee empowerment, flexibility and responsiveness. He discontinued many of Schloss's personal initiatives and he and his new management team began to change the corporate culture by empowering line and staff employees in every function and level. Customer focus took on a new meaning in the Deli Select Line of products. Employees were empowered and encouraged to take a customer view of quality. By monitoring defect rates, as well as the traditional yield figures using SPC, employees were able to identify problems and determine how they could be corrected. Thus, under the new managers, customer focus was sharpened (employees defined customer specifications for the product and its packaging, and then measured it), quality leadership was broadened and decentralized, fact-based management was consistently practiced (through SPC) and employee participation was extended and focused on business issues.

HF-K has come a long way toward implementing TQM. Since TQM is a "race with no finish line," then TQM has probably not been fully adopted, yet. One area that was not mentioned was supplier partnerships. HF-K should seek to involve suppliers in their TQM effort. This would help to increase quality of their products, reduce inspection, and reduce cost.

II. The Case of the Stalled Quality Program

There appear to be two problems that have surfaced in this case. These are: 1) attempting to "inspect quality into" the product by defining quality in terms of rejection rates and productivity levels; and 2) a disagreement over visual (somewhat subjective) quality standards. The first is more serious than the second.

The first problem should be treated by training line employees to be responsible for their own quality. This will also mean that the role of the inspectors must be changed to technical consultants and quality auditors, rather than "traffic cops" whose job is to catch "lawbreakers."

The second problem should be handled by determining what the customer's requirements are for the "visual" attributes in question. The problem solving process must include fact-based management. Data must be gathered to define what is a "quality" item versus what is a "defective" item. Everyone from workers to managers to inspectors should agree on the standard and how to recognize it. Models of various types of defects should be collected and studied. Individuals who must make the judgments must be "calibrated" to the same standards.

CHAPTER 5

Focusing on Customers

Teaching Notes

This chapter focuses on customer satisfaction. This is a topic that was thought to be out of the area of responsibility of human resources and production/operations managers until the TQM movement got under way. It was formerly reserved for a few specialists in "consumer behavior" within the "marketing research" discipline. The focus on TQM has helped to change this attitude. Students who are not marketing majors need to be made aware of this important refocusing of management's attention. Objectives of this chapter are to:

• Raise students' awareness that satisfying customers is perhaps the most important competitive goal of any business.

• Emphasize the concept of *moments of truth* when a customer comes in contact with an employee of the company and forms perceptions and is satisfied or dissatisfied with the quality of service by comparing their expectations with actual outcomes.

• Study the leading practices for achieving customer satisfaction include: thoroughly understanding customer needs and expectations, understanding the linkages between customer needs and design/production/delivery processes, making extraordinary commitments, managing the customer relationship process effectively, measuring customer satisfaction, and acting on the results.

• Learn the important classification scheme known as the "Kano model" which segments customer requirements into dissatisfiers, satisfiers, and exciters/delighters.
• Survey the tools for gathering customer information and classifying customer requirements.

• Understand requirements for customer relationship management including: establishing commitments, developing customer-focused service standards, training and empowering customer contact employees, and effectively dealing with complaints.

• Explore requirements for customer satisfaction measurement to include both performance and importance measures that will provide useful information to improve a company's operations and products to further satisfy its customers.

ANSWERS TO QUALITY IN PRACTICE KEY ISSUES

Customer Focus at Granite Rock

1.   The importance of these factors could vary for different customers. According to the surveys that Granite rock uses customers rank the characteristics as follows:

Rank	Item	Assumed Reason
(1)	On-time delivery (c.)	Waiting time for labor crews is very costly in construction.
(2)	Product quality (f.)	Concrete or other materials failure can cost time and money.
(3)	Scheduling (d.)	Schedule changes are common in construction. Responsiveness by a company such as Granite Rock is valuable.
(4)	Problem resolution (a.)	Customers demand fairness and prompt attention to problems.
(5)	Price (e.)	Price (especially for high-quality) product is a consideration but ranks pretty far down the list.
(6)	Credit terms (g.)	Credit terms are probably fairly "standard" across all firms.
(7)	Salespeople's skills (b.)	Customers and salespeople probably have equivalent knowledge about the product, so such skills are "taken for granted"

2.   The customer importance survey is designed to determine the quality and service factors and their relative ratings for Granite Rock's product line. The customer report card is designed to get feedback on the relative quality of suppliers in that region, after the customers have done business with them. The relationship is that the dimensions on each survey are basically the same.

There is probably enough information on the two surveys to provide a rough estimate of the importance/performance matches and gaps. However, a more detailed questionnaire to determine the company's performance might be needed to "fine-tune" the analysis.

Waiting Time and Customer Satisfaction at Florida Power and Light

1.   People who are waiting almost invariably overestimate the time that they have waited when they have no objective means of measurement. As FP&L found, people were willing to wait longer and more patiently when they had an estimate of the required waiting time. For organizations that are trying to set standards, two conclusions may be drawn: a) people don't like to be made to wait, so try to minimize waiting time, and b)

if waiting time is inevitable, try to provide an estimate of the length of the wait for customers.

2.   FP&L's analysis went beyond the "rules of thumb" given above and classified the interactions between waiting times and customer satisfaction. In summary, they found:

> a. Customer satisfaction generally decreased as the length of wait increased.

> b. Customers were generally willing to wait longer if they had an estimate of the amount of time that they would have to wait.

> c. If customers were given a choice of waiting or calling back later, they had higher levels of satisfaction.

> d. Customers expected to wait different lengths of time, depending on the type of service that they were trying to receive.

With analysis to "tailor" to these findings to specific firms, these general ideas might be tested and used in any business where people place orders over the telephone.

ANSWERS TO REVIEW QUESTIONS

1.   The four key customer-related goals of any business are:

- To satisfy its customers.
- To achieve higher customer satisfaction than its competitors.
- To retain customers in the long run.
- To gain market share.

2.   Customer satisfaction occurs when products and services meet or exceed customer expectations. Loyal customers spend more, refer new clients, and are less costly to do business. Poor quality products and services, on the other hand, lead to customer dissatisfaction in the form of complaints, returns, and unfavorable word-of-mouth publicity. Dissatisfied customers purchase from competitors.

3.   A "moment of truth," in a service industry, is the moment when a customer comes in contact, either directly (i.e. face-to-face, by telephone) or indirectly (i.e. by letter or fax), with an employee of the company. This is the make-or-break moment for customer satisfaction. Problems result from unkept promises, failure to provide full service, service not provided when needed, incorrectly or incompletely performed service, or failure to convey the correct information.

4.   *Expected quality* is true customer needs and expectations, that is, what the customer assumes will be received from the product. *Actual quality* is the outcome of the process

and what is delivered to the customer. *Perceived quality* is actual quality minus expected quality. If the amount of actual quality provided is equal to or more than the expected quality, the customer perceives positive satisfaction. If the amount of actual quality provided is less than the expected quality, the customer perceives negative or **dis**-satisfaction.

In the customer-driven quality cycle, (1.) expected quality is identified, and (2.) translated into product/service specifications (design quality) to produce (3.) output. Customer perceptions concerning the output (perceived quality) are then measured as being positive or negative, and necessary improvements are continually built into the first three steps of the process.

5.   The five leading practices of businesses that practice customer focused quality are:

1. They understand both near-term and longer-term customer needs and expectations (the voice of the customer) and employ systematic practices for gathering customer needs and managing the information.
2. They understand the linkages between the voice of the customer and design, production, and delivery processes.
3. They make commitments to customers that promote trust and confidence in their products and services.
4. They have effective customer relationship management processes by which customers can easily seek assistance, comment, complain, and receive prompt resolution of their concerns.
5. They measure customer satisfaction, compare the results relative to competitors, and use the information to evaluate and improve internal processes.

Samples of each of these can be found in the text.

6.   A company can expect to encounter external customers, which, as previously mentioned, may include both consumers and other companies within the "chain of customers," and internal customers, people or divisions within the company who receive products or services from suppliers within the company. If an organization remembers that its customers include both its employees and the public, then it consciously maintains a work environment conductive to the well-being and growth of all employees.

7.   In AT&T's customer-supplier model, Your Suppliers provide Inputs into Your Process. The Process then provides Outputs to Your Customers. The Customers provide Requirements & Feedback on Your Process, and you in turn provide Requirements & Feedback to Your Suppliers.

8.   Customers should be segmented because of and according to their different requirements and expectations. A company usually cannot satisfy all customers with the same products or services.

9.   The five key dimensions of quality in service industries are:

1. *Reliability*--The ability to provide what was promised, dependably and accurately.
2. *Assurance*--The knowledge and courtesy of employees, and their ability to convey trust and confidence.
3. *Tangibles*--The physical facilities and equipment, and the appearance of personnel.
4. *Empathy*--The degree of caring and individual attention provided to customers.
5. *Responsiveness*--The willingness to help customers and provide prompt service.

10.   Noriaki Kano, a Japanese professor, has suggested three classes of customer requirements:
a. *Dissatisfiers*--Requirements that are *expected* in a product or service. If these features are not present, the customer is dissatisfied.
b. *Satisfiers*--Requirements that customers say they want, but secretly do not expect. Fulfilling these requirements creates satisfaction.
c. *Exciters/delighters*--New or innovative features that customers do not expect. The presence of unexpected features leads to high perceptions of quality.

The focus, then, of quality management is to continually research and determine these requirements and develop them to their fullest extent.

11.   The major methods of gathering customer information include:

▪ *Comment cards and formal surveys*--These are easy ways to solicit information on customer satisfaction and perceptions of the importance of various quality dimensions. However, only a small percentage of customers regularly respond to such surveys.
▪ *Focus groups*--A focus group is a panel of individuals (customers or non-customers) who answer questions about a company's products and services as well as those of competitors. Focus groups offer a substantial advantage by providing the direct voice of the customer to an organization. A disadvantage of focus groups is their higher cost of implementation compared to other approaches.
▪ *Direct customer contact*--In customer-driven companies, top executives commonly visit with customers personally. This approach also works well with the rank-and-file employees.
▪ *Field intelligence*--Any employee who comes in direct contact with customers can obtain information simply by engaging in conversation, observing, and listening to customers. The effectiveness of this method depends on a culture that encourages open communications with superiors.
▪ *Study complaints*--These allow companies to learn about product failures and service problems. The downside, is that you hear of customer dissatisfaction only after the fact.

12.   Affinity diagrams and tree diagrams are used to organize customer requirements into logical categories. Teams use affinity diagrams to sift through large volumes of data, and identify key quality issues and their elements. Tree diagrams show hierarchical structures of facts and ideas, are used in designing implementation plans for projects.

13.   Extraordinary commitments are those that promise exceptional, uncompromising quality and customer satisfaction, and back that promise with a payout intended to fully recapture the customer's good will. Examples can be found within the text.

14.   *Service standards* are measurable performance levels or expectations that define the quality of customer contact. Service standards include technical standards such as response time, or behavioral standards. Companies need to communicate, continually reinforce, and implement a process for tracking employee adherence to service standards.

15.   Good customer relationship management depends on the quality of training of customer-contact personnel. Companies committed to customer relationship management ensure that customer-contact employees understand the products and services well enough to answer any question, develop good listening and problem recovery skills, and feel able to handle problems. Empowering employees allows them to make decisions on their own to satisfy customers, who dislike being transferred to a seemingly endless number of employees to obtain information or resolve a problem.

16.   By resolving complaints quickly, companies may retain a customer, and furthermore cut down negative word-of-mouth advertising about the problem. Complaints also provide a source of product and process improvement ideas.

17.   By measuring customer satisfaction, a company can learn how pleased or dissatisfied its customers are with products or services. It can discover customer perceptions of how well the business is doing in meeting customer needs, discover areas for improvement, and also track trends to determine if changes actually result in improvements.

18.   Typically, only firms that are more customer-sensitive than most recognize the need to analyze their customer satisfaction surveys to determine the relationship between *importance* and *performance* (the FP&L Quality in Practice incident is an excellent example). The concept simply recognizes that certain key quality characteristics are of major significance to customers, while others are of little or no interest. If companies do not perform well on the significant characteristics, customer perceive that the organization has poor quality, even if they perform exceptionally well on most other dimensions.

The classic story is told of an interdisciplinary operations research team consulting for a hotel. They studied its guests and the importance of various quality characteristics and found that guests were extremely sensitive to the amount of time that they had to wait for elevators. However, an anthropologist on the team who looked at the phenomenon pointed out that people were very concerned with their appearance. Therefore, the hotel installed mirrors in the elevator lobbies on all floors and complaints dropped dramatically even though the average waiting time did not change! This shows that *important* characteristics may be replaced in the customers' perception by more important characteristics, under certain conditions.

ANSWERS TO DISCUSSION QUESTIONS

1.   Until faced with a crisis, firms may fail to recognize the importance of customers for various reasons -- long running success in the marketplace, a dominant market share, seeing the product from an "internal" perspective, failure to train employees to be sensitive to customers, lack of in-depth knowledge of the product or the systems for producing it, and failure to heed warnings of quality declines or competitive threats.

2.   The answers will vary here, depending on students' perspectives. Some examples may be registering for classes; paying fees; coming in contact with advisors, food service, or housing personnel; and day-to-day contacts with professors in the classroom.

3.   This question should generate a great deal of discussion about who are the "customers" in a university setting. The customer-driven quality cycle may be seen as applying to anything from registration processes to program and course design.

4.   This question is a follow-on from the previous question. You may want to address the question in terms of how **you** or your **college** implements customer oriented practices in the classroom.

5.   This is a "hands on" exercise for the student.

6.   This question anticipates the "personal quality" case study in Chapter 11, which you may wish to read before assigning this question.

7.   Once again, the question of "who is a customer?" must be addressed. The publics with which a college or university interacts are important input for this discussion. They include students, employers, faculty, administrators, parents, the state and federal government, public and private organizations, and the general public.

8.   See Review Question 9, above, for the five key dimensions of service quality from which to begin discussion. Understanding the entire retail banking service system should be emphasized.

9.   See Review Question 10, above, for a definition from which to begin discussion.

10.   The answers will vary here, depending on students' perspectives.

11.   This is a "hands on" applied exercise for the student group.

ANSWERS TO CASE QUESTIONS

I. The Case of the Missing Reservation

1. Although it is difficult to speculate on the amount of "empowerment" that a restaurant hostess/manager might have, it is apparent that she did not attempt to "move heaven and earth to satisfy a customer" as employees are empowered to do at Ritz-Carlton. In this situation the manager might have seated Mark and Donna and their party and then made "back-up" plans, such as setting up another table for other guests who arrived a little later. She might also have provided some compensating factor, such as giving the party 25% off on their bill.

2. Different people have a higher and lower tolerance for poor service. Most people would not have taken the time to write and send a letter as Mark did. They would simply not return to the restaurant the following year. Once again, the response from the hotel was less than adequate. The letter was "delegated" to the "quality person,"indicating a lack of leadership and commitment of the hotel manager. The response letter was polite, but simply stated the facts without apology for any possible part of the mistake, and there was no offer of service, refund or other compensation for inconvenience.

II. Western America Airlines

1. An affinity diagram could be constructed by putting each of the customer service requirements on a 3" x 5" card and clustering items that were similar to each other under a category heading. Category headings might include: reservations, baggage handling, facilities and preflight service, aircraft, amenities, food service, and inflight service. See the diagram on the next page where customer service items are matched with categories.

2. Once the Affinity Diagram has been developed, the design of a customer survey questionnaire would be straight-forward. Sections could be included for each of the designated categories of: reservations, baggage handling, facilities and preflight service, aircraft, amenities, food service, and inflight service. Questions could be constructed on a scale of 1-7 or 1-10, with 1 = Very poor and 7 = Outstanding. For example, in baggage handling, the questions might include:

```
                                  Very
                                  Poor                        Outstanding
                                  1       2       3       4       5       6       7
Convenience of baggage check-in   +-------+-------+------+-------+-------+-------+


                                  1       2       3       4       5       6       7
Timely baggage claim on arrival   +-------+-------+------+-------+-------+-------+
```

	Very Poor						Outstanding
	1	2	3	4	5	6	7
Responsiveness/ability to solve problems & answer questions	+-------+-------+------+-------+-------+-------+						

	1	2	3	4	5	6	7
Overall quality of service provided	+-------+-------+------+-------+-------+-------+						

Note that questions on overall satisfaction might be appropriate for each of the categories. Also, questions about the courtesy of the service personnel might be appropriate in any category where there is face-to-face contact of employees with customers.

AFFINITY DIAGRAM FOR WESTERN AMERICA AIRLINES

Reservations

courteous reservation personnel

reservation calls answered promptly

correct explanation of fares and schedules

ability of reservation agents to answer questions

Baggage handling

convenient baggage check-in

timely baggage claim upon arrival

ability to solve baggage claim problems

Facilities and Preflight Service

timely & accurate communication of pre- boarding information

efficient ticket line & waiting procedures

convenient ground transportation

courteous, efficient gate personnel

efficient seat selection process

courteous, efficient sky cap

provide assistance for passengers with special needs

courtesy of ticket counter personnel

convenient parking close to terminal

Food Service

quality food

good beverage selection

sufficient quantity of food

Amenities

good selection magazines and newspapers

interesting Western American in-flight magazine

good variety of audio/visual programming

Aircraft

appealing interior appearance

seats in good condition

clean lavatories

Aircraft (Continued)

good quality audio/visual system

in-flight telephone access

comfortable seating and leg room

quality public address system in-flight

Inflight Service

ability to solve problems, answer questions in flight

efficient, attentive attendants

flight attendants with good attitudes

flight attendants know airline programs & policies

timely, accurate flight information (in-flight)

III. Valentine Laboratories

1. Key customers are patients who independently care for themselves at home and professionals who care for patients in a hospital/ambulatory setting. Other customers might include insurance companies and families of heart patients.

    Customer requirements include high reliability, no side effects or special drugs, ease of use for self-administration, portability, easy filter disposal and maintenance, (in certain markets) special ordering and distribution services, high levels of customer service, technical support, and education. The customer requirements and major process areas model suggests that the key product/service requirements are product quality, sales representation, training/education, and order/delivery. Product/service quality, price, and image all contribute to customer perceptions of value.

    Other critical success factors include meeting international and regulatory requirements, understanding different countries' reimbursement policies, and meeting the individual needs of different market segments.

2. Customer satisfaction is determined by third party measurement surveys and internal reports. Surveys are blind and include competitors to ensure objectivity and validity. Surveys focus on the **principal** market segment, the **secondary** segment, and **geographical** segments. Customer retention studies help to understand why competitors are chosen. Internally, Valentine uses customer focus groups, validation by sales management and customers, and external third party reviewers. Results are used to plan continuous improvement actions.

3. Valentine Laboratories has clearly identified the key attributes of customer satisfaction through its major process areas model. Regression analysis has determined that buying behavior is significantly related to the 52 attributes. Thus, understanding of customer requirements and their impact on the business is indeed based on factual data.

    The company uses multiple methods for understanding customer satisfaction. Third party surveys ensure a factual basis, particularly relative to competitors. The frequency of surveys suggest an on-going, systematic effort. Since all survey methods are focused on both customer segments and multiple geographic regions provides evidence that they are well deployed. However, it is not clear if the basic approach is reactionary or proactive, because issues sought in the various surveys, how all the data acquired are aggregated and compared to gain a consistent understanding of customer perceptions, and how it is used to improve products and services and the company direction have not been specified.

    Valentine Laboratories is focused on improvement and soundly evaluates its survey approaches down to individual process attributes. They attain a high level of refinement by expanding the number of MPAs, changing the rating scale and respondents. Monitoring customer dissatisfaction indicators provides another method of identifying improvements.

CHAPTER 6

Leadership and Strategic Planning

Teaching Notes

This chapter centers on leadership and planning as the basis of all managerial activities relating to total quality management. Leadership is the "driver" for an effective TQM focus. A basic understanding of leadership concepts and their importance is vital for manager and workers at every level in a TQM focused organization. Strategic planning and management has become more important in organizations that aspire to high quality levels, so leaders must understand how to "deploy" plans and quality efforts throughout the organization.

The Japanese approach planning in a much different way than we do it in the West. They may spend 60-70% of the total time related to a project on planning. This frequently allows them to perform the task in a relatively short period of time, with much less effort absorbed in correcting mistakes and redesigning products.

Students should be encouraged to focus on what to do, how to do it, when to do it, and how leadership must actively be involved in doing it as they look at strategic quality planning and management. Key objectives for this chapter should include:

• To define leadership as the right to exercise authority and the ability to achieve results from the people and systems under one's authority. Leaders create clear and visible quality values and integrate these into the organization's strategy.

• To discuss the five core leadership skills of: vision, empowerment, intuition, self-understanding, and value congruence.

• To study the five major perspectives from which leadership research has been developed: the trait approach, the behavioral view, the contingency approach, the role approach, and new perspectives such as transactional theory. These contemporary theories are based on contingency approaches, and include Fiedler's model, Vroom and Jago's model, and a variety of others.

• To emphasize that a critical role of leadership is strategic management. Strategy is the pattern of decisions that determines and reveals a company's goals, policies, and plans, and is determined through strategic planning.

• To define the process and content of planning for quality in organizations. Steps in strategy formulation begin with determining the organization's mission, vision, and guiding principles. These lead to goals and strategies that set the direction for achieving the mission.

• Key practices for effective strategic planning include active participation by both top management and lower-level employees, a strong customer focus, supplier involvement, and well-established measurement and feedback systems.

• Deploying strategy effectively is often done through a process called hoshin kanri, or policy deployment that emphasizes organization-wide planning and setting of priorities, providing resources to meet objectives, and measuring performance as a basis for improving it.

• The seven management and planning tools help managers to implement policy deployment and are useful in other areas of quality planning. These tools are the covered in the chapter.

ANSWERS TO QUALITY IN PRACTICE KEY ISSUES

Teaching the Buffalos to Fly: Johnsonville Foods

1.   Although the strategic management process at Johnsonville is not discussed in detail, it would appear that Stayer is setting the direction and cultural norms for the company, but he is relying on employees at all levels to do the day-to-day planning and control that is a vital part of strategy implementation. He is attuned to the need for a leader to help set the mission, vision and values of the organization, in order for strategic goals to mesh with the overall direction of the firm.

2.   Stayer's management style seems to be that of the *transformational leader* under the "emerging theory" category. He takes a long-term perspective, focuses on customers, promotes shared vision and values, works to stimulate the organization intellectually, invests in training, takes risks, and treats employees as individuals.

3.   The answer to whether other organizations could duplicate the leadership style of Stayer at Johnsonville Foods depends on the situation. The characteristics of Johnsonville's environment, leadership, and attitude of the led are unique. However, the general

characteristics of a *transformational leader* can be learned and practiced in other organizations and environmental settings. McGregor pointed out in his Theory X-Y approach that workers will usually respond in kind to the way in which they are treated. If leader assume that employees really feel that work is as natural as play, that they have a broad range of talents, and that they do not need to be coerced and controlled in order to achieve results, then workers will tend to take on more responsibility. If workers are not treated in that fashion then they will become dependent and rule-bound.

Leadership at Rubbermaid, Inc.

1. The mission and extremely detailed management principles seem to fit the basic requirements for a TQM focus, including customer focus, employee involvement and continuous improvement. The first and last of those TQM principles are included in the mission statement. The middle principle (employee involvement) is spelled out in the management principles under the sub-category of "**For our associates**."

2. Strong leadership helps to keep the company focused. The first item under the sub-category of "**For our associates**" is: "we will strive to have management lead by example." Obviously, when Gault met with the trucker on the trucker's schedule, that sent a message to managers and other employees in the company that he was serious about empowerment and quality.

3. Executive leadership contributes to the management principles in the various categories in the following ways:

    • Consumers - leaders must provide resources for the search for newer and value-added products and must take the lead in standing behind every product.

    • External customers - leaders must see that products are designed in a way that will meet the needs of the ultimate consumer so that they will provide viable markets which customers (wholesalers and retailers) can tap. In addition, customers must be listened to and heard and company policies must be set to benefit these direct customers.

    • Suppliers - long-term partnerships and objective, ethical dealing with suppliers is not possible without leadership from the top.

    • Associates - Gault set the example to managers in his treatment of the truck driver. Listening, learning, empowerment, and reward structures cannot be changed without the active involvement of leadership.

    • Communities and governments - communities and governments generally look to top management of an organization to be the "spokesperson" and "figurehead" for the firm, using Mintzberg's role terms. By acting ethically and being corporate good citizens, leaders can promote a positive image of the corporation in the community.

• Shareholders - it is interesting to note that the traditional shareholder interest in return on investment and timely communication of performance not mentioned until the last two items on the list. The earlier items cover development of human and wise use of other resources, as well as leadership depth and strategic direction. If executive leadership is to keep shareholders happy, shareholders must understand and support the long-term vision of managers **and** see the payoffs in the form of ROI and market share growth.

• Everyone - executive leadership, as stated earlier must set the tone and be an example if integrity and high ethical standards are to be upheld.

Strategic Quality Planning at the Stroh Brewery Company

1.   Stroh's customers are not specifically "spelled out," but it is assumed that they are distributors who sell the beer to retail chains and outlets. The consumer is the beer-drinking public, although a specific segment or geographical region is also missing from their mission and vision statements. (It is hinted at in the "national advertising," regional and national marketing, and future international marketing statements in their strategy).

Stroh puts growth, prosperity and a dynamic motivated "marketing" organization that meets the needs of its shareholders first in its Vision. However, meeting or exceeding the needs of their customers is the focus of their Mission.

2.   Together, Stroh's mission and values support customer focus (mission), employee involvement (values -- teamwork) and continuous improvement through the sharing of ideas among "employees, suppliers, wholesalers, and retailers."

ANSWERS TO REVIEW QUESTIONS

1.   *Leadership* is the right to exercise authority and the ability to achieve results from those people and systems under one's authority. Strong leadership is necessary to successfully implement a quality process. Leaders may seek to motivate employees and develop enthusiasm for quality with rhetoric, but taking strong, decisive, and personal action to implement quality changes makes a bigger impression on employees.

2.   The five core leadership skills exhibited by effective leaders, as described by Byrd, are *vision, empowerment, intuition, self-understanding,* and *value-congruence.*

Leaders are visionaries, anticipating and striving for the future, not reaching back into the past. They empower and encourage employees to participate in quality improvement efforts, and develop cross-functional teamwork and customer-supplier partnerships. They must be willing to follow their own intuition and make difficult decisions that will help the organization to be successful. They must be able to identify their own strengths and weaknesses, and understand their relationships with employees and within the organization. Value-congruence occurs when leaders integrate their basic assumptions and beliefs about the nature, mission, and relationships of the organization into the company's management system. Specifically, values include trust and respect for individuals, openness, teamwork, integrity, and commitment to quality.

3.   The leading practices of top managers in TQM-based operations include:

• Managers create a strategic vision and clear quality values--revolving around customers, both external and internal--that serve as a basis for business decisions at all levels of the organization.
• Managers set high expectations, and motivate employees to do things they (the employees) do not believe they can do.
• Managers demonstrate substantial personal commitment and involvement in quality, often in a missionary-like fashion. By "practicing what they preach," they serve as role models for the entire organization.
• Managers integrate quality values into daily leadership and management.
• Managers sustain an environment for quality excellence.

Examples of each can be found in the text.

4.   The five common perspectives from which leadership theory is studied are:

a) the trait approach--Involves discerning how to be a leader by examining the characteristics and methods of recognized leaders.

b) the behavioral approach--Attempts to determine the types of leadership behaviors that lead to successful task performance and employee satisfaction.

c) the contingency approach--Holds that there is no universal approach to leadership. Rather, effective leadership behavior depends on situational factors (i.e. who is leading, who is led, and what is the situation) that may change over time.

d) the role approach--Suggests that leaders perform certain roles as par to the situation.

e) emerging theories--Enhance or extend current theory by attempting to answer questions raised, but not answered, by traditional contingency approaches. For example, Attributional Theory states that leaders' judgement on how to deal with subordinates in a specific situation is based on their attributions of the internal or external causes of the behaviors of followers.

5.   Although a fully developed comparison of Fiedler's theory with the Vroom-Jago model is beyond the limited scope of the summary in this text, it can be said that Fiedler's model focuses on the characteristics of the leader, the led and the situation, with an emphasis on the *situational* factors that result in effective leadership. Vroom and Jago's model is focused on the *decision-making* situation, not the characteristics of the leader and led in the situation. Thus a) the quality of the decision, b) the degree of acceptance of the decision, and c) the time frame within which the decision must be made are key variables for the Vroom-Jago model.

6.   Transformational Leadership Theory explains the impact of leadership in a TQM environment. According to this model, leaders adopt many of the skills and practices discussed in Questions 2 and 3. They take a long-term perspective, focus on customers, promote a shared vision and values, work to stimulate their organizations intellectually, invest in training, take some risks, and treat employees as individuals.

7.   A strategy is a pattern or plan that integrates an organization's major goals, policies, and action sequences into a cohesive whole. Formal strategies contain three elements:

   1. Goals to be achieved.
   2. Policies that guide or limit action.
   3. Action sequences, or programs, that accomplish the goals.

8.   Strategy-making (to paraphrase Mintzberg) is the process of capturing the insights of managers based on hard and soft data and synthesizing it into a vision of the direction which the business should pursue. Thus *strategic quality planning* is a systematic approach to setting quality goals. Planning for quality management requires an understanding of the importance of quality and the need for awareness of the total quality concept -- quality of design and conformance -- as well as an understanding of the planning process. Planning sets the direction and tone for future quality-related activities. *Strategic quality planning* should become synonymous with *strategic business planning* because more and more companies are finding that quality drives financial and marketing success.

9.   The leading practices for effective strategic planning include:

   • Top management and employees all actively participate in the planning process.
   • They use customer wants and needs to drive the strategy.
   • They involve suppliers in the strategic planning process.
   • They have well-established feedback systems for continuous measurement and re-evaluation of the planning process.

10.   The vision statement is a statement of guiding values, principles, and direction of expected growth of an organization or some segment of it, and is generally developed by key managers and others who are responsible for planning and carrying out that vision. Vision statements may be developed at any level within the organizational hierarchy from

top to bottom. This is a very worthwhile activity, as long as the statements are coordinated so as to fit with those of the next higher level and the overall organization's vision.

The purpose, or mission, of the organization is a statement of "why the organization is in business." In the past, the purpose of the organization was frequently stated in terms of products or services produced or profitability to stockholders. TQM-focused firms are now stating their purpose in terms of their customer focus and their commitment to strive for higher levels of quality.

Values, or guiding principles, guide the journey to that vision by defining attitudes and policies for all employees, which are reinforced through conscious and subconscious behavior at all levels of the organization. The mission, vision, and guiding principles serve as the foundation for strategic planning. They must be articulated by top management and others who lead, especially the CEO. They also have to be transmitted, practiced, and reinforced through symbolic and real action before they become "real" to the employees, and the people, groups, and organizations in the external environment that do business with the firm.

11.   The steps in the planning process are shown in Figure 6.2. Once the company's mission, vision, and guiding principles have ben determined, the organization must assess the gap as to where it is now, and where it wants to be as described in its vision. Using this assessment, it must then develop goals, strategies, and objectives that will enable it to bridge this gap.

12.   Key business factors include:

   • the nature of a company's products and services, its principle customers, major markets, and key customer quality requirements
   • position in market and competitive environment
   • facilities and technologies
   • suppliers
   • other factors, such as the regulatory environment, industry changes, etc.

Key business drivers, those strategic elements of a business that drive the major elements of the quality system (i.e. strategic planning) must be developed in consistency with these factors.

13.   *Hoshin kanri,* known as *policy deployment* or *management by planning* in the U.S.A., is the Japanese process of deploying management strategy. Companies have various definitions for policy deployment. They all emphasize organization-wide planning, setting priorities, providing resources to meet objectives, and measuring performance as a basis for improving performance. Essentially, it is a TQ-based approach to executing a strategy.

14.   *Catchball* is the term for the negotiating process used within an organization to determine long- and short-term quality objectives. Leaders communicate mid-term objectives and measures to middle-managers who develop short-term objectives and recommend necessary resources, targets, and roles/responsibilities. Catchball is not an autocratic, top-down management style. It marshals the collective expertise of the whole organization and results in realistic and achievable objectives that do not conflict.

15.   Policy deployment is a planning and implementation method that ties improvement activities to long-term strategies of the organization. It is driven by data, supported by documentation, emphasizes company-wide planning, and includes setting of priorities for improvement. It is somewhat similar to MBO, but has a different focus. First, MBO focuses on the performance of the individual employee, while policy deployment focuses on the organization as a whole. Objectives in MBO are tied to performance evaluation and rewards. Second, MBO objectives do not support the company's objectives, but are set independently. Third, the focus of MBO is as a control mechanism between supervisors and subordinates. Fourth, MBO objectives usually are not emphasized in daily work, but are brought out only at performance review time.

16.   The seven management and planning tools include:

1. *Affinity diagrams*--This is a tool for organizing a large number of ideas, opinions, and facts relating to a broad problem or subject area, i.e. a vision statement.
2. *Interrelationship digraphs*--Identifies and explores casual relationships among related concepts or ideas. It shows that every idea can be logically linked with more than one idea at a time, and allows for "lateral thinking" rather than "linear thinking."
3. *Tree diagram*--Maps out the paths and tasks necessary to complete a specific project or reach a specified goal.
4. *Matrix diagrams*--These are "spreadsheets" that graphically display relationships between ideas, activities, or other dimensions in such a way as to provide logical connecting points between each item.
5. *Matrix data analysis*--Takes data and arranges it to display quantitative relationships among variables to make them more easily understood and analyzed.
6. *Process decision program chart*--A method for mapping out every conceivable event and contingency that can occur when moving from a problem statement to possible solutions.
7. *Arrow diagrams*-- Arrow diagrams are another name for PERT/CPM project planning diagrams. Students who have had a basic operations management course may be familiar with the term *network diagrams* for project planning and scheduling.

ANSWERS TO DISCUSSION QUESTIONS

1.   By saying that leadership is the "driver," we try to emphasize the critical nature of leadership at every level for successful TQM. The answer to Review Question 3, above, elaborates on the practices of top managers in leading TQM focused organizations.

Without strong commitment of leaders at every level, a TQM system may not survive, and it certainly will not grow and flourish.

2.   See Review Question 2, above as a basis for developing the answer to this question.

3.   Answers will vary, depending on the experiences of the students.

4.   See Review Question 4, above as a basis for developing the answer to this question.

5.   Deming demanded that leadership play a consistent role as the "driver" of quality in every organization. All of his 14 Points were addressed to top management. Points 1, 2, 7, 9, 11b, and 14 were specific to top management practices, leadership, and corporate action. All of the other points pointed out how managers must change the systems and the organizational culture in order to encourage and permit a change to a total quality organization.

6.   The answer to this question will require that students "go beyond" the textbook and research the Fiedler model, in detail. A principles of management or organizational behavior text will have Fiedler's "Model of the Effects of Leadership Styles on Leader Performance According to Situational Conditions" and sufficient detail for this answer. Although Fiedler's situational model is not discussed in detail in the chapter, other sources show that the "situational conditions" consist of the leader (called the "leader position power" variable by Fiedler), the led (called the "leader-member relations" variable), and the situation (called "task structure"). Because tasks become less structured in a TQM environment (in contrast to rigid, highly structured tasks in traditional organizations), leader position power is weakened (the first line employees are "empowered"), but leader-member relations are typically good (due to high quality communications and shared commitment). Thus, a "relationship-oriented" leader is better qualified than a "task-oriented leader" in this situation.

7.   The mission statement of an organization (or an individual) defines the reason for its existence and answers the question "Why are we in business?". Vision tells the direction in which the organization (or person) intends to move and addresses the question of what the organization should plan for. Values, or guiding principles, guide the journey and tell what the organization (or person) stands for -- e.g. what are their important beliefs and attitudes? The mission, vision and values statements should address the anticipated quality that the organization (individual) will strive to attain, how it (the person) plans to reach it, and how it (the person) will behave during the journey. Several of Stephen Covey's books provide individual mission statements that students may wish to review.

8.   Xerox used its Leadership Through Quality strategy as a focal point for major changes in organizational quality. To ensure that managers (leaders) "got the message" of the importance of quality Xerox redefined its promotion standards to ensure that managers supported and demonstrated quality in order to be promoted.

9.   This is a "hands on" library exercise for the student.

10.   The criteria developed by the MBNQA committee as a standard against which to measure award applicants can provide a guide to improving the planning processes of many organizations. As will be pointed out in a later chapter, the section in the award criteria on Strategic Quality Planning examines: (1) the company's planning process for achieving or retaining quality leadership; (2) how the company integrates quality improvement planning into overall business planning; and (3) the company's short-term and longer-term plans to achieve and/or sustain a quality leadership position. The impact of these requirements is four-fold and incorporates the elements of the planning process presented earlier in Figure 6.3. It requires that strategic thinking be done about: (1) the <u>mission, vision, and purpose</u>, represented by goals for quality leadership that must be set by the organization; (2) the level of competition in the <u>environment</u>, and how to exceed the quality levels of competitors in order to be a "world class" producer; (3) how to <u>take action steps</u> to develop data, information, and analysis (<u>control systems</u>) for <u>evaluating</u> customer requirements, process capabilities, competitor and benchmark data, and supplier capability to meet <u>objectives</u> contained in goal-based plans; and (4) how to evaluate and improve goal-setting and strategic planning processes, themselves.

11.   This mini-project can help students to understand the importance of planning as a significant component of total quality management.

12.   Most colleges and universities now have a mission statement and strategy. It will be interesting to determine if they have a *policy deployment* process in place. See the next chapter for details on this process.

13.   a. The first statement is a vague, general statement that will be of little use to the organization.
        b. The second statement is more specific than the first, although it is also very general in tone.
        c. The third statement is the most specific and is a customer focused vision of the future state of the firm; it specifies the customers, including employees, shareowners and communities in which the organization does business. It would need to be even more specific in order to be operationalized.

14.   This is a "hands on" exercise for the student.

ANSWERS TO CASE QUESTIONS

I. Corryville Foundry Company

1.   The current mission statement of Corryville Foundry appears to lack focus. It doesn't tell why the company is in business, other than to "improve return on investment." Therefore, it is not adequate to provide the strategic direction necessary for CFC to move forward. Using this mission statement CFC could be making light bulbs or personal computers rather than castings.

2.   The mission statement could be improved by including a definition of products or services, types of markets, important customer needs, or distinctive competencies. The mission statement might be:

> CFC's mission is to produce superior customized cast metal products for markets in the midwestern United States using teamwork and unique advanced technology in order to meet or exceed customer requirements, while still providing an above average return to our shareholders.

Their vision might be:

> CFC's vision is to be an outstanding company that leads the industry in quality, technological innovations, service, and productivity. We will strive to accomplish our vision by embracing superior customer focus, flexibility, adaptability, innovation, employee involvement and teamwork, with a constant awareness that productivity, cost effectiveness, and competitive pricing are vital to business profitability and success.

Their values seem to be:

- Quality and service using a Deming philosophy
- Teamwork
- Financial accountability
- Competitiveness
- Pride in workmanship

II. Blue Genes Corporation

In general, this case presents examples of effective approaches to strategic planning and deployment, but is rather thin on providing specific information as to how these approaches are implemented. Discussion should focus on these issues. Students might explore alternative approaches that might be more effective. The instructor might challenge the students to come up with more effective approaches. Insight can be gained by examining the Strategic Planning category in the Baldrige criteria.

1.   Blue Genes' Quality Planning Process revolves around customer focused strategy teams and capability focused strategy teams to help prioritize and focus customer needs in developing strategies. A matrix representation shows the interaction of these two types of teams in the planning process. Key inputs include company challenges, lead signs, and key quality requirements, as well as the company mission statement, quality definition and strategic intent. The long term strategies lead to short term tactical quality plans which are aligned through measurements and key indicators. Feedback provides a means to improve the process. Apparently, there is a high level of employee involvement in the process at all levels of the organization.

   a. Customer requirements are identified by New Product Committees and Research and Development. Senior scientists and consulting firms provide information to project future industry capabilities that may benefit customers. However, there is little information about how customer requirements are determined. The roles of the New Product and R&D Committees are not described. Thus, it is not clear how effective these approaches are.

   b. Competitive product evaluations and industry forums provide information about the competitive environment, which are communicated to appropriate strategy teams and management by Market Research and Competitive Assessment groups. However, the company does not seem to proactively anticipate future competitive issues.

   c. Financial and market risks are evaluated through contingency planning and multi-path development and by cost/benefit and make/buy analyses. Customer focused teams review products and processes to verify fit with company capabilities. No information is provided on how Blue Genes considers societal risk or how risk reviews are conducted. This precludes understanding how effective the approaches really are.

   d. Capability Focused Teams ensure consideration of company resources during the planning process, for example, by matching needed human resource needs with available skills. However, specific information on the approaches used is not provided, and it is not clear that this approach is consistently deployed throughout the company.

   e. Each Strategy Team analyzes supplier capabilities needed to support their activities. Teams include representatives of critical suppliers. This help ensure that supplier capabilities are indeed available.

2.   Operational performance improvement is addressed in two ways: by reengineering work processes to improve customer focus, and by improving productivity, cycle time, and waste reduction. It is unclear how these activities are integrated into the planning process other than brainstorming sessions, how resources are allocated to achieve improvements, or how reengineering activities are tied to customer requirements.

3.   Involving many individuals and units in the planning process paves the way for smoother deployment of plans. All managers are involved, and top managers hold small group

meetings to include every employee to obtain feedback. Communication to suppliers is accomplished in various ways. The key method of deployment is the translation of SQP to TQP via individual goals and measurements. This helps to ensure alignment throughout various levels in the company. Apparently there is ongoing of commitment of resources to the SQP, however, it is not clear how lower-level resources are committed.

4.   This is an area to which few companies pay much attention. Usually, an approach remains static for some time. A TQM philosophy focuses on constant improvement of all processes. In this area, Blue Genes conducts an appraisal of its planning process that includes all participants in strategy teams and individual satisfaction levels. This information is evaluated by the QPP facilitation team. Several examples of improvements in the process and its overall level of sophistication suggest that the approach to evaluation and improvement has been effectively used for some time.

CHAPTER 7

Quality in Product and
Process Design

Teaching Notes

This chapter investigates the concepts and techniques used to design products and services to meet customer needs. As a quality concept, design is a "rising star," because managers and people in key quality positions in organizations are just beginning to appreciate the importance and competitive power of high design quality. In this chapter we present some "hair-raising" adventures that center on both good and bad designs. These examples and "stories" should prove to be exciting to students. A good video clip that could be shown with this chapter is the "In Search of Excellence" segment on 3M Corporation, a company that has a "world class" reputation for fostering design and innovation "champions." Key objectives for this chapter should include:

• To introduce the concepts of quality of design and quality of conformance in production, which determine the ultimate performance, reliability, and value of a product. Product and process design must be coordinated to ensure a quality product.

• To explore the product development process consisting of idea generation, preliminary concept development, product/process development, full-scale production, product introduction, and market evaluation.

• To review several leading practices in closely coordinated and highly effective product design and development processes.

• To consider the advantages and results of simplifying designs and a key concept of design for manufacturability.

• To introduce three new design directions - the internal need for design for manufacturability, the environmentally conscious need to "design for disassembly" and the need to be legally aware of the impact of design practice in order to avoid legal liability for design failures. Genichi Taguchi's definition of quality as the loss that a product causes to society after being shipped has been used to demonstrate the economic value of meeting nominal specifications rather than simply staying within tolerances and can be tied into environmental concerns.

• To discuss how and why customers and engineers/designers speak different languages. Quality function deployment (QFD) is a technique to ensure that the voice of the customer is carried through the design and production process, and the major planning document in QFD (the House of Quality) can provide a planning structure for relating customers' needs to technical specifications.

• To explore the differences in approach required in designing services, such as consideration of physical facilities, processes, and procedures; behavior; and professional judgment.

• To understand how design reviews, value analysis/value engineering, and concurrent engineering enhance the project management capabilities of multifunctional teams and help to remove organizational barriers between departments, thus reducing product development time.

ANSWERS TO QUALITY IN PRACTICE KEY ISSUES

Quality Function Deployment at Digital Equipment

1.   DEC developed an automated purchasing system for non-computer literate customers by using a modified form of the QFD process. They first anticipated the voice of the customer by brainstorming a set of ideas for service. They then questioned potential customers about these ideas and asked them to add their own. They developed a matrix, but did not use the typical QFD weighting exercise to assess the importance of the customer attributes to their matching counterpart characteristics. The second house of quality consisted of determining high-level design features for each function that had been specified. It included distribution channels, pricing, selling service and hardware, as well as the software design. The third house of quality involved the need to resolve alternative design issues. Here they looked at alternatives for the technology, procedures, and methods used to create the product. These might include such features as pointing devices such as mice, cursors, touch screens, etc. The fourth house of quality matched the technology, methods, and procedures with people, time, equipment, building facilities, and money needed to complete the project. A prototype was developed and test-marketed to allow assessment of the other three houses before the fourth house was completed. Many of the similarities and differences of DEC's QFD process to the traditional theory were pointed out above. Essentially, they attempted to "streamline" the process in order to do concurrent engineering of the product (actually, a service with technological capabilities), and they took into account the many "intangible" factors of the process inherent in software design.

2. It may <u>appear</u> that marketing's role has been eliminated, but it could simply have been translated into another form. If the engineers are to do traditional marketing work of performing surveys, prototype testing, and developing advertising, they must either be cross-trained to do these functions themselves, or they must bring marketing people into their area to assist in the process of effectively performing them.

ANSWERS TO REVIEW QUESTIONS

1. Product design and development consists of idea generation, initial screening and economic analysis, preliminary product design and development, prototype testing, final product design, pilot runs and release to production.

2. Nominal specifications are the ideal specifications or the target values which manufacturing seeks to meet in a product. Tolerances are the permissible variations in a dimension or other quality characteristics of a product, and are based on the difficulty of consistently meeting a targeted quality level in a product specification.

3. It is extremely important to try and reduce the leadtime between idea generation and release to production, because competition is doing so, and thus the competitive edge is gained or lost in the so-called time-to-market of products and services. The problems incurred in speeding up the process are well known. If done too hastily, the result will be the need to revise or scrap the design, cost increases or project over-runs, difficulty in manufacturing the product, early product failure in the field, customer dissatisfaction, and/or lawsuits due to product liability.

4. The key practices that organizations employ for efficient and effective product development include the following:

    □ They address all product and service quality requirements early in the design process, taking into account cost and manufacturability, supplier requirements, and legal and environmental issues.
    □ They ensure that quality is built into products and services and use appropriate engineering and statistical tools and approaches during the development process.
    □ They fully understand customer requirements and translate them into product and service design requirements.
    □ They develop linkages between product design requirements and process requirements.
    □ They manage the product development process to enhance cross-functional communication and reduce product development time.

5. Traditional products, such as hand tools, and hydraulic pumps require less sophisticated processes and procedures than do "modern" products, such as "high tech" multi-geared bicycles, semiconductors and fighter aircraft. Some characteristics related to traditional products include: simplicity, low precision, limited need for interchangeability, used in

a natural environment, long life of new designs, largely designed on empirical science, usually low volume production, and cause of field failures usually due to manufacturing errors. Some parallel characteristics related to modern products are: complex, dynamic products (not simple), high precision, extensive need for interchangeability, used in an unnatural environment, short life of new designs, product usually designed on a highly scientific (rather than empirical) basis, often high volume of products produced, and field failure usually due to design weakness.

6..   Management considerations in design are related to technical considerations, but revolve around the strategic variables of production and sales. Management is vitally interested in cost factors, time-to-market, manufacturability, quality, environmental (design for disassembly, for example), and product liability issues. Technical concerns include systems design, parameter design, robustness of design, tolerance design, and losses from the process due to failure to center on design specifications (such as suggested by the Taguchi Loss Function).

7.   The concept of design for manufacturability is the process of designing a product so that it can be produced efficiently at the highest level of quality. Its goal is to improve quality, increase productivity, reduce lead time (time to market, as well as manufacturing time) and maintain flexibility to adapt to future market conditions.

8.   Key design practices include: 1) analyze all design requirements to assess proper dimensions and tolerances, determine process capability, identify and evaluate possible manufacturing quality problems, select manufacturing processes that minimize technical risks, and evaluate processes under actual manufacturing conditions.

9.   Product liability should be of concern because of the damage that hazardous designs can do to consumers of the product, first. Also, liability lawsuits can do major damage to the financial health of an organization, as well as its image and reputation in the marketplace. Records and documentation relating to the design process are the best defense against liability lawsuits. These would include records on prototype development, testing, and inspection results.

10.   Design for disassembly has become an important concept because of concern for the environment. Students should be encouraged to look for examples in the popular press, although they will have to have "sharp eyes" since this is being stress in more environmentally conscious countries, such as Germany, more than in the U.S.

11.   Genichi Taguchi proposed three principle tools for quality engineering -- system design, parameter design, and tolerance design. System design relates to the process of applying scientific and engineering knowledge to produce a basic functional design. It involves a search for the best available technology, considering functional influences, technological influences, and economics of production. Parameter design looks at the way that performance of the product is affected by manufacturing imperfections, environmental

factors, and human variations in operating the product. Tolerance design is the process of determining tolerances around the nominal settings identified by parameter design.

12.   Although Taguchi methods are used as a part of all three of the above principle tools, they have widest application in the <u>parameter design</u> tool area. Taguchi proposed the use of statistically designed experiments for use in designing parameters appropriately. He simplified the experimental design process to concentrate on critical factors, while de-emphasizing their interactions, thus reducing the number of required experiments. Parameter design experiments are aimed at reducing variability caused by manufacturing variations, as opposed to the traditional focus on optimizing the mean value of a particular characteristic.

13.   Signal to noise ratio is a concept that Taguchi adapted from electrical engineering that measures the sensitivity of the effect (the signal) to the noise factors.The signal is measured by a mean value and the variability of the signal is the noise. The S/N ratio is equivalent of the ratio of the mean to the standard deviation. It incorporates the controllable and uncontrollable factors. High signal to noise ratios mean that the sensitivity to noise factors is low.

14.   Taguchi defines quality in economic terms as the avoidance of "loss a product causes to society after being shipped, other than any losses causes by its intrinsic functions." These include 1) failure to meet customer expectations, 2) failure to meet performance characteristics, and 3) harmful side effects caused by the product. He proposes measuring these losses in monetary units and relating them to quantifiable characteristics.

15.   The Taguchi loss function differs from the traditional loss function that is based on specifications and tolerances since it shows that losses begin as soon as the actual value obtained from a process begins to move away from the target specification. (Refer to Figures 7.3 and 7.4). A process may be operating well within specification limits, but losses will be incurred unless the process can be made 100% accurate. The traditional loss function only recognizes losses that are incurred for product units that fall outside of specifications. This is often referred to as the "goalpost mentality."

16.   The Japanese have developed the concept of *quality function deployment* (QFD) to ensure that customers' requirements are met throughout the design process, and also in the design of production systems.   QFD is basically a philosophy and a set of planning and communication tools that focuses on customer requirements in coordinating the design, manufacturing, and marketing of goods.

17.   A major benefit of QFD is improved communication and teamwork between all areas in the production process, such as between marketing and design, between design and manufacturing, and between purchasing and suppliers.   Product objectives are not misunderstood or misinterpreted during the production process. QFD helps to determine the causes of customer dissatisfaction, and is a useful tool for competitive analysis of

product quality by top management. Productivity improvements also result, the time for new product development is significantly reduced. QFD allows companies to simulate the effects of new design ideas. This allows them to bring new products into the market sooner and gain competitive advantage.

18. The QFD process requires that the "voice of the customer" be probed. *Customer attributes* must be defined. These are the needs and desires that fall into the dissatisfier, satisfier, and delighter categories. Second, *counterpart characteristics* must be identified. The next step is to relate the *counterpart characteristics*, which are the technical specifications required to translate the voice of the customer into technical language, to the *customer attributes*. Then competing products should be evaluated to determine how they measure up to the customers' needs and your own technical specifications. The last two steps are to evaluate characteristics in order to develop targets for product design or improvement, and to decide which counterpart characteristics to deploy in the remainder of the production process. Although one functional group may take the lead in developing each step of the process, **all** groups should be involved in every step of building the House of Quality. For example, the initial phase of assessing customer attributes may be developed by marketing research personnel, but unless engineering personnel are in on the design of the interview/questionnaire effort, critical questions may not be asked. Once prototype models are developed, customers should be surveyed to determine if they like or dislike the way that various features have been designed.

19. Process planning is similar to product planning and must be done concurrently with product development. To design a production process, engineers must analyze the product, select appropriate technology, select specific production processes, select equipment and lay out the production or service facility. These steps are similar to the product design sequence listed in question 1, above. Today, design engineers and planners must "build in" quality considerations into the process, as well as into the product.

20. An economic optimum level of quality is based on the mistaken concept that quality increases production costs. The traditional economic "trade-off" theory of quality holds that increasing the cost of quality assurance activities (such as inspection and prevention costs) results in decreasing the cost of non-conformance (such as rework, repair and warranty costs) and total quality costs, up to a point. Beyond the theoretical "optimum" the total cost of quality begins to rise again as diminishing returns are encountered. Increasing quality assurance costs are incurred to bring about smaller and smaller increases in the quality level. The Japanese have a different theory that causes them to stress "the modern view", explained in Question 4, above. They believe that the increased emphasis on prevention and continuous improvement will allow the total cost of quality to fall lower and lower as 100% conformity of products is approached.

21. The Japanese concept of Zero Quality Control is based on three principles of:
    a. Source inspection - checking for factors that cause errors, not looking for defects "after the fact."

b. 100% inspection made possible through poka-yoke (mistake proofing).

c. Immediate action - operations are stopped when a defect or error is discovered and are not re-started until the source of the mistake is corrected.

22.   Poka-yoke is a technique for avoiding human error at work. It is based on the concepts of prediction -- recognizing that a defect is about to, or might occur -- and detection -- realizing that the defect has occurred. There are numerous examples of the use of poka-yoke type designs, especially in the workplace. For example, punch press operators typically wear safety cords connected to wrist bands. If they don't move their hands away when to press is descending, the cords will pull their hands back, automatically.

23.   Design of services may use some of the same processes and concepts as are used in manufacturing, but the nature of the "service product" is different. Services include physical facilities, processes and procedures. They must take into account people's behavior and professional judgment. Too much or too little emphasis on processes, procedures, behavior or judgement may result in a perception of poor quality. The design can be approached using the three dimensional classification scheme presented in the Haywood-Farmer model discussed in the chapter. The three factors of "degree of customer contact and interaction," "degree of labor intensity," and degree of customization" must be considered and balanced accordingly.

24.   The concept of backward chaining involves starting with outputs--customer requirements-- and moving backward through the production process to identify the key steps needed to produce each output, stopping when the process reaches the supplier input stage.

25.   Poka-yoke in services is a new and exciting concept. For example, banks will now routinely ask that customers send them a verification form indicating that the customer has received the card in the mail. If the form is not received within the allotted time period, they assume that the card was probably stolen, and follow up to see if that was the case. Similar follow-ups are being done by department stores when appliances are installed. Customers are called to verify that the installation was done satisfactorily. A final example is in the design of ATM machines that will only accept a credit card that is inserted with the magnetic strip down. Some banks even put a reminder on the machine to keep the customer from making a mistake.

26.   Design reviews are intended to ensure that all important design objectives have been taken into account during the design process. It is supposed to stimulate discussion, raise questions, and generate new ideas and solutions to problems.

Preliminary, intermediate, and final design reviews are typically held at various stages of the design project. The categories of issues considered includes: 1) function of the product, including: conformance to customer requirements, completeness of specifications, manufacturing costs, and process capability; 2) value and appearance; 3 marketing considerations; 4) make or buy decisions; 5) environmental conditions and product testing;

6) reliability requirements, including testing plans and liability issues; 7) engineering documentation; and 8) scheduling of the design and development process.

27.   *Value engineering* and *value analysis* are tools used by quality engineers to analyze every function of every component of a product system or service to determine how that function can be accomplished most economically without degrading the quality of the product or service. Value engineering comes first, because it is used to avoid costs by looking at the product or service before production begins. Value analysis is used for cost reduction during production.

28.   *Concurrent engineering* is also called *simultaneous engineering*. It is the process in which all major functions involved in getting a product to market are continuously involved with the product development form conception through sales. It typically involves teams of from 4 to 20 people including every specialty in the company. The teams are charged with the responsibility of determining the character of the product, analyzing product functions, performing a design for manufacturability study to determine if the design can be improved, designing an assembly sequence, process and methods; and designing a factory system that fully involves workers in production strategy to attain low inventory and integration with vendor's methods and capabilities.

ANSWERS TO DISCUSSION QUESTIONS

1.   One of the authors was actually involved in this type of process at both the program level and the course level. He attempted, with some success, to use TQM principles and tools in the design process. The process should begin with customer needs and expectations (expected quality), and end with what the customer sees and believes the quality of the product to be (perceived quality). Expected quality is what the customer assumes will be received from the product as a reflection of the customer's needs. Perceived quality is the customer's measure of satisfaction in the product, the "feel" for its quality. Between these two extremes, the product is in the hands of the producer.

The first task of the producer (university administrators and faculty) is to identify customer needs and expectations. The university must focus on the key dimensions that are reflected in specific customer needs. If these expectations are not identified correctly or are misinterpreted, then the final product will not be perceived to be of high quality by customers. A university has two primary customers (and many other customer groups). The primary customers are the students and the employers of graduates.

Technical requirements determine the design quality of the product. Process (or course) designers' perceptions of customers' needs can often differ from their actual needs. For instance, the "average" customer might need course content that is general enough for use in any organization. A "design" decision might be made in a computer course to teach Fortran, rather than a common spreadsheet program. If the intent is to prepare business (not engineering) students to work in business organizations, then the "product (student who graduates)" may be said to "fail prematurely" under normal use. If course designers never have an opportunity to interact with customers (employers), the probability that they will not understand or misinterpret the expected quality is greatly increased.

Next, product designs are transferred to people or organizational units responsible for delivering the service. Poor attention to customer needs can affect the perceived quality. For example, if the system is not designed to assure conformance to the technical specifications, then the actual quality produced may not be the same as the design quality. The fundamental equation that relates these different levels of quality is: perceived quality = actual quality - expected quality.

3.   This exercise is designed to further students' awareness of the breadth of the "quality movement" and help them confirm that the theory of quality is being applied in a practical setting in business and industry.

4.   Customer attributes and technical requirements might be:

Attributes	Technical Requirements

a. Coffee:

Attributes	Technical Requirements
Flavor	Grind - flake, coarse, or fine
Smell	Roasting
Color	conditions
Ease of use	Packaging
Value	Price/size

b. Cooler:

Attributes	Technical Requirements
Size	Capacity
Weight	Material
Durability	Strength
Price	Manufacturing
Features	costs

c. Registration:

Attributes	Technical Requirements
Convenience	Time, dates, methods
Speed	Process standards
Costs	Fees
Accuracy	Error prevention

Construction of the matrix is left to the student.

5.   This is a "hands on" exercise for the student groups.

6.   This is a "hands on" homework exercise for the student.

7.   Answers will vary, depending on the experience of the students.

8.   Answers will vary, depending on the experience and interests of the students.

9.   Traditionally, there have been high "walls" built between design engineers and manufacturing engineers. In fact, in many companies, there is a saying that Design develops the product requirements and "throws the new design over the wall" for Manufacturing to make. The implication is that neither side has wanted to talk to, or cooperate with, the other. Quality assurance personnel may be able to "bridge the gap" or "tear down the walls" between these groups by focusing on the needs of the organization to design a product with the customer in mind, where the customer can be seen as the immediate group (Manufacturing) by the design engineers, as well as the ultimate customers or consumers of the finished product.

10. a) Legal Sea Foods designs their process to include major steps of: 1) Supplier specifications (fresh, local products from government certified beds) carefully monitored. 2) Closely controlled initial processing (cutting and filleting in an environmentally controlled facility with an in-house microbiology laboratory) that assures high quality raw materials. 3) Acceptance and in-process inspections (total of eight) that are consistently performed. 4) Customer-focused order taking and processing (cooked to order and delivered individually) using teamwork to assure freshness at the customers' tables.

   b) Legal Sea Foods would probably fall in Block 7 or 8 on the three dimensional classification of service. It would certainly **not** be in Block 6 with the fast food services!

   c) The list of customer requirements from which a House of Quality could be constructed might include: 1) Taste (flavor, texture); 2) Visual appeal (appearance, portions); 3) Health factors (nutrition, calories); 4) Service (knowledge, attentiveness, appearance, friendliness, timing); 5) Value (competitive price, perceived quality/price relationship).

SOLUTIONS TO PROBLEMS

1.   The Taguchi Loss Function is: $L(x) = k (x - T)^2$

   $\$3 = k (0.009)^2$
   $k = 37,037.$

   $\therefore L(x) = k (x - T)^2 = 37037 (x - T)^2$

2.   For a specification of 75 ± 5 mv:

  a) $L(x) = k (x - T)^2$
      $\$300 = k (5)^2$
      $k = 12$

  b) $EL(x) = k (\sigma^2 + D^2) = 12 (2^2 + 0^2) = \$48$

3.   For a specification of $2.000 \pm .002$ mm and a $4 scrap cost:

$\overline{x} = 2.00008; \quad D = 2.00008 - 2.00 = 0.00008$
$\sigma = 0.00104$

  a) $L(x) = k (x - T)^2$
     $\$4 = k (0.002)^2 ; \quad$ Therefore, $k = 1,000,000$

  b) $EL(x) = k (\sigma^2 + D^2) = 1,000,000 (0.00104^2 + 0.00008^2) = \$1.088$

4.   (This problem requires the use of concepts of calculus.)

$I = [p - C(q) - m] D(q)$

Therefore: $dI/dq = [p - C(q) - m]D'(q) - D(q)C'(q) = 0$

For the firm to remain in business, $p - C(q) - m$ must be greater than 0. Given this, at the point where $Di/dq = 0$, we must have $C'(q) > 0$, in order for a solution to exist. This point may be called q^*. The value of q, called q_0 that minimizes $c(q)$ must satisfy $C'(q_0) = 0$. Therefore, $q_0 < q^*$.

5. a)   The Taguchi Loss function is:

$L(x) = k (x - T)^2$
$400 = k (25)^2$
$k = 0.64$
So, $L(x) = 0.64 (x-T)^2$

  b) $\$1.50 = 0.64 (x-120)^2$

     $2.34 = (x - 120)^2$

     $(x - T)_{Tolerance} = \sqrt{2.34} = 1.53$ volts

     $\therefore \quad x = 121.53$

6. The best way to prioritize the voice of the customer would be to have a focus group of typical customers, such as craftspeople, "do-it-yourselfer's", hobbyists to provide input on how they used the screwdriver and what their priorities were. Below is one possible configuration of the matrix. Students may come up with other variations.

**HOUSE OF QUALITY MATRIX
FOR A SIMPLE SCREWDRIVER**

	Price	Interchg Bits	Steel Shaft	Rubber Grip	Rachet Capabil.	Plastic Handle	Priority
Easy to use		●		△			
Doesn't rust	○		●				
Durable	●		●			△	
Comfortable				●			
Versatile	○	●			●		
Inexpensive	●		○	△	○	△	

7. For a glider the following customer attributes and counterpart characteristics might be:

Attributes	Technical Requirements
Ease of assembly	"Design for assembly"
	Simple instructions
Easy to fly	"Launch" mechanism
Flight characteristics	Wing, tail, body design
Durability	Quality of wood
Value	Price/durability ratio

Construction of the matrix is left to the student.

8. a) The information in the scoreboard that applies to QFD the customer attributes are listed as row headings: (1) Competitive Rates, through (5) Courteous, knowledgeable personnel. The equivalent to counterpart characteristics would be the bases for scoring, such as "Based on number of institutional representatives that customers had to deal with," listed at the bottom of the table, below the "weighted score" line.

b)   To develop a House of Quality, the available information would give a good start; however, more information would needed about the relationships between attributes and counterpart characteristics and the interrelationships between those characteristics. Also, the relative priorities of customers and the selling points would have to be determined.

c)   In attempting to develop a competing mortgage loan service, current or prospective companies could look at the strengths of the strongest product (National Mortgage) and attempt to meet or exceed the excellence of the customer attributes there. They could also look at the attributes that aren't well covered by any product, such as (4) Single point of contact, and try to develop a product that would fill the gap, if customers consider the attribute(s) to be very important to this product.

ANSWERS TO CASE QUESTIONS

Case I. A Case of Failure in Product Development

If the Ford case is a classic in automotive turnaround stories, the GE rotary compressor case is a classic one of a company "shooting itself in the foot," instead of proving "quick on the draw." It should be pointed out that GE has apparently solved this particular problem and is now selling the compressors to some Japanese manufacturers.

1.   Several factors contributed to the product development disaster. First, the managers and design engineers were concentrating on reducing the noise level of the compressor, and may not have paid sufficient attention to prototype testing and results. Second, they designed the compressor to require extremely tight tolerances. Third, they also rejected the opportunity to use the expertise of a retired GE consultant in compressors and the opportunity to develop the product as a joint venture with a Japanese firm. Fourth, they did not conduct the usual series of field tests for new products, due to time pressures to "get the product out." Finally, they ignored warning signs, discovered by technicians after laboratory tests under simulated field conditions, that the compressors had wear problems and perhaps had not been tested rigorously enough.

2.   Two of the techniques of quality engineering, design reviews and experimental design, might have helped to improve the compressor design and avoid the multi-million dollar disaster that occurred. Design reviews could have been used to develop the initial strategy and consider problems at each stage from preliminary review to intermediate review to final review. At the second stage, lower level employees might have been able to voice their concerns and receive a hearing from middle or top level managers, rather than having their opinions "filtered out" by first line supervisors. Obviously, the experimental design was not well planned. At least _some_ field testing should have been implemented,given the differences between air conditioner and refrigerator rotary compressor characteristics, and the fact that refrigerators are used in such widely varying physical environments.

3.   It might be hoped that GE learned to use a systematic and well developed design process in the future, perhaps based on the design review approach.

Case II. BurgerMate Corporation

The House of Quality for BurgerMate's competition is developed below. As the analysis of customer responses shows, there are several strong relationships between the customer requirements and their associated technical requirements of value versus price; nutrition versus calories; and sodium versus percent fat, for example. The technical requirements must be placed on a somewhat more equal basis, which would best be shown as units/ounce, except for the percent fat value. These are shown in the table below.

Company	Price/oz.	Calories/oz.	Sodium/oz.	% Fat
Grabby's	$ 0.264	89.46	104.72	15
Queenburger	$ 0.206	73.67	120.11	16
Sandy's	$ 0.214	75.45	122.20	23

The deployment strategy this analysis would suggest is that BurgerMate should try to increase its size and visual appeal, while reducing the cost per ounce. At the same time, it should build on the strength of the nutrition trend keeping the sodium and % fat low, as did Grabby's, and slightly reducing the number of calories per ounce to be more competitive.

Solution to Burger Mate Case

		Price	Size	Calories	Sodium	% Fat	Importance 1 2 3 4 5	Compet. Evaluation 1 2 3 4 5	Selling Points
Taste	Moistness		Δ			Δ		G/Q S	
	Flavor	O		Δ	Δ	⊙		S G Q	*
Visual	Visually Appealing	O	⊙					G S Q	*
Healthy	Nutritious	Δ		⊙	⊙	⊙		Q S G	*
Value	Good value	⊙	O					Q S G	*
Compet. Evaluation: Grabby's		3	3	4	5	5			
Queenburger		5	5	5	3	4			
Sandy's		4	4	5	3	3			
Targets		$0.13 per oz	8.0 oz.	80 per oz.	NC	NC			
Deployment		*	*	*					

⊙ = Very strong relationship

O = Strong relationship

Δ = Weak relationship

CHAPTER 8

Measurement and Strategic Information Management

Teaching Notes

This chapter develops facets of measurement and strategic information. These concepts may be somewhat difficult for students to grasp, at first. This may be especially true if you have accounting or finance majors in the class, or practicing accountants in a seminar. Two compatible views of quality costs are presented in the chapter, which do, however, disagree with the "conventional" views of accountants and many economists. These are the Taguchi loss function concept and the concept of accounting for quality costs with a focus on four categories of cost. Key objectives are:

• To focus on the role of measurement and the broad scope of management by fact in the total quality management process.

• To develop the relationship between price, market share, cost, quality, and profits.

• To point out flaws in traditional economic and accounting models which may lead to misunderstanding of the causes, effects, and importance of quality costs.

• To develop the Taguchi loss function and accompanying concepts.

• To categorize the four classes of quality costs and show how they can help to translate quality issues into the language of management -- money.

• To define and provide examples of several tools used to measure, analyze, and allocate quality costs, including the relatively new accounting technique of "activity-based" information, or costing.

ANSWERS TO QUALITY IN PRACTICE KEY ISSUES

Data and Information Management at Xerox

1.   Xerox captures data from suppliers to customers to answer the question, "What information can help to meet both internal and external customer requirements?" Systems for collecting data include the Automated Installation Quality Reporting system, the Technology Readiness system, and systems for tracking defects and measure customer complaints, product development and delivery leadtimes and administrative competence.

2.   Xerox has a series of systems that seem ideal for gathering data needed for interlinking. To interlink them, they should develop quantitative models of cause and effect relationships between external and internal performance criteria -- for example, the relationship of customer satisfaction measures to internal process measures.

The following objectives of interlinking might be set in order to make useful information available to Xerox's management:

- Focusing management attention on key performance measures that do make a difference, such as those from the Automated Installation Quality Reporting System
- Predicting performance such as customer satisfaction levels, using data from customer reports of product reliability.
- Setting target standards for performance, such as repair response time and efficiency or billing accuracy.
- Requiring areas such as marketing and operations to coordinate their data analysis efforts in the efforts to gather and evaluate data required for product development.
- Making wise decisions faster than competitors do, using the information provided by the Technology Readiness system
- Seeing relationships among performance variables that competitors miss.
- Enhancing communication within the organization based on good data analysis and measurement by fact.

3.   Operability in the form of some of the criteria listed might be measured as follows:

Feature	Possible Measure
Auto jam clearance	Number of jams not cleared/time period
Document handling	Number of documents handled/time period by type
Easy-load paper	Time required to install standard package of paper
Easy-load toner cartridge	Time required to replace toner cartridge and put machine back in service

Quality Cost Reporting at NAP Consumer Electronics Corporation

1.   NAPCEC collects quality cost data by plant, product and quality cost category. Reports are in statement format and report quality costs in the traditional categories of prevention, appraisal, internal failure and external failure costs. An interesting feature is that each of the categories are shown with planned, actual and variance amounts. The same cost categories are further cross-tabulated against planned, actual and prior year figures as a percent of manufacturing standard costs. A separate report, based on direct labor, is prepared showing the relationship between appraisal cost, failure cost, and total direct labor cost by product line.

2.   In order to budget for warranty, testing, and repairs, NAPCEC must gather information using account numbers 400-460, shown in Table 8.4. These external failure costs can then be analyzed, and realistic targets can be set for reducing failure costs based on systemic improvement of quality.

ANSWERS TO REVIEW QUESTIONS

1.   Data at the individual level provide workers with information to continually evaluate and, if necessary, correct the performances of machines and processes. At the process level, data collected through systematic measurement describe process performance and identify areas for improvement. At the organizational level, quality and operational performance data, along with relevant financial data, provide the basis for strategic planning and decision making.

2.   Inspection and measurement provide data, usually in the form of quality and operational performance data. Quality-related data provide input needed for strategic planning, the design of products and services, human resource management, and process improvement. Operational performance data help managers determine if they are doing the right job, if they are using resources effectively, if they are improving, where problems are occurring, and where corrective action is needed.

The disadvantages of inspection and measurement are that they are often used incorrectly, and may end up reducing quality and the effectiveness of operational performance. In the example given, a company discards all product introduction projects which could not be realized in under six months. In doing so, one type of quality data (benefits of faster marketing time) supersedes another (benefits of more fully-developed products), so that customer requirements are met in time performance (customers have new products in a shorter time), but not product performance (products do not perform as fully as customers would like).

3.   The leading practices used by companies for successful quality data and information management include:
     a. They develop a comprehensive set of performance indicators that reflect internal and

external customer requirements and the key factors that drive the business.

b. They push responsibility for inspection, measurement, and analysis down to the lowest levels of the organization using sound analytical methods to support analysis and decision making.

c. They assure that data are reliable, accessible, and widely visible throughout the organization.

d. They logically link key external indicators to internal indicators.

e. They continually refine information sources and their uses within the organization.

4. Effective data and information management should address the following aspects:

a. Supplier performance: The inputs to the production system.

b. Product and service quality: The outputs of the system and the core processes that create products and services.

c. Business and support services: The functions and processes that support a company's core manufacturing or service capabilities.

d. Company operational performance: Customer-related and financial data for top level planning.

5. *Nonconformity* has replaced *defect* because of the negative connotation of *defect* and its potential implications in liability suits. For example, the dust buster which will not turn on has a nonconformity in its manufacture. The dust buster which not only turns on but has sufficient pressure to suck out your eyebrows has a serious defect.

6. *Attribute measurement* involves the measurement of a quality characteristic that is either present or absent in the unit or product under consideration. Attributes assume values of: conformance or nonconformance, within or out of tolerance, complete or incomplete, etc.

   Variable measurement involves the measurement of values on a continuous scale, for instance, length or weight. Variable measurements are concerned with the *degree* of conformance to specifications.

   Examples of both measurement forms are provided within the text.

7. The two fundamental mistakes companies often make in collecting data are: (1). not measuring key characteristics critical to company performance or customer satisfaction, and (2). taking irrelevant or inappropriate measures. In the first case, the company often fails to meet customer expectations to the fullest extent and possibly loses competitive advantage. In the second case, the company directs attention to areas that are not important to customers, thus wasting time and resources.

8. Key business factors are those strategic elements of a business that drive all major elements of the quality system: strategic planning, design and management of process quality, human resources development and management, and information and analysis.

Key business factors include:

a. The nature of a company's products and services.
b. Principle customers.
c. Major markets.
d. Key customer quality requirements.
e. Position in market and competitive environment.
f. Facilities and technologies.
g. Suppliers.
h. Regulatory environment.
i. Other factors, such as new company thrusts, industry changes, etc.

9. The process of determining useful performance measures is as follows:
    ■ Identify all customers of the system and determine their requirements and expectations.
    ■ Define the work process that provides the product or service.
    ■. Define the value-adding activities and outputs that compose the process.
    ■ Develop performance measures or indicators.
    ■ Evaluate the performance measures to insure their usefulness.

10. Quality cost programs are valuable to managers because it translates poor quality and its results into the language that managers use and understand -- money. It serves purposes such as 1) evaluating the importance of quality problems, 2) identifying areas for cost reduction, 3) aiding in budgeting and cost control activities, and 4) serving as a scoreboard to evaluate the degree of success in achieving quality objectives.

11. The four categories of quality costs are: prevention costs, appraisal costs, internal failure costs, and external failure costs. The first are costs incurred to prevent non-conformances, the second are costs incurred in measurement and data analysis, the third are costs of unsatisfactory quality that is found prior to the product leaving the organization, and the fourth is the cost of allowing defective products or services to be delivered to customers. Examples are training costs in the prevention category, inspection costs in the appraisal category, scrap and rework costs in the internal failure category, and replacement and warranty costs in the external failure category.

12. Quality cost measures are collected with great difficulty in most organizations. Some costs are available from the cost accounting system, but because many costs are too late, too aggregated and too distorted for use in their normal form for quality cost determination. However, standard cost and other reporting systems are the starting point and can provide information on direct labor expenses, overhead, scrap costs, warranty expenses, product liability costs, and maintenance, repair, and calibration costs for test equipment. By use of functional categorization of costs and adoption of the newer accounting approaches, such as <u>activity-based costing</u> it may be possible to obtain more accurate approximations of true costs of quality.

13.   Index numbers can be used to measure and interpret variations in quality costs. If costs can be collected into each of the four categories (prevention, appraisal, internal and external failure) then they can be related to a relevant <u>base</u> to form a relative index. For example, we could determine the relative cost of quality as a fraction of labor costs, manufacturing costs, or dollars of sales for each appropriate period (month, quarter, or year). By comparing the indices over a period of time, it is possible to determine if quality costs are increasing decreasing, or remaining stable despite changes in levels of the indices or the absolute cost of quality that are reported.

14.   Quality costs in services are generally less "uniform" than in manufacturing firms because customers frequently place differing demands for service on the organization, even when they are using the same basic product. Often project costs are collected for customized services and can form the basis for quality cost reporting.

15.   The 12 steps suggested by the NAA for establishing a quality cost reporting system basically deal with planning and organizing the study (steps 1-4), cost definition, identification, report formats, and procedures (steps 5-9), and data collection, system debugging, and system expansion and maintenance (steps 10-12). The steps are important to ensure that a systematic design is established, and to verify that the output from the business process meets the needs of the "customers."

16.   Pareto analysis is based on a concept developed by economist Vilfredo Pareto in Italy, and popularized by Joseph Juran, sometimes known as the 80-20 rule. It can be used to determine the 20%, or so, of significant causes that may contribute up to 80% of quality costs in a given cost category. If these causes can be established and corrected, substantial quality cost reduction is frequently possible in a short time.

17.   The data in the table indicate that substantial quality costs are being incurred for inspection and other appraisal activities, as well as for scrap and rework. Despite these efforts, relatively high external failure costs are also being experienced. The cure for these problems is to spend much more on prevention costs, thus reducing costs that is currently being wasted in the other three categories.

18.   As in question 17, too much money is being lost due to scrap and rework. Too little is being spent "up front" in areas of equipment design and vendor quality surveys. Investment in prevention might reduce many of the other quality costs.

19.   Activity-based costing (ABC) is a new accounting concept that may revolutionize the field of cost accounting. Many activities use resources that aren't closely related to the number of units that are produced, thus distorting the traditional cost accounting systems that were designed when products required a high component of labor and a relatively low level of overhead. Activity-based costing is designed to allocate overhead dollars to the activities that use them. In the traditional system, costs were assigned to cost centers and overhead costs were allocated based on the number of labor hours or machine hours used by each

center. In the ABC system, the expenses are assigned to the activities that use them. So, if the parts department requires more data processing support, the cost will be allocated to that activity, rather than "spread" on the basis of labor hours in the shop. This has substantial implications for quality costs. It is much easier to see where costs are being incurred and what the impact of quality improvement efforts might be on those costs.

20. A company's efforts are wasted if collected data are not available to the right employees when needed. In most companies, data are accessible to top managers and others on a need-to-know basis. In TQM-focused companies, quality-related data are accessible to everyone. Many companies accomplish this through on-line computer networks supplemented by local processing capabilities.

21. *Interlinking* is the term that describes the quantitative modeling of cause and effect relationships between external and internal performance criteria--such as the relationship of customer satisfaction measures to internal process measures. Examples are provided in the text.

22. The objectives and benefits of interlinking include:
• Screening out weak or misleading performance measures.
• Focusing management attention on key performance measures that do make a difference.
• Predicting performance such as customer satisfaction levels.
• Setting target standards for performance.
• Requiring areas such as marketing and operations to coordinate their data analysis efforts.
• Making wise decisions faster than competitors do.
• Seeing relationships among performance variables that competitors miss.
• Enhancing communication within the organization based on good data analysis and measurement by fact.

ANSWERS TO DISCUSSION QUESTIONS

1. The answers will vary here, depending on students' choice of restaurants from which they gather data. Note that many of the internal performance characteristics that relate to the pizza restaurant example in the body of the chapter would also apply to other restaurants, regardless of type.

2. Without going into all of the problems of what is wrong with course and instructor evaluations, it can be said that at least four major flaws are common in most systems, as well-intended as they may be: a) they typically lack customer (student) input and customer focus; b) they are too general and fail to take into account the mission or objectives of the course, department, college or university; c) only in rare cases have their validity and reliability been statistically shown; and d) evaluations do not typically focus on improvement.

3.   Most university departments keep many statistics, but have few customer-oriented measurement systems in place. It is not uncommon for universities to know exactly how many students they graduate each year, but to have no information on how many have obtained jobs. Admissions departments can tell how many students they have admitted, but are unable to tell how long it takes for the admission decision to be made (sometimes **months** after the completed application and paperwork has been received).

       "Time to market" is a statistic that many businesses are beginning to question. Statistics indicate that it takes an average of about five years for the typical student to obtain an undergraduate degree in the U.S. Can that cycle time be reduced by better advising, reducing overlap between courses, cutting out unnecessary requirements, and better advising to ensure that students take full loads and don't switch majors every few semesters?

4.   Answers will vary, depending on the experience and interests of the students.

5.   This "field" exercise is designed to further student awareness of the breadth of the "quality movement" and to help them to confirm that the theory of quality is being applied in practical settings in business and industry.

6.   The key to the quality implications of this information technology is the "machine-human" interface." If the humans who input the data on prices or those who program the system are not accurate, the scanners simply improve the ability to make mistakes faster. Stores are now experimenting with having customers scan their own items and pay the totals, without requiring the use of checkout clerks. If successful, perhaps the store would institute some type of sampling inspection to ensure that customers were not cheating the store out of large amounts of revenue.

7.   This question can be used to test students' ability to apply the definition of attributes and variables. The following are divided into attributes or variables:
       a. Attribute (discrete units- people)
       b. Variable (continuous variable - time)
       c. Variable (same as b.)
       d. Attribute (same as a.)
       e. Variable (same as b.)

8.   This question can be used to test students' ability to apply the definition of attributes and variables in another service operation. The following are divided into attributes or variables:
       a. Variable (continuous variable - time)
       b. Attribute (discrete units- errors)
       c. Attribute (discrete units- enquiries)
       d. Variable (same as a.)
       e. Attribute (same as b.)

9.   This field exercise is designed to further student awareness of the breadth of the "quality management" and to help them to confirm that the theory of quality is being applied in practical settings in business and industry.

10.   In the cheese-making process, customer requirements of full weight, wholesomeness (lack of contamination, excessive chemical additives, or inferior content, such as excessive water), smell and taste might all be customer related measures that could be interlinked with internal measures.

11.   This field exercise is designed to further student awareness of the breadth of the "quality management" and to help them to confirm that the theory of quality is being applied in practical settings in business and industry.

12.   The four categories of quality costs can be applied to colleges and universities, as well as other organizations. Internal failure could be the costs of scrapped and reworked materials, from poorly designed laboratory tests to reprinting class schedules that were printed with serious errors in them. An example of an external failure cost is one that might be incurred in correcting an erroneous handout that an instructor had given to a professional development seminar and had to mail out to participants, after the seminar was over. Appraisal costs include all costs incurred in testing students before admission (SAT, GMAT tests), during the teaching process (examinations), and at the end of their programs (senior assessment exams). Examples of prevention costs are those incurred to teach people how to improve their quality, such as sending people to quality seminars. It would be difficult (but certainly not impossible) to measure many of these quality costs.

13.   Juran, Crosby, and Deming are all correct, based on their own perspectives. Juran and Crosby focus on the tangible costs of internal failure, appraisal, and prevention costs, many of which can be objectively measured. Although some external failure costs such as the cost of a product recall, can be measured, the cost of loss of customers, and even some internal failure costs, such as losses from poor employee morale and fear, can never be measured.

14.   Spreadsheet programs can be used to develop the database, compute the indices, print reports of quality costs in a tabular and graphical form, and calculate "what-if" cases for management decision-making purposes.

15.   This is one of those "gray areas" that depend on the situation. Managers typically want to know the justification for an expensive purchase of equipment, whether it is quantitative or qualitative. Thus, a quality department will probably have to "manage by facts" in their requests. What "quantitative" information do they have that tells them that competitors have this testing capability? What are the costs versus benefits of the proposed purchase in quantitative and in qualitative terms?

SOLUTIONS TO PROBLEMS

1.   Since no values for percentages of sales attributable to quality costs were indicated, it is not possible to calculate an index base for the various cost categories. However, it is possible to draw some general conclusions from the data. The data show that both internal and external failure costs are too high for Product A, appraisal costs are too high for product B, and both internal failure and appraisal costs are too high for Product C. Managers of all product lines should put more emphasis on prevention and attempt to reduce costs in other categories.

2.   The composite index for quality costs shows that total quality cost has been stable at $0.07/total sales $. Internal failure rates have been reduced substantially, from $168.20 in the first quarter to $66.40 in the fourth quarter. External failure rates have shown improvement in the fourth quarter, dropping from $42.80 in the third quarter to $28.60 in the fourth. Increases in prevention and appraisal expenditures have apparently led to improvements in failure costs. The overall index has fallen slightly. Management should maintain or increase the level of prevention and appraisal in an effort to reduce quality costs, especially failure costs. See table, below.

Quality Cost Indices

Quarter	1	2	3	4
Total Sales	$4120.00	$4206.00	$4454.00	$4106.00
External failure	40.80	42.20	42.80	28.60
Internal failure	168.20	172.40	184.20	66.40
Appraisal	64.20	67.00	74.20	166.20
Prevention	28.40	29.20	30.20	40.20
Total quality costs	$ 301.60	$ 310.80	$ 331.80	$ 301.40
Qual. cost/Total sales $	0.07	0.07	0.07	0.07
External failure	0.010	0.010	0.010	0.007
Internal failure	0.041	0.041	0.041	0.016
Appraisal	0.016	0.016	0.017	0.040
Prevention	0.007	0.007	0.007	0.010

3.   The data and bar chart show that the company is spending too much on appraisal and internal failure cost and too little on prevention. Improvement efforts should concentrate on the categories of proofreading, press downtime and correction of typos.

Cost Element	Amount ($ Thousands)	Category
Proofreading	710	Appraisal
Quality planning	10	Prevention
Press downtime	405	Int. failure
Bindery waste	75	Int. failure
Checking & inspection	60	Appraisal
Customer complaint remakes	40	Ext. failure
Printing plate revisions	40	Int. failure
Quality improvement projects	20	Prevention
Other waste	55	Int. failure
Correction of typos	300	Int. failure

Totals	Amount ($ Thousands)
Appraisal	770
Prevention	30
Internal failure	875
External failure	40

Histogram of Quality Losses

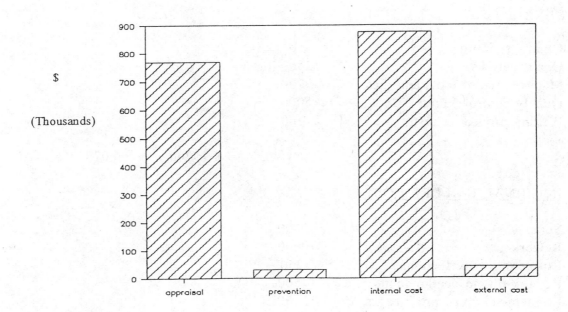

4.   The largest costs are internal failure (56.6%) and appraisal (27.1%). More must be done in quality training, a component of prevention (currently 7.8%), if failure, appraisal, and overall quality costs are to be controlled. External failure costs are 8.6% of quality costs, so screening methods are working fairly well. Note that the above proportions are fractions of the total quality costs of $ 247,450.

Quality Cost Categories

Cost Elements	Costs	Subtotal	Proportion
APPRAISAL			
Incoming test & inspection	7500		
Inspection	25000		
Test	5000		
Laboratory testing	1250		
Design of Q.A. equipment	1250		
Material testing & insp.	1250		
Insp. equipt. & calibration	2500		
Formal complaints to vendors	10000		
Setup for test & inspection	10750		
Laboratory services	2500		
		$ 67000	0.271
PREVENTION			
Quality training	0		
Quality audits	2500		
Maintenance of tools and dies	9200		
Quality control admin.	5000		
Writing proced. & instr.	2500		
		$ 19200	0.078
INTERNAL FAILURE COSTS			
Scrap	35000		
Rework	70000		
Correcting imperfections	6250		
Rework due to vendor faults	17500		
Problem solving - prod. engrs.	11250		
		$140000	0.566

Cost Elements	Costs	Subtotal	Proportion
EXTERNAL FAILURE COSTS			
Adjustment cost of complaints	21250		
		$ 21250	0.086
Total costs		$247450	

5. See table, below, and figure for Pareto analysis.

Category	Cost Element (Ranked by $ Lost)		Percent	Cumulative %
1	Rejected paper	$560,000	61.1	61.1
2	Custom. complaint	125,000	13.6	74.7
3	Odd lots	79,000	8.6	83.3
4	High matl. costs	67,000	7.3	90.6
5	Downtime	38,000	4.1	94.7
6	Excess inspection	28,000	3.1	97.8
7	Testing costs	20,000	2.2	100.0
	Total costs	$917,000		

Conclusion: Approximately 75% of the losses are attributable to "rejected" [an interesting side note is the term used in the industry for <u>rejected</u> or waste paper incurred during production; it is called "broke"] and "customer complaints." These are the most important cost elements and should be the primary targets for quality improvement elements.

Problem 8-5

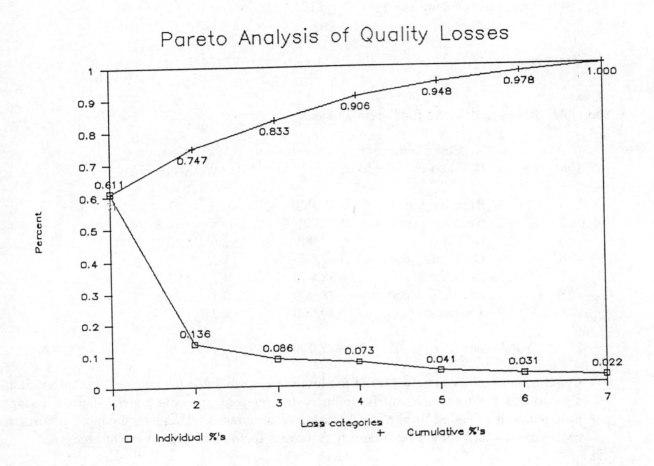

Pareto Analysis of Quality Losses

ANSWERS TO CASE QUESTIONS

CASE I. Ultra Productivity Fasteners Company, Part I

Key business factors:

• UPF supplies fasteners to two major customers: appliance and automotive.

• Key customer requirements are rapid response to design and manufacture and technical assistance (appliance market); JIT delivery, consistently meeting specifications; ease of use; durability.

• Durability and JIT delivery are especially important to automotive customers.

• The market is extremely competitive; UPF is one of three major suppliers.

• UPF has 2 major plants and one smaller one.

Performance indicators:

Supplier quality: metal composition; hardness

Product and service quality: breaking strength; dimensionality; conformance to specifications; on-time shipment; order entry error rate; invoice errors; responsiveness to technical assistance requests; design lead time

Business support services: (a variety of support measurements in marketing, accounting, packaging, etc. might be specified)

Company operational results: customer satisfaction; complaints received and resolved; market share; financial performance; production cost; productivity; cost of quality

These performance measures should be reported by product line and by plant.

CASE II. The Hamilton Bank Cost of Quality Report

A detailed report should be prepared as an internal or external quality consultant to the bank. An analysis of the data found in the table for the case might include:

| | Quality Cost Categories | | |
Cost Elements	Costs	Subtotal	Proportion
APPRAISAL			
1. Run credit checks	26.13		
Loan Payment & Loan Payoffs			
1. Receive & process (2 items)	1058.92		
Inspection			
2. Review documents	3021.63		
4. Prepare tickler file, etc.	156.75		
5. Review all output	2244.14		
		$ 6507.57	0.496
PREVENTION			
10. Conduct training	1366.94		
		$ 1366.94	0.104
INTERNAL FAILURE COSTS			
Scrap and Rework			
3. Make document corrections	1013.65		
6. Correct rejects	425.84		
7. Reconcile incomplete collateral reports	78.34		
9. Compensate for system downtime	519.38		
Loan Payment or Payoff			
2. Respond to inquiries - no coupon	783.64		
2. Research payoff problems	14.34		
		$2820.85	0.215

EXTERNAL FAILURE COSTS

8. Respond to dealer calls, etc.   2418.88

                                              $ 2418.88   0.185

Total costs $13114.24

1.   As one would hope, the external failure costs for the bank are not <u>extremely</u> high at $2418.88 However, they do represent 18.5 % of the total quality costs. The process of working with dealers should be investigated to determine if it can be simplified, better communications established, and problems avoided, in the future.

2.   The highest cost category is in appraisal costs at $ 6507.57 and 49.6% of total quality costs. If the categories of "document review" and "review all output" can be reduced without compromising the quality of the lending procedure, these costs could be greatly improved.

3.   The largest internal failure costs are being incurred in the document correction and "Respond to inquiries - no coupon areas." There is also a fairly substantial cost of quality for the "Compensate for system downtime" category. These should be investigated to determine if procedures can be improved in order to reduce costs.

4.   In the prevention area, it appears that not much attention is being given to the need for this activity. If training could be given in quality improvement techniques, as well as time spent on quality planning and improvement, then the other cost categories might be reduced with only a modest increase in prevention costs.

CHAPTER 9

Process Management and Continuous Improvement

Teaching Notes

This chapter introduces the tools and concepts of the Japanese *kaizen*, or continuous improvement, philosophy. Students may have some difficulty in understanding how frequent, gradual changes over the long term can be successful in our "quick fix" society. Key objectives for this chapter should be to assist students:

• To understand what a problem is, and the need for careful, systematic, and yet, creative problem-solving.

• To learn the process of creative problem-solving, based on mess finding, fact finding, problem finding, idea finding, solution finding, and implementation.

• To practice using the Deming-Shewhart Cycle of plan, do, study, act, and how it is being applied to problems around the world.

• To compare the concepts of Juran's breakthrough approach with Crosby's managerial/behavioral 14 step improvement process.

• To become familiar with and apply (some, if not all of) the "seven QC tools" for quality problem-solving.

• To be exposed to the definitions and uses of the "new seven" tools for improvement.

ANSWERS TO QUALITY IN PRACTICE KEY ISSUES

Applications of Quality Improvement Tools at Rotor Clip

1.   Once the seam problem was understood, several steps could be taken to prevent recurrence of the problem. First, metallographic testing could be done to ensure that defective product didn't get into the process, second, Rotor Clip should work with the supplier on the new material to test out its properties and to help them to develop consistent quality controls that would meet Rotor Clip's specifications.

2.   In the freight charge example, Rotor Clip should work with customers for a reasonable period of time to develop alternatives to expedited shipments. However, if they want that type of service, in the long term Rotor Clip should provide it, but the customers should be shown the cost data and be required to pay extra for expedited shipments that lead to chronic high costs.

3.   In the case of the advertising department's use of scatter diagrams, they could use them to test out the effectiveness of certain promotions in certain market areas. If a promotion or advertising campaign was directly related to sales increases or market share changes, it could then be extended over all territories. Top management could use the tool to set budget priorities based on heaviest funding for the advertising techniques that seemed to be providing the largest payoffs.

Process Improvement at Boise Cascade

1.   The real benefits from flowcharting the claims process were: a) understanding the complexity of the process; b) realizing why the process took months to complete; c) concluding that many steps added no value to the process; and d) helping team members to build confidence in each other and fostering mutual respect. Obviously, these benefits could be attained by any team that seriously studied the processes that team members were involved with.

2.   The old flowchart had 27 individual steps (some of which were actually sub-processes, themselves). The new process is a model of simplicity with only 5 steps.

In the old process, there appeared to be numerous approval steps and unnecessary filing, coordination and signatures that were required to process each claim. It appears that under the old method, sales representatives did not have the training nor the power to settle claims without consultations with product managers, who often had to send the claim to "the mill" for research, or had to request more information through the sales representative from the customer. Even after that information was received and the claim had been approved, the sales representative had to send the adjustment request form to a manager for signature. If the manager did not have "signing authority" for that amount, it had to be sent to a higher level manager before the signature authorizing payment could be obtained. It often cost more to process the claim than the value of the claim, itself.

The new process shows the effects of training and empowerment. The sales representative has been trained to handle the claims process single-handedly. Thus, approvals, unnecessary paperwork, and costly delays have been eliminated.

3.   There seems to have been an upward shift in the percentage of claims processes within 48 hours during the second year, when compared to the first year. The approximate average in the first year may have been about 70%. Except for three months during the fall and winter of 1992, the percentage processed was in the 80% range. The averages appear to be statistically different. They might be tested using a statistical test for significance.

ANSWERS TO REVIEW QUESTIONS

1.   Process management involves planning and administering the activities necessary to achieve a high level of performance in a process, and identifying opportunities for improving quality and operational performance, and ultimately, customer satisfaction. The importance of process management lies in its focus on prevention of defects and errors, and elimination of wasteful procedures, resulting in better quality and improved company performance through shorter cycle times and faster customer responsiveness.

2.   Innovation generally represents the focus of Western management, results in large, short-term, and radical changes in products or processes. It is what Juran termed the "breakthrough" approach. Kaizen, (see question 8,below, for details), the current "buzz word for continuous improvement, is focused on small, gradual improvements over a long term. People, not technology, is the principal focus. Kaizen is a process-oriented way of thinking rather than a results-oriented approach that is so characteristic of Western management thought.

3.   The leading practices of companies recognized for superior process management include:

1. They control the quality and operational performance of key processes used to produce and deliver products and services.

2. They identify significant variations in processes and outputs, determine root causes, make corrections, and verify results.

3. They continuously improve processes to achieve better quality, cycle time, and overall operational performance.

4. They set "stretch goals" and make extensive use of benchmarking and reengineering to achieve breakthrough performance.

4.   The three components of any control system are a standard or goal, a means of measurement of accomplishment, and a way to compare actual results with the standard, along with an appropriate method of feedback of results to form the basis for corrective action. Such a system can be seen at work in an airline that measures on-time arrivals, by stating that the airplane must arrive within 15 minutes of the time shown in the printed schedule. Each airplane is then monitored, with its precise arrival time being recorded. Statistics are then reported to pilots, station agents, and government agencies, who keep records and feed back the information for correction to pilots and schedulers for action.

5.   *Preliminary control* is designed to ensure that everyone knows how outcomes will be measured and standards evaluated. *Concurrent control* involves immediate measurement and feedback of results, with correction of deviations taking place in a timely fashion. *Feedback control* involves the adjustment of the control system, itself, as standards become obsolete or objectives change. Top managers are most concerned with preliminary control and performance on feedback controls. Middle managers are concerned with all three areas, but are responsible for developing control systems and maintaining standards for concurrent control. First-line managers are most concerned with concurrent control and have only a secondary interest in preliminary and feedback control.

6.   Operator-controllable processes have three requirements: 1) the operator has to have a means of knowing what is expected of him or her through clear instructions and specifications; 2) he/she must have a means of determining their actual performance via inspection or measurement; 3) they must have a means of making corrections if they discover a variance between what is required (specification) and their actual performance. The implications of operator-controllable requirements is that management must provide (generally with operator assistance) the necessary instructions and specifications, the tools and assistance needed to set up a measurement system, and the training and empowerment to allow operators to take corrective action when there is an error or defective process in operation.

7.   *Work simplification*, a program developed by Allan Mogensen, is designed to train workers in the simple steps necessary to analyze and challenge the work they are doing, and thus make improvements when necessary. *Planned methods change*, created by Proctor & Gamble, seeks not only to improve processes, but also to replace or eliminate unnecessary operations. This approach relies on forming teams of employees to study the operations, establish dollar goals as to how much of their cost they would try to eliminate through planned change, and provide positive recognition for success.

8.   One of the key differences between managerial attitudes in Japan and the United States is encompassed in the old cliche: "if it ain't broke, don't fix it." In other words, much of Western management is focused primarily on <u>maintaining</u> technical and operating functions. Japan, on the other hand, has a distinctive focus toward <u>improving</u> them. The improvement of quality should be a <u>proactive</u> task of management, not simply a reaction to problems and competitive threats. Often in the West, quality improvement is viewed

simply as improvements in <u>product</u> quality. In the kaizen philosophy, improvement in all areas of business enhance the <u>quality of the firm</u>. Thus, any activity directed toward improvement falls in the Kaizen umbrella. Financial investment is minimal. Everyone, not just top management, is involved in the process; many improvements result from the know-how and experience of workers. The essence of kaizen is simple and just plain common sense.

9.   *Stretch goals*, also called *breakthrough objectives*, are urgent, short-term goals for improving products or services which force a company to think radically, different, to encourage major improvements and well as incremental ones. Such goals apply to all areas of a company.

10.   Benchmarking is measuring your performance against that of best-in-class organizations, determining how they achieve their performance levels, and using the information to improve on your own targets, strategies, and implementation. In a business school, the dean could determine which schools of business in the region or nationally were doing the best job in recruiting excellent students and faculty, delivering excellent undergraduate or graduate programs, or providing outstanding performance in research or community service. He or she could then use these as benchmark criteria for improvement. In the classroom, individual professors could benchmark their classroom teaching methods against others in the school, in the university (not necessarily in business courses), and at other universities.

11.   *Reengineering* has been defined as "the fundamental rethinking and radical redesign of business processes to achieve dramatic improvements in critical, contemporary measures of performance, such as cost, quality, service, and speed." Reengineering's incremental improvement and breakthrough improvement are not incompatible, but rather are complementary approaches that fall under the TQM umbrella; both are necessary to remain competitive. It has been suggested that TQM support is needed for successful reengineering. Reengineering alone is often driven by upper management without the full support or understanding of the rest of the organization, and radical innovations may end up as failures. The TQM philosophy encourages participation and systematic study, measurement and verification of results that support reengineering efforts.

12.   According to Kepner and Tregoe, a problem is a deviation between what should be happening and what is happening that is important enough to make someone think that the deviation ought to be corrected. This definition can be directly applied to quality assurance, since there are often standards that have been defined to state when a problem will exist, such as when a part has a dimension outside of specification limits, or a painted panel has too many defects per square foot.

13.   Structured, semi-structured, and ill-structured problems can be used as categories to classify how much information is available about the "gap" that exists between the present and desired state of a problem situation. For structured problems, we have complete

information about the problem. For ill-structured problems, we have a great deal of uncertainty and "fuzziness" about the information. Semi-structured problems fall in between. This means that the structured problems can usually be solved by routine, programmable decision-making techniques, while the ill-structured problems must be solved with more qualitative, creative techniques.

14. The Deming cycle consists of four steps: plan, do, study, act. It is related to the creative problem-solving process in that the six steps of the Osborn/Parnes process: 1) understanding the "mess"; 2) finding facts; 3) identifying specific problems; 4) generating ideas; 5) developing solutions; and 6) implementation are very close to Deming's steps.

15. Juran defines *breakthrough* as any improvement which takes an organization to unprecedented levels of performance. Breakthrough is focused on attacking chronic losses, or in Deming's terminology, common causes of variation. All breakthroughs follow a common sequence of discovery, organization, diagnosis, corrective action, and control. The steps in the process are: a) Proof of the Need; b) Project Identification; c) Organization for Breakthrough; d) The Diagnostic Journey; e) The Remedial Journey; f) Holding the Gains. Juran's program is cast in traditional organizational structures and uses specific techniques and methods for problem identification, diagnosis, and remedy.

16. Crosby's program for quality improvement consists of 14 steps. His quality improvement program is a formal, company-wide program with a heavy emphasis on motivation. It differs from Deming's focus on a generic problem-solving process that can be understood and performed by individuals or groups at all levels of an organization, and Juran's specific methods and focus on "breakthrough" approaches to problem-solving.

17. The four major components of any problem-solving process are:
   a. Redefining and analyzing the problem.
   b. Generating ideas
   c. Evaluating and selecting ideas.
   d. Implementing ideas.

18. The six steps of the Osborn/Parnes process are 1) understanding the "mess"; 2) finding facts; 3) identifying specific problems; 4) generating ideas; 5) developing solutions; and 6) implementation. Each of these steps is explained in detail under the PROBLEM-SOLVING METHODOLOGY FOR QUALITY IMPROVEMENT heading in the body of the chapter.

19. Messes arise from several sources:
   • A lack of knowledge of how a process works.
   • A lack of knowledge of how a process <u>should</u> work.
   • Errors in performing the steps involved in the process.
   • Waste and complexity.
   • Excess variation. Deming and Juran strongly advocate reducing variation.

20.   Work sampling can be used to help a manager understand the nature of activities being performed and opportunities for improvement. The example cited in the chapter involved thirty clerical and professional people in a Hewlett-Packard office taking telephone orders. Sixty-five percent of the activities were classified as non-productive work. The supervisor immediately made changes in the work procedures to improve the processing of returns and a task force was formed to reduce the number of products returned.

21.   Quality-related problems in service organizations can be identified using some of the same indicators of "messes" as are found in any organization, including:

   • Lots of work-in-process. Many stacks of paper and "stuffed" file drawers.
   • Many people walking around, standing in line (at the copier?), or idle while waiting for something.
   • Work areas that are in disarray, dusty boxes, bookcases full of dusty binders, etc.
   • People who can give only a brief, vague definition of what they're working on and why it is important.
   • Humorous signs taped to the walls, relating to the slow process, or lack of progress.
   • Supervisors and managers pacing around trying to find out what's going on, ascertain who made a critical mistake, or expedite late orders. Also, see the answer to question 11, below.

22.   The first step in data collection is to develop operational definitions for all quality measures that will be collected. For example, what does it mean to have "on-time delivery?" Does this mean within one day of the promised time? One week? One hour? What is an error? Is it wrong information on an invoice, a typographical mistake, or either? Clearly, any data are meaningless unless they are well defined and understood without ambiguity. The Juran Institute suggested ten important considerations for data collection that are listed in the chapter.

23.   A *run chart* is a line graph in which data are plotted over time. The vertical axis represents the measurement. The horizontal axis represents the time scale. A *control chart* is a run chart to which two horizontal lines, called *control limits*, are added: the *upper control limit* and the *lower control limit*. Control limits are chosen statistically so that there is a high probability that points will fall between these limits if the process is in control. Control patterns make it easier to interpret patterns in a run chart, and draw conclusions about the state of control.

24.   Check sheets are simple, flexible devices that can be tailored to fit the type of data collection that is required. Thus, the objective is to design a form which may be interpreted with little or no additional processing. Some examples given in the chapter were those that had class intervals of data or specifications listed, so that the number of observations could be tallied on the sheet according to the class, defect category, or range within which the observations fell. Another type was used to locate defects on sketch of the part that was being inspected.

25. Problem detection methodology is often used in services to detect and isolate critical problems. Customers assess each problem along key dimensions, such as frequency and bothersomeness, with estimates of a particular problem. Managers then try to concentrate on those problems that are especially bothersome or have frequencies associated with higher levels of "bother." The techniques does have limitations brought about by difficulty in using customer ratings to develop an accurate and appropriate rating system.

26. Methods that may be used for idea finding include brainstorming, checklists, and rewording of problem statements in different ways.

27. *Brainstorming* is a technique in which people are encouraged to generate a large number of ideas through combination and enhancement of existing ideas. No criticism is permitted and radical ideas are encouraged, often triggering other good ideas.

28. A *cause-and-effect diagram* is a diagram used for tracing the routes of materials, machines, methods, and measurements to identify the sources of problems and possible solutions for them. There are two basic types of cause-and-effect diagrams. *Dispersion analysis* involves identifying and classifying possible causes for a specific quality problem. *Process classification* diagrams are based on a flowchart of the process. The key factors that influence quality at each step are drawn on the flowchart.

29. *Scatter diagrams* are the graphical plot of points used for regression analysis. While they do not provide rigorous statistical analysis, they often point to important relationships between variables. Typically, the variables in question represent possible causes and effects obtained from Ishikawa diagrams.

ANSWERS TO DISCUSSION QUESTIONS

1. Processes need to be *repeatable* (the process must recur over time) so that enough data can be gathered to show useful information. They must also be *measurable* so that patterns about the process performance can be made clear. This ability to "predict" performance then leads to ability to detect out-of-control conditions and helps in the search for improvements. Examples of the types of processes that are repeatable and measurable will vary according to student understanding and interests.

2. The answers will vary here, depending on students' perspectives.

3. Typically, examinations are a means of control (or appraisal, in quality cost terms). They could be used as a means for gathering data to discover areas for improvement. An advantage of the "English system" of examinations is that classroom examinations are separated from comprehensive examinations. Classroom examinations (if they are given) are <u>developmental</u>, and have no direct bearing on class rank or the comprehensive exam "grade." The comprehensive examinations are not prepared by individual professors. Therefore, professors are seen more as "tutors," "lecturers," or "mentors" in the classroom

setting as opposed to "quality control" police.

4.   Common causes and special cause variations exist as follows:

Process	Common Causes	Special Causes
College exam	Type of examination, textbook, handout materials, room temperature, lighting, amount of study done by students preparing for exam.	Disruption in the exam (e.g. fire alarm), exam question that draws on special knowledge unavailable to all students, exam pages missing and not detected
Grilling hamburger	Heat of grill, single chef	Multiple grills, differences between common ingredients, chefs, differences introduced by meat from different sources, different spices used.
Meeting scheduled appointment	Weather in the area, normal traffic in vicinity of meeting, lack of a central meeting location, single source of meeting notices	Flat tire on car, message not sent in time, need to send substitute representative, multiple meeting notices creating confusion

5.   It is obvious that Company A does not use a TQM approach and that there is no control process in place. The three elements of an adequate control system appear to be lacking, since there is no visible standard for processes (data sheets not mentioned, in-process inspection is nonexistent, no temperature control on dryers), valid means of measurement (such as calibrated timing devices, pin gages for operators, adequate lighting) are absent, and the means of correction of quality problems have been ignored (no solder analysis, poor housekeeping, etc.). In contrast, Company B appears to exhibit a model TQM approach to quality control and assurance. The recommendation to Company A is obvious: benchmark the quality control and assurance processes against the standard set by Company B. The hard part is getting managers at Company A to acknowledge that they have a problem, to be trained in what is to be done, and then to do it.

6.   As indicated in the answer to Review Question 8, above, the kaizen philosophy, improvement in all areas of business enhance the <u>quality of the firm</u>. Thus, any activity directed toward improvement falls in the Kaizen umbrella. Applying this concept to the classroom would mean that students would search for improvement opportunities in every area, from study skills to improving the quality and readability of their written reports, as well as the professor's handouts.

7. .   Answers will vary, depending on the faculty interviewed and the interests of the students.

8.   Processes might include accounting, budgeting, purchasing, training and development and research. Institutions that might be benchmarked might be hospitals (accounting), banks (budgeting), retail stores (purchasing), consulting firms (training and development) and pharmaceutical firms (research and development).

9.   Answers will vary, depending on the exam preparation processes of the students.

10.   The Deming cycle of plan, do, study, act could be applied to any personal processes from preparing for a case presentation, to getting to class or work on time, to improving the quality of a term paper.

11.   Answers will vary, depending on the experience and desperate situations of the students.

12.   Some typical problems that might be addressed by students could include, "In what ways might I...?" a) improve my grade in my Quality Management course; b) Make an "A" on my next exam; c) Complete my term project with high quality and before the deadline?"

13.   The "seven tools" are:

♦ Flow charts
♦ Run charts and control charts
♦ Check sheets
♦ Pareto diagrams
♦ Histograms
♦ Cause and effect diagrams
♦ Scatter diagrams

This question is designed to encourage students to think about their own "personal quality" approaches and to discover for themselves that they can apply TQM tools.

14.   The important quality characteristics for this drive-through window are: the machinery, materials, methods, and people. The machinery must work well, e.g. most important is the speaker system by which the order is transmitted and received, the bell and its operating system must work well, the menu sign must be readable and conveniently placed, the order computer/cash register must be working properly to give the total bill, and all the

necessary equipment in the food preparation area must also be working properly. The "materials" used in order taking are few, however, the sign must be kept up-to-date with the latest prices and selection of menu items. The method currently being used is shown on the flowchart, and possible improvements are discussed in the next paragraph. The people who take the order must be trained to be courteous, friendly, accurate, and knowledgeable, or the system's quality will suffer.

Possible improvements to the system might include installation of a second window, so that the order is taken at the first window, money is collected there, and the pickup is made at the second window. A radio transmit/receive unit linking the customer at the sign to the employee wearing a headset could increase the ability of the employee to hear the order and to move around to assemble the order while the customer is driving through. Automatic order entry of standard selections might be built into the menu board with push buttons (similar to an automated teller machine in a drive-through banking operation). This would probably need to be coupled with personal assistance from employees for special orders via a speaker system.

15.   Answers will depend on the level of detail to which students analyze their routines.

16.   A checksheet for a high school student who is getting poor grades on math quizzes would contain information related to time spent studying, numbers of problems attempted and solved correctly for homework, completeness of class notes, scheduled assignments completed, and number and frequency of chapters read. A checklist table might look like:

Category	Monday	Tuesday	.. Sunday	Totals
Time - End	9:30	10:30	9:15	Avg. 9:00
" - Start	9:00	11:00	8:00	Avg. 8:30
" - Hours	0.5	0.5	1.25	3.5 hrs. / Avg 0.5 hr
Problems - Tried	\\\\	⊬⊤⊤ \\\	⊬⊤⊤ \\\\	42 total 6 avg.
Problems - Correct	\\\	⊬⊤⊤	\\\\	21 total 3/day avg.
Assign- ments Com- pleted	1 out of 2	1 out of 2	3 out of 4	Average of 2 out of 3
Number of chapters read/assgn	0.5 out of 1	0.5 out of 1	None	2 out of 3

17.   Problem detection methodology is often used in services to detect and isolate critical problems. Customers assess each problem along key dimensions, such as frequency and bothersomeness, with estimates of a particular problem. Managers then try to concentrate on those problems that are especially bothersome or have frequencies associated with higher levels of "bother." The techniques does have limitations brought about by difficulty in using customer ratings to develop an accurate and appropriate rating system.

18.   See the cause and effect diagrams, below, for a, b, and c as examples.

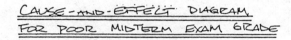

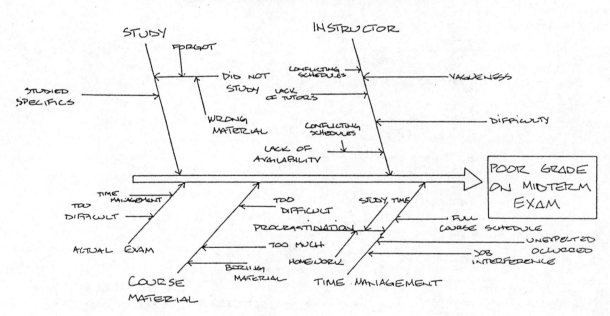

Question 18.

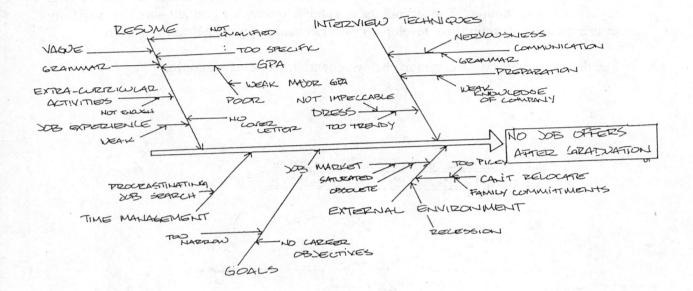

CAUSE-AND-EFFECT DIAGRAM
FOR LACK OF JOB OFFERS

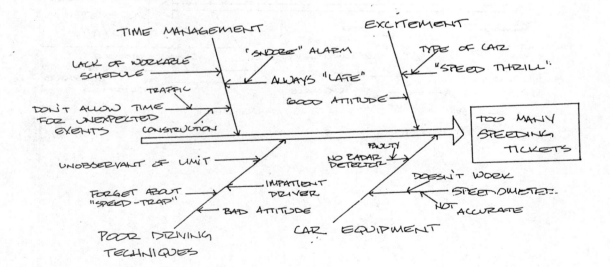

CAUSE-AND-EFFECT DIAGRAM FOR
EXCESSIVE SPEEDING TICKETS

19.   Answers will vary, depending on the experience and interests of the students.

20.   The solution to this comprehensive case project is left up to the ingenuity of the student teams.

21.   The PepsiCo flowchart explicitly contains three of the elements of Deming's plan-do-study-act cycle. Planning involves a customer focus, analysis of the current steps in the process, and proposing an improved process, with process measures. "Doing" involves pilot testing the new process, implementing stabilizing it, and continuously improving it (repeating the cycle). After the pilot test, it is assumed that one would study the results for flaws or necessary corrections before full implementation takes place. This is not stated explicitly. In contrast with the Deming cycle, there is a definite **customer focus** that is a unique part of the planning process.

PepsiCo's process has several features that are similar to the Juran improvement program, as well. The process flowchart seems to emphasize the steps in the *diagnostic journey, the remedial journey, and holding the gains* that Juran developed.

22.   See flowchart, below, for the summary of the process. The most serious problem from the standpoint of customer service is the fact that there may be as much as a 12-hour delay before an order reaches the supervisor for error checking, and another 3-4 hours may be required before entry into the computer. There was obviously too much checking and handling of the order, and much of the checking occurred many hours after the customer and order information had originally been taken. Several suggestions for improvement could include: a) process small batches of orders (perhaps within 1-2 hours, or less); b) have built-in error checking, perhaps through direct entry of telephone orders into the computer; c) also, at the time the order is taken, process information need for customer verification and setup of new accounts; d) only have the phone department supervisor audit or sample orders for errors; e) develop a computerized method of matching orders and invoices, so that manual verification is not required; f) if order verification and proofreading is a vital step, then a have an exceptions report generated after step (e), with proofreading required for printing information that cannot be computerized.

Question 22.

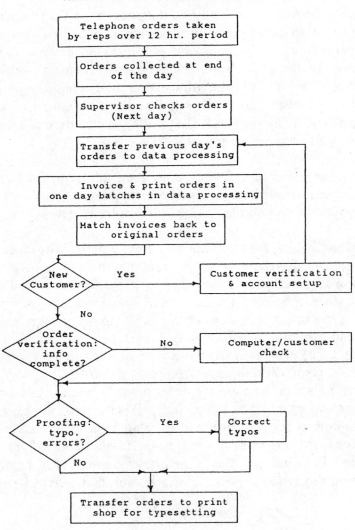

CATALOG ORDER FILLING PROCESS

23.   The solution to this process analysis problem is left up to the student.

24.   For the Welz Business Machines case problem, a comprehensive analysis is required.

a. & b. See the cause and effect and Pareto diagrams, below.

c. The cause and effect diagram and the Pareto analysis help to determine where the problem of long telephone waiting may lie and point the way to some possible solutions. First, the Pareto diagram shows that the two major categories that account for most of the customer problems are no operator (operators short-staffed) and no receiver (receiving party not present). These reasons account for 73.1% of the customer complaints about long waits. The causes for these problems for phone service representatives seem to be that peak periods are not well-staffed and there is no lunch break coverage. For the "no receiver" category, the sales representatives who are frequently out of the office seem to have no "back up" people who stay to receive calls.

Possible solutions are to bring in extra phone representatives for peak morning and afternoon periods, and either "stagger" lunch breaks or bring in extra representatives, then. The sales representatives, and/or their supervisors, should attempt to develop cross-training, so that everyone in the office is equally well-trained, sales representatives should be scheduled to be "on call" in the office at certain times, and communications should be set up in such a way that phone reps and sales reps work to coordinate customer service and communications, perhaps even giving the phone reps pager access to reach sales reps in the field.

CAUSE AND EFFECT DIAGRAM - WELZ CASE

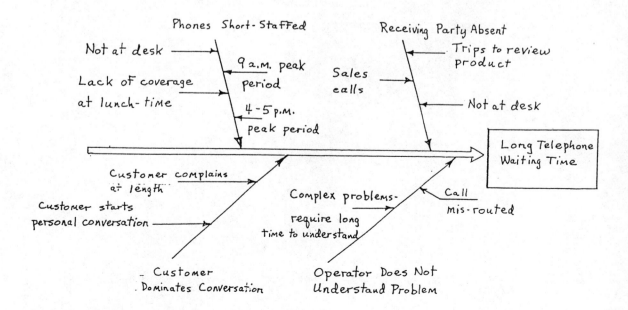

Question 24.

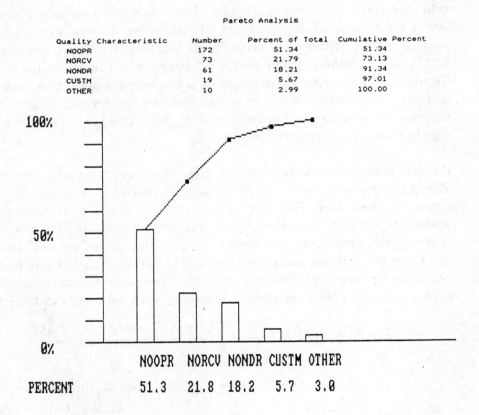

Pareto Analysis

Quality Characteristic	Number	Percent of Total	Cumulative Percent
NOOPR	172	51.34	51.34
NORCV	73	21.79	73.13
NONDR	61	18.21	91.34
CUSTM	19	5.67	97.01
OTHER	10	2.99	100.00

	NOOPR	NORCV	NONDR	CUSTM	OTHER
PERCENT	51.3	21.8	18.2	5.7	3.0

25.   The Circle H "case" problem is designed to give students a "feel" for the types of challenges that are faced by quality auditors, who must act as "detectives" to determine **what** problem exists before they can recommend **how** it is to be fixed. In this case, there are many questions raised by the data from the customer survey. The main question in this case is "how to define the problem." answers to associated questions are:

   a. A number of questions about the problem must be raised, and appropriate data must be gathered inside and outside the company, before the solution can be found. Among these are:

   • How many people were included in the survey at the three former customer's companies, from which the survey data was compiled? What were their titles and what <u>specifically</u> did they say about the three top complaint categories?
   • If detailed information on complaint categories is available from the customers, what data can they provide on the way in which the packaging was inconvenient (wrong sizes, way the order was packed and shipped from the plant, etc.)? What data is available on delivery and restocking time? Has this changed recently, or was it always "too slow"? What information can be provided about the lack of availability of preferred items? Was their customer representative aware that this was a problem? What was done to communicate and handle the problems?
   • What internal company information is available from the shipping department on the way the product is packed before sending the product to the customer? Have customer preferences in packaging been communicated to shipping?
   • What information is available from the ordering and production control departments on the former customers' preferences for certain products versus production scheduling and run sizes? Are these products running into capacity bottlenecks, constantly sold out, or delayed during production due to chronic production problems?

   b. The same type of questions used above could be extended to the investigation of whether the credit approval process significantly affected the order processing time. Specifically, you would need to know when the customers became aware of the fact that delivery and restocking were "too slow." Then the following line of investigation should be taken in the company, by asking:

   • What information is available from <u>all</u> affected departments on the <u>complete</u> process used to enter and process orders, up to and including the new delay for credit checking of restock orders, and how are controls set up to ensure that the orders are shipped in a timely and complete fashion?
   • Were any of the former customers involved in the delinquent accounts receivable category? Was there a way to avoid having <u>every</u> restock order to be scrutinized by the credit department, such as having a code on the order for "good" customers and a separate code for "delinquent" customers?

c. If there are problems in order processing and accounts receivable, as there appear to be, the next step is to analyze their processes, determine what controls are in place, find out why the controls aren't giving satisfactory results, and organize a team composed of representatives from both departments to take quick corrective action.

SOLUTIONS TO PROBLEMS

1. From the histogram, below, it appears that the waiting time is concentrated in the 2 periods from 3.02 up to 12.53 seconds. The histogram tells us that the times are concentrated on the lower end of the scale, but there are some long waiting times (specifically 6 out of 20 observations, or 30% of the total).

    NOTE: The histograms in this and the next problem are not in the format of histograms presented in this chapter of the text. They are reproduced directly from the Quality Management Analyst software and may require some "translation" to avoid confusion, when presented to students.

```
        Minimum value:          3.00000
        Maximum value:         22.00000
        First quartile:         6.50000
        Median:                 8.00000
        Third quartile:        14.50000
        Average:               10.15000
        Variance:              30.76579
        Standard Deviation:     5.54669
        Range:                 19.00000
        No. of observations    20

            Histogram

    Cell  Upper Limit  Frequency
    ----  -----------  ---------
     1       -1.74        0     |
     2        3.02        1     |*
     3        7.77        7     |*******
     4       12.53        6     |******
     5       17.28        3     |***
     6       22.04        3     |***
     7      infinity      0     |
```

2. See the histogram for a graphical summary. Running time is fairly evenly distributed. Frequencies rise to a peak in the 10.14 - 14.95 hour category and then fall from there.

```
        Minimum value:          4.20000
        Maximum value:         27.50000
        First quartile:         8.90000
        Median:                12.40000
        Third quartile:        15.40000
        Average:               12.54500
        Variance:              31.39313
        Standard Deviation:     5.60296
        Range:                 23.30000
        No. of observations    20

            Histogram

    Cell  Upper Limit  Frequency
    ----  -----------  ---------
     1        0.54        0     |
     2        5.34        2     |**
     3       10.14        5     |*****
     4       14.95        7     |*******
     5       19.75        4     |****
     6       24.55        1     |*
     7      infinity      1     |*
```

3. See the Pareto diagram, below. We can conclude from this diagram that 49.2% of the problems are with unclear charges and another 34% are due to long delays, for a total in the top two categories of 83.2%. These are the categories that should be improved first.

Error Category	Frequency	%
Unclear charges	9650	49.23
Long delays	6672	34.04
Shipping errors	1960	10.00
Billing errors	867	4.42
Delivery errors	452	2.31
Totals	19601	100.00

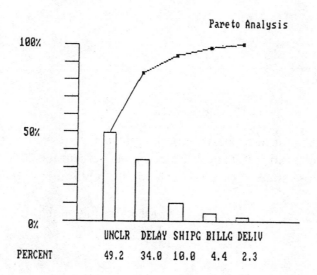

* Scale values do not sum to 100% due to rounding errors.

4.   The scatter diagram, below, (really, a regression plot from the Quality Management Analyst software) shows an interesting, and perhaps counter-intuitive result. As the production rate increases, the defect rate decreases. This could be because of the "learning curve" effect in that as operators become more skilled and familiar with the process and production runs are longer, the defect rate can be improved.

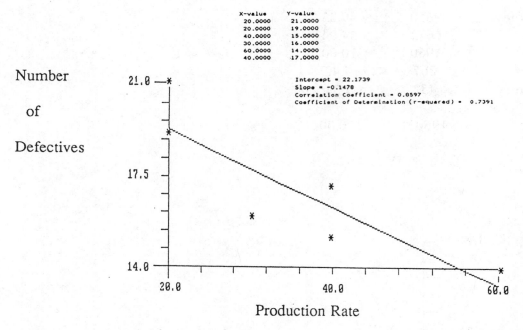

5.   On the control chart (a modified p-chart), below, ignoring control limits, we see that on day 20 and 21, the number of defects (and associated percentage of defects) was very high. Other than that, the process appears to be stable, without excessive variations or trends up or down.

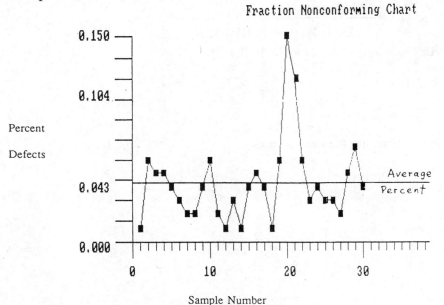

ANSWERS TO CASE QUESTIONS

Case I. The State University Experience

1.   The prospective student experienced a number of service quality defects in trying to navigate "the system" at State College. First, the tour guide was not well trained, thus creating a poor initial impression.

The admissions process obviously needed improvement. The application form was confusing, a transcript was lost, the choice of major by the applicant was miscoded, and the confirmation form contained redundant information that had been requested on the previously submitted application form.

The billing and financial aid process were also uncoordinated. The systems for payment seemed to have some unresolved problems, which created errors and confusion.

2.   To fix the problems with the systems at State University, administrators should begin with customer focus. They need to understand the problems of the average 18-25 year old prospective student, and design their processes to be user-friendly. This would require them to chart the processes (such as admissions, financial aid and billing), analyze them for unnecessary steps and overlap (such as the same information required on the application and the acceptance form), gather data on the problems and perhaps analyze them using Pareto analysis, and redesign the system to simplify it. With this approach, customer satisfaction could certainly be improved.

Case II. Ajax Insurance

1.   Ajax has identified its key processes, which are "owned" by teams. These teams have end-to-end responsibility for all aspects of these processes. At a high level, Ajax strives to ensure that each team has the right number and mix of people to meet customer requirements within cycle time standards. Associates are trained and held accountable for their activities through customer-driven quality measures and standards, primarily timeliness and accuracy. These are measured through information systems or by sampling on a daily, weekly, or monthly basis as appropriate. Clear standards are provided for each key process. Counts on labor-intensive activities are maintained and forecasted by type of customer and service. Personnel from pools can be shifted to different activities to smooth the workload.

Teams are empowered to act on process upsets. Other appropriate managers or associates may join the teams as necessary. A seven step process is used to resolve out-of-control conditions. Root causes that lie outside the process are resolved with external customer input. Processes that remain out of control for more than 3 weeks are facilitated by QA and process improvement teams, which may recommend various improvements. Improvement memos document important information for continuous improvement.

Generally, Ajax has an effective process control approach based on well-defined processes, clear customer-based standards, measurements, and team-based action plans. Particularly notable is the involvement of external customers to improve problems whose root causes lie outside the processes themselves. However, standards for all key customer requirements for each process are not fully described (for example, policy production or timeliness of new business information. In addition, it is not clear how measurements or observations are used to maintain control.

2.   Process improvement teams and managers analyze customer satisfaction data and other measures as part of their process improvement approach. The on-line inventory provides a useful categorization of improvement opportunities. One might question why Quality Assurance, rather than process improvement teams and managers themselves, maintains the inventory of improvement opportunities. Process analysis, benchmarking, new technology analysis, and other approaches are used to support improvement efforts. Examples of efforts are provided. However, this description does not provide enough information to conclude that Ajax is effectively improving processes or that improvement initiatives are widely deployed. For example, it is not clear how stretch targets are used for improvement. The large number of potential improvement items in the inventory suggests that the company spends more time seeking opportunities rather than making the actual improvements themselves.

CHAPTER 10

Human Resource Management for Quality

Teaching Notes

This chapter provides an overview of one of the most important sub-systems in TQM - the human resources sub-system. The human resources area is undergoing wrenching change as organizations try to improve or keep their people motivated, enhance quality and productivity, and downsize the organization to remain competitive and profitable. Students may have had prior courses in management, organization behavior, or personnel and human resources management, and may thus feel that they are "experts" in this area. You should point out that companies which embrace the TQM philosophy are now adopting a <u>unique</u> HRM perspective. In some ways, this perspective "goes against the grain" of the traditional HRM approaches, while taking advantage of much of the behavioral research that has never been well-implemented in business organizational practices. Key objectives for this chapter should include:

• To establish the differences between traditional HRM practices, that have tended to focus primarily on tasks and duties of HRM personnel, as opposed to quality-related individual development and enhancement of employee involvement in problem-solving and decision-making activities using team approaches.

• To provide definitions and historical insight into the multi-faceted nature of HRM and to lay out the characteristics of a progressive, sometimes radical, approach to HRM when it is blended with the TQM philosophy.

• To point out the need for companies that adopt the blended TQM/HRM approach to align their quality philosophy and measurement systems with HRM objectives, individual motivational approaches, leadership development, employee selection and retention, training and development, appraisal and compensation practices.

• To briefly review theoretical concepts of motivation and leadership and to show how they may be effectively applied in a TQM environment. To that end, and important d) is to be made between <u>process</u> and <u>content</u> theories of motivation and leadership. Most undergraduate and many graduate students have never had this distinction pointed out to them, so they rely on the oversimplified concepts of Maslow's Hierarchy of Needs to explain complex motivational behavior.

• To develop the concept that industrial engineering and union/management relations must undergo changes in order to be compatible with the new HRM/TQM approach.

• To introduce the idea that the HRM/TQM approach requires that an effective and progressive compensation system depends on a policy of equitable rewards that reinforce group achievements and a system of individual pay linked to skills and mastery.

ANSWERS TO QUALITY IN PRACTICE KEY ISSUES

<u>Human Resource Management at Disneyland</u>

1. Disney has build TQM concepts into the HRM function by recognizing the importance of individual and group efforts to the success of their business. They work to develop the core HRM concepts of "motivation, pride, dedication, responsibility, and reward into their human resources practices. This allows them to offer the characteristics of cleanliness, courtesy, and friendliness that customers equate with "service quality" at theme parks like Disneyland. It also pays off in the long run, because employee loyalty helps uphold quality standards, while keeping training and development costs down.

2. As a service firm, Disney has the usual challenges of:
    (a) The intangible output of service systems.
    (b) The fact that behavioral aspects of management, such as motivation, are critical to quality control and enhancement in Disney's service business.
    (c) Service organizations, such as Disney, handle a large volume of transactions, which increases the opportunity for error.
    (d) Inspection cannot be used as a means of quality control in many aspects of Disney's operations, since their services are consumed as they are created and cannot be inventoried.
    (e) Because Disney provides services that are labor intensive, quality cannot be "automated" into the process.
    (f) The service delivery system is often very time sensitive, and customers and Disney workers must often interact for delivery of quality service.

Taking Care of People at FedEx

1.   Human resource (HR) activities at FedEx are an integral part of the people-service- profit corporate philosophy. By having policies and practices in place that show that people are to be treated fairly and are important, FedEx shows its commitment to quality service. Apparently top management believes that the profits will follow if people and service are emphasized.

2.   The processes at FedEx include the GFTP process for grievance handling, the SFA employee leadership survey, the Open Door Policy, FXTV, formal reward and recognition programs, extensive training (especially the Leadership Institute) and the Quality Academy. Customer focus is supported by these processes because top managers have realized that employees, as well as paying customers, are *their* customers, as well. For employees to serve the ultimate customer, they must feel that management cares about their opinions, needs for proficiency and personal empowerment. Participation and teamwork is supported especially well by FXTV, the formal reward and recognition program, training (including the Leadership Institute), and the Quality Academy. Continuous improvement is encouraged by the GFTP, the SFA survey, the Open Door policy and (again) extensive training. All are interrelated, so it is difficult to say how much impact any single process has on the overall outcome of TQM at FedEx.

ANSWERS TO REVIEW QUESTIONS

1.   The impact of F.W.Taylor on quality and productivity has been profound. Taylor developed his "scientific management approach" primarily to improve efficiency and productivity of manual workers. However, under the pressure to achieve productivity improvements, quality eroded. Labor unions became stronger and adversarial relations developed between labor and management as the "push" for productivity intensified. The Taylor system failed to make use of the knowledge and creativity of the workforce.

2.   According to Byars and Rue:

"Human resource management (HRM) encompasses those activities designed to provide for and coordinate the human resource of an organization... Human resource management is a modern term for what has been traditionally referred to as personnel administration or personnel management."

Human resource functions include determining the organization's human resource needs; recruiting, selecting, developing, counseling, and rewarding employees; acting as a liaison with unions and government organizations; and handling other matters of employee well-being."

Human resource managers still perform the traditional tasks of "personnel management," such as: interviewing job applicants, negotiating contracts with unions, keeping time cards on hourly employees, and teaching training courses, but the scope and importance of their area of responsibility has changed dramatically. These managers are taking on a <u>strategic</u> role in their organizations. They're also being required to plan for the development of the <u>corporate culture</u>, as well as day-to-day operations involved with maintenance of HRM systems. In organizations that are committed to a Total Quality Management philosophy, both the <u>process and content</u> of the human resource department -- the way that it carries out its mission and responsibilities -- is rapidly changing.

3.   The traditional HRM approach versus the TQM/HRM viewpoint is summarized in Table 10.1. The traditional norm in many industries over the years has been the formal, contractual approach to human resources management. It is identified with the "labor relations" (with or without union involvement) and "industrial engineering" perspectives, within the framework of the personnel management systems. It has frequently led to rigid work rules, labor unrest, and a "we-versus-they" mind-set as management and labor attempted to get or keep the upper hand.

However, the TQM/HRM approach has been used recently by many small, medium, and a few large firms to develop a more cooperative, productive, flexible, and innovative work environment. This approach is in the spirit of the "human relations approaches," although it does not deny the necessity of developing human resource, industrial engineering and labor relations systems to meet organizational needs.

4.   The TQM-based HRM practices used by leading companies include:

• Integration of human resource plans with overall quality and operational performance plans to fully address the needs and development of the entire work force.
• Empowerment of individuals and teams to make decisions that affect quality and customer satisfaction.
• Continual improvement of key personnel management processes such as recruitment, hiring, training, performance evaluation, and recognition.
• Maintenance of a work environment conductive to the well-being and growth of all employees, and measurement of employee satisfaction.
•   Promotion of ongoing employee contributions through individual and group participation.

5.   Business strategy has to be considered when a TQM/HRM quality approach is being developed because the strategy determines the HRM structure, and the HRM mission and goals must support the organization's strategy and mission. The typical competitive strategy used by organizations that do not find themselves in highly unstable or very stable environments, but tend to fall somewhere in between, is the quality enhancement strategy. The profile of employee behaviors necessary for firms pursuing a strategy of quality enhancement is (1) relatively modest and predictable behaviors, (2) a more long-term or intermediate focus, (3) a modest amount of cooperative, interdependent behavior, (4) a high concern for quality, (5) a modest concern for quantity of output, (6)

high concern for process (how the goods or services are made or delivered), (7) low risk-taking activity, and (8) commitment to the goals of the organization.

In firms that attempt to gain competitive advantage through a quality-enhancement strategy, the key HRM practices include (1) relatively fixed and explicit job descriptions, (2) high levels of employee participation in decisions relevant to immediate work conditions and the job itself, (3) a mix of individual and group criteria for performance appraisal that is mostly short-term and results-oriented, (4) relatively egalitarian treatment of employees and some guarantees of employment security, (5) extensive and continuous training and development of employees.

In general, managers must make choices in the five areas that affect the design and operation of the HRM system: planning, staffing, appraising, compensating, and training and development. Each of these five areas has dimensions that can be viewed on a continuum from a structured environment with rigid practice to an unstructured environment with flexible practices.

6. Empowerment simply means giving people authority and power to make decisions, gain greater control over their work, and thus more easily satisfy customers. Successful empowerment of employees requires that:

- Employees be provided education, resources and encouragement.
- Policies and procedures be examined for needless restrictions on the ability of employees to serve customers.
- An atmosphere of trust be fostered rather than resentment and punishment for failure.
- Information be shared freely rather than closely guarded as a source of control and power.
- Workers feel their efforts are desired and needed for the success of the organization.
- Managers be given the support and training to adopt a "hands off" leadership style.
- Employees be trained in the amount of latitude they are allowed to take.
- Managers relinquish some power, but also obtain new responsibilities for hiring and developing people capable of handling empowerment, for encouraging risk-taking, and for recognizing achievements.

7. Meeting and exceeding customer expectations begins with hiring the right people. Managers look for new employees displaying enthusiasm, resourcefulness, creativity, and the flexibility to learn new skills rapidly. Good interpersonal skills are also necessary. Customer-focused employees should exhibit calmness under stress, optimism, initiative, and a people-orientation, the ability to listen well, and the ability to analyze, prevent, and solve problems.

Career development is also changing because of TQM. As managerial roles shift from directing and controlling to coaching and facilitating, managers who must deal with cross-functional problems benefit more from horizontal movement than from upward movement in narrow functional areas. Thus, career development expands learning opportunities and creates more challenging assignments rather than increasing spans of managerial control.

8.   Performance appraisal is an exceedingly difficult HRM activity to perform. Dissatisfaction with conventional performance appraisal systems is common among both managers, who are the appraisers, and workers, who are the appraisees. Literally dozens of research studies and analyses by experts have pointed out the problems and pitfalls of performance appraisal. The controversy is over whether the conventional approach can be improved, or whether a radical approach, such as suggested by Deming is the "right" answer.

The "conventional" school says that a formal process is necessary and desirable, but can be improved upon. The "Deming followers" school says that a formal process is unnecessary and should be eliminated due to flaws in any such process. Although the "anti-appraisal" supporters are growing in number, theirs is the more controversial viewpoint, and would require radical changes in both the appraisal and compensation practices of most organizations. The "anti's" are strict followers of W. Edwards Deming, who has condemned performance appraisal process as one of the "seven deadly diseases" of management. Deming literally suggests that management eliminate the use of performance appraisal because it is statistically unsound.

There is no one right answer to the question of whether conventional performance reviews should be eliminated, or not. Obviously, a TQM-oriented organization must face the question of what they reward and how they will do so. Performance appraisals are most effective in a TQM environment when they are based on the objectives of the work teams that support the organization. In this respect, they act as a diagnostic tool and review process for individual, team, and organizational development and achievement. The performance appraisal can also be a motivator when it is developed and used by the work team itself. Quality improvement is one of the major dimensions on which employees are evaluated, and many companies use peer review, customer evaluations, and self-assessments as part of the appraisal process. Other companies are replacing performance evaluation all together with personal planning and development systems; the thrust of the process is to develop each individual to the fullest.

9.   Quality and related training and education improve and/or enhance the knowledge and skills employees need to do their jobs efficiently and effectively. Training includes quality awareness, leadership, project management, communications, teamwork, problem solving, interpreting and using data, meeting customer requirements, process analysis and simplification, waste and cycle time reduction, error-proofing, and other educational issues affecting employee effectiveness, efficiency, and safety. In many cases, education also provides job enrichment skills and job rotation that enhance employees' career opportunities.

Companies should assess the specific training needs of employees. All employees need basic skills and quality orientation. Advanced topics differ among employee categories and functions. Companies committed to TQM invest heavily in training. Specific approaches vary by company size and requirements. Large companies often have in-house training staffs with state-of-the-art facilities while small companies may send employees to public seminars. Continual reinforcement of lessons learned in training programs is essential. Companies must develop approaches for evaluating training effectiveness.

10.   The topics of motivation, leadership, performance review, and training and development all ultimately lead to the question of "what's in it for me?" or, "what is the reward structure?" for each individual in every organization. Without willing, sustained individual effort, coordinated team efforts, and the sum total of the individual efforts that meet organizational goals, TQM is an impossible dream. Extrinsic and intrinsic rewards are the key to sustained individual efforts. A well-designed pay and benefit system can provide excellent extrinsic motivation. The design of the job itself is the key to intrinsic rewards and has been discussed earlier. An emerging **commitment model** is replacing the **control model** for HRM. The commitment model is most compatible with our TQM/HRM model described earlier. It is by no means easy to make the transition to the TQM/HRM approach to compensation. In the long run, managers may have no choice but to move to the TQM/HRM model, due to the aging workforce, the need for general skills in broadly defined jobs, the trends toward group problem-solving and team efforts, and continual economic pressures from foreign and domestic sources.

11.   Key practices that lead to effective employee recognition and rewards include:
        a. Giving both individual and team awards.
        b.   Involving everyone, including both front-line employees and senior management.
        c. Tying rewards to quality based on measurement objectives, rewarding for behavior, not just results.
        d. Allowing peers and customers to nominate and recognize superior performance.
        e. Publicizing team and individual recognition extensively.
        f. Making recognition fun.

In managing quality, it is important to separate individual compensation, i.e. pay and promotion, from the performance appraisal. One way to do this is through gainsharing, where all employees, regardless of rank, share savings equally. Another way to separate compensation from performance is to have pay tied closely to the acquisition of new skills. This can be done within the context of a continuous improvement program in which all employees are given opportunities to broaden their work-related competencies.

Team incentives, gain sharing, and pay for skills should not be installed if individualized measures, such as bonus systems and individual incentive systems are left in place. If management is not willing to spend resources in training employees so that they can continuously improve their skills, then they might as well not install such innovative pay systems. Management needs to be <u>very</u> careful about sending "mixed messages" when they design their reward systems.

12.   The model, developed by Bounds and Pace, describes how individual activities of selection, performance, appraisal, development, and reward can be tied to the identical activities system within the overall company for a viable HRM process. For example, a high quality individual cannot be selected unless the HRM recruiter has determined what the relative goals and objectives of the system or organization are, and how an individual's skills and characteristics will help to enhance the quality of that organization or department. To avoid the drawbacks of individual performance appraisal, HRM systems that are geared primarily toward individuals must be modified to encourage and reward individuals to support team initiatives. Finally, in system development and organizational improvement, HRM managers must encourage individual development activities that support and enhance the systems.

13.   A simple definition of motivation is response to a felt need. Thus, there are three components of motivation: 1) the felt need, 2) the stimulus that produced that felt need, 3) and the response to the stimulus.

14.   The distinction between process and content theories of motivation is extremely important. Process theories deal with the "dynamics" of motivation, while content theories focus on a static "snapshot" of motivation characteristics. The content theories of Maslow, Herzberg, and McGregor focus primarily on a single aspect of behavior, such as the priority of human needs (Maslow), application of needs within organizations (Herzberg's Two-Factor Theory), or managerial attitudes about worker's needs (McGregor's Theory X-Y). Vroom's and Porter and Lawler's models look at the dynamic process of how people make choices, based on their personal characteristics and organizational contingencies in order to obtain rewards. Environmentally based theories are designed to alter the environment in which employees find themselves, with a goal of providing a more supportive climate within which individuals will be motivated to work..

15.   The Porter and Lawler model draws on expectancy theory and provides some insights into motivation that may be used to enhance quality management. The model states that, depending on the actions of management, the expectations of the employees, and the actual outcomes, a certain quantity and quality of employee motivation in the organization will result. Implications that may be *cautiously* drawn from the model are that motivation of employees is somewhat related to the Deming philosophy. Actions taken toward empowering workers to make important decisions about quality, eliminating blame for uncontrollable variation, recruiting employees who will be committed to meeting quality standards, providing adequate training and education to employees, changing the role of supervisors to coaches and teachers, keeping workers informed of management decisions that affect quality, and providing the opportunities to participate in solving quality problems can all have a positive effect on motivation.

16.   The Hackman and Oldham job characteristics model can be used to design motivating potential into a job, thus enhancing quality. Their approach to task design help to explain

the motivational properties of tasks by tying together human and technical components of jobs. In the model, shown in Figure 10.5, the five core job characteristics of task significance, task identity, skill variety, autonomy, and feedback from the job can all be related in some way to quality. For example, the job of data entry operator in a computer center was formerly designed using a highly specialized "pool concept" where operators received work assigned at random from all departments. Also, groups of operators were designated to enter data while others did nothing but "verify" (re-key data) to check for accuracy. High error rates, low productivity, absenteeism, and turnover were experienced in the center. When the job was redesigned, using Hackman and Oldham's concepts, substantial improvement in quality, productivity, and measures of employee satisfaction resulted. The redesign involved cross-training on data entry and verification skills for all operators, assignment of work from individual departments to specified operators, and more control over work elements. This provided for a greater feeling of task identity and significance, an opportunity for greater use of skills, and more autonomy and feedback from "customers" in the departments that sent work to the center.

17.   Union-management relations are being affected by TQM in the workplace. In the past, there was a highly structured, "rules-based," generally adversarial relationship between the parties. The emphasis on teamwork, employee empowerment, and flexibility is requiring a new look at the traditional ares of: a) work operations ad design; b) pay systems; c) training; and d) system governance. Unfortunately, while many companies and unions seem to be willing to consider fresh points of view, the NLRB's recent rulings seem to have raised the possibility that forming and using teams will be more difficult in the future because of restrictions that suggest that they must be representative *organizational* units, free from *management control*, and difficult to set up in *non-union environments* without the company agreeing to bringing in a union.

ANSWERS TO DISCUSSION QUESTIONS

1.   Answers will vary, depending on the existing trade climate and international awareness of the students.

2.   This is a library exercise that will encourage the interested student to research one particular branch of HRM and tie in the findings to quality management issues.

3.   Business strategy may be responsible for determining how easily a firm can shift from a traditional to a TQM/HRM quality approach. Strategy determines the HRM structure, and the HRM mission and goals must support the organization's strategy and mission. The typical competitive strategy used by organizations that find themselves in between a highly unstable or very stable environment, is the quality enhancement strategy. The profile of employee behaviors necessary for firms pursuing a strategy of quality enhancement is (1) relatively modest and predictable behaviors, (2) a long-term or intermediate focus, (3) a modest amount of cooperative, interdependent behavior, (4) a high concern for quality, (5) a modest concern for quantity of output, (6) high concern

for process (how the goods or services are made or delivered), (7) low risk-taking activity, and (8) commitment to the goals of the organization.

In an attempt to gain competitive advantage through a quality-enhancement strategy, the key HRM practices include: (1) relatively fixed and explicit job descriptions, (2) high levels of employee participation in decisions relevant to immediate work conditions and the job itself, (3) a mix of individual and group criteria for performance appraisal that is mostly short-term and results-oriented, (4) relatively egalitarian treatment of employees and some guarantees of employment security, (5) extensive and continuous training and development of employees.

In general, managers must make choices in the five areas that affect the design and operation of the HRM system: planning, staffing, appraising, compensating, and training and development. Each of these five areas has dimensions that can be viewed on a continuum from a structured environment with rigid practice to an unstructured environment with flexible practices.

4.   The answers will vary here, depending on students' perspectives on relevant organizations.

5.   The answers will vary here, depending on students' perspectives.

6.   Students may be empowered to do anything that does not fall within the exclusive responsibility or technical expertise of the professor. They could develop "regulations" about the conduct of the classroom, participate in determining delivery methods, grade peers on activities like group case presentations and internal operations of their groups on teamwork dimensions, and participate in an advisory role to the professor in activities such as exam formatting and content delivery .

7.   Companies are increasingly asking colleges and universities to take on more responsibility for teaching TQM principles an other common business practices **before** the students reach them. This would indicate that in the future, if colleges and universities do not form a closer customer-supplier partnership that companies may simply set up their own accredited colleges and recruit trainable high school students that will be sent to their own "in-house" colleges.

8.   This controversial subject is left to the brave professors and eager students among our readers who wish to tackle the issue of how to change our traditional grading system in the U.S.

9.   See Review Question 8, above, for a definition from which to begin discussion. Understanding the system should be emphasized.

10.   The answers will vary here, depending on students' perspectives.

11.   The Xerox training strategy seems to have several advantages, including the basic quality values of customer focus, teamwork, top management leadership, and repeatable and measurable processes. Disadvantages are its "lock step" nature which might lack flexibility to meet local needs, and Mass training which may not be closely tied to the problems that people need to work on. The approach would tend to work in more highly structured businesses and those that have the financial resources to do extensive training.

12.   This student project is related to the concept of empowerment in Discussion Question 6, above.

13.   See Review Question 11, above, for a definition from which to begin discussion. Understanding the system should be emphasized.

14.   See Review Question 14, above, for a definition from which to begin discussion. The answers will vary here, depending on students' perspectives.

15.   This exercise is a "field" research project to encourage the students to go out and talk to "real world" managers to ascertain their level of knowledge and use of quality management concepts.

16.   Simple theories, such as those of Maslow, Herzberg, and McGregor provide a "snapshot" view of a limited number of dimensions of motivation. Complex models, such as Bandura's are "richer" and more dynamic, thus helping explain "real world" conditions and phenomena more fully.

17.   See Review Question 17, above, for an overview of the issues from which to begin assignment or discussion.

ANSWERS TO CASE QUESTIONS

Case I. HD Corporation

It is obvious that HD Corporation is suffering from a disease called "the paralysis of analysis." They are so caught up in their systems that they don't understand the need for either a customer focus or an employee emphasis. As plant manager, the first task would be to raise awareness of both of these issues. The first might be accomplished by bringing in a focus group of customers and determining their thoughts and feelings about the strengths and weaknesses of the products and services that the company provides. The summarized findings should be widely distributed.

Then to address the second issue, an anonymous employee survey might be taken to determine the employees' feelings about quality-related aspects such as customer focus, quality emphasis in the plant, participation (or lack of it) and the needs for training and development of the first-line managers and themselves.

Management should examine and analyze the data. They should decide what they are willing to do and how far they will go in changing the "corporate culture." Once the data was gathered and summarized, management and employee representatives should sit down, discuss the findings and what it means and begin to talk about options and possible solution.

Case II. Joy Industries

PPD's human resource strategy is based on the Corporate Quality Goal of achieving total customer satisfaction through employee involvement. The strategy has four key strategic components which specific plans and approaches identified with each of them. Long term plans are also presented. However, the integration with overall quality and operational performance plans is not clear. There is no clear linkage with overall business strategy nor specific description of how these plans will support overall strategy. The HR strategy is linked to manufacturing capabilities and requirements at different plants; however, specific developmental needs of the entire workforce are not identified clearly. Very little information is provided as to how plans include the issues listed in the first question.

PPD uses a variety of approaches to improve its HR plans and practices: benchmarking, studying Baldrige winners, employee feedback, and HR experts. The GMT reviews all HR goals to assure alignment with stretch goals and business plans, using a variety of performance indicators. PPD appears to clearly identify improvements based on data and information that address its key strategies and goals. However, how benchmarking and other approaches are used for improvement is not clearly described.

The company collects information for evaluating and improving its HR processes at three levels: QIT locations, divisional, and corporate. The scope and variety of information that is acquired suggests a high level of refinement of knowledge about HR processes. However, little specific information is provided as to how improvement is conducted. It is not clear how improvement initiatives are tied with company business directions. Another key issue is *integration*. It is not clear whether the information is used consistently among all the company's sites or addressed globally as a corporation. No information is provided as to how differences between union and non-union plants or between manufacturing and support personnel are addressed.

In summary, while a lot of information is gathered, it is not clear that it is being deployed consistent with business strategies or throughout the multiple sites and functions within the company.

CHAPTER 11

Employee Involvement and Participative Management

Teaching Note

This chapter focuses on the important topic of employee involvement and participative management. It covers the history of quality circles, employee participation, and involvement for two reasons. Students should know that the team concept, which the Japanese called "quality control circles, (QCC's)" was developed in the U..S. long before Ishikawa started circles in Japan, and the idea has been used successfully for many years in pioneering American companies, such as Lincoln Electric, Maytag, and Procter and Gamble. Second, the "roots" of employee involvement teams come from an interdisciplinary blend of behavioral psychology/sociology, engineering, and management science concepts that contribute to its richness and diversity. Understanding EI should help bridge the gap between the "quants" and the "touchy-feely" people who are interested in TQM. Key objectives for this chapter are:

• To establish the importance of participative problem-solving approaches as a way to build bridges between individuals and groups with diverse backgrounds.

• To show the interdisciplinary nature of EI and its history.

• To summarize the Japanese contribution to the development of QCC's and their adapting of problem-solving techniques that provided tools for team members to use.

• To appreciate why Quality Circles (QC's) in the U.S. in the 1980's had limited success.

• To define and clarify the concept of self-managed work teams.

• To describe how firms have overcome earlier QC problems to develop successful EI programs.

• To suggest ways in which EI programs have, or can measure results, based on principles developed by effective organizations.

ANSWERS TO QUALITY IN PRACTICE KEY ISSUES

Total Employee Involvement at Burroughs Wellcome Co.

1.   The steps involved in developing B.W. Co.'s Total Employee Involvement concept began with investigation of quality circles in 1981, with the installation of six pilot teams. They did parallel the steps shown in Figure 11.3 fairly closely. After initial leader and team training, these teams set about identifying and solving problems in their own work areas. The voluntary teams got off to a rather slow start, but soon picked up speed. The initial patience of the steering committee was rewarded, and the program was approved for expansion to the point where, in five years time the number of circles had grown to 63, and projected annual savings were over $1 million. Little was mentioned of the initial facilitator or leader training, but leader/facilitator length of service became an early threat to the program and its growth. After that, two other issues of management support and need for efficient documentation and administration were overcome. The second through fourth stages of evolution of employee involvement as management and hourly worker "buy-in" took place, employee ownership was developed, and movement toward complete "self management" of the EI process is evident.

2.   It seems that the 10-year success of the E.I. program at B.W. Co. is based on the concept of continuous improvement and evolution of the program toward self-management by employees, and adoption of the idea by management that this participative approach is a "way of doing business." These results seem to be well correlated with results from various participation studies cited in the chapter. The EI program at B.W. Co. has had a positive effect on job satisfaction, has had strong support in a"hi tech," research-based firm, it has been shown to enhance group effectiveness, it is positively related to the fact that ideas are implemented quickly, and it did take time and money (and patience) to get the quality circle process under way, initially.

RIT/USA Today Quality Cup Awards

1.   Process management involves planning and administering the activities to achieve a high level of performance in a process, and identifying opportunities for improving quality and operational performance, and ultimately, customer satisfaction. A team from the U.S. Steel Gary Works visited customers' plants and revised their process to reduce rejects, which decreased from 2.6% to 0.6% after their suggestions were adopted. A team from Norfolk General Hospital cut out 14 wasted steps from a 40 step process, reducing the turnaround time for X-rays, CAT scans and other radiological tests from 72.5 to 13.8 hours. The administrative team at Wilkerson Middle School in Birmingham set up a peer reading program for sixth grade students that helped increase their reading scores by 21-31% over a year's time in 6th, 7th, and 8th grades. A Pacific Bell team investigated causes for

cable-related service outages and found that 41% of them were caused by contractors cutting cables with backhoes. They developed a publicity and enforcement process to raise contractor awareness of the problem. The result was a 24% reduction in cable damage in 1993, saving Pacific Bell $6 million. The important focus of process management in on preventing defects and errors, and eliminating wasteful procedures, resulting in better quality and improved company performance through shorter cycle times and faster customer responsiveness.

2.   Criteria for evaluating excellence of Quality Cup applications might include asking:

■ If the company provided adequate education, training in the amount of latitude they are allowed to take, resources and encouragement to their teams?

■ Whether team members showed evidence of a dedication to serving customers?

■ Whether teams systematically gathered information and organizations shared it freely rather than closely guarding it as a source of control and power?

■ If the information that was gathered was systematically analyzed and used to shed light on the problem and potential solutions?

■ If their managers gave support, but adopted a "hands off" leadership style to "empower" teams to come to their own conclusions on the proposed solution?

■ Was the solution implemented in a timely fashion with management support, and did the team follow up to see if the results were satisfactory?

■ What results were attained in the form of improved customer satisfaction, reduced scrap and rework, shorter cycle times, improved performance, and/or cost savings or profit increases?

In addition to corporate and team information, the application information should include a systematic description of the problem solving process. This might include the *problem definition phase* which would require a description of how the problem was discovered, the training process that the team members went through, and some aspects of how the team was managed, guided and supported. The *analysis phase* might include descriptions by teams of how the data was gathered (with special emphasis on customer input), what techniques were used to analyze it and what the results showed. The *decision phase* would include alternative solutions that were considered, why the final solution was chosen and who had to review and approve the recommendation. The *implementation phase* would describe how and who implemented the recommendation, what followup was done on the solution to ensure that it worked correctly, and would show the measurable results that were attained.

ANSWERS TO REVIEW QUESTIONS

1. EI offers many advantages over traditional management practices, including:

    (1) replacing the adversarial mentality with trust and cooperation.
    (2) developing the skills and leadership capability of individuals, creating a sense of mission and fostering trust
    (3) increasing employee morale and commitment to the organization
    (4) fostering creativity and innovation, the source of competitive advantage
    (5) helping people understand quality principles and instilling them into the corporate culture
    (6) allowing employees to solve problems at the source immediately
    (7) improving quality and productivity

2. First, the team concept, which the Japanese called "quality control circles," was developed and put into practice in the U.S. and other countries (such as Germany in the 1800's at the Zeiss Company) long before Ishikawa started circles in Japan. Also, the idea of team approaches to problem-solving has been used successfully for many years in a few pioneering American companies, such as Lincoln Electric, Maytag, and Procter and Gamble. Second, the "roots" of employee involvement teams come from an interdisciplinary blend of behavioral psychology/sociology, engineering, and management science concepts that contribute to its richness and diversity. (See the answer to question 6 for an additional historical summary.)

3. The levels of employee involvement and their primary outcomes, respectively, are:

    a. Information sharing--Conformance
    b. Dialogue--Acceptance
    c. Special problem solving--Contribution
    d. Intra-group problem solving--Commitment
    e. Inter-group problem solving--Cooperation
    f. Focused problem solving--Concentration
    g. Limited self-direction--Accountability
    h. Total self-direction--Ownership

4. Total quality leaders use key practices to foster employee involvement in their organizations:

    ■ They involve all employees at all levels and in all functions.
    ■ They use suggestion systems effectively to promote involvement and motivate employees.
    ■ They emphasize and support teamwork throughout the organization.
    ■ They monitor the extent and effectiveness of employee involvement.

5. Personal initiative involves individual employees taking action to spot and fix problems, contribute to a company's goals, and bring about change. If employees can develop a personal commitment to quality, they will persist in tasks, do them better, and commit to the goals and objectives of the organization.

6. Dessler's Keys To Commitment include the following:

    ▪ People-first values--A total management commitment to employees that includes such things as fair treatment, written policies, hiring and indoctrination processes, managers who will "walk the talk" in everyday actions, and elimination of trust barriers such as timeclocks.
    ▪ Double-talk--A catchy way of saying that communication must flow up the organization as well as down.
    ▪ Communion--Efforts to encourage people to take pride and develop a sense of ownership and belonging in their organization.
    ▪ Transcendental meditation--Articulation and development of the ideologies, missions, and values, and communication mechanisms they require.
    ▪ Value-based hiring--Careful attention to the hiring process by articulating the corporate values carefully, advertising widely, thorough interviewing, and rigorous training.
    ▪ Securitizing--Lifetime employment without guarantees, meaning that the company will do whatever it can to maintain permanent employment security through such practices as giving bonuses only when the company is profitable, and "sharing the pain" by salary and work-week reductions during economic downturns.
    ▪ Hard-side rewards--Pay plans that support employees and provide incentives for them to help themselves while they help the organization.
    ▪ Actualizing--Giving employees the opportunities and incentives to use a wide variety of skills and knowledge to accomplish their jobs.

    In the current corporate world, where corporation-employee relationships are being redefined, these "Keys to Commitment" are meant to provide employees with the senses of job security. It will be easier for employees to commit to TQM principles and corporate goals if their current and future position in the company is not viewed with uncertainty

7. Suggestion systems must be carefully planned and executed. Management should encourage submissions with no restrictions, acknowledge all of them and respond promptly, evaluate the suggestions carefully, reward employees, and monitor the suggestions that are implemented. Employees also need training in how to identify problems and develop solutions.

    As with many quality improvement methods, the Japanese have succeeded with suggestion systems, while American firms have frequently botched the job. This is due to a variety of reasons. Most U.S. suggestion systems emphasize cost savings, or favor significant, innovative ideas. This focus excludes fair consideration of long-run suggestions for improving quality or productivity. Where the Japanese actively solicit employee suggestions, U.S. managers take a passive approach, putting up a few suggestion boxes and waiting. Many U.S. companies do not provide time for employees to develop suggestions during the regular work day.

8.   The key success factors for suggestion systems include:

   ○ Management must first, and always foremost, be involved in the program. Involvement should begin at the top and filter down through all levels until all employees participate.
   ○ Push decision making regarding suggestion evaluation to lower levels.
   ○ Gain union support by pledging no layoffs due to productivity gains from adopted suggestions.
   ○ Train everyone in all facets of the suggestion system. Improve problem solving capability by promoting creative problem solving through the use of seven basic statistic tools.
   ○ Ensure that all suggestions are resolved in one month.
   ○ Ensure that all suggestors are able to personally describe their idea to a supervisor, engineer, or manager.
   ○ Promote pride in work, and quality and productivity gains from suggestions, rather than the big cash awards possible.
   ○ Remove ceilings on intangible suggestion awards. Revise evaluations of intangible suggestions to value them more on par with tangible suggestions.
   ○ Remove restrictions prohibiting suggestions regarding a worker's immediate work area.
   ○ Continuously promote the suggestion program, especially through supervisor support.
   ○ Trust employees enough to make allowances for generation, discussion, and submittal of suggestions during work hours.
   ○ Keep the program simple.

9.   A team is a small number of people with complementary skills who are committed to a common purpose, set of performance goals, and approach for which they hold themselves mutually accountable.

Teams provide opportunities to individuals to solve problems that they may not be able to solve on their own. Teams may perform a variety of problem-solving activities, and may also assume many traditional managerial functions. Effective teams are goal-centered, independent, open, supportive, and empowered.

10.   The most common types of teams are:

   - Quality circles--Teams of workers and supervisors that meet regularly to address workplace problems involving quality and productivity.

   - Problem-solving teams--Teams whose members gather to solve a specific problem and then disband.

- Management teams--Teams consisting mainly of managers from various functions like sales and production that coordinate work among teams.
- Work teams--Teams organized to perform entire jobs, rather than specialized, assembly line-type work. When work teams are empowered, they are called self-managed teams.
- Virtual teams--Relatively new, these team members communicate by computer, take turns as leaders, and jump in and out as necessary.

11.   Employee Involvement (EI) refers to participative team approaches currently being applied to problem solving and decision making in various organizations. These approaches involve transforming the culture of the entire organization to tap the creative energies of all employees. EI allows individuals "to discover their own potential--and to put that potential to work in more creative ways....People develop in themselves pride in workmanship, self-respect, self-reliance, and a heightened sense of responsibility."

12.   A quality circle is a small group of employees from the same work area who meet regularly and voluntarily to identify, solve, and implement solutions to work-related problems. Characteristics of quality circles include:

(1) Quality circles are small groups, ranging from 4 to 15 members. Eight members is considered the norm.
(2) All members come from the same shop or work area. This gives the circle its identity.
(3) The members work under the same supervisor, who is a member of the circle.
(4) The supervisor is usually, though not always, the leader of the circle. As leader, he or she moderates discussion and promotes consensus. The supervisor does not issue orders or make decisions. The circle members, as a group, make their own decisions.
(5) Voluntary participation means that everyone has an opportunity to join.
(6) Circles usually meet once every week on company time, with pay, and in special meeting rooms removed from their normal work area.
(7) Circle members receive training in the rules of quality circle participation, the mechanics of running a meeting and making management presentations, and techniques of group problem solving.
(8) Circle members, not management, choose the problems and projects that they will work on, collect all information, analyze the problems, and develop solutions.
(9) Technical specialists and management assist circles with information and expertise whenever asked to do so. Circles receive advice and guidance from an adviser who attends all meetings but is not a circle member.
(10) Management presentations are given to those managers and technical specialists who would normally make the decision on a proposal.

13.   Quality control circles were an outgrowth of the postwar education effort in Japan. Japanese manufacturers considered quality control to be the responsibility of all employees, including management and line workers. In postwar Japan, everyone from top managers on down were being trained in basic quality concepts using nationwide radio

broadcasts. This quality improvement effort and the cultural bias toward group activity resulted in the formation of the quality control circle concept, attributed to Dr. Kaoru Ishikawa of the University of Tokyo.

Evidence exists that quality circle concepts were used by some U.S. firms in the late 1960's. The quality of worklife programs developed in the early 1960's were related to circle concepts but tended to emphasize behavioral interventions, reorganization of groups or tasks, or efforts to build or enhance morale. The quality circle movement became established in the U.S. after a team of managers for Lockheed Missiles visited Japan in 1973 to view quality control circles in action, and returned with a favorable review of the scheme. Quality circle programs began to catch on after Lockheed implemented its own highly successful circle program.

14.   A self-managed team is defined as "a highly trained group of employees, from 6 to 18, (maybe a little older), on average, fully responsible for turning out a well-defined segment of finished work. The segment could be a final product...or a service. It could also be a complete but intermediate product or service." Whereas the quality circle team is concerned mainly with finding and solving problems, the employees in a self-management team are encouraged to take on many of the roles formerly held only by management.

15.   Self-managed teams exhibit the following characteristics:

• They are empowered to share various management and leadership functions.
• They plan, control, and improve their own work processes.
• They set their own goals and inspect their own work.
• They often create their own schedules and review their performance as a group.
• They may prepare their own budgets and coordinate their work with other departments.
• They usually order materials, keep inventories, and deal with suppliers.
• They frequently are responsible for acquiring any new training they might need.
• They may hire their own replacements or assume responsibility for disciplining their own members.
• They take responsibility for the quality of their products and services.

16.   Numerous factors have been noted in the failure of quality circles programs. The failures of many programs have been based on false hopes of management for finding a panacea for all the ills that plagued U.S. businesses in the 1970's. Management believed that quality circles would only require limited support and commitment but would be a quick fix to quality problems. Deming's philosophy says that inadequate funding of the program, lack of proper training, resistance of staff or middle managers, and lack of proposal implementation by management are all elements of the management system beyond the control of the workers. Without support, workers quickly lose interest and initiative. It is likely that many of the early quality circle failures would have been avoided had managers understood and followed the Deming philosophy of culture change as a necessity for successful implementation of TQM.

17.   Fairly standard procedures exist for establishing EI team programs and training participants. Initially, there should be a period of investigation, reflection, and soul searching before buying into the concept of EI teams. The process begins with investigation of the history and philosophy of EI. After gathering this information, managers must examine the organization's goals, objectives, and culture to evaluate readiness to install quality circles. Once readiness has been established, and it has been decided to move ahead, most organizations find it best to establish a steering committee made up of a group of interested, committed line and staff members. If a union exists, union representation in the steering committee is needed. The steering committee establishes policies and procedures for the quality circle program and chooses a person or persons to be the facilitator(s). Facilitator(s), leaders and team member training is done. Initial projects are chosen by pilot teams, alternative solutions are investigated, the best solution is chosen and presented to management and the steering committee. After this pilot process and successful solutions to problems are presented by pilot teams, the decision is made as to whether to expand, stabilize or abort the EI program.

18.   Peter Scholtes suggests ten ingredients for a successful team:

(1) Clarity in team goals-- A team must agree on a mission, purpose, and goals.
(2) An improvement plan--A plan guides the team in determining schedules and mileposts by helping the team decide what advice, assistance, training, materials, and other resources it may need.
(3) Clearly defined roles--All members must understand their duties and know who is responsible for what issues and tasks.
(4) Clear communication--Members should speak with clarity, listen actively, and share information.
(5) Beneficial team behaviors--Teams should encourage members to use effective skills and practices to facilitate discussions and meetings.
(6) Well-defined decision procedures--Teams should use data as the basis for decisions and learn to reach consensus on important issues.
(7) Balanced participation--Everyone should participate, contribute their talents and share commitment to the team's success.
(8) Establish ground rules--The group outlines acceptable and unacceptable behavior.
(9) Awareness of group process--Team members exhibit sensitivity to nonverbal communication, understand group dynamics, and work on group process issues.
(10) Use of the scientific approach--With structured problem-solving processes, teams can more easily find root causes of problems.

19.   Keys to overcoming resistance, held by managers as organizational leaders, are early involvement by all parties, open and honest dialogue, and good planning. They must believe in workers and their ability to contribute. Managers, must also show commitment to the practices of EI, such as training, rewards, and recognition.   Some specific suggestions include:

○ Design the change process to include significant management involvement in its implementation.

○ Create significant dissatisfaction with the status quo, stimulating a need for change (For many companies, the crisis is already present).

○ Provide support to raise comfort levels with the new concepts.

○ Be consistent in the pursuit of participative management, continuously modeling the desired behavior.

○ Be intolerant of insubordination, and deal immediately and decisively with flagrant resisters.

20. Donovan has recommended seven steps in the design of SMTs during a transition from a quality circle type of program. The steps involved include:

(1) Create a work unit responsible for an entire task.
(2) Establish specific measures of the work unit's output.
(3) Design multi-skilled jobs.
(4) Create internal management and coordination tasks.
(5) Create boundary management tasks.
(6) Establish access to information.
(7) Establish support systems.

It does not make much difference if an organization has previous EI experience. The requirements to transform an existing organization to a team approach aren't considerably different from ones used to develop a start-up work-team organizational structure, with one exception, as noted in the text. Careful, systematic planning for both work-design and coordination issues is required for successful introduction of self-managed teams.

21. Because many activities of EI team programs are intangible and difficult to measure, EI program coordinators and facilitators have generally avoided setting up an explicit measurement system. Despite the difficulties of measurement, there are many reasons that it should be performed, including the need to:

(1) Convince management to begin an EI program.
(2) Convince management to continue its support of the EI program.
(3) Convince workers that it's worthwhile to continue the EI program.
(4) Decide whether to implement a costly improvement project proposal from a team.
(5) Assess the need to modify an EI program to improve its effectiveness.
(6) Choose an EI program installation over some other competing program (based on cost/benefit results)
(7) Justify budgeting limited funds to the EI program.
(8) Choose a "winning" team to appear at a local, regional, or national EI convention from within an organization.
(9) Calculate financial rewards for team suggestions.

(10) Satisfy management expectations for measurement.

22. Edward E. Lawler differentiated between the traditional Japanese-style TQM philosophy and the sociotechnical employee involvement philosophy. Lawler argued that the TQM approach, as he defined it, is more structured and driven by a philosophy that assumes management direction and involvement, structured planning processes, and continuous improvement of processes through problem-solving and incremental change. In contrast, the employee involvement approach is focused on various aspects of job design, organizational design, pay systems, and organization change. It is more effectiveness-oriented and less efficiency oriented than the structured TQM approach.

ANSWERS TO DISCUSSION QUESTIONS

1. See Review Question 16, above as a starting point for this discussion.

2. To move from level 1 to level 8 requires increasing levels of commitment by management and employees who share a common vision of where they want the organization to develop and change. The major obstacles would be resistance to change, lack of leadership commitment, or fear of changing from the familiar to the unknown.

3. EI in universities has typically been started in administrative areas, such as purchasing, accounting, facilities, security departments. As with all TQM efforts, if more support is available from top administrators, it is more likely that the EI process will be successful.

4. EI in the classroom would require considering how to empower students to solve problems in their own areas of expertise while still giving the professor authority to use his/her expertise for the benefit of "customer-clients" in the class. This might be done by developing an advisory board of students who could give advice and feedback to the professor during the academic term.

5. This field exercise is designed to further student awareness of the breadth of the "participative movement" and to help them to confirm that the theory of quality is being applied in a practical setting in business and industry.

6. Opinions may vary, depending on students' perspectives.

7. Students will always have had positive and negative experiences with teams, in their university classes and during part time or full time work periods. Problems invariably involve coordination and balancing the workload of team members. Successes often occur as a result of the shared experiences and synergistic problem solving abilities of teams.

8. Students' perspectives will vary. The Semco example in the text is about as "perfect" an example as is available. Of course the argument can (and will) be made "that's a case from another culture; it could never be done in the U.S. (or Canada, India, Mexico.)

9. The work content and labor effectiveness of EI teams cannot be effectively measured using time and motion studies because the tool doesn't fit the nature of the work being done. Time studies are meant to be used to set standards on routine, repetitive jobs, where each element of the work can be specified in a process sheet and work elements are uniform in content and duration, except for predictable variations. EI teams are formed to manage projects to improve work within or across the boundaries of their immediate work areas. They must use "project management" skills to deal with unique non-routine, non-repetitive problem solving projects, similar to the content of many managerial jobs.

10. The question of "people-oriented" managers and the requirement for "hard" measures of success of quality control circles in Japan is only a contradiction when looked at through "western eyes." In Japan, the group is the smallest unit of society, so what your group does reflects on you, as a member of the group. The manager of a group wants very much for the group to succeed, just as every group member wants it to succeed. Therefore, there is no conflict between the manager and the group members because they want to not only meet, but exceed the "quota" for the <u>group</u> that was set by the upper level manager, who also wants to see his "<u>group</u>" (company) succeed. In contrast, quotas are sometimes seen as de-motivating in the U.S., because we react as individuals, saying "how much more will <u>I</u> get paid, if <u>I</u> make <u>my</u> quota?" If there's no financial, or at least tangible reward, then people will refuse to be forced to meet the quota, unless there's a threat for not making the lowest acceptable level of quota.

11. The issue of rewards is one of the most controversial of the employee involvement/participative management movement. Most EI programs in the U.S.A. have operated on the assumption that EI activities and results provide sufficient intrinsic rewards to team members and that financial incentives are either unnecessary or actually a detriment to program success. Some writers have been vocal in their disagreement with this conventional wisdom. They have stated that the long-term success of EI programs depends on giving the circle members a share in the savings that they have generated.

Although a clear, unequivocal policy recommendation cannot be made on the applicability of incentive systems to EI programs, the following three points should be considered:

(1) Historical precedence exists for giving workers a share in increased productivity and cost production.
(2) Some research evidence suggests that financial rewards that are tied to and result from meeting clear objectives are effective in motivating workers to increase output.
(3) Many of the early developers of EI insisted that the programs be seen as representing a change in management style rather than "merely" as a program. However, the fact remains that from a budgetary perspective, they must and will be seen as programs that can be cut out or supported, depending on results.

12. See Review Question 22 for a starting point to answering this discussion question.

13.   This field research project should probably be a "graduate level" one. If you are located outside of a metropolitan area, a challenge may be to find more than one or two organizations that have an employee involvement process that is over three years old. Research has shown that the programs that have been in operation for three or more years are likely to survive over an extended period. Also, because you may not want to "wear out your welcome" with "target" companies, you may wish to give this as a group case assignment, with only one group going to each targeted local company for an interview.

14.   As mentioned in the case Mack became both complacent about their external reputation for quality, and they lost the "team spirit" that had formerly prevailed in the company. This may have been due to the business environmental changes, but management was partly to blame for not meeting their responsibility to continuously improve their management systems, stay in contact with their customers, and listen to their employees.

15.   See the Answers to Case Questions for the way teams contributed to Mack's recovery.

ANSWERS TO CASE QUESTIONS

Case I. The Frustrated Team Builder

Problem Development

There is no definitive solution to this case. However, by asking the "5 Whys," root causes should surface, including:

1. Bob Greenshades, the AP2 supervisor was too involved in day-to-day crises to attend the first TQM training session and was too distracted to get much out of the second session that he did attend.

2. George Key, the accounting superintendent, and James Jones, the AP1 supervisor were too busy, and not able to clear their calendars for the second training session.

3. The AR2 team chose an advanced, complex, and cross-functional project to work on as the pilot project for their team.

Two major environmental problems may have affected the results of the AP2 team in this situation: limited management support and lack of empowerment of the AP2 team.

The key problems to be addressed are: 1) obtaining management support and 2) getting the AP2 team out of the impossible dilemma of having chosen the "wrong" problem.

Recommendations for Salvaging EI

Actually, Trent has done a creditable job, with 2 out of 3 teams presenting very successful projects. The danger is that the AP2 group may resent their peers' successes and undermine future accomplishments of the EI process. Trent should talk to Bob about the dangers, request his full support for the EI process, and assess the situation to determine what is "bogging down" the process of completing the project that the team has started. If the problem is complex, he might recommend that the team be given only part of the problem to complete. If the problem might be solved by the team with the help of more training, Trent should try to facilitate that. If the problem is the personality or competence of Bob, then Trent might seek guidance from George Key, the accounting superintendent.

Case II. A Personal TQM Project

This approach, developed and published by Roberts and Sergesketter, has been used for several semesters by one of the authors (Lindsay) as a class assignment with both undergraduate and graduate students in a Production and Operations Management course and a Quality Management course. Student response at the end of the term has been overwhelmingly positive. Answers are based on experiences in these classes.

1. The graphical analysis tends to show an initial, often dramatic drop in total weekly defects over the first three or four weeks. Later in the semester, regression often occurs because of exam weeks or project assignments coming due. The final several weeks of the semester seem to show another drop in the scatter diagram, possibly because the final project report comes due and people want to "look good."

2. Sergesketter's results are widely observed in students' charts. Students are encouraged after submitting the mid-term project report to assess their strengths and weaknesses and to drop and add items that may be too easy or too impossible to attain. However they are required to continue to track a minimum of 8 goals (4 academic and 4 non-academic).

3. Some students are very wary of revealing their defects to others, or discussing how they are doing except in very general terms. Other are more open to the process, and often get significant help from their peer is reaching or exceeding their goals.

4. The personal TQM project can help the students to understand how difficult it is for managers to break "bad habits" of producing defective parts, plot data systematically, and take corrective action based on facts. Thus, "Quality in Daily Work" can refer to "getting to class on time" or producing fewer defective computer chips. "Zero Defects" in the factory can be as difficult as "Zero Defects" on the next exam. "Casting Out Fear" is related to the idea that managers don't fire employees for producing a defective item if it is beyond their control. Similarly, the professor should assign grades for this project based on whether the students write excellent reports that are well-documented and analyzed, not on whether their defect totals went down an certain amount over the term, or whether students were pleased or angry with their own results.

Users of this text should feel free to contact me for further details.   **- Bill Lindsay**

CHAPTER 12

Quality Management Evaluation and Assessment

Teaching Notes

A key to attaining an in-depth understanding of TQM as a system is to thoroughly understand the Baldrige criteria (or individual states', European, Canadian and/or Deming quality awards, depending on where you do business) and their importance. The ISO 9000 quality standards have become so pervasive in international and even domestic business that anyone who is working on quality-related activities in production and many service businesses that have international customers or operations will have to be familiar with those criteria. This chapter provides a comparison of the awards, analysis of criteria, and some excellent case examples of how they are used. Key objectives should be:

● To understand the concept and importance of the three types of quality audits.
● To appreciate the advantages and limitations of supplier certification audits and why ISO 9000 certification is replacing this practice.
● To contrast the methods of quality system audits using the Baldrige criteria versus the use of ISO 9000 criteria.
● To provide an overview of the ISO 9000 global quality systems standards and to understand its strengths and limitations.
● To explore the Malcolm Baldrige National Quality Award criteria, understand its seven key components, and compare and contrast it with state quality award and ISO 9000 criteria.
● To investigate the Deming Prize, European Quality Award, and Canada Awards for Excellence criteria to see their similarities and differences.

ANSWERS TO QUALITY IN PRACTICE KEY ISSUES

The Payoff from Baldrige at Texas Instruments

1.   The preparation of the mock Baldrige Award application at Texas Instruments (TI) was obviously extremely valuable. Two primary benefits were attained by this exercise. First, it required people at TI to focus on the need for quality in staff functions, as well as in line manufacturing operations. Second, it helped to dispel the argument in the Defense Systems & Electronics Group that: "Total quality is fine for the XYZ organization's type of business, but it won't work in **our** defense contract type of business."

     Other companies can and have attained similar results by applying the Baldrige criteria to their operations. Many of these companies do not follow through to apply and attempt to win the Baldrige award, but they still obtain major benefits from this activity.

2.   Competing for the Baldrige award is indeed a "stretch" for many small businesses. Consequently, there have only been six small business winners between 1988 and 1994, and there have never been more than one in any single year (even though up to two may be awarded in that category). The problem occurs because resources for doing many of the required Baldrige quality activities are limited. For example, information and analysis (criterion #2) is required, which means that people must design collection systems, gather the data, and analyze it for meaning and improvement ideas. This can be costly. Another potentially costly area is in the design of jobs, compensation systems, and training required for a top notch human resource development and management activity (criterion #4). Many small organizations would prefer to continue to do things the way that they've always done, rather than face the prospect of making these sorts of changes which assume that a "long run" payoff will be obtained.

The Ford Q1 Award

1.   The overall thrust of the Ford Q1 award is to certify vendors from within and outside the company through use of a comprehensive audit process, with the objective of building a roster of supplier who are known to provide high quality products and service to Ford. The company provides criteria, assessment factors, and scoring guidelines, as well as assistance in helping suppliers or potential suppliers to meet their quality standards. The basis for the analysis is in a review of five quality areas of the quality system, process capability, internal quality indicators, customer satisfaction, and management commitment. The five categories of Ford's Q1 process appear to be similar in content to the seven Baldrige categories. The scoring system Ford appears to be very similar to Baldrige, although a 0-10 scale is used instead of a percentage scale as used by the MBNQA.

2.   As with any quality assessment, if a company is serious about improving its quality, an "outside" evaluation, whether Ford's Q1, Baldrige, or another can help to show where the strengths and weaknesses of the company's quality program are. Eventually, most

manufacturing companies and many service businesses may be required to undergo some type of quality assessment process to remain in business. The use of 5 or 7 categories is less important than the fact that trained quality professionals (such as Ford's) have come in to a company and have given an objective quality assessment of the entire system.

Florida Power and Light

1. FP&L is a service organization that produces and sells an "intangible product," electricity. Since it is a utility, it is subject to many factors that affect quality, such as customer perceptions of service, government regulation of rates, the fact that it must provide its product 24 hours per day, seven days per week, and must deal with a variety of unique external environmental factors such as weather, impact of generating and distribution facilities on the environment, etc. It is similar to an oil refinery or a city water department in that it is a continuous process with "flows" of product through "conduits" (wires, instead of pipes are used by FP&L). However, it is different in that it is a "high visibility" organization that impacts every individual and business in its service area in a substantial way.

2. "Policy deployment" helped focus FP&L's quality effort and disseminate TQM throughout the organization. It emphasized setting priorities in the areas of improved reliability, customer satisfaction, and employee safety. Departments were required to determine projects in priority order, work on only the three highest priorities, and develop solutions to problems in great detail.

3. Although not discussed in detail, it is obvious that cross-function and other forms of QIP teams helped in the "deployment" of the quality process that was a major factor in helping the company to win the Deming Prize. Part of the requirement for the Prize is that individual employees must be able to intelligently answer questions about where they"fit" in the organization's total quality efforts. Such questions from the Prize examination team as: What are your main accountabilities? What are the important priority issues for the company? What indications do you have for your performance, your target, and how are you doing today compared to your target? must be answered by individuals and groups. These questions can only be answered if teams and individuals are thoroughly trained and the culture supports the total quality effort.

4. The major lesson that FP&L learned after winning the Deming Prize was that the quality improvement process can become a bureaucratic "program" that is mechanical an inflexible. FP&L went on to show that financial results can be attained while continuing to use quality improvement principles and practices.

ANSWERS TO REVIEW QUESTIONS

1. A quality audit is a systematic, independent examination and evaluation to determine if quality activities comply with planned arrangements, whether these arrangements are

implemented effectively, and whether they are suitable to achieve objectives. Issues are addressed by quality audits and benefits that are provided by focusing on these issues include: management involvement and leadership, improvement of product and process design, better product control, enhanced customer and supplier communications, improved quality improvement programs, more employee participation, enhanced education and training, and consistent and higher quality information.

2.   *Policy audits* check written procedures and policies against standards and specifications. This audit usually involves reading manuals, records, and similar documents, and tells whether people in the organization know what they are supposed to be doing. *Practice audits* check actual practices against procedures or accepted good practices. *Product audits* involve evaluation of the product as to whether or not it conforms to specifications. This type of audit is used by many companies to evaluate a new supplier.

3.   See the answer to Question 1, above.

4.   Supplier certification programs are designed to rate vendors on their capability to provide quality materials in a timely and cost-effective manner. After thorough investigation (a supplier certification audit), vendors who are certified as having high quality products and processes will be allowed to send product directly into their customer's production or service process with no receiving inspection (periodic audits are usually required). This provides recognition and motivation for continuous improvement for the "Certified Vendor." It also provides advantages to the customer of: higher quality, lower cost, elimination of ongoing, routine inspection, improved delivery, and ability to reduce the number of suppliers used.

5.   To standardize quality requirements for countries within the E.E.C. common market and those wishing to do business with those countries, a specialized agency for standardization, the International Organization for Standardization (ISO), founded in 1946 and composed of representatives from the national standards bodies of 91 nations, adopted a series of written quality standards in 1987. These standards have been recognized by about 100 countries, including the U.S. and Japan. In some foreign markets, companies will not buy from noncertified suppliers. Thus, meeting these standards is becoming a requirement for international competitiveness.

6.   The ISO 9000 standards define three levels of quality assurance:

> - Level 1 (ISO 9001) provides a model for quality assurance in firms that design, develop, produce, install, and service products.
> - Level 2 (ISO 9002) provides a quality assurance model for firms engaged only in production and installation.
> - Level 3 (ISO 9003) applies to firms engaged only in final inspection and test.

Two other standards, ISO 9000 and ISO 9004, define the basic elements of a comprehensive quality assurance system and provide guidance in applying the appropriate level. ISO 9004, specifically, guides the development and implementation of a quality system. It examines each of the elements of the quality system in detail and can be used for internal auditing purposes. Together, these standards are referred to as the ISO 9000 series.

7.　　The key requirements of ISO 9000 include:

■　*Management responsibility*--Management establishes and publicizes its policy, objectives, and commitment to quality and customer satisfaction. It designates a representative with authority for implementing and maintaining the standard, defines the responsibility, authority, and relationships for all employees whose work affects quality, and conducts in-house verification and review of the quality system.

■ *Quality system*--The company must write and maintain a quality manual that meets the criteria of the applicable standard (9001, 9002, or 9003), which defines conformance to requirements.

■ *Contract review*--The company must review contracts to assess whether requirements are adequately defined and whether the capability exists to meet requirements.

■ *Design control*--The company must verify product design to ensure that requirements are being met and that procedures are in place for design planning and design changes.

■ *Document control*--The company must establish and maintain procedures for controlling documentation through approval, distribution, change, and modification.

■ *Purchasing*--The company must have procedures to ensure that purchased products conform to requirements.

■ *Purchaser supplier products*--Procedures to verify, store, and maintain purchased items must be established.

■ *Product identification and traceability*--The company must identify and trace products during all stages of production, delivery, and installation.

■ *Process control*--The company must carry out production processes under controlled conditions. The processes must be documented and monitored, and workers must use approved equipment and have specific criteria for workmanship.

■ *Inspection, measurement, and test equipment*--The company must maintain records at all stages of inspection and testing

■ *Inspection and test status*--The company must label products throughout all stages of production.

■ *Control of nonconforming product*--Procedures should insure that the company avoids inadvertent use of nonconforming product.

■ *Corrective action*--The company should investigate causes of nonconformance and take action both to correct the problems and prevent them in the future.

■ *Handling, storage, packaging, and delivery*--The company should properly handle, store, and deliver products.

■ *Quality records*--The company should identify, collect, index, file, and store all records relating to the quality system.

■ *Internal quality audits*--The company's system of internal audits determines whether its activities comply with requirements.

- *Training*--Procedures are needed to identify needs and provide training of employees.
- *Servicing*--The company must perform service as required by its contracts with customers.
- *Statistical control*--Procedures should identify statistical techniques used to control processes, products, and services.

8   The ISO 9000 standards have evolved into a criteria for companies (customer and supplier) who wish to "certify" their quality management or achieve "registration" through a third-party auditor, usually a laboratory or some other accreditation agency (called a registrar). Rather than a supplier being audited for compliance to the standards by each customer, the register certifies the company, and this certification is accepted by all of the supplier's customers.

The registration process includes *document review* by the registrar of the quality system documents or quality manual; *preassessment*, which identifies potential noncompliance in the quality system or in the documentation; *assessment* by a team of two or three auditors of the quality system and its documentation; and *surveillance*, or periodic re-audits to verify conformity with the practices and systems registered. Recertification is required every three years. Individual sites--not entire companies--must achieve registration individually. All costs are borne by the applicant, so the process can be quite expensive.

9.   In addition to improving internal operations, the most important reasons why companies seek ISO 9000 certification include:

a. *Meeting contractual obligations*--Some customers now require certification of all their suppliers. Suppliers that do not pursue registration will eventually lose customers.

b *Meeting trade regulations*--Many products sold in Europe, such as telecommunication terminal equipment, medical devices, gas appliances, toys, and construction products require product certifications to assure safety. Often, ISO certification is necessary to obtain product certification.

c. *Marketing goods in Europe*--ISO 9000 is widely accepted within the European Community. It is fast becoming a *de facto* requirement for doing business in the region.

d. *Gaining a competitive advantage*--Many customers use ISO registration as a basis for supplier selection. Companies without it may be at a market disadvantage.

10.   The purposes of the Malcolm Baldrige Award are to:

▫ Help stimulate American companies to improve quality and productivity for the pride of recognition while obtaining a competitive edge through increased profits.
▫ Recognize the achievements of those companies that improve the quality of their goods

and services and provide an example to others.

□ Establish guidelines and criteria that can be used by business, industrial, governmental, and other enterprises in evaluating their own quality improvement efforts.

□ Provide specific guidance for other American enterprises that wish to learn how to manage for high quality by making available detailed information on how winning enterprises were able to change their cultures and achieve eminence.

11.   The Baldrige Award framework has four basic elements:

■ Senior executive leadership sets directions, creates values, goals, and systems, and guides the pursuit of customer value and company performance improvement.
■ The system comprises a set of well-defined and well-designed processes for meeting the company's customer and performance requirements.
■ Measures of progress establish a results-oriented basis for channeling actions to delivering ever-improving customer value and company performance.
■ The basic aims of the system are the delivery of ever-improving value to customers and success in the marketplace.

The above summarizes the importance of the seven categories used by examiners to assess the quality of candidates. The seven categories in the Baldrige Award criteria include:

1. *Leadership*
2. *Information and Analysis*
3. *Strategic Planning*
4. *Human Resource Development and Management*
5. *Process Management*
6. *Business Results*
7. *Customer Focus and Satisfaction*

12.   See Figure 12.1 and discussion in the chapter.

13.   See Tables 12.3 and 12.4 and discussions in the chapter.

14.   In assessing Baldrige Award applications, key strengths and common weaknesses are evident. Most companies that apply have strong senior management leadership, are driven by the needs of customers and the marketplace, and have high expectations. The firms have strong information systems that provide an excellent basis for assessing the state of quality. They link external customer satisfaction measurements with internal measurements such as process quality and employee satisfaction. Strong firms invest heavily in human resource development, and EI is continuing and expanding.

Common weaknesses among firms that do not score well include:

□ Weak information systems.

◻ Delegation of quality responsibility to lower levels of the company.
◻ A partial quality system, e.g., strong in manufacturing but weak in support services.
◻ An unclear definition of what quality means in the organization.
◻ A lack of alignment among diverse functions within the firm; that is, not all processes are driven by common goals or use the same approaches.
◻ Failure to use all listening posts to gather information critical to decision making.

Baldrige award administrators have been disappointed to find that few organizations practice *total quality*. Many lack a quality vision or do not translate vision into a business strategy. They emphasize the negatives of quality--defect reduction, ignoring customers.

15. Many companies use the Baldrige Award criteria to evaluate their own quality programs, set up and implement TQM programs, communicate better with suppliers and partners, and for education and training. Using the award criteria as a self-assessment tool provides an objective framework, sets a high standard, and compares units that have different systems or organizations. The award addresses the full range of quality issues and can help those setting up new systems to obtain an complete picture of TQM. The award criteria assist companies with internal communications, communications with suppliers, and communications with other companies seeking to share information. Finally, the award examination is being used for training and education, particularly for management, because it summarizes major issues that managers must understand.

16. The Baldrige Award program differs considerable from the ISO 9000 registration process. First, the Baldrige Award emphasizes competitiveness, specifically excellence in customer value and operational performance. Its purpose is to share competitiveness learning, and its quality definition is customer-driven. ISO 9000 measures conformity to quality practices as specified by the registrant's own quality system. Its purpose is to provide a common basis for assuring buyers that specific practices conform with the providers' stated quality systems. Its quality definition is conformity of specified operations to documented requirements, assuring customers that a registered supplier has a documented quality system and follows it. The Baldrige Award is a form of recognition, but is not intended as a product certification. ISO 9000 focuses primarily on repetitive processes, while Baldrige focuses on service excellence. Baldrige winners are required to share their quality strategies, while ISO 9000 members are not under this obligation.

17. JUSE defines companywide quality control (CWQC) as follows:

"a system of activities to assure that quality products and services required by customers are economically designed, produced and supplied while respecting the principle of customer-orientation and the overall public well-being. These quality assurance activities involve market research, research and development, design, purchasing, production, inspection and sales, as well as all other related activities inside and outside the company. Through everyone in the company understanding statistical concepts and methods, through their application to all aspects of quality assurance, and through repeating the cycle of rational planning, implementation, evaluation, and action, CWQC aims to accomplish business objectives."

18.   In comparing the framework of the European Quality Award with the framework of the Baldrige award, several key differences are apparent. For the European Quality Award, results--including customer satisfaction, people (employee) satisfaction, and impact on society--constitute a higher percentage of the total score. These results, like the Baldrige Award, are driven by leadership and the quality system. The three criteria of people satisfaction, impact on society, and business results are somewhat different.

People satisfaction refers to how employees feel about the organization, including the working environment, perception of management style, career planning and development, and job security. Unlike Baldrige Award category 4.0, it is an independent results category. The impact on society category focuses on the perceptions of the company by the community at large and the company's approach to the quality of life, the environment, and the preservation of global resources. The European quality Award criteria places greater emphasis on this category than is placed on the public responsibility item in the Baldrige Award criteria. The business results criterion addresses the financial performance of the firm, its market competitiveness, and its ability to satisfy shareholders' expectations. Other nonfinancial areas of performance, such as order processing time, new product design lead time, and time to break even are also considered.

ANSWERS TO DISCUSSION QUESTIONS

1.   A quality audit for a class might be developed by adapting the criteria used in the Baldrige Award to fit conditions in the class. This would provide the frame of reference from which a questionnaire could be constructed. To conduct such an assessment, an "outside examiner" such as a businessperson or faculty member familiar with quality would have to be engaged. Class members and the professor ("top management") would have to do a self-assessment and then call in the quality auditor to verify the results.

2.   A supplier certification program would require a great deal of time and coordination, since there would have to be agreements on both sides of what constituted a "quality" high school graduate from a college preparatory program who would be an excellent applicant for university admission to any program.

3.   This is an exercise for an advanced student. See Chapter 6 on affinity diagrams.

4.   See Review Question 16 as a starting point for this comparison.

5.   This is an exercise for an advanced student.

6.   This is a form of the House of Quality type matrix. See Chapter 7 for examples.

7.   This could be an extremely interesting and useful exercise for students in a part time MBA program, who may be called upon at some point to prepare a plant, division, or firm for ISO certification. The exercise is designed to further student awareness of how quality is being applied in a practical setting in business and industry.

8.   See Discussion Question 1 on the development of a quality audit for a class.

9.   The Deming Prize is a nationwide (later extended to other countries) award for quality that recognizes individuals, factories, divisions, and small businesses for quality excellence. It has 10 measurement categories that are related to CWQC based on statistical quality control concepts. Some of these are policy/objectives, organization, information, analysis, quality assurance, effects, and future plans. The MBNQA has 7 criteria, including a number that are in the Deming Prize criteria. Some of these are strategic quality planning, information and analysis, human resource utilization, quality assurance, and quality results. Interestingly, customer satisfaction and leadership are included in the MBNQA criteria, but not in the Deming Prize requirements.

10.   The answer to this question will vary by location.

ANSWERS TO CASE QUESTIONS

Case I. World-Wide Appliances

1.   Harold needs to determine his objectives before deciding whether to hire a consultant. If the consultant is to be a "full service" advisor, then he/she must be familiar with the phases of the registration process, including document review, preassessment, assessment, and surveillance. Harold should look for someone with experience, "credentials" (as an auditor), and the ability to train employees and managers in the basics of the ISO system.

        If Harold decides to do the training himself, he will have to be trained in the ISO 9000 requirements. Then he will have to train workers and managers on the philosophy and requirements of ISO. This should include the need for manager and worker support, the phases listed above, the detailed requirements for calibration and documentation, and a separate advanced training process for internal auditors.

2.   The "bundling" audit technique has some advantages, but a number of limitations. The advantages are that it will not require major disruption of operations while the audit is being conducted. If the audit teams are made up of different people for each small area, this will provide opportunities for many people to be involved as auditors. This can help to "cross-fertilize" good quality practices and improvements across the plant.

        The disadvantages include the cost for additional auditor training and the probable lack of consistency in the audits and their results. Some audit teams may be very diligent, and other could be lax. Also, it will be difficult for separate teams to consistently apply the quality standards in the same way in each area. Close coordination and frequent meetings between the teams will be required.

Case II. Ultra-Productivity Fasteners: Part II

SAMPLE BALDRIGE RESPONSE - VERSION A

Strengths

a +   Lots accepted at test and shipments reliability index show generally improving trends over the past four years.

a +   Order entry error rates and invoice errors have decreased in the past 2 years.

Areas for Improvement

a -   Results for key appliance customer requirements of rapid response and technical assistance are not reported.

a -   Only five months of data are available for delivery satisfaction index, and it is not clear whether the competitive comparison represents the best competitor.

a -   Results do not clearly differentiate between customer segments or among production facilities.

a -   Shipments reliability index is below industry average.

b -- No comparisons with industry leaders, best competitors, or benchmarks are provided.

Score: 20

SAMPLE BALDRIGE RESPONSE - VERSION B

Strengths

a +   Lots accepted at test - dimensional show consistent improvement over the past four years

a +   Lots accepted at test - hardness show improving levels, particularly for the Louisville plant

a +   Shipments reliability index and delivery satisfaction index show improving trends.

a +   Order entry error rates and complaints resolved on first contact exhibit a decrease approaching benchmark levels

a +   Invoice error rates show positive trends.

b +   Several key quality indicators are close to benchmark levels or exceed best competitors in both key industry sectors.

Areas for Improvement

a -   Results for key appliance customer requirements of rapid response and technical assistance are not reported.

Score: 70

CHAPTER 13

Organizing and Implementing TQM

Teaching Notes

This chapter focuses on the process of organizing as it applies to quality functions. The organizing concept is one that students may find easier to grasp than the cost of quality or even planning for quality. However, you should point out that the "safe" concept of organizations is rapidly changing, as organizations and individuals are shaken out of their complacency by events that surround them, today. The strict hierarchy of the conventional organizational "pyramid" is giving way to the "matrix" organization, self-managed teams, massive part-time employment, and attempts to align the corporate culture with the total quality management, global marketplace, and "lean and mean" concepts that look ahead to the 21st Century. Key objectives are:

• To introduce the process of organizing as a way to define work in order to establish lines of authority, improve efficiency, quality of work, and communication.

• To point out the importance of corporate culture and how it and quality are impacted by organization structure, and vice versa.

• To develop the need to view organization for quality at the organizational level, the process level, and the individual level, all working to meet the needs of customers.

• To understand the components of a quality organization from design through quality assurance; understand description of the organization through tools such as organization charts, position descriptions, procedures, etc.; and understanding task design as the key to the way that quality can be "built in" to the tasks of individuals.

• To raise awareness of the fact that future organizations are likely to be highly self-managed, innovative and will be subjected to rapid change requiring a a holistic quality philosophy and structure to support it.

ANSWERS TO QUALITY IN PRACTICE KEY ISSUES

Changing the Organizational Architecture at Xerox

1.   Many of the organizational context factors swayed Xerox's decision to go into the insurance business in the 1980's and influenced their obvious lack of success, such as:

   (1) Company operational and organizational guidelines. Standard practices from Xerox's history caused the company to be organized and operated in a rigid, bureaucratic fashion.
   (2) Management Style: The management team style at Xerox in the 1980's was very formal, not democratic.
   (3) Customer influences: Xerox's customers were primarily large corporations and government agencies. Thus, service specifications or administrative controls were dominated and/or mandated by customers. Another powerful customer group was the stockholders, and they were not happy about Xerox's loss of market share and profitability. This led to the decision to diversify.
   (4) Company size was **huge!** This influenced the ability to maintain formal systems and records, but also was thought of as a "plus" for the decision to go into the insurance business.
   (5) Xerox did not have a very diverse product line, although copiers were complex products. It later proved true that an organization suitable for the manufacture and servicing of a small number of highly sophisticated products could not adapt very well to producing a high volume of standard insurance products.
   (6) Stability of the product line was a problem for Xerox at this time. Frequent changes in their core copier products made more control, more product innovation, and more changes to the quality system necessary at this time. It wasn't really a good time to get into a completely new line of business like insurance.
   (7) Xerox recognized that they had a major problem with quality in the early 1980's, but they were not able to become *financially stable* until the late 1980's. Quality managers need to recognize that their programs must fit within the overall budget of the firm.
   (8) Xerox lacked skilled personnel in both quality management skills and in insurance industry skills. If skilled personnel are not available, it may be necessary to use less skilled people as a substitute. The lack of certain skills may require other people, such as supervisors, to assume duties they ordinarily would not be assigned.

2.   The new organization structure is a **radical** change for Xerox. It resembles the matrix type most closely. It does have certain characteristics that are similar to the line-staff organization. This can be seen in the integrated R&D, strategic services, and geographic customer operations groups and divisions. It is not as radical as the description of the Semco organization, however.

3.   The success of the new organization structure depends on Xerox's people meeting Allaire's goals of being "more entrepreneurial, more innovative and more responsive to the marketplace." The structure does seem to have the advantage of incorporating teamwork

and a *process*, as opposed to a *functional* structure for product-market divisions. Xerox continues to have a TQM focus in their operations and customer focus.

4.   The TQM concepts that are evident in this organizational design are customer focus, teamwork (and empowerment), a cross-functional *process* approach, and although it is not specifically mentioned, a concern for continuous improvement. The continuous improvement concern is implied by their interest in innovation, as well as the fact that they have tried to continue improving on quality and organization design since winning the Malcolm Baldrige award.

Quality Organization at the IRS

1.   Total quality management is integrated throughout the Cincinnati Service Center of the IRS via the QIP program and its associated processes. The two forms of organization that are critical to this activity are (1) the Quality Council and sub-councils and (2) the QIP teams. The council(s) provide guidance, support, and dissemination of information through training, implementation of suggestions, newsletters, and quality-related activities. The QIP teams receive standard "quality team" training and develop improvement projects such as the redesign of equipment (tax cart), improvement of processes (the ELF initiative), and submission of "quick-fix" suggestions ("Captain Q's" collection boxes around CSC).

2.   Obviously, the organization structure of the QIP process fits the organization of the IRS, which is a highly structured government agency. The very nature of the organization precludes it ever attaining the level of "empowerment" of people and innovativeness of a Semco. However, through a team approach to problem-solving, together with some internal "quality of worklife" planning, the CSC is continuing to make progress toward significant quality improvement. They seem to be both effective and efficient in meeting their objectives at CSC.

ANSWERS TO REVIEW QUESTIONS

1.   Companies decide to adopt TQM for two basic reasons: a) as a reaction to competition that poses a threat to its profitable survival; and b) as an opportunity to improve. The first reason is most prevalent. When faced with a threat to survival, a company effects cultural change more easily; under these circumstances, organizations generally implement TQM effectively.

2.   The dangers of a "one-dimensional" quality approaches lie in the lack of complete understanding and the tendency to imitate--the easy way out. Imitation of TQM efforts made by one successful organization may not lead to good results in another; most successful companies have developed their own unique TQM approaches to fit their own requirements. Also, companies may attempt only a partial commitment, adopting quality practices in some areas but not others. Successful TQM implementation requires a

readiness for change, a total change in thinking and practice, the adoption of sound practices and implementation strategies, and an effective organization.

3.   "Corporate culture" is the way an organization does things. The way of doing things at a company is important for effective quality control since the processes of production generally have the greatest effect on quality output. A dysfunctional corporate culture is one in which shared values and behavior are at odds with the organization's long-term health. If the quality of a company's product or service is low, there is usually a flaw somewhere in the corporate culture.

Studies show that change is easier in corporate cultures that emphasize customer satisfaction and continuous improvement; in other words those that embrace TQM principles. Traditional organizations are generally ill-prepared to accept change, not only with respect to TQM.

4.   Pieters has suggested several ways in which a corporate culture change to a TQM environment can be made permanent. These include:

• Making involvement in TQ a required part of people's responsibility. Making it voluntary implies that it is less important than things that are required.
• Using the existing organization to implement TQ. Special task forces and committees can disband; TQ should be part of the permanent organization.
• Ensuring everyone spends at least one hour per week working on quality issues. Enforcing this rule gets people accustomed to the idea of devoting time to quality and keeps other priorities from crowding out TQ.
• Changing the measurement and information systems. Without appropriate measurements and information systems, quality cannot become a fabric of the organization.

5.   Studies of highly successful companies suggest that certain key practices in their organizational culture have contributed to their success.

■ They focus on quality through strategic planning, which is deployed throughout the organization.
■ They have the commitment and involvement of top management.
■ They integrate customer satisfaction across functions.
■ They emphasize employee participation and training.
■ They customize their quality efforts.
■ They link quality to financial returns.

6.   "Quality engines" are the individual strengths that drive the quality activities of each Baldrige Award-winning company. The quality engine customizes the quality effort of the organization's culture and provides focus. They differ because of the company's strategic focus and mission, indicating that each company has different needs and requirements.

7.   The Coopers and Lybrand Quality Maturity Profile matrix can be used to assess the level of a firm's maturity in relation to typical measures of the firm's quality effort: approach, role of top management, quality responsibility, process, customer relations, supplier relations, quality cost, training, and transition strategy. Once the level of a firm's maturity in each of these categories has been obtained, an organization can design a program to implement quality practices that will take each element from its current level to the level of excellence.

8.   The Best Practices study, by Ernst and Young, found that best practices depend on the current level of performance of a company, and that trying to implement all the practices of world-class organizations can actually waste time and money, not help. The study used two performance measures: ROA (return on assets: after tax income divided by total assets) and VAE (value added per employee: sales less the costs of materials, supplies, and work done by outside contractors). Low performers--those with less than two percent ROA and $47,000 VAE--can reap the highest benefits by concentrating on fundamentals, i.e. identifying and improving processes to better serve customer and market demands. Medium performers--those with ROA's from two percent to 6.9 percent and VAE between $47,000 and $73,999--achieve the most benefits from meticulously documenting gains and further refining practices to improve value added per employee, time to market, and customer satisfaction. High performers--with ROAD and VAE exceeding seven percent $74,000 respectively--gain the most from using self-managed teams and cross-functional teams that concentrate on horizontal processes such as logistics and process development.

The best practices can be related to the Deming philosophy in that profound understanding of processes and systems was always advocated by Deming. This is shown in Points 3, 5, and 9. of his 14 Points. In 3 he advocated using inspection for improvement of processes and cost reduction (concentrating on the "fundamentals" for low-performing companies); Point 5 requires improving constantly and forever the system of production and service (documenting the gains for medium performers, as well as other process refinements); and more emphasis on advanced teamwork and horizontal processes (for high performers), as suggested in Point 9 -- optimize toward the aims and purposes of the company the efforts of teams, groups, and staff areas.

9.   "Return on quality" is becoming increasingly important as a measure of value added by the investment in improved quality. Companies are now attempting to assess the financial impact of quality, just as they do for an investment in new equipment or in employee training and development. Some ways to implement a process with a high ROQ include:

        o Starting with an effective quality program.
        o Calculate the cost of current quality initiatives
        o Determine the key factors that keep or drive away customers
        o Focus on quality efforts likely to improve customer satisfaction at a reasonable cost.
        o Roll out successful programs after pilot-testing the most promising efforts and

eliminating the ones that don't have a big impact.
o Improve programs continually.

10. Senior managers must ensure that their plans and strategies are successfully executed within the organization. The ten managerial roles, defined by Mintzberg, that leaders must play include (1) figurehead, (2) leader (3) liaison, (4) monitor, (5) disseminator, (6) spokesperson, (7) entrepreneur, (8) disturbance handler, (9) resource allocator, (10) negotiator. The importance of each role is contingent on the environmental and organizational factors that face managers who must lead, i.e. the industry or environment surroundings of the organization, its age and size, etc.

Senior managers' responsibilities include the following tasks:
a. Ensure that the organization focuses on the needs of the customer.
b. Cascade the mission, vision, and values of the organization throughout the organization.
c. Identify the critical processes that need attention and improvement.
d. Identify the resources and tradeoffs that must be made to fund the TQM activity.
e. Review progress and remove any barriers to progress.
f. Improve macroprocesses in which they are involved, both to improve the performance of the process and to demonstrate their ability to use quality tools for problem solving.

Middle managers currently find themselves monitoring progress, disseminating information and suggestions between local and distant line, staff, and outside experts, and acting as a spokesperson inside and outside the firm. Technology development requires that managers constantly scan the environment to be aware of technological developments that may threaten or enhance the operations of the company. Systems and process integration means optimizing the system to meet strategic goals such as customer service, and using tools of quality measurement and continuous improvement. Samuel suggests that transforming middle managers into change agents requires a systematic process which dissolves traditional management boundaries and replaces them with an empowered and team-oriented state of accountability for organizational performance. Middle managers must also show that they support total quality, by listening to employees as customers, creating a positive work environment, implementing quality improvements enthusiastically, challenging people to develop new ideas and reach their potential, setting challenging goals and providing positive feedback, and following through on promises. These changes are often difficult for middle managers to accept.

The work force implements quality policies. This requires ownership that goes beyond empowerment and gives employees the right to a voice in deciding what needs to be done and how to do it. It is based on a belief that what is good for the organization is also good for the individual and vice-versa.

Labor's role is first to recognize the need for changing its relationship with management and then to educate its members as to how cooperation will affect the organization. This information includes what its members can expect, and how working conditions and job security might change. At the same time, management must realize that the skills and knowledge of all employees are needed to improve quality and meet competitive challenges. Management must be willing to develop a closer working relationship with labor and be ready to address union concerns and cultivate trust.

11. Organizing is the process of assigning work and responsibility to functions and individuals along with the appropriate delegation of authority. Organizing links the planning process with the execution process. Organization is the integral part of the quality planning process in which individuals and groups decide what tasks must be performed and who will carry them out. The three principle reasons for organizing are as follows:

   a. To establish lines of authority.
   b. To improve efficiency and quality of work through synergism.
   c. To improve communication.

12. The key contextual factors that affect the organizational structure of a company and the quality organization include:

   - Company operational and organizational guidelines. Standard practices that have developed over the firm's history can dictate how a company organizes and operates.
   - Management Style: Refers to the way the management team operates. Management style might be formal or informal, or democratic or autocratic.
   - Customer influences: Occasionally, customers can wield a great deal of power, for example, if the "customer" is a government agency, such as the IRS or the FDA. Thus, specifications or administrative controls may be mandated by customers.
   - Company size: This influences the ability to maintain formal systems and records.
   - Diversity and complexity of product line: An organization suitable for the manufacture of a small number of highly sophisticated products may differ from an organization required to produce a high volume of standard products.
   - Stability of the product line: Frequent changes in products make necessary more control and changes to the quality system.
   - Financial stability: Quality managers need to recognize that their programs must fit within the overall budget of the firm.
   - Availability of personnel: If skilled personnel are not available, it may be necessary to use less skilled people as substitutes. The lack of certain skills may require other people, such as supervisors, to assume duties they ordinarily would not be assigned.

13. Commonly used types of organization structure include the line organization, the line-and-staff organization, and the matrix organization. The line organization is a functional form, having departments that are responsible for marketing, finance, and operations. In this type of organization, quality planning and assurance usually are part of the responsibility of each operating manager and employee at every level. In practice, this organization structure is not generally successful except when used in small firms.

The line and staff organization is the most prevalent type of organization structure for medium-sized to large firms.   In such organizations, line-departments carry out the functions of marketing, finance, and production for the organization.   Staff personnel, including quality managers and technical specialists, assist the line managers in carrying out their jobs by providing technical assistance and advice.   In the line and staff organization, quality managers and inspectors may take on the role of guardians of quality instead of technical experts who assist line managers and workers in attaining quality.

In a matrix-type organization, each project has a project manager and each department that provides personnel for project work has a technical or administrative manager. Quality assurance technicians might be assigned to the quality assurance department for technical and administrative activities, but attached to Project A for day-to-day assignments. For advantages and disadvantages of the matrix, see below.

14. The first task to be performed in the quality assurance department is to get everybody to agree on a quality philosophy. Operating checks and balances must also be installed to ensure that conformance to quality standards is maintained at a high level. Quality managers at this level must ensure that measurement, control, and improvement activities are carried out in timely and cost-effective ways. The appraisal activity must be addressed in the areas of inspection, testing, development of procedures, training of operators and inspectors, maintenance of test equipment, and reporting of quality levels and results.

Generally a quality assurance organization must be structured in such a way as to:

(1) Define the company quality purposes.
(2) Establish the objectives that the organization must achieve to support the purposes.
(3) Determine the basic work activities that must be accomplished in meeting the organization objectives. Classify these work activities into a number of basic functions.
(4) Combine these basic functions into job packages that pass the screen of the seven "acid-test" questions listed in the text.
(5) Consolidate the job packages into an organization component or components best suited to specific company requirements, recognizing the particular character of the organization component that has been created.
(6) With this in mind, locate the component in that segment of the larger company organization where it can do its job and achieve its objectives with maximum effectiveness and economy and a minimum of friction. Establish the relationships with other organization components that are necessary to the organization objectives.

15. Committees have their place as part of the organization structures of companies that embrace a TQM philosophy. Well-managed committees can be used to transmit information, and gain support for decisions. If misused, they can block progress, foster dissention, and diffuse responsibility to the point of meaninglessness. It should be noted that the power to make decisions cannot reside within a committee. Decision power in a committee can lead to a very poorly run and disorganized way of handling business, as

seen with the United States Congress, where so many good ideas "die in committee." Committees should have power only to recommend decisions to be made in any situation.

16.   Numerous barriers to successfully implementing total quality in organizations include:

☐ Lack of consistent top management support.
☐ Inadequate knowledge and understanding about TQM
☐ Fear and resistance to change.
☐ Lack of a long-term focus.
☐ Politics and turf battles.
☐ Employee apathy.
☐ Inadequate planning.

17.   Implementation of TQM is often attempted without a full grasp of its nature. Certain mistakes are made repeatedly. Some of the more common mistakes include:

+ TQM is regarded as a "program," despite the rhetoric that may be made to the contrary.
+ Short-term results are not obtained, so management loses interest -- often no attempt is made to get immediate results, or they believe that savings lie only in the distant future.
+ The process is not driven by a focus on the customer, a connection to strategic business issues, and support from senior management.
+ Structural elements in the organization block change--such as compensation systems, promotion systems, accounting systems, rigid policies and procedures, specialization and functionalization, and status symbols such as offices and perks.
+ Goals are set too low. Management does not shoot for stretch goals.
+ The organizational culture remains one of "command and control" and is driven by fear or game-playing, budgets, schedules, or bureaucracy.
+ Training is not properly addressed. Too little training is offered to the work force. Training may be of the wrong kind, such as a focus on tools and not problems.
+ The focus is mainly on products, not processes.
+ Little real empowerment is given and is not supported by actions.
+ The organization is too successful and complacent. It is not receptive to change and learning, and clings to the "not invented here" syndrome.
+ The organization fails to address three fundamental questions: Is this another program? What's in it for me? How can I do this on top of everything else?
+ Senior management is not personally and visibly committed and actively participating.
+ An overemphasis on teams for cross-functional problems which leads to the neglect of individual efforts and local improvements.
+ Employees believe that more data are always desirable,"paralysis of analysis."
+ Management fails to recognize that quality improvement is a personal responsibility at all levels of the organization.
+ The organization does not see itself as a collection of interrelated processes making up an overall system. Individual processes and the overall system need to be understood.

18.   Perceived crises in implementing TQM programs arise from two sources. The first is change. TQM requires significant changes to an organization, in methods, processes, attitudes, and behavior. Organizations need time for this realization to set in, and sometimes change is painful. Everyone from line workers to top managers must assume new roles and new responsibilities. The second cause of a quality crisis is rising expectations. As people become knowledgeable about what a quality organization should look like, they become more sensitive to problems within the organization and in their own behavior. This sensitivity can cause anxiety. Such situations can be avoided through proper training. At the beginning of the process, expectations should be kept simple. Everyone needs to recognize that setbacks will occur as a normal evolution. Managers should be trained to use interpersonal skills so that they can manage the human issues associated with change. First-year projects should be simple and have a high probability of success. All improvements, no matter how small, should be documented and publicized. Progress should be reviewed periodically, and goals revised accordingly.

19.   Senge defines a learning organization as "an organization that is continually expanding its capacity to create its future. For such an organization, it is not enough merely to survive. 'Survival learning,' or what is most often termed 'adaptive learning' is important--indeed it is necessary. But for a learning organization, 'adaptive learning' must be joined by 'generative learning,' learning that enhances our capacity to create."

        Organizations cannot count on succeeding in the long run if they merely have committed leaders who use TQM principles for strategic planning and policy deployment, practice TQM in daily operations, and use it for continuous improvement of the current process. These adaptive activities are called "first generation" TQM. Senge advocates developing a learning organization with a new approach to leadership. Instead of the adaptive approach to learning, leaders must use a generative approach--constantly anticipating the needs of customers to the point of anticipating products or services they would value but have never experienced and would never think of asking for. Leaders must develop the ability to integrate creative thinking and problem solving throughout the organization.

20.   One of the worst things an organization can do is to downsize shortly after implementing TQM. A much better approach is to downsize first, then use TQM as an opportunity to re-energize the company and make it more efficient. TQM tools can be used to build a new strategy for the company. Employees must recognize that TQM is not a separate effort, but the core approach for managing the business. Involved employees are more easily able to overcome the anxiety that accompanies downsizing. If it is inevitable, management must do everything possible to separate downsizing from TQM efforts.

ANSWERS TO DISCUSSION QUESTIONS

1.   TQM concepts can apply to individual schools and school systems some of the same ways as in business. They require a change in philosophy to include customer focus, leadership from the top, continuous improvement, development of an information system to support

management by fact, and appropriate changes in infrastructure, such as employee empowerment and consistent reward systems. Many school systems are adopting TQM, so students should be able to locate models of excellence in almost any community.

2.   This exercise is designed to further student awareness of how the "quality movement" is being implemented in business and industry.

3.   This field exercise improves awareness of TQM implementation in business and industry.

4.   See Review Questions 7 and 8 above as a basis for developing the hierarchy requested.

5.   Small and large companies may differ in ways in which they can implement TQM, due to availability of financial and human resources. See Chapter 12 on the Baldrige Award.

6.   Answers will vary, depending on the companies reviewed and the interests of the students.

7.   See Review Question 16 as a springboard for discussion for this question.

8.   See Review Question 16 as a springboard for discussion for this question.

9.   Amazingly, many colleges and universities would not be classified by Senge as "learning organizations." To do so, they would have to begin to practice what they teach. For example, colleges of business and engineering would have to go beyond just teaching about TQM to applying it to their academic and administrative processes, as well.

10.   To equate TQM with cost reduction is to erect a barrier to effective implementation. The narrow view of TQM means that "Total" quality management cannot be taken seriously. TQM must affect every level of the organization, requires an internal and external customer focus, teamwork, and continuous improvement.

ANSWERS TO CASE QUESTIONS

Case I. The Parable of the Green Lawn[1]

1.   This parable shows that many of the common failings of TQM transformation efforts and attempts to improve business processes are common to everyday experiences away from the job, as well. As "Pogo," the character who played the title part in a 1960's and '70's cartoon series used to say, "We have met the enemy, and he is us!"

2.   Many common problems encountered on the path to TQM are contained in this story:

---

[1] Source: James A. Alloway, Jr. "Laying the Groundwork for Total Quality," *Quality Progress*, 27, 1, January, 1990, p. 67.

- Equating higher price with higher quality
- Jumping right into a program without first preparing the groundwork
- Trying to treat the symptoms, rather than the causes
- Never having enough time to do the job right the first time but always having enough time to do it over
- Judging performance by isolated incidents
- Copying tools and programs from others without understanding your own process and how to apply the tools
- Blaming other and things beyond your control when efforts fail
- Equating expected results with money and time rather than on effective use of resources
- Believing that islands of success will spread without preparation rather than realizing that a successful operation will be overcome by an unsuccessful one if left unattended
- Drifting from one program to another, hoping for a solution
- Trying to purchase technological solutions to problems
- Automating a process without first understanding it completely

Case II. Equipto, Inc.

1. In launching a major effort to change the corporate culture, a great deal of planning needs to be done. At Equipto, a personable middle manager was chosen as division TQM director. Three days of training was given to top management. Then division managers chose in-house facilitators and local consultants to give three to five days of quality training. Teams were pretty much on their own to develop projects during the first year.

   Things might have gone better if managers and workers had been given just in time (JIT) training on TQM principles and tools, while they were learning to use them. Also, if managers had been required to use the tools and approaches, and report on results at the same time that subordinates were using them, it could have been very reinforcing,

2. Details were not given on the content of the training, but it is likely that it was more team based than SPC oriented because of Bob Green's influence on the decision. Up-front training was very popular in the 1980's (and still is in some organizations). However, the advantage of JIT training is that team members can immediately put their skills into practice and see results. Some momentum may have been lost by the "large scale" training effort. Also, people want to see some results before they will "buy into" a new approach.

3. SPC should be introduced to operating levels of employees fairly soon after they have learned problem solving skills in their teams, in most cases. However, training and use must be tailored to the needs of employees, so JIT training is preferable to up-front training. Employees need to learn the basics of measurement and control, in addition to instruction on teamwork, how to improve processes, and how to solve problems. It was probably past time for Equipto to do so, since many of their customers probably were technical people who could talk intelligently about motor specifications and may have been concerned about the impact of TQM on their products.

4. It is certainly possible for TQM to be implemented successfully and to have market conditions to turn down. TQM is no guarantee of corporate financial success. However, if there is "constancy of purpose" in the installation and application of a TQM process, long-run success has a much higher probability with TQM than without it. For example, Wallace Corporation was a Baldrige award winner, but it had to declare Chapter 11 bankruptcy due to the drop in oil prices and foreclosure by banks on their business loans.

5. The company should "stay the course" with its TQM focus. Frequently, corporations that institute a TQM process quit too early, thus damaging employee morale and losing momentum in quality efforts. Rather than a sudden, wrenching change, Harry Rule should introduce JIT training in SPC. He should not scrap EI teams, but should have local and corporate steering committees to channel the efforts of the teams toward a balanced emphasis on problem solving and control and performance.

Case III. The Downsizing Dilemma

1. Organizations that have had a successful TQM process in place for an extended period are beginning to find that <u>human</u> and other resources are being used more efficiently and effectively. The dilemma is: what to do with the excess people that are no longer needed?

2. If downsizing becomes necessary, there are a number of avenues that might be explored in order to perform it in a total quality manner. As mentioned in the text, it is not a good practice to closely connect downsizing with the TQM process. The first step is to examine the organization's objectives for the future and the system effects of losses of employees. The approach of "cutting 20%, across the board" is rarely wise or successful.

    Large corporations can often reduce the ranks through attrition, early retirement incentives, and internal placement on new jobs or within new or growing divisions. Small organizations must be more creative to avoid downsizing or reduce its impact. Some companies have asked the employees for ideas and have been surprised by their flexibility. Thus, such ideas as reducing the workweek and pay of everyone, including managers, can often relieve the pressure if the business is only temporarily in a slump. Some companies have even hired out employees to other firms to give them work until business improved. Others send line employees out to work as sales people in the field.

CHAPTER 14

Quality Assurance and Control

Teaching Notes

This chapter describes concepts and methods of inspection of products and services. Specifications and tolerances, aspects of metrology, and process capability are covered. Students should be warned that while inspection is essential to quality control, it is only a means to the end. Inspection does not guarantee quality. Quality cannot be inspected into products or services.

The chapter Appendix also reviews basic statistical concepts and techniques relevant to statistical process control (SPC). These topics are covered in business or engineering statistics course that students should have had prior to the one using this text. Key objectives for this chapter include:

• To establish the importance of inspection as the "bridge" between quality of design and conformance. Proper use of inspection is highlighted as an auditing and improvement tool.

• To help students appreciate the importance of specifications, tolerances, and planning processes needed to assure quality in operations within an organization.

• To introduce concepts of measurement, gauging, metrology, and calibration.

• To help students to understand the concept of process capability and its effects on quality and conformance to specifications.

• To explore the concept of six sigma quality, coined by Motorola.

• To introduce the concept of statistical measurement of service quality.

• To review definitions and concepts of statistics, and relate them to quality control applications.

ANSWERS TO QUALITY IN PRACTICE KEY ISSUES

Quality Assurance for an International Wine Producer

1.   Detailed process flowcharts were developed for the production of two representative wines. Activities were then grouped into four categories -- operations, inspections, transportations, and storage. These were then used to develop a four-level hierarchy of product quality characteristics and key quality factors. These went from broad categories at the first level down to detailed quality factors on every material and production process and the inspection points on the flowcharts at which every quality factor may be controlled. For the two pilot products over 2200 factors were identified.

  This method could be used for the development of a quality assurance process for pizza by flowcharting the processes as above. The hierarchy that would be developed might be similar to that of this case. The categories of operations, inspections, transportations, and storage would certainly apply to pizza preparation processes. At level one, the broad categories of content, baking and packaging and delivery could be used. Further down at level 4, the characteristic of "excellence of crust" might be analyzed in detail. At this level, materials (what goes into the dough) and processes (rising time, shaping, oven temperature and time, etc.) would have to be considered. Quality factors could then be set so that "excellent crusts" would be highly likely to result from the content and process that was consistently used.

2.   Process capability was found to be a factor that had to be carefully analyzed by J. Boutaris and Sons. After critical quality characteristics and processes were identified, they were monitored for several weeks under controlled conditions to determine process capability. It was found that some specifications were too tight and others were unnecessarily strict, requiring them to be loosened. In some cases suppliers had to be contacted to require them to improve quality. This was done over a period of time in order to give them a chance to comply with the change in specifications and to promote continuous improvement.

  The general lessons to be learned include the needs to: a) carefully define processes, critical quality characteristics, and specifications; b) measure process capability to determine conformance to specifications; c) adjust specifications, if necessary; d) get suppliers involved in the quality improvement effort; and e) promote continuous improvement.

A Process Capability Study

1.   The key to the calculation of an estimated process capability for this case is to calculate an estimated standard deviation for each condition. Using the simplifying assumption that the sample standard deviation is a good approximation of the population standard deviation will allow us to make a reasonable estimate, even though for the cases of the

small sample sizes of 30 or 35 that assumption would be open to argument by statisticians.

We will concentrate on the calculation of C_p for only case (a) and (e), since it is obvious that the capability became drastically worse during the experimental stages from (b) to (d). Reading the data from the histograms, we can use the calculation of the sample standard deviation with grouped data from the chapter. The frequency histogram for condition (a) shows:

Group	mp, x	Frequency	fx	fx²
1	45	3	135	6075
2	50	6	300	15000
3	55	0	0	0
4	60	16	960	57600
5	65	4	260	16900
6	70	22	1540	107800
7	75	6	450	33750
8	80	23	1840	147200
9	85	5	425	36125
10	90	10	900	81000
11	95	0	0	0
12	100	5	500	50000
			7310	551450

$$\bar{x} = \frac{\Sigma fx}{n} = \frac{7310}{100} = 73.1$$

$$s = \sqrt{\left(\frac{\Sigma fx^2}{n-1}\right) - \left(\frac{\Sigma(fx)^2/n}{n-1}\right)} = \sqrt{\left(\frac{551450}{99}\right) - \left(\frac{7310^2/100}{99}\right)} = 13.138$$

$$\therefore c_p = \frac{UTL - LTL}{6\sigma} = \frac{100 - 50}{6(13.138)} = 0.63; \text{ not acceptable}$$

The frequency histogram for condition (e) shows:

Group	mp, x	Frequency	fx	fx²
1	60	2	120	7200
2	65	0	0	0
3	70	12	840	58800
4	75	7	525	39375
5	80	11	880	70400
6	85	3	255	21675
			2620	197450

$$\bar{x} = \frac{\Sigma fx}{n} = \frac{2620}{35} = 74.857$$

$$s = \sqrt{\left(\frac{\Sigma fx^2}{n-1}\right) - \left(\frac{\Sigma(fx)^2/n}{n-1}\right)} = \sqrt{\left(\frac{197450}{34}\right) - \left(\frac{2620^2/35}{34}\right)} = 6.241$$

$$\therefore \; C_p = \frac{UTL - LTL}{6\sigma} = \frac{100 - 50}{6(6.241)} = 1.34; \text{ not outstanding,}$$
$$\text{but much better}$$

2.   The process used here was obviously a systematic process of problem-solving similar to the one suggested in Chapter 9. The first step was a) to understand the "mess." A Pareto-like approach found that 50% of the defective items were due to dimensional problems on one diameter of the valve stem. Next, b) find facts on the process capability; c) specific problems were identified: overadjustment by the operator, and lack of ability of the machine to hold tolerances; d) ideas on machine adjustments and improvements were generated; e) solutions were implemented, with the machine being adjusted and later overhauled; f) as Deming said, "Do it over, again and again." [Step 7, added to the process, is continuous improvement].

ANSWERS TO REVIEW QUESTIONS

1.   James A. Sears has listed seven situations that could cause an organization to maintain the traditional inspection function in operations areas despite the fact that a total quality concept had been adopted:

(1) Quality conformance may be required by government regulations.
(2) Customer requirements specify an independent inspection activity.
(3) Critical parts or materials require close scrutiny by an independent inspection function to prevent economic losses from defective items.

(4) Centralized inspection is needed to accomplish testing using expensive inspection equipment in a timely and cost-effective fashion.

(5) Inspection and testing activities require specialized skill or in-depth training for the person performing the work.

(6) Strategically placed inspection personnel may be able to give early warnings of potentially catastrophic situations before they cause major damage.

(7) Management audit and review requirements may necessitate an impartial inspection and quality.

2. Gauges can generally be divided into two basic categories: variable gauges and fixed gauges. Variable gauges are adjusted to measure each individual part or dimension being inspected. Fixed gauges are preset to a certain dimension, and parts are classified according to whether or not they meet this dimension.

There are several types of variable gauges in use. Line graduated gauges have graduated spacings representing known distances. They include rulers and tapes, various types of inside and outside calipers, and micrometers. Dial, digital, and optical gauges show variations using a mechanical, electronic, or optical system to obtain dimensional readings.

Types of fixed gauges include plug gauges, ring gauges, snap gauges, and gauge blocks. Plug gauges are used to measure the inside diameters of bores. Ring gauges are used to measure outside diameters of parts using a go/no-go principle. Snap gauges, like ring gauges, are used to measure the outside diameters of parts, but have an open-ended construction so that they can snap onto the diameter of the part. Gauge blocks are special types of fixed gauges designed to be used as a precision measurement standard for calibration of other measuring and inspection instruments.

3. A variety of automated testing and measuring equipment has been introduced in recent years. Processes can now be continuously monitored for correct temperature and timing. Monitors and scanners can automatically store data for later analysis. Handheld micrometers can run "instant" process capability studies from readings taken on the shop floor. The expensive coordinate measuring machine is a highly accurate and sophisticated instrument with digital readouts. Computer vision systems can read symbols, identify objects, measure dimensions, and inspect parts for flaws. In quality control applications, vision systems are used to measure, verify, or inspect parts for dimensional tolerances, completeness of assembly, or mechanical defects.

4. The methods for the efficient collection, organization, and description of data are called *descriptive statistics*. *Statistical inference* is the process of drawing conclusions about unknown characteristics of a population from which the data were taken. *Predictive statistics* is used to develop predictions of future values based on historical data. The three differ in approach, purpose, and outcomes. Descriptive statistics simply summarize and report on existing conditions, inference helps to make decisions about population

characteristics based on sample data. Predictive statistics attempt to look into the future and state what <u>will be</u> the results, if certain assumptions hold. All three of these can be important to a manager who is trying to describe the current characteristics of a process, or make inferences about whether a process is in control, or predict future values of instrument readings in order to determine whether it is properly calibrated.

5.   A *population* is a complete set or collection of objects of interest. A *sample* is a subset of objects taken from a population.

6.   The *central limit theorem* is extremely useful in that it states (approximately) that a *sampling distribution* can be defined as the distribution obtained by taking a large number of samples of size n from any population with a mean μ and a standard deviation σ, and calculating their means. The mean of the sample means for this probability distribution will approach μ, and the standard deviation of the distribution will be $\sigma/\sqrt{n}$, as larger and larger sample sizes are taken. The CLT is extremely important in any SQC techniques that require sampling.

7.   The *standard error of the mean* is the (estimated) standard deviation of the population σ divided by $\sqrt{n}$. The standard deviation is, of course, a measure of variability within a population, where the standard error of the mean is a measure of the standard deviation within the sampling distribution.

8.   Traditional inspection practices typically involves heavy inspection of incoming materials and final product, with some off-line inspection of work in process. As materials and components are received, they are routed to a staging area where each part of some sample is inspected for conformance to specifications. There is no trust in the suppliers' ability to do what they are paid to do--supply conforming items. The modern viewpoint of inspection is that quality is everyone's responsibility, not just that of the guy standing at the end of the assembly line. The new role of inspection is a means to an end, not the end in itself. Product specifications provide the basis for achieving quality in the production system. When materials and components are received, occasional inspection might be used to audit compliance. However, the suppliers themselves should be required to provide documentation and statistical evidence that they are meeting required specifications. Within manufacturing, inspection should be conducted in a statistical fashion and performed by the workers on the production line so they have immediate feedback that can be used for process adjustment. This modern use of inspection fits Deming's philosophy very well, specifically, his point #3, "Understand the purpose of inspection, for improvement of processes and reduction of costs."

9.   *Acceptance inspection* is inspection of raw materials, parts, or components upon receipt from vendors, at any point in the production process, or after final production to decide whether or not to accept the item. The steps in an acceptance sampling plan include: a) the receiving stage, where the lot is received for inspection; b) sample selection, which involves drawing the sample for inspection; c) inspection and analysis, which requires

measuring and analyzing critical characteristics of the items in the sample; d) comparison of results with criteria, which allows the inspector to determine if items meet or fail to meet the specifications; and e) acceptance or rejection decision, which determines whether the materials in the lot are acceptable or not acceptable for use.

10. Acceptance sampling is no longer the preferred method of quality control, because companies that practice the TQM philosophy know that quality cannot be "inspected into" a product. If the supplier can demonstrate that they have a stable process, then quality at a known (and acceptable) level will always be received. If the supplier's process is not stable, then the purchaser should ask why, and work to help the supplier to achieve that goal. The burden of supplying high quality products should be placed on suppliers, not their customers. Thus, acceptance sampling should only be a temporary measure.

11. Inspection serves as the control function that ties together quality of design with quality of conformance. Pyzek stated that one should try to control all process factors that cause variation in product features. Thus the guidelines for selection of indicators for inspection include:

    • Indicators that are closely related to cost or quality
    • Indicators that are economical to measure
    • Indicators that show measurable variation
    • Indicators that provide information that help the organization to improve quality

12. In determining where to locate inspection stations, one must consider trade-offs between the explicit costs of detection, repair or replacement and the implicit costs of unnecessary additional investment in a nonconforming item if inspection is not performed. Several rules of thumb have been proposed for the location decision.

    (1) Locate before all processing operations, such as before every machine or assembly operation.
    (2) Locate before relatively high cost operations or where significant value is added to the product.
    (3) Locate before processing operations that may make detection of defectives difficult or costly, such as operations that may mask or obscure faulty attributes.
    (4) Locate after operations likely to generate a high proportion of defectives.
    (5) Locate after the finished product is completed.

13. For critical quality characteristics, 100% inspection is usually required. While it provides the best assurance of conformance to specifications, it is not always perfect because of such problems as human error, faulty measuring equipment, and use of incorrect standards. It is not often practical because of the time, effort, and costs involved. Clearly, it cannot be used when testing is destructive.

Sampling procedures are useful in dealing with large quantities of noncritical quality characteristics. Sampling is more economical than 100% inspection but it is subject to a higher degree of risk. It has been shown that sampling inspection is generally superior to 100% inspection because of its ability to overcome systematic forms of human error.

14.   The challenges of visual inspection are that they are performed by humans, subject to a variety of interpretation, often require considerable training, and are frequently found to have high error rates. Human factors in inspection are extremely varied, due to the strengths and weaknesses of the species. The physical, environmental and system factors that surround inspectors have their effects on inspection. Some of these factors include: a) complexity of the parts or process, b) defect rate, c) repeated inspections, d) inspection rate. Ways to improve inspection are suggested in the body of the chapter.

15.   *Accuracy* is defined as the closeness of agreement between an observed value and an accepted reference value or standard. Accuracy is measured as the amount of error in a measurement in proportion to the total size of the measurement. One measurement is more accurate than another if it has a smaller relative error.

Precision is defined as the closeness of agreement between randomly selected individual measurements or results. Precision, therefore, relates to the variance of repeated measurements. A measuring instrument having a low variance is said to be more precise than another having a higher variance.

Reproducibility is the variation in the same measuring instrument when it is used by different individuals to measure the same parts. Causes of poor reproducibility include poor training of the operators in the use of the instrument or unclear calibrations on the gauge dial.

16.   *Calibration* is the comparison of a measurement device or system having a known relationship to national standards to another device or system whose relationship to national standards is unknown. Calibration is necessary to ensure the accuracy of measurement and hence to have confidence in the ability to distinguish between conforming and nonconforming production. Measurements made with uncalibrated or inadequately calibrated equipment can lead to erroneous and costly decisions.

17.   *Process capability* is the range over which the natural variation of a process occurs as determined by the system of common causes. It is the ability of the combination of people, machines, methods, materials, and measurements to produce a product or service that will consistently meet design specifications. Process capability is measured by the proportion of output that can be produced within design specifications; in other words, it is a measurement of the uniformity of the product.

18.   A process is in control, if, to use Deming's terms, it is subject only to common causes, and no special causes are present. Thus if the process is operating in a stable fashion, it may not be operating within specifications at all, since the specifications may have been set without regard to process capability.

19.   A *process capability study* is a carefully planned study designed to yield specific information about the performance of a process under specified operating conditions. Three types of studies are often conducted. A peak performance study is focused on determining how a process performs under actual operating conditions. A process characterization study is designed to determine how a process performs under actual operating conditions. A component variability study has the goal of determining the relative contribution of different sources of total variation. The steps involved in making a process capability study are listed in the chapter.

20.   The *process capability index*, Cp, is defined as the ratio of the specification width to the natural tolerance of the process. Cp relates the natural variation of the process with the design specifications in a single, quantitative measure.

21.   The concept of *six sigma* was popularized by Motorola, when they set that as a stretch goal for "every process to have six sigma (6 σ) capability by 1992." In practical terms, it means shrinking the process variation to half of the design tolerance, while allowing the mean to shift as much as 1.5 σ from the target. The area under the curve beyond the 6 σ ranges (the tolerance limits) is only 3.4 parts per million.

22.   A few examples of service standards might be: a) on-time arrivals and departures for busses; b) customer compliments versus complaints for tours; c) merchandise returns for a department store; d) power outage hours or incidents for an electrical utility; and e) return visits for a hotel or motel.

23.   The two factors that influence sampling procedure are the method of selecting the sample and the sample size. Methods include simple random sampling, stratified sampling, systematic sampling and cluster sampling. Sample size is dependent on the amount of variation in the population (measured by σ) and the amount of error that the decision maker can tolerate at a specified confidence level.

24.   The basic questions that must be addressed in a sampling study are:

a. What is the objective of the study?
b. What type of sample should be used?
c. What possible error might result from sampling?
d. What will the study cost?

All of these questions are inter-related, and only the last two are quantifiable. Anyone making a decision regarding these questions needs to have some understanding of the options, relative accuracy, and cost tradeoffs of each potential alternative in sampling studies. The long-run consequences of making a wrong choice in the design of a sampling study can be quite serious. For example, if a pharmaceutical firm makes a substantial error in the design or execution of a sampling study on a new drug, the result could be felt in the direct costs of running a correct study, the likelihood that customers would sue the company for injury suffered in taking the drug, or for the lack of any substantial benefit coming from having taken an ineffective drug. In addition, the firm's reputation could be permanently damaged.

25.   Methods of sample selection, listed previously, include: simple random sampling, stratified sampling, systematic sampling and cluster sampling. Simple random sampling is useful where one needs to gather information from a moderately large, homogeneous population of items. For example, if a MBA director wished to find out the attitudes of 300 MBA students toward various policies, procedures, and services provided to the students, s(he) might use a simple random sample to determine who the survey should be sent to. A stratified sample could be used by an automobile insurance company to determine accident rates of customers, stratified according to their various ages. An auditor might use a systematic sampling to sample accounts receivable records by choosing every 50th record out of a file cabinet. Cluster sampling could be used by management analysts within city government to determine satisfaction levels of residents on a neighborhood by neighborhood (cluster) basis. Judgment sampling should be avoided, except as a way to gather preliminary, impressionistic data before beginning a true sampling study.

26.   Systematic errors in sampling can come from bias, non-comparable data, uncritical projection of trends, causation, and improper sampling. Ways of avoiding these systematic errors are thoroughly discussed early in the chapter. Basically, careful planning of the sampling study, awareness of possible systematic error causes, and careful execution of the study can help one to avoid most of the common errors listed above.

SOLUTIONS TO PROBLEMS

1.   a) Currently, $p = 2 / 10,000 = 0.0002$ error rate

b) For $C_1 = \$0.25$ and $C_2 = \$25.00$

$p = C_1 / C_2 = 0.25 / 25 = 0.01$ or   1 error /100
electronic components

Therefore, it would not pay the manufacturer to 100% inspect these components since the error rate would have to be 1/100 to break even on the cost.

The answer to the question of how much is saved or lost per radio is subject to the assumptions. Obviously, the expected number of defective components per radio is: 0.0002 X 60 = 0.012. Also, it would cost $0.25 X 60 = $15.00 to inspect each component prior to assembly of the radio. If you assume that it costs $25 to <u>find and repair</u> each defective component, regardless of the number of components in the radio, then the expected <u>savings</u> from avoiding the repairs would be: 0.012 X $25 = $0.30 per radio. Therefore, the <u>loss</u> from 100% inspection would be $15.00 - 0.30 = $14.70.

2.   For C_1 = $0.25 and C_2 = $500.00

$p = C_1 / C_2$ = 0.25 / 500 = 0.0005 <u>or</u> 0.5 errors/1000 transactions

3.   Accuracy of:

       Instrument A   Instrument B

$$100 \times \frac{0.06 - 0.05}{0.05} = 20\% \quad 100 \times \frac{0.054 - 0.05}{0.05} = 8\%$$

Instrument B is more accurate.

The frequency distribution, taken from the QMA printout, shows that Instrument A is more precise than Instrument B.

Instrument A is a better instrument, since it is likely that it can be adjusted to center on the nominal value of 0.

```
Instrument A                              Instrument B

Minimum value:        0.05000      Minimum value:        0.04000
Maximum value:        0.07000      Maximum value:        0.07000
First quartile:       0.06000      First quartile:       0.04000
Median:               0.06000      Median:               0.05000
Third quartile:       0.06000      Third quartile:       0.07000
Average:              0.06000      Average:              0.05400
Variance:             0.00004      Variance:             0.00016
Standard Deviation:   0.00667      Standard Deviation:   0.01265
Range:                0.02000      Range:                0.03000
No. of observations   10           No. of observations   10

      Histogram                          Histogram

ell  Upper Limit  Frequency        Cell  Upper Limit  Frequency
--   -----------  ---------        ----  -----------  ---------
1                              :    1        0.03        0     :
2      0.05         2         :**   2        0.04        0     :
3                              :    3        0.05        3     :***
4      0.06         6         :*****  4      0.06        3     :***
5                              :    5        0.07        4     :****
6      0.07         2         :**   6        0.08        0     :
7    infinity       0         :    7      infinity      0     :
```

4.

$\bar{x}_1 = (\Sigma\Sigma M_{ijk}) /nr = 29.721 / 30 = 0.9907$

$\bar{R}_1 = (\Sigma M_{ij}) / n = 0.280 / 10 = 0.028$

Use this method to calculate values for operator

$\bar{x}_2 = 29.901 / 30 = 0.9967;\ \bar{R}_2 = 0.380/ 10 = 0.038$

$\bar{x}_D = \max\ \{\bar{x}_i\} - \min\ \{\bar{x}_i\} = 0.9967 - 0.9907 = 0.0060$

$\bar{\bar{R}} = (\Sigma \bar{R}_i) / m = (0.028 + 0.038) / 2 = 0.033$

$D_4 = 2.574$; $UCL_R = D_4\ \bar{\bar{R}} = (2.574)\ (0.033) = 0.0849$, all ranges below

$K_1 = 3.05$; $K_2 = 3.65$ (from Table 13.2)

$EV = K_1\bar{\bar{R}} = (3.05)\ (0.033) = 0.10065$

$OV = \sqrt{(K_2\bar{x}_D)^2 - (EV^2/nr)} = 0.0119$

$RR = \sqrt{(EV)^2 + (OV)^2} = 0.1014$

Equipment variation = 100 (0.10065 / 0.12) = 83.88%
Operator variation   = 100 (0.0119 / 0.12) = 9.92%
R & R variation   = 100 (0.1014 / 0.12) = 84.50%

$\therefore$ Concentrate on reducing equipment variation

5.   The mean, $\mu = 10.75$; the standard deviation, $\sigma = 0.1$

$$Z = \frac{x - \mu}{\sigma} = \frac{11 - 10.75}{0.1} = 2.5$$

$$P(x > 11) = 0.5000 - P\left(Z > \frac{x - \mu}{\sigma}\right)$$

$P(Z > 11) = 0.5000 - P\ (\ Z > 2.5\ ) = 0.5000\ -\ 0.4938 = 0.0062$
(Using Normal Table, Appendix A)

6.   (Using the Standard Normal Distribution Table, Appendix A)

$$z = -1.88 = \frac{20 - \mu}{0.7} \quad ; \quad \therefore \quad \mu = 21.316$$

7.   The mean, $\mu = 16.05$; the standard deviation, $\sigma = 0.03$

$$P(x < 16.0) = 0.5000 - P\left(Z > \frac{x - \mu}{\sigma} \right)$$

$$Z = \frac{x - \mu}{\sigma} = \frac{(16.0 - 16.05)}{0.03} = -1.67$$

$P(Z < 16.0) = 0.5000 - P(-1.67 < Z < 0) = 0.5000 - 0.4525 = 0.0475$
(Using Normal Table, Appendix A)

$$P(x > 16.1) = 0.5000 - P\left(Z > \frac{x - \mu}{\sigma} \right)$$

$$Z = \frac{x - \mu}{\sigma} = \frac{(16.10 - 16.05)}{0.03} = 1.67$$

$P(Z > 16.1) = 0.5000 - P(0 < Z < 1.67) = 0.5000 - 0.4525 = 0.0475$
(Using Normal Table, Appendix A)

8.

Group	mp, x	Frequency	fx	fx²
1	37.5	1	37.5	1406.25
2	37.8	4	151.2	5715.36
3	38.1	9	342.9	13064.49
4	38.4	29	1113.6	42762.24
5	38.7	30	1161.0	44930.70
6	39.0	15	585.0	22815.00
7	39.3	7	275.1	10811.43
8	39.6	3	118.8	4704.48
9	39.9	2	79.8	3184.02
		100	3864.9	149393.97

$$\bar{x} = \frac{\Sigma fx}{n} = \frac{3864.9}{100} = 38.649$$

$$s = \sqrt{\left(\frac{\Sigma fx^2}{n-1}\right) - \left(\frac{\Sigma(fx)^2/n}{n-1}\right)} = \sqrt{\left(\frac{149393.97}{99}\right) - \left(\frac{3864.9^2/100}{99}\right)} = 0.443$$

9.

Class	mp	f	Cumulative Freq.	Cumulative Relative Freq.
1	37.5	1	1	.01
2	37.8	4	5	.05
3	38.1	9	14	.14
4	38.4	29	43	.43
5	38.7	30	73	.73
6	39.0	15	88	.88
7	39.3	7	95	.95
8	39.6	3	98	.98
9	39.9	2	100	1.00

It can be seen from the normal probability plot below, that there is a fairly close fit with a normal distribution, although some variation is evident in the center of the distribution.

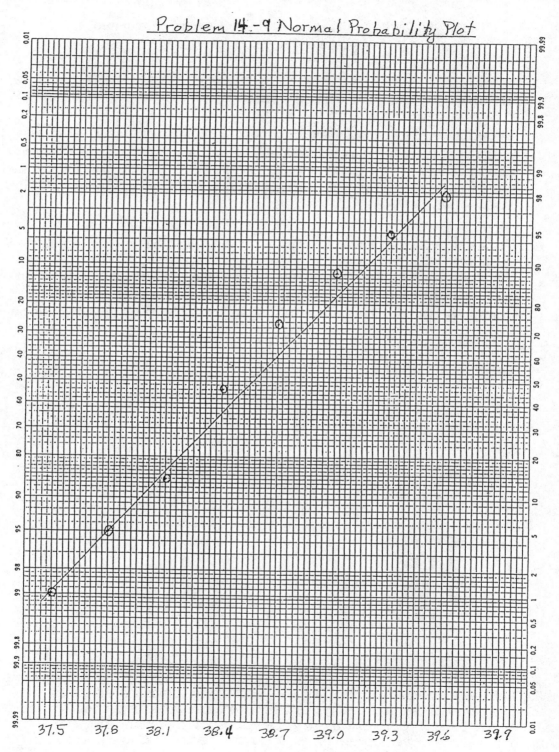

Problem 14-9 Normal Probability Plot

Probability Scale x 90 Divisions

Weights of Castings (Kg.)

10. $c_p = \dfrac{UTL - LTL}{6\sigma} = \dfrac{40.5 - 36.9}{6(0.443)} = 1.35$; not satisfactory

$c_p = \dfrac{40.5 - 36.9}{6\sigma} = 2.0$; Therefore, $\sigma = 0.3$ would be required, instead of the current $\sigma = 0.443$

11.   a) See accompanying line and bar charts[1].

b) For line 1, the data are skewed to the left, but the mean is at 2.3167, instead of being centered at 0. This indicates that a number of parts are likely to fall outside the upper tolerance limit of +5 (0.05 in decimal form). For line 2, the data are also skewed to the left, but the mean is -0.9833. This indicates that a number of parts will fall outside the lower tolerance limit of -5.

c) The data show a vary obvious overlapping distribution, with a significantly higher mean for line 1, and a negative value of the mean for line 2. There is less variability of the data for line 1, also. If such data are combined, the resulting distribution may appear to be quite normal, with a mean of 0.6583, but with a wide variability (s = 2.1431). In reality, by centering the process, it's capability could be improved considerably.

---

[1] In this and succeeding chapters we will occasionally use STATPAD and SAMSPAD, Lotus 1-2-3 based templates provided by kind permission of John A. Clements. Further information on Lotus 1-2-3 based software packages may be obtained from him at Professional Applications Development, 6 Country Lane, Douglassville, PA 19518, telephone (215)689-8787.

Problem 14-11

STATPAD PRINTOUTS:[2]

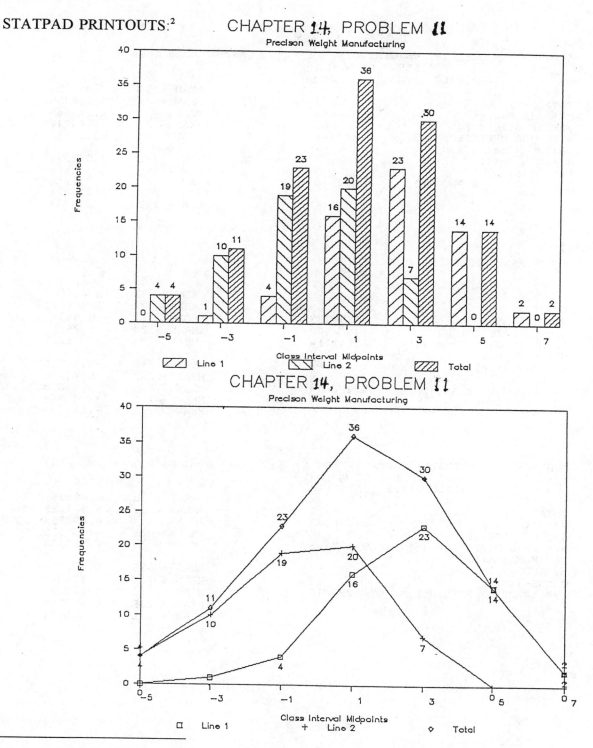

[2] Reprinted from STATPAD - Statistical templates for use with Lotus 1-2-3 by kind permission of John A. Clements.

```
* DESTAT1 * DESCRIPTIVE STATISTICS 1        No. of data rows =        60
              * TITLE * CH 14-11 A
          VARIABLE TITLE    LINE1
                              X               MEAN + 3s    7.962799
TOTAL (T)                    139              MEAN + 2s    6.080755
MEAN (X bar)            2.316666              MEAN         2.316666
SAMPLE SIZE (n)               60              MEAN - 2s   -1.44742
STANDARD DEVIATION (s)  1.882044              MEAN - 3s   -3.32946
MAXIMUM (max)                  7
MINIMUM (min)                 -2              MEAN + 3SE   3.045579
RANGE (r)                      9              MEAN + 2SE   2.802608
STD ERROR OF MEAN (SE)  0.242970              MEAN         2.316666
                                              MEAN - 2SE   1.830724
                                              MEAN - 3SE   1.587754


* DESTAT1 * DESCRIPTIVE STATISTICS 1        No. of data rows =        60
              * TITLE * CH 14-11 B
          VARIABLE TITLE    LINE2
                              X               MEAN + 3s    5.446008
TOTAL (T)                    -59              MEAN + 2s    3.302894
MEAN (X bar)           -0.98333              MEAN        -0.98333
SAMPLE SIZE (n)               60              MEAN - 2s   -5.26956
STANDARD DEVIATION (s)  2.143114              MEAN - 3s   -7.41267
MAXIMUM (max)                  3
MINIMUM (min)                 -6              MEAN + 3SE  -0.15330
RANGE (r)                      9              MEAN + 2SE  -0.42998
STD ERROR OF MEAN (SE)  0.276674              MEAN        -0.98333
                                              MEAN - 2SE  -1.53668
                                              MEAN - 3SE  -1.81335


* DESTAT1 * DESCRIPTIVE STATISTICS 1        No. of data rows =       120
              * TITLE * CH. 14-11 C
          VARIABLE TITLE    LINE1&2
                              X               MEAN + 3s    8.480369
TOTAL (T)                     79              MEAN + 2s    5.873023
MEAN (X bar)            0.658333              MEAN         0.658333
SAMPLE SIZE (n)              120              MEAN - 2s   -4.55635
STANDARD DEVIATION (s)  2.607345              MEAN - 3s   -7.16370
MAXIMUM (max)                  7
MINIMUM (min)                 -6              MEAN + 3SE   1.372384
RANGE (r)                     13              MEAN + 2SE   1.134367
STD ERROR OF MEAN (SE)  0.238016              MEAN         0.658333
                                              MEAN - 2SE   0.182299
                                              MEAN - 3SE  -0.05571
```

12.   For $\bar{x}$ = 0.5750; σ = 0.0065

$C_p = \dfrac{UTL - LTL}{6\sigma} = \dfrac{0.582 - 0.568}{6(0.0065)}$ = 0.359; not satisfactory

13. $\bar{x}$ = 0.5748, σ = 0.00239

$C_p = \dfrac{UTL - LTL}{6\sigma} = \dfrac{0.582 - 0.568}{6(0.00239)}$ = 0.976; The capability is outside the tolerance limits.

14.   a)   Data set 1: $\bar{x}$ = 1.7446; s = 0.0163; 3s = 0.0489

Data set 2: $\bar{x}$ = 1.9999; s = 0.0078; 3s = 0.0234

Data set 3: $\bar{x}$ = 1.2485; s = 0.0052; 3s = 0.0156

Part 1 will not consistently meet the tolerance limit since its ± 3s value is greater than the tolerance limit. Parts 2 and 3 are well within their tolerance limits, since their ± 3s values are smaller than the stated tolerances.

Note: Students may not have been exposed to advanced statistics. It may be necessary to explain how to calculate the $\sigma_{Process}$ using the variances of each of the data sets.

b) $\bar{x}_T$ = 4.9930 ; Estimated $\sigma_{Process} = \sqrt{s_1^2 + s_2^2 + s_3^2}$ =

$\sqrt{0.0163^2 + 0.0078^2 + 0.0052^2}$ = 0.0188

Process limits: 4.9930 ± 3(0.0188) or

4.9366 to 5.0494 vs. specification limits of
4.919 to 5.081 for a confidence level of 0.9973.

The parts <u>will</u> fit within their combined specification limit with a 0.9973 confidence level.

15.   Specification for answer time is : $0.04 \le \mu_1 \le 0.14$
Specification for service time is: $0.20 \le \mu_2 \le 0.70$

($\bar{x}_1$ = 0.1023, s_1 = 0.0183), ($\bar{x}_2$ = 0.5044, s_2 = 0.0902)

($\bar{x}_T$ = 0.6076, s_T = 0.0920)

$Z = \dfrac{0.84 - 0.6067}{0.0920}$ = 2.54   P(Z > 2.54) = 0.0055 that time
                                                                                                     will exceed upper limit

$Z = \dfrac{0.24 - 0.6067}{0.0920} = -3.99$ $P(Z < -3.99) = 0.00$ that time
will exceed lower limit

Therefore, the percent outside is: 0.0055, or 0.55 %

16. Note: The values below were coded to simplify input into the computer, as follows. (See accompanying printouts and histogram). They represent variations in thousandths of inches above and below the nominal value of 24.

Classes	mp	Frequency
-0.030 to -0.025	-0.0275	1
-0.025 to -0.020	-0.0225	0
-0.020 to -0.015	-0.0175	3
-0.015 to -0.010	-0.0125	5
-0.010 to -0.005	-0.0075	13
-0.005 to 0.000	-0.0025	19
0.000 to 0.005	0.0025	23
0.005 to 0.010	0.0075	17
0.010 to 0.015	0.0125	10
0.015 to 0.020	0.0175	5
0.020 to 0.025	0.0225	3
0.025 to 0.030	0.0275	1
		100

$\bar{x} = 24.0014$; s = 0.0097

Specification limits for the process are: $23.97 \le \mu \le 24.03$

$Z = \dfrac{24.0300 - 24.0014}{0.0097} = 2.95$ $P(Z > 2.94) = (0.5 - 0.4984) = 0.0016$ that
items will exceed upper limit

$Z = \dfrac{23.9700 - 24.0014}{0.0097} = -3.24$ $P(Z < -3.24) = 0.00$ that time
will exceed lower limit

Therefore, the percent outside is: 0.0016, or 0.16 %

$C_p = \dfrac{UTL - LTL}{6\sigma} = \dfrac{24.030 - 23.970}{6\,(0.0097)} = 1.031$

$$C_{pu} = \frac{UTL - \bar{x}}{3\sigma} = \frac{24.030 - 24.0014}{3\ (0.0097)} = 0.983$$

$$C_{pl} = \frac{\bar{x} - LTL}{3\sigma} = \frac{24.0014 - 23.970}{3\ (0.0097)} = 1.079$$

The process capability indexes are slightly out of tolerance for the upper index, and within minimum limits for the lower and overall index. This indicates that the process may be minimally adequate, if it can be centered on the nominal dimension of 24. However, the ideal situation would be to launch process improvement studies so that the capability indexes could be more than doubled.

17. $\bar{x} = 99.6767$, $\sigma = 2.1666$

$\bar{x} \pm 3\ \sigma = 99.6767 \pm 3(2.1666)$ <u>or</u> 93.177 to 106.177

Insufficient data is given to specifically calculate process capability. However, if the specification limits are **assumed** to be 100 ± 6.5 pounds (e.g. $\pm 3\sigma$).

$$C_p = \frac{UTL - LTL}{6\sigma} = \frac{106.5 - 93.50}{6\ (2.1666)} = 1.000$$

$$C_{pu} = \frac{UTL - \bar{x}}{3\sigma} = \frac{106.5 - 99.6767}{3\ (2.1666)} = 1.050$$

$$C_{pl} = \frac{\bar{x} - LTL}{3\sigma} = \frac{99.6767 - 93.5}{3\ (0.0097)} = 0.950$$

Conclusion: The process capability should be adequate if the process can be centered. Currently, it is not centered. However, the DESTAT[3] normal probability plot, below, shows that the data vary considerably from a normal distribution, especially for values above the mean. This puts the assumptions of any process capability computations in doubt.

---

[3] Reprinted from STATPAD - Statistical templates for use with Lotus 1-2-3 by kind permission of John A. Clements.

Problem 14-16

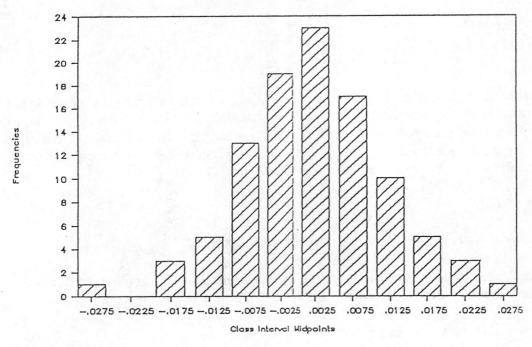

Problem 14-17

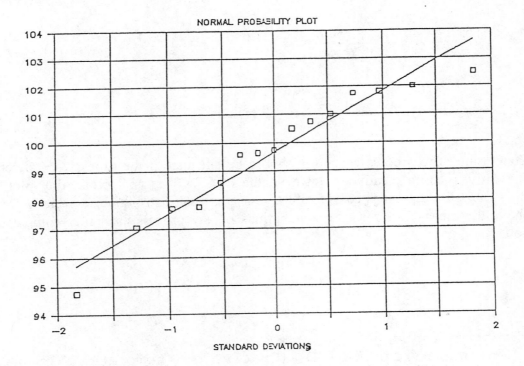

18. $\bar{x} = 50.25$; $\sigma = 1.5$

(a) $C_p = \dfrac{UTL - LTL}{6\sigma} = \dfrac{54.25 - 46.25}{6\,(1.5)} = 0.889$

$C_{pu} = \dfrac{UTL - \bar{x}}{3\sigma} = \dfrac{54.25 - 50.25}{3(1.5)} = 0.889$

$C_{pl} = \dfrac{\bar{x} - LTL}{3\sigma} = \dfrac{50.25 - 46.25}{3\,(1.5)} = 0.889$; Conclusion: The process does not have adequate capability at this time.

(b) $C_p = \dfrac{54.25 - 46.25}{6\,(1.5)} = 0.889$

$C_{pu} = \dfrac{54.25 - 50.0}{4.5} = 0.944$

$C_{pl} = \dfrac{50 - 46.25}{4.5} = 0.833$; Conclusion: The process still does not have adequate capability at this time.

(c) $\sigma^2_{new} = 0.81\,(2.25) = 1.8225$ $\therefore$ $\sigma_{new} = 1.35$

$C_p = \dfrac{54.25 - 46.25}{6\,(1.35)} = 0.988$

$C_{pu} = \dfrac{54.25 - 50.25}{3\,(1.35)} = 0.988$

$C_{pl} = \dfrac{50.25 - 46.25}{3\,(1.35)} = 0.988$; Reducing the variance brings the c_p and c_{pu} almost to the point of minimal adequacy, provided the process can be centered.

19. $C_p = \dfrac{UTL - LTL}{6\sigma} = 2.0 = \dfrac{5.60 - 5.20}{6\sigma} = \dfrac{0.4}{6\sigma}$; Therefore, $\sigma = 0.033$

$C_{pu} = \dfrac{UTL - \bar{x}}{3\sigma} = \dfrac{5.60 - \bar{x}}{3\sigma} = 2.0$; Therefore, we get: $\bar{x} = 5.4$

$C_{pl} = \dfrac{\bar{x} - LTL}{3\sigma} = \dfrac{\bar{x} - 5.20}{3\sigma} = 2.0$; Therefore, we get: $\bar{x} = 5.4$

20. $\overline{x}$ = 0.2085; s = 0.0039; $\overline{x}$ ± 3s = 0.1968 to 0.2202

21.
Cells	Frequency
0.202-0.204	1
0.204-0.206	3
0.206-0.208	17
0.208-0.210	15
0.210-0.212	11
0.212-0.214	2
0.214-0.216	0
0.230-0.232	1

See attached frequency histogram. Note that the outlying point should be investigated for an assignable cause.

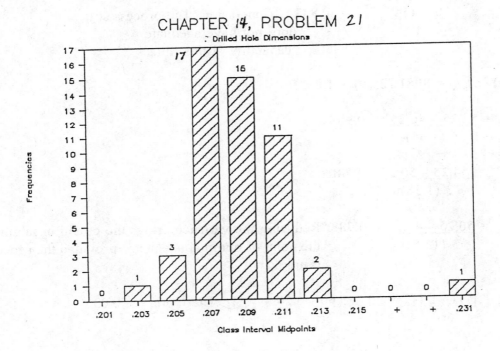

CHAPTER 14, PROBLEM 21

Drilled Hole Dimensions

22. $C_p = \dfrac{UTL - LTL}{6\sigma} = \dfrac{0.215 - 0.205}{6(0.0039)} = 0.427$

$C_{pu} = \dfrac{UTL - \bar{x}}{3\sigma} = \dfrac{0.215 - 0.2085}{3(0.0039)} = 0.556$

$C_{pl} = \dfrac{\bar{x} - LTL}{3\sigma} = \dfrac{0.2085 - 0.205}{3(0.0039)} = 0.299$

$C_{pk} = $ Min $(C_{pu}, C_{pl}) = 0.299;$ Conclusion: the process does not have adequate capability at this time.

23.   To draw a simple random sample of class members in order to do a project that required in-depth interviews on their attitudes and beliefs about quality, you would first have to count them and assign a sequential number to each person. For example, if there are 20 people in the class, after assigning each of them a number, enter the table in Appendix C at random, say, Row 3. If you wished to draw a 25% (1 out of every 4 students) sample, you would select 5 names, as shown:

Sequence	Random Number	Action	Sequence	Random Number	Action
1	55	Reject	12	76	Reject
2	95	Reject	13	16	Reject
3	75	Reject	14	65	Reject
4	72	Reject	15	35	Reject
5	43	Reject	16	40	Reject
6	83	Reject	17	10	Accept
7	86	Reject	18	22	Accept
8	50	Reject	19	66	Reject
9	99	Reject	20	44	Reject
10	11	Accept	21	60	Reject
11	19	Accept	22	14	Accept

Notice that a large number of random numbers have to be examined in order to obtain the five subjects to be used in the study.

24.   Using Table 14.7, for a population of 2,000 the sample size required for a critical 1% rate, with a 99% confidence level is <u>approximately</u>: 400 (use 98.9% confidence, critical rate of 1%).

25.   The proper sample size for a sorting error rate of 0.022, a 95% confidence level and a 0.01 allowable error is:
$n = (z_{\alpha/2})^2 \, p \, (1-p) / E^2 = (1.96)^2 \, (0.022)(0.978) / (0.01)^2 = 826.56$, use 827

ANSWERS TO CASE QUESTIONS

Case I. Acme Parts Ltd.

a.   The first part of the analysis requires that a standard process capability study be done. Although it may stretch credibility to think that a team doing a capability study would use "second-hand" data, it does show that it may be hard to differentiate between items produced by two different processes or inspected by two different inspectors. Process capability results from the Quality Management Analyst software are shown below.

These data show that the process has a rather low overall capability, with $C_p = 0.53141$ and a total of 11.5% of the values falling outside of the specification limits of .05 - .10

```
            PROCESS CAPABILITY ANALYSIS

Mean =       0.07726              Minimum value:       0.04850
Standard deviation =    0.01568   Maximum value:       0.10500
6 sigma =     0.09409             First quartile:      0.06500
                                  Median:              0.08000
Lower specification limit =    0.05000   Third quartile:    0.09050
Upper specification limit =    0.10000   Average:           0.07726
                                  Variance:            0.00025
Mean - 3 * sigma =    0.03021     Standard Deviation:  0.01568
Mean - 2 * sigma =    0.04590     Range:               0.05650
Mean - 1 * sigma =    0.06158     No. of observations   60

Mean + 1 * sigma =    0.09294              Histogram
Mean + 2 * sigma =    0.10862
Mean + 3 * sigma =    0.12430     Cell  Upper Limit  Frequency
                                  ----  -----------  ---------
Process capability index, Cp:    0.53141    1      0.0407       0
  Lower capability index, Cpl:   0.57941    2      0.0511       3   ***
  Upper capability index, Cpu:   0.48341    3      0.0616       9   *********
              Cpk:               0.48341    4      0.0720      12   ************
                                            5      0.0825      11   ***********
Fraction below lower specification:  0.0411  6      0.0929      15   ***************
Fraction above upper specification:  0.0735  7      0.1034       8   ********
                                            8      0.1138       2   **
                                            9      infinity      0
```

b.   With the new information, it appears that much of the work on the process capability analysis has been negated. The data provides a poor approximation of the <u>true</u> process capability. Questions that might be asked would be:

   • Since it appears that the measurement process, *itself* is in question, can we gather valid process data, now?

   • Is it within our charter to do an R&R study and fix any problems before going back to the process capability study?

   • Do we need expertise, equipment, etc. to conduct the R&R study?

   • Can we use the data that has been gathered to do the R&R study, even though it is not the right data for the process capability study?

   Assuming that the team decides to go on with the R&R study and delay the process capability study, then the data that has been gathered might be used to analyze the conditions and possible need for gauge calibration and correction steps.

c.   Calculations for the repeatability and reproducibility (R&R) study are as follows:

$$\bar{x}_1 = (\Sigma\Sigma M_{ijk}) /nr = 2.3378 / 30 = 0.0779$$

$$\bar{R}_1 = (\Sigma M_{ij}) / n = 0.1030/ 15 = 0.0069$$

Use this method to calculate values for operator 2

$$\bar{x}_2 = 2.2974 / 30 = 0.0766; \quad \bar{R}_2 = 0.0945/ 15 = 0.0063$$

$$\bar{x}_D = \max \{\bar{x}_i\} - \min \{\bar{x}_i\} = 0.0779 - 0.0776 = 0.0013$$

$$\bar{\bar{R}} = (\Sigma \bar{R}_i) / m = (0.0069 + 0.0063) / 2 = 0.0066$$

$$D_4 = 3.267 ; \quad UCL_R = D_4 \bar{\bar{R}} = (3.267) (0.0066) = 0.0216, \text{ all ranges below}$$

$$K_1 = 4.56 ; \quad K_2 = 3.65 \text{ (from Table 14.1 in the text)}$$

$$EV = K_1\bar{\bar{R}} = (4.56) (0.0066) = 0.0301$$

$$OV = \sqrt{(K_2\bar{x}_D)^2 - (EV^2/nr)} = \sqrt{[(3.65)(0.0013)]^2 - [(0.0301)^2/30]} = \sqrt{- 0.0000077}$$

NOTE: According to the *Measurement Systems Analysis Reference Manual* published by the Automotive Industry Action Group (AIAG), Troy MI, 1990, p. 44:

> "... if a negative value is calculated under the square root sign, the [OV] defaults to zero (0)."

$$RR = \sqrt{(EV)^2 + (OV)^2} = \sqrt{(0.0301)^2 + (0)^2} = 0.0301$$

Therefore, in this case, RR = EV

% Equipment variation (related to tolerance) = 100 (0.0301 / 0.05)   = 60.2%
Operator variation (related to tolerance)   =   0%
R & R variation (related to tolerance)   = 60.20%

$\therefore$ Concentrate on reducing equipment variation, not operator variation.

<u>Total Variation</u> (TV) = $\sqrt{(RR)^2 + (PV)^2}$, where PV is Part Variation

$PV = R_p \, K_3$

R_p = Range of part averages for the entire sample: 0.1013 to 0.0516 = 0.0497

K_3 = 1.45 from Table 14.9

PV = (0.0497) (1.45) = 0.0721

Thus TV = $\sqrt{(RR)^2 + (PV)^2} = \sqrt{(0.0301)^2 + (0.0721)^2} = 0.0781$

% OV = 0

% EV = % RR, related to TV = 100 (0.0301 / 0.0781) = 38.5

% PV, related to TV = 100 (0.0721 / 0.0781) = 92.3

NOTE: The sum of the above percentages will not add to 100.

Based on the "rules" for process capability given in the text, it can be assumed that the equipment and the process need to be improved, since none of the percentages fall below the 30% or 10% minimums. The operators are consistent in their measurements, so their methods are not in question at this point.

Worn or faulty gauges should be discarded and the rest should be calibrated.

CHAPTER 15

Fundamentals of Statistical Process Control

Teaching Note

This chapter presents the basic concepts of statistical process control. These include purposes, control charting techniques, design and analysis of charts, managerial requirements for implementation of SPC, and SPC considerations within service organizations. Key objectives for this chapter should include:

• To establish the importance of statistical process control as a means to give workers the information that they need on when a process should be adjusted and when it should not be adjusted.

• To introduce the common control charts for variables and attributes, show how they can be constructed, and describe their use in organizations.

• To introduce and practice analysis of control chart patterns for out-of-control conditions, and also how modified control limits may be used for highly capable processes.

• To help students to understand the managerial factors that contribute to successful implementation of SPC, including top management commitment, a champion, good initial projects, training, and an accurate measurement system.

• To explore the unique possibilities for use of SPC in service organizations. There, measurable variables and attributes must be identified, and statistical techniques that were developed in manufacturing settings must be translated and used for non-manufacturing applications.

ANSWERS TO QUALITY IN PRACTICE KEY ISSUES

Using SQC for Process Improvement at Dow Chemical Company

1.   The charts show "before and after" results of the application of SPC to two key process characteristics: drier operation and neutralizer excess alkalinity. In the first characteristic, the x-bar chart showed an obvious pattern of "hugging the control limits, or mixture, before SQC improvements were introduced. In addition, the range was very wide and occasionally out of control. After operator retraining, these problems were virtually eliminated. In the charts for the second characteristic, points appeared to hug the centerline and the mean value was rather high on the x-bar chart, while the R-chart seemed to exhibit large variability. After SQC improvements were introduced the process average was greatly reduced, as was the variability.

2.   Since the process capability is high, the company might decide to go to switch from control charting on a regular basis to modified control limits, which would reduce the cost and frequency of taking samples for control charts.

Process Capability Analysis at John Deere

1.   For the data given in Figure 15.33 we get:

$\bar{\bar{x}} = 875.27580$; $\bar{R} = 0.12133$; n = 3

$\bar{\bar{x}} \pm A_2 \bar{R} = 875.27580 \pm 1.023 \,(0.12133) = 875.15168$ to 875.39992

R-chart: : $UCL_R = D_4 \bar{R} = 2.574 \,(0.12133) = 0.31230$

$LCL_R = D_3 \bar{R} = 0$

Estimated $\sigma = \bar{R} / d_2 = 0.12133/1.693 = 0.071666$

It appears that there is some slight rounding error in the above figures versus those given on the CAIR report. However, they agree until about the fourth decimal place.

2.   The data show that the capability of this machine is extremely good, standing at 23.79. It is estimated that 100% of the product will be within specifications as long as the machine remains in adjustment.

3.   Deere has strict guidelines for process conditions, materials, operators, inspectors, and repeatability during capability tests because they want to ensure that no "special causes" are allowed to enter into the test and bias the results.

ANSWERS TO REVIEW QUESTIONS

1.   *Statistical process control* is a methodology using control charts for assisting operators, supervisors, and managers to monitor the output from a process to identify and eliminate special causes of variation. The advantages of using it are a) that it can help to reduce scrap and rework, increase productivity, determine process capability, predict yield from a process, and provide evidence that processes are in control to customers who may ask for it.

2.   The two basic reasons for using SPC are that it provides us with the information needed so that we can know when to take action to correct a process, and so that we'll know when to <u>leave the process alone</u>.

3.   Consistent quality is important in a production process because, without it, survival is not possible in a highly competitive marketplace. SPC provides the means to prove that a process is capable of producing <u>consistently</u> high quality items.

4.   A process is said to be *in statistical control* when variation in the process are due only to common causes (no special causes are present).

5.   In making process control decisions, managers face different decisions with differing risks. If a process is initially under control, and decisions about whether to adjust the process are made based on sample data, the risk of a Type I or Type II sampling error must be assessed. If a manager decides to adjust a process due to sample information, a Type I error may be made if the process is actually in control but the sample came from the high or low end of the population data. A Type II error may be made if the sample data shows no problem, but the process should actually have been adjusted.

6.   Histograms should not be used as the sole method for making process capability studies, since they do not show a progression of data over a period of time. Instead, they plot frequencies against dimensions, thus showing how the data is clustered, rather than how it occurred in a process, over time.

7.   The three primary applications of control charts are to: a) establish a state of statistical control, b) monitor a process and signal when it goes out of control, and c) determine process capability.

8.   *Variables data* is data such as length, time, weight, etc. that is measured along a continuous scale. *Attributes data* assumes only two values: good-bad, pass-fail, etc. and is measured by counting. The x-bar and R charts are used to chart and analyze variables data; the p-chart is the most commonly used one to chart and analyze attributes data.

9.   x-R charts are developed by taking a number of samples (usually 25-30) of a certain size (usually 3-10 items per sample) from a process that is thought to be in statistical control and calculating the sample means and ranges. Using standard statistical methods, the grand mean (mean of the sample means) and average range (R-bar), are calculated and used as center-lines for the segments of the x-bar - R chart. Based on these values, and tabulated parameters for control limits, the control limits for the sample x-bar and R values are established. Then the sample values are plotted on their respective charts. Any values that fall outside of either the calculated x-bar or R limits, or other indicators discussed in the next question, below, mean that the process is not <u>in control</u>. Assignable causes must be determined, the out-of-control samples must be discarded,and the control chart characteristics must be re-calculated.

10.   The characteristics that one looks for in interpreting control charts are those that indicate whether or not the process is remaining in control, or whether *assignable causes* have crept into throw the process out of control. These might be detected through using the rules of thumb of: 1) one point outside of a control limit; 2) two out of three consecutive points in the outer one-third region; 3) four out of five points in the outer two-thirds region, or 4) eight consecutive points on the same side of the centerline. Such out-of-control indicators may be traced to causes such as: one-time events (calculating error, power surges); sudden shifts in process average (new operator, inspector, or machine setting); cycles (day vs. night shifts, gauge variations, seasonal effects); trends (tool wear, operator fatigue, improving operator skills); hugging the centerline (taking samples from several machines, miscalculation of control limits).

11.   Shop floor personnel should use control charts to take steps to ensure that defective products are not produced. If corrective action is possible, on the spot, it should be taken. If not, the shop floor employee should take suitable action, stopping the process, if necessary, in order to prevent further defects from occurring.

12.   Modified control limits are used when the process capability is good. They should be used only if it is not practical to investigate every isolated point that falls outside of control limits, but these points are still well within specifications. Standard practice is to use them when process capability is at least 60 - 75 percent of tolerance.

13. Control charts can be used to determine process capability by calculating the limits for individual items and then determining the percent of items likely to fall outside, according to standard statistical estimates.

14. Control limits apply to samples of a given size and refer to sample means and ranges. Specification limits apply to individual items that are produced by a process, so are not average values.

15. There are many risks and costs associated with using control charts. Theses are affected by sample size, sampling frequency and control limits. Guidelines, such as those in the body of the chapter, listed in Table 15.5, are available for setting control limits that consider such risks and costs.

16. A defect is a non-conformance to a specific standard. A defective part or product is one that exhibits one or more non-conformances (it has one or more defects).

17. A p-chart is easier to construct than a x-R chart. A number of samples (usually 25, or more) are gathered of a specified size (say, 100 items). The sample can be of virtually any size, as long as it's consistent, although larger sample sizes are generally preferable for attributes, as opposed to smaller samples for variables. Then the defective items are counted and the sample proportion (number of defectives divided by the total sample size) is calculated. The average proportion (p-bar), is calculated and used as the centerline for the p-chart. The standard error of p is calculated using a standard error formula. Control limits for the p-chart are established simply by adding and subtracting 3 times the standard error to the average proportion. If any points fall outside the control limits, or if other indicators that the process is out of control exist, then assignable causes are determined, the out of control points are discarded, and the parameters and control limits are recalculated.

18. *Rational subgroups* is a concept of selecting samples in such a way that it is likely that the same system of common causes and special causes apply to all the items in the group. If assignable causes are present, the chance of observing differences between samples should be high, while the chances of observing differences within samples is low.

19.   The tradeoffs that exist when selecting sample size for a control chart affect accuracy, cost, and production rates. Small samples are desirable because they require less time and cost to gather and there is less possibility of within sample variation due to special causes. Large samples are more costly, but allow smaller changes in process characteristics to be detected with high probability.

20.   Control limit location is closely related to Type I and Type II errors. If a special cause is signaled by the control chart, but isn't present, it's a Type I error. If a special cause is not signaled by the chart, but it is present, then a Type II error has been made. The wider the control limits, the less chance there will be for points to fall outside, so there is a smaller chance of making a Type I error. Type II errors, depend on the width of the control limits, the degree to which the process is out of control, and the sample size. Wider control limits increase the risk of making a Type II error for the same sample size.

21.   Economic tradeoffs must always be considered when designing a control chart. The only way to reduce both the Type I and Type II error, simultaneously, is to increase sample size or frequency. Of course, this will always result in higher sampling costs.

22.   The application of SPC in short production run situations requires that adjustments be made in conventional control charting practices. This is necessary because samples to compute control limits may be difficult or impossible to collect. Thus three methods of compensation are typically used: 1) tables of special control chart constants for control limits can compensate for short production runs with limited number of samples; 2) data may be coded by subtracting the nominal value from the actual to measure deviations from target specifications, regardless of the product or number of units; or 3) data can be transformed so that it is independent of the unit of measure.

23.   There are several factors that are necessary for the successful implementation of SPC. They include: a) top management commitment, SPC project champions, a focus on addressing one problem at a time, education and training of all employees, and verification that gaging and measurement systems provide the necessary level of accuracy, repeatability, and reproduceability before implementing SPC.

24.   Applications of control charts to service organizations are many and varied. They are summarized in Table 15.6.

       An interesting example is the way control charts were used at the IBM facility at Kingston, NY, used control charting in an employee feedback (Speak Up!) program to monitor response time, in a medical examination program to monitor and improve process time, and in a purchasing department to monitor and improve nonconforming documents. All of these cases showed that both variables and attributes data could be gathered, charted and analyzed for improvement potential in a service environment.

25.   The lessons learned by Uniroyal in implementing SPC were in the categories of what <u>not</u> to do, and later <u>what</u> to do. In the first stage, they educated people, but did not really use SPC as a part of the way that they did business. In the second stage, a six-step process was put into place, including defining the process, identifying characteristics to study, determining ability to measure the characteristic, performing capability studies, studying actual process performance, and implementing process control. It took a long period of time to do it right, after taking a long time to do it wrong. The moral to the story was: don't get tired!

26.   Students should be encouraged to look at some service operations that may not currently be using control charting. They can then use their imagination to list 10 applications of control charts in service organizations that were not in this chapter. For .example, at an airport they could see that on-time arrival of airplanes, percentage of bags mishandled, average check-in time at counters, average unloading time of airplane baggage, etc. <u>could</u> all be control charted, even though the airline may not be doing so at this time. In an accounting department average collection period or errors in invoices could be charted.

SOLUTIONS TO PROBLEMS

Author's Note: In this chapter we will use printouts and summarized solutions taken from the Quality Management Analyst software, wherever feasible. The numbers for solutions taken from the QMA software will sometimes appear to be slightly different from those produced on a hand calculator, due to rounding differences.

1.   Results from 30 samples of 3 show that the R chart is apparently in control. However, on the x-bar chart, samples 11-18 (8 points on the same side of the mean) are more than one standard deviation away from the centerline. Assignable causes should be determined, one or more of these data points should be removed, and control limits should be recalculated.

Problem 15-1

a)

```
Minimum value:        2.69000
Maximum value:        4.48000
First quartile:       3.25000
Median:               3.56500
Third quartile:       3.77000
Average:              3.52600
Variance:             0.17355
Standard Deviation:   0.41659
Range:                1.79000
No. of observations   90
```

Histogram

Cell	Upper Limit	Frequency	
1	2.53	0	:
2	2.78	2	:**
3	3.03	9	:*********
4	3.28	12	:************
5	3.53	18	:******************
6	3.78	27	:***************************
7	4.03	8	:********
8	4.28	9	:*********
9	4.53	5	:*****
10	infinity	0	:

b)

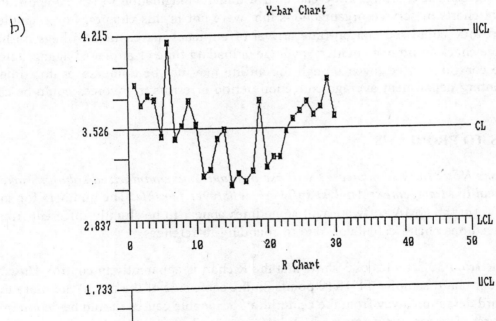

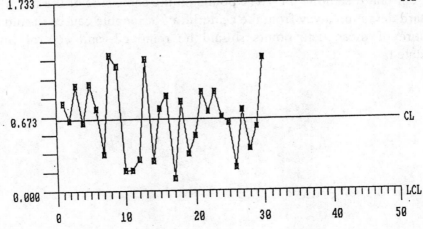

2.   For the Center Lines, $CL_{\bar{x}}^{-}$: $\bar{\bar{x}} = 480$; $CL_{\bar{R}}$: $\bar{R} = 34$

Control limits for the x-chart are: $\bar{x} \pm A_2\, \bar{R}$

$UCL_{\bar{x}}^{-} = \bar{\bar{x}} + A_2\, \bar{R} = 480 + (\ 0.483)\ 34 = 496.422$

$LCL_{\bar{x}}^{-} = \bar{\bar{x}} - A_2\, \bar{R} = 480 - (\ 0.483)\ 34 = 463.578$

For the R-chart:

$UCL_R = D_4\, \bar{R} = (2.004)\ 34 = 68.136$

$LCL_R = D_3\, \bar{R} = 0$

Estimated $\sigma = \bar{R}/d_2 = 13.418$

3.   For the Center Lines, $CL_{\bar{x}}^{-}$: $\bar{\bar{x}} = 5.42$; $CL_{\bar{R}}$: $\bar{R} = 2.0$

Control limits for the x-chart are:

$\bar{\bar{x}} \pm A_2\, \bar{R} = 5.42 \pm (0.577)\ 2.0 = 4.27$ to 6.57

For the R-chart: $UCL_R = D_4\, \bar{R} = 2.114(2.0) = 4.23$

$LCL_R = D_3\, \bar{R} = 0$

Estimated $\sigma = \bar{R} / d_2 = 2.0 / 2.326 = 0.86$

4.   See control chart, below.

For the Center Lines, $CL_{\bar{x}}^{-}$: $\bar{\bar{x}} = 95.398$; $CL_{\bar{R}}$: $\bar{R} = 0.665$

Control limits for the x-chart are:

$\bar{\bar{x}} \pm A_2\, \bar{R} = 95.398 \pm (\ 0.729\ )\ 0.665 = 94.913$ to 95.883

For the R-chart: $UCL_R = D_4\, \bar{R} = (2.282)\ 0.665 = 1.518$

$LCL_R = D_3\, \bar{R} = 0$

Problem 15-4

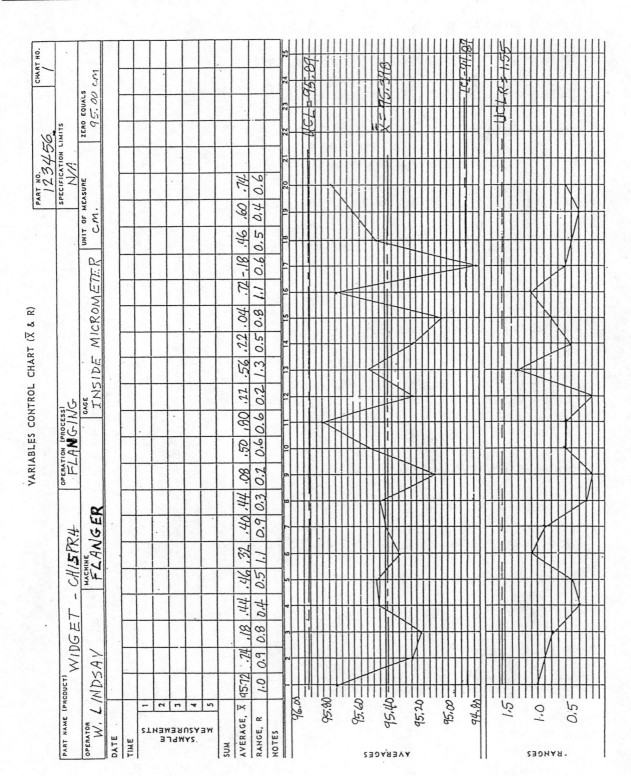

VARIABLES CONTROL CHART (X̄ & R)

PART NAME (PRODUCT) WIDGET – CHISPRA			OPERATION (PROCESS) FLANGING											PART NO. 123456				CHART NO. 1										
OPERATOR W. LINDSAY			MACHINE FLANGER				GAGE INSIDE MICROMETER							SPECIFICATION LIMITS N/A													
										UNIT OF MEASURE CM.				ZERO EQUALS 95.00 cm														
DATE																												
TIME																												
SAMPLE MEASUREMENTS	1																											
	2																											
	3																											
	4																											
	5																											
SUM																												
AVERAGE, X̄	95.72	.74	.18	.44	.46	.32	.40	.44	.08	.50	.80	.12	.56	.22	.04	.72	–.18	.46	.60	.74									
RANGE, R	1.0	0.9	0.8	0.4	0.5	1.1	0.9	0.3	0.2	0.6	0.6	0.2	1.3	0.5	0.8	1.1	0.6	0.5	0.4	0.6									
NOTES																												

AVERAGES

UCL = 95.89
X̄ = 95.398
LCL = 94.87

96.00
95.80
95.60
95.40
95.20
95.00
94.80

RANGES

UCLR = 1.55

1.5
1.0
0.5

5.   See data and control charts, below.

For the Center Lines, $CL_{\bar{x}}^- : \bar{\bar{x}} = 402.92$; $CL_R^- : \bar{R} = 33.20$

Control limits for the $\bar{x}$-chart are:

$\bar{\bar{x}} \pm A_2 \bar{R} = 402.92 \pm 1.023 (33.20) = 368.96$ to 436.88

For the R-chart: $UCL_R = D_4 \bar{R} = 2.574 (33.20) = 85.46$

$LCL_R = D_3 \bar{R} = 0$

Throw out outliers #16, #23, revise.

For the $\bar{x}$-chart:

$\bar{\bar{x}} \pm A_2 \bar{R} = 400.29 \pm 1.023 (30.96) = 368.62$ to 431.96

For the R-chart: $UCL_R = D_4 \bar{R} = 2.574 (30.96) = 79.69$

$LCL_R = D_3 \bar{R} = 0$

Sample	Observations			Mean	Range
1	414.0000	388.0000	402.0000	401.3333	26.0000
2	408.0000	382.0000	406.0000	398.6667	26.0000
3	396.0000	402.0000	392.0000	396.6667	10.0000
4	390.0000	398.0000	362.0000	383.3333	36.0000
5	398.0000	442.0000	436.0000	425.3333	44.0000
6	400.0000	400.0000	414.0000	404.6667	14.0000
7	444.0000	390.0000	410.0000	414.6667	54.0000
8	430.0000	372.0000	362.0000	388.0000	68.0000
9	376.0000	398.0000	382.0000	385.3333	22.0000
10	342.0000	400.0000	402.0000	381.3333	60.0000
11	400.0000	402.0000	384.0000	395.3333	18.0000
12	408.0000	414.0000	388.0000	403.3333	26.0000
13	382.0000	430.0000	400.0000	404.0000	48.0000
14	402.0000	409.0000	400.0000	403.6667	9.0000
15	399.0000	424.0000	413.0000	412.0000	25.0000
16	460.0000	375.0000	445.0000	426.6667	85.0000
17	404.0000	420.0000	437.0000	420.3333	33.0000
18	375.0000	380.0000	410.0000	388.3333	35.0000
19	391.0000	392.0000	414.0000	399.0000	23.0000
20	394.0000	399.0000	380.0000	391.0000	19.0000
21	396.0000	416.0000	400.0000	404.0000	20.0000
22	370.0000	411.0000	403.0000	394.6667	41.0000
23	418.0000	450.0000	451.0000	439.6667	33.0000
24	398.0000	398.0000	415.0000	403.6667	17.0000
25	428.0000	406.0000	390.0000	408.0000	38.0000

Control Chart Calculations for file: CH16PR5

X-Bar Chart

Upper control limit =	436.8836
Center line =	402.9200
Lower control limit =	368.9565

R-Chart

Upper control limit =	85.4568
Center line =	33.2000
Lower control limit =	0.0000

Estimated standard deviation for process capability (Rbar/d2) =   19.6102

Problem 15-5

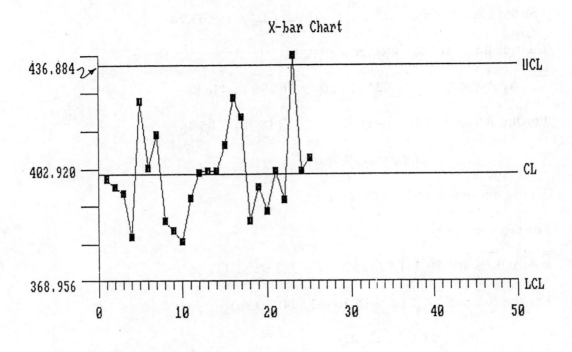

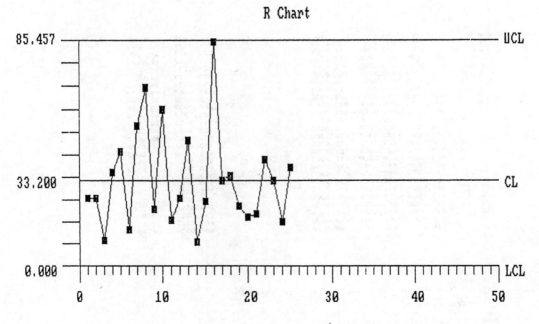

Problem 15-5: Revised x̄-chart and R-chart

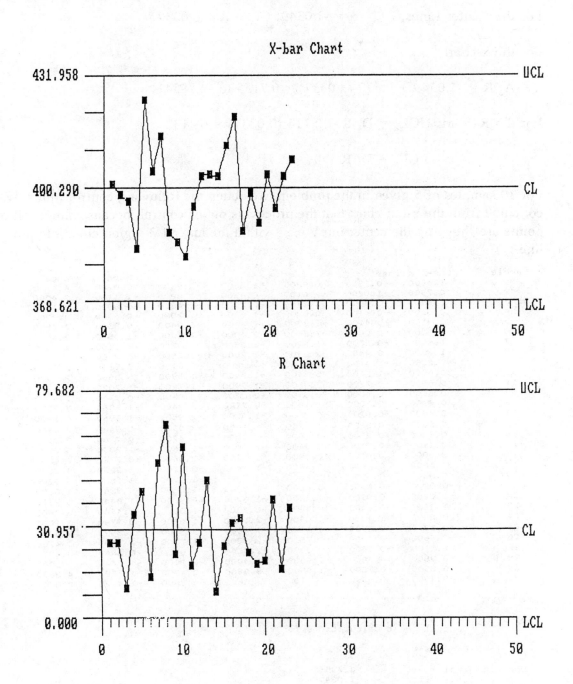

6.   See data and control charts, below.

For the Center Lines, $CL_{\bar{x}}$: $\bar{\bar{x}} = -1.0349$; $CL_{\bar{R}}$: $\bar{R} = 3.0337$

For the x-chart:

$\bar{\bar{x}} \pm A_2 \bar{R} = -1.0349 \pm 0.577 (3.0337) = 0.7155$ to -2.7854

For the R-chart: $UCL_R = D_4 \bar{R} = 2.114 (3.0337) = 6.4132$

$$LCL_R = D_3 \bar{R} = 0$$

For 30 samples of 5 given in the problem, we obtain the following control limits. We can conclude from the x-bar chart that the process is out of control, because almost all of the points are "hugging the center line" (e.g., within the inner 1/3 region closest to the center line.)

Sample	Observations					Mean	Range
1	1.4500	-0.1500	-0.9300	-1.5500	-2.9600	-0.8280	4.4100
2	0.7900	-1.0200	-2.6100	-0.8500	-1.8900	-1.1160	3.4000
3	1.0800	-0.5400	-1.3400	-2.0300	-1.4800	-0.8620	3.1100
4	0.3200	-0.4100	-0.5200	-1.8700	-1.7000	-0.8360	2.1900
5	0.2100	0.4100	-1.0900	-1.4400	-2.3400	-0.8500	2.7500
6	-0.1200	0.0000	-1.5600	-2.4000	-1.1900	-1.0540	2.4000
7	1.6600	-0.5000	-1.6200	-2.2500	-2.8700	-1.1160	4.5300
8	-1.2800	0.4400	-2.2900	-1.2000	-1.7500	-1.2160	2.7300
9	-0.2300	-1.4100	-0.1500	0.3300	-2.6100	-0.8140	2.9400
10	0.6500	-1.2100	-0.5400	-1.7400	-1.5900	-0.8860	2.3900
11	0.5500	-0.7700	-2.0800	-1.9900	-1.7200	-1.2020	2.6300
12	-0.6100	-0.4000	-0.8100	-2.0700	-0.9900	-0.9760	1.6700
13	0.0100	-0.5000	-1.1000	-0.7100	-3.2400	-1.1080	3.2500
14	-0.4600	-0.8200	-1.2800	-1.3700	-2.0500	-1.1960	1.5900
15	0.8000	-0.5200	-1.7700	-1.1600	-2.0900	-0.9480	2.8900
16	0.8400	-0.3900	-0.1600	-1.5000	-2.4700	-0.7360	3.3100
17	0.4100	-0.9100	-2.0400	-2.6000	-1.2600	-1.2800	3.0100
18	-0.3000	0.0100	0.0900	-1.1200	-2.5400	-0.7720	2.6300
19	-0.1600	0.4400	-0.6400	-1.9400	-3.8100	-1.2220	4.2500
20	-0.8300	0.5900	-1.6800	-2.7300	-1.1900	-1.1680	3.3200
21	-0.0200	-0.8300	-0.6800	-1.5200	-1.5800	-0.9260	1.5600
22	-0.0200	0.8100	-1.4200	-1.6200	-2.9700	-1.0440	3.7800
23	1.2600	-0.6400	-0.4400	-0.7300	-1.8000	-0.4700	3.0600
24	0.0000	1.1300	-1.0900	-2.0400	-1.8900	-0.7780	3.1700
25	-0.1300	-0.2700	-1.4100	-1.4000	-3.5500	-1.3520	3.4200
26	-0.6600	-0.9700	-0.7500	-2.1300	-1.7300	-1.2480	1.4700
27	1.2100	-0.2800	0.3300	-2.3800	-1.6100	-0.5460	3.5900
28	-0.9800	0.4000	-1.8500	-2.4000	-2.8900	-1.5440	3.2900
29	0.3900	-0.1200	-1.5500	-3.9900	-2.4900	-1.5520	4.3800
30	-0.4500	0.6300	-1.5700	-2.3600	-3.2600	-1.4020	3.8900

Control Chart Calculations for file: CH16PR6

X-Bar Chart

```
Upper control limit =       0.7155
        Center line =      -1.0349
Lower control limit =      -2.7854
```

R-Chart

```
Upper control limit =       6.4132
        Center line =       3.0337
Lower control limit =       0.0000
```

Estimated standard deviation for process capability (Rbar/d2) =   1.3042

Problem 15-6

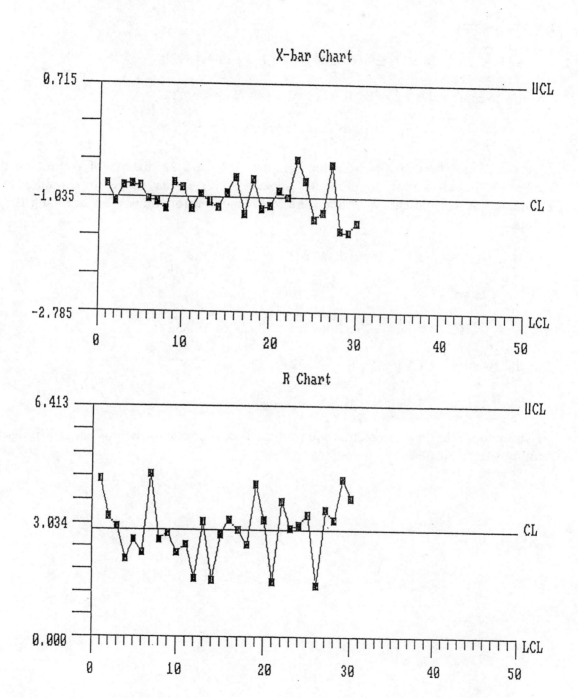

7.   See data and control charts below.

a) For the Center Lines, $CL_{\bar{x}} : \bar{\bar{x}} = 10.5850$; $CL_{\bar{R}} : \bar{R} = 0.4304$

For the $\bar{x}$-chart:

$\bar{\bar{x}} \pm A_2 \bar{R} = 10.5850 \pm 0.729\ (0.4304) = 10.2712$ to 10.8988

For the R-chart: $UCL_R = D_4\ \bar{R} = 2.282\ (0.4304) = 0.9822$

$$LCL_R = D_3\ \bar{R} = 0$$

b) We can see from the R-chart that samples 4, 8, and 22 are out of control on their ranges. Although sample number 14 appears O.K. on its range, it should also be eliminated as not typical. We obtain the following control limits after dropping these 4 points:

New Center Lines: $CL_{\bar{x}} : \bar{\bar{x}} = 10.5871$; $CL_{\bar{R}} : \bar{R} = 0.3362$

For the $\bar{x}$-chart:

$\bar{\bar{x}} \pm A_2 \bar{R} = 10.5871 \pm 0.729\ (0.3362) = 10.3421$ to 10.8322

For the R-chart: $UCL_R = D_4\ \bar{R} = 2.282\ (0.3362) = 0.7672$

$$LCL_R = D_3\ \bar{R} = 0$$

c) The additional data shows that the process is still operating within control limits. See "composite" control charts below.

Problem 15-7(a)

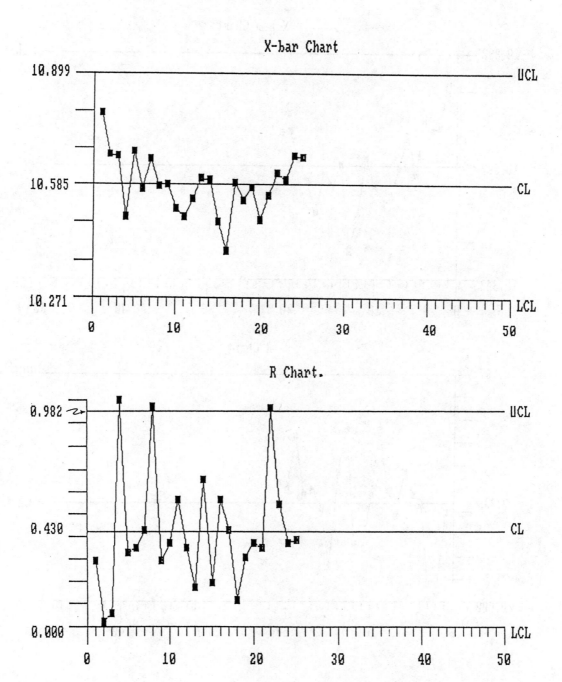

Problem 15-7(b): Revised x̄-chart and R-chart

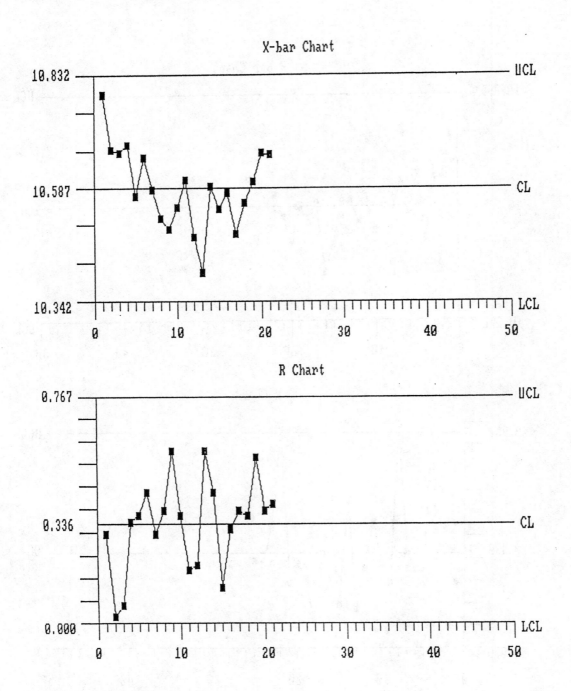

Problem 15-7(c): Composite control charts with new sample data

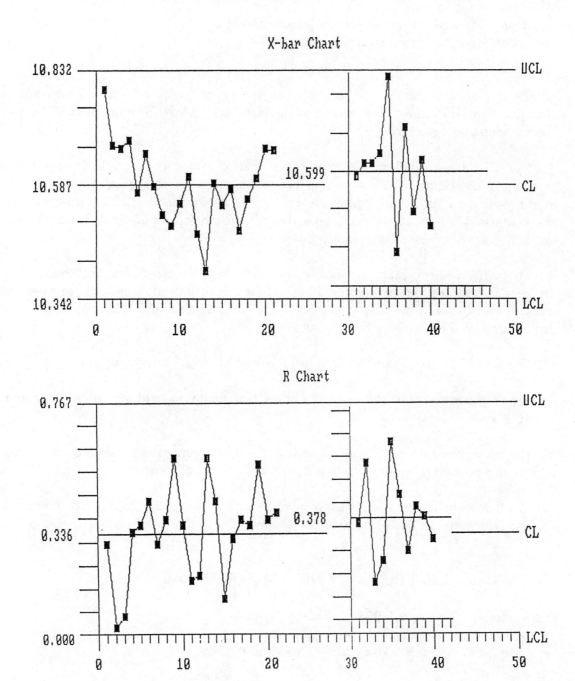

8.　　a) Two points outside upper control limit.
　　　b) Process is in control
　　　c) Mean shift upward in second half of control chart.
　　　d) Points hugging upper and lower control limits.

9.　　a) The first control chart shows an out-of-control process with a definite downward <u>trend</u>. The last 4 out of 5 points are below one standard error away from the mean. The process needs adjustment upward.

　　　b) The second control chart shows an out of control condition, with the first eight points above the centerline. Then there appears to be a sudden shift in the process average, putting the next six points <u>below</u> the centerline. It is possible that the process is being **over-adjusted**. It needs to be centered and then watched for out-of-control indications with no unnecessary operator intervention.

　　　c) The third control chart shows the data hugging the centerline, indicating that the process is possibly out of control. If the process has multiple machines or operators, a control chart should be constructed for each machine to avoid "masking" the variation brought on by mixing data from several sources.

　　　d) The fourth control chart shows a process that is stable and <u>in control</u>.

　　　e) The fifth control chart shows an out of control condition, with a point above the upper control limit.

　　　f) The sixth control chart shows that seven out of eight of the most recent points are below the centerline, indicating that the process is out of control.

　　　g) The last control chart shows too many points close to the upper and lower control limits, indicating an out of control condition.

10.　　For the Center Lines, $CL_{\bar{x}} : \bar{\bar{x}} = 0.0756$;　$CL_{\bar{R}} : \bar{R} = 0.0046$

　　　Estimated $\sigma = \bar{R} / d_2 = 0.0046 / 2.326 = 0.0020$

　　　$\bar{\bar{x}} \pm 3\ \sigma_{est} = 0.0756 \pm 3\ (0.0020) = 0.0696$ to 0.0816

　　　The limits above apply to <u>individual items</u>, only.

　　　Individual items can only be plotted on x-charts.

Although extraneous to the question of how individual values should be plotted on x-charts, students may need an explanation of x-bar and R-chart results for comparison with the above. These are provided as a "bonus" for you, should you wish to use them.

For the $\overline{x}$-chart:

$\overline{\overline{x}} \pm A_2 \overline{R} = 0.0756 \pm 0.577\,(0.0046) = 0.0729$ to 0.0783

For the R-chart: $UCL_R = D_4 \overline{R} = 2.114\,(0.0046) = 0.0097$

$LCL_R = D_3 \overline{R} = 0$

The limits above apply to <u>sample groups</u> of 5 items each.

<u>Problem 15-10</u>

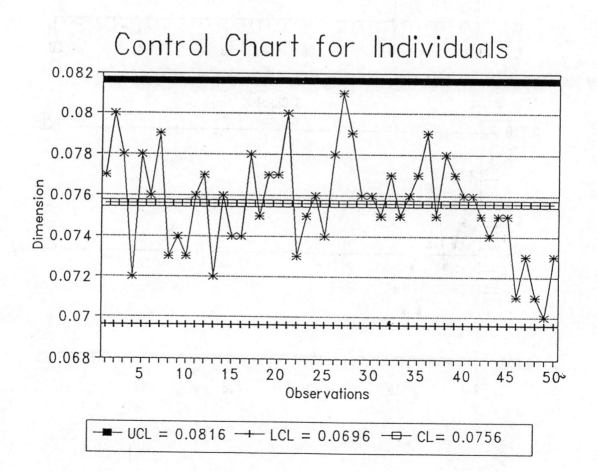

Control Chart for Individuals

UCL = 0.0816   LCL = 0.0696   CL = 0.0756

Problem 15-10: x̄-R chart for Sample Groups

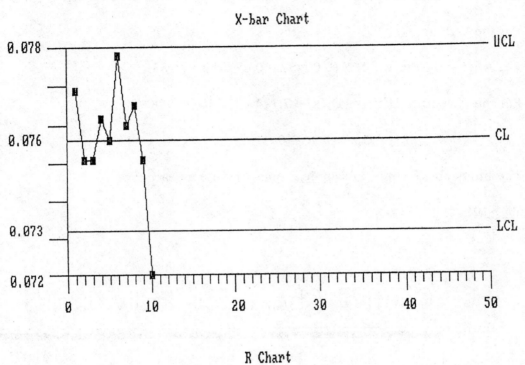

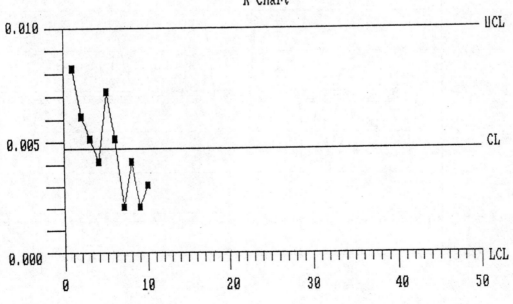

11. $s = 0.00243$;   Estimated $\sigma = \bar{R} / d_2 = 0.0046 / 2.326 = 0.0020$

Since we are not given other information on the specification limits, the assumption may be made that the "spread" of the specification limits are $\pm 3 \sigma_{est} = 0.012$

$$C_p = \frac{\text{USL - LSL}}{6\sigma} = \frac{0.012}{6(0.00243)} = 0.82$$

$$\text{Estimated } C_p = \frac{0.012}{6(0.0020)} = 1.0$$

However, because the process is not currently centered on 0.0756, calculation of the C_{pu} would show more than 1% of the product would fall outside the upper specification limit.

The reason that s differs from σ_{est} is merely the fact that the standard deviation is calculated including all the data in the sample, while the average range, a less accurate measure of variablity, is used to calculate σ_{est}.

Minimum value:	0.07000	
Maximum value:	0.08100	
First quartile:	0.07400	
Median:	0.07600	
Third quartile:	0.07700	
Average:	0.07560	
Variance:	0.00001	
Standard Deviation:	0.00243	
Range:	0.01100	
No. of observations	50	

PROCESS CAPABILITY ANALYSIS

Mean =   0.07560
Standard deviation =   0.00243
6 sigma =   0.01460

Lower specification limit =   0.06900
Upper specification limit =   0.08100

Mean - 3 * sigma =   0.06830
Mean - 2 * sigma =   0.07073
Mean - 1 * sigma =   0.07317

Mean + 1 * sigma =   0.07803
Mean + 2 * sigma =   0.08047
Mean + 3 * sigma =   0.08290

Process capability index, Cp: 0.82211
Lower capability index, Cpl: 0.90432
Upper capability index, Cpu: 0.73990
Cpk: 0.73990

Fraction below lower specification: 0.0033
Fraction above upper specification: 0.0132

12.   For the Center Lines, $CL_{\bar{x}}$: $\bar{\bar{x}}$ = 46.175; $CL_{\bar{R}}$: $\bar{R}$ = 5 45

For the x-chart: $\bar{\bar{x}} \pm A_2 \bar{R}$ = 46.175 ± 0.577 (5.45) = 43.030 to 49.320

For the R-chart: $UCL_R = D_4 \bar{R}$ = 2.114 (5.45) = 11.521

$$LCL_R = D_3 \bar{R} = 0$$

The limits above apply to <u>sample groups</u> of 5 items each.

Estimated $\sigma = \bar{R} / d_2$ = 5.45 / 2.326 = 2.343

The problem asks that students perform a process capability analysis. This is only justified if the process is in control. The fact that the process is thought to be normally distributed does not establish that it is <u>in control</u>. The x-bar chart shows that the process is, in fact, out of control. The % outside calculation can be performed as follows. Note the warning given below, however.

<u>Percent outside Specification Limits (41 to 51)</u>

<u>% Below LSL</u>: $Z = \dfrac{LSL - \bar{\bar{x}}}{\sigma}$

$Z = \dfrac{41 - 46.175}{2.343}$ = - 2.21 ; P(Z < -2.21) = (0.5 - 0.4864) = 0.0136 that items will exceed lower limit

<u>% Above USL</u>: $Z = \dfrac{USL - \bar{\bar{x}}}{\sigma}$

$Z = \dfrac{51 - 46.175}{2.343}$ = 2.06 ; P(Z > 2.06) = (0.5 - 0.4803) = 0.0197 that items will exceed upper limit

Therefore, the percent outside is <u>calculated</u> as: 3.33 %

Although the % outside calculations <u>seem</u> to show that the process has a relatively small % outside specifications, it should be noted that the x-bar chart shows that the process is not even **close** to being in control. Hence, the % outside calculation is going to generate questionable results.

Problem 15-12

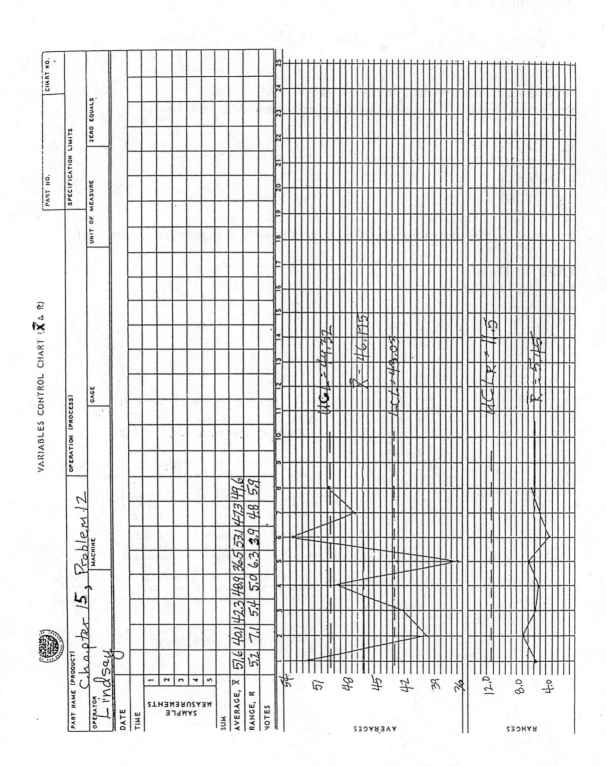

13. Referring back to problem 5, and using n = 23, after discarding points #16 and #23 from the original data set:

Estimated $\sigma = \overline{R} / d_2 = 30.957/1.693 = 18.285$

14. With data from Problem 5 and USL = 500, LSL = 300:
See QMA Process Capability Analysis and calculated data, below.

C_p = 1.772
C_{pl} = 1.778
C_{pu} = 1.767
C_{pk} = 1.767

% outside = 0% indicating that the process is well within specification limits.

URL $_{\overline{x}}$ = 476.813
LRL $_{\overline{x}}$ = 323.187

Minimum value: 342.00000
Maximum value: 444.00000
First quartile: 390.00000
Median: 400.00000
Third quartile: 410.00000
Average: 400.28986
Variance: 353.70887
Standard Deviation: 18.80715
Range: 102.00000
No. of observations 69

PROCESS CAPABILITY ANALYSIS

Mean = 400.28986
Standard deviation = 18.80715
6 sigma = 112.84290

Lower specification limit = 300.00000
Upper specification limit = 500.00000

Mean - 3 * sigma = 343.86841
Mean - 2 * sigma = 362.67556
Mean - 1 * sigma = 381.48271

Mean + 1 * sigma = 419.09701
Mean + 2 * sigma = 437.90415
Mean + 3 * sigma = 456.71130

Process capability index, Cp: 1.77238
Lower capability index, Cpl: 1.77751
Upper capability index, Cpu: 1.76724
Cpk: 1.76724

Fraction below lower specification: -.0000
Fraction above upper specification: -.0000

Problem 15-14: Calculation Worksheet
(Reverse side - ASQC Control Chart form.)

CALCULATION WORK SHEET _____ *Chapter 15, Problem 14*

CONTROL LIMITS				LIMITS FOR INDIVIDUALS
				COMPARE WITH SPECIFICATION OR TOLERANCE LIMITS

SUBGROUPS INCLUDED _____ *All* ⟵ ——— *#16, #23 Removed*

$\bar{R} = \frac{\Sigma R}{k} = \frac{712}{23}$ = 30.957 _____ •

$\bar{\bar{X}} = \frac{\Sigma \bar{X}}{k} = \frac{9206.67}{23}$ • 400.290 _____ •

$\bar{X}'$ (MIDSPEC. OR STD.) • 400

$A_2\bar{R} = 1.023 \times 30.957 =$ _____31.669_____ x = _____

$UCL_{\bar{X}} = \bar{\bar{X}} + A_2\bar{R}$ • 431.959 •

$LCL_{\bar{X}} = \bar{\bar{X}} - A_2\bar{R}$ • 368.620 •

$UCL_R = D_4\bar{R} = 2.574 \times 30.957 =$ 79.683 x •

$\bar{\bar{X}}$ • 400.290

$\frac{3}{d_2}\bar{R} = 1.772 \times 30.957 =$ _____54.856_____

$UL_X = \bar{\bar{X}} + \frac{3}{d_2}\bar{R}$ • 455.146

$LL_X = \bar{\bar{X}} - \frac{3}{d_2}\bar{R}$ • 345.434

US • 500

LS • 300

US − LS • 200

$6\sigma = \frac{6}{d_2}\bar{R}$ • 109.712

MODIFIED CONTROL LIMITS FOR AVERAGES
BASED ON SPECIFICATION LIMITS AND PROCESS CAPABILITY.
APPLICABLE ONLY IF: US−LS > 6σ.

US • 500   LS • 300

$A_M\bar{R} = 0.749 \times 30.957 =$ _____23.187_____ $A_M\bar{R}$ • _____23.187_____

$URL_{\bar{X}} = US - A_M\bar{R}$ • 476.813 $LRL_{\bar{X}} = LS + A_M\bar{R}$ • 323.187

FACTORS FOR CONTROL LIMITS

n	A_2	D_4	d_2	$\frac{3}{d_2}$	A_M
2	1.880	3.268	1.128	2.659	0.779
3	1.023	2.574	1.693	1.772	0.749
4	0.729	2.282	2.059	1.457	0.728
5	0.577	2.114	2.326	1.290	0.713
6	0.483	2.004	2.534	1.184	0.701

NOTES

15.
$$\overline{p} = \frac{p_1 + p_2 + p_3 + \dots p_k}{k}$$

So, CL_p^- : $\overline{p}$ = 68/2500 = 0.0272

$$s_p = \sqrt{[\,(\overline{p}\,)(\,1 - \overline{p}\,)\,]\,/\,n}$$

$$s_p = \sqrt{[\,(0.0272)\,(0.9728)]/100} = 0.0163$$

Control limits:

$$UCL_p = \overline{p} + 3\,s_p$$

$$UCL_p = 0.0272 + 3(0.0163) = 0.0761$$

$$LCL_p = \overline{p} - 3\,s_p$$

$$LCL_p = 0.0272 - 3(0.0163) = -0.0217, \text{ use } 0$$

16.
$$\overline{p} = \frac{p_1 + p_2 + p_3 + \dots p_k}{k}$$

So, initially, CL_p^- : $\overline{p}$ = 0.13 (see printout)

$$s_p = \sqrt{[\,(\overline{p}\,)(\,1 - \overline{p}\,)\,]\,/\,n}$$

$$s_p = \sqrt{[\,(\overline{p}\,)(\,1 - \overline{p}\,)\,]\,/\,n} = \sqrt{[\,(0.13)\,(0.87)]/200} = 0.0238$$

Control limits:

$$UCL_p = \overline{p} + 3\,s_p$$

$$UCL_p = 0.13 + 3(0.0238) = 0.2014$$

$$LCL_p = \overline{p} - 3\,s_p$$

$$LCL_p = 0.13 - 3(0.0238) = 0.0586$$

See initial data and control chart, below.

Problem 15-16: Initial p-chart

Sample	Number Nonconforming	Fraction Nonconforming
1	22	0.110
2	32	0.160
3	24	0.120
4	20	0.100
5	18	0.090
6	24	0.120
7	24	0.120
8	30	0.150
9	18	0.090
10	26	0.130
11	32	0.160
12	46	0.230
13	30	0.150
14	24	0.120
15	22	0.110
16	22	0.110
17	28	0.140
18	32	0.160
19	20	0.100
20	26	0.130

Control Chart Calculations

Fraction Nonconforming Chart

Upper control limit =	0.2013
Center line =	0.1300
Lower control limit =	0.0587
Standard deviation =	0.0238

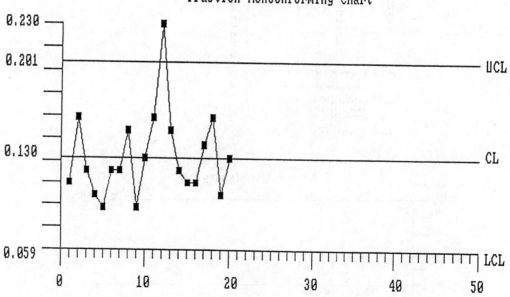

Fraction Nonconforming Chart

16. (Continued)

Revised $CL_{\bar{p}}$: $\bar{p}$ = 0.1247 (after sample 12, with a fraction defective of 0.23 was removed),

$$s_p = \sqrt{[\,(\bar{p})\,(1 - \bar{p})\,]\,/\,n} = \sqrt{[\,(0.1247)\,(0.8753)]/200} = 0.0234$$

$$UCL_p = \bar{p} + 3\ s_p = 0.1247 + 3(0.0234) = 0.1948$$

$$LCL_p = \bar{p} - 3\ s_p = 0.1247 - 3(0.0234) = 0.0546$$

See data and control chart, below, after sample 12 was removed.

Problem 15-16: Revised p-chart

Sample	Number Nonconforming	Fraction Nonconforming
1	22	0.110
2	32	0.160
3	24	0.120
4	20	0.100
5	18	0.090
6	24	0.120
7	24	0.120
8	30	0.150
9	18	0.090
10	26	0.130
11	32	0.160
12	30	0.150
13	24	0.120
14	22	0.110
15	22	0.110
16	28	0.140
17	32	0.160
18	20	0.100
19	26	0.130

Control Chart Calculations

Fraction Nonconforming Chart

Upper control limit =	0.1948
Center line =	0.1247
Lower control limit =	0.0546
Standard deviation =	0.0234

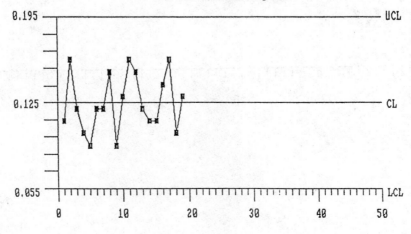

Fraction Nonconforming Chart

17.   <u>Initial</u>

$$\bar{p} = \frac{p_1 + p_2 + p_3 + \cdots p_k}{k}$$

$CL_{\bar{p}}$: $\bar{p} = 0.53 / 25 = 0.0212$

$s_p = \sqrt{[(\bar{p})(1 - \bar{p})] / n} = \sqrt{[(0.0212)(0.9788)/100}} = 0.0144$

$UCL_p = \bar{p} + 3 s_p = 0.0212 + 3(0.0144) = 0.0644$

$LCL_p = \bar{p} - 3 s_p = 0.0212 - 3(0.0144) = -0.0022$, use 0

Throw out #9 and #23, out-of-control values, revise.

<u>Revised</u>

$CL_{\bar{p}}$: $\bar{p} = 0.3795 / 23 = 0.0165$

$s_p = \sqrt{[(\bar{p})(1 - \bar{p})] / n} = \sqrt{[(0.0165)(0.9835)]/100} = 0.0127$

Control limits:

$UCL_p = \bar{p} + 3 s_p = 0.0165 + 3(0.0127) = 0.0546$

$LCL_p = \bar{p} - 3 s_p = 0.0165 - 3(0.0127) = -0.0217$, use 0

Problem 15-17: Initial

Sample	Number Nonconforming	Fraction Nonconforming
1	3	0.030
2	3	0.030
3	3	0.030
4	2	0.020
5	0	0.000
6	3	0.030
7	0	0.000
8	1	0.010
9	7	0.070
10	3	0.030
11	2	0.020
12	0	0.000
13	0	0.000
14	4	0.040
15	1	0.010
16	2	0.020
17	4	0.040
18	0	0.000
19	1	0.010
20	1	0.010
21	0	0.000
22	2	0.020
23	8	0.080
24	2	0.020
25	1	0.010

Control Chart Calculations

Fraction Nonconforming Chart

Upper control limit =	0.0644
Center line =	0.0212
Lower control limit =	0.0000
Standard deviation =	0.0144

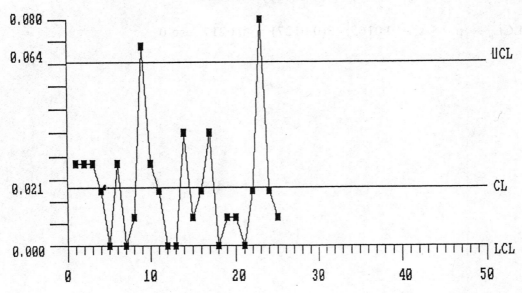

Fraction Nonconforming Chart

Problem 15-17: Revised

Sample	Number Nonconforming	Fraction Nonconforming
1	3	0.030
2	3	0.030
3	3	0.030
4	2	0.020
5	0	0.000
6	3	0.030
7	0	0.000
8	1	0.010
9	3	0.030
10	2	0.020
11	0	0.000
12	0	0.000
13	4	0.040
14	1	0.010
15	2	0.020
16	4	0.040
17	0	0.000
18	1	0.010
19	1	0.010
20	0	0.000
21	2	0.020
22	2	0.020
23	1	0.010

Control Chart Calculations

Fraction Nonconforming Chart

Upper control limit =	0.0548
Center line =	0.0165
Lower control limit =	0.0000
Standard deviation =	0.0127

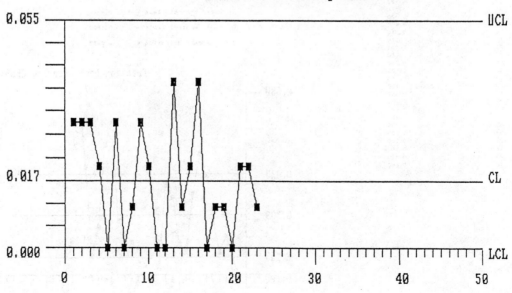

Fraction Nonconforming Chart

18.   <u>Initial</u>

$$\overline{p} = \frac{p_1 + p_2 + p_3 + \ldots p_k}{k}$$

$CL_{\overline{p}}$: $\overline{p} = 7.22 / 25 = 0.2888$

$$s_p = \sqrt{[(\overline{p})(1 - \overline{p})]/n} = \sqrt{[(0.2888)(0.7112)/100} = 0.0453$$

Control limits:

$$UCL_p = \overline{p} + 3\ s_p = 0.2888 + 3(0.0453) = 0.4247$$

$$LCL_p = \overline{p} - 3\ s_p = 0.2888 - 3(0.0453) = 0.1529$$

See initial p-chart, below.

Throw out all 43 and over, and revise.

<u>Problem 15-18: Initial p-chart</u>

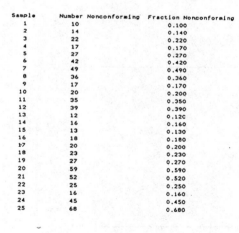

Sample	Number Nonconforming	Fraction Nonconforming
1	10	0.100
2	14	0.140
3	22	0.220
4	17	0.170
5	27	0.270
6	42	0.420
7	49	0.490
8	36	0.360
9	17	0.170
10	20	0.200
11	35	0.350
12	39	0.390
13	12	0.120
14	16	0.160
15	13	0.130
16	18	0.180
17	20	0.200
18	23	0.230
19	27	0.270
20	59	0.590
21	52	0.520
22	25	0.250
23	16	0.160
24	45	0.450
25	68	0.680

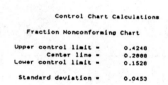

Control Chart Calculations

Fraction Nonconforming Chart

Upper control limit = 0.4248
Center line = 0.2888
Lower control limit = 0.1528

Standard deviation = 0.0453

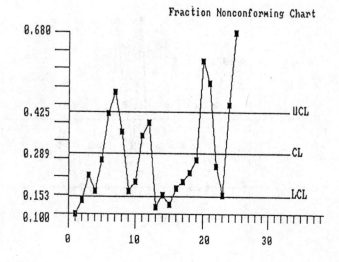

Fraction Nonconforming Chart

18. (Continued) CL_p: $\bar{p} = 4.490 / 20 = 0.2245$

$$s_p = \sqrt{[(\bar{p})(1-\bar{p})]/n} = \sqrt{[(0.2245)(0.7755)/100}} = 0.0417$$

Control limits:

$$UCL_p = \bar{p} + 3\, s_p = 0.2245 + 3(0.0417) = 0.3496$$

$$LCL_p = \bar{p} - 3\, s_p = 0.2245 - 3(0.0389) = 0.0994$$

Throw out all over 35, revise again.

Problem 15-18: First revised p-chart

Sample	Number Nonconforming	Fraction Nonconforming
1	10	0.100
2	14	0.140
3	22	0.220
4	17	0.170
5	27	0.270
6	42	0.420
7	36	0.360
8	17	0.170
9	20	0.200
10	35	0.350
11	39	0.390
12	12	0.120
13	16	0.160
14	13	0.130
15	18	0.180
16	20	0.200
17	23	0.230
18	27	0.270
19	25	0.250
20	16	0.160

Fraction Nonconforming Chart

Upper control limit =	0.3497
Center line =	0.2245
Lower control limit =	0.0993
Standard deviation =	0.0417

Fraction Nonconforming Chart

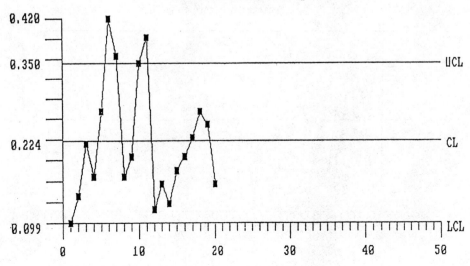

18. (Continued)   Final Revised

CL_p^- : $\overline{p}$ = 2.9696 / 16 = 0.1856

$s_p = \sqrt{[(\overline{p})(1-\overline{p})]/n} = \sqrt{[(0.01856)(0.8144)]/100}$ = 0.0389

Control limits:

$UCL_p = \overline{p} + 3 s_p = 0.1856 + 3(0.0389) = 0.3023$

$LCL_p = \overline{p} - 3 s_p = 0.1856 - 3(0.0389) = 0.0689$

Problem 15-18: Final revised p-chart

Sample	Number Nonconforming	Fraction Nonconforming
1	10	0.100
2	14	0.140
3	22	0.220
4	17	0.170
5	27	0.270
6	17	0.170
7	20	0.200
8	12	0.120
9	16	0.160
10	13	0.130
11	18	0.180
12	20	0.200
13	23	0.230
14	27	0.270
15	25	0.250
16	16	0.160

Control Chart Calculations

Fraction Nonconforming Chart

Upper control limit =	0.3023
Center line =	0.1856
Lower control limit =	0.0690
Standard deviation =	0.0389

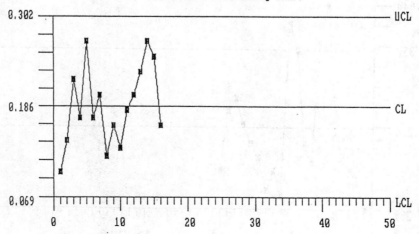

Fraction Nonconforming Chart

19. Note that the values obtained with a hand calculator will differ slightly from those obtained from the QMA software. QMA uses the average sample size to calculate all p values and for the p-bar calculation.

The p-chart constructed from data taken from the patient satisfaction questionnaire shows:

<u>Initial</u>

a) The <u>average</u> sample size $\bar{n}$ = 258.75

$$\bar{p} = \frac{p_1 + p_2 + p_3 + \dots p_k}{k}$$

$CL_{\bar{p}}$: $\bar{p}$ = 0.966 / 20 = 0.0483,

$s_p = \sqrt{[(\bar{p})(1 - \bar{p})]/n} = \sqrt{[(0.0483)(0.9517)]/258.75} = 0.0133$

$UCL_p = \bar{p} + 3\ s_p = 0.0483 + 3(0.0133) = 0.0882$

$LCL_p = \bar{p} - 3\ s_p = 0.0483 - 3(0.0133) = 0.0084$

Point #19 is out of limits and another point, #7 is barely within limits. After deleting these points, we get:

<u>Revised</u>

The revised <u>average</u> sample size $\bar{n}$ = 258.83

$CL_{\bar{p}}$: $\bar{p}$ = 0.7812 / 18 = 0.0434,

$s_p = \sqrt{[(\bar{p})(1 - \bar{p})]/n} = \sqrt{[(0.0434)(0.9566)/258.83} = 0.0127$

$UCL_p = \bar{p} + 3\ s_p = 0.0434 + 3(0.0127) = 0.0815$

$LCL_p = \bar{p} - 3\ s_p = 0.0434 - 3(0.0127) = 0.0053$

The process is now considered under control.

Problem 15-19: Initial p-chart

```
Sample     Number Nonconforming   Fraction Nonconforming
   1              10                     0.039
   2              11                     0.043
   3               8                     0.031
   4              10                     0.039
   5               7                     0.027
   6              15                     0.058
   7              22                     0.085
   8               9                     0.035
   9              12                     0.046
  10               6                     0.023
  11              13                     0.050
  12              14                     0.054
  13               9                     0.035
  14              16                     0.062
  15              10                     0.039
  16              16                     0.062
  17              11                     0.043
  18              17                     0.066
  19              26                     0.100
  20               8                     0.031
```

```
            Control Chart Calculations

         Fraction Nonconforming Chart

    Upper control limit =        0.0883
             Center line =        0.0483
    Lower control limit =        0.0083

    Standard deviation =         0.0133
```

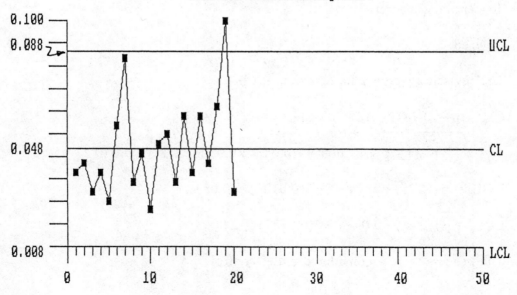

Fraction Nonconforming Chart

Problem 15-19: Revised p-chart

Sample	Number Nonconforming	Fraction Nonconforming
1	10	0.039
2	11	0.042
3	8	0.031
4	10	0.039
5	7	0.027
6	15	0.058
7	9	0.035
8	12	0.046
9	6	0.023
10	13	0.050
11	14	0.054
12	9	0.035
13	16	0.062
14	10	0.039
15	16	0.062
16	11	0.042
17	17	0.066
18	8	0.031

Control Chart Calculations

Fraction Nonconforming Chart

Upper control limit =   0.0813
Center line =   0.0434
Lower control limit =   0.0054

Standard deviation =   0.0127

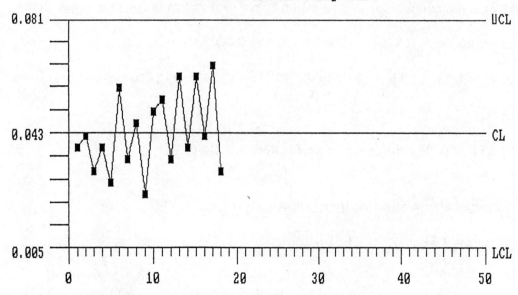

Fraction Nonconforming Chart

20. a. The control chart shown in the figure below was constructed. Parameters for the charts were calculated as:

For the Center Lines, $CL_{\bar{x}} : \bar{\bar{x}} = 3.9376$; $CL_R : \bar{R} = 0.00077$

For the $\bar{x}$-chart:

$UCL_{\bar{x}} = \bar{\bar{x}} + A_2 \bar{R} = 3.9376 + 0.577 (0.00077) = 3.9380$

$LCL_{\bar{x}} = \bar{\bar{x}} - A_2 \bar{R} = 3.9376 - 0.577 (0.00077) = 3.9372$

For the R-chart: $UCL_R = D_4 \bar{R} = 2.114 (0.00077) = 0.0016$

$$LCL_R = D_3 \bar{R} = 0$$

The control chart establishes that the process is in control.

   b. The limits above apply to sample groups of 5 items each.
% outside calculations are based on specification limits for individual items.

Estimated $\sigma = \bar{R} / d_2 = 0.00077/2.326 = 0.00033$

$\therefore c_p = \dfrac{UTL - LTL}{6\sigma} = \dfrac{3.9380 - 3.9375}{6(0.00033)} = 0.253$; very poor capability

The % outside calculation is performed as follows.

Percent outside Specification Limits (3.9375 to 3.9380)

% Below LSL: $Z = \dfrac{LSL - \bar{\bar{x}}}{\sigma}$

$Z = \dfrac{3.9375 - 3.9376}{0.00033} = - 0.30$; $P(Z < -0.30) = (0.5 - 0.1179) = 0.3821$
that items will exceed lower limit

<u>% Above USL</u>: $Z = \dfrac{USL - \bar{\bar{x}}}{\sigma}$

$Z = \dfrac{3.9380 - 3.9376}{0.00033} = 1.21$; P(Z > 1.21) = (0.5 - 0.3869) = 0.1131
that items will exceed upper limit

Therefore, the percent outside is <u>calculated</u> as: 49.52 %

Obviously, the problem lies in the fact that the process is not capable of producing good end caps that consistently fall within specification limits. It is also obvious that the Bell Vader Company needs to analyze the process to determine what may be done to make it capable. This could include investigation of the current materials, equipment, machining methods, etc. It is recommended that the process be improved, and/or that new equipment be purchased in order to improve capability and reduce costs.

Problem 15-19. x̄-R Chart for Bell Vader Case

End Cap Control Chart

PART NAME (PRODUCT): End cap
OPERATION (PROCESS): Bore
OPERATOR:
MACHINE:
GAGE: Bore gauge

PART NO. 21819
SPECIFICATION LIMITS 3.9375 - 3.9380
ZERO EQUALS
UNIT OF MEASURE .0000

Low value - 3.9374
High value - 3.9380

$\bar{X} = 3.9376$
$R = .00077$

Sample	1	2	3	4	5	6	7	8	9	10	11	12	13	14	15	16	17	18
Date/Time	15	77	12	19	70	73	77	75	78	12	20	12	79	74	76	12	15	80
Measurement 1	75	77	76	76	70	73	77	75	78	76	70	81	79	74	76	80	75	80
Measurement 2	76	80	76	78	76	72	78	76	79	77	78	77	76	84	82	81	84	75
Measurement 3	77	79	82	70	77	82	79	79	80	81	75	78	78	79	74	75	78	75
Measurement 4	79	83	74	73	78	75	77	70	76	81	76	70	70	84	81	78	80	76
Measurement 5	75	80	75	76	74	74	75	75	71	75	80	80	70	75	75	76	74	70
Average, X̄	3.9376	3.9380	3.9377	3.9374	3.9375	3.9375	3.9377	3.9375	3.9377	3.9376	3.9378	3.9378	3.9378	3.9379	3.9375	3.9376	3.9378	3.9375
Range, R	.0004	.0006	.0008	.0008	.0008	.0010	.0004	.0004	.0009	.0010	.0010	.0006	.0009	.0010	.0007	.0006	.0006	.0010
Notes																		

Averages scale: 3.9385, 3.9380, 3.9375, 3.9370
UCL, LCL

Ranges scale: 0.0015, 0.0010, 0.0005, 0.0000
UCL

21.   See data and control charts below.

a) For the Center Line, $CL_{\bar{x}} : \bar{\bar{x}} = 0.0481$; $CL_{\bar{R}} : \bar{R} = 0.1035$

For the x-chart:

$\bar{\bar{x}} \pm A_2 \bar{R} = .0481 \pm 0.729\,(0.1035) = -0.0273$ to 0.1236

For the R-chart: $UCL_R = D_4 \bar{R} = 2.282\,(0.1035) = 0.2362$

$LCL_R = D_3 \bar{R} = 0$

b) We can see from both the x-chart and the R-chart that the process is "hugging the centerline" creating an out of control condition on the means and their ranges. The cause for this condition may be judged from the structure of the data. It appears that each of the heads on the molding machine has a separate distribution of data. Thus, control charts should be prepared for each head, rather than treating the data as if it came from the same population.

<u>x</u>-R Chart for Problem 15-21

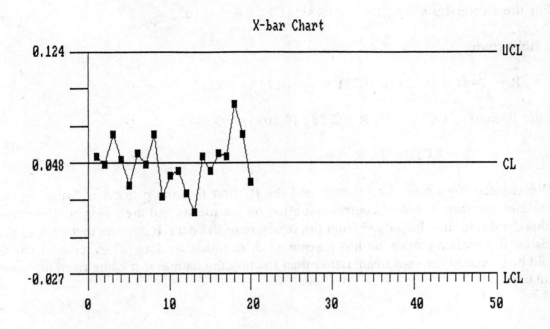

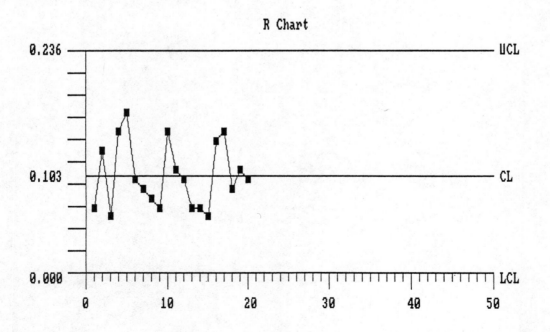

ANSWERS TO CASE QUESTIONS

Case I. Dean Door Company

This case is designed to test the students' abilities to apply SPC principles, to interpret the results effectively, and see "beyond the data." The key points are summarized below:

1. Students should be able to apply the formulas from Chapters 15 to construct an x-bar and R-chart and to determine the state of control, remove out-of-control points, and compute new control limits.

2. A key aspect of the case is to recognize potential differences among operators. This requires going beyond the computations and using the data for diagnosis. The astute student might even take a different approach and stratify the data by operator to study differences among them. Although the key result (concerning operator Cameron) can be gleaned by cross-comparing the control chart with Table 15.8, a stratified analysis would clearly show the source of the problem.

3. It is critical that process capability calculations be performed *after* the process is brought into control by removing out-of-control points.

4. The fact that process capability is extremely good means that the company should not be concerned, but should devote its attention to improving training of any substitute operators and using SPC as an audit tool.

5. The additional data indicate that the process tends to drift after some time. The student should speculate on the possible reasons for this.

Detailed Solution and Data Analysis

Since the data are variables data, the first step is to construct x-bar and R-charts and determine if the process is in control. Figure DDC-1 (from the QMA software) shows the mean, range and control limits for the original set of 30 samples. Using these data, the grand mean is 29.9919 and the average range is 0.0737. Since the sample size is 5, $D_4 = 2.114$ and $A_2 = 0.577$. The control limits are

$$UCL_R = 2.114 \, (0.0737) = 0.1558$$
$$LCL_R = 0$$

$$UCL_{\bar{x}} = 29.9919 + 0.577(0.0737) = 30.034$$
$$LCL_{\bar{x}} = 29.9919 - 0.577(0.0737) = 29.949$$

Figure DDC-2 shows the averages and range charts with these control limits. The range chart seems well in control; however, the x-bar chart has three points below the lower control limit. Inspecting the production records, we see that when each of these samples were taken, a different operator, "Cameron" was running the cutting operation. Apparently this was a substitute for operator "Dana" who was absent. Hence, these data may be construed as a special cause. (The company should determine if "Cameron" was knowledgeable about the operation and equipment or needs additional training.)

These data that show defective products must be removed from consideration and new control limits must be computed before capability can be assessed. Deleting these samples, recompute the new averages as:

$$\bar{\bar{x}} = 30.000$$

$$R = 0.0692$$

These lead to the new control limits:

$UCL_R = 2.114 \ (0.0692) = 0.1463$
$LCL_R = 0$
$UCL_{\bar{x}} = 30.0003 + 0.577 \ (0.0692) = 30.040$
$LCL_{\bar{x}} = 30.0003 - 0.577 \ (0.0692) = 29.960$

The new control charts are shown in Figure DDC-3. The process now appears to be in control.

Process capability may now be evaluated. An estimate of the standard deviation from the revised control chart statistics is

$R/d_2 = 0.0692/2.326 = .02975$

The six-standard deviation spread is $30.000 \pm 3 \ (0.02975)$, or 29.911 to 30.090. (If one computes the standard deviation of the raw data after the three samples are deleted, the actual standard deviation is found to be 0.0296, so the estimate is very close.) The variation is well within the specifications of 29.875 and 30.125. This can also be seen by computing the process capability indexes:

$C_p = 0.250 \ / \ [6 \ (0.02975)] = 1.40$
Since the process is centered exactly, $C_{pl} = C_{pu} = C_{pk} = 1.40$ also. This means that the process is highly capable of meeting the specifications.

FIGURE DDC-1

Sample	Observations					Mean	Range
1	30.0460	29.9780	30.0260	29.9860	29.9610	29.9994	0.0850
2	29.9720	29.9660	29.9640	29.9420	30.0250	29.9738	0.0830
3	30.0460	30.0040	30.0280	29.9860	30.0270	30.0182	0.0600
4	29.9970	29.9970	29.9800	30.0000	30.0340	30.0016	0.0540
5	30.0180	29.9220	29.9920	30.0080	30.0530	29.9986	0.1310
6	29.9730	29.9900	29.9850	29.9910	30.0040	29.9886	0.0310
7	29.9890	29.9520	29.9410	30.0120	29.9840	29.9756	0.0710
8	29.9690	30.0000	29.9680	29.9760	29.9730	29.9772	0.0320
✱ 9	29.8520	29.9780	29.9640	29.8960	29.8760	29.9132	0.1260
10	29.9870	29.9760	30.0210	29.9570	30.0420	29.9966	0.0850
11	30.0280	29.9990	30.0220	29.9420	29.9980	29.9978	0.0860
12	29.9550	29.9840	29.9770	30.0080	30.0330	29.9914	0.0780
13	30.0400	29.9650	30.0010	29.9750	29.9700	29.9902	0.0750
14	30.0070	30.0240	29.9870	29.9510	29.9940	29.9926	0.0730
15	29.9790	30.0070	30.0000	30.0420	30.0000	30.0056	0.0630
16	30.0730	29.9980	30.0270	29.9860	30.0110	30.0190	0.0870
17	29.9950	29.9660	29.9960	30.0390	29.9760	29.9944	0.0730
18	29.9940	29.9820	29.9980	30.0400	30.0170	30.0062	0.0580
19	29.9770	30.0130	30.0420	30.0010	29.9620	29.9990	0.0800
20	30.0210	30.0480	30.0370	29.9850	30.0050	30.0192	0.0630
✱ 21	29.8790	29.8820	29.9900	29.9710	29.9530	29.9350	0.1110
22	30.0430	30.0210	29.9630	29.9930	30.0060	30.0052	0.0800
23	30.0650	30.0120	30.0210	30.0240	30.0370	30.0318	0.0530
✱ 24	29.8990	29.8750	29.9800	29.8780	29.8770	29.9018	0.1050
25	30.0290	30.0110	30.0170	30.0000	30.0000	30.0114	0.0290
26	30.0460	30.0060	30.0390	29.9910	29.9700	30.0104	0.0760
27	29.9930	29.9910	29.9840	30.0220	30.0100	30.0000	0.0380
28	30.0570	30.0320	29.9790	30.0270	30.0330	30.0256	0.0780
29	30.0040	30.0490	29.9800	30.0000	29.9860	30.0038	0.0690
30	29.9950	30.0000	29.9220	29.9840	29.9680	29.9738	0.0780

✱ *Out of control*

Control Chart Calculations for file: C15DEAN

    X-Bar Chart

Upper control limit =   30.0344
        Center line =   29.9919
Lower control limit =   29.9494

        R-Chart

Upper control limit =   0.1558
        Center line =   0.0737
Lower control limit =   0.0000

Estimated standard deviation for process capability (Rbar/d2) =   0.0317

Control Chart Calculations for file: C15DN2CC

    X-Bar Chart

Upper control limit =   30.0402
        Center line =   30.0003
Lower control limit =   29.9603

        R-Chart

Upper control limit =   0.1463
        Center line =   0.0692
Lower control limit =   0.0000

Estimated standard deviation for process capability (Rbar/d2) =   0.0298

FIGURE DDC-2

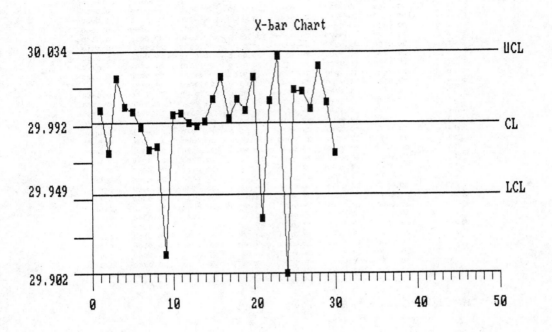

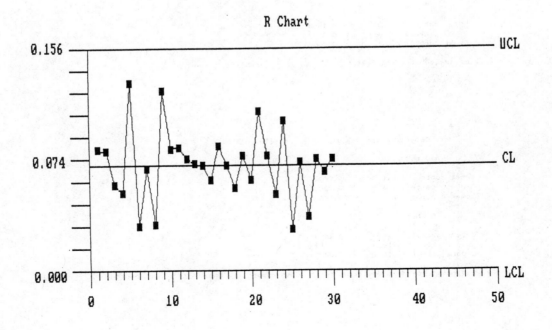

FIGURE DDC-3

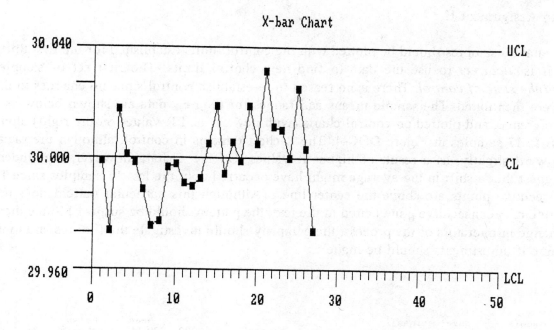

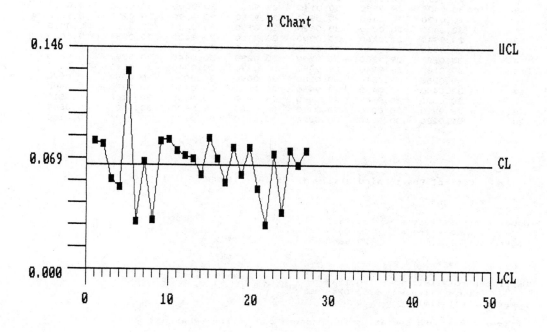

Dean Door Company Case (Continued)

Solution to Assignment II

The additional 20 samples should be plotted with the control limits established for the first thirty samples. It is *incorrect* to use the data to find new control limits. The first set of samples *established the state of control.* There is no reason to re-establish control since no changes to the process were mentioned. The sample means and ranges for the new data are shown below as a point of reference, and plotted on control charts (with new x and R values on the right) along with the first 27 samples in Figure DDC-4. The R-chart remains in control, although the range shifted upward slightly, as a result of higher R values. On the x-chart, however, the student should suggest that a shift in the average might have occurred over the last 11 samples since 11 of 12 consecutive points are above the center line. (Although this particular pattern does not meet the rule of 8 consecutive points cited in the text, the pattern should be suspect.) Since there was no change in operators or the process, the company should investigate the fixtures and tools to determine if adjustments should be made.

Sample	Observations					Mean	Range
1	29.9700	30.0170	29.8980	29.9370	29.9920	29.9628	0.1190
2	29.9470	30.0130	29.9930	29.9970	30.0790	30.0058	0.1320
3	30.0500	30.0310	29.9990	29.9630	30.0450	30.0176	0.0870
4	30.0640	30.0610	30.0160	30.0410	30.0060	30.0376	0.0580
5	29.9480	30.0090	29.9620	29.9900	29.9790	29.9776	0.0610
6	30.0160	29.9890	29.9390	29.9810	30.0170	29.9884	0.0780
7	29.9460	30.0570	29.9920	29.9730	29.9550	29.9846	0.1110
8	29.9810	30.0230	29.9920	29.9920	29.9410	29.9858	0.0820
9	30.0430	29.9850	30.0140	29.9860	30.0000	30.0056	0.0580
10	30.0130	30.0460	30.0960	29.9750	30.0190	30.0298	0.1210
11	30.0430	30.0030	30.0620	30.0250	30.0230	30.0312	0.0590
12	29.9940	30.0560	30.0330	30.0110	29.9480	30.0084	0.1080
13	29.9950	30.0140	30.0180	29.9660	30.0000	29.9986	0.0520
14	30.0180	29.9820	30.0280	30.0290	30.0440	30.0202	0.0620
15	30.0180	29.9940	29.9950	30.0290	30.0340	30.0140	0.0400
16	30.0250	29.9510	30.0380	30.0090	30.0030	30.0052	0.0870
17	30.0480	30.0460	29.9950	30.0530	30.0430	30.0370	0.0580
18	30.0300	30.0540	29.9970	29.9930	30.0100	30.0168	0.0610
19	29.9910	30.0010	30.0410	30.0360	29.9920	30.0122	0.0500
20	30.0220	30.0210	30.0220	30.0080	30.0190	30.0184	0.0140

```
              Control Chart Calculations for file: C15DN3CC

                  X-Bar Chart

       Upper control limit =     30.0511
               Center line =     30.0079
       Lower control limit =     29.9647

                  R-Chart

       Upper control limit =      0.1583
               Center line =      0.0749
       Lower control limit =      0.0000

       Estimated standard deviation for process capability (Rbar/d2) =      0.0322
```

FIGURE DDC-4

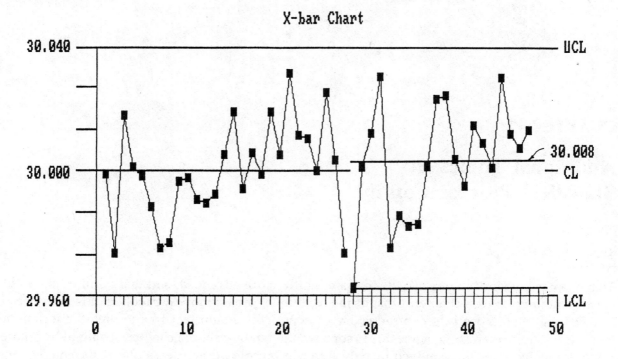

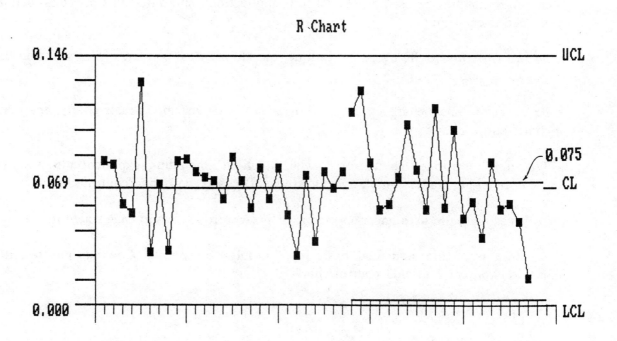

CHAPTER 16

Additional Topics in Statistical Process Control

Teaching Notes

This chapter develops topics in SPC that are a little more advanced, and that build on the basics covered in the previous chapter. Most of the techniques are no more difficult, and in many cases, **less** difficult than those in the introductory chapter. You should feel free to pick the techniques that are the most interesting, since this is somewhat a "smorgasbord" chapter. It should be pointed out that the Japanese have moved heavily into precontrol and are de-emphasizing conventional control charting. Perhaps you should plan on covering precontrol as one of the topics from this chapter. Key objectives for the chapter include:

- To establish the purpose of this chapter as providing an overview of several SPC techniques that may be used in general SPC applications, and others that are for situations that need special tools.

- To learn to choose the proper technique, based on an assessment of the situation that needs to be under control.

- To cover the basic characteristics and uses of $\bar{x}$-s charts, individuals charts, np-charts, c-charts and u-charts.

- To briefly introduce charts for special situations, including exponentially weighted moving average charts, cumulative sum (cusum) charts, and zone control charts.

- To investigate the uses and importance of pre-control for short manufacturing runs.

- To "dig into" the statistical basis for the rules for points showing out-of-control conditions on conventional control charts.

ANSWERS TO QUALITY IN PRACTICE KEY ISSUES

Using a u-chart in a Receiving Process

1.   The average number of packing slip errors can be obtained by taking the square root of the sum of the errors and dividing by the total number of packing slips reviewed.

For the u-chart conditions: 62 samples; total n = 5129, number of defects = 479

$\bar{u}$= 479/5129 = 0.09339

Control limits must be calculated for <u>each</u> sample, since each sample size is different, hence the "ragged" appearance of the upper control limit on the u-chart in figure 16.19. A typical calculation for one set of control limits for the first individual sample is:

$$\bar{u} \pm 3 \sqrt{\bar{u}/n} \;=\; 0.09339 \pm 3\sqrt{(0.09339/87)} =$$

$$0.09339 \pm 3(0.03276) = -0.00489 \text{ to } 0.1917 \text{ } \underline{or} \text{ } 0 \text{ to } 0.1917$$

The first five values give us:

Smpl.	n	c	u = c/n	3 σ	UCL	LCL
1	87	15	0.1724	0.0983	0.1917	0
2	79	13	0.1645	0.1032	0.1965	0
3	92	23	0.2500*	0.0956	0.1890	0
4	84	3	0.0357	0.1000	0.1934	0
5	73	7	0.0959	0.1073	0.2007	0

* This value is out of control.

2.   A separate chart for each category would help to pinpoint the contributing factors for out-of control conditions. For example, in sample 3 with 23 errors, which categories contributed the most to this problem? Also, construction of several charts would help to establish which categories were stable and which fluctuated over a wide range. The decision as to whether the time and effort required to keep separate charts would depend on the improvement objectives of Cincinnati Belting. If they wanted to improve one category at a time, perhaps they should continue with the above chart, and add one for "purchase order errors". Later, they could replace the latter chart with one for "quantity errors," etc.

ANSWERS TO REVIEW QUESTIONS

1.   The s-chart is sometimes used in place of the R-chart because the sample standard deviation is more sensitive to changes in process variability, especially for larger sample sizes. In addition, modern calculators, computers, and automated process monitoring have reduced the computational effort required and have reduced the need for simpler measures, such as the range.

2.   A chart for individual measures may be particularly useful in small batch production, where only a few items are produced. It is also useful to measure individual items in automated processes where data is easily obtained. Some useful areas for charting individuals are in HRM areas such as absenteeism and turnover, accounting data on shipments and orders, or in recording the results of physical or chemical analyses of production processes.

3.   The moving range is used as a measure of variability to accompany control charts for individuals (sample size of one). It is a moving average of ranges, and is obtained by finding the absolute difference between the highest and lowest value of a sequence of numbers, e.g. $n = 2$, or $n = 3$, etc. The moving range is interpreted just as the standard R-chart, but it must be done with caution, since successive range values are correlated, and may thus indicate an out-of-control condition that doesn't exist.

4.   Median charts are easier to use on the factory floor than $\bar{x}$ charts because the median of an odd sample size of, say, 3 or 5 items can be obtained by inspection, rather than having to perform any calculations. It is limited by not being as efficient as the mean, thus causing the value of the data to be diluted, somewhat.

5.   A np-chart is a chart that shows the number of items from a sample that are non-conforming. This is in contrast to the p-chart which shows the <u>fraction</u> of a sample that is non-conforming. The np-chart is frequently easier for shop floor personnel to understand and use, since it refers to a count of items, rather than a percentage of items.

6.   C-charts are used to monitor and control the <u>number</u> of defects when the group size for the sample remains constant. For example, if a sample of 30 toy boats is taken from a production line each hour and the defects on all thirty boats are counted, then the average, c, would be obtained by: # Defects / 30. A u-chart is used to measure defects per standard unit of measure, such as defects per square foot or per square inch.

7.   A quality rating system is often used to measure internal quality, or the quality of items supplied by vendors. Categories can be set up, ranging from very serious to not serious deficiencies. A series of points (demerits), ranging from 100 for each very serious deficiency down to 1 for the "not serious" category can be assigned. When the rating is done, the results can be plotted on a c-chart or u-chart, depending on the units or area being measured.

8. Zone control charts have been proposed as a simpler alternative to $\bar{x}$ charts. The standard control chart is divided into 8 segments (4 above, 4 below the center line). Each point on the chart is assigned a numeric value, depending on which zone it falls in. A numeric score is accumulated to tell the observer whether the process is in or out of control, thus eliminating the need for more complete interpretation using the standard $\bar{x}$ chart rules.

9. Pre-control is a method that is useful when there are short manufacturing runs, or where operators do not have time to record, calculate or plot data. It should only be used where a process is in good statistical control. It can be shown that the technique is statistically accurate, but it only applies to the initial operating conditions at the beginning of a production run, or when intermittent sampling takes place. The technique should not be used unless the process is under control because samples are not taken as the product is produced, so process variability and shifts cannot be detected. If the process deteriorates, sampling frequency is increased; if it is stable, sampling frequency is reduced.

10. Control limits are chosen to ensure that only a small percentage of points representing values of a statistic obtained from a random sample, such as the mean value or sample proportion, will fall outside of this range by chance, if the population parameter remains constant. When upper and lower control limits of $\pm 3\sigma$ are chose, there is less than a 0.3% probability of points falling outside the upper and lower control limits by chance alone, if the process parameter has not changed.

11. Historically, the value for probability limits of $z_{\alpha/2} = 3$ has been used in the U.S., whereas in Britain, $z_{\alpha/2} = 3.09$ is used. The limits are used to determine upper and lower ranges on control charts, thus giving limits of $\mu \pm 3\sigma_x$ for variables control charts.

12. The null hypothesis for a control chart is that the mean, proportion, or other parameter of the population has not shifted vs. the alternative hypothesis that the parameter has shifted. This hypothesis is implicitly tested when samples are taken, plotted on control charts, and interpreted as to whether the process has gone out of control.

13. The number of runs test can be used to develop decision rules for determining out-of-control conditions by performing a two-tailed test of the following hypothesis.

H_0: the sequence is random
H_1: the sequence is not random

If a test statistic, z, calculated from the observed number of runs, falls above or below the critical value for the normal distribution using a specified Type I error factor, then the null hypothesis can be rejected, thus stating that the run of values occurred due to some assignable cause, rather than by chance alone.

SOLUTIONS TO PROBLEMS

1. $CL_{\bar{x}} = 2.122$; $CL_{s} = 0.111$

$\bar{\bar{x}} = (\Sigma \bar{x}) / k = 42.44 / 20 = 2.122$

$\bar{s} = (\Sigma s) / k = 2.22/20 = 0.111$

$UCL_{\bar{x}} = \bar{\bar{x}} + A_3\bar{s} = 2.122 + 1.427 (0.111) = 2.280$

$LCL_{\bar{x}} = \bar{\bar{x}} - A_3\bar{s} = 2.122 - 1.427 (0.111) = 1.964$

$UCL_{s} = B_4\ \bar{s} = 2.089 (0.111) = 0.232$

$LCL_{s} =\ B_3\ \bar{s} =\ \ \ \ 0 (0.111) = 0$

Points appear to be "hugging" the Center Line for both the x-bar and s-chart, so there is reason to suspect that the process is out of control.

See x-s chart, below.

Problem 16-1

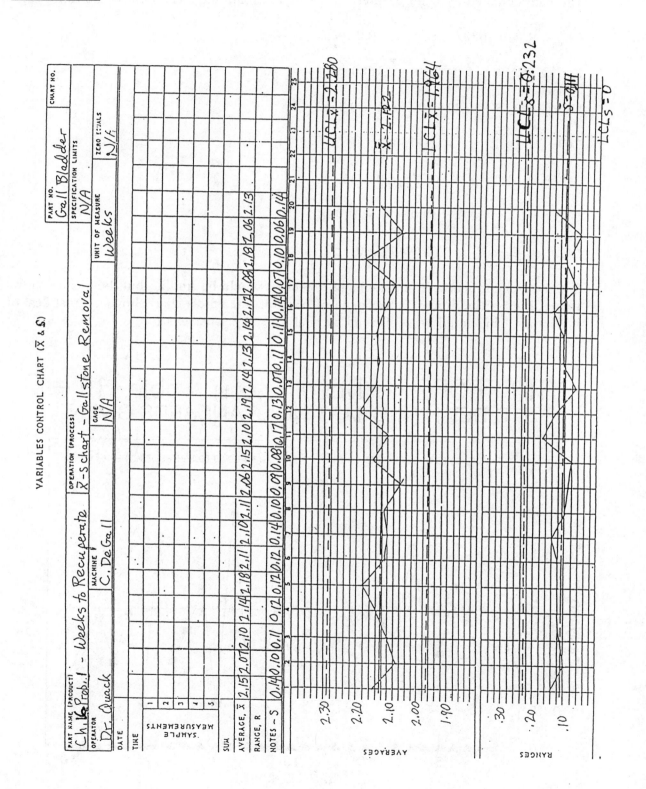

2.   The data obtained by from chapter 15, Table 15.1, and the s chart show the following:

$CL_R = \overline{R} = 0.1680;$ $CL_s^- = \overline{s} = 0.0717$

$\overline{R} = (\Sigma R) / k = 5.04 / 30 = 0.1680$

$UCL_R = D_4 \overline{R} = 2.114 (0.1680) = 0.3552$

$LCL_R = D_3 \overline{R} = 0 (0.1680) = 0$

$\overline{s} = (\Sigma s) / k = 2.1498 / 30 = 0.0717$

$UCL_s^- = B_4 \overline{s} = 2.089 (0.0717) = 0.1498$

$LCL_s^- = B_3 \overline{s} = 0 (0.0717) = 0$

See the s-chart, below. The patterns of a R-chart would be similar, but the s-chart shows tighter limits. The process may be out of control, since the s-chart shows a great deal of instability. This could be confirmed by analyzing the x-bar chart.

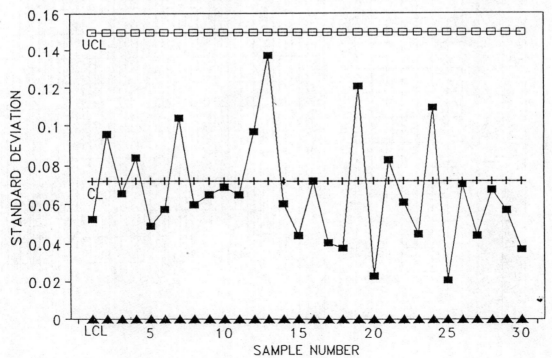

CH16 PROB2 — Data From Table 15—1
STD DEV'N (s) CHART NO STANDARDS GIVEN

<u>Problem 16-2</u>

STATPAD PRINTOUTS:[4]

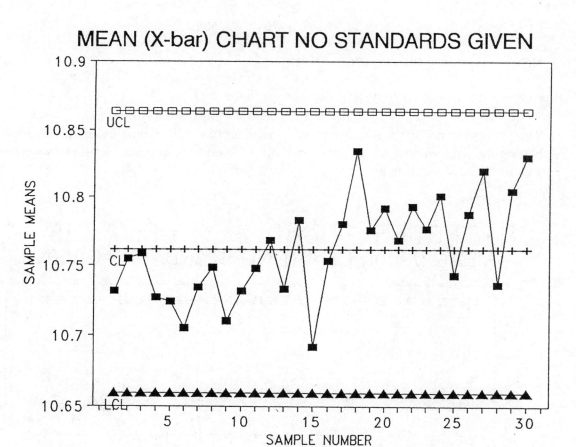

MEAN (X-bar) CHART NO STANDARDS GIVEN

─────────

[4] X-BAR & S charts were reprinted from STATPAD - Statistical templates for use with Lotus 1-2-3 by kind permission of John A. Clements.

3.   The data from chapter 15, problem 1 on the $\bar{x}$-s chart show:

$CL_{\bar{x}} = \bar{\bar{x}} = (\Sigma \bar{x}) / k = 105.78 / 30 = 3.526$

$CL_{s} = \bar{s} = (\Sigma s) / k = 11.9087 / 30 = 0.3970$

$UCL_{\bar{x}} = \bar{\bar{x}} + A_3\bar{s} = 3.5260 + 1.954 (0.3970) = 4.3017$

$LCL_{\bar{x}} = \bar{\bar{x}} - A_3\bar{s} = 3.5260 - 1.954 (0.3970) = 2.7502$

$UCL_{s} = B_4\,\bar{s} = 2.568 (0.3970) = 1.0195$

$LCL_{s} = B_3\,\bar{s} = \quad 0 (0.3970) = 0$

The process is probably out of control, due to a "run" of 8 points below the Center Line, beginning with sample 11 on the x-bar chart. There also appears to be instability on the s-chart. [See $\bar{x}$-s charts.]

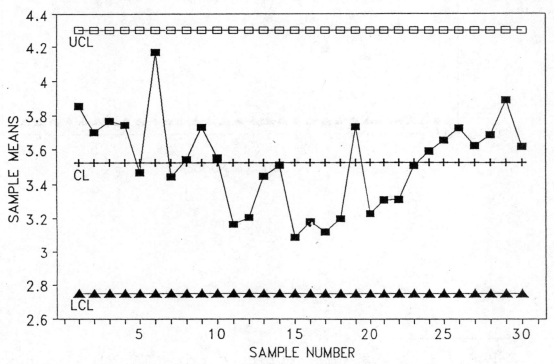

CH **16** PROB3 — Data From Prob **15** —1
MEAN (X-bar) CHART NO STANDARDS GIVEN

Problem 16-3

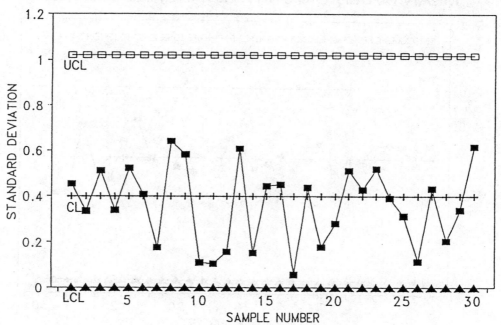

CH **16** PROB3 — Data From Prob **15** –1
STD DEV'N (s) CHART NO STANDARDS GIVEN

4.   The data from chapter 15, problem 6 on the $\bar{x}$-s chart shows:

$$CL_{\bar{x}}^{-} = \bar{\bar{x}} = (\Sigma\, \bar{x}) / k = -31.047/30 = -1.0349$$

$$CL_{s}^{-} = \bar{s} = (\Sigma\, s) / k = 37.227 / 30 = 1.2409$$

$$UCL_{\bar{x}}^{-} = \bar{\bar{x}} + A_3\bar{s} = -1.0349 + 1.427\,(1.2409) = 0.7359$$

$$LCL_{\bar{x}}^{-} = \bar{\bar{x}} - A_3\bar{s} = -1.0349 - 1.427\,(1.2409) = -2.8057$$

$$UCL_{s}^{-} = B_4\, \bar{s} = 2.089\,(1.2409) = 2.5922$$

$$LCL_{s}^{-} = B_3\, \bar{s} = \quad 0\,(1.2409) = 0$$

* The process is probably <u>not</u> under control, since points appear to be "hugging" the Center Line on the x-bar <u>and</u> s-charts. [See charts.]

Problem 16-4

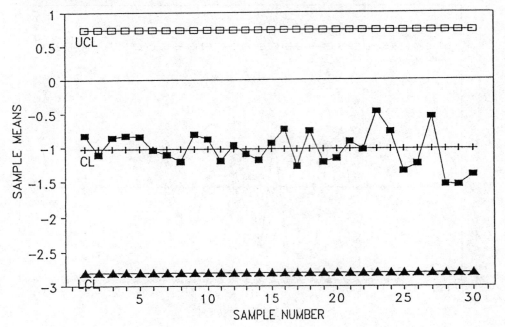

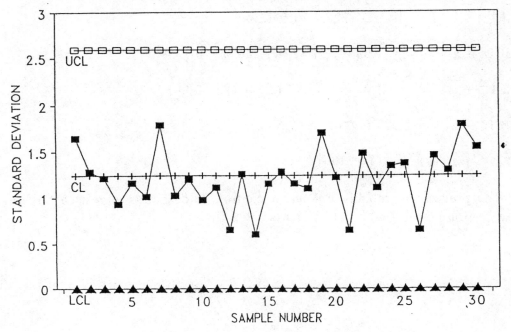

5.   a) X-chart for individuals and two-period moving range calculations:

$\bar{x} = 11.56, \quad \bar{R} = 1.37$

Control limits on x:

$$UCL_x = \bar{x} + 3\,(\bar{R}\,/\,d_2) = 11.56 + 3(1.37)/1.128 = 15.20$$

$$LCL_x = \bar{x} - 3\,(\bar{R}\,/\,d_2) = 11.56 - 3(1.37)/1.128 = 7.92$$

Control limits on R: $UCL_R = D_4\,\bar{R} = 3.267\,(1.37) = 4.48$

$$LCL_R = D_3\,\bar{R} = 0\,(1.37) = 0$$

Ranges 12 and 13 are out of limits. Point 13 is also out of limits on the x-chart.

b) 3-period moving range calculations are:

$\bar{x} = 11.56$ (from above)

Control limits on R: $UCL_R = D_4\,\bar{R} = 2.574\,(2.12) = 5.46$

$$LCL_R = D_3\,\bar{R} = 0\,(2.12) = 0$$

The 3-period R-chart shows two points out of control.

The summary of data and charts for the 2 and 3-period moving ranges and x-chart for individuals is shown below.

Problem 16-5: Calculations and x-chart

MOVING RANGE CALCULATIONS

Mean Calculation

$$x\text{-bar} = \frac{254.30}{22} = 11.56$$

Two Period Range Calculations

$$R\text{-bar} = \frac{28.7}{21} = 1.37$$

Three Period Range Calculations

$$R\text{-bar} = \frac{42.3}{20} = 2.12$$

Number	Observation	2-Period Moving Range	3-Period Moving Range
1	9.00		
2	9.50	0.50	
3	8.40	1.10	1.10
4	11.50	3.10	3.10
5	10.30	1.20	3.10
6	12.10	1.80	1.80
7	11.40	0.70	1.80
8	11.40	0.00	0.70
9	10.00	1.40	1.40
10	11.00	1.00	1.40
11	12.70	1.70	2.70
12	11.30	1.40	1.70
13	17.20	5.90	5.90
14	12.60	4.60	5.90
15	12.50	0.10	4.70
16	13.00	0.50	0.50
17	12.00	1.00	1.00
18	11.20	0.80	1.80
19	11.10	0.10	0.90
20	11.50	0.40	0.40
21	12.50	1.00	1.40
22	12.10	0.40	1.00
Totals	254.30	28.70	42.30

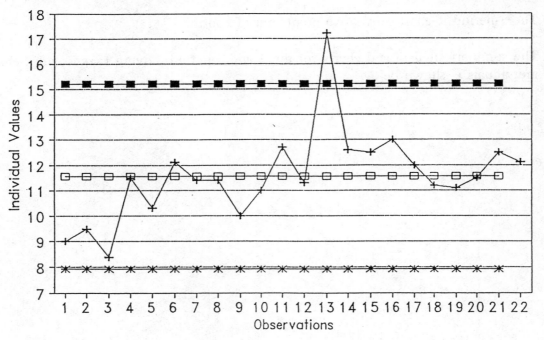

CH 16 PROB5 — X CHART FOR INDIVIDUALS

UCL-x = 15.20   LCL-x = 7.92   CL-x = 11.56

<u>Problem 16-5 (a)</u>

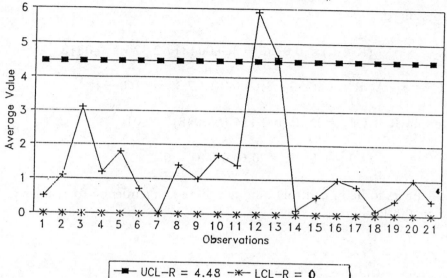

<u>Problem 16-5 (b)</u>

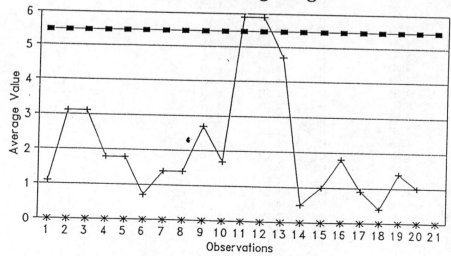

6.   Using data from chapter 15, problem 10, as individual measures, with 5 sample moving ranges, the calculations for the x-chart for individuals and R-chart show:

From the data summary, below: $\bar{x}$ = 0.0756; $\bar{R}$ = 0.0048

Control Limits on $\bar{x}$:

$$UCL_x = \bar{x} + 3\ (\bar{R} / d_2) = 0.0756 + 3(0.0048) / 2.326 = 0.0818$$

$$LCL_x = \bar{x} - A_2\ \bar{R} = 0.0756 - 3(0.0048) / 2.326 = 0.0694$$

Control limits on R: $UCL_R = D_4\ \bar{R} = 2.114\ (0.0048) = 0.0101$

$$LCL_R = D_3\ \bar{R} =\ 0\ (0.0048) = 0$$

The process appears to be in control, although there is a tendency for values to "hug" the Center Line on the R-chart.

MOVING RANGE CALCULATIONS

Number	Observation	5-Period Moving Range	Number	Observation	5-Period Moving Range
1	0.077		26	0.078	0.005
2	0.080		27	0.081	0.007
3	0.078		28	0.079	0.007
4	0.072		29	0.076	0.007
5	0.078	0.008	30	0.076	0.005
6	0.076	0.008	31	0.075	0.006
7	0.079	0.007	32	0.077	0.004
8	0.073	0.007	33	0.075	0.002
9	0.074	0.006	34	0.076	0.002
10	0.073	0.006	35	0.077	0.002
11	0.076	0.006	36	0.079	0.004
12	0.077	0.004	37	0.075	0.004
13	0.072	0.005	38	0.078	0.004
14	0.076	0.005	39	0.077	0.004
15	0.074	0.005	40	0.076	0.004
16	0.074	0.005	41	0.076	0.003
17	0.078	0.006	42	0.075	0.003
18	0.075	0.004	43	0.074	0.003
19	0.077	0.004	44	0.075	0.002
20	0.077	0.004	45	0.075	0.002
21	0.080	0.005	46	0.071	0.004
22	0.073	0.007	47	0.073	0.004
23	0.075	0.007	48	0.071	0.004
24	0.076	0.007	49	0.07	0.005
25	0.074	0.007	50	0.073	0.003
				3.782	0.223

$$\text{x-bar} = \frac{3.782}{50} = 0.0756$$

$$\text{R-bar} = \frac{0.2230}{46} = 0.0048$$

Problem 16-6

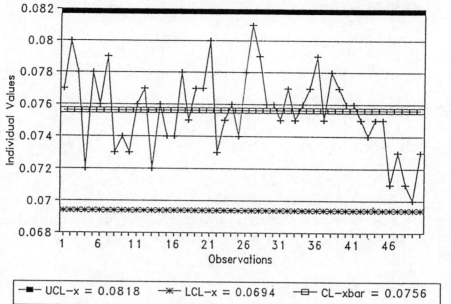

CH**16**PROB6 — X CHART FOR INDIVIDUALS

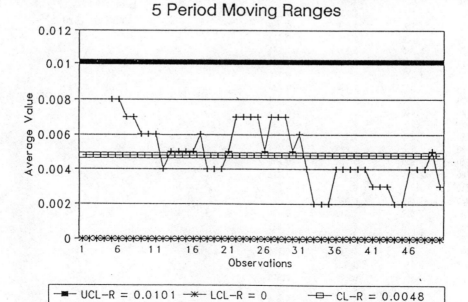

CH**16** PROB6 — R CHART FOR MOVING RANGES
5 Period Moving Ranges

7.   Using data from chapter 15, problem 1, the median chart shows:

$$\overset{\approx}{x} = 3.605; \quad \tilde{R} = 0.715$$

Control Limits on $\overset{\approx}{x}$:

$$UCL_x = \overset{\approx}{x} + A_5 \tilde{R} = 3.605 + 1.265 \, (0.715) = 4.510$$

$$LCL_x = \overset{\approx}{x} - A_5 \tilde{R} = 3.605 - 1.265 \, (0.715) = 2.705$$

Control Limits on R:

$$UCL_R = D_6 \tilde{R} = 2.745 \, (0.715) = 1.963$$

$$LCL_R = D_5 \tilde{R} = \quad 0 \, (0.715) = 0$$

The process appears to be out of control, with 8 points on the same side of Center Line beginning with observation 11. Also, there appears to be a great deal of instability in the R-chart.

MEDIAN CHART CALCULATIONS

Number	Median Obsrvs.	Ordered Data	Ranges	Ordered Range
1	3.640	2.840	0.820	0.110
2	3.610	3.050	0.650	0.190
3	3.610	3.110	0.980	0.190
4	3.610	3.120	0.630	0.210
5	3.280	3.150	0.990	0.270
6	4.320	3.280	0.770	0.290
7	3.510	3.280	0.330	0.330
8	3.380	3.370	1.250	0.340
9	3.640	3.380	1.150	0.380
10	3.610	3.380	0.190	0.510
11	3.120	3.440	0.190	0.590
12	3.150	3.510	0.290	0.630
13	3.440	3.550	1.210	0.630
14	3.590	3.590	0.270	0.650
> 15	2.840	3.600	0.770	0.690 <
> 16	3.280	3.610	0.880	0.740 <
17	3.110	3.610	0.110	0.750
18	3.050	3.610	0.830	0.770
19	3.680	3.610	0.340	0.770
20	3.370	3.620	0.510	0.820
21	3.630	3.630	0.910	0.830
22	3.550	3.640	0.740	0.880
23	3.800	3.640	0.910	0.910
24	3.800	3.650	0.690	0.910
25	3.650	3.680	0.630	0.980
26	3.770	3.770	0.210	0.990
27	3.380	3.800	0.750	1.150
28	3.600	3.800	0.380	1.210
29	4.080	4.080	0.590	1.230
30	3.620	4.320	1.230	1.250

Median for obsv. = $\dfrac{(3.600 + 3.610)}{2} = \dfrac{7.210}{2} = 3.605$

Median for ranges = $\dfrac{(0.690 + 0.740)}{2} = \dfrac{1.430}{2} = 0.715$

<u>Problem 16-7</u>

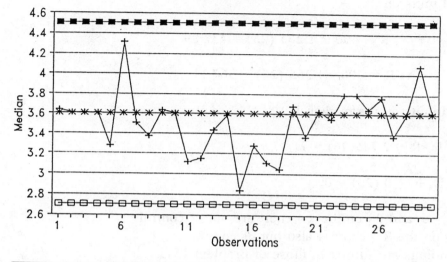

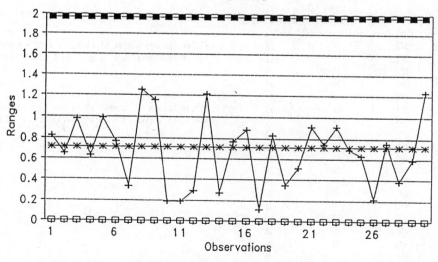

8.   The data summary, below, and the median chart constructed from data taken from chapter 15, problem 5 shows:

$$\approx \atop x = 400; \ \tilde{R} = 26$$

Control Limits on $\overset{\approx}{x}$:

$$UCL_x = \overset{\approx}{x} + A_5 \tilde{R} = 400 + 1.265 \,(26) = 432.89$$

$$LCL_x = \overset{\approx}{x} - A_5 \tilde{R} = 400 - 1.265 \,(26) = 367.11$$

Control Limits on the median R:

$$UCL_R = D_6 \tilde{R} = 2.745(26) = 71.37$$

$$LCL_R = D_5 \tilde{R} = 0 \,(26) = 0$$

Points 5, 16, and 23 on the $\tilde{x}$ - chart are out of control.
Point 16 on the R - chart is also out of control.
These findings are similar to those of problem 15-5.

MEDIAN CHART CALCULATIONS

Number	Median Obsrvs.	Ordered Data	Ranges	Ordered Range
1	402	372	26	9
2	406	380	26	10
3	396	382	10	14
4	390	390	36	17
5	436	392	44	18
6	400	394	14	19
7	410	396	54	20
8	372	398	68	22
9	382	400	22	23
10	400	400	60	25
11	400	400	18	26
12	408	400	26	26
13	400	400	48	26
14	402	402	9	33
15	413	402	25	33
16	445	403	85	35
17	420	406	33	36
18	380	406	35	38
19	392	408	23	41
20	394	410	19	44
21	400	413	20	48
22	403	420	41	54
23	450	436	33	60
24	398	445	17	68
25	406	450	38	85

Median for odd number of items is middle-most one is an ordered set; e.g., the 13th observation = 400

Median for an odd number of ranges is also the middle-most item; the 13th observation is 26

Problem 16-8

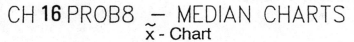

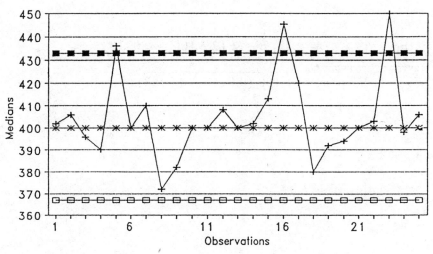

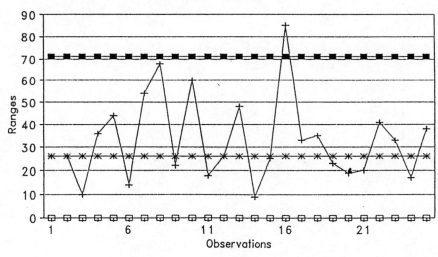

9.   Using data from chapter 15, problem 17, we get:

$$\overline{np} = \frac{y_1 + y_2 + y_3 + \dots y_M}{M}$$

<u>Initial</u>

So, $CL_{\overline{np}}$: $\overline{np} = 53 / 25 = 2.12$; $\overline{p} = 2.12 / 100 = 0.0212$

$s_{\overline{np}} = \sqrt{[n\,(\,\overline{p}\,)(\,1 - \overline{p}\,)\,]} = \sqrt{100\,(0.0212)\,(0.9788)} = 1.44$

Control limits:

$UCL_{\overline{np}} = \overline{np} + 3\,s_{\overline{np}}$

$UCL_{\overline{np}} = 2.12 + 3(1.44) = 6.44$

$LCL_{\overline{np}} = \overline{p} - 3\,s_{\overline{np}}$

$LCL_{\overline{np}} = 2.12 - 3(1.44) = -2.20$, use 0

Values for samples 9 and 23 are out of limits. Eliminating these points, we get revised control limits shown after the initial control chart, below.

<u>Problem 16-9: Initial</u>
STATPAD PRINTOUTS:[5]

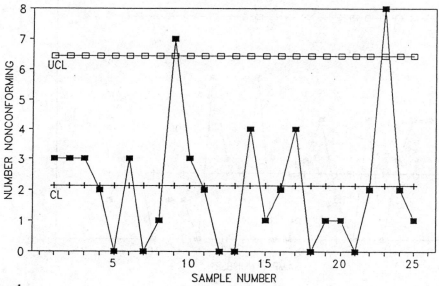

CH **16** PROB9 — Data From Prob. **15** –17
np CHART

<u>Revised</u>

So, $CL_{\overline{np}}$: $\overline{np}$ = 38 / 23 = 1.65; $\overline{p}$ = 1.65 / 100 = 0.0165

$s_{\overline{np}} = \sqrt{[n\,(\,\overline{p}\,)(\,1 - \overline{p}\,)\,]} = \sqrt{100\,(0.0165)\,(0.9835)}$ = 1.274

Control limits:

$UCL_{\overline{np}} = \overline{np} + 3\ s_{\overline{np}}$

$UCL_{\overline{np}} = 1.65 + 3(1.274) = 5.47$

$LCL_{\overline{np}} = \overline{p} - 3\ s_{\overline{np}}$

$LCL_{\overline{np}} = 1.65 - 3(1.274) = - 2.172$, use 0

The $\overline{np}$ chart, below, shows that all points are now in control.

---

[5] np charts were reprinted from STATPAD - Statistical templates for use with Lotus 1-2-3 by kind permission of John A. Clements.

<u>Problem 16-9: Revised</u>

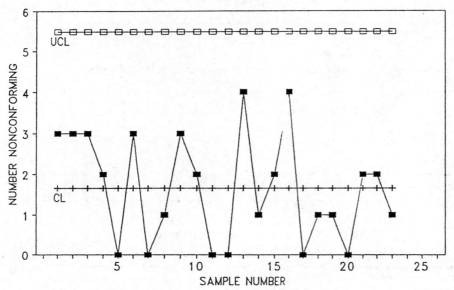

CH **16** PROB9 — Data From Prob. **15** −17
np CHART

10.   Using data from chapter 15, problem 18, we get:

$$\overline{np} = \frac{y_1 + y_2 + y_3 + \dots y_M}{M}$$

<u>Initial</u>

So, $CL_{\overline{np}}$: $\overline{np}$ = 722 / 25 = 28.88; $\overline{p}$ = 28.88 / 100 = 0.2888

$s_{\overline{np}} = \sqrt{[n\,(\overline{p})(1 - \overline{p})]} = \sqrt{100\,(0.2888)\,(0.7122)}$ = 4.53

Control limits:

$UCL_{\overline{np}} = \overline{np} + 3\,s_{\overline{np}}$ = 28.88 + 3 (4.53) = 42.48

$LCL_{\overline{np}} = \overline{p} - 3\,s_{\overline{np}}$ = 28.88 - 3 (4.53) = 15.28

After identifying and correcting the assignable causes, through the same process and iterations used in Problem 15-18, the <u>final</u> revised values are shown after the <u>initial</u> printout, below. Note that 9 observations (all values of 35 or over) were dropped.

Problem 16-10: Initial

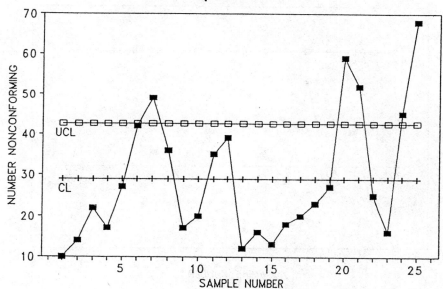

CH**16**PROB10 — Data From Prob. **15**−18
np CHART

Revised

So, $CL_{\overline{np}}$: $\overline{np}$ = 297 / 16 = 18.56; $\overline{p}$ = 18.56 / 100 = 0.1856

$s_{\overline{np}}$ = $\sqrt{[n\,(\,\overline{p}\,)(\,1 - \overline{p}\,)\,]}$ = $\sqrt{100\,(0.1856)\,(0.8144)}$ = 3.89

Control limits:

$UCL_{\overline{np}}$ = $\overline{np}$ + 3 $s_{\overline{np}}$

$UCL_{\overline{np}}$ = 18.56 + 3(3.89) = 30.23

$LCL_{\overline{np}}$ = $\overline{np}$ - 3 $s_{\overline{np}}$

$LCL_{\overline{np}}$ = 18.56 - 3 (3.89) = 6.89

Problem 16-10: Revised

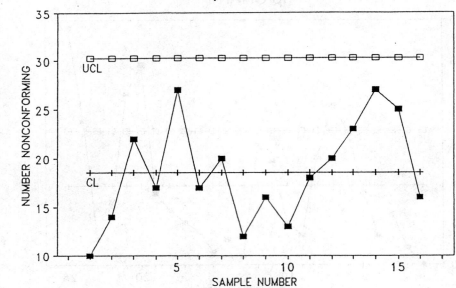

CH **16** PROB10 — Data From Prob. **15**−18
np CHART

11.   For the u-chart conditions: 25 samples; n = 9, number of defects = 400

Center Line for the u-chart: $\bar{u}$ = 400 / 225 = 1.78

$\bar{u} \pm 3 \sqrt{\bar{u}/n}$ = 1.78 ± 3 $\sqrt{(1.78/9\ )}$ = 1.78 ± 1.33 = 0.45 to 3.11

Center Line for the c-chart: $\bar{c}$ = 400/25 =16

$\bar{c} \pm 3 \sqrt{\bar{c}}$ = 16 ± 3 $\sqrt{16}$ = 16 ± 12 = 4 to 28

12.   For the c-chart: Number defective = 176; number of samples = 10

Center Line for the c-chart: $\bar{c}$ = 176/10 = 17.6

$\bar{c} \pm 3 \sqrt{\bar{c}}$ = 17.6 ± 3 $\sqrt{17.6}$ = 17.6 ± 12.59 = 5.01 to 30.19

See c-chart, below.

<u>Problem 16-12</u>
STATPAD PRINTOUT[6]

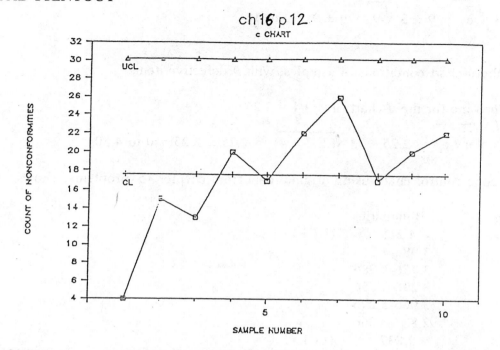

ch 16 p 12
c CHART

COUNT OF NONCONFORMITIES

SAMPLE NUMBER

* CCHART *   QC CHART FOR NONCONFORMITIES (c)
                    * TITLE *   ch16 pr12
No of sample cols =
      CENTER LINE c   10
            17.6
      CURRENT avg c   Samples analysed
            17.6   10
                              NOTES

SAMPLE NUMBER (#) DATA	1	2	3	4
COUNT OF NONCONFORMITIES IN SAMPLE	4	15	13	20
UCL c	30.185	30.185	30.185	30.185
CENTER LINE c	17.6	17.6	17.6	17.6
3=Out of Ctrl	1	1	1	1

	6	6	7	8	9	10
	17	22	26	17	20	22
	30.185	30.185	30.185	30.185	30.185	30.185
	17.6	17.6	17.6	17.6	17.6	17.6
	1	1	1	1	1	1

---

[6]   c-charts were reprinted from STATPAD - Statistical templates for use with Lotus 1-2-3 by kind permission of John A. Clements.

13.   For the c-chart: Center Line = average number of defects = 9

$$\bar{c} \pm 3 \sqrt{\bar{c}} = 9 \pm 3 \sqrt{9} = 9 \pm 9 = 0 \text{ to } 18$$

14.   For the u-chart conditions: 4 samples, with 9 defective items.

Center Line for the u-chart: $\bar{u} = 9/4 = 2.25$

$$\bar{u} \pm 3 \sqrt{\bar{u} / n} = 2.25 \pm 3 \sqrt{(2.25 / 4)} = 2.25 \pm 2.25 = 0 \text{ to } 4.50$$

15.   The zone control chart, using <u>original</u> data from chapter 15, problem 1 shows:

Zone	Boundaries	
D	> 4.215	(UCL)
C	3.986-4.215	
B	3.756-3.986	
A	3.296-3.756	
B	3.066-3.296	
C	2.837-3.066	
D	< 2.837	(LCL)

The process went out of control at point 16 and remained out of control through point 18. Assignable causes should be determined and control limits recalculated.

Problem 16-15 Zone Control Chart

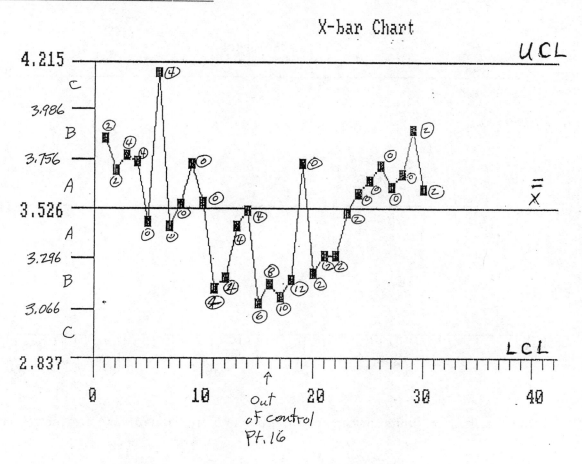

16.   The zone control chart, using final, revised data from chapter 15, problem 5 shows:

Zone	Boundaries	
D	> 431.958	(UCL)
C	421.402-431.958	
B	410.846-421.402	
A	389.734-410.846	
B	379.178-389.734	
C	368.621-379.174	
D	< 368.621	(LCL)

All points are in control

Problem 16-16 Zone Control Chart

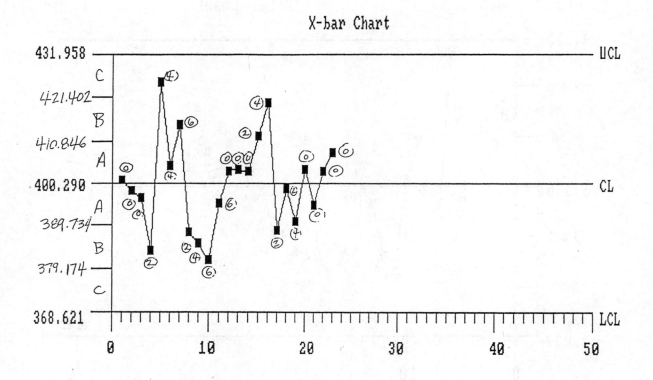

X-bar Chart

17.   If the specification limits for chapter 16, problem 5 are 9.0 and 12.0, pre-control shows:

```
                          Green
Red |_Yellow_|_____+_____|_Yellow_| Red
              Nominal = 10.5
     LTL=      9.75                  11.25      UTL=
     9.0                                        12.0
```

Where: UTL = Upper tolerance limit
       LTL = Lower tolerance limit

Part	Value	Zone
1	9	Red/Yellow
2	9.5	Yellow

Pre-control should not be applied to this process. Obviously, too much variability exists, with numerous points out of specification limits. The process should first be brought under control.

18.   For $Z = \pm 2.75$, $P(Z > 2.75) = P(Z < -2.75)$
        From the normal probability table: $0.5000 - 0.4970 = 0.003$;

        Therefore, the % outside $= 100 \times 2(0.003) = 0.6\%$

19. $\dfrac{\alpha}{2} = \dfrac{0.04}{2} = 0.02$; From the normal probability table, $P(Z) = 0.4800$

        Therefore, $Z_{0.02} = 2.05$, since it was the closest table value to 0.4800.

20.   The solution to this problem is left as an exercise for advanced computer-literate students.

21.   Using the binomial formula:

$$\text{Probability (acceptance)} = \sum_{x=0}^{n} f(x) = \text{and } f(x) = \binom{n}{x} p^x (1-p)^{n-x}$$

        11 in a row $= (0.5)^{11}$ $\qquad\qquad = 0.049\%$

        10 of 11 $\quad = \binom{11}{10}(0.5)^{10}(0.5)^{1} = 11(0.5)^{11} = 0.539\%$

        9 of 11 $\quad = \binom{11}{9}(0.5)^{9}(0.5)^{2} = 55(0.5)^{11} = 2.695\%$

        8 of 11 $\quad = \binom{11}{8}(0.5)^{8}(0.5)^{3} = 165(0.5)^{11} = 8.085\%$

        7 of 11 $\quad = \binom{11}{7}(0.5)^{7}(0.5)^{4} = 330(0.5)^{11} = 16.17\%$

        9 out of 11 points are statistically significant ($p < 0.05$).

ANSWERS TO CASE QUESTIONS

I. Murphy Trucking, Inc.

The Billing Study - Part I

The first assignment requires the construction of a p-chart, since we are interested in the proportion of bills in error. The calculations are shown below. The average proportion of bills in error is 0.63 and the standard deviation is 0.108. Using the formulas for a p-chart, the lower and upper control limits are, respectively, 0.306 and 0.954. The control chart is shown in Figure MTI-A.

$$CL_p^- : \quad \bar{p} = 252 \ / \ 400 = \bar{p} = 0.63$$

$$s_p^- = \sqrt{[(\bar{p})(1 - \bar{p})/n]} = \sqrt{(0.63)(0.37)/20} = 0.108$$

Control limits:

$$UCL_p^- = \bar{p} + 3 \ s_p^- = 0.63 + 3 \ (0.108) = 0.954$$

$$LCL_p^- = \bar{p} - 3 \ s_p^- = 0.63 - 3 \ (0.108) = 0.306$$

Perhaps the most surprising finding is that the process appears to be under control! See the control chart constructed below. However, improvements definitely need to be made. Although the process is in control, an error rate of 63 percent is clearly unacceptable. The capability of the process is specified by the control limits, since they are 3 standard deviations on either side of the average. This can be interpreted to mean that error rates only as low as 31 percent and as high as 95 percent might be reasonably expected. Thus, further analysis is warranted.

<u>Figure MTI-A</u>

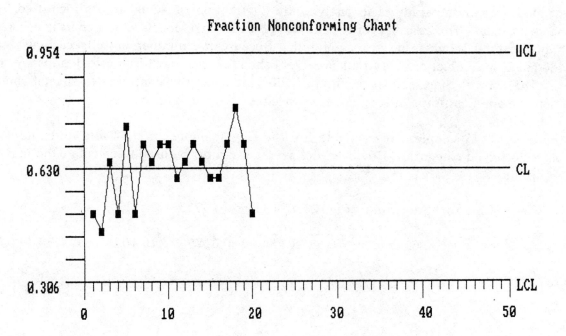

Fraction Nonconforming Chart

Sample	Number Nonconforming	Fraction Nonconforming
1	10	0.500
2	9	0.450
3	13	0.650
4	10	0.500
5	15	0.750
6	10	0.500
7	14	0.700
8	13	0.650
9	14	0.700
10	14	0.700
11	12	0.600
12	13	0.650
13	14	0.700
14	13	0.650
15	12	0.600
16	12	0.600
17	14	0.700
18	16	0.800
19	14	0.700
20	10	0.500

Control Chart Calculations for file: murphycc

Fraction Nonconforming Chart

Upper control limit =	0.9539
Center line =	0.6300
Lower control limit =	0.3061
Standard deviation =	0.1080

The Billing Study - Part II

The second part of the study is to analyze the distribution of actual errors identified by the management team. The analysis consists of two phases. First, construct a u-chart is constructed to study the total number of errors per bill. Because the number of bills each day varies considerably, individual control limits are established for each day. The calculations are shown below. The control chart, shown in Figure MTI-B, is clearly in control. No special causes of variation are apparent; thus, management must attack the common causes.

For the u-chart: 25 samples are available; for the Day 1sample, n = 54 total bills, number of defects = 36 for all categories. However, the average u must be used to calculate the individual control limits.

Center Line for the u-chart: $\bar{u}$ = 1233 / 1965 = 0.6275

$\bar{u} \pm 3 \sqrt{\bar{u}/n}$ = 0.6275 $\pm$ 3 $\sqrt{(0.6275)/54}$ = 0.6275 $\pm$ 3 (0.1078) = 0.3234 to 0.9509

Figure MTI-B

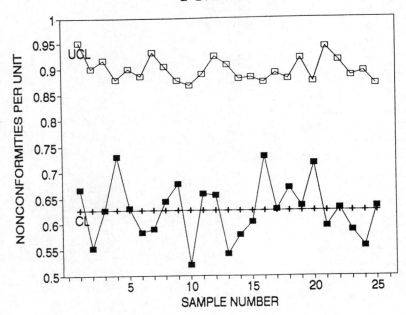

If each error category is summed, we may construct a Pareto diagram of the distribution of errors by category as shown in Figure MTI-C. By examining the nature of the errors, you should realize that many of the errors, specifically categories 1, 2, 3, 6 and 7, can easily be recognized by the driver, while the other categories are "true" billing errors. Nearly seventy percent of the errors fall into this category. This suggests that an increased focus on driver training and awareness could reduce a majority of the errors. The customers also should be informed of their role in providing correct information to reduce the scope of the problem.

Figure MTI-C

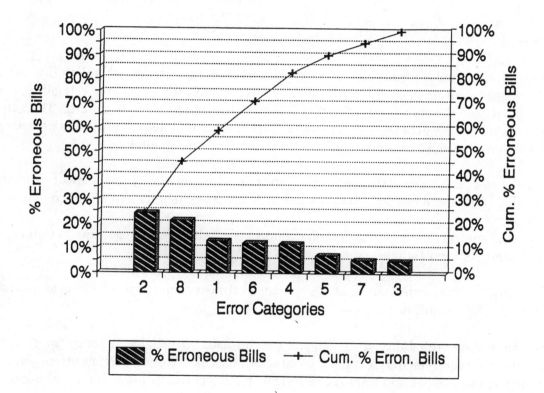

Murphy Trucking, Inc.
Distribution of Billing Errors

Murphy Trucking, Inc.
Distribution of Billing Errors

Error Cat.	Erroneous Bills	Proportion of Total Errors	Cumulative Bill. Errors	Cum. Proportion of Total Errors
2	300	24.331%	300	24.331%
8	264	21.411%	564	45.742%
1	159	12.895%	723	58.637%
6	151	12.247%	874	70.884%
4	147	11.922%	1021	82.806%
5	87	7.056%	1108	89.862%
7	63	5.109%	1171	94.972%
3	62	5.028%	1233	100.000%
	1233			

CHAPTER 17

Reliability

Teaching Notes

This chapter is designed to provide an overview of the importance of reliability in our increasingly quality-conscious world. Students may have an intuitive "feel" for reliability, since most have experienced the frustration of early product failure at one time or another. Thus, there is some immediate interest generated by the topic. This chapter will help to differentiate between "shades of meaning" of the basic concept. Key objectives of this chapter should be:

• To develop the basic definitions and terms used in reliability assessment, including reliability, functional failure, reliability failure, inherent reliability and achieved reliability.

• To assist students in understanding the concepts of failure rate, mean time to failure, and mean time between failures.

• To introduce the mathematical and graphical treatment of the product life characteristics curve and the reliability function.

• To show how reliability management can be used to provide a focus on customer performance requirements, economic considerations, costs, etc., and reliability engineering can be used to analyze and improve technical characteristics through the use of numerous reliability assessment and enhancement techniques.

• To consider the special and increasingly important needs for software reliability.

ANSWERS TO QUALITY IN PRACTICE KEY ISSUES

Testing Audio Components at Shure Bros., Inc.

1.   For the home environment, Shure uses the cartridge drop test and cartridge scrape test. For P.A. systems, they use the microphone drop test and barrel tumble. For mobile application, the two above tests, plus the stair tumble test would be applicable. Finally, for the professional recording and sound reinforcement, the microphone drop, barrel tumble, perhaps the stair tumble, and outside weathering tests would be appropriate. The purpose of the tests is to simulate actual operating conditions so that the products can sustain accidents and rough handling and perform effectively over a useful life. Quality characteristics that are studied are reliability and performance.

Software Quality Assurance at Los Alamos National Laboratory

1.   Los Alamos National Laboratory (LANL) developed a new approach that was designed to deliver a more reliable, maintainable software product in a shorter period of time. This was done by integrating QA into the development process. Modules included project planning, peer reviews of software products, availability of current sets of procedures and guidelines, cost-effective testing procedures, accurate measures of actual efforts, and reliable project estimating tools.

2.   While the use of a separate testing group may seem to conflict with the TQM principle that each person should be responsible for his/her own quality, this use of a testing group seems to leave much responsibility for high quality in the hands of the designers. The purpose for the test group is to find unintended problems and breakdowns of the complex programs that are being written. Obviously, programs that are too complex to be written by one individual are too complex to be "debugged" by an individual, as well. The team approach has been used to encourage finding and solving unanticipated problems of the kind unlikely to be isolated by designers.

ANSWERS TO REVIEW QUESTIONS

1.   Reliability has grown increasingly important among the quality disciplines due to safety needs of consumers, the search for competitive advantage by companies, growing consumer awareness, and rising expectations and the difficulty of achieving high reliability in more sophisticated and complex modern products.

2.   *Reliability* is the probability that a product, piece of equipment, or system performs it intended function for a stated period of time under specified operating conditions. There are four key components of this definition, including probability, time, performance and operating conditions. All of these have to be considered in a comprehensive definition of reliability. <u>Probability</u> allows comparison of different products and systems, <u>time</u> allows us to measure the length of life of the product, <u>performance</u> relates to the ability of the

product to do what it was designed to do, and <u>operating conditions</u> specify to amount of usage and the environment in which the product is used.

3.   A *functional failure* is one incurred at the start of the product's life due to defective materials, components or work on the product. A reliability failure is one that is incurred after some period of use. For example, if a new TV set suffers a blown picture tube during the first week, it's a functional failure. There was obviously a defect in the manufacture of the tube. If the vertical hold feature of the set goes out (perhaps 3 days after the 1 year warranty is up), that is a reliability failure. It should reasonably be expected to last much longer than one year, but it didn't.

4.   *Failure rate* is defined as the number of failures per unit of time during a specified time period being considered. For example, if 15 TV sets were tested for 500 hours and there were two failures of picture tubes, the failure rate would be: $2 / (15 \times 500) = 1 / 3750$ or 0.000267.

5.   The cumulative failure rate curve plots the cumulative percent of failures against time on the horizontal axis. The failure rate curve, discussed in more detail below, is obtained by determining the slope of the failure rate curve at a number of points to obtain the instantaneous failure rate (failures per unit time) at that point. A plot of these values yields the failure rate curve.

6.   The product life characteristics curve, is the so-called "bath-tub curve" because of its shape. It is actually the <u>failure rate</u> curve, described above. Such curves can be used to understand the distinctive failure rate patterns of various designs and products, over time.

7.   The *reliability function* represents the probability that an item will <u>not</u> fail within a certain period of time, T. It is directly related to the cumulative distribution function: $F(T) = 1 - e^{-\lambda T}$, that yields the probability of failures. Since $F(T)$ is the probability of failure, the reliability function, $R(T)$ can be defined as the complement, e.g. probability of <u>not</u> failing:

$$R(T) = 1 - (1 - e^{-\lambda T}) = e^{-\lambda T}$$

It can also be expressed using the mean time to failure (MTTF) value θ as: $R(T) = e^{-T/\theta}$

8.   The reliability of series, parallel, and series parallel is relatively easy to compute, given the reliability of components in each system. For the series system, $R_S = R_1 R_2 R_3$. Thus reliabilities are multiplicative.

For a parallel system, the relationships are a little more complex, since the units are designed to use redundant components, so that if one unit fails the system can continue to operate. The system reliability is computed as:

$$R_S = 1 - [(1 - R_1)(1 - R_2)(1 - R_n)]$$

For series-parallel systems, the equivalent reliabilities of each parallel sub-system is calculated, successively, until there are no more parallel sub-systems. The system is then reduced to a serially equivalent system in which all component reliabilities can be multiplied to get the final reliability value.

9.   *Reliability engineering* is the discipline concerned with the design, manufacture, and assurance of products having high reliability. It uses methods such as standardization, redundancy, study of the physics of failure, reliability testing and burn-in to achieve the objectives of developing more reliable products. Details are given in the chapter.

10.   Methods of reliability testing include: life testing, accelerated life testing, environmental testing and vibration and shock testing. In life and accelerated life testing the product is tested until it fails. The latter speeds up the process by overstressing the item to hasten its eventual failure. Environmental and shock tests are performed to determine the product's ability to survive and operate under adverse conditions of heat, cold, or shock.

11.   *Latent defects* are frequently found in electronic devices, such as semi-conductors. The term refers to the fact that a certain small proportion of the units will have defects which show up during the early life of the product, perhaps the first 1,000 hours of operation. Then the remaining components, after the "infant mortality" period has passed, the remaining components may operate for <u>years</u> without many failures.

12.   *Failure mode and effects analysis* (FMEA) and *fault tree analysis* are analytic tools designed to discover ways in which products may fail and to attempt to prevent them from occurring. FMEA is used to identify the ways in which failure may occur, to estimate the effect and seriousness of the failure, and to recommend corrective actions that designers may take. Fault tree analysis is a logical procedure that begins with a list of potential hazards and works back to develop the possible causes and origins of the failure. It shows logical relationships between failures and causes in an attempt to avoid any potential dangers that can be uncovered.

13.   Effective reliability management requires that steps be taken to define customer performance requirements; determine economic effects and relate them to reliability requirements; define the environmental conditions under which the product will be used; select the components, designs and vendors to be used; determine the reliability requirements for the machines to be used to manufacture the products; and finally, to analyze field reliability data as a method for quality improvement.

14.   Reliability in computer software is becoming more critical as many of our products and services depend on microprocessor technology, from telephone systems to electric power switching to automobile control systems. Software reliability is difficult to attain because of the wide variety of programmer skills, small project staffs, software naive customers, poorly defined customer objectives, high turnover rate for programmers, externally generated constraints, hardware complexities, and poor quality of existing programs.

15.   *Configuration management* is a process for designing and maintaining software by keeping tight controls on the set of software components that make up a complex software system. It provides an effective means of incorporating changes during development and use. It includes the steps of establishing approved baseline designs for computer programs, maintaining control over all changes in the baseline program, and providing traceability of baselines and changes with a paper trail.

16.   *Maintainability* is the totality of design factors that will enable maintenance to be accomplished easily. Design issues for maintainability include: access of parts for repair, modular construction and standardization, and diagnostic repair procedures.

17.   *Availability* is the probability that equipment is not down due to failure. The two types of availability are *operational availability* and *inherent availability*. The former is the ratio of mean time between maintenance (MTBM) to MTBM plus mean downtime. The latter is the ratio between MTBF and MTBF plus meant time to repair (MTTR). Operational availability is useful to operations managers who are concerned with whether equipment is available for use,or not. Inherent availability is based on theoretical considerations. For example MTBF and MTTR assume no preventive maintenance downtime, not waiting time, etc, since these cannot be estimated. Thus this ratio is useful for design purposes, where the other must be used in the field.

SOLUTIONS TO PROBLEMS

1.   See sketch of reliability function, below.

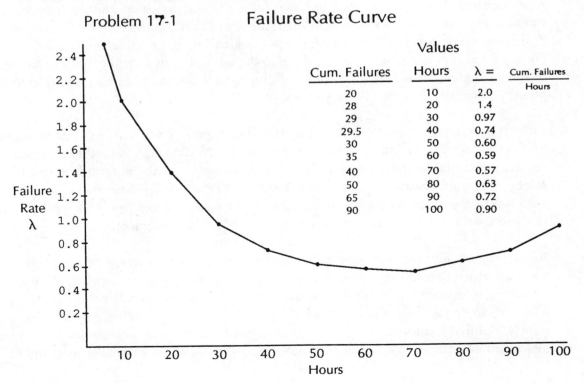

Problem 17-1   Failure Rate Curve

Values			
Cum. Failures	Hours	$\lambda = $	$\dfrac{\text{Cum. Failures}}{\text{Hours}}$
20	10	2.0	
28	20	1.4	
29	30	0.97	
29.5	40	0.74	
30	50	0.60	
35	60	0.59	
40	70	0.57	
50	80	0.63	
65	90	0.72	
90	100	0.90	

2. From 0 - 50, slope = 30 / 50 = 0.6
    From 50 - 100, slope = (90 - 30) / (100 - 50) = 1.2
    From 0 - 100, slope = 90 / 100 = 0.9

3. a) $P(x > 1300) = 0.5 - P(1200 < x < 1300)$

$$P(1300 < x < 1300) = P\left(Z < \frac{1300-1200}{60}\right) = P(0 < Z < 1.67) = 0.4525 =$$

Therefore, $P(x > 1300) = 0.5 - 0.4525 = 0.0475$ should survive beyond 1300 days.

b) $P(x < 900) = P\left(Z < \frac{900-1200}{60}\right) = P(Z < -5)$ Without even attempting to look the value up in the table, it is obvious that the probability of such an occurrence is practically zero.

c) This distribution looks approximately like:

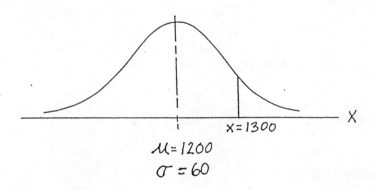

d) Let x_w be the limit of the warranty period.
   $P(x < x_w) = 0.10$; $Z = -2.33$, for $Z = \frac{x-1200}{60} = -2.33$, $x_w = 1060.2$ hours for the warranty limit.

4. $\lambda = \dfrac{2}{[(3 \times 500) + 40 + 220]} = \dfrac{2}{1760} = 0.00114$ failures / hour

5.
$$\lambda = \frac{3}{[(7 \times 200) + 8 + 54 + 162]} = \frac{3}{1624} = 0.00184 \text{ failures/hr.}$$

6.   The reliability function is $R(T) = 1 - F(T) = e^{-\lambda T}$

$\lambda = 0.001;\ R(T) = P(x < 800) = 1 - e^{-0.001(800)} = 0.55$

7. $R = e^{-\lambda T}$ $0.90 = e^{(-\lambda)\,500}$

$\ln 0.9 = -500\,(\lambda)$

$-0.105 = -500\,\lambda$

$$\lambda = \frac{\ln 0.9}{-500} = \frac{0.105}{500} = 0.0002 \text{ failures per hour}$$

Time - t	Failures - F(T)	Survivors - R(T)
100	0.02	0.98
200	0.04	0.96
300	0.06	0.94
400	0.08	0.92
500	0.10	0.90

8.   For $\theta = \dfrac{1760}{2} = 880$ hours; For $\theta = \dfrac{1624}{3} = 541.3$ hours

9.   For $\theta = \dfrac{4500}{2} = 2250$ hours

10. $\lambda = \dfrac{1}{1000} = 0.001$ failures / hr.

11.   Mean days between breakdown = 14, s = 3, 260 days per year
For no preventive maintenance: 260/14 = 18.6 breakdowns per year
18.6 breakdowns/year X $500 /breakdown = $9286
For a 1% chance of breakdown, let x be time between maintenance

$\dfrac{x - 14}{3} = -2.33$, $x = 7.01$ days

260/7.01 = 37.09 maintenance checks

$$37.09 \text{ X } \$100 \text{ / check } = \quad \$ 3709.00$$
$$+ \; 0.01 \text{ X } 37.09 \text{ x } \$500 = \quad \underline{185.45}$$

TOTAL $ 3894.45

For a 10% chance of breakdown, let x be time between maintenance

$$\frac{x-14}{3} = -1.28 \;, \qquad x = 10.16 \text{ days}$$

260/10.16 = 25.59 maintenance checks

$$25.59 \text{ X } \$100 \text{ / check } = \quad \$2559$$
$$+ \; 0.1 \quad \text{X } 25.59 \text{ X } \$500 = \quad \underline{1280}$$

TOTAL $ 3839

Therefore, we may conclude that preventive maintenance is worthwhile.

12.   Example of typical calculations for the table:

Maintenance every 25 hours: 2080/25 X $50   = $4160
Every 30 hours: (2080/30 X $50) + (30 X 2080/30 X 0.2) = $3882.67

Time Between Inspections	Number of Inspections Per Year	Probability of Failure Before Next Inspection	Insp. Cost	Failure Cost	Total Cost
93	83.2	0	$4,160	0	$4,160
30	69.3	0.2	$3,467	$ 416	$3,883
35	59.4	0.6	$2,970	$1,069	$4,039
40	52	0.9	$2,600	$1,404	$4,004

For no preventive maintenance, with MTBF = 34 hours. Expect 61.2 failures/yr.

Cost of maintenance: 2080/34 X $30 = $1,836; Therefore, do no maintenance.

13.   MTBF = (0.5)(0.20)+1.5(0.1)+2.5(0.1)+3.5(0.15)+4.5(0.2)+5.5(0.25) = 3.3 wks

52/3.3 = 15.76 failures/year

Time between Maintenance	Failure Expense	Maintenance Expense	Total
1 wk	0.20 X 52 X $1500 = $15,600	52 X 100 = $5,200	$20,800
2 wk	0.30 X 52/2 X $1500=$11,700	26 X 100 = $2,600	$14,300
3 wk	0.40 X 52/3 X $1500=$10,400	17.3 X100= $1,730	$12,130
4 wk	0.55 X 52/4 X $1500=$10,725	13 X 100 = $1,300	$12,025
5 wk	0.75 X 52/5 X $1500=$11,700	10.4 X100= $1,040	$12,740
6 wk	1.00 X 52/6 X $1500=$13,000	8.7 X100= $ 870	$13,870

15.76 X $1500   = $23,640/year, with no maintenance. Therefore, perform maintenance every 4 weeks for minimum cost.

14.   The reliability of the parallel R_{cc} is calculated as follows

$R_{cc} = 1 - (1 - 0.9)^2 = 0.99$
$R_a R_b R_{cc} R_d = (0.95)(0.98) (0.99)(0.99) = 0.9125$

15.   Supplier 1: $R_a R_{bc} = (0.95) [1 - (1 - 0.80)(1 - 0.90)] = 0.931$
Supplier 2: $R_a R_{bc} = (0.92) [1 - (1 - 0.86)(1 - 0.93)] = 0.911$
Supplier 3: $R_a R_{bc} = (0.94) [1 - (1 - 0.90)(1 - 0.85)] = 0.926$

16.   a) $R_a R_b R_c = (0.60)(0.75)(0.70) = 0.315$

b) $R_{aa} R_{bb} R_{cc} = [1 - (1 - 0.60)^2] [1 - (1 - 0.75)^2] [1 - (1 - 0.70)^2] =$
(0.84) (0.9375) (0.91) = 0.717

17.   a) $R_t R_m R_g = (0.99)(0.98)(0.99)(0.96) = 0.922$

b) $R_t R_m R_{eg} = (0.99)(0.98)(0.99)[1 - (1 - 0.96)^2] = 0.959$

18.   a) $R_T = 0.90$

b) Since these are parallel systems, $R = 1 - (1 - 0.90)^2 = 0.99$

ANSWERS TO CASE QUESTIONS

I. Automotive Air Bag Reliability

1.   The actuators in the mechanical air bag system act as a "trigger" to start the deployment of the air bag after the sensor has noted a sudden deceleration of vehicle. By putting in two actuators in parallel, there is built-in redundancy. In case one actuator fails the other will perform the action. This increases the overall reliability of the air bag system.

2.   a) For the AMS system (Figure 17.14), one must first calculate the equivalent reliability of the parallel actuators, and then calculate the overall (series) system reliability, as follows:

The reliability of the parallel actuators -- R_{aa} -- is calculated as follows

$$R_{aa} = 1 - (1 - 0.985266)^2 = 0.999783$$

The reliability of the entire *sensor* mechanism -- $R_b R_{aa}$ -- is calculated as follows

$$R_S = R_b R_{aa} = (0.999993)(0.999783) = 0.999776$$

Finally, the system reliability is calculated as

$$R_S R_e R_p R_f R_b R_c = (0.999776)(0.999986)(0.999986)(0.999994)(0.999975)(0.999999)$$
$$= 0.999716$$

b) The EMS system (Figure 17.15) also has several parallel components, but subsystem reliabilites are indicated on the diagram, so the overall system reliability may be calculated as

$$R_S R_{bc} R_e R_d R_{spac} = (0.999239)(0.998318)(0.957124)(0.982782)(0.999892)$$
$$= 0.938246$$

c) The ES system (Figure 17.16) also has several parallel components, and subsystem reliabilites are indicated on the diagram. It is the most complicated system of all, having 12 components and subsystems, some of which contain numerous components and subsystems, themselves. To simplify calculations, each *line's* reliability, from the flow process chart, will be calculated. Then, the overall system reliability will be calculated.

Line 1: Consisting of the "Start" through the "Regulator" steps

$$R_S R_c R_p R_a R_r = (0.998919)(0.998019)(0.996439)(0.999905)(0.994825)$$
$$= 0.988155$$

Line 2: Consisting of the "Pins and connections" through the "PCB and components"

$$R_{pc}R_fR_{fc}R_pR_{PCB} = (0.999574)(0.974324)(0.982386)(0.988661)(0.991532)$$
$$= 0.937896$$

Line 3: Consisting of the "Diagnostic circuits" through the "End"

$$R_{cc}R_{spac} = (0.999762)(0.999788) = 0.999550$$

The overall system reliability may be calculated as

$$R_{L1}R_{L2}R_{L3} = (0.988155)(0.937896)(0.999550) = 0.926370$$

3. The graph of the data is shown in "Systems Reliability by Type", below. It appears that when repairability is taken into account, that EMS is slightly superior in reliability to AMS. It is obvious that the ES system is noticeably less reliable throughout its useful life.

Automotive Airbag Reliability Case

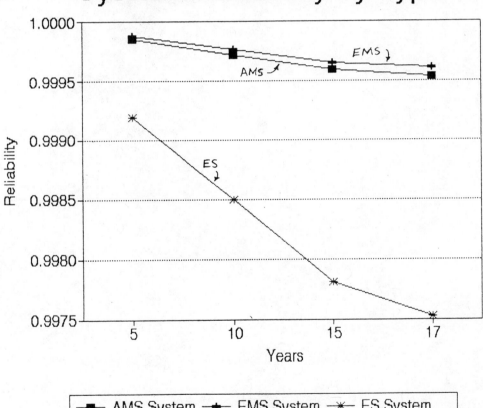

APPENDIX A

Baldrige Award Case Supplement

We have included in this Instructor's Manual the 1995 case study – Colony Fasteners, Inc. – used to train Examiners for the Malcolm Baldrige National Quality Award evaluation process. This case was also used in many state award examiner training programs. Included with the case is a copy of the 1995 Baldrige criteria and the evaluation notes describing the strengths and weaknesses of each item in the criteria. All this information is in the public domain and may be copied freely.

Instructors should note that the Award criteria are modified each year. A single free copy may be obtained by any individual by contacting the Baldrige Award office as described in Chapter 12 of the text. Bulk copies may be ordered from ASQC at (800) 248-1946. Examiner case studies used in training are usually published in late summer of that year and can be purchased from ASQC.

The case study is highly appropriate for MBA classes, although the full case can become quite tedious and boring. Thus, we suggest that different student groups be assigned only one item in a particular category to evaluate in order to obtain a feel for the assessment process. Instructors might discuss each category as the individual topics are discussed in class. For example, you might discuss Category 7 (Customer Focus and Satisfaction) in conjunction with Chapter 5 in the text. In this case, it would be appropriate to review the Baldrige Award as described in Chapter 12 first. The alternative is to use the case after covering the material in Chapters 5 through 12 of the book.

A useful reference to help the instructor interpret the criteria and responses is *Baldrige Award Winning Quality: How to Interpret the Malcolm Baldrige Award Criteria* by Mark Graham Brown, White Plains, NY: Quality Resources (current edition). This is available through ASQC Quality Press at the toll-free number listed above.

In assessing the case, the numerical scores are not as important as the comments. After some experience, most students will arrive at scores generally close to the "expert" scores (which are not always representative of the consensus of all examiners). It is important that the evaluation be done in groups to achieve consensus, similar to the way the actual evaluation is done. It is important to remember that a 50% score is representative of a sound approach – winners generally do not exceed 750 points in the entire evaluation. In assessing the case, strengths are usually easy to identify. However, students will typically have a difficult time with the "Areas for Improvement." These generally represent issues in which the applicant does not fully address the scope or nature of the criteria: issues that are not clear, or are missing from the response. Remember, the criteria are nonprescriptive. Thus, comments should not suggest specific approaches but relate to failure to fully address the criteria items.

CASE STUDY

Table of Contents

CASE STUDY

Overview

History and Nature of Our Business

Colony Fasteners, Inc. (CFI), is the world leader in the design and manufacture of fasteners. It has a distinguished history as the oldest fastener manufacturer in the United States, steeped in tradition dating back to 1877. The company started as a supplier of bolts, screws, rivets, and staples to the U.S. Army in the decade after the Civil War ended. Its original founders were two brothers, James and Thomas Pote, who served in the war as armorers. During their service, they were constantly frustrated with the quality and durability of the fasteners used for the artillery and undercarriages. They saw the need to supply a higher quality product to the Army and mobilized around the opportunity. With their background, experience, and service connections, they founded Colony Fasteners in Philadelphia, Pennsylvania.

The two brothers began the business with a credo founded in quality.

To All Customers, We Promise Service, Satisfaction, and Value.

To this day, this credo hangs in every CFI location worldwide. They instilled this spirit into employees, customers, and suppliers from the very beginning, believing that if they, and all their employees, lived true to these words, a successful enterprise would emerge. Today's business success is living testament that their vision was clear.

Originally, the product lines were limited to the types of fasteners used by the Army. Quickly they expanded their products as new markets and customers were identified. Significant opportunities occurred in supplying the U.S. Navy's shipyards in Philadelphia and the surrounding areas. The company saw rapid growth with the defense building booms during the many wars and conflicts.

Significant growth occurred after World War II and during the Korean War. Offshore expansion began utilizing the tremendous leverage of inexpensive labor and facilities. Product lines grew when business segmentation began to occur. In the mid-'50s, CFI reorganized, establishing three significant business sectors: Consumer Products, Commercial and Automotive, and Defense and Aerospace. Each sector served a very distinct market. Customer segmentation occurred with new approaches to customer satisfaction emerging. Strong partnerships had been forged with the various branches of the defense establishment; ties to the automotive industry were deeply rooted; and CFI was leading the

commercial market. Figure 0.2 shows how CFI is segmented according to business markets. Included in the business segments is the Corporate Support Sector, which is the organizational unit responsible for all corporate functions, such as Information Systems and Human Resources.

The Nuclear and Specialty sector was established in the late '50s with the advancement of the nuclear power industry and requirements for exotic materials and manufacturing processes. It was also the expansion of the aerospace environment that drove the requirement for special types of fastener devices that included explosive components and special processing. Fasteners with strain gages embedded in the products were introduced by CFI.

During the '50s, CFI took a hard look at how it addressed its customers' needs. There were many staff members that had seen the successes of process control and began exploring new methods of process improvement and control. They were early converts of the teachings emerging from the universities and technology-based companies. During these years, many engineers and managers versed in quality principles, who are today's quality leaders and visionaries, were brought in to teach and share process improvement methodologies.

The '60s and '70s were business heydays. Growth was dramatic, with the defense and automotive sectors leading the contributions. Technology advancements were happening at blinding speed. Up to this time, CFI was a privately held company. In 1972, with growth and expansion driving the corporate direction, CFI went public on the New York Stock Exchange (NYSE symbol – CFI).

This was also a time when some of the customer focus was lost. The demands of new technology, growth and new market development, and the rapid expansion of the defense and aerospace business put a veil in front of the customer awareness. CFI lost ground relative to its customer satisfaction levels.

In the mid-'80s, it became apparent that something had happened. Customers were no longer first in the list of critical business priorities — or at least, so it seemed. Senior management at CFI stood back, reflected on the company's roots and determined that if this course continued, it would lose entirely its eroding market position. Ultimately, the company could suffer irreparable damage.

Senior management defined the elements of change in how the company would operate. Customers would again be placed first and foremost in everything employees do. Some of the old approaches to customer satisfaction were reinstalled. The notion of "Back to Basics" began to drive the company the way it was originally founded. These changes fortunately occurred in the mid-'80s. CFI's customers noticed the change in how they were being serviced and how their needs were again a driving force in the business relationships.

Customer Base

CFI's customer base is worldwide and extends from prime contractors for spacecraft manufacture to the average homeowner using its products to repair a lawnmower.

Each sector at CFI has a major customer base that it supplies. A brief description follows:

Consumer Products Sector — major customers include a large base of distributors, wholesalers, jobbers, and retail outlet chains.

Commercial and Automotive Sector — the major automotive manufacturers around the world are customers of CFI. The largest users of CFI products include the "Big 3" in the U.S. and the "Big 2" in Japan. Most of the smaller manufacturers in the U.S., Europe, South America, and Japan are also consumers of the same products supplied the major automotive manufacturers.

Defense and Aerospace Sector — literally all manufacturers of airframe, spacecraft and defense products purchase or contract CFI fabricated fasteners. Because the products are so specialized in construction and require extensive testing and qualification, CFI dominates this market.

Nuclear and Specialty Sector — there are few manufacturers in this market to contest CFI's presence. Most manufacturers of defense related aircraft use CFI products from this sector (e.g., explosive bolts for ejection systems). The nuclear power market is well served by the products from CFI. They are in almost all nuclear installations around the world.

Major Markets Served by CFI

Today, CFI is strong, reflecting a growth pattern that is unparalleled in its industry. The company is represented in all major industrialized countries in the world with manufacturing locations spanning from Asia to South, Central, and North America, and to European-Economic Community (EEC) countries.

Products range from exotic to ordinary. CFI has products sitting on the moon, embedded in spacecraft heading out of this solar system, and holding together deep sea mining equipment 20,000 feet below the ocean's surface. Explosive products are included in most aircraft life-critical pilot ejection systems and in 85% of all automotive passive airbag restraint

systems. Each and every nuclear reactor in the U.S. and most in the free world have CFI fasteners at critical locations in their systems. The defense sector provides fasteners to all branches of the U.S. military and most of the armies of the free world. CFI fasteners are used in critical locations from the compressor turbines of jet engines to the wheel studs supporting most of the rolling armament around the world. The ordinary products include pins, bolts, nuts, rivets, and screws used to assemble a wide variety of household products, from refrigerators and lawn mowers to cabinet hinges.

CFI's markets are segmented into 4 distinct sectors. Each sector serves a worldwide customer base that is serviced by a network of distributors, wholesalers, jobbers, and retail sales outlets. The four sectors are:

Consumer Products Sector — designs and manufactures simple screws, rivets, pins, and bolts of inexpensive materials and are sold at low cost for all types of uses.

Commercial and Automotive Sector — designs and manufactures fasteners used in industrial products and by all major automotive manufacturers.

Defense and Aerospace Sector — designs and manufactures high quality, high performance fasteners for special products used in airframe, spacecraft and defense products.

Nuclear and Specialty Sector — designs and manufactures fasteners for nuclear reactors, fusion devices and radiation hardened products. Also includes fasteners of extremely complicated design, materials, and applications like explosive bolts for ejection systems on fighter aircraft.

Quality Requirements

CFI's visibility occurred before the extensive scandal erupted concerning counterfeit bolts and fasteners illicitly distributed throughout the industry. It helped to prevent serious tainting of CFI's reputation. The scandal was a wake-up call to the industry and its customer base. CFI used this opportunity to further its already established reemergence of customer orientation. The scandal drove Congressional passage of the Fastener Quality Act of 1990 (FQA) for new regulations in the industry and placed a pall over all suppliers in varying degrees. Many of the data included in this application reflect this turbulent time in the industry.

Four years ago, a major customer initiated the need for suppliers to be oriented to the Malcolm Baldrige National Quality Award (MBNQA) Criteria, and CFI began proliferating the six sigma approach to its supplier base. This reinforced and placed further emphasis on CFI's process controls which had already begun in the '50s. Six sigma is now used in mainstream product production, support services, business services, and outreach to CFI's supplier base.

Position in the Industry

CFI is the leader in our industry. Because it has been in existence since the late 1800s, many strong bonds have been established between it and its customers. These bonds and partnerships contribute to its position in the industry. In many areas of the industry, CFI has hundreds of competitors, such as the Consumer Products sector. Most of these competitors are small and have a limited life span of five to 10 years. In the Commercial and Automotive areas CFI is a leader, but has strong competition from off-shore manufacturers supplying competitive products at very low prices. Some of these competitors have been in business for a very long time and have demonstrated their staying power. They are the ones offering the greatest challenge to maintaining and growing our current market share position. CFI has been supplying the defense industry for over 100 years and has clearly demonstrated in this market its willingness to meet ever changing and very demanding requirements. While there are many competitors, most of them are short lived and are driven through contract awards. CFI is the largest U.S. supplier of products to this market segment. Nuclear and Specialty sector products are driven, almost exclusively, by contracted specification and requirements. CFI has few competitors in this market segment. It has the leadership position in a small field of specialty fastener manufacturers. Often, the small manufacturer accepts a contract for specialty products then subcontracts the work to CFI because of our manufacturing capabilities and demonstrated design knowledge.

Employee Base

CFI has a unique culture, one that is recognized throughout the world by its customers and competitors alike. It is open, communicative, and constructively challenging. Employees openly talk and challenge each other. Managers and executives seek to ensure the highest quality products, in the least amount of time, and with the highest value for the customer. It is the highest embodiment of an "open door policy" seen in our benchmarking efforts on human resources and organizational development. Teams are actively involved throughout the world, driving CFI to excellence with a minimum of organizational barriers.

Figure 0.1 shows the growth, in terms of employees since the company's formation in the late 1870's. The

shift to off-shore labor is responsible for the transition between the U.S. and non-U.S. workers. The employee base at CFI contains hourly, salary non-exempt, and salaried contributors (approximately 61%, 18%, and 21% respectively). Most hourly workers have completed high school or its equivalent (92%). A large percentage (56%) of the salary non-exempt have some college education, a two-year degree or technical school credentials. Salaried employees have an expectation of being college graduates. While the majority of them have bachelors (83%), masters (32%), and doctorate degrees (14%), the small number (17%) are actively pursuing their academic goals using CFI's education support package.

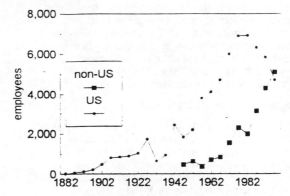

Figure 0.1, Employee Growth History

Today's employees live a common vision while driving for higher levels of performance. The original credo of the two brothers forms the basis for all actions, internally and externally.

Major Equipment, Facilities and Technologies

World headquarters is in Philadelphia with manufacturing locations worldwide including (by sector): Consumer Products (Juarez, Mexico; Sao Paulo, Brazil; Xiang, China; El Paso, TX); Commercial and Automotive (Dearborn, MI; Milwaukee, WI; Macon, GA; Jacksonville, FL; Oyama, Japan; Nagoya, Japan); Defense and Aerospace (Philadelphia, PA; Santa Ana, CA; Los Angeles, CA; Boston, MA); and Nuclear and Specialty (Los Angeles, CA; Philadelphia, PA; Salt Lake, UT [specializing only in explosive fasteners]; and Berlin, Germany). Other locations include sales offices in most major U.S. cities and significant cities around the world, a regulatory office in Washington D.C., and regional sales hubs (East Coast office is Philadelphia, PA; West Coast office is Los Angeles, CA; Great Lakes office is Detroit, MI; Southeast office is Dallas,

CASE STUDY

TX: Asia/Pacific office is Tokyo, Japan; Europe office is Calais, France). Note that the majority of employees assigned to a sales hub are located out of small offices and their homes to more conveniently locate them with their customers.

Supplier Base

CFI's supplier base is predominately composed of raw material suppliers and distributors. They supply materials such as wire, rod and bar stock, explosive components, and lubricants. Many supplier additionally provide the materials and equipment needed to turn the raw materials into sellable products. These include: cutting tools, small and large manufacturing equipment, protective equipment for the employees, and equipment used to test and evaluate the quality of the finished products. Some services are contracted by CFI such as maintenance, cafeteria, health services, and temporary workforce employees. Each supplier is expected to perform according to contract. They are measured and managed using these contract expectations.

Regulatory Environment

CFI is in a highly regulated industry in some market segments. Because it supplies products to the defense, aerospace, and nuclear market it is bound by a wide variety of requirements and regulations associated with each one. Additional regulations and requirements are imposed on CFI for the products it manufactures and markets outside of the United States.

Environmental regulations and requirements are similar to most manufacturing operations. CFI is regulated on the amount and type of effluents and waste discharge, safety considerations for its workers, and community safety activities.

There are some unique regulations and requirements imposed on the Salt Lake facility due to its processing of explosive materials. These include employee and community safety, testing and evaluation operations, and registration of some devices with bureaus of the U.S. and foreign governments.

Other Factors

The corporation started a profit-sharing program with its employees in the late 1980s. The approach annually splits corporate profits over a specified profitability value, pending a Board of Directors review: 50% for the corporation and 50% for the employees. The worldwide employee base shares equally in the division of its 50%.

In today's daily operations CFI is always focused on the future, especially in terms of customer needs and expectations and operational results. Throughout this application this is evident in the graphs, tables, and figures. Many of these show 1995 values: these represent the best foresight of the 1995 expected results.

CASE STUDY

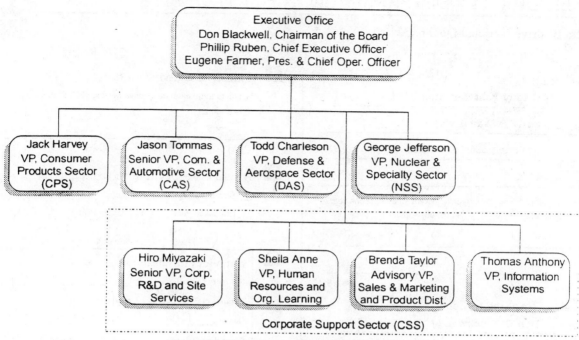

Figure 0.2, Senior Management Organization

CASE STUDY

1995 ELIGIBILITY DETERMINATION FORM *Page 1 of 7*

Malcolm Baldrige National Quality Award

1 Applicant

Name   Colony Fastener, Inc. (CFI)

Address   3147 S. Naval Way

Philadelphia, PA 22222

USA

Has the applicant officially or legally existed for at least one year?
(Check one.) X Yes ___ No (Briefly explain.)

2 Highest-Ranking Official

Name   Don C. Blackwell

Title   Chairman of the Board

Address   3147 S. Naval Way

Philadelphia, PA 22222

USA

Telephone No. (215) 555-3289

3 For-Profit Designation

Is the applicant a for-profit business?
(Check one.)   X Yes ___ No

4 Size of Applicant

Total number of employees ____ 9941 ____

Percent employees in the U.S. and/or territories ____ 56 ____

Percent physical assets in U.S. and/or territories ____ 73 ____

Total number of sites ____ 21 ____

Sales Preceding Fiscal Year *(Check one.)*
___ 0-$1M   ___ $10M-$100M   X $500M-$1B
___ $1M-$10M   ___ $100M-$500M   ___ Over $1B

5 Industrial Classification

List up to three most descriptive two-digit SIC Codes
(See page 28.)

____ 33 ____   ____ 34 ____   _____

6 Award Category / Pilot Program (Check one.)

X Manufacturing ___ Service   ___ Small Business

___ Education Pilot   ___ Healthcare Pilot

7 Supplier and Dealer Networks

Number of Suppliers ____ 788 ____

Number of External Sales Organizations:

Dealers ____ 0 ____   Distributors ____ 0 ____

Franchises ____ 0 ____   Other (Type/Number) ____ 0 ____

8 Percent Customer Base

Is over 50% of the sales of the applicant to customers outside of the applicant's organization, its parent company, or other companies with financial or organizational control of the applicant or parent company? (Check one.)

X Yes ___ No (Briefly explain.)

OMB Clearance #0693-0006
Expiration Date: June 30, 1997

This form may be copied and attached to, or bound with, other application materials.

Malcolm Baldrige National Quality Award

9 | Site Listing and Descriptors

a. Address of Site	b. Relative Size Percent of Applicant's		c. Description of Products or Services
	Employees	Sales	
Philadelphia, PA 3147 S. Naval Way	8.2%	11.4%	Headquarters, design, manufacture (defense, aerospace, nuclear, specialties), and sales hub (includes small offices and home-based offices)
El Paso, TX 103 E. 93rd Avenue	0.9%	3.3%	Design, manufacturing (consumer)
Dearborn, MI 651 Ford Place	9.2%	13.6%	Design, manufacturing (automotive)
Milwaukee, WI 9210 Riverview Industrial Park	2.1%	11.1%	Design, manufacturing (commercial, automotive)
Macon, GA 1142 W. Front Street	4.1%	4.2%	Manufacturing (commercial)
Jacksonville, FL 1616 E. Airport Place	2.9%	5.0%	Manufacturing (commercial)
Santa Ana, CA 13421 S. Edinger Avenue	7.8%	5.2%	Manufacturing (aerospace)
Los Angeles, CA 8190, 8192, & 8211 E. Freeway	17.7%	12.1%	Design, manufacturing (defense, aerospace), sales hub
Boston, MA 111 Loop Drive	0.8%	0.9%	Design, manufacturing (defense)
Salt Lake City, UT 10 CFI Circle	1.7%	2.0%	Manufacturing (specialty-explosive type)
Detroit, MI 938 W. Center Avenue	0.6%	0.0%	Sales hub (includes small offices and home-based sales offices)
Dallas, TX 4247 El Rancho Court	0.5%	0.0%	Sales hub (includes small offices and home-based sales offices)
Washington, DC 601 W. 3rd Street	<0.1%	0.0%	Regulatory office

1Provide all the information for each site except *where multiple sites produce similar products or services For such multiple site cases, see page 11.*

This page may be copied and attached to, or bound with, other application materials.

ix

Malcolm Baldrige National Quality Award

9 Site Listing and Descriptors

a. Address of Site	b. Relative Size — Percent of Applicant's		c. Description of Products or Services
	Employees	Sales	
Foreign Locations Juarez, Mexico Sao Paulo, Brazil Xiang, China Oyama, Japan Nagoya, Japan Berlin, Germany Tokyo, Japan Calais, France	43.4%	31.2%	Manufacturing and sales hubs

1 Provide all the information for each site except where multiple sites produce similar products or services. For such multiple site cases, see page 11.

This page may be copied and attached to, or bound with, other application materials.

x

10 Business Factors

Provide a brief description of the following key business factors:

a. Nature of the applicant's business (products, services, and technologies); conclude with a list of major competitors

Products range from the bland to the exotic. CFI has products sitting on the moon, embedded in spacecraft heading out of this solar system, and holding together deep sea mining equipment 20,000 feet below the ocean's surface. Explosive products are included in most aircraft life-critical pilot ejection systems and in 85% of all automotive passive airbag restraint systems. Each and every nuclear reactor in the U.S., and most in the free world, have CFI fasteners at critical locations in their systems. The defense sector provides fasteners to all branches of the U.S. military structure and most of the armies of the free world. The fasteners are used in critical locations from the compressor turbines of jet engines to the wheel studs support most of the rolling armament around the world. The sublime products include pins, bolts, nuts, rivets and screws used to hold together a large variety of household products, from refrigerators to lawn mowers to cabinet hinges.

Major competitors include:
- Special Performance Products (SPP)
- Critical Life Components, Inc. (CLC)
- Worldwide Pins Corp. (WP)
- Top Flight Hardware, Inc. (TFH)

Major customers include:
- Big 3 U.S. Automotive Mfgrs.
- Big 2 Japanese Automotive Mfgrs.
- All major airframe manufacturers
- Top defense contractors and their tiered sub-contractors

b. Nature of major markets (local, regional, national and international); conclude with a list of major customers

CFI's markets are segmented into 4 distinct sectors. Each sector serves a worldwide customer base that is serviced by a network of distributors, wholesalers, jobbers and retail sales outlets. The four sectors are:

Consumer Product Sector — designs and manufactures simple screws, rivets, pins, and bolts of inexpensive costs.

Commercial and Automotive Sector — designs and manufactures fasteners used in industrial products and by all major automotive manufacturers.

Defense and Aerospace Sector — designs and manufactures high quality, high performance fasteners for special products used in airframe, spacecraft and defense products.

Nuclear and Specialty Sector — designs and manufactures fasteners for nuclear reactors, fusion devices and radiation hardened products. Also includes fasteners of extremely complicated design, materials, and applications like explosive bolts for ejection systems on fighter aircraft.

Malcolm Baldrige National Quality Award

10 **Business Factors** (Continued)

c. Importance of suppliers, dealers, distributors, and franchises; conclude with a list of major suppliers

Suppliers are critical to CFI's ability to satisfy customer needs and expectations. The large percentage of the invested cost of CFI's products is the raw material used for fabrication. Suppliers are included in product design, validation, qualification, and analysis of field failures.

CFI uses a worldwide network of distributors, wholesalers, jobbers and retail sales outlets to move its products from manufacturing to actual usage. This delivery chain is vital to CFI success. Through several forums and types of communication vehicles, their inputs are used to improve the delivery cycle, increase customer satifaction and improve profitability for every link in the delivery chain.

Major suppliers include:
- Southern States Steelmill
- Tilken Steel Supply
- Alacon Aluminum Foundry
- Nippon National Mill
- Precise Explosive Corporation
- Wilmont Wire, Inc.
- Northern Rod & Bar Distributor

11 **Subsidiary Designation**

Is applicant a subsidiary, business unit, division, or like organization? ___Yes (Continue) __X__ No (Go to Item 12.)

a. Parent Company

Name _____

Address _____

_____

_____

Highest Official _____

Title _____

Number of worldwide employees of the

parent company _____

b. Does applicant comprise over 25% of the worldwide employees of the parent company? (Check one.)

___Yes ___No

c. Does the applicant consist of more than 50% of the worldwide sales of the parent company? (Check one.)

___Yes ___No

d. Is the applicant's parent company or another subsidiary of the parent company intending to apply? (Check one.)

___Yes (Briefly explain.) ___No ___Don't know

11 **Subsidiary Designation** (Continued)

e. Name the document supporting the subsidiary designation.

_____

_____

Include a copy of the document with this application. See instructions on page 12 for limit on materials to be submitted.

f. Briefly describe the organizational structure and management links to the parent company.

g. Do other units within the parent company provide similar products or services? (Check one.)

___Yes (Briefly explain.)   ___ No

h. Briefly describe the major business support functions provided to the applicant by the parent company or by other units of the parent company.

12 Ownership by a Holding Company

Is the applicant owned by a holding company?
___Yes (Continue)   X No (Go to Item 13.)

a. Holding Company

Name _____

Address _____

_____

_____

Highest Official _____

Title _____

b. Is the holding company or another unit of the holding
company intending to apply? (Check one.)

___Yes (Briefly explain.) ___No ___Don't know

c. Briefly describe the organizational structure and
management links to the holding company.

d. Do other units within the holding company provide similar
products or services? (Check one.)

___Yes (Briefly explain.) ___No

13 Use of Supplemental Sections

Does the applicant have a single or related product and
service lines served by a single quality system?
X Yes (Go to Item 14.)   ___No (Continue)

a. Number of Supplemental Sections proposed

_____

b. Briefly describe which products and services are to be
included in the Application Report and in each
Supplemental Section.

13 Use of Supplemental Sections (Continued)

14 Fee (See page 3 for instructions.)

Enclosed is $ 50.00 to cover the eligibility determination.

Make check or money order payable to:

The Malcolm Baldrige National Quality Award

15 Eligibility Inquiry Point

Name Sheila Anne

Title VP, Human Resources & Organizational Learning

Mailing Address 3147 S. Naval Way

Philadelphia, PA 22222

Overnight
Mailing Address SAME

Telephone No. (215) 555-1713

Telefax No. (215) 555-2004

16 Signature, Authorizing Official

X *Don C. Blackwell*   Date March 1, 1995

Name Don C. Blackwell

Title Chairman of the Board

Address 3147 S. Naval Way

Philadelphia, PA 22222

USA

Telephone No. (215) 555-3289

DO NOT WRITE BELOW THIS LINE

Note: This form will be returned to you with the eligibility determination indicated below. An approved 1995 Eligibility Determination Form must be submitted as part of each copy of the 1995 Application Package.

☒ Manufacturing   ☐ Education Pilot
☐ Service   ☐ Healthcare Pilot
☐ Small Business   ☐ Ineligible

Eligible
3/10/95
James Harris

For Official Use Only

CASE STUDY
1995 APPLICATION FORM

Malcolm Baldrige National Quality Award

1 Applicant

Name Colony Fastener, Inc. (CFI)

Address 3147 S. Naval Way

Philadelphia, PA 22222

USA

2 Award Category/Pilot Program (Check one.)

X Manufacturing ___ Service ___ Small Business

___ Education Pilot ___ Healthcare Pilot

3 Highest-Ranking Official

Name Don C. Blackwell

Title Chairman of the Board

Address 3147 S. Naval Way

Philadelphia, PA 22222

USA

Telephone No. (215) 555-3289

4 Official Inquiry Point

Name Sheila Anne

Title VP, Human Resources & Organizational Learning

Mailing Address 3147 S. Naval Way

Philadelphia, PA 22222

Overnight Mailing Address SAME

Telephone No. (215) 555-1713

Telefax No. (215) 555-2004

5 Application Components

1995 Eligibility Determination Form with confirmation ___X___
(check)

1995 Application Report only ___X___
(check)

1995 Application Report and _____ Supplemental Sections
(number)

6 Fee (See page 3 for instructions.)

Enclosed is $ 4,000 to cover one
Application Report and ___X___ Supplemental Sections.

Make check or money order payable to:

The Malcolm Baldrige National Quality Award

7 Release Statement

We understand that this application will be reviewed by members of the Board of Examiners or the Pilot Evaluation Team. Should our company be selected for a site visit, we agree to host the site visit and to facilitate an open and unbiased examination.

We understand that the company must pay reasonable costs associated with a site visit. If our company is selected to receive an award, we agree to share information on our successful performance and quality strategies with other U.S. organizations.

8 Signature, Authorizing Official

Date **March 28, 1995**

X _Don C Blackwell_

Name Don C. Blackwell

Title Chairman of the Board

Address 3147 S. Naval Way

Philadelphia, PA 22222

USA

Telephone No. (215) 555-3289

OMB Clearance #0693-0006
Expiration Date: June 30, 1997

This form may be copied and attached to, or bound with, other application materials.

CASE STUDY

Glossary of Terms and Abbreviations

	Description
360˚ review	an employee's annual review process that uses data and information from management, peers, and subordinates
6 sigma, or 6σ	a statistical measurement and analysis process used to determine process capability

- A & B -

ANSI	American National Standards Institute
APAC	Asia-Pacific sales and marketing geographical region covering southeast Asia and the pacific rim
AR	action required, a notation for assigning and accepting responsibility for follow-up action
ASMF	American Society for Mechanical Fastening
ASQI	American Society for Quality Improvement
ASTP	American Society of Training Professionals
b'mark	shorthand nomenclature for benchmarking used in many graphs in figures throughout application
BIC	best-in-class
Benchmarking	process of identifying the best practices in a specific area and the levels of their resulting output
BKM	best known methods
BUM	business update meeting, a method used to periodically communicate key corporate messages

- C & D -

CA	corrective action
CAFD	computer-aided fastener design
CAM	Colony assessment methodology
CAP	corrective action plan
CAR	corrective action request
CAS	commercial and automotive sector
CBT	computer-based training
CEO	Chief Executive Officer
Certification	supplier qualification process

C/F	the concept and feasibility phase of the new product development process
CFC	chlorofluorocarbon
CFI	Colony Fasteners, Inc.
CFIAA	CFI Achievement Award; CFI's Nobel prize
CFIOPEC	CFI operations, philosophy, and economics; a course that all new employees must attend to accelerate their cultural acclimation to CFI
CFIQA	CFI Quality Award
CFIUS	CFI university system
CIS	corporate information system
CO	corporate objective
COB	Chairman of the Board
CODB	cost of doing business, a metric used for analyzing business success
COOP	Chief Operating Officer and President
COS	cost of sales, measure of productivity for direct labor
C_p	ratio between the full distribution of a process and its allowable specification limits
C_{pk}	the single sided ratio (worse case) between the one-sided distribution of a process and its allowable specification limits
CPD	customer promised date
CPS	Consumer Products Sector
CQE	customer quality engineer
CPR	cardiopulmonary resuscitation
CSA	current situation analysis, an approach to data and information aggregation and analysis
CSO	corporate strategic objective
CSR	customer service representative
CSS	corporate support sector
CTD	California technology development
Customer Window	an analytical tool which quantifies subjective data using two crossed axes and related scoring

CASE STUDY

Cycle Time   time it takes to complete a process from beginning to end

DAS   defense and aerospace sector

Design Rules   the detailed design requirements for CFI fastener products used during the new product design process

DFM   design for manufacturability

DFQR   design for quality and reliability

DMR   discrepant material report

DOC   Department of Commerce

DOD   Department of Defense

DOE   design of experiments

DPM   defects per million opportunities

- E & F -

EAP   employee assistance program

EBP   executive bonus plan

ECA   environmental compliance audit

ECBP   employee cash bonus plan

EDI   electronic data interchange

EHS   environmental, health, and safety

EIA   engineering information architecture

E-mail   electronic mail system

Empowerment   chartering employees to make important decisions and participate in key business decisions; based on the principle that employees know their job best and that decisions should be made at the lowest possible levels

EOL   end-of-life, the last phase of the product life cycle

EPA   Environmental Protection Agency

HRDS   human resources data system

ERT   emergency response team

EVT   the engineering and validation test phase of the new product development cycle

EO   executive office with triad leadership; consists of the COB, CEO, and COOP.

Fab   fabrication plant (manufacturing location)

Fastened Together   company newspaper

FDR   final design review

FQA   Fastener Quality Act, 1990

FDS   financial data system

FSE   field sales engineer

- G & H -

G&A   general and administrative

GPTW   great place to work, one of CFI's core values

GRP   graduate rotation program

GSS   general site services

HR   human resources

HRET   human resources evaluation team

- I, J, K & L -

IFI   Industrial Fastener Institute

IS   information systems

ISO 9000   an international set of standards for quality system elements

JIT   just-in-time; usually reserved for supplier-customer delivery processes

K-12   kindergarten through 12th grade, usually for corporate engagements with external primary schools

LAN   local area network

LPD   linked policy deployment

- M & N -

MBNQA   Malcolm Baldrige National Quality Award

MBO   management by objective

MBP   management by planning

MBTI   Myers-Briggs Type Indicator; a type of behavior analysis tool that describes preferred behaviors of the individual taking the instrument

MDS   marketing data system

MRB   material review board

MRC   management review committee

NAFTA   North American Free Trade Agreement

NASA   National Aeronautics and Space Agency

NCOS   non-cost of sales, measure of productivity for indirect labor

NDT   non-destructive testing

NIH   not-invented-here; a syndrome of constantly reinventing processes because the owner of the new process has to leave a new design

NRC Nuclear Regulatory Commission

NSS Nuclear and Specialty Sector

NVLAP National Voluntary Laboratory Accreditation Program

NWG natural work group

NWT natural work team

- O, P, Q & R -

ODC ozone depleting compound

ODS operations data system

OEM original equipment manufacturer

OSHA Occupational Safety and Health Administration

PAR product acceptance review

Partners several meanings: (1) customers; (2) suppliers; (3) internal customers/suppliers; (4) business engagements - domestic and foreign; and (5) government and regulatory agencies.

PAS performance against schedule

PCCP preferred customer certification program

PDR preliminary design review

PC personal computers, often nodes on a LAN

PDCA plan, do, check, act; a process used to methodically analyze a process and improve it

PDR preliminary design review

PDT product development team

PIT process improvement team

Plan the strategic, tactical, and operating plan that results from semi-annual execution of the MBP process

PLBP product line business plan

Plating an electrochemical process of coating one metal with another material, usually a different metal

PM preventative maintenance

PMA process maturity acceptance phase of the new product development process

POR plan of record; the annual financial operating plan

PRP peer recognition program

PTP pass through partnerships is an approach used to communicate lessons learned upstream and downstream

PVT process validation test

Q'Link an electronic communication vehicle used to communicate quality messages and plans around the world

QAT quality action team

QFD quality function deployment

QIT quality improvement team

QLS quality leadership system

QST quality steering team

R&D research and development

RCA root cause analysis

ROI return on investment

- S & T -

SAT safety awareness team

SBI safety bulletin incident

SCP supplier certification process

SCQI supplier continuous quality improvement

SCS supplier certification system

Sectors business units of the corporation: product sectors

SFE Society of Fastener Engineers

SIT safety improvement team

SLRP strategic long-range plan

SMDE single minute die exchange

SMP survey of management practices

SNE salaried non-exempt employees

SO strategic objective

SOR sector operations review

SPC statistical process control

SRS supplier rating system

Tactic one of the levels of a strategic plan as defined by MBP

TAM total available market

TDS technical data system

TESS training and education support system

CASE STUDY

Top Hat Award	recognition program at the local level within a business sector
Total Quality	performance to CFI corporate values
TQE	total quality excellence
TPT	throughput time

- U, V & W -

UMB	University Management Board
Upset	a process used to minimize material loss during fastener heading
USSR	United Soviet Socialist Republics
VA/NVA	value-add/non-value-add; an analysis tool that identifies non-value added activities
Values	six key concepts on which CFI behaviors are based
VOC	has two meanings: voice of the customer; and vendor of choice
VRP	vendor rating plans
WAN	wide-area-network

- X, Y & Z -

ZBB	zero-based budget, a process that determines which strategic plan elements are going to receive funding for the coming period

CASE STUDY

1.0 LEADERSHIP

1.1 Senior Executive Leadership

CFI customers increasingly expect world-class performance across the board in everything from product quality, delivery, service, support, and pricing.

In the corporation's early years of existence, the co-founding brothers instituted clear quality goals for CFI. Based primarily upon historic product knowledge, these goals drove early plans for making steady progress toward the best manufacturing performance possible. CFI's maturing focus on modern manufacturing methods, combined with efforts to strengthen product leadership and customer partnerships, led to today's dominant position. CFI is poised for tomorrow's challenges.

1.1.a(1) Creating and reinforcing values and expectations

From CFI's inception, senior executives held themselves responsible and accountable for the quest in being the best. Today, the senior staff drives the application of world-class goals and benchmarks, customer inputs, and third-party quality standards to the development and execution of business plans. Through quarterly visits with customers, suppliers, and partners around the world, senior executives gather data about CFI and world-class competition. Additionally, CFI's senior executives and their direct reports conduct monthly and weekly meetings with customers to collect information about customer satisfaction levels and to stay current on customer recognized world-class standards.

Since the very beginning, CFI's unwavering credo has been:

To All Customers, We Promise Service, Satisfaction, and Value.

This is translated into CFI's mission, to do an outstanding job for shareholders, customers, and employees. Each group represents a distinct set of interests and expectations that are kept in balance by CFI's senior executives for sustained success. Shareholders expect a fair return on their investment. Customers expect advanced performance solutions with superior quality and service, competitive pricing, on-time delivery, and organizational responsiveness. Employees expect challenging jobs, the means to be successful, and recognition for their contributions and accomplishments.

To ensure that CFI achieves its mission and serves these unique interests, a dynamic foundation of corporate values and key business strategies has been established by CFI's senior executives. The values describe how the company's employees act, and the strategies define what business goals they will aggressively pursue.

There is constancy of purpose and clarity of vision in CFI's values. They are slightly adjusted on a periodic schedule to maintain behavioral balance as the company matures. Today, CFI has six values that represent its corporate culture — ones that define how its employees behave and what customers can expect in its employee's performance. Table 1.1.1 shows the values, what they mean to the leadership team, and the behaviors that are expected of management and employees alike.

Five key business strategies have been developed by the leadership team to continuously challenge CFI to meet customer's requirements. In other parts of this application, these will also be identified as the corporate objectives, especially as they are used for the strategic planning process.

These are reviewed and changed annually according to the business needs and challenges. They form the core of CFI's strategic plan. They are:

➤ To deliver products to customers on time and defect free (6 sigma levels).

➤ To be recognized as the producer of highest value fasteners.

➤ To be the technology leader in the introduction of revolutionary fastener products.

➤ To protect the environment at all worldwide locations and set benchmark levels of compliance.

➤ To be recognized as number one in employee satisfaction at all worldwide locations.

Total quality at CFI means performance according to its values, business strategies, and customer requirements. Performance to its values allows creation of a total quality environment and performance of a great job for customers. Performance to its business strategies keeps the company focused on doing the right things and supports its mission of doing a great job for CFI shareholders. To do a great job for customers, CFI strives to perform effectively and responsively to all of their requirements.

Senior executives continuously monitor and reinforce performance to company values through feedback from employees, operations reviews, performance reviews, internal assessment processes, customer feedback, third-party surveys and assessments,

CASE STUDY

Table 1.1.1, CFI Values and Behaviors

Value (It means to us ...)	Behaviors (We strive to ...)
Results - We are results oriented.	Set challenging goals; Execute flawlessly; Focus on output; Assume responsibility; Confront and solve problems.
Risk Taking - To succeed we must maintain our innovative environment.	Embrace change; Challenge the status quo; Listen to all ideas and viewpoints; Encourage and reward informed risk taking; Learn from our successes and mistakes.
Customer Orientation - Partnerships with our customers and suppliers are essential to our mutual success.	Listen to our customers; Communicate mutual intentions and expectations; Deliver innovative and competitive products and services; Make it easy to work with us; Serve our customers through partnerships with our suppliers.
Quality - Our business requires the continuous improvement of our performance to our Mission and Values.	Set challenging and competitive goals; Do the right things right; Continuously learn; Develop and improve; Take pride in our work.
Great Place To Work - A productive and challenging work environment is key to our success.	Respect and trust each other; Be open and direct; Work as a team; Maintain a safe workplace; Recognize and reward accomplishments; Be an asset to the community; Have fun!
Discipline - The complexity of our work and tough business environment demands a high degree of self-discipline and cooperation.	Properly plan, fund, and staff projects; Pay attention to detail; Clearly communicate intentions and expectations; Make and meet commitments; Conduct business with uncompromising integrity and professionalism.

independent external surveys, and ongoing training. Examples of these include:

➤ In 1994 CFI, conducted its biannual worldwide employee survey to measure performance to corporate-wide values. Several changes were made by the leadership team due to the feedback of survey respondents, including:
  ● Simplifying the description of company values;
  ● Modifying CFI's performance appraisal system;
  ● Changing some of the basic employee training; and
  ● Improving the strategic planning system.

➤ All levels of management are retrained every year in developing and delivering annual performance reviews for all employees. This training includes guidelines for measuring employee performance to the six values.

➤ CFI actively seeks customer information on how well it is performing to its values. Focus teams use a common assessment instrument to regularly conduct a self-audit program.

➤ Independent external surveys also provide key data used in monitoring CFI's performance to customer requirements. In a recent *Industry Age* survey released in January 1995, commercial and automotive customers rated CFI as number one among all suppliers in quality, reliability, product line coverage, and company reputation.

➤ Third-party assessments are typified in the use and interpretation of the MBNQA Criteria as they relate to CFI's business. As seen in Figure 1.1.2, CFI adopted the MBNQA model and realigned the elements to better match its culture, behaviors and business operations. CFI actively uses local, state, and national award programs as a forum to invite experts into its organizations to assess and respond to its systems.

➤ Performance is monitored through extensive surveys on company values. This ongoing focus provides feedback on how well the values are role modeled and the extent to which they drive day-to-day activities.

1.1.a(2) Setting directions and performance goals

The senior management team at CFI drives the corporation in strategic directions using a wide variety of approaches. As a market leader, it is vital to set clear directions, ones that strategically drive to new levels of customer satisfaction, product quality, and operational results.

The approaches used by the senior leadership team include:

➤ Active customer relationships used to derive the next set of expectations and insights into where the marketplace is heading.

➤ Sponsorship of critical benchmark studies, ones that bring into the corporation unique approaches that would contribute to improvements at the sector and corporate levels.

➤ Review of competitive intelligence assembled using a formal data and information gathering methodology that strives to reinforce the company's belief in ethical behavior.

➤ Evaluation of governmental directions acquired via the dedicated office in Washington, DC, and at other key DOD and NASA locations.

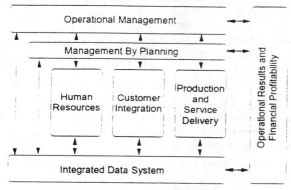

Figure 1.1.2, CFI Business Model

The CFI approach to strategic planning is explained in greater detail in Item 3.1, but an introduction here aids understanding of the planning and review cycle. Management By Planning (MBP) is the CFI approach for policy deployment. It is a top-down, cascaded, and validated approach that identifies the critical strategic objectives, strategies, tactics, and projects required to secure continued corporate success. Data and information inputs about CFI's current situation integrate with key organizational management structures into short- and long-range plans (Figure 3.1.1). Using the notion of cascaded reviews (Figure 3.1.5), communication of the strategic and tactical plans is transferred to all layers of the organization. The strategic plans enable any employee, whether a manager or individual contributor, to look upward into the plan to its sponsoring objectives or downward into the plan to identify the activities enabling success. The structure of the plans contain owners, leading or lagging indicators, and goals for success. These are used at all reviews as a common platform.

1.1.a(3) Reviewing company performance

Senior executives are intimately involved in measurement, assessment, and review of all facets of CFI operations. They actively participate in periodic reviews at the corporate and sector level. They drive reviews of new proprietary product development programs for high profile customers. All of this information is used to manage the business sectors for higher yields and increased contributions to market share growth.

If a business sector or geography shows a decline in performance, the senior manager teams with key leaders in the organization to identify units requiring improvement. They ensure that adequate steps are taken to accelerate continuous improvement and reverse the worsening conditions. In many instances, they collect specialists from other parts of the operation to focus on the opportunity and deliver appropriate solutions. CFI is a highly matrixed and networked organization that mobilizes quickly when needed. Figure 1.1.3 shows a high-level mapping of cross-functional support from organizations within the Corporate Support sector with the business sector organizations. Organizational barriers are minimized using philosophies centered on the six values, especially quality, customer orientation, and results. Issues are always driven to closure using the lowest possible levels of employees. CFI recognizes that employees embedded in the affected operation often know more about the root cause than outsiders. CFI utilizes this advantage as corrective action teams are assembled. There are times when problems cut across sector boundaries, or impact the entire corporation, that require members of the executive office to actively participate in problem resolution.

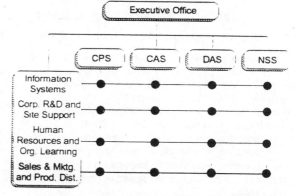

Figure 1.1.3, Cross-Functional Support Organization

CASE STUDY

1.1.b *Evaluate and improve the leadership system*

At CFI the senior leadership team actively reviews its approaches to lead, plan, and provide strategic guidance. CFI seeks to identify its best leaders and to drive improvements into the management system and its players. There are several methods used to provide insight into how well the managers are performing. These include the following:

➤ A 360° review of all senior managers on an annual basis. Inputs are derived from subordinates, peers, and superiors. At the executive office level, this includes semi-annual review by designated members of the Board of Directors (BOD). Annual reviews of the entire senior management team are conducted by the BOD in conjunction with the annual corporate financial review.

➤ Employee surveys are performed biannually with 100% of the corporation participating. Contained in the survey are cross-referenced questions targeted at determining the effectiveness of company leadership.

➤ System effectiveness assessments using various models are conducted on all sectors of the corporation. Contained in the instruments are areas that address the effectiveness of management approaches and the styles used by the leadership team.

➤ Many personality and behavior assessment tools are used to aid personal development of the senior management team and its individual members. Examples include the Myers-Briggs Type Indicator (MBTI), Survey of Management Practices (SMP) assessment, and Quality Leadership Surveys (QLS).

1.2 Leadership System and Organization

1.2.a *Organizational focus on the customers*

The CFI values drive the way all employees act and behave. One of the critical values is customer orientation. We use it to focus our energies on integrating our customers' needs throughout the organization. The entire management system, from planning and execution to individual performance review, includes key elements of customer needs and expectations - both internal and external. Because we have a cohesive approach to integrating our customers, we continue to increase our ratings and market share.

Another critical value is quality. Leading the implementation of that value is the setting of challenging and competitive goals. Pride in being the best has become instilled throughout our workforce Active comparisons and benchmarking have shown all levels in the organization how we compare and are used as the basis for setting targets which will result in CFI "being the benchmark" in all key areas.

In the process of cascading our goals throughout the organization, a key element in achieving the performance objectives is for each layer of the organization to take pieces of appropriate objectives. The organizations decide how much they can each contribute to the objectives so that the end result, when aggregated, will meet or exceed the objective.

Organizationally, our four major product sector structure enables us to focus those entire organizations on the unique requirements and expectations of their customers. Within each of those organizations, a mirroring of major customer organizations occurs whenever possible with dialog occurring at several levels between CFI and its counter-part customers.

1.2.b *Communication of values and expectations*

A wide range of communication activities are used to continually project quality values, objectives, goals, and expectations throughout the CFI organization. Among these are the following:

➤ New-hire orientation is frequently taught by senior management, providing all employees with a detailed presentation of the CFI values and what they mean to the senior leadership of the company.

➤ Management training courses and curriculums offer extensive information and experiential learning on applying and role modeling the CFI values. These courses are designed, in various forms, for all levels of managers.

➤ The CFI culture workshop is propagated throughout the organization and taught monthly for all new employees. It provides an in-depth presentation of the corporation's values, behaviors, and culture

➤ Business update meetings (BUMs) are quarterly meetings presented to all employees worldwide The agenda of these meetings is to openly communicate changes and the status of the corporation. Typical topics include the resurrection of Back-to-Basics, competitive threats, new product developments, and interpretations of CFI values in relation to recent business course changes.

➤ One-on-one meetings are core to CFI's culture, providing an opportunity for employees to raise issues important to them with their managers and supervisors. The schedule and agenda are set by the employees, with a guideline that these one-on-one meetings should occur at least monthly to maintain an open communication line.

➤ Informal communication sessions are used to disseminate our values. Examples of these informal meetings include open meetings by factory managers to communicate how they perceive and deploy our values. Business sector managers lead "open door days" that are used for individual employees to discuss their concerns and issues with the senior managers of their businesses.

➤ Printed media provide a formal method of communicating values, objectives, and goals. These include newsletters, posters, brochures, and magazines, all helping to promote better understanding of CFI values. Examples include: *Fastened Together*, which is the company's core magazine containing all types of messages; Voice of the Customer (VOC), which describes the customer perspective of our products and services; and *Q'Link*, which is the company's quality communication vehicle. Voicemail is used by the senior executive team to communicate real-time messages to all locations around the world using global broadcast capabilities.

1.2.c Performance reviews and assessment

CFI's business sectors and corporate support sector have systematic and disciplined approaches for reviewing performance to plans and goals. These include the following:

➤ Annual reviews which cover yearly performance and address long-range plans.

➤ Quarterly reviews focusing on cost review and performance to the annual plan.

➤ Monthly reviews analyzing CFI's performance to productivity, design, and annual plans and goals. These ensure that corrective actions are taken for opportunities identified in the weekly and daily reviews.

➤ Daily and weekly reviews targeting external customer input, internal quality results, and process corrective actions.

➤ Vendor of choice (VOC) reviews enabling management to monitor CFI's performance to customer requirements and expectations.

➤ Sector operation reviews (SOR) focusing on our performance to the annual plan and corporate plans at the business sector level.

Table 1.2.1, Operational Reviews

Type	Leader	Freq.
POR	All Mgrs.	Monthly
PAS	Program and Project Leaders	Monthly
PLBP	Product Mgrs.	Quarterly
SLRP	EO and Sector Mgrs.	2x/year
MBP	All Mgrs.	Monthly
Program	Program Mgrs.	Monthly
Project	Project Mgrs.	Per Plan
QST	EO	Quarterly
QIT	Sector Mgrs.	Monthly
QAT	Team Leaders	Per Plan
MRC	Team Leaders	Per Plan
Cust. Focus Mtg.	Sector and Program Mgrs.	Quarterly
Design Reviews	Program Mgrs.	Per Plan

Table 1.2.1 provides an insight into the types and frequencies of reviews, who typically participates, and who controls the agenda.

1.3 Public Responsibility and Corporate Citizenship

1.3.a(1) Risks, regulatory and legal requirements planning

CFI is engaged in an industry with heavy involvement of regulatory agencies, defense system accountabilities, and product liability considerations.

Regulatory agencies include the U.S. Departments of Commerce (DOC), Defense (DOD), and Environment, OSHA, EPA, Nuclear Regulatory Agency (NRC), state and local nuclear regulatory agencies, and foreign governmental agencies. A large part of CFI's revenue base comes from defense-related fastener production. Regulations involve the purchasing and overview infrastructures of all major defense contractors, other non-U.S. national defense departments, and industry regulations for defense products. Product liability considerations come from all product sector customers. The magnitude ranges from minimal financial impact to severe life-critical liability.

CASE STUDY

CFI uses several approaches to assess the risks inherent in our business. These include the formalized product and process risk assessments (used during the design process), new business financial return-on-investment (ROI) analysis, product market assessment, environmental risk evaluations and planning sessions, regulatory scenario simulations, business simulations, and product level "business wargame" simulations. These are integral to the new business acquisition and management process.

All inputs provide current situation analysis information for strategic planning sessions at various times throughout the year.

Of specific mention is the anticipated implementation of the Fastener Quality Act. CFI's planning process started with an analysis of the proposed regulations issued by the U.S. Department of Commerce. CFI has taken many actions to align our practices with the regulations and has a plan to implement the requirements of the final regulations.

1.3.a(2) Societal responsibilities for products and operations

CFI is extremely aware of its responsibility to the global society concerning its manufacturing process and its products. CFI strives to lead all competitors in each of the countries it operates in, regardless of the requirements, from the most lax to the most stringent.

Annually, in each sector, an environmental planning session is held where projections are made of emerging requirements for the 2, 5, and 10 year horizon.

CFI's processes are regularly reviewed with the goal to reduce costs, improve throughput, increase efficiency, and minimize the negative impact to its surrounding communities.

Specific considerations are given to the by-products of CFI's processes. The by-products include solid waste, scrap material, effluents, airborne contaminants, and ancillary waste products. Each site has a committee dedicated to reviewing the outputs in each area and the results of environmental planning sessions, and looking for ways to minimize the impacts. Examples include the Los Angeles (CA) site and the amount of reduction it has attained in the effluents it releases to the surrounding communities. At the Philadelphia (PA) site, they have reduced by over 300% the amount of solid waste being delivered to the local landfill. Regardless of the geographic locations of each site, CFI strives to be a leader in its community, geographic location, and the nation and,

wherever possible, drive business sectors to achieve and exceed the most stringent requirements.

1.3.a(3) Legal and ethical conduct

As part of its values, CFI expects all employees to conduct themselves with uncompromising integrity. A Code of Conduct Handbook is published, which is reviewed with all employees annually at their performance reviews. CFI conducts 4 hours of legal training on ethical behavior for all new employees, and over 40 hours are required for senior management, procurement personnel, customer contact employees, and project managers.

Evidence of the effectiveness of this training is the lack of any inquiries, challenges, or sanctions over the actions or conduct of any of our employees. This is especially noteworthy in light of the counterfeit fastener scandal that rocked the U.S. fastener industry in the late 1980s and the continued use of substandard (non-CFI) products in the foreign markets CFI serves.

1.3.b Community corporate citizenship

We recognize that our responsibility for quality excellence extends to the communities in which CFI does business. To promote a greater awareness of quality in partnership with public agencies and organizations, employees from CFI participate in a variety of programs. Among these are:

➤ CFI cosponsors the 45th Annual Fastener Reliability Testing Institute Conference at Bainmear University in California.

➤ Employees present a wide variety of papers at conferences around the world. In 1994, there were over 235 quality-oriented papers or significant presentations given at conferences, symposiums, and retreats. All employee efforts to participate in these activities are funded by CFI.

➤ CFI donates more than $500,000 in grants to local schools to support advancements in science, engineering, and technical vocations.

➤ CFI has been a principal sponsor of the Pennsylvania Quality Award. The CEO is on the Foundation's Board of Directors and three executives are members of the Board of Examiners.

CASE STUDY

2.0 INFORMATION AND ANALYSIS

2.1 Management of Information and Data

The CFI data system model is shown in Figure 2.1.1. At the core of the model is the worldwide data and information system and its five major database structures according to the sectors they support. Drawing data and information from the information system are the sectors, utilizing them to create unique applications and data structures. These, while unique, are accessible using various local area network and wide-area network technologies. The architecture and measurement of the effectiveness of this data system are the responsibility of the CSS Information Systems Group.

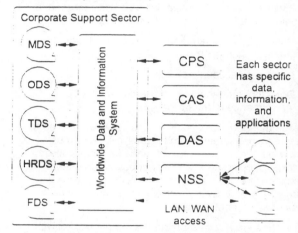

Figure 2.1.1, CFI Data System Model

2.1.a Selection of data

CFI recognizes that the selection of proper data is essential to manage, monitor, and control the total business. It is important to collect all necessary data but not to collect too much data which would overload the process and result in lack of focus and concentration on the essential issues.

Data collected are related to the four product sectors and the one corporate support sector and are structured to lead to excellence in the five key business strategies of the company. Senior management determines which top-level data should be common to uniformly drive the excellence in the five key business strategies across the corporation, and which should be unique to ensure excellence in the sectors.

Foremost in the data selection process is a customer focus. The data collected provide information to

reinforce the customer delight actions in each of the five business strategies.

The top-level data are decomposed to successively lower levels throughout the sectors down to the team level. Since employee involvement through teams is a key corporation strength, collection, analysis, and use of data at this level are the cornerstones to effectively managing by fact. The strong linkage of data up through all organizational levels enables appropriate action to be taken at the lowest possible level, as well as identification at all levels of connectivity and impacts to the five business strategies. From the team level upward, internal and external customers and suppliers are linked into the data stream to achieve the strong customer focus.

Benchmarking visits with process observations are utilized and adapted in the data selection and analysis review process as a vehicle to continually improve data management.

2.1.a(1) Types of data collected

Since the company depends heavily on process control of all products and support services, C_{pk}'s are prominent in the data items collected. This is true for both product-related as well as support service data. Some examples of the types of data collected are shown in Table 2.1.1. The sample data displayed are categorized in the business driver areas.

Each sector utilizes teams of concerned employees who are responsible for the selection of the data to be collected. These teams consist of users, developers, customers, suppliers, and Information Systems (IS) experts. They formally meet every Friday afternoon at 1:00 PM and hold informal meetings when special circumstances occur. The formal meetings are documented and ensure that each data task is often reviewed for continual improvement.

2.1.a(2) Reliability and access of data

Data reliability is ensured by several means. CFI realizes that if data used for analysis of processes are not the best, best results will not happen. Most of the data are collected by automatic means and directly filed in the data system to ensure reliability.

Software utilized within the data system is designed to analyze the data as it is collected and immediately provide a flag if a large or significant variation occurs or erroneous entrees are made. The flag alerts the operators to immediately review the situation as to the existence of poor data or a possible change in the process. The data teams regularly review the number of flags that occur for each data item. This reflects on both data collection and the actual process

CASE STUDY

performance. By flagging wide variations. erroneous data inputs are corrected. and this results in further data reliability.

Table 2.1.1, Business Related Driver Areas

Customer Related	Fig.
Response Time to Customer Queries	7.2.1
All Sector Customer Satisfaction	7.4.1
CAS Composite Customer Satisfaction	7.4.2
Technological Leader	7.4.5
CAS Customer Satisfaction	7.4.4
Customer Complaint Calls	7.4.6
Customer Retention	7.4.3
Product and Service Performance	
Percent Process Yield by Product	6.1.2
Type	6.1.1
Percent of Critical Processes $C_{pk} > 1.5$	6.1.3
Operations Yield	6.1.4
Warranty Returns	6.1.5
Customer Problems Resolved in 24	
Hours	6.1.6
On Dock Performance	
Internal Operations	
Operations Quality	6.2.3
Operational Productivity Non-Product	6.2.2
Product Design Cycle Time	6.2.8
Product Setup Cycle Time	6.2.9
Information Systems	6.2.10
Reduction in Solid Wastes	6.2.11
Employee Safety Record	6.2.13
Training Hours Per Employee	6.2.18
Employees Engaged in Teams	6.2.21
Corporate Citizenship Engagements	6.2.22
Supplier Performance	
Supplier Base Transitions	6.3.1
Supplier Receiving History	6.3.2
Certified Supplier Quality	6.3.3
Financial Performance	
Annual Sales Volume	6.2.5
Market Share	6.2.6
Profit Margin	6.2.7
Sector Gains and Losses in Market	7.5.5–
Share	7.5.8

Daily, IS personnel back up all the data to ensure that loss does not occur if power outages or other disruptions occur. Weekly IS personnel also verify data accuracy through the use of automatic diagnostic routines.

Data are managed on a companywide Information Systems network using PC terminals for local use and a centralized mainframe in Philadelphia connected by satellite links. The local PC terminals are linked in local area networks so that all employees have access to real-time data anywhere in the world. In all locations, a minimum of 90% of the employees have a PC terminal readily at hand. Thus, data are accurate and reliable, real-time, and readily accessible.

Passwords, updated monthly, and authorized entry lists are randomly checked to verify security.

2.1.b Improvement of the data system

Semiannually, a formal top-down data review occurs. Starting at senior management and cascading through all levels of the organization. including customers and suppliers, the following questions are asked:

➤ Has the current data enabled us to make decisions and set priorities?

➤ Is the data actionable?

➤ Does the data enable us to determine the performance of the process?

Recommended changes from these reviews are fed to a Data Management Team for analysis. This multi-functional team, composed of management, process teams, IS, customers, and key supplier personnel, using the five business strategies as a guide to ensure data continuity, makes appropriate changes in the data management system.

The formal data review process is supplemented with informal data updates by IS management teams (with representatives from all sectors) which result from benchmarks and the continuous improvement process. Figure 6.2.10 shows the improvements over the last ten years in the data systems.

2.1.b(1) Scope of information and data

In the data management team's formal analysis, as well as team activities within continuous improvement. one of the items addressed is whether the right data are reaching the right people. The teams analyze whether the results data show process outputs of importance to customers and whether in-process data enable prediction of output to gauge the performance of the process. Additionally, teams assess whether the recipients of the data are the appropriate persons for taking action on the data. As a means of canceling collection of data which is no longer of value, an additional consideration is: "Is this data being used?" CFI has found these analyses to be extremely valuable for ensuring that the right data gets to the right people while preventing data overload.

2.1.b(2) Use and analysis of data

With the aim of continual improvement of processes, improved C_{pk}'s are the desired result. However, the teams are continually refining the collection techniques to improve data reliability and timeliness as well as the effectiveness of the resulting data analysis.

At the top level of the company, Pareto and quadrant analyses are primary tasks at the team level. Cause-and-Effect Diagrams, the "5 Whys," and Pareto Charts are the most frequently used analysis tools.

The continuous improvement of C_{pk}'s across all functions, products, and support services is an indicator of the success of the process being utilized.

Figure 6.1.1 shows the improvement in the percent of critical processes exceeding a C_{pk} of at least 1.5.

A technique widely used among the team members is electronic mail (E-mail) where all members are in an ongoing communication link. Many times a team member comes to work in the morning to find a solution or a well-defined occurrence that can be utilized to improve a process by reducing variability and cycle time.

2.1.b(3) Feedback from users

At the weekly meetings of the teams responsible for the data to be collected, users not assigned to the team are invited on a random basis and anyone interested has an open invitation. These non-team members are solicited to express concerns and make suggestions as to methods to make the data more available and useful to them.

All process operators, and this includes support functions, utilize their PC terminals to communicate with the other team members by electronic mail with addresses pre-loaded by name and function. Thoughts that occur to them on an ongoing basis, regardless of the time of day or circumstances, are easily captured and recorded for review and action.

An address is available to all employees on E-mail soliciting comments on data timeliness, accuracy, and clarity.

Many employees have PCs at home that are networked to the company data systems. These employees were helped in the purchase of the equipment. The company paid one-half the purchase cost and arranged for the purchase through the company, which reduced the cost another 15% as a result of the buying leverage. Additionally, the company pays for a dedicated telephone line to the employee's home to enable unencumbered communication service.

With communication capabilities in place, comments are continually received by the data teams. Many comments by electronic mail are received during the night-shift operations from employees with ideas that occur at home.

The comment may be as simple as "I don't understand the data." Whatever the comment, appropriate actions are taken. These comments often result in actions by the teams to request training sessions either on-the-job or in the classroom if the situation appears to be widespread. Often the teams will do the training design and sometimes the training itself.

The data are collected for the convenience of the users. All data teams realize the purpose of their existence is to be responsive to the user and for the improved operations of the company resulting in a greater personal profit share for the accomplishment.

2.2 Competitive Comparisons and Benchmarking

2.2a How required information is selected

CFI has pursued an aggressive benchmarking process since 1989 when Xerox, a Malcolm Baldrige National Quality Award (MBNQA) winner, demonstrated its success in using the technique. Since that time, many metric comparisons have been made. Most importantly, process changes have been accomplished that have significantly reduced variability and simplified processes throughout the company.

Early in the benchmarking process, training courses were established that described the total concept with the desired results. The training included process mapping techniques and how to modify processes to result in superior performance in cycle time reduction, quality improvement, and reduced variability.

To emphasize the importance of this new concept, a formal activity was initiated called *Pass Through Partnerships* (PTP). This concept is also utilized in working with suppliers and is described further in Item 5.4.

PTP is a process where complete cooperation between companies is established, and information that is non-proprietary is openly shared. As the process has matured, the partners have revised what was considered to be proprietary after realizing more

CASE STUDY

is to be gained than lost in almost every information exchange.

The benchmarking activities were started in the Philadelphia headquarters. Quickly, responsibility was transferred to each of the four product sectors and corporate support sector, retaining a strong coordinating function to ensure full utilization of information access and to ensure focus on the real business issues. Each sector shares in the information gained by any of the sectors through the data systems.

The critical processes are identified during the strategic planning process and are continually monitored for continually improving results.

2.2.a(1) Needs and priority determination

The strategic planning process identifies areas of the business where competition is great and the market share is low. The planning process causes the businesses to review capabilities in comparison with competitors in the marketplace by collecting data primarily from public domain information. Analysis of this information is used in establishing goals and stretch targets and setting benchmark priorities.

The initial step in determining benchmark partnership needs is to make improvements in areas that will have the most immediate effect on the business or to provide a longer term capability that is necessary for continual growth.

The initial priority in benchmarking is to determine if the "best practice" is within one of the CFI sectors. If not, then outside benchmarking partners are searched for and found.

In the rapidly growing automotive market, the strategic plan indicated that the Commercial and Automotive Sector was not adequately responding to customer delivery demands of short-term increases in product quantities with little or no lead time. It was pointed out by the mutual customer that Hubler Electric was responsive in delivering electrical connectors overnight.

An arrangement with Hubler allowed a benchmarking team to review how the short-term increase was accomplished. The process was reviewed in detail. CFI's processes for storing and handling raw materials and the area layout were modified. Paperwork processes were also changed. CFI now can respond to doubling the delivery quantity on the next shift after a request, compared to what had been 14 days. This is one example of process improvement as a result of the PTP process. The

overall improvement in delivery-on-dock results is seen in Figure 6.1.6.

Each business sector establishes its own priorities for functions to benchmark. After individual sector priorities are established, a master priority list is formulated. Each sector takes lead responsibility for two to three specific functions to benchmark. The ten or more functions are typically both product-related and non-product-related. Each year, this list is reviewed, and the top 10 functions are reestablished. Additional issues are added on an emergency basis if business conditions dictate. This usually adds about five more for each sector each year.

2.2.a(2) Criteria for information

Although the strategic planning process identifies the basic need, each specific instance requires different information. Gaps in knowledge of competitor performance or results are the highest targets for gathering information. The second highest priority targets are processes which are critical competencies for our businesses. Within those critical competencies, our top priority is to determine our competitors' performance and then find those companies outside our industry whose process performance is better than ours and our competitors. Once found, CFI establishes a new partnering relationship to learn and understand how their processes are designed and perform.

2.2.a(3) How data are used

After the benchmark partnership is established, a team consisting of persons familiar with the process being examined and trained in the benchmark process is sent to observe in detail the process being used along with the metrics utilized. The team typically consists of a representative from Engineering, Operations, Information Systems from interested sections, plus members of Headquarters Administration to help ensure consistency and alignment with corporate directions.

The team, after the investigations, then returns to the home facility and modifies applicable processes, making changes and modifications to result in a simplified process with less variability, better quality, and reduced cycle time. The new process is documented and provided to the other business sectors within CFI through the corporate coordinator and the data system.

Team members are often called on to travel to another plant in another sector in order to ensure optimum application of the specific process steps. The process steps for the investigation and adaptation of processes from other companies have been well established from many repeat actions and are well documented. There is no longer a not-invented-here (NIH) attitude at CFI as far as applying processes from others.

Many support service process changes have been utilized across the company with few internal modifications. This demonstrates the confidence the various groups have built in the overall process. The result has been the multiplying of improvements of many routine common steps across the company. There have been many improvements in many applications with little additional costs.

2.2.a(4) Stretch targets

When conducting benchmark comparison analysis, both current and future gaps are established considering costs, process disruption, criticality of processes, and impact on other processes when setting stretch targets.

Process changes that have resulted from learning from other organizations in the PTP process have resulted in significantly improved results within CFI. Often the review of an individual process has resulted in modifying only a small part of an established process. Only a few individual steps are improved, and yet the overall results are substantially better.

In a heat treating process for fasteners for the Nuclear and Specialty sector, the PTP supplier being examined was treating the bolts in a manner that resulted in significantly better performance. Detailed examination showed that the improvement was primarily in the device that loaded and unloaded the bolts although the heating and quenching were not as good as what CFI was using. By changing only the handling device, we were able to achieve an overall tenfold improvement, five times better than the total process that was reviewed for benchmarking.

Besides the process improvements noted, metrics are gained that are utilized for goals to be attained. Many stretch goals have been selected through the PTP process.

Benchmarking successes have encouraged teams to be totally unencumbered with the past and to accept new processes that can be totally or partially applied.

2.2.b How the process is improved

A good measure of the results of the benchmarking process is seen during the annual strategic plan update. Competitive comparisons that are reviewed at that time show changes as the result of the improved processes throughout the organization.

Market share increases, increased sales, and increased profits all relate to the benchmarking activities.

Measurements for competitive comparisons and benchmark metrics of best-in-class companies are continuously plotted for many activities. As actual results move toward the established stretch goals and best-in-class measures, satisfaction with results and methodology is determined. If the rate of change in the indicators is not aggressive enough to close the defined gap, changes activities are initiated for the process.

Since 1989 when the benchmarking activities started, the process has matured and grown. Initial benchmark partners were often selected on the basis of convenience of location or personal knowledge of some influential person in the potential partner. Today partners are selected on an objective basis of having the potential to significantly help the various businesses in their various processes. Best-in-class goals are utilized in the assessment and comparison of process results.

Similarly, experience has shown the importance of public domain searches before beginning formal benchmarking visits. This has been of significant help in the selection of the right benchmarking partners.

As processes have improved, the expectations have also improved. As more people have become familiar with what the benchmarking process can contribute, and as results have improved in the financial characteristics, there is more dissatisfaction with the present status and increased enthusiasm in doing things even better. The profit sharing by the employees is a great motivator.

2.3 Analysis and Use of Company-Level Data

2.3.a Data integration, analysis, review, and use

As is explained in Item 2.1, CFI recognizes the value of data to manage the business on the basis of facts. With a centralized mainframe at the Philadelphia Headquarters, data are beamed through satellite to all facilities, which in turn network the PC terminals, real-time, to make accurate data available to whomever needs it and is entitled to the specific information, including those employees that have home PCs linked to the company.

The company's five business strategies are constantly updated on the mainframe with the latest information with weighted values derived from various data inputs. The information is printed out at each facility on

CASE STUDY

Monday morning for posting on a prominent bulletin board giving all employees worldwide the latest status toward the business strategies.

The mainframe has five basic data systems that are integrated for cross-communications, calculations, and analysis. The systems are separately available for the specific functions who have the need for the data through passwords.

The separate data systems are:

➤ Marketing Data System (MDS)
➤ Operations Data System (ODS)
➤ Technical Data System (TDS)
➤ Human Resources Data System (HRDS)
➤ Financial Data System (FDS)

Each system has:

➤ Data bases for the basic information required for that function of the business.

➤ Specific analytical tools required to manipulate the data for the required purposes.

➤ Matrices for each of the four sectors, with each sector using an access code for identification of the ownership of the data.

In addition, each facility has local area networks with PC terminals for local monitoring and control. Data are down-loaded from the mainframe and up-loaded constantly.

2.3.a(1) Understanding of customers and markets

The *Marketing Data System* (MDS) contains inputs drawn from customer surveys, individual customer inputs gathered in various ways, and customer complaints fed through quality reports, product replacement data, Marketing, Service Centers, field sales engineers (FSEs), and other organizational contacts.

Product delivery promises, new product design status, production status, and delivery dates are readily available from the system. Sales personnel at remote locations can interrogate a satellite channel for product delivery status. Inventory status of completed products is also available for delivery information for sales representatives. This is discussed more fully in Item 7.1.

Customer inputs are continually collected by various contacts and continuously fed into the MDS.

Built into the MDS software for this system is an analysis of markets giving competitor's names with their respective market shares in each of the four sectors of the business. Market share changes are

maintained in the data base for five years to enable forward projections.

Any open customer complaints or other open issues are flagged for anyone opening the system so everyone is aware that some issue requires action. The data base stores the problem resolution information and maintains the time required for resolution for two years.

2.3.a(2) Operational performance and capabilities

The *Operations Data System* (ODS) contains all production information including purchased material status and inventories. Production status, including productivity measurements, cycle times, and quality issues such as scrap, is determined through software programs performing statistical analysis on various data groups. On-dock deliveries completed compared to promise are retained for three years.

Because of the importance of process control to the company, individual processes have calculated C_{pk}'s on the basis of information fed into the data base. This information is retained at the local facility with only summary information, such as the percentage of processes that have a C_{pk} of at least 1.5, being sent back to the mainframe. However, if the detailed information is desired, it is possible to call up the details.

Local control is primarily utilized for the *Human Resource Data System* (HRDS) which monitors employee characteristics such as retention, time off with specific reasons such as accidents, and accumulated training courses scheduled, in process, or completed. Data concerning team participation and recognition for outstanding accomplishments are some of the types of information accumulated. Various software programs are installed to provide specific analysis of the data to show trends and variations. Periodic employee survey results are maintained for four years. Summary data are transferred back to the mainframe for overall company statistics.

The *Technical Data System* (TDS) is primarily for the use of Engineering with technical specifications and the capacity to provide mathematical calculations required in new process control initiations. Design of Experiments (DOE) is a widely used technique, and the data system contains the information structure to facilitate the task.

The *Financial Data System* (FDS) provides management with real-time financial characteristics such as sales, inventories, profits, and cash flow. The data from facilities around the world are presented at headquarters as well as the sectors in real-time and are reliable to make timely management decisions on the basis of the financial data presented.

The data in the five data systems are continually correlated to improve the overall accuracy and reliability of the information. This is especially critical because, as seen in Figure 2.1.1, sectors create many individual, or unique, data applications using information derived from the worldwide data and information system. For instance, as customer comments and product quality information integrate, discrepancies may occur. If this happens, the IS function immediately investigates to determine if there really are discrepancies, and if so, why and what corrective actions can be put in place to prevent future occurrences.

2.3.a(3) Competitive performance

Competitive performance information and data are primarily contained in the MDS. As is pointed out earlier, market share and competitor accomplishments are available. Competitor prices and product capability are compared with CFI prices and product capability from which projected costs and performance gaps are estimated from marketing inputs.

With historical data resident in the data system, meaningful trend information is available and can be examined at any time. The dynamics of the marketplace dictate that data systems are required for management to understand the present, observe the changed trends from the past, and predict trends in the future.

2.3b Relating performance changes to financial changes

CFI is a company that is process oriented and customer focused. All sectors of the company continually show their focus through close attention to process and reduced variability in all functions. Figure 6.2.1, Operational Productivity, Products, and Figure 6.2.2, Operational Productivity, Non Products, show the results of operational improvements. Figure 6.2.4, Scrap Material, indicates a dramatic reduction in scrap that results in reduced product cost and increased profitability.

The attention to process improves responsiveness and quality, reduces costs, and builds customer respect and loyalty. The highly integrated data systems provide timely, accurate data worldwide. The data systems furnish the information needed by all functions to accomplish the tasks of continuous improvement.

Customer attitudes are important and of great concern, and are always factored into management decisions concerning new products, new markets, and new and upgraded facilities. Balancing customer attitudes with ongoing required investments in new products and operational facilities is a major management task. The extensive data system provides the information to make these decisions. Category 7.0 explains in more detail how customer attitudes and desires are folded into the data base for future considerations and priority establishment.

The company has been financially successful due to its ability to balance the priorities of customer needs, internal needs, and available resources. Sales increases are becoming more difficult with the downturn of the defense business and the low level of ongoing nuclear activities. The continually increasing profit margins are directly attributable to lower costs, primarily due to better performance of processes.

Total employee numbers are about constant with increases in non-U.S. workers as the company is responsive to customers in other countries desiring non-U.S. labor content. Figure 0.1 shows the relationships. Fall off in U.S. labor has been handled with attrition, and no write off has been necessary as the result of termination pay.

The annual strategic planning process establishes plans for the year for each of the four sectors. Basic information for this planning is established in the data systems and furnished as inputs to the planning process.

Within the company plans, each sector executive has contributing plans. With the policy deployment concept, sector managers have the authority to execute the plans and make modifications as market forces change during the year.

When the USSR collapsed and the eastern markets opened, the company was one of the first fastener companies to establish contacts through the European office in Calais, France. Through the data systems, management was able to determine what investments in Marketing personnel were necessary to initially penetrate the eastern market, yet remain within established guidelines for the yearly plan. Although the magnitude of the opportunity was great enough that top management approval would have been required, this was not necessary since the information on the yearly plan was readily available in the data systems.

Although yearly strategic plans are carefully set, the market dynamics of all large companies dictate that modifications are required during the year. A strong

CASE STUDY

extensive data base utilizing up-to-date
communications and data transfer techniques is
essential. CFI has such a system that has served the
company well.

CASE STUDY

3.0 STRATEGIC PLANNING

3.1 Strategy Development

3.1.a(1) Customer requirements and expectations

CFI's goal is to provide world-class fastening and assembly solutions to meet or exceed customer requirements for advanced products, superior quality, competitive pricing, on-time delivery, and responsive service and support. To accomplish this, CFI is committed to an ongoing process of defining world-class targets that best serve customers and developing plans to achieve them.

CFI's executive staff is responsible for developing the corporation's overall strategic direction. This corporate direction provides the company's five key business strategies for meeting customer requirements. Figure 3.1.1 illustrates CFI's strategic planning process. This process is a closed-loop system which encourages continuous improvement to CFI's plans.

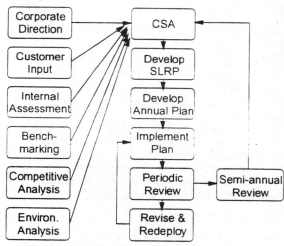

Figure 3.1.1, Management By Planning Process

CFI integrates the corporate direction, customer surveys, internal assessments, benchmarking information, competitive analysis, supplier capability, and environmental factors to formulate both long- and short-range plans. Because total quality requirements are so fully integrated into both types of plans, separate quality plans are not distinguished within them.

CFI relies on many sources for obtaining customer information on current and future requirements, which are product, service, and relationship oriented. Among these are CFI-directed customer surveys and focus groups, third-party directed customer surveys, customer forums, customer visits. and customer partnership feedback (see Figure 7.1.1).

The strategic long range plan (SLRP) is a three to five year plan that outlines world-class goals for achieving customer requirements. This is consistent with the planning window of the majority of customers in the aerospace, automotive, nuclear, and explosive markets. These goals are expressed as CFI's strategic objectives. Using the SLRP as a framework. CFI's annual plan is formulated. Additionally. all CFI business sectors develop annual plans specific to their business needs, in support of CFI's corporate plan. The annual plan includes financial data, operating performance indicators, and the goals to be accomplished during the next year.

Figure 3.1.2 describes the annual planning cycle that provides CFI with its long- and short-term plans. Each of the planning segments receive discussion in Item 3.1, but a high-level summary provides an understanding of the strength of CFI's system. The full cycle includes the following steps: (1) accumulation of information about the business and competition (current situation analysis); (2) integration of the information into product line business plans (PLBP); (3) using this to create the SLRP; (4) this information feeds the development of the strategic and tactical management plans (MBP); (5) building the annual operating plans and budgets (annual plans); and (6) culminating in the next year's operating plan and budget (locked POR).

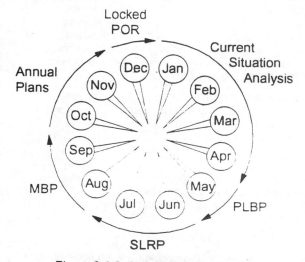

Figure 3.1.2, Annual Planning Cycle

One of CFI's most significant improvements has been the evolution of the formalized Management By Planning (MBP) process. MBP links the SLRP,

CASE STUDY

PLBP, the annual plan. MBOs, projects, and tactics in an integrated, closed-loop feedback system.

The essence of the plan is stated in the MBP format. MBPs at CFI consist of:

➤ Concise, measurable objectives that describe what will be done.

➤ An accompanying set of key results that defines how objectives will be accomplished.

The MBP process was developed in response to customer expectations and needs, and business needs. CFI participates in Bueland's Total Quality Excellence (TQE) assessment. Other tools and supporting approaches include benchmarking and internal assessment which were piloted, refined, and maintained by CFI's Quality Technology Group. MBP integrates world-class features found through benchmarking U.S. and Japanese companies, such as policy deployment and planning. To improve the annual planning process, data are collected through one-on-one discussions, surveys of training effectiveness, and polls of the network of CFI's total quality managers.

CFI's strategic objectives from the SLRP and annual plan are deployed to all of the corporation's business sectors, as noted in Figure 3.1.4, where each department formulates its specific tactics and projects to support the achievement of these long- and short-range goals. Strategies, tactics, and projects are continually reviewed and revised as needed to ensure that goals are met. Figure 3.1.5 provides a view of the cascade review process. Strategic Objective progress to plan is reviewed with CFI's president, Eugene Farmer, during monthly operations reviews, which enable the business units to optimize resource utilization and improve their plans.

In preparation for the SLRP and the annual plan, individuals and teams are assigned by CFI staff to review current and projected customer needs to identify competitive gaps in CFI performance. Data are gathered through such means as internal and supplier assessments to compare current quality levels and capabilities with external benchmarks. Figures in Category 6.0 show examples of CFI's quality goals as compared against world-class benchmarks.

3.1.a(2) Competitive environment

A primary element in developing CFI's strategic plans and objectives is the current situation analysis, which collects and analyzes information to set business direction. This analysis is the first step in the strategic quality planning process and is followed by the SLRP

and annual plan. Information used in the analysis is continually reviewed for changes, and plans are adjusted accordingly. Figure 3.1.1 shows the Current Situation Analysis (CSA) phase of the annual planning process.

Competitive and benchmark data are used to measure CFI's performance against world-class levels both within and outside the industry to ensure that customer expectations are met or exceeded. CFI routinely collects and analyzes information on competitors who produce comparable products and services. Product data on technical capabilities, product portfolios, manufacturing performance, and quality levels are analyzed. Also examined are service data in such categories as pricing, field support, guarantees, warranties, and shipment throughput time. CFI's approach to benchmarking is described in detail in Item 2.2.

CFI's executive staff identifies changes in the corporate direction. The overall corporate directions are used as the framework for CFI to develop long- and short-range objectives, initiatives, and goals.

3.1.a(3) Risks: financial, market, technological, and societal

Each proposed strategy for CFI's products and services is analyzed to determine key sensitivities of approach in influencing increases in market share, environmental impacts (both beneficial and adverse), complexity of production, and degree of new technology required with near- and long-term financial impacts. Each of these factors is weighted based on company strategic objectives and integrated to provide a summary score of the risk of each approach. This risk factor is combined with other factors in establishing company strategies.

3.1.a(4) Company capabilities

Process capabilities, which are based on periodic annual internal assessments, are used to review CFI capabilities, provide data on performance, and identify priorities for improving competitive position. This information may take the form of performance indicators, C_{pk} metrics, or anecdotal information. Data are gathered from employee feedback as well as from evaluation of the previous year's plan results.

3.1.a(5) Supplier and partner capabilities

Supplier capabilities are key elements to the strategic quality planning process. CFI reviews supplier capabilities and incorporates supplier quality initiatives, such as CFI's Supplier Continuous Quality Improvement (SCQI) approach. In addition, the SCQI approach is key to the Corporate Materials Group's annual plan for its suppliers.

3.1.b Strategy translation into actionable plans

The results of these assessments allow us to analyze past, current, and future quality levels in light of world-class performance and customer expectations. As mentioned before, the MBP is a planning process that generates a strategic and tactical plan. Figure 3.1.3 shows the natural linkage from the corporate objectives (CO) through strategic objectives (SO), strategies, tactics, and finally projects. Projects are where all of the work is accomplished. However, from an organizational and employee perspective, it is important for anybody at CFI to be able to look at the work he or she is doing and be able to recognize how it connects and supports the attainment of one or more of the corporate objectives, and ultimately the profitability of the company.

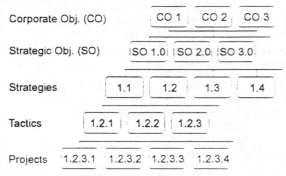

Figure 3.1.3, MBP Breakdown and Deployment

Figure 3.1.4 shows the methodology used to develop the cascaded corporate objectives. It notes the "catchball" process used to start at the top and develop a tentative set of next-level objectives or plans, and those members of CFI who are the targeted owners respond and negotiate what the action, metrics, and goals will be. When this step is complete, the results are locked in. Then the process repeats itself on the next lower level until it has been negotiated all the way to the project level.

CFI's SLRP and annual plans are communicated and deployed in several ways throughout each CFI sector. Special meetings are held each year to provide the information contained in these plans to all levels of employees across each business sector. At least once a year the internal publication *Fastened Together* publishes the corporate values and strategic objectives from each major business sector within CFI. Business update meetings (BUMs) are held for all employees on a quarterly basis to outline corporate

and sector goals, as well as the performance to those goals and corresponding indicators. Quarterly MBPs are also formulated at all exempt levels to ensure the support of annual CFI objectives. Additionally, CFI's open communication style promotes the deployment of the plans and goals within the corporation, through such means as posters, bulletin boards, communication kiosks, and frequent one-on-one discussions.

CFI's plans and goals are communicated to suppliers primarily through supplier partnerships. Plans outlining supplier requirements are transmitted from CFI's Corporate Materials Group, which also monitors suppliers to ensure that they continuously meet overall quality plans.

Figure 3.1.4, Cascaded MBP Plan Development

Projects are prioritized and funded on an annual basis, using zero-based budget (ZBB) methodology. Projects are ranked in order of priority based on their importance in meeting the overall plan. Resources are allocated accordingly, including staffing and budget requirements. This process ensures that adequate resources are allocated to provide a high level of quality to all projects. Projects are initiated and terminated on the basis of the current situation analysis. Additionally, a yearly departmental budget is formulated to allocate direct spending (e.g., training, employee recreation, materials, and capital) and indirect spending (e.g., facilities allocation) dollars, which are reviewed against the plan on a monthly basis.

Figure 3.1.5 shows how the elements of MBP are reviewed and the information is aggregated into the next higher level of review. Tactics and projects are reviewed within each business sector on a daily to bimonthly basis, depending on scope, complexity and urgency. Additionally, CFI president Eugene Farmer conducts monthly operations reviews for all business sectors. These reviews are designed to evaluate

CASE STUDY

progress to plan and provide real-time feedback, ensuring timely alteration or redeployment as needed.

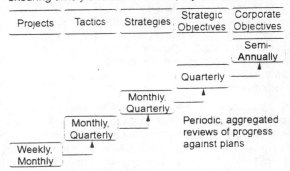

Figure 3.1.5, Aggregated MBP Review Process

3.1.c Evaluation and improvement of planning processes

CFI's strategic planning system and goal-setting processes have been enhanced for greater effectiveness and productivity as the business has evolved. In addition, CFI significantly improved our annual planning process, reducing it from six months to three. To focus more efficiently on customer requirements, CFI has changed the MBP evaluation process. Previously, MBPs included "stretch goals" with an acceptable achievement rate of 70%. Today, our MBPs target 100% achievement of objectives and key results, ensuring that commitments to our customers are met.

3.2 Strategy Deployment

3.2.a(1) Key operational requirements, performance measures and deployment

The foremost quality and operational goal for CFI is to do a great job for customers, and goals for achieving the highest levels of quality are driven by customer requirements. Table 3.2.1 summarizes CFI's customer requirements and key business strategies as described in Item 1.1. To collect these data, we use indicators derived from benchmarking, as well as feedback from our customers, gathered through a customer-perception rating system. Our goal is to be the number one supplier in supporting all of our customer requirements. The customer rating system is the most effective form of external, third-party validation used to confirm our progress toward that goal.

The next Items are presented in reverse order to better reflect CFI's process for strategic planning: long-range plans are formulated first, followed by short-range plans.

3.2.a(2) Organizational alignment between suppliers, partners, and organizational units

CFI drives alignment between its suppliers, partners and sectors by actively integrating them into the SLRP cycles that happen throughout the year. For the suppliers, the PTP approach is used to link all key suppliers (e.g., either technology based or primary source) into the design and manufacturing cycles.

Table 3.2.1 illustrates the linkage between CFI objectives as they translate into partner expectations, activities, and projects. The linkage is through the periodic MBP plans. In the more advanced and mature suppliers and partners, CFI has pushed its MBP process into their operating systems to further strengthen its linkages and gain greater leverage.

3.2.a(3) Productivity, waste, and cycle time improvements

Refer to Table 3.2.1 for planned improvements in the areas of productivity, waste and scrap, and cycle time reductions in setup, design, and order lead time.

3.2.a(4) Resources to accomplish short- and long-term plans

The resources required to accomplish the short- and long-term plans are identified in Table 3.2.1. These resources are determined using the MBP, PLBP, SLRP, and ZBB processes noted in Item 3.1.

3.2.b Two to five year objectives, measures, and comparisons

CFI uses the customer requirements and business strategies noted in Item 1.1 to build long-term strategic objectives outlined in Table 3.2.1. These strategic objectives, which in turn support customer requirements and key business strategies, have primary owners responsible for ensuring that they are met. CFI senior staff measures success in achieving objectives through a set of indicators and goals.

CFI's managers and support organizations also develop a set of strategies for their organizations to support overall CFI strategic objectives. Figure 3.1.4 illustrates how the corporate quality, operational, and customer goals cascade down into the organizations using some of the review processes noted in Table 1.2.1.

For example, using Corporate Objective CO3 from the corporate MBP (Table 3.2.1) outlines the major goals and indicators required for each sector to meet the overall objective. Not seen in this high level summary of goals are the strategic objectives, strategies, and tactics which have identified owners and are measured by indicators and goals derived from

CASE STUDY

benchmark data, customer input, competitive information, and organizational requirements.

As customers demand an ever-increasing level of performance from their suppliers, CFI must respond to those expectations. Table 3.2.1 outlines the high-level operational goals necessary to meet customer requirements for the 1995 to 1998 time frame. These goals reflect both world-class and best-in-class benchmarks for a three-year period and have targets to meet or exceed all competitive benchmarks in this time frame. The process for defining these world-class benchmarks and competitive benchmarks is described in Item 2.2.

CASE STUDY

Table 3.2.1, CFI Corporate Objectives, Strategic Objectives, and Strategies

Corporate Objectives		Strategic Objective Goals				
		CPS	CAS	DAS	NSS	CSS
CO1	Deliver 6 sigma products to customers on time	➤ Drive 100% of critical processes to C_{pk} > 2.0	➤ Drive 100% of critical processes to C_{pk} > 1.8	➤ Drive 100% of critical processes to C_{pk} > 1.7	➤ Drive 100% of critical processes to C_{pk} > 1.5	➤ Identify critical processes.. 80% to C_{pk} > 1.8
CO2	Be recognized as the highest value producer of fasteners	➤ Customer value matrix of > 9/7 (†)	➤ Customer value matrix of > 8/8	➤ Customer value matrix of > 8/9	➤ Customer value matrix of > 8/9.4	➤ Customer value matrix of > 8/9 (‡)
CO3	Be the technology leader in the introduction of revolutionary fastener products	➤ Introduce 3 major product lines in 1995 ➤ > 3 patent awards	➤ Drive > 11 design wins in automotive ➤ intro. 6 new product lines ➤ > 11 patent awards	➤ Drive 8 major sub-contractor design wins ➤ > 7 patent awards	➤ Win all nuclear bids ➤ > 5 patent awards ➤ introduce 1 new product line	➤ Engage > 6 process benchmark activities ➤ Develop best-in-class IS ➤ Implement HR transition plan
CO4	Protect the environment at all worldwide locations with benchmark-level results	➤ Eliminate CFCs by 1995 ➤ Reduce effluents by 50% in 1995 ➤ Reduce solid waste by 30%	➤ Eliminate CFCs by 1995 ➤ Reduce effluents by 60% in 1995 ➤ Reduce solid waste by 20%	➤ Reduce CFCs by 60% in 1995 ➤ Reduce effluents by 50% in 1995 ➤ Reduce solid waste by 45%	➤ Reduce CFCs by 50% in 1995 ➤ Reduce effluents by 50% in 1995 ➤ Reduce solid waste by 55%	➤ Reduce solid waste by 60% ➤ Increase electronic information usage by 100%
CO5	Be recognized by our employees as number one in employee relationships at all worldwide locations	➤ Score > B on employee survey in all six values	➤ Score > B on employee survey in all six values	➤ Score > B on employee survey in all six values	➤ Score > B on employee survey in all six values	➤ Score > B on employee survey in all six values

(†) The customer value matrix is seen in Figure 7.4.4 of this application. The first number represents the "satisfaction with product cost" axis, the second number represents the "product fitness for use" axis.

(‡) For the Corporate Support Sector customers include both internal and external customers and partners. The first number represents the horizontal axis and relates to "service and support availability", the vertical axis represents "service and support quality."

CASE STUDY

4.0 HUMAN RESOURCE DEVELOPMENT AND MANAGEMENT

4.1 Human Resource Planning and Evaluation

CFI's total quality leadership is driven by "our employees, who are our fundamental strength; by our commitment to their development and well-being; and by the shared goals of customer support, productivity, and continuous improvement." The Human Resources Strategic Long Range Plan (HR SLRP) embodies these principles. The plan was developed through analysis of the company SLRP, projection of the future environment, and consideration of various CFI human resource data and survey results.

4.1.a(1) Changes in work design

Key strategies in the plan addressing changes in the work design include:

➤ Increasing self-directed work teams to enhance flexibility and innovation.

➤ Increasing self-audits to reduce cycle time.

➤ Implementing flexible manufacturing to enhance work force flexibility and utilization.

➤ Reducing an additional management layer within one year to enable rapid response to changes.

➤ Increasing use of core competency skill teams across sectors to rapidly deploy resources in response to changes.

➤ Achieving a 20% virtual work force buffer through part-time and contract employees to achieve flexibility in meeting work demands without impacting the core work force.

4.1.a(2) Employee development

Key strategies in the plan addressing employee development include:

➤ Expanding the breadth of skills of all employees to achieve a multi-skilled core work force.

➤ Training a specialist cadre on advanced product and process technologies to lead change.

➤ Developing and publishing long-term projections of skill needs by each year of the planning horizon. These skill projections will be integrated with individual employee development plans to retrain personnel with declining skills.

➤ Developing a "buy" category of skill needs to be filled through part-time and contract hires where long-term needs for the skill set are not cost effective for full-time core employees.

From a career development perspective, CFI will increase the number of managers attending its core management development program by approximately 210 per year. Since late 1992, over 730 managers have participated in this program. CFI also enhances and strengthens dual career ladders for managers and individual contributors.

4.1.a(3) Changes in compensation and recognition

Leadership at CFI means committed performance to values, business strategies, and customer requirements. These goals are incorporated into annual, quarterly, and monthly objectives. Key results are developed by managers and employees in support of their business groups' direction. Objectives, along with goals for enhancing and developing capabilities required to continuously improve performance, also form the basis of individual performance assessment.

Performance to objectives is measured through a performance appraisal system that rewards quality over quantity. This is accomplished through a compensation system that is based on merit. For example, all salary exempt (SE) and salary non-exempt (SNE) personnel are evaluated on quality and quantity, but weighting assigned to quality is 50% greater than that for quantity. Competitively increased pay raises for employees acquiring greater skills and accepting additional responsibilities on teams are critical changes to how CFI addressed compensation in prior years.

Employees influence the development and improvement of performance measurements through their input on surveys. An example is the feedback from our 1994 culture survey, which resulted in a revamping of CFI's exempt performance management system.

We share our financial success with employees and provide them with incentives to achieve quality results through an Employee Cash Bonus Program (ECBP) based on company profitability. Historically, this amounts to approximately 10 days pay and is distributed after fiscal quarter two and quarter four closing. Additionally, 15 percent of our employees are identified for exceptional contribution to the group's success. This designation earns them a bonus payout that is 60% greater than the standard payout. Plans are to increase the level of 15% to 25% in the next two years. CFI also has another bonus plan that has 44% of our exempt employees, managers, and individual contributors involved. It is called the Executive Bonus Program (EBP), whose targets are developed to support sector business performance. Traditionally, the EBP offers bonus amounts equivalent to 20% to 45% of executives base annual salary.

Sixty-five percent of all exempt employees participate in CFI's Stock Option Program (SOP). These data compare to 51% participation in competitive companies and not more than 10% participation in many other industries. Starting in 1995, CFI will contribute one-half of every dollar an employee contributes to the SOP. A stock participation plan is open to all employees, providing a sense of ownership and commitment to CFI's success.

In addition to performance-based increases, between 10% and 20% of our employees are promoted annually, being recognized for increased performance and enhanced capabilities. In 1995, career planning guidance will be revised to increase emphasis on employee growth and gaining multi-skills capabilities and an expanding variety in work assignment.

CFI rewards outstanding achievements by individuals and teams in corporate, sector, and department programs through the CFI Achievement Award (CFIAA).

Each CFI sector also conducts its own Sector Recognition Award (SRA) program to acknowledge accomplishments that deserve sector-wide recognition, including cash awards and a public ceremony within the sector. In addition, managers extend less formal, more spontaneous recognition, such as movie tickets, dinner for two, and gift certificates, to reward quality efforts.

Many awards are peer generated, such as the monthly Peer Recognition program in the Dearborn (MI) facility, the Employee of the Month program in the Milwaukee (WI) location, the Quarterly Top Hat Award in Human Resources, and those given at monthly shift meetings suck as the Profuse Thanks program in Salt Lake City (UT).

Although teams are a way of life at CFI, recognition of individual performance was the rule in the past. Starting in 1985, a significant shift occurred, reflecting the desire on the part of employees and managers to recognize total team performance. A good example of this change in emphasis is renaming of the traditional Individual Achievement Award at CFI to the CFI Achievement Award (CFIAA). Team awards are often cross-functional, cross-organizational, and multilevel in composition. Figure 6.2.19 shows the CFI awards delivered to teams and individuals

between 1985 and 1994 (with 1995 projected). Plans are to promote stronger linkage of all recognition activities to the five key corporate strategies.

4.1.a(4) Recruitment

Supporting human resource's strategic objectives is a focused set of improvement strategies, tactics, and projects with quarterly goals. For example, CFI will increase the number of entry- to mid-level professional positions filled by new college graduates from 45% to 75% by 1995. In addition, CFI will double the number of hires by its Graduate Rotation Program (GRP), and increase to 6% and 15%, respectively, its non-Asian minority and technical female hires.

Other strategic goals include:

➤ Doubling the number of key external experienced hires from our External Sourcing program.

➤ Decreasing the cost per hire.

➤ Increase both offer and accept rates by more than 10% to 70% and 80%, respectively.

Improvement tactics and goals targeting the Great Place To Work (GPTW) value include:

➤ Evaluation of expanding employee wellness programs.

➤ Strategies, in the areas of post-retirement benefits, child-care and elder care.

➤ Implementation of alternate starting times to provide greater flexibility for single parent and "two-working parent" families.

Also in support of this value, a direction will be implemented on skill-based pay that will enhance career development and empowerment of multi-skilled non-exempt employees. We will also make recommendations and deploy the best-known methods for reward and recognition of teams and individuals.

Other items on the improvement agenda that will increase quality hires in the future are:

➤ Partnerships with local schools and universities, including involvement in education and the kindergarten through 12th grade (K-12) level through employee tutoring.

➤ Assistance to outside institutions in math and science curricula development.

➤ Sponsorship of local and national math and science competitions.

4.1.b(1) Assessment of employee development

Most employee-related data come from:

- ➤ Continuous surveys conducted on corporate, sector, and factory levels.
- ➤ Management-hosted employee lunches.
- ➤ One-on-one meetings conducted at the sector, factory, and department levels.

The employee perception survey process is conducted biannually and typically includes questions regarding employee and department morale, job satisfaction, reward and recognition, management effectiveness, training effectiveness, quality of communication, and opportunities for career growth. Improvement plans are developed collaboratively between managers and employees, and customized to meet the changing needs of employees and their organizations.

These data are correlated with the company goals and analyzed via Pareto charts to establish those factors most important for employee development.

4.1.b(2) Linkage to key results

A multi-functional, multi-sector Human Resources Evaluation Team (HRET) meets on a quarterly basis to assess whether human resource strategies and practices are making a positive contribution to the performance of the business. Additionally, the HRET determines if there are best practices occurring in individual sectors which should be expanded to other sectors. In this assessment, the HRET conducts a multi-variable correlation of the business with human resource results. These correlations have, over time, established definitive correlations between company results and human resource initiatives and actions. For instance, technical and quality training has been shown to be responsible for approximately 60% of the contributions to reduction in cycle time and 73% of the contributions to improvements in quality. Similarly, increases in involvement have contributed 67% of the improvements in cycle time and 83% of the improvements in quality. Reverse correlations show that involvement has reduced turnover by 14% and increased employee satisfaction by 43%, which has cut employee overhead costs by 11%.

4.1.b(3) Ensuring reliable information

Another element of the HRET responsibility is to validate the reliability of the information. Each of the correlation models is validated semi-annually to ensure that the variables used are still those important to the business and provide a true reflection of performance. The team also conducts an accuracy spot-check of data inputs on a quarterly basis to verify that the information received is accurate and complete. Changes to the process and/or changes to data collection occur as necessary based on this analysis. This is in addition to the automated data reliability checks performed by IS personnel and systems noted in Item 2.1.

4.2 High Performance Work Systems

CFI honors employees and teams worthy of corporate-wide recognition. The CFIAA typically recognizes major accomplishments in customer support, quality, productivity improvements, and technical innovation and is considered CFI's "Nobel Prize." Winners receive CFI common stock and a plaque to commemorate the accomplishment. The award is presented at highly visible, sector-wide meetings and is widely publicized in a special edition of the corporate newspaper *Fastened Together*.

4.2.a(1) Creation of opportunities for initiative

CFI's founding objective was to create a company culture that not only provided diverse opportunities for employee contributions, but that also actively involved employees in all aspects of their work. CFI's value of results orientation requires employees to identify, understand, and confront problems directly and constructively to achieve timely resolution. Implicit in these behaviors is ongoing communication and feedback at all levels. Over time, employee involvement has evolved into a living part of the company culture. It is reflected in a wide array of management practices and other processes that offer all levels of employees every possible opportunity to have ownership of projects and tasks, be accountable, and make a difference.

Employees contribute to the accomplishment of CFI's quality and business objectives through a number of formal and informal employee involvement mechanisms, including:

- ➤ Teams and task forces, which can be either long- or short-term teams, typically are led by a "content expert," are formed ad hoc, and are disbanded once an effective resolution is implemented and verified. Forums for improvement include task forces, material review boards, project teams, and problem-solving teams.

- ➤ A decentralized suggestion program fosters both "all-purpose" and functionally specific suggestion programs to expedite timely feedback and implementation of inputs. For example, the Defense and Aerospace Sector safety suggestion program features suggestion boxes and a "safeline" for confidential, phone-in use. Inputs are

CASE STUDY

reviewed weekly by a review committee for applicability and effectiveness. Feedback is provided to the employee who made the suggestion immediately after the meeting. With this example, there has been a very high implementation rate, exceeding 87% in 1994, as seen in Figure 6.1.23.

➤ Self-audit teams are employed across all CFI sectors. The teams are designed to evaluate internal operations and make necessary adjustments to support customer and internal audit requirements. The results of internal self-audits can be seen in Figure 6.2.24.

CFI's culture values employees' skills, knowledge, and performance over formal position. CFI's principal goal is for decisions to be made at the level where they are executed whenever possible for all categories of employees. To help improve and speed up the decision-making process, we have systematically removed layers of management over the past five years. All CFI organizations are now at three to five levels from top to bottom, compared to seven to nine levels four years ago.

Because of the increasing complexity and competitive nature of our business, we believe that most tasks benefit by cross-functional and multilevel team efforts. Specific plans for developing such ongoing teams are different for each organization, but all focus on bringing together the necessary experts for solving problems and empowering them to take action. Examples include:

➤ *Self-sustaining manufacturing vision at Sao Paulo, Brazil, facility* - In the fall of 1990, Sao Paulo announced a three-year plan to evolve its traditionally managed structure of hourly production operators into approximately 50 facilitated teams. These teams will assume many routine supervisory and technical tasks, such as basic troubleshooting and line inventory management. In 1992, all 700+ employees participated in an eight-hour empowerment workshop to kick off the process.

➤ *"Three-Level Factory" vision* - In 1993, the Juarez, Mexico, facility initiated a plan to evolve its total organization into a three-level structure featuring the following:

Level 1 - A Factory Steering Committee, made up of the plant manager and his staff.

Level 2 - Five peer support teams of middle managers and supervisors.

Level 3 - Approximately 40 natural work teams (NWTs) of all operators, technicians, and engineers who run each operation. Each NWT has an associated Performance Improvement Team (PIT), which focuses on continuous improvement for the operation. Over 200 PIT members received eight hours of orientation training that included extensive business information.

➤ *Product (or Process) Development Teams (PDTs)* - PDTs are formed for developing and bringing new products into the market. Members are cross-functional and include product design and manufacturing engineers, marketing and planning personnel, and often customers and suppliers.

Expectations that employees should be involved and empowered are embedded in CFI culture. Employees perform their work as teams, and the company focuses on, acknowledges, and rewards the accomplishments of the team effort versus tracking the extent and effectiveness of involvement. Examples of PDT accomplishments include the following:

(1) Between 1989 and 1993, employee involvement teams across the General Site Services and Customer Support Services groups reduced expenditures by $17.4 million through cost savings, reductions, and cost avoidance.

(2) The Hybrid Rivet Product Development Team, which was cross-organizational and cross-site that included Oyama, Japan, Boston, MA, and Berlin, Germany. It was responsible for CFI's fastest product introduction thus far. The team used a modular design process to take the multi-material rivet from initial product implementation plan to available samples in three weeks.

(3) The Rivet-With-Mastic (RWM) Task Force successfully reduced throughput times from eight weeks in 1989 to three weeks in early 1994. The team won a CFI Achievement Award in the fourth quarter of 1994.

Results achieved through employee involvement are also reflected in recognition awards, which show the effectiveness of teams in action. Employees are evaluated on both individual performance and support of group actions and goals. Individual development plans address the improvement needs of specific team members.

CASE STUDY

Several point-in-time "monitors" of team activity across organizations have supported our belief that employee involvement is continuously growing. Examples include the following:

➤ *Sample of quality improvement teams* - Between June 1988 and March 1989, CFI's Quality Technology Group received abstracts documenting the success of 224 performance improvement teams across CFI's domestic sites.

➤ *Surveys of current team activity* - A survey was administered to all CFI organizations in January 1994 to estimate the number of active teams for CFI's 1994 MBNQA application. At that time, almost 400 multilevel and cross-functional teams were reported. Another survey in January 1995 reported more than 550 active teams throughout CFI, and results showed that "teams" are broadly defined to include any variety of problem-solving team, project team, improvement team, or natural work group.

These are dynamic snapshots of team activity, as empowered employees are continually creating new ad hoc teams and disbanding old ones as needed. A current review also indicates that more than 95% of all decisions are now made through a team process.

4.2.a(2) Fostering flexibility

Flexibility and mobility are critical to the success of CFI and its employees as the company deploys personnel both to accommodate technological and business changes, and to support employee career development goals. Areas of major focus since the mid-'80s and key components of the HR SLRP have formalized the CFI redeployment process and its integration with an enhanced internal staffing capability.

Through this process, CFI's Macon (GA) operation has successfully redeployed 324 employees, including 218 salary non-exempts (SNEs), for a total of 91% of those desiring placement. The redeployment process includes a comprehensive move package, formal career assessment, workshops on interviewing and resume development, retraining and funding for internal and external opportunities, and assimilation assistance for relocating employees.

Additionally, to keep pace with continuously increasing performance expectations and emerging skills, training needs are often addressed by training groups or functional content experts as described in Item 4.3. Strong relationships with community colleges and universities have resulted in customized training that enhances the skill set of current CFI employees, while also ensuring a supply of externally qualified employees. Similar relationships are being established with high schools to help them better equip students with fundamental skills before entering the work force.

For example, in Los Angeles (CA), CFI's ongoing relationship with the community college system produced a customized training program for computerized fastener designers that has continually evolved in response to changing technology demands. CFI's partnership with the Technical-Vocational Institute of Los Angeles resulted in the development of an associate's degree program in metallurgical technology. CFI employees also support such institutions by assisting with curriculum development and by teaching courses. In addition, CFI offers cooperative fellowships and part-time work opportunities to qualified students.

4.2.a(3) Ensuring effective communications

CFI believes that meaningful employee involvement must be supported by freely and openly sharing information about business operations with all employees. Examples of forums for disseminating business information include:

➤ Business update meetings (BUMs) are accomplished worldwide on a quarterly basis. CFI executives and senior managers update employees on performance to goals and plans through corporate overviews. The corporate information is enhanced with sector and factory specific information. The combined presentations cover the financial performance data, competitive analysis, and new product strategies. Employees are encouraged to raise concerns and make inputs during these meetings.

➤ Immediate information access is enabled through:

  ● Written publications distributed on all "information kiosks" located at key spots throughout all CFI buildings worldwide.

  ● The issuance of internal press releases before they are available externally.

  ● Through a wide range of sector or function specific magazines distributed monthly or quarterly. Information technology is driving CFI communication methods toward being electronically available 24 hours a day, all year, worldwide.

➤ Voice mail is widely used to communicate between sites as well as within sites. Electronic mail also provides widespread communication.

CASE STUDY

4.2.b Compensation reinforcing work effectiveness

The most effective means of evaluating recognition and performance measurement systems is to survey CFI's internal customers — the managers who administer the systems and the employees who are reviewed and rewarded by the processes. Vehicles for soliciting this feedback have been discussed in Item 4.2. Changes were made to our exempt performance management system as a result of employee feedback from the 1993 culture survey. Employee performance ratings were reduced from five to three — outstanding, successful, and improvement required — reaffirming the efforts of the majority of our employees, who fall into the middle category.

We also introduced a component called "trending," which evaluates an employee's rate of change relative to his or her peers. It stresses the necessity of achieving a rating at least equal to one's peers by continuously improving one's performance. Managers were trained on the new system, and all exempt employees, including managers, were surveyed on the process. Results indicated that the concepts were good, but the content needed improvement. A task force was formed to refine the basic components, and revised training was delivered to all managers and exempt employees. Exempt employees will be re-surveyed for feedback in the second quarter of 1995.

Additionally, CFI's Defense and Aerospace Sector is currently soliciting feedback and assistance from its employees on enhancements to the recognition process. The HR SLRP includes a reevaluation of the most effective methods for rewarding individual and team performance.

4.3 Employee Education, Training, and Development

4.3.a(1) Key performance objectives

CFI defines quality education and training as all training that provides employees with the skills and knowledge to support business strategies and values. CFI presently uses five different organizations or methods to meet education and training needs. Each one's approach for assessing training needs is specific to its target constituency and training type.

Functional area training departments, such as the manufacturing training departments or General Site Services (GSS) training, deliver specialized functional skills necessary for job performance. This training focuses on the skills required within the specific function. For example, the Corporate Information Services (CIS) training group offers skills training for its programmers, operators, and analysts. Training in

Statistical Process Control (SPC) and Design of Experiments (DOE) is offered through functional training departments, which allows "how-to" application of the subject matter.

Training needs are driven by the operation's specific business needs and the assessment of proficiency against the required skill level. An example is Philadelphia's (PA) approach for just-in-time delivery of team orientation training to over 200 employees on PITs, described in Area 4.2a. Functional area training departments either assist and qualify employee content experts to develop and deliver the training, or contract directly with external resources.

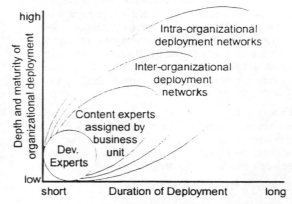

Figure 4.3.1, Training Deployment Approach

Figure 4.3.1 shows the deployment methodology used to embed skills and training throughout CFI. In the beginning development experts provide training in selected "early adopter" organizations. At this time the duration of deployment is low and the organizational maturity is also low. Both conditions requiring intensive, highly competent training from the content experts. The next phase is where the content expert develop additional content experts who are assigned to each business unit — in the same context as an internal consultant. These additional experts enable wider deployment throughout the organization. This cascaded deployment continues as the new content experts train additional inter- and intra-organizational experts (those employees assigned to a business area but capable of floating to other business areas).

4.3.a(2) Employee progression

Employees are asked annually to update their career enhancement forms. This is done independently of the performance appraisal and merit pay review cycles to ensure that focus is provided on helping employees to plan how to increase their worth to the

CASE STUDY

company. All employees are provided with "Careers at CFI" which describes potential career paths employees may pursue. For all employees, after completion of their career enhancement forms, an analysis called "My Career at CFI" is provided with alternatives in training, education, and potential work assignments employees can follow to enhance their progression. It is the employees' decision whether or not to accept the recommendations and enroll in training and education. Enrollment and tracking of training are accomplished through the automated Training and Education Support System (TESS). TESS feeds to employees updates to their "My career at CFI" analysis after completing training, education classes, or changes in work assignment. TESS also notifies employees when changes are made to their profile following their annual performance review. The employee satisfaction survey, exit interviews, and focus group discussions show that this methodology is viewed very favorably by employees as fully enabling them to plan their careers.

4.3.b(1) Determining training needs

CFI University has defined committees of cross-organizational training employees to benchmark CFI training systems against companies both within and outside of the fastener industry in five areas:

➤ Curriculum development;
➤ Training tracking systems;
➤ Measurements and evaluation systems;
➤ Professional development; and
➤ Interactive technology.

Each committee's results and subsequent system improvements have been incorporated into the "common architecture" across every college in the CFI University system. Figure 4.3.2 show the CFI University Deployment system. In the figure are the development arm, various colleges, type of delivery mechanisms and methods used to assess training effectiveness. All of this infrastructure is supported by the TESS system. The structural interaction of committees and colleges provides the building blocks for CFI to create a world-class training and development system over the next three years that will integrate all CFI training activity. The following improvements have begun in 1994-1995:

➤ CFI University's Curricula Development Committee has created a competency-based curricula development model that will be used to establish curricula for all functionally based colleges. When all colleges are operational, every discipline will have skill-based curricula, enabling all employees

to identify the courses they need to make performance improvements on the job.

➤ During CFI's 1993 Baldrige assessment effort, weaknesses were identified in CFI's system for measuring training effectiveness. To address these, cross-organizational teams have been dedicated as full-time resources for development of a CFI training evaluation system. This system requires that our training workshop students demonstrate learned behaviors on the job and will be deployed to six workshops in 1995. Line managers will verify that the system meets their needs before implementation.

➤ CFI's deployment of TESS offers significant administrative improvements for the company's decentralized training environment as follows:

➤ TESS tracks all training that employees take through any training resource.

➤ TESS provides information on any discipline's curriculum, as well as on training plans, career development, degree tracking, and certifications.

➤ All employees have access to TESS directly via on-line capabilities to learn about available training opportunities, understand their skill requirements, and register for courses.

4.3.b(2) Training delivery

Components training focuses on the highly technical aspects of design, assembly, test, and production, including equipment engineering training for engineers and technicians, and process-flow training. Training needs are triggered by the introduction of new processes or technology, or by customer feedback. Components training employs a pool of technical content experts who develop and deliver training to all components' manufacturing organizations and who certify on-site content experts to deliver training programs.

Corporate Education and Development is the source for training on CFI's corporate culture and values, management development, and administrative service development. This group provides employees with a variety of courses to help them understand performance to CFI values, beginning with a new-hire orientation on their first day, titled "What Makes CFI -- CFI?" Other core orientation programs available to all employees include "CFI Culture," "All About CFI," and "CFI Operations, Philosophy, and Economics" (CFIOPEC).

CASE STUDY

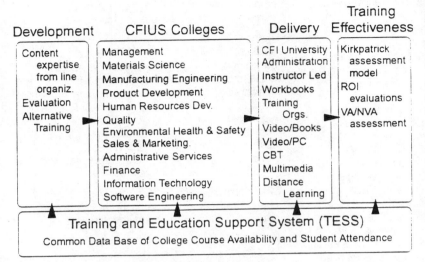

Figure 4.3.2, CFI University Deployment

Employees are also encouraged to attend and time is provided for them to take courses that teach specific practices to support CFI values, such as "Effective Meetings" and CFI's "Management By Planning." Management development programs, available to all levels of management, emphasize the importance of role modeling behaviors that support CFI values.

Corporate Education and Development recruits and trains personnel at each site to deliver its training programs. Organizations may arrange to have courses delivered to intact teams on a just-in-time basis, which facilitates immediate application of the subject matter to real workplace situations. Training needs are triggered by corporate surveys or through the CFI University system described below.

Extended education through external trade schools, colleges, and universities is encouraged to enhance employees' professional development. CFI provides on-site degree programs wherever resources are available, such as the program with Treadwall University at Philadelphia (PA). If classes are offered off-site, CFI pursues an active partnership with the school, such as the relationship between the Los Angeles (CA) facility and the Orange County Technical Vocational Institute.

External training consultants may be utilized by any training or non-training organization in three situations:

➤ When subject expertise is not available internally;
➤ When it is more cost-effective to train externally; or
➤ When internal resources cannot respond to needs.

Employee training plans are jointly developed by the individual and the immediate supervisor, and may utilize any of the above resources. To continuously improve our overall process of delivering appropriate training to all employees, CFI created the integrated CFI University System (CFIUS) in 1989. An executive Management Review Committee (MRC) was established to ensure that CFI's total training investment supports business objectives and strategies. A rotating CFI executive staff member serves on the MRC for corporate leadership and guidance. Training managers identified for each business group or geography make up the CFI University Management Board (UMB). Quarterly meetings with the executive MRC ensure a closed-loop system that integrates total training activities with company business objectives and needs.

CFI University is composed of functional "colleges," which include training personnel from organizations across the company. Each college is chartered to identify the key skills and knowledge necessary for the quality execution of all jobs within its functional area, including total quality competencies identified by CFI's Quality Technology Group. The identified competencies form the bases of curricula for every discipline at CFI. The first of 12 planned colleges, Management Development, was formed in 1990. The colleges of Quality, Product Development, Finance, Information Technology, Materials, Manufacturing, Engineering, and Human Resources Development have been established since then.

CFI believes that effective on-the-job reinforcement of knowledge and skills involves:

➤ Designing performance objectives into courses, based on what students need to know.

➤ Evaluating whether courses have accomplished their performance objectives.

➤ Reinforcing the new performance on the job.

Examples of this process include:

Operator skills training - All manufacturing operator certifications are performance based. Behavioral checklists are used to ensure that operators demonstrate skill competency while running their equipment in the actual workplace before they are certified to operate the equipment alone.

Multimedia training and information systems - CFI training increasingly incorporates multimedia instructional tools so that information can be reinforced after the learner leaves the classroom. For example, computer systems training offered by Planning Systems Training includes screen and report guides with field definitions for the user's workplace computer screen. In another example, components training interviews process-flow students six months to one year after completing the course to determine its impact on their job performance and to evaluate gains in job competency.

Post-tests and simulation practice - An example of post-tests used in conjunction with effective training design is Los Angeles' (CA) Technician Training on CFI's ultra-pure high carbon manufacturing process. Each complex task is broken down into a natural progression of skill requirements grouped into modules. Technicians must pass a post-test before progressing to the next module, thus reinforcing content and measuring knowledge for eventual task performance in the workplace.

Simulation practice - Planning Systems Training uses simulation practice to introduce new features of CFI's central planning system. Teams of planners are trained at each site and practice skills in an on-line simulation of the actual system before the new system features are implemented in the workplace. "Peer trainers" are also trained at each site, with backup videos made of the training session for reinforcement of skills on the job.

4.3.b(3) Training reinforcements

At the beginning of each training session, instructors are required to detail what skills, knowledge, and capabilities employees will possess at course completion. A copy of this is provided to each attendee's supervisor, who incorporates an evaluation of the employee's capability in using the new skill or knowledge into the employee's performance appraisal. After the year-end performance review, the training department analyzes the results to determine the effectiveness of the training and makes changes in the curricula, instruction, or delivery method accordingly.

4.3.b(4) Training evaluation and improvement

In general, CFI considers a wide variety of training activities to be quality focused, including customer-oriented training and courses on team effectiveness and interpersonal skills, and CFI culture and values training. Several factors have influenced quality education at CFI. In the early to mid-1980s, training on SPC was added to benchmark CFI's quality against that of leading Japanese companies, and in response to the expectations of major customers. By the mid-1980s, structured problem-solving training and employee teamwork were deployed throughout CFI. To support CFI's current business objectives, training is increasingly focused on cycle-time reduction and benchmarking.

In addition, New-Employee Orientation Training has been systematically revised to reflect CFI's continuous improvement philosophy. Our current orientation program presents our corporate values and culture, total quality philosophy, business products, policies, and procedures. Training plans are then developed for new employees, who receive an average of 51 hours of functional and operations-specific orientation.

With almost 5% of CFI's annual payroll applied to training, the company spends more than three times the national average on professional training. Between 1986 and 1994, the number of training hours per CFI employee increased by 55%. This can be seen in Figure 6.2.18.

Total CFI dollars invested in training (which we consider to be a key trend reflecting total quality education and training) increased 24% between 1989 and 1994, to $26.3 million. CFI's training and development investment levels increased from 2.6% of total payroll in 1989 to 4.9% in 1994, compared to a major competitor's investment of total payroll in 1994 of 3.4%. Moreover, CFI's training and development investment per employee increased from $1,725 per employee in 1989 to $2,025 per employee in 1994. CFI's investment per domestic employee was $2,460 in 1994. This compares to a 1994 U.S. average training expenditure of $471 per employee for companies with 10,000 to 20,000 employees.

To speed delivery and aid application and retention, both SPC and structural problem-solving training are delivered primarily "just in time" to intact teams encompassing virtually all employees.

4.4 Employee Well-Being and Satisfaction

4.4.a(1) Well-being improvement activities

Several of the sectors, including the Defense and Aerospace Sector (DAS) and the Nuclear and Specialty Sector (NSS), are involved in using materials that could be dangerous to employee health. Therefore, inherent in the process improvement

CASE STUDY

process are efforts to address both the reduction and elimination of materials hazardous to employees and the safe use of the materials if elimination cannot be achieved. When any process requires the use of hazardous materials, metrics are established to track the reduction in those same materials. This gives continuing visibility and priority to the elimination of all hazardous materials. Secondly, all accidents or incidents involving hazardous materials are given a "red flag." Immediately, a team is created to eliminate the root cause of the problem. This includes reengineering the process to eliminate hazardous material usage. Benchmarking of processes of other companies is a high priority when it is determined that they have reduced or eliminated the use of hazardous materials where CFI has not.

Maintaining a safe work environment is also one of our prime thrusts. Again, when accidents or incidents happen, an improvement team is formed whose responsibility is to perform root cause analysis (RCA) for the accident or incident. The team is responsible for developing permanent improvements to prevent recurrence in the future. When improvements are implemented, members from the safety organization validate that the improvement will eliminate the RCA determined cause before the improvement team is disbanded.

To proactively prevent accidents or incidents, Safety Awareness Teams (SATs) in each plant conduct regular safety audits of the work spaces to ensure that they are maintained in a safe condition. Safety "tickets" are written up on each violation. The supervisor of the area has the responsibility of correcting the discrepancies to the satisfaction of members of the SAT before the ticket is closed. Quarterly, the SAT in each plant analyzes the data on violations to determine if there are systemic issues. Violation summaries from other sectors are also reviewed to determine if there are emerging or corporate-wide issues. If systemic issues are noted, process improvement teams are formed to implement actions to prevent problems.

4.4.a(2) Improvement requirements

The corporate value of making CFI a "Great Place To Work," which states that employees are its fundamental strength, embodies the company's commitment to employee well-being and morale. Employee feedback, the changing demographics of the work force, industry trends, and recognition of the merging of work and personal lives continuously drive CFI to enhance its comprehensive program of employee benefits and services. During the past few years, for example, an employee assistance program,

recreation centers, a child care resource and referral network, and flexible start times have been introduced.

Major goals and methods impacting employee satisfaction and well-being include the following:

➤ Enhancement of an internal staffing capability to facilitate redeployment and career planning, thorough training, and upgraded systems and capabilities.

➤ Continued focus on management development through training and assessment of management skill through culture surveys, management practice surveys, and demonstrated learning.

➤ Maintenance of a leadership position in benefits while maintaining costs and providing excellent customer service.

Improvement in the quality of environmental, health, and safety (EHS) issues affecting employees is pursued at a number of levels within CFI. Integrated throughout CFI, from R&D groups to manufacturing and beyond, EHS provides a "built-in" quality improvement process that assesses the impact of new process, product, and equipment introductions. CFI also champions EHS improvements across the industry through equipment vendors, and has published extensive EHS performance standards in a Fasteners Supplier Handbook.

The Safety Improvement Team (SIT) fosters and directs EHS improvements and accident/incident reductions. The SIT established a Safety Bulletin Incident (SBI) program to report and investigate accidents and incidents. This programs ensures that incidents meeting predetermined criteria are formally investigated. It reviews findings, conducts RCA, and communicates corrective action among all CFI sites for purposes of elimination and prevention.

By analyzing trends and incidents, CFI safety committees make significant contributions to quality improvement. Safety suggestion systems and telephone hot lines support employee involvement in safety.

CFI's EHS group responds to illness and injury, and is proactive in promoting wellness through employee health fairs, cardiopulmonary resuscitation (CPR) training, and publication of health-related newsletters. This group routinely conducts medical monitoring for employees working with chemicals, reviews results with employees, and analyzes and acts on the aggregate test results. Each building also has an emergency response team, whose members receive extensive emergency-preparedness training.

CASE STUDY

In 1994, CFI achieved a number of results based on ongoing ergonomic assessments. These include the implementation of a number of workcell improvements at the Boston (MA) site and a corporate strategy to provide improved ergonomic designs for new CFI offices that are currently being deployed.

Key improvement goals for EHS are:

➤ A 45% reduction in solvent-based incidents by 1996.

➤ Elimination of all ozone-depleting compounds by 1997.

➤ A 50% hazardous waste reduction by 1996.

➤ A 60% reduction in 1995, cumulative trauma injuries.

4.4.b Services, facilities, and activities

CFI offers a variety of special services to support employee health, satisfaction, and well-being. A key service is the Employee Assistance Program (EAP), which provides confidential, 24-hour treatments and referrals for mental health, chemical dependency, and general living problems for all CFI employees and dependents.

Recreational facilities and showers were opened at all domestic sites in the late '80s, and CFI sponsors many employee sports teams, on-site aerobic classes, wellness programs, and stress management workshops.

A special program for domestic employees involves the granting of a nine-week sabbatical every seven years. This is in addition to their regular vacation accrual. The non-U.S. sites have comparable programs, but they are structured differently due to the local laws and customs of the country.

A child-care resource and referral program, parental leave-of-absence policy, and pre-retirement counseling were introduced in 1989. CFI also provides 100% tuition reimbursement and a wide range of professional development support that specifically targets its diverse work force, including the Asian Network, Women in Technology Group, Black Student Network, New College Graduate Network, and Diversity Task Force.

To address the disproportionate rising cost of home ownership in California, CFI implemented a first-time home buyers' loan program, amounting up to $30,000 of employee mortgage loans. This amount is loaded at the IRS minimum allowable interest rates over a five year loan horizon. Another example of CFI's commitment to the health and well-being of employees was the broad-based effort to assist affected employees after the devastating earthquakes and riots in California, floods in Georgia, and natural calamities in Xiang, China. CFI immediately formed task forces after the events to meet employee needs, including housing arrangements, van or transportation pools for commuting from restricted areas, counseling sessions, and employee contributions, grants, and loans to address material damages.

4.4.c Determining employee satisfaction

Employee satisfaction is determined most extensively through regularly conducted surveys, focus groups, and other communication forums. Examples of these methods include the following:

➤ One-on-one interviews with the agendas being controlled by the employees.

➤ Employee participation in the periodic employee culture survey that is delivered to all employees.

➤ Business update meetings for general communication and questions concerning business concerns.

➤ Various assessment methods and tools that include 360 degree input to managers, collective assessment of team dynamics, and individual learning and behavioral styles.

Examples of employee feedback and CFI's response - which include improvements to the performance appraisal system, and implementation and recreation centers and child-care resources have all been discussed in other areas-to-address.

CASE STUDY

5.0 PROCESS MANAGEMENT

CFI utilizes process design, monitoring, and control as a basic strategy for the business. The company has determined that increased quality and productivity with minimized costs is the result of such actions.

CFI closely follows the Motorola concept of 6 sigma (6σ), using the capability index of $C_p = 2$ and C_{pk} of 1.5 considering a 1.5 sigma variation shift of the mean.

To meet the process capability of $C_p = 2$, three sigma limits of the process are 0.5 of the 6σ specification limits of the particular process step. This concept is carried throughout the organization in products and non-product service support functions, and with suppliers.

A C_{pk} of 1.5 results in 3.4 parts per million (ppm) outside the specification limits.

If the mean of the process moves 1.5σ, the mean would be 4.5σ from a limit and is shown as C. For an individual item, $C_{pk} = C / (0.5 B) = 4.5 / 3 = 1.5$.

If the mean of the in-control process shifts 1.5σ, the results are that 3.4 parts per million will be outside the specification limit. If the mean shifts only 1σ, the result will be .39 ppm, and with no shift, .002 ppm.

The aims of the processes are to hold the mean at the center, but it may shift 1.5σ and still have only 3.4 ppm outside the specification limit for the individual process step.

CFI has used this approach successfully, and the customers and suppliers understand the concept and participate in the fruits of the results. As is described in this Category, process teams continually reduce process variability. Many processes have been subjected to several years of improvement.

As the individual process variations become less, the possibility for mean shifts becomes greater. Although the operators and responsible teams strive to hold the means, some movement usually results.

Another aspect of the approach used is that the customers, both internal and external, through the many contact opportunities have understood the need for moving out specification limits. The limits are expanded not to deliver products and services over a wider range, but to allow process capabilities of at least $C_p = 2$.

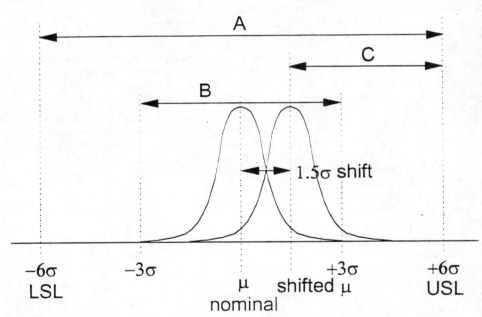

Figure 5.0.1, C_p and C_{pk} Relationships

Figure 5.0.1 shows this relationship and the calculations of C_p and C_{pk}. This figure is from a Motorola publication, "The Nature of Six Sigma Quality," by Mikel Harry, Ph.D.

The in-control process of ±3σ is shown as B. The specification limits of ±6σ are shown as A. The capability index $C_p = 2$ represents A / B = 6 / 3 = 2.

Industry specifications are generally wider than customers desire, and it is customary for producers to deliver to tighter tolerances, often as tight as one-half to one-quarter of industry standards.

CFI has led discussion in the industry and with customers to utilize the process capability approach

CASE STUDY

rather than tighter limits. With wider tolerances, more processes operate with C_{pk}'s of 1.5 or more.

5.1 Design and Introduction of Products and Services

5.1.a How products and delivery processes are designed

5.1.a(1) Translation of customer requirements

The design process is handled in a slightly different manner for products in each of the four sectors due to different product requirements. However, both internal as well as external customer satisfaction is always considered as the prime driver for new or improved processes. Another driver is for manufacturability which is processed in a program called Design for Manufacturabilty (DFM).

Inputs from the concerned functions convert customer requirements into product and service design requirements. This ensures customer needs are recognized as the basic reason for any changes, improvements, or new concepts.

A very important input to the design process is through the field sales engineer (FSE) who brings detailed customer knowledge to the design process. The FSE has spent a lot of time in the customer facilities, has talked to customer employees, and has firsthand information about the needs and expectations.

The FSEs and marketing representatives make recommendations in conjunction with suppliers for the selection of appropriate materials for an application that results in reduction of waste material. The results of effective material selection provide reduction in material wastage, as shown in Figure 5.1.1.

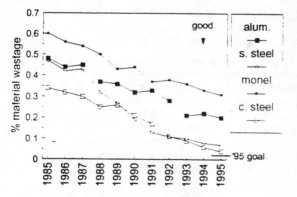

Figure 5.1.1, Wastage Reduction

In the Consumer Product Sector (CPS), industry standards are utilized for configuration, and CFI

processes are used. Commercial and Automotive Sector (CAS) parts are a combination of both standards and user specifications. DAS products are designed to military specifications with CFI processes.

The listening post activities described in Area 7.1.c are utilized to better understand customer requirements for the introduction of new products and services.

A brief, high level summary of the product design cycle at CFI is capsulated below and in Figure 5.1.2. The first activity in the cycle focuses on a new concept and its feasibility of design and production. Customers provide detail designs which are reviewed, evaluated, and concurred by CFI sector product teams. After agreement by the customer and CFI, the order is accepted. The first review is a Preliminary Design Review (PDR) where dimensions, materials and suppliers are screened for capabilities, proper design margins, and safety allowances. At this PDR, preliminary processes are presented for customer concurrence, and PTP relationships are established between CFI, the customer, and associated suppliers.

During the engineering and validation test activity phase (EVT), the new product is fully engineered and tested according to product specifications. Design capability margins and reliability are ensured. The final results of the design and its testing are reviewed at the Final Design Review (FDR). The initial production processes have been designed and checked for capability and verification that a process capability of $C_p = 2.0$ is attainable. The process itself and the limit specifications provided by knowledgeable customers, are considered.

The production validation testing (PVT) activities follow the FDR. In this set of activities, the initial processes are put into place and early production begins. Processes are constantly reviewed, analyzed, and tuned to ensure that proper capabilities are attained. The results of these activities are reviewed during the product acceptance review (PAR). This is the final review before a new product is put into full scale production. Once in full production, the product goes into the phase focused on process maturity acceptance (PMA). This is where process capabilities are constantly reviewed, production output is ramped up, and product maturity begins.

In each sector, customer requirements are fulfilled, suppliers are consulted, and, if applicable, customers approve the design.

In the Technical Data System (TDS), statistical techniques are maintained in the Engineering Information Architecture (EIA). All designed products are subjected to a DOE analysis for assurance that the design is robust and that applied environmental conditions will not adversely affect the reliability or the performance of the product in the end-use conditions. The DOE is contained in the Design for Quality and Reliability (DFQR) section of the EIA.

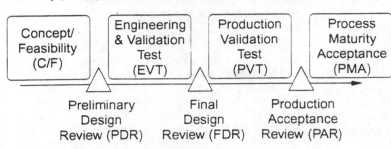

Figure 5.1.2, Product Design Cycle

Each sector maintains its own design capability, and all procedures and processes are documented and maintained. All sectors use the two design review process steps noted in Figure 5.1.2, but they modify and adjust them according to the particular design program requirements.

Within each sector, designs are documented in a single file that ensures coordination for the many designs utilized when they are formalized and placed under configuration control. These files are summarized for the review of other sectors for the possibility of adaptation or overlap. The complete files are always available to other sectors if desired.

An important link between customers and CFI during new product design, as well as other times where close communication is required, is the Electronic Data Interchange (EDI). Data are transferred between both suppliers and customers of CFI. EDI is also utilized between the engineering organizations and the factories to facilitate transfer of information at a high degree of accuracy, which is particularly important with the factories spread worldwide. The manual transfer of data would take considerably more time and be subject to many errors.

Another important communications tool with outside customers and suppliers is the voice mail hook-up where the outside organizations are treated as an arm of CFI.

5.1.a(2) Requirements translated into processes

As stated earlier, CFI maintains a strategy that all processes must maintain a C_p of 2.0 or greater.

Production process changes for new products are usually modifications of those used for similar

products. However, before FDRs can be approved, objective data must be presented demonstrating the distribution pattern of the material in the specific process steps. It must reference the measured sigma compared with the tolerance limits determined for that particular step. Usually the variation is well within the capability index of two and often has a margin of three or more. The design review team determines what characteristics will be measured and when the measurements will be accomplished.

Each of the process steps is documented with the sampling plan that is used to ensure that process variability is monitored and maintained. The sample size, frequency of sampling, and parameters to be checked are listed. The sampling proves the distribution to be in control, and the sigma are automatically calculated by the Operations Data System (ODS).

5.1.a(3) How all requirements are addressed early in the design cycle

Design reviews vary in scope depending on the complexity of the product and whether the changes are minor or major. In all cases, the reviews are accomplished with all concerned organizations.

Typically the functions represented in the design review are Engineering, Manufacturing, Quality, Logistics, Marketing, Field Service, and Purchasing, as well as supplier representatives and customers. At the PDR, all customer and CFI requirements are reviewed. All design reviews are documented, and the results maintained in the TDS.

The Computer Aided Fastener Design (CAFD) process embedded in the EIA is utilized for consistency and completeness.

Suppliers are included in the early design phase. CFI realizes that the suppliers provide the basic raw materials crucial to product and process consistency. This includes the chemicals used for cleaning, plating, and other process steps. Suppliers are often able to recommend better materials to meet customer requirements such as expected environments, the strength or other special needs, and the workability in the drawing, upsetting, and threading processes.

This careful selection of materials is part of the data used by the customer for consideration of allowing broadened specifications.

CASE STUDY

5.1.b How processes are reviewed prior to launch

The FDR provides data that show that the materials or services subjected to the specific processes meet the criteria of a distribution by attaining at least one-half the specification limit for the specific process step.

Many designs are modifications to existing products, and the established processes have been subjected to a continuing improvement process over several years. The process teams have the experience and knowledge, along with the data systems described in Category 2.0, to fully understand where the processes might need possible additional modification. The Design for Quality and Reliability (DFQR) process establishes assurance that production processes have been fully considered prior to a production launch.

Inputs to the design reviews come from functional organizations and are used to determine the necessary actions by the design team. These inputs are furnished by the functional representative on the design team who also provides two-way communications into the functional organizations. This ensures that all levels of employees have reviewed the designs to ensure that any details have not been overlooked.

5.1.c How processes are evaluated and improved

Within each department of each sector, processes are maintained by teams assigned the responsibility of designated processes. This same approach is used in the support service departments as well as the production departments. These teams continually review the status of processes to ensure that the relationship between the element being acted on and the limits assigned is within at least a C_{pk} of 1.5.

In the few cases when the $C_p = 2.0$ is not attainable initially, teams continue to work on improvements to the process steps in various ways including benchmarking, R&D, reengineering, and examining similar processes within CFI. Customers are also contacted to relate to process capability indices rather than the use of expanded specification limits if the design permits. Special summary reports are structured for those processes with C_p's of less than 2.0 and reported in the departmental reviews.

Every quarter, a review of the design process in each sector is accomplished. Representatives from the functional areas in the design process as well as corporate representatives review past data for results in quality and cycle time.

To ensure continuous improvement, goals are set for improvement and reviewed for attainment at the next meeting. If improvements have not been attained, assignments are established with specific dates set for accomplishment.

One success of this approach is shown in Figure 6.2.8. Design cycle time improvement results have occurred in all sectors with NSS still showing the greatest improvement opportunity primarily due to the extreme customer and regulatory requirements.

At monthly departmental reviews for action teams, various characteristics are compared to goals set, and process teams report, on a rotating basis, the results of their activities. They report on how many of the processes have a C_{pk} of 1.5 and how many exceed that figure. Team recognition is awarded to the top five teams each month in each department.

Teams are continually examining processes in their areas of responsibility and looking for better ways to accomplish the task. Benchmark activities are extensively used for comparison with other organizations that use alternative techniques that result in less variability, shorter cycle time, or lower cost.

Although each sector has different products, many processes are similar. This gives the teams during monthly reviews opportunities to compare process steps and results. In the case of support services, the differences in needs of the organizations are less, and usually the modified processes can be applied directly.

5.2 Process Management: Product and Service Production and Delivery

5.2a How the company maintains performance in production

5.2.a(1) Key processes

In the production of fasteners, all production processes are considered important because each and every process contributes to the quality, cycle time, and cost of the products. CFI has maintained the concept that all production processes will be at least a C_{pk} of 1.5.

The key processes that produce the products and services supplied to the customers are shown in Figure 5.2.1.

The principal requirements for the key processes are as follows:

Receiving Material Check - The receiving material check varies with the material, end customer requirements, and status of the supplier of that material. When the supplier is a key supplier that has been certified through the PTP process, the checking process only identifies the material and any certifications required by the end customers, as is usually required in the Nuclear and Specialty Sector. The PTP partner continually feeds statistical data through the EDI communication capabilities.

Other materials from non-certified suppliers will have chemical analysis or checks of physical properties. These checks are on a statistical sampling basis unless otherwise demanded by the individual customer. It is the primary goal of all sectors to reduce this effort as suppliers are certified through training and proven performance.

In handling incoming materials, bar codes are utilized to reduce cycle time and improve accuracy. Certified suppliers are provided with special bar code strips that identify the material, lot number, and required statistical process results information.

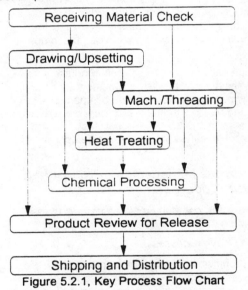

Figure 5.2.1, Key Process Flow Chart

Drawing and Upsetting - The drawing process typically changes the materials that are received in spools, such as wire, to the proper diameter for the particular fastener. The controls on this process vary with the end requirements of size tolerance, strength, material coatings, or other special customer needs.

The upsetting process forms the heads on the end of the fastener as with bolts or rivets. Some upsetting as in the drawing process requires precise temperature and environmental controls. Each situation is clearly defined during the design cycle, and the process is controlled to maintain the C_{pk} that was qualified during the process design drawing reviews.

These processes are dependent on lubricants used during the metal forming operations. Productivity gains have resulted from changes in lubricants as a result of supplier inputs and benchmarking visits.

Machining and Threading - Most of the fasteners produced use machining and thread cutting or rolling. Differences lie in the size, materials, and end use of the product.

The processes involved include the type of machine. usually with high levels of automation, and the type of cutting tools used with the requirement of adequate sharpness, and required coolants. Threading is accomplished in a variety of ways depending on the physical characteristics and the customer end use.

During the machining operations. the operators are empowered to monitor the process and are expected to halt the process if excessive variations occur. The operators use optical comparators on a regular basis. On a periodic basis, technicians from the labs select random samples for a complete analysis.

Process steps are handled during the process design with the sampling and assurance of the proper distributions to ensure the C_{pk} as determined in the design of the process.

Heat Treating - Heat treating is considered a key process because of the critical nature of the end use where the safety of people is usually involved.

The heat treating process includes chemicals. temperature controls, and various quenching techniques. The heat treating process is highly automated with little intervention by operators and, therefore, with less chance for process variability. The processes are certified during the design cycle as explained in Item 5.1, to ensure an index of at least $C_{pk} = 1.5$.

Chemical Processing - Chemical processing is vital to customers who use fasteners in environments hostile to the materials used. The amount and type of protection vary by the sector and the specific customer.

The process requirements may be plating which includes the chemicals used and the configuration of the baths with the times, temperatures, and agitation required. The process might be a dipped coating or a coating applied by an electrostatic process.

Processes have individual steps, each of which contribute to the end result. Each individual process step was defined during the design process, and the process steps were documented to result in a $C_{pk} = 1.5$. During the process, performance sampling

CASE STUDY

procedures are followed and documented in the ODS. Periodic audits of the production areas and data system ensure ongoing compliance of the chemical processing system.

Product Review for Release - This key process is for assurance that all processes have been applied to the proper materials for the proper customers. With the facilities distributed around the world delivering to customers around the world, and with the large number of products, overall reviews are necessary.

Production control of all products is centrally controlled in the ODS. Bar codes are used extensively to result in rapid, accurate records. Problems are seldom discovered. However, to ensure customer satisfaction, this process is retained.

Shipping and Distribution - The distribution system is a key process for CFI due to the necessity of delivery to customers throughout the world from the 16 manufacturing facilities in various countries.

Customers have become increasingly demanding of just-in-time deliveries. CFI has learned to balance off-shore manufacturing to stage products in warehouse sites at strategic locations close enough to major customers to meet just-in-time requirements.

To accomplish these actions, a multi-layer distribution system has been developed. This system provides bulk shipments from manufacturing facilities directly to large customers as well as distributed warehouses. In turn, warehouses ship directly to customers as well as secondary facilities where materials from all sectors are accumulated. This is particularly important for the Consumer Products Sector.

As a result, the distribution system requirements of accuracy of records and protection of parts are essential. The concept of $C_{pk} = 1.5$ is maintained with processes being determined with sampling used to ensure minimized variability. Automatic counting utilizes sensitive scales and bar codes with the automatic stocking process being computer controlled.

5.2.a(2) Measurement plan

During the design cycle, every process is designed and proven before the design is released. The process certification consists of demonstrated success that the process has a capability of at least a C_{pk} of 1.5. As products are processed, distributions are automatically calculated via the ODS to ensure that the sigma is remaining as was initially determined to be necessary.

When it is discovered that the distribution is out-of-control or the variability has increased, the process is immediately stopped by the operator who is empowered and expected to halt the process. The team that has the responsibility for the specific process is immediately convened, and it requests any technical capabilities that are needed to rectify the process problem. Design engineers, suppliers, quality engineers, data analysts, or whoever can contribute to the solution are utilized by the process team leader. The Plan, Do, Check, Act (PDCA) process is exercised at this time. After the root cause has been determined, the solution is installed, the process restarted, and the data taken once again.

The sample frequency is tripled, and no more deviations can be experienced for the next five shifts in order for the sampling frequency to go back to normal. The process team reviews the data records to determine any similar processes throughout the company. If any are found, the responsible teams are immediately notified in the other three sectors.

Another key service deliverable is the service of FSEs who perform in close liaison with customers solving problems and providing a vital link back to the various CFI businesses.

5.2.b How processes are improved

5.2.b(1) Process analysis and research

The assigned process teams are always on the alert to improve processes in order to reduce variability and increase capability. Benchmarking and communicating with other functions in the company have proven to be a fertile area for improvement ideas.

Employee operators are aware of distributions that begin to spread. They alert the appropriate team if the capability number drops although it may still be over the C_{pk} of 1.5.

For common processes, a section of the common R&D division researches processes for both improvements as well as totally new approaches. This information is available to the process teams in all sectors through the data system.

As a result of the data system providing information worldwide, any time a process shows improvement, the information is available to the other plants regardless of the sector affiliation. At the annual Recognition Celebrations, the process teams are recognized for the increases in capability indexes that they have accomplished.

CASE STUDY

5.2.b(2) Benchmarking

As has been pointed out earlier, benchmarking has proven to be one of the better methods for improving process characteristics including simplification, reduced variation, and reduced cycle time.

When a benchmark partner in the PTP process is selected for a particular review, the process team members make the partners fully aware of their own process with the specific measurements used to measure the process. During the visit, the partner's process is examined in detail with careful observance to incremental improvement data. Often, only a part of the process may be the superior part, and only that particular segment may be utilized.

5.2.b(3) Use of alternative technology

Technology has resulted in many improvements. Design engineers and process teams are always aware of opportunities to apply new techniques, equipment, and approaches to process control.

As an example of applying a new technique, a recent improvement in the DAS was the result of better temperature control of bolts that had a heat treating requirement. One of the process teams learned of a new electronic method that used very high frequency radiation to heat bolts in a protective container. This new method reproduced the temperature variation to within ±0.3 degrees centigrade where with past equipment would only reproduce to ±1.0 degrees. This order of magnitude improvement resulted in a new C_p of 2.1 against the earlier C_p of 1.8.

With this change, the process capability was improved to the point that heat treating testing was eliminated. Only the regular sampling required to determine that the process is in control is used. The new technology was developed for a drug manufacturing process, but an alert process team member visualized the application to heating individual bolts.

5.2.b(4) Information from customers

CFI maintains close customer relationships as described in Items 7.2 and 7.3. Some customers also manufacture fasteners although none has the broad range of products of CFI. These customers have provided benchmark partnerships, PTPs, that have resulted in many process improvements.

Other customers have helped in service areas such as stocking and delivery techniques. Customers want just-in-time deliveries, and CFI is dedicated to provide the service. In several instances, customers have suggested solutions and improvements to CFI's service deliveries by describing and demonstrating how cycle times could be reduced, and in many cases have provided better protection for the product. This has been most prevalent in the CAS where customers are more mature in ways of handling products and delivering just-in-time.

With many teams in action throughout the company in all sectors, internal customer feedback has been the source of many applications of improved processes and reduced cycle time.

Stock handlers in CPS provided an idea to handle large skids of product by using air to lift the skid for better maneuverability. A base with air outlets on the bottom connecting to an air line permitted a lone stock handler to move skids weighing greater than one ton around the shipping floor.

5.3 Process Management: Support Services

In this Item, several examples are discussed that are representative of the total company. The process concept of the company, as is described in Items 5.1 and 5.2, encompasses the support service functions as well. Formal procedures are utilized in the support service areas in a similar fashion to those used in the product and service portions of CFI.

The support functions now use measurements in parts per million (ppm) rather than percent. They are tied to the production facilities with EDI, and they design and monitor their processes to the goals of $C_p \geq 1.5$. The support functions are also connected to customers, both internal and external, as well as suppliers, with voice mail capabilities. This improvement in communications reduces cycle times, improves accuracy, and results in lower costs.

5.3.a How support services processes are designed

5.3.a(1) How key requirements are determined

Each support service makes a determination of the key processes needed for support of its delivered products. The department determines the mission of its function as a result of the strategic planning process, and the departmental plans stem from the strategic plan and from discussions with employees in the function.

Planning teams are formed during the data gathering phase for the strategic plan, and priorities are established in the order of importance to the business aims of the sector. The cognizant team lists all of the requirements for specific actions with the agreement of the team as to what are the key requirements to establish priorities.

CASE STUDY

5.3.a(2) How requirements are translated into processes

Process teams are utilized in the support service functions as they are in the product and service producing functions. These teams are also trained in process mapping, problem solving, and benchmarking. Processes are flowcharted, compared to similar processes, and fully documented.

Processes in the support functions are structured with specific limits for each step, and the process is measured to determine the sigma for the controlled process. These processes are also expected to attain a capability index of $C_p \geq 2$. Dialog with internal customers result in limits that are more easily defined. The process steps are documented, and the necessary measurements are included. This includes the sampling plan with the specific parameters to be checked.

As an example in the CAS, the Accounting Department designed an accounts payable process to be more responsive to small suppliers who require regular cash flow to maintain their continuous improvement processes.

An Accounting Department team met with suppliers and Purchasing to determine the best method for submitting invoices. It also met with the material receiving organization to determine the fastest, most accurate methods of verifying material acceptance. The results are shown in Figure 5.3.1.

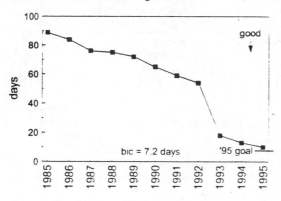

Figure 5.3.1, Time to Pay Invoices

A new process was designed and installed selecting limits in cycle time for each step in the paying process. The resulting sigma was determined to ensure that the process operated at $C_p \geq 2.0$. Sampling plans were installed to ensure that the process would remain "in-control."

Another process that has been significantly improved is the reduction in time to close the books at the end of each month. This required the efforts of a cross-functional team composed of members from Accounting, Operations, IS, Marketing, and Human Relations. The team met weekly and continues to meet to maintain the rate of improvement. The results of this activity are shown in Figure 5.3.2.

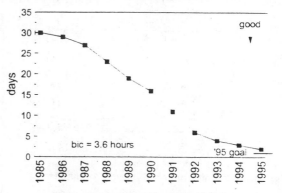

Figure 5.3.2, Days to Close the Books

5.3.a(3) Requirements addressed early in the design

Most of the processes in the functional support organizations are established and changed using the continuous improvement methodology by the assigned process teams.

New processes usually evolve from new technology and new techniques to go with additional requirements. An example of this has been the upgrading of the IS process. As the company has grown and expanded around the world, significant additional demands were placed on the system. At the same time, both hardware and software with additional capabilities had become available.

To take advantage of the new capabilities and to meet growing requirements, a significant amount of coordination with all the sectors, suppliers, and customers was needed. Facilities around the world were consulted to ensure adequate inputs for requirements and agreement of acceptable internal data system cross-communications and available data outputs.

The new IS system was completely designed before going on line in 1989. The system was installed with measurements concerning response time and availability for data inputs. Limits were established, and the resulting sigma operated within the required process capability considerations.

CASE STUDY

The system went on line with few problems, a real tribute to the many teams that worked together to structure the system. It could also be a tribute to the work of designing the process to the requirements of the internal customer and determining the capability of the process to operate within the set limits.

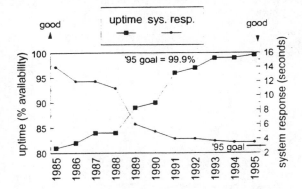

Figure 5.3.3, Information Systems Availability

Figure 5.3.3 shows the success of the system for availability and improved response time. This has been accomplished during a period of sales growth and increased dependence on the data system.

5.3.b How the company maintains performance

5.3.b(1) Key processes and requirements

Some key processes in support areas are contained in Table 5.3.1. These are highlights of a wealth of additional processes.

Each of these representative key processes has principal requirements that are determined by assigned teams in the areas of the process. For example, the requirements of the Financial Data System (FDS) are concerned with accuracy, time to generate reports, containment of all costs and revenues, and timely output reports that are clear and understandable by those receiving the reports.

The planning teams use an established methodology to the approach of reviewing processes. Each key process has established measurements with goals of continuous improvement assigned. Processes are reviewed through process mapping using questions like: "Is the process step needed?"; "Is it accomplishing the requirement?"; or "Can it be done better by modification of equipment or operator training?" This same methodology is repeated in all functions, by all teams, to ensure continuous improvement.

As an example, preventive maintenance (PM) is a function that has a significant effect on the overall operations. When the maintenance is performed on time, the production equipment performs better. Figure 5.3.4 shows the results of improved maintenance over the last ten years with machine downtime approaching 1.0%.

Table 5.3.1, Key Company Processes

Area	Processes	Figure
Accounting	Time to Pay Invoices	5.3.1
	Sales Volume	6.2.5
	Profit Margin	6.2.7
	Days to Close Books	5.3.2
Marketing	Market Share	6.2.6
	Customer Complaint Calls	7.4.6
	Lead Time to Order Fulfillment	6.1.7
R&D	Design Cycle Time	6.2.8
	Product Setup Cycle Time	6.2.9
Human Resources	Employees Engaged in Teams	6.2.21
	Training Hours per Employee	6.2.18
	Team and Individual Awards	6.2.19
Administration	Corporate Citizenship Engagements	6.2.22
	Information Systems	6.2.10
Operations	Preventive Maintenance	5.3.4
	Operational Productivity, Non-Products	6.2.2

The measurement plan in the service and support areas is very similar to those in the product areas. All process steps are designed with a documented process. The steps are continually assessed to be in control with a calculated sigma to ensure a C_{pk} of 1.5 or better.

As in production, the process steps have specific plans for the frequency of sampling as well as the parameters to be measured. In support areas, usually the measurement is for cycle time, with accuracy and costs also measured. Examples of the reduction in cycle times are the invoice payment cycle and "days to close the books" indicators shown in Figures 5.3.1 and 5.3.2.

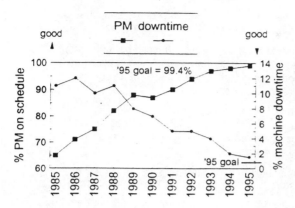

Figure 5.3.4, Preventive Maintenance

5.3.b(2) The measurement plan

Support functions require continual training of employees involved in statistical techniques to ensure their comfort and competence with these types of measurements. The process control applications in support functions have normally been heavily weighted toward measuring and controlling paper handling and administrative type processes. This has proven to be a significant driver in increased organizational performance resulting in less cycle time and lower operating costs.

5.3.c How processes are improved

5.3.c(1) Process analysis and research

Support processes are analyzed to define the steps for measurement improvement. Research is accomplished primarily when new techniques or equipment are utilized such as the data system redesign with new computer capabilities.

Similar techniques are used in the engineering areas where new workstations have become available. Word processing techniques have completely superseded all typing duties. The application of bar coding techniques is a good example of improving data input cycle time and accuracy.

Process teams in all functions are continually investigating new capabilities that often require additional training. If required, the teams arrange for and sometimes perform the training.

5.3.c(2) Benchmarking

Benchmarking activities have been mentioned in several areas. CFI has discovered the advantages of benchmarking in the goal-setting mode and the more important advantage of process review capability and improvements.

Benchmarking has been utilized to a high degree in support areas. A real advantage is that new processes have applicability in most sector businesses. The major difference in support processes from product processes is that we generally go outside our industry to find high performance processes.

A new process, such as preventive maintenance which was described earlier, can be used in the same manner for many facilities in the company. As was also stated earlier, the NIH factor has been overcome, and processes learned in a benchmark study are frequently used "as-is" in many support organizations.

5.3.c(3) Use of alternative technology

Alternative technology has been addressed in many areas in the field of personal computers. As new equipment with significantly greater capability and many new software programs become available, teams are continually investigating and evaluating their applicability. Due to the rapid changes in costs and capabilities, comparisons are ongoing.

Voice mail is used extensively in the support functions. Communications have been vastly improved, and actual paper use has almost been eliminated. Bar codes are used in the support areas for routing of reports and documents.

Process teams in the support functions are continually researching and reviewing ideas for the application of alternative technologies. Inputs for ideas and actions derive from benchmarking visits of organizations outside the fastener industry, visits to trade shows, internal visits to other sectors, and combing business periodicals. Monthly meetings are utilized to measure progress and emphasize the need for improvements.

5.3.c(4) Information from customers

CFI is focused on outside customers and has always maintained a good dialog with them. Although much of the information transferred relates to products for both today and in the future, many times support processes are covered in customer discussions. Usually this concerns an interface condition, such as billing or credits, and sometimes occurs as a result of a visit where an observation can lead to improvements.

Internal customers are also solicited for information, and actions are often taken as a result of their observations and suggestions.

Most of the sectors have utilized the PTP technique of having internal suppliers and customers meet at a regular time (such as Friday afternoons at 3:00 PM) to

CASE STUDY

discuss mutual needs and services. These meetings allow better understanding between the parties and result in continually improved, more effective services.

All sectors of the company are encouraged to take advantage of customer inputs. The NSS recently learned of a better process to tabulate and maintain records of audits required by the Nuclear Regulatory Commission. The process utilized a portable device that transferred records by radio directly from the auditor to the records retention area. The device also produced a bar code strip that would be attached to the material.

This was faster and more accurate, with less overall cost, and was an application of new technology provided by an outside customer. In turn, this process was picked up by the CPS as a method of inventory counting where counts from the end of the production line are fed into the data system immediately. Upon receipt in the stockroom, a verification count would either accept the count or immediately alert the material handlers of possible misplaced material.

5.4 Management of Supplier Performance

CFI recognizes the importance of suppliers to the success of the business in all sectors and has established a process called Pass Through Partnerships (PTP) to share lessons learned to improve quality, reduce cycle time, and pass on technology advances.

Figure 5.4.1, Supplier Certification Process

This process establishes special relationships with suppliers. It fosters sharing of benchmark information, provides training in process control concepts, and periodically holds seminars in "lessons learned." When suppliers qualify with their processes attaining C_{pk}'s > 1.5 and pass other requirements to show the capabilities will be maintained, they become "Certified" and their products are not subject to receiving inspection at any of the CFI facilities. Figure

5.4.1 shows a high-level view of the supplier certification process.

Certified Suppliers receive special bar code strips to attach to products delivered. This simplifies the incoming process and results in the suppliers receiving payment earlier.

Certified Suppliers are connected with EDI, which provides them with product specifications and production requirements information as soon as CFI makes needs determinations.

The supplier certification program is shared with all sectors to minimize costs of developing suppliers.

Figure 6.3.1 shows the growth in PTP partners and the increase in Certified Suppliers.

5.4.a Summary of company requirements

5.4.a(1) Principal requirements for key suppliers

CFI presently has 420 suppliers for both raw materials for products and materials integrated into salable products. Key materials are metals such as aluminum, carbon steel, stainless steel, monel, and brass. Chemicals for processing and cleaning are also considered to be key materials.

Quality, delivery, and price are all very important for the following reasons:

Quality - The foundation of CFI has been built in quality and continues to be a driving force in the competitive markets. Due to the nature of the products, the raw materials establish the foundation for output product quality.

Delivery - A percentage of customers are purchasing proprietary parts and depend on CFI to deliver on time. If delivery were to be interrupted, customer's deliveries would be quickly affected as most customers are utilizing just-in-time concepts with little material in stock.

Price - Price is always important as competitors are emerging on a daily basis. Although customers understand quality and dependable on-time delivery, they are continually concerned about price. Fasteners are usually considered a "C" item and expected to be a very low price.

Utilizing the process control philosophy with process capability measurements, CFI passes the same requirements on to suppliers. Suppliers are expected to have their processes measured and to have a C_{pk}

CASE STUDY

of 1.5 or greater. This includes the support services at the suppliers.

CFI has a business strategy to be the technology leader in the introduction of revolutionary fasteners and has established a supplier base with similar goals. These knowledgeable suppliers have simplified the transfer of understanding of process control capability techniques.

5.4.a(2) How the company determines performance

Through the PTP and supplier certifications with process capability techniques in which many suppliers participate, incoming product quality is ensured. Many suppliers are part of large companies and have participated in similar programs with other customers.

In some cases, suppliers are not certified and alternative suppliers have not yet been developed to replace them although an active program is in process. For suppliers not certified, product inspection is performed on all incoming materials. These inspections consist of samples of chemical analysis and physical properties. The measurements to be sampled are determined during the design process to maintain material capabilities that are utilized in the production process. In addition to quality requirements, price and delivery are also important and are consistently monitored by the purchasing group.

5.4.a(3) How performance is fed back

The PTP program is structured with a series of meetings with involved suppliers that occur a minimum of quarterly. These meetings are held with all concerned sectors represented to minimize the number of meetings of the company.

The number of suppliers in the PTP program is shown in Figure 6.3.1. Also shown is the number of Certified Suppliers.

For suppliers in the PTP program, all have the EDI link to receive real-time feedback on their performance. In addition, most have electronic mail connectivity for regular communications with CFI.

For suppliers not in the formal PTP program, information is mailed to them from the Purchasing organization once per quarter in the form of a printout from the ODS. This Supplier Rating System (SRS) information is automatically compiled, and rejection rates are presented along with supplier receipt information.

If any lot rejection rate exceeds 250 ppm, the supplier is flagged with a Supplier Corrective Action Request (SCAR). A specific site visit is made to resolve the problem by determining the root cause and developing a Corrective Action Plan (CAP).

5.4.b How the company improves supplier performance

5.4.b(1) Improve suppliers' abilities

As described earlier in the application, CFI utilizes several programs to improve suppliers' capabilities. The PTP program for participating suppliers has many ways to help.

A Cost of Doing Business (CODB) factor has been established for all suppliers which calculates the costs to CFI due to suppliers' failure to meet requirements, such as the costs to return lots which fail to meet specification. The CODB factor is used in subsequent procurements to give preference to high performing suppliers.

Annually, a planning meeting is held with the top 40 volume suppliers to develop plans for improvements. In this planning meeting, action plans with targets are developed for both CFI and the supplier for the upcoming year. These action plans and targets are fed into the company's annual planning process.

CFI has provided supplier training and recognition as incentives to improve. The data systems discussed in Category 2.0 explain how data are available, timely, and accurate.

If the incentives and help are not enough for improvement to occur, the supplier may well become one of those in the supplier base reduction plan.

5.4.b(2) Improve procurement

The PTP program provides a two-way dialog with individual suppliers. This gives them the opportunity to point out situations where the purchasing process can be improved.

Last year, CFI started a Preferred Customer Certification Program (PCCP). Our principal suppliers have helped develop a set of criteria for rating whether we are the customer of choice. These criteria include: timeliness, quality, clarity of communication, and supplier satisfaction. Quarterly Survey Inc., an independent contractor, sends all CFI suppliers a survey. Analysis is conducted on the survey and ratings are established similar to the PTP program. Action plans are established by a multi-functional internal team to improve our procurement and supplier management process. Results of the survey and action plans are fed to all suppliers.

In 1994, one of the suppliers that had not attained certification, Salter Inc., explained in a memo that it

CASE STUDY

was not provided a detailed set of reasons why its product, a special washer, was being rejected. The investigation by the process team determined that the washer specification had been modified for use in another sector. Further analysis proved that a second supplier of the same washer had agreed to the change and had been shipping to a tighter specification. The purchasing procedures were modified, and Salter was able to make the changes and the rejections stopped.

5.4.b(3) Minimize costs of inspection

The process control capability concept is directed toward reduced costs in receiving inspection. In the case where suppliers have processes greater than a C_{pk} of 1.5, they also can cease final inspection. Thus, the thrust of capability studies is directed toward lower costs and reduced lead-times.

The suppliers who have achieved certification send process performance data through the EDI system to CFI. When this data shows that the supplier is attaining a C_{pk} of at least 1.5, then all inspections and audits are suspended for that supplier. As long as the data continue to show the processes are under control, no audits or inspections are conducted. Further, if the supplier takes prompt actions for processes which are drifting out of control, inspections and audits are not resumed. Our PCCP survey results indicate that all suppliers find this proactive approach very helpful and meaningful.

CASE STUDY

6.0 BUSINESS RESULTS

6.1 Product and Service Quality Results

6.1.a Levels and trends in product and service

One of CFI's business strategies is to deliver 6 sigma products on time. The quality of the product delivered is directly related to the C_{pk}'s of processes at the various facilities. Category 6.0 describes how the various sectors have met that challenge.

Figure 6.1.1 shows the results of sectors that are operating with C_{pk}'s of at least 1.5 and showing improvements over the last ten years.

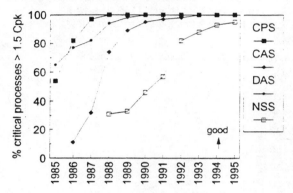

Figure 6.1.1, Percent of Critical Processes > 1.5 C_{pk}

The improved C_{pk}'s translate to improved product quality.

Process yields vary for each type of product in each sector. To demonstrate the differences, a chart from the CPS is shown for four different products. The yields are related to the complexity of the part and the processes used and are shown in Figure 6.1.2.

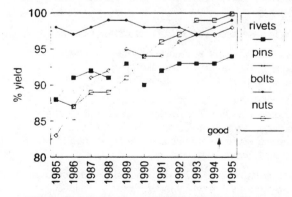

Figure 6.1.2, Process Yield by Product Type

The improved process capabilities have shown overall results in the yields. Figure 6.1.3 shows the yields by sector.

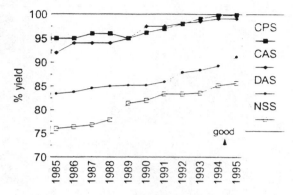

Figure 6.1.3, Operations Yield

The Consumer Products Sector has the highest percentages of processes operating with high C_{pk} values as the company has more flexibility in setting limits. DAS and NSS customers are continually attempting to get the most out of all products pushing processes to their limits, making process capabilities less, and thus yields are lower.

Problems with customers often relate more to mistakes in quantities or the wrong product shipped than defective parts. These situations result in most of the warranty returns. Figure 6.1.4 shows the reduction in warranty returns over the last ten years for each of the four sectors.

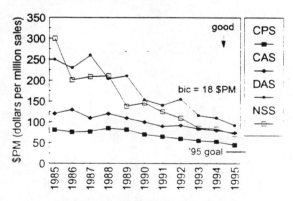

Figure 6.1.4, Warranty Returns

The highest warranty returns are in DAS with just under 0.01% of sales with CPS running under 0.005% of sales.

Significant to customers is the resolution of problems when they do occur. Figure 6.1.5 shows for the same ten years, over 90% of the problems are resolved for all sectors except the Defense and Specialty Sector, with the Commercial and Specialty Sector being over 98%.

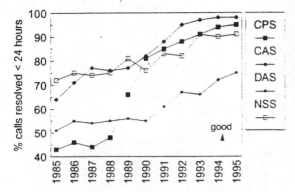

Figure 6.1.5, Problem Calls Resolved Within 24 Hours

The DAS is still low as a result of solving paperwork problems with defense contract administrators and the extensive checking that is required. Typically, warranty returns represent only about one-fourth of the problems, and the problem calls reflect about this same percentage.

On-time delivery, part of one of the five key business strategies, is shown in Figure 6.1.6.

Figure 6.1.6, On Dock Performance

For many years, CFI maintained that delivery was the date a product was shipped from the CFI facility. Customers explained that, from their standpoint, the date the material arrived at their dock is all that mattered. In 1990, CFI changed the measuring point and the performance degraded until new processes were established to meet the customers' expectations.

Meeting the promised on-dock delivery to the customer is very important to CFI. On-dock performance for the Commercial and Automotive Sector approximates 100%. NSS shipments are around 99% often due to the unreasonable dates requested by their customers and the promise by CFI to try and make a very short-time delivery. Nuclear requirements are sometimes changed during production due to changes in government regulations.

Another important matter is delivery with very short lead times. Customers expect immediate delivery with an order, and the company has responded.

Figure 6.1.7 shows significant improvement over the last ten years. The exception is NSS where few speculative product actions can be taken prior to order receipt.

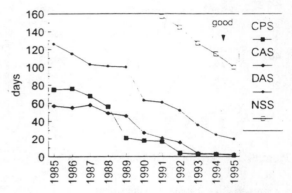

Figure 6.1.7, Lead Time to Order Fulfillment

NSS remains higher than the other sectors due to business characteristics; however, progress is substantial. The remaining three sectors have experienced outstanding results.

6.2 Company Operational and Financial Results

6.2a Levels and Trends in Operational Results

Results information is presented in three separate groups. The figures are representative, and space limitations preclude the inclusion of more.

The first grouping is from the operations area, the second shows financial results, and the third, service and support functional results. Some figures show comparisons and some figures are comparison figures by themselves.

Operations - Figure 6.2.1 demonstrates productivity improvements over ten years for product-related operations. Productivity has consistently improved in all sectors for the last ten years. This is the result of

CASE STUDY

team actions in all product areas and due in large measure to the efforts in improving the process capabilities.

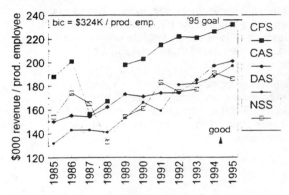

Figure 6.2.1, Operational Productivity, Products

Figure 6.2.2 shows the increases in productivity in non-product functions. As is discussed in Item 5.3, the same actions are taken in the support functions to improve processes and attain C_{pk}'s of 1.5, or better, as are taken in the product areas. This has improved the productivity over the last ten years in all sectors. This improvement in the support service areas has given CFI significant advantages in cost over the competition who has not kept pace in the support areas.

The recent improvement in CPS results is due to moving off-shore production work and the significant reduction in support personnel that has been customary in the U.S.

NSS has lagged as a result of regulation requirements that will not allow reductions even when process capability studies show that checking functions can be eliminated.

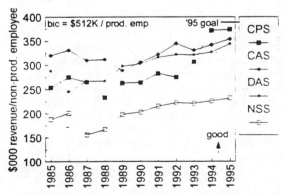

Figure 6.2.2, Operational Productivity, Non-Products

Figure 6.2.3 demonstrates the substantial improvement in overall quality of all the sectors in all actions. This figure is a compilation of quality figures throughout the company and is the information figure provided to top management for their assessment of the total company. This figure demonstrates the power of the process capability approach.

The corporate quality index accounts for problems within the production facility as well as customer complaints and problems. The index is structured so that 100 indicates organizational excellence with no problems being identified.

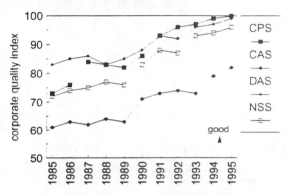

Figure 6.2.3, Operations Quality

Another measure of operations is the scrap report. Figure 6.2.4 shows the significant reduction in scrap for the total company. This figure is compiled for the entire company and is another indication of the results of the approach to have all process steps operating with a C_p of at least 2.0.

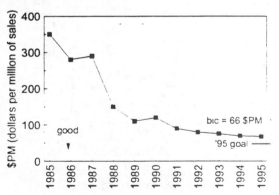

Figure 6.2.4, Scrap Material

Another operational result is shown in Figure 5.3.2. This accomplishment described in Item 5.3 demonstrates the success of a rigorous preventive

47

CASE STUDY

maintenance program aimed at improving machine downtime.

Financial - As a result of pleasing customers with good products on time, business has continued to increase, and sales volume has increased as shown on Figure 6.2.5. Although NSS sales volume has reduced and DAS is about the same, overall company sales have continued to increase.

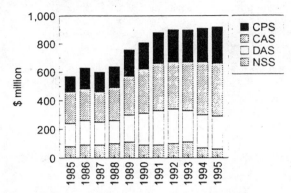

Figure 6.2.5, Worldwide Annual Sales Volume

The increase in market share is shown on Figure 6.2.6. It shows total available market (TAM) share growth in all sectors including NSS. The DAS has continued to increase in spite of the reduction in defense dollars. This is a real measure of the success of CFI with its customers.

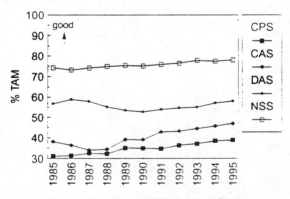

Figure 6.2.6, Worldwide Market Share

The best-indication of success for any company is sustained profit results over continuing years. CFI has experienced an impressive increase in profit margins across all products except DAS. The DAS profit margin has been dropping due to the extreme pressures from both competitors and the Government buyers. Since supply to the defense industry was a core business during the establishment of the

company, CFI will continue to remain a dominant supplier to the country in spite of eroding profit margins and diminished market opportunity.

Figure 6.2.7 shows that profit margins have increased directly as a result of the capability process techniques. Figures 6.1.1 indicate an increased number of critical processes attaining process capabilities over 1.5.

The leverage of increased volume with increased productivity and lower costs results in better profit margins. DAS profitability has fallen off due to customer price pressures and reduced business opportunities.

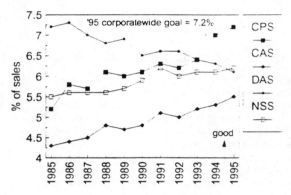

Figure 6.2.7, Profit Margin

Service Support - The overall productivity data for the non-product functions are shown in Figure 6.2.2. More detailed measurements displaying **accomplishments in service support areas by figures in the following areas:**

- ➤ *Engineering*
- ➤ *Information Systems*
- ➤ *Environmental*
- ➤ *Human Relations*
- ➤ *Administration*

Engineering - Engineering function accomplishments are displayed in two figures. Figure 6.2.8 shows the reduction in product design cycle time over ten years for each sector. All sectors have been significantly reduced over the last ten years. NSS creates product designs in a difficult area of ever-changing requirements due to the constant change in regulations. However, the improvement has been substantial.

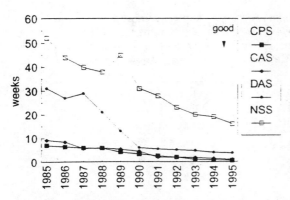

Figure 6.2.8, Product Design Cycle Time

Another measure of the improvement in the engineering function has been the reduction in product setup cycle time. With the continual needs of customers for shortened time for deliveries and shorter production runs, engineering resources have been directed toward reducing the setup time for different products.

The single minute die exchange (SMDE) program was instigated in 1989. This program moved the engineering organizations toward reducing the time for product set-ups and has resulted in significantly reduced cycle time as seen in Figure 6.2.9.

This reduction has allowed CFI to be more responsive to the customer and yet be more productive with less inventory for both cost and product obsolescence reasons.

In 1993, NSS suffered a setback in reducing setup time when significantly more stringent requirements were placed on x-ray results that must be taken, interpreted, and passed before a product could be moved from the production fixtures.

Through some very successful benchmark visits and discussions within the nuclear industry, the setup times are once more being reduced.

Figure 6.2.9, Product Setup Cycle Time, dramatically shows this experience.

Information Systems - Information systems as described in Category 2.0 are an essential element in the operation of the business as the data systems tie together the total company and provide the information required to manage the worldwide facilities on the basis of facts.

As data requirements have increased, the demands on the data system have also increased. To address this opportunity, teams from all functions work together utilizing new technologies and new equipment to increase the capability and availability of the varied data systems, both at the corporate level and within the individual sectors.

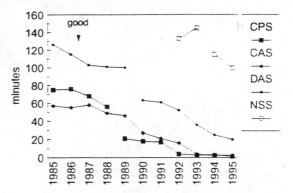

Figure 6.2.9, Product Setup Cycle Time

Figure 6.2.10 shows how the availability has increased and the response time has decreased at a time when the demands of the system have been expanding at a great rate.

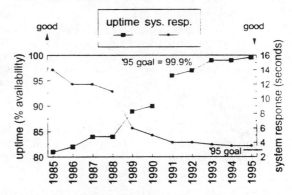

Figure 6.2.10, Information Systems Availability

Environmental - Another of the company's business strategies is to protect the environment at all worldwide locations, setting the benchmark for others to follow. An example of environmental responsiveness is shown in Figure 6.2.11 which shows the reduction in solid wastes over the last ten years.

Solid waste is a significant problem. Many resources are expended in handling the various wastes including metal cuttings, chemical deposits, paper of all types, and wood from receiving materials from overseas shipments.

CASE STUDY

The various solutions have been attained by team actions in all locations and in all sectors. Many examples of success are passed on to other organizations. Benchmarking PTPs, along with discussions with suppliers and customers, have led to the results shown.

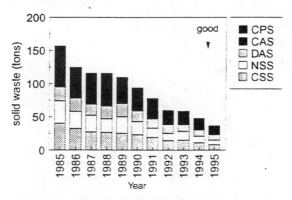

Figure 6.2.11, Reduction of Solid Waste

CFI has established itself as the benchmark with the corporate goal of being compliant to the tightest goals around the world for all facilities.

Liquid wastes have been reduced 97% over the last five years through the use of substitute materials such as water soluble cleaning solutions. Vapor emissions have been reduced 95% during this same period of time.

Another example of how the company is protecting the environment around the world is the effort to reduce the amount of material that requires recycling through more efficient use of material. This reduction is shown in Figure 6.2.12.

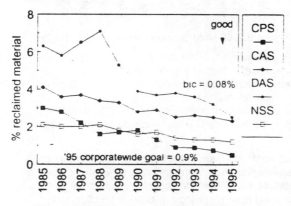

Figure 6.2.12 Percent Reclaimed Material

Human Relations - Many favorable accomplishments have resulted from efforts in the Human Resources function, and several programs in effect are discussed in Category 4.0.

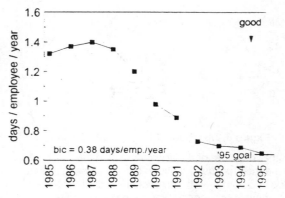

Figure 6.2.13, Lost Work Day Cases

One example of success in this function is shown in Figure 6.2.13. This figure demonstrates the reduction in lost days of work due to accidents. The number of cases corporatewide in the United States has been significantly reduced from a high of 1.4 in 1987 to under 0.7 in 1994 and nearing the benchmark of 0.38. This reduction indicates the results of the company's efforts to emphasize safety through training, invest in equipment, and constantly remind employees about safety concerns.

Additional accomplishments in the Human Resources function are shown in Figures 6.2.14 through 6.2.21. Workers compensation, although not yet attaining the benchmark, has been reduced every year for the last six years, as illustrated in Figure 6.2.14.

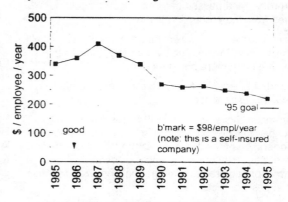

Figure 6.2.14, Workers Compensation

A composite picture of employee satisfaction and working relationships is created using Employee

CASE STUDY

Survey Results, Figure 6.2.15. with Figure 6.2.16. Employee Turnover. and Figure 6.2.17, Employee Years of Service. These key indicators point to the facts that employees are well satisfied with the way they are respected and compensated for their accomplishments.

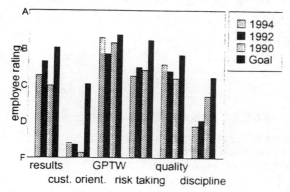

Figure 6.2.15, Employee Survey Results

CFI is considered a good company to work for, and since 1988 many employees have demonstrated this statement with presenting CFI with low turnover rates and increases in the average employee longevity. These are seen in Figures 6.2.16 and 6.2.17, respectively. Note the reduction in salary exempt longevity in Figure 6.2.17 is indicative of many long-term employees retiring (e.g., W.W.II and Korean War veterans).

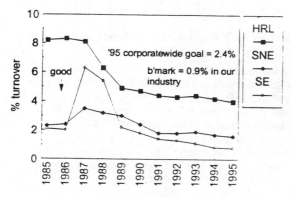

Figure 6.2.16, Employee Turnover

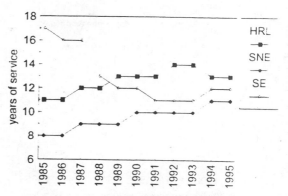

Figure 6.2.17, Employee Years of Service

The hours of training per employee are reflected in Figure 6.2.18.

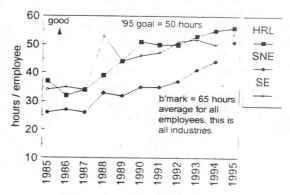

Figure 6.2.18, Training Hours per Employee

Recognition of individuals and teams is shown in Figure 6.2.19.

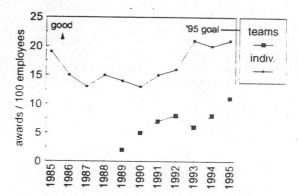

Figure 6.2.19, Team and Individual Awards

Figure 6.2.20 demonstrates that activity and team growth have been substantial over the last five years.

CASE STUDY

Figure 6.2.20, Recognized Individuals in Teams

In Figure 6.2.21, the growth rate of the percentage of employees who actively participate in teams can be seen. It is critical to note that while percentages are shown, they are approximate. The use of teams is so embedded in CFI that it is difficult to accurately measure and indicate.

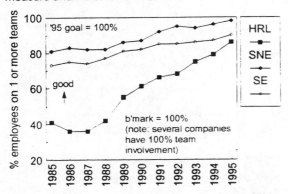

Figure 6.2.21, Employees Engaged in Teams

Administration - Figure 6.2.22, Corporate Citizenship Engagements, shows the increase in contacts outside the company by employees. The activity level indicates that an average of about two engagements are made every working day.

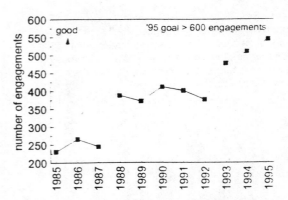

Figure 6.2.22, Corporate Citizenship Engagements

Figure 6.2.23 shows growth in the rate of implementation of employee suggestions with the 1995 goal increasing to approximately 88%.

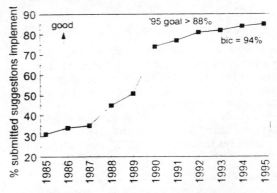

Figure 6.2.23, Suggestion Implementation Rate in DAS

Self-assessments are a way of life at CFI. Results of self-assessments are measured in corrective action requests (CARs) focused on internal operations. Figure 6.2.24 shows the trend of how many self-assessments result in internal CARs. The critical counterbalance to this indicator is the number of internal self-assessments has been increasing over this same period. Today CFI conducts 360% more self-assessments than it did in 1985.

CASE STUDY

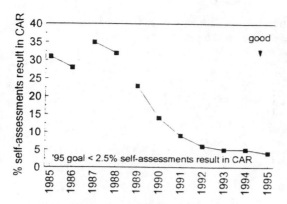

Figure 6.2.24, Self-Assessment Results

6.3 Supplier Performance Results

6.3a Levels and trends of supplier results

In this Item, representative figures are shown. Each sector maintains similar figures that are standardized to enable management to make comparison decisions between the sectors.

Each sector maintains the measures of its own suppliers, and the measures are listed for key supplies. There are 155 suppliers that deliver 80% of the suppliers by dollar volume. These suppliers are distributed in the sectors as shown in Table 6.3.1. The values provided for 1990 and 1994 are supported by an intermediate growth trend for Certified Suppliers consistent with the end values.

Table 6.3.1, Supplier Segmentation

Sector	Suppliers	Certified	
		1990	1994
CAS	83	60	80
CPS	33	15	30
DAS	28	20	27
NSS	11	4	11

CFI has a very active supplier participation program called PTP that is described in Item 5.4. The number of PTP suppliers are shown in Figure 6.3.1, Supplier Base Transitions.

The participation of approximately 100 suppliers in the PTP is a reflection of progress from the start of the program in 1988.

In Item 5.4, supplier relationships were discussed as well as the techniques that CFI uses in dealing with suppliers, working to attain process capabilities of C_{pk}'s of 1.5, or greater.

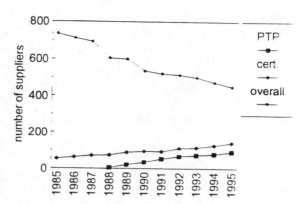

Figure 6.3.1, Supplier Base Transitions

Figure 6.3.1, Supplier Base Transitions. shows the number of Certified Suppliers. These suppliers have demonstrated the ability to design. measure. and maintain processes of C_{pk} of 1.5. or more. and to maintain the process sigma at the defined level.

Delivery of parts is crucial when proprietary products are used by customers of CFI. The supplier's delivery on-time as promised is needed and is continually monitored.

Figure 6.3.2 shows the percent of materials or services received on time. The figure compares raw material, services, and G&A. The raw material indicates the greatest improvement since that segment has received the most emphasis over the last four years.

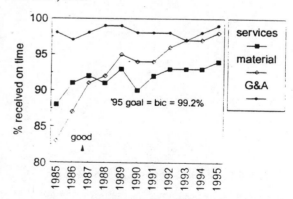

Figure 6.3.2, Supplier Receiving History

CFI has a very active program to reduce the number of suppliers. The goal is to reduce the 420 suppliers today by 6% per year. Figure 6.3.1 also shows the number of suppliers as they have been reduced over the past 10 years.

CASE STUDY

Certified Suppliers are treated differently from non-Certified Suppliers in the manner that their materials are handled upon receipt. Certified Suppliers are given bar code strips to affix to the packages. The material is only identified with the bar code scan after an examination for shipping damage. No inspection of the product occurs.

The results of the incoming material checks are shown in Figure 6.3.3.

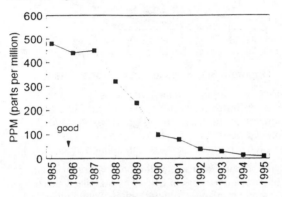

Figure 6.3.3, Certified Supplier Quality

Non-certified suppliers' materials are sampled in the incoming area for physical properties and chemical analysis. The results of these inspections are shown in Figure 6.3.4.

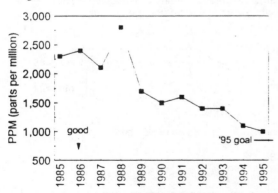

Figure 6.3.4, Non Certified Supplier Quality

These results show great improvement over the ten-year period and are now at .04% with the benchmark being .03%. The aim of CFI is to have all major suppliers certified and cease all incoming inspection.

Figure 6.3.5 demonstrates how suppliers have improved over the past ten years as measured by the need for CFI to make requests for corrective action. This improvement is the result of many actions,

including the establishment of the PTP program, certifications, and the reduction in the number of suppliers.

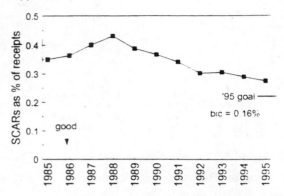

Figure 6.3.5, Supplier Corrective Action Requests

Figure 6.3.6 shows that the number of corrective action requests that have been made of suppliers are being closed in shorter and shorter cycle times. The lower axis is in time of closure in days, with a shift of the closure cycles being observed from 1985 to 1995 (projected). The program with suppliers has paid off with improved relationships, better quality, lower cycle time, and improved customer relationships due to supplier improvements.

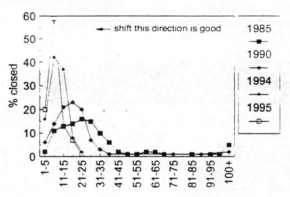

Figure 6.3.6, Velocity of CAR Closure

CASE STUDY

7.0 CUSTOMER FOCUS AND SATISFACTION

7.1 Customer and Market Knowledge

CFI uses a closed communications loop to collect, analyze, and utilize data from and about customers. The center of the loop is the Marketing Data System (MDS) which is described in Category 2.0. This worldwide system provides the focal point for all marketing actions. The system contains listening posts to continually gather information about customers and potential customers and their needs and expectations.

The closed-loop process is continually improved by evaluating the process and feeding back modifications and improvements to make the process more accurate and responsive, with greater focus on the customer.

The process loop is shown in Figure 7.1.1, Customer Expectation Determination Process.

7.1.a Determining expectations and requirements

In keeping with the business strategy of being the highest value producer of fasteners, it is essential for CFI to be continually abreast of customer expectations and to be aware of any changes in requirements that might be coming in the near term as well as the future.

7.1.a(1) How customer groups are determined

The company is organized into four sectors that have distinctive customer bases. Within each product sector, there are variations of the customers that must be considered.

Consumer Products Sector - Consumer products are marketed primarily through distributors. The products are sold through wholesale and retail stores to individuals who make the final satisfaction determination. In this market, new competitors are emerging every day.

In spite of intense competition with some suppliers entering the market with very low priced products, the market has been growing steadily. Many customers of higher end, more profitable products were influenced to buy through their outstanding experience with our consumer products. For this reason, CFI continually pursues excellence in products and complete satisfaction of the end customer as well as the distributors, wholesalers, jobbers, and retailers of the products.

To continually expand its market, CFI is always comparing results with those of its competitors. It is always aware of those who are not customers and what their expectations might be. Through surveys and other

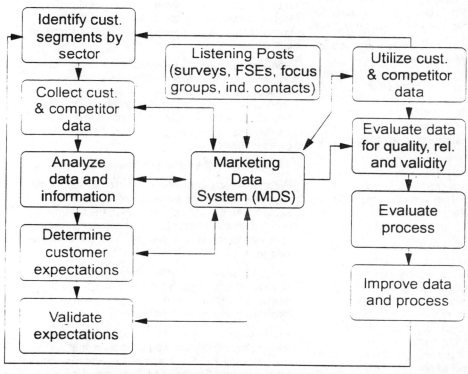

Figure 7.1.1, Customer Expectation Determination Process

CASE STUDY

listening posts described, those potential customers are always identified and characterized.

Commercial and Automotive Sector - This sector has two major segments of customers, the commercial consumers using CFI products in everyday industrial use and the automotive customers with high volume, short lead-time, and special design needs.

The first segment of CAS customers are commercial users that procure through distributors, sales representatives, and commercial supply houses. The second segment is the automotive customers which consist of the Big 4 in the U.S. and the Big 3 in Japan as well as most of the European automakers. These customers are most concerned about consistency of products and responsiveness in delivery. They traditionally practice just-in-time manufacturing with little inventory and rapidly changing delivery requirements.

Although using the same quality level of products, these two segments have differing needs, and competitors approach each in a different manner. CFI has to be aware of these needs and respond to both segments accordingly. Price, delivery, and quality are all important in varying degrees with these customers.

Again, it takes more than CFI's present customers to expand markets and increase market share — CFI must gain customers from competitors. Automotive customers are a good source of competitor information as they usually use competitor facts to leverage CFI actions. This information is recorded in the Marketing Data System which directly feeds the competitive intelligence efforts, product designs, and strategic planning efforts.

Defense and Aerospace Sector - The customers in this sector are also divided into two segments, defense and aerospace. They are similar in nature as they primarily buy to Military Specifications and usually to lowest price.

This sector had the severe problem with counterfeit parts in the 1980s when substandard bolts with insufficient strength were delivered from distributors. This incident resulted in many of our defense and aerospace customers refusing to buy through distributors, and they now require certifications and firm proof of the quality of the product. CFI has responded, and the episode ended to CFI's advantage. The number of competitors has lessened, and the cost of extra proof of compliance has helped the competitive situation.

As a result of the formalized bidding process in this sector, competitors are easier to identify, and the

differences in offerings are exposed in the bidding process.

Nuclear and Specialty Sector - The Nuclear and Specialty Sector has its customers partitioned into two major segments.

The first, Nuclear, are those customers procuring products to meet the strict nuclear regulations with their required inspections, audits, and proof of materials and certified processes. Competitors are fewer in this segment, and the total market continues to shrink as a result of environmental difficulties and global pressures concerning industry safety.

The second customer segment in this sector, Specialty, buys very special products made according to unique requirements and unusual specifications We find that competition with these customers is less. Most competitors do not have the technical capabilities in equipment and people to adequately respond to the requirements.

This sector has few competitors, and we meet on limited competitive occasions and know the representatives well. However, it is still important to vigorously pursue the few customers of these competitors to determine their expectations now and in the future.

Some of our specialty products are unique (e.g., underwater explosive bolts for deep submersible vehicles), and competitors have difficulty copying our product. CFI takes advantage of this situation with these unique products by selling purchase agreements where the total price of all fasteners can be competitive.

7.1.a(2) How information is collected

With the diverse customer base in each sector, the approach is different yet similar for each of the sectors. An example of one sector, the Commercial and Automotive Sector (CAS), is representative of how information is collected and analyzed in all the sectors.

The CAS has many methods to determine customer needs and requirements. A few examples are described to show how the type and depth of information are assembled for analysis.

Professional societies have groups collecting and assembling information about products that are important to CFI. For instance, the American Society for Mechanical Fastening (ASMF) maintains a considerable number of standards for widely varied fastener applications. CFI is very active in the subcommittees that survey the industry for new applications and develop more demanding requirements.

CFI sales representatives are continually visiting and exchanging information with major automotive companies around the world to determine what is occurring with present products and what changes are going to be necessary in the future.

Outside sales representatives who handle CFI products for commercial customers provide weekly reports to CFI of their observations with their customers, especially showing how the present products perform and what changes are needed.

Another important input from customers comes from field service representatives. These individuals have constant contact with industrial and automotive customers and usually are involved with situations that show the best or the worst of the company. From the regular weekly reports that go into the Marketing Data System (MDS), as well as informal discussion inputs that are also placed in the data system, customer opinions are captured.

Customer surveys are contracted out to universities and colleges across the country. These surveys, directed and financed by CFI, go to all users of the products of CFI. This includes customers as well as non-customers. Included are some competitors, who also happen to be customers.

Data from all inputs are collected in the MDS (described in Category 2.0). The accumulated data are aggregated and compared against each input to determine the objectivity and validity. From this data bank of information, which is available to all employees, customer requirements and expectations are accurately determined.

7.1.a(3) Specific features and importance determination

When the various inputs are collected in the MDS, trends become apparent, and engineers and marketing representatives note them for indication of necessary changes, future modifications, or new products.

A team is formed of representatives from Engineering, Sales, Production, and Administration to assemble focus groups in the areas where the data indicate changes are occurring.

Focus groups are formed from various customers who provide information to define requirements for product modifications and additions. These focus groups are utilized to generate priorities that are then reviewed

and modified by CFI employees using the other data that have been collected.

Thus, the engineering group has collected and analyzed data from many inputs and is able to maintain a direction for each of the products. This information is fed into the yearly strategic plan or into interim product modifications if that is the best course to take to maintain customer satisfaction.

7.1.a(4) How other data are collected

The MDS is a comprehensive data collection and analysis system that collects all types of marketing information. With preprogrammed analysis, the MDS presents the data in forms that Marketing can readily utilize.

These data include market share, competitor comparisons, product performance and comparisons, and customer comments. Customer focus group inputs are added to this information as described above. Thus, the loop is closed and a comprehensive analysis is portrayed. If any of the data do not seem to fit together, the formed teams utilize the questionable information in discussions with the various focus groups.

Information also goes out to various contact personnel, such as field sales and service representatives, for their concurrence or revisions. It is also recognized that it is important to keep these groups fully informed so that they maintain a completely involved perspective.

7.1.b Addressing future requirements

It is also important how individuals collecting the information are trained to listen carefully and pass on essential information without distortions and personal biases.

Sales representatives have received an enhanced course in customer listening. This training is built on the standard course that all CFI employees have attended. To learn to listen is essential in discussions with outsiders to understand what they are trying to say. In the case of future products, the statements may be somewhat vague as customers are talking about something that does not exist although there is a real problem situation or difficulty.

CFI continually monitors the business environment as well as the physical environment. The company has business strategies in each of these areas. The company is the benchmark in the world for environmental protection. To remain in this leading position, CFI must be continually aware of requirements and changes in the regulations around the world. This requires the listening posts to be proactive in searching out new laws and regulations regardless of the geographic location or particular situation.

CFI is also the leader in innovative technology. To maintain this position requires the technical organizations of engineering to follow the latest technical writings and patent filings and attend the major trade shows. This includes the *Fastener Technology International Journal* and the International Trade Show.

When new innovative products are ready for launch, customers who are leaders in the field are provided early production parts to evaluate and stress in real-life applications. This is one method used to ensure adequate value for the uses intended and to look for improvement opportunities.

When significant orders are lost, a "won/lost" analysis is performed to determine the cause and establish process changes to ensure that future losses will not occur. As part of this process, focus groups are formed of lost customers.

With the market becoming smaller in some areas, as noted in the Defense and Aerospace Sector, and the company planning to expand market share, each and every lost customer is very important. The reason for loss or defection must be determined, and corrective processes must be established.

Earlier in this application, the counterfeit bolt scandal that rocked the industry in the 1980s was mentioned. Such a situation results in the whole industry needing to reassess the way it does business and handles products in production and distribution. CFI has made a commitment so that a critical situation will not happen to its products.

CFI has always been in the forefront with the latest in technology in the fastener industry. Customers often seek CFI's help when they have a particular problem that does not seem to have a good solution. CFI prides itself in being able to provide solutions in these instances.

Another important task of the listening posts is to determine potential customers who may not be aware of CFI's technical capabilities. Each sector representative in all the various listening posts is always on the lookout for business for other sectors. Employee profit sharing covers the total company. It is to the advantage of each individual to improve the company's profitability and be a part of the strategic growth process.

7.1.c How the company evaluates and improves

Although CFI feels that the knowledge of the marketplace is understood and that customer requirements and expectations are well known, the company realizes that the customer awareness process must be continually improved to remain successful and to continue to grow. A closed loop system is utilized as shown in Figure 7.1.1.

The listening post function continually evaluates the adequacy, timeliness, and reliability of the information being received and utilized for decision making. The output of the focus groups has resulted in several improvements in the process.

The focus groups have directly faced the issue of the best methods for the listening post to use and have recommended specific training sessions that have been included in the training program for customer contact personnel.

The network of inputs does a good job of determining customer expectations. It also accomplishes a purpose of indicating where the process can be improved. The MDS has been a help in assembling data on a real-time basis with analysis indicating where data are missing or do not appear to track so adjustments can be made.

An example of how the continuing improvement process is utilized involves the surveys mentioned that are contracted to universities and colleges. These are continually improved by soliciting comments from those who do not respond. One of the requirements placed by CFI on the institution making the survey is to personally contact any person or organization that does not answer using the question, "Why did you not answer?" Responses that indicate problems with the structure or method of questioning are used in the reengineering of the survey to make it more effective.

CFI continually reviews the processes used to determine customer satisfaction. No single process is best but a combination of all is required. It is important to continually examine each process individually to make improvements.

In the annual strategic planning process, opportunities for comparing projected changes are exposed. In the case of significant changes in direction or of customer attitudes and opinions, the total customer satisfaction determination process is reviewed for modifications and improvements.

CASE STUDY

7.2 Customer Relationship Management

7.2.a How the company provides easy access to customers

CFI realizes that sometimes a customer may wish to contact someone even if the situation is not necessarily critical. Other times the situation might be critical and need an immediate answer.

To accommodate all situations, customers have several means to contact the company. During the initial customer contact by a salesperson, the person contacted is given information on how to reach a responsive individual at CFI for future reference.

Toll-free "800" numbers are provided for both telephone and fax. The telephone numbers provide access to a group of service contact personnel who are on duty 24 hours per day, every day. The fax numbers are for a machine at the desk of the appropriate on-duty service person. Each facility also has computers that receive electronic mail and EDI communications.

Voice mail is extensively utilized at CFI. Customers and PTP suppliers are listed in the company phone book and have access to the CFI telephone system. EDI is used for many customers who are interconnected with appropriate data systems.

Managers of the facilities around the world have given their home phone numbers to major customers to call if they feel that they have not received a proper response or escalation of an issue is required. The on-duty service person has been instructed to give the appropriate manager's number so the customer has an opportunity to escalate a question of issue to a higher level if they feel it is necessary.

All large shipments have a tag affixed with a postage-paid card self-addressed to the originating location. The cards have a series of boxes to be checked indicating possible problems and a space for written comments if desired. All distributors, wholesalers, and jobbers have a supply of these cards available and insert one in each CFI customer shipment. This approach is an important way to ensure that customers can provide questions and feedback to the company.

The customer service functions in each facility and in each sector are consolidated in a Service Center area. The people who staff these posts 24 hours a day, are on teams who meet weekly to establish the service standards to all meet the criteria of totally satisfying the caller.

Customer contact personnel are aware that customers have been given the appropriate home phone number of the facility manager. Their responses must reduce, and eliminate, the need for any customer to escalate an issue to the manager.

Some representative service standards are expressed in finite numbers, and these are as follows:

➤ response time to answer the phone;
➤ time to respond to the problem;
➤ time to resolve critical and urgent problems; and
➤ problem escalation to the manager.

A representative set of service standard charts from the Commercial and Automotive Sector is shown in Figures 7.2.1 through 7.2.5.

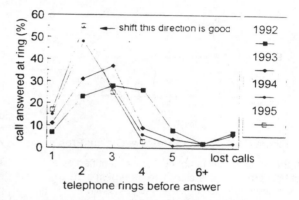

Figure 7.2.1, Response Time to Answer Telephone Calls

In Figure 7.2.1, the distribution displayed shows the peak is two rings and the majority is within three rings. The goal is to have all calls answered within two rings.

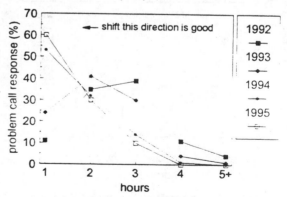

Figure 7.2.2, Time to Respond to Problem Calls

Figure 7.2.2 shows how CFI has shortened the cycle time to respond to customer problem calls. In 1992, the peak of the distribution was three hours to provide responses. Projected 1995 results show the advancement of the curve to where approximately 90% of the problem calls are answered within the two hour response goal.

Figure 7.2.3 reinforces the advancement of CFI's critical problem response for its customers. The goal is to close all critical problems in two hours, and CFI is projected to achieve 100% of its goal. A 93% attainment of the goal was demonstrated in 1994.

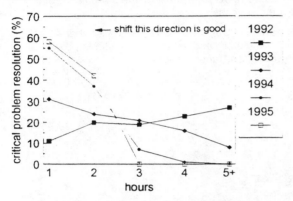

Figure 7.2.3, Time to Resolve Critical Problems

If the problem call is not customer identified as a critical problem, it is classified as urgent. CFI's commitment to its customers is to close these problems in 24 hours or less. Figure 7.2.4 shows how CFI is advancing on this goal. In 1994, 79% of urgent problems were closed in 24 hours or less, with 1995 projections to be 94% urgent problem closure in 24 hours.

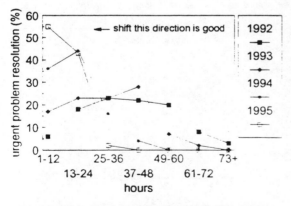

Figure 7.2.4, Time to Resolve Urgent Problems

It is critical for customers to have the freedom to escalate their problems to appropriate managers if they have not been satisfied with the results offered by the customer contact personnel. CFI measures the effectiveness and empowerment of the customer contact personnel by the number of calls escalated to managers. CFI continues to lower the number of calls escalated, as shown by the trend in Figure 7.2.5.

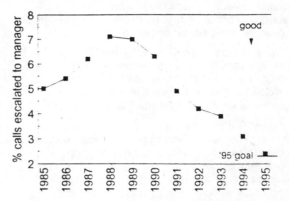

Figure 7.2.5, Problem Escalation to Manager

If it is necessary to transfer a call to another number for additional information, the first receiver of the call does not get off the line until the second person has responded and is also on the line. This is called a warm transfer.

The service standard is that no more than two transfers will be made and three individuals maximum can handle a single call. Each call transfer is a "warm transfer" such that the transferring person stays on line with the customer, introduces the incoming CFI contact, and summarizes the topic and expectation for the transferred call. Training is continually added to provide the customer contact personnel additional skills to be able to handle more of the calls themselves.

The data for all service standards are tracked in the MDS, and the results are posted in the Service Center each morning. The teams who set the standards also have established goals such as the two rings in the example given in Figure 7.2.1.

Comparisons with other facilities in the sector are included, and the best results in the company are also noted as internal benchmarks.

7.2.b How the company ensures all calls are resolved

The MDS is an essential part of the complaint resolution process. All complaints are logged into the system whether they are formal or informal. The responsiveness and accuracy of problem resolution are the result of rapid, accurate inputs. All formal comments are directed to the Service Center at each facility, and the customer contact personnel on duty log the information in a format that is standardized throughout the company.

Complaints or comments, formally or informally received in the field are input into the MDS by means of portable computers using cellular phones. The information use an identical format despite its remote origin.

Complaints are categorized into critical and urgent. Critical issues are immediately assigned to a field sales engineer for immediate answers. These critical issues are to be resolved within two hours.

Urgent issues are assigned to field sales representatives in a revolving manner such that each input has an individual immediately assigned. Urgent issues, all issues that are not critical, are to be resolved within 24 hours.

Once in the data system, comments are automatically aggregated with all other comments. The analysis program in the system presents the data in Pareto distribution charts and correlation analysis. These data are retained for future comparisons.

Each morning at the product meeting, the individual assigned to handle the comment or complaint that was received reports on the status. The assigned individual is expected to fully understand the situation and offer the progress, or status, at that time.

The date for complete resolution is placed in the MDS. Any date that takes longer than two days to resolve is flagged. At each day's meeting, all open issues are reviewed. If an instance misses the assigned date, a double flag is applied, the issue is escalated, and an expert is immediately assigned to help with the solution.

The issue is not completely resolved until the solution is filed in the MDS. Once in the data system, the information is immediately available throughout the world, as described in Category 2.0.

7.2.c How the company follows up with customers

CFI utilizes several techniques to follow up with customers. To better ensure customer satisfaction, additional surveys are performed. On a random basis, one of the universities is contacted to perform a special survey with selected customers who are selected because of past specific problems with delivery, cost, or loss of an order.

To ensure that problem resolutions are prompt and complete, five customers from the Service Center comment list are selected. Monthly, a private visit by the facility manager is arranged. From these visits, the problem resolution is ensured, customer satisfaction is investigated, and a relationship is further established.

Feedback comes from visits such as these and also from the mail-back cards described in Area 7.2.a. Sample cards are selected each month, and the manager places a call to the person who filled out the card. This person might be a receiving clerk or a manager. Feedback is obtained and the information placed in the MDS.

A fourth way that customer follow-up is performed is by management handling the telephones in the Service Center. The individuals are expected to meet the established service standards and handle any situation that arises. This provides the manager a good evaluation of how customers rate the company and fosters improved relationships with that specific customer. This time at the phone is often at a time during the night or early in the morning. Each manager is expected to take on this assignment for two hours every two weeks.

7.2.d How the company evaluates and improves customer relationships

7.2.d(1) Service standards improved

Service standards are improved in a three-step process that consists of multiple inputs, an action focus group, and follow-up results. Table 7.2.1 provides a brief outline of how service standards are reviewed and changed.

7.2.d(2) Aggregation of customer comments

The MDS and the ODS contain all the information concerning customer comments and complaints, both formal and informal, as discussed earlier. The data systems aggregate the data input from standard formats. Output reports place the information in a Pareto distribution for ease of action initiation.

Reports are automatically generated in the data system and are downloaded every four hours or more frequently when specifically requested. When the reports are received, actions are taken throughout the company.

Field sales engineers are assigned specific products and facilities. Sales representatives are assigned specific customers. These two groups take action if the reports involve their products, facilities, or customers.

Any time a product appears on a report three times in a three-month period, the central engineering group is involved. The monthly meetings of each department

CASE STUDY

within each sector include in the agendas the status of the customer complaints and the corrective actions accomplished to solve the problem permanently.

Table 7.2.1, Setting Service Standards

Inputs	Feedback gathered from customers that have been contacted by supervisors
	Comments gathered by managers talking to customers
	Field sales engineers with information from customers and employees
Action	Focus groups are formed with the Service Center employees who meet weekly to receive inputs. The groups determine actions to be taken
Results	The results of the focus groups can take several forms. They may determine to modify standards or establish new standards. Often the decisions are that additional training is necessary in the areas of customer interface or problem solving. The results can lead to additional training concerning products.

7.2.d(3) How knowledge about customers is accumulated

The MDS is designed around the ability to understand the customer. The data system accepts data from many inputs, aggregates and sorts, and outputs reports in the form for users to be able to immediately take action.

Information about customers is collected through listening posts as seen in Figure 7.1.1. Information comes from many areas, such as: surveys, FSEs, focus groups, and individual contacts.

The information about customers comes from many people in different organizations in different parts of the world. Surveys taken by third parties of Industrial Fastener Institute (IFI) and contracted universities and colleges form the basic information. This aggregated data and information includes the following:

➤ Information is collected from customer contact representatives with direct constant contact. These are the sales representatives who are assigned to and should know that customer best. The field sales engineers are also very close as

they spend considerable time at the customer's facilities working with the people at all levels in the customer's organization.

➤ Service Center contacts have knowledge as a result of discussions concerning problems or answering requests for information. Although the information is not as direct, it becomes more useful when combined with the other data collected and aggregated in the data system.

➤ Customer contact reports are reserved from all levels of management when managers perform site visits or customer calls.

➤ Design engineers get involved with customers when developing a new product or working on an ongoing problem. and their knowledge is added.

➤ Suppliers are another good source of information as they are often also a supplier to the customer and usually a supplier to competitors of CFI.

➤ Benchmarking investigations often involve customers to examine various processes for analysis and incorporation.

With these many inputs to the data system, a complete picture is developed, and this aggregated knowledge provides CFI with the ability to understand the customer needs and expectations.

7.3 Customer Satisfaction Determination

7.3.a How the company determines customer satisfaction

7.3.a(1) Description of processes

The primary process for determining customer satisfaction is through surveys. Although inputs are obtained from sales representatives and field sales engineers, the consistency and validity are not as certain as those obtained from third party surveys.

The IFI performs a complete survey of the total fastener industry twice a year. Individual companies participating are not directly identified.

CFI contracts with nine universities and three colleges to conduct 12 surveys a year. one each month. each by a different institution. The CFI sponsored surveys are sent to both customers and non-customers. From a competitive information view, the questions are structured so that distinctions are possible to decode the IFI survey to identify the major participants.

In addition, CFI directly conducts one or two surveys each year. These surveys are specialized and conducted to obtain specific information or information that is needed in a very short time. These limited

CASE STUDY

surveys are not used in the primary process of determining customer satisfaction.

The two types of surveys are objective as they are performed by a third party, and the validity is checked by the comparison of information between the two separate surveys.

The mail back cards are another source of input to the process. They have limited reliability as not all customers fill them out and return them. Although these data may be limited, they are used with caution concerning the statistical validity of aggregated information they present.

The measurement scales for the two primary surveys are different. IFI uses a 1 to 10 scale with 10 being the best for the various questions. CFI has its surveys use an "A", "B", "C", "D", and "F", as respondents are more able to understand the meanings of the letters and can personally relate to the scores.

To make the scores comparable between the surveys, 9 or 10 are considered an "A", 8 or 7 a "B", 6 or 5 a "C", 4 or 3 a "D", and 2 or 1 an "F". The customer satisfaction charts shown throughout Category 7.0 are presented with the letter designations. All sectors use the same designations and maintain charts of customer satisfaction. Examples of these charts are provided in Items 7.4 and 7.5.

7.3.a(2) Customer future behavior

Future customer behavior is very important to the marketing organization, and inputs are continually investigated. Sales representatives are in constant contact with the purchasing function and the manufacturing organizations to solicit information about upcoming orders.

The field sales engineers also are in contact with the customers and often with other levels in the organization that have a different view. The combination of this information provides insight into future possible actions. The field sales engineers also communicate with representatives from other fastener suppliers and obtain competitor information.

The best information comes from surveys that ask several questions leading the customers to discuss their reorder likelihood from the same supplier.

They are asked the following typical questions:

➤ Are you satisfied with your present supplier?

➤ Do you have any reason to change suppliers?

➤ Do you know of any supplier that can furnish the same value as your present supplier?

➤ Do you expect to continue using your present supplier?

➤ Would you recommend your present supplier to others looking for a fastener provider?

Tabulation of the answers provide a look at the future expected business from those customers.

For the IFI survey, it is necessary to identify the customer, which is not furnished by the IFI report. This is accomplished by comparing information from the CFI-sponsored surveys which provide the essential correlation.

Combining the survey information with the information provided by the sales representatives and the field sales engineers, CFI is able to predict with some certainty from which customers to expect reorders.

One of the prime responsibilities of the sales representative is to determine future business and to be aware if competitors are gaining or holding share. Any problem situations reflect negatively on CFI, and the sales representatives are always on top of any customer problem resolutions. All information about the customer is recorded in the MDS.

7.3b Satisfaction relative to competitors

7.3.b(1) Company-based studies

CFI utilizes several methods to determine customer satisfaction relative to competitors. The best, most objective, and most valid are the surveys performed by the contracted universities and colleges.

These surveys are sent to a long list of major fastener users, some of whom are known to be good customers of competitors. The information returned provides insight into how satisfied the customers are with the competitor suppliers. This information is completely objective and valid as the surveys are not identified as to the sponsor or provider. The information gathered is shared with all participants so the competitors receive the same information although not coded to specific companies.

Some other methods utilized by CFI to determine competitor results are through field sales engineers. These employees have good contacts with customers and also with competitor representatives.

CFI purchases competitors' products on the open market and performs analytical tests. The information is valuable; however, caution is applied because it is not void of CFI bias which might compromise its objectivity.

CASE STUDY

The information is added to the survey results for validation. If it reinforces and correlates with other information, it is accepted.

7.3.b(2) Studies by independent organizations

Customer satisfaction must be earned and retained while competitors are constantly trying to gain customers from CFI. The information flow concerning how well competitors are doing is actively pursued. Information about competitor success with customer satisfaction comes from third party surveys, customers of CFI, and suppliers.

IFI performs semi-annual surveys of the total fastener industry. The survey covers a wide range of customers and is totally objective and valid as far as any supplier to the fastener industry is concerned. In the survey, several questions are asked about the satisfaction levels and how the various fastener suppliers react to customer needs.

The outputs of the surveys provide direct comparison information about relative customer satisfaction. CFI utilizes this information and reports to the employees the successes and issues in the pursuit of total customer satisfaction.

The automotive industry has strong ties to suppliers and maintains extensive records concerning the quality of parts with delivery and cost information. These reports compare suppliers of industries such as fasteners and provide comparison information.

CAS customers provide these reports to CFI, and the information is compiled in the MDS data bank.

The nuclear industry has fewer suppliers and limited customers. The industry publishes reports from product users that compare sources in the area of customer satisfaction. This source of information gives input that can be compared to other data and normally agrees with other sources.

Suppliers are another source of information concerning customer satisfaction as they provide materials and supplies to the fastener industry, and their customers are the competitors of CFI.

7.3.c How the company evaluates and improves the satisfaction determination process

The process of determining customer satisfaction is constantly evaluated and examined for modification and improvement. This activity is performed in the listening post function in the marketing organization.

The basis for the examination of the process is the comparison with competitor activities described earlier. The listening post group examines areas where competitors are ahead and specific actions taken by competitors to give them any advantages.

The Marketing organization forms focus groups to address these issues and obtain additional data to establish reasons and determine modifications to the process.

Specific areas examined are in gains and losses of customers. The data bank of customer complaints and field contact information is utilized in the assessment of customer dissatisfaction.

The results of the focus group activities are published monthly by the Marketing Management Group. The information is reviewed by the business management team and distributed.

The results of these activities have led to the establishment of an ongoing approach to identify customer satisfaction criteria and arrange them in a model that assigns weight to each of the inputs to relate to performance of the business.

This modeling activity has resulted in changes to the surveys sponsored by CFI and modified the directions for representatives of the organization to take when pursuing information concerning customer satisfaction information.

These activities are ongoing and continually modify the process in an ever-improving cycle.

7.4 Customer Satisfaction Results

7.4.a Current levels and trends of satisfaction

As is described in the application, CFI is very concerned about customer satisfaction and utilizes several inputs for determining the status of customer attitudes.

An overall chart for customer satisfaction by sector is shown in Figure 7.4.1, for a ten-year period. This chart compares all the sectors against the grading score of "A", "B", "C", "D", and "F", as explained earlier. This is the composite of IFI surveys, third party surveys (universities and colleges), customer inputs to Service Centers, and field sales engineers.

This chart shows that DAS has reached the goal and CAS has the most opportunity to improve. The ten-year trend is positive.

Another measurement is the trend over time for each sector with comparisons to the best competitor for that sector, the goal for the sector, and the benchmark. Figure 7.4.2 shows CAS Composite Customer Satisfaction for a ten-year period with the comparisons.

CASE STUDY

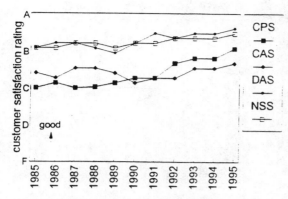

Figure 7.4.1, All Sector Customer Satisfaction

A measure of customer satisfaction is how well customers stay with the company and are retained. There are many reasons why customers leave. Some are quality related, some are financial, and some are due to business conditions beyond the control of either company.

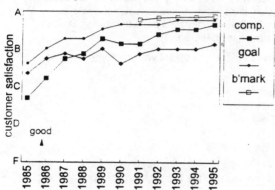

Figure 7.4.2, CAS Composite Customer Satisfaction

Each sector is measured in a similar manner.

Due to CFI's size, length of company history, and diversity of products and customers, all the situations have been experienced. However, the end result has been an increase in retention in all the sectors over the last ten years. Figure 7.4.3 shows the improvement for each sector with varying competitive and market driven forces.

These results show that, in spite of decreasing total markets in the Defense and Aerospace Sector and the Nuclear and Specialty Sector, customers have been retained. This again is the result of the success of CFI in customer focus and process-oriented business.

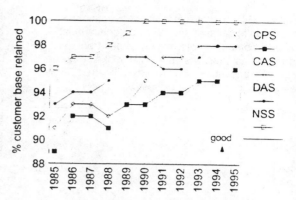

Figure 7.4.3, Customer Retention

As has been mentioned several times in this application, CFI has five key business strategies. Customer satisfaction is considered to be indicative of the successful accomplishment of these goals. The goals are as follows:

First - *To deliver products to customers on time and defect free (6 sigma levels).* The accomplishment is shown by Figure 6.1.6, meeting the on dock promise.

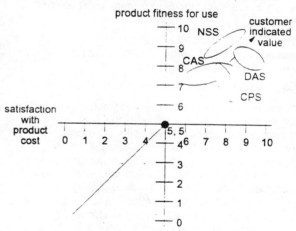

Figure 7.4.4, Customer Satisfaction - Perceived Value

Second - *To be recognized as the producer of highest value fasteners.* This is shown in Figure 7.4.4. This figure shows the four sectors in the upper right quadrant, reflecting high satisfaction and high quality. Our customers define this as high value. The information for this chart comes from aggregating many of the inputs that have been explained in this application.

Third - *To be the technology leader in the introduction of revolutionary fastener products.* Figure 7.4.5 is the

CASE STUDY

result of CFI's aggressive technology roadmap yielding an increasing number of patents annually. The best competitor information comes from the Industrial Fasteners Institute which looks at a wide range of competitors. The results show that CFI is clearly ahead of the next closest competitor.

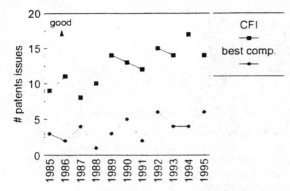

Figure 7.4.5, Technology Leadership

Fourth - *To protect the environment at all worldwide locations and set benchmark levels of compliance.* Results in protecting the environment are shown in Figure 6.2.11.

Fifth - *To be recognized as number one in employee satisfaction at all worldwide locations.* Employee satisfaction is reflected in Figure 6.2.15.

7.4.b Customer dissatisfaction

Customer dissatisfaction can be portrayed in several ways. However, each sector uses the same measurement, customer complaints. Customer complaints include all customer concerns whether they are product or service related, or concerned with the conditions of how CFI is conducting its business. Process, service and business complaints are often timely, where some product related complaints can be delayed by weeks, or months, due to shipping, warehousing, or distribution lead time.

Customer complaints are a standard measurement that is the same for all sectors. Figure 7.4.6 shows the reduction in the last ten years for all the sectors in spite of the improved methods of communication such as fax, voice mail, E-mail, and the availability of "800" number telephone service.

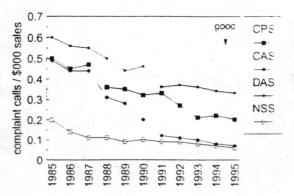

Figure 7.4.6, Customer Complaint Calls

7.5 Customer Satisfaction Comparison

7.5.a Current levels and trends of satisfaction compared to competitors

CFI has utilized many paths to understand customers and how they enjoy doing business with the company. Through its surveys, personal contacts, and the extensive data systems, a considerable volume of information is collected.

CFI measures each sector with customers in five areas:

➤ Delivery
➤ Price
➤ Quality
➤ Responsiveness
➤ Ease of business

These measures are compared with goals, benchmarks, and the best competitor for each sector.

This information is shown for 1994, and the goals for 1995 for each of the sectors are illustrated in Figures 7.5.1 through 7.5.4.

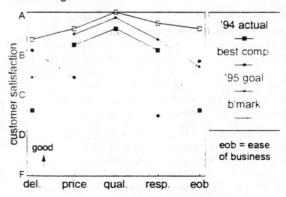

Figure 7.5.1, CPS Customer Satisfaction

CASE STUDY

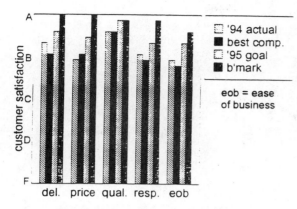

Figure 7.5.2, CAS Customer Satisfaction

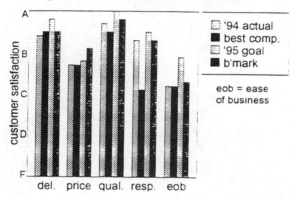

Figure 7.5.3, DAS Customer Satisfaction

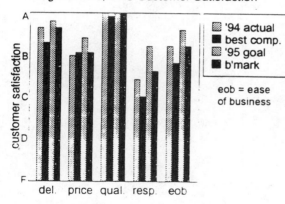

Figure 7.5.4, NSS Customer Satisfaction

7.5.b Trends in gaining or losing market share to competitors

Market share is an end result of the total business activity. It reflects on all aspects of business including price, quality, delivery, and customer relationships.

Markets increase and decrease as the result of international financial changes. However, market share is related to the individual business. CFI has performed well in market share in all sectors. Some competitors are more formidable than others, and we track the three best competitors for comparison.

Each sector is compared to its three best vendors, and this information is shown in Figures 7.5.5 through 7.5.8 as compared to the total available market.

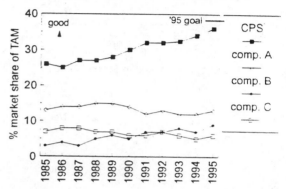

Figure 7.5.5 Gains and Losses in Market Share CPS

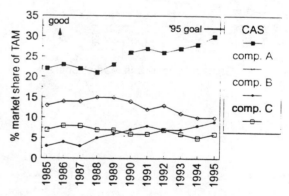

Figure 7.5.6 Gains and Losses in Market Share CAS

CASE STUDY

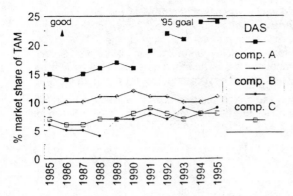

Figure 7.5.7 Gains and Losses in Market Share
DAS

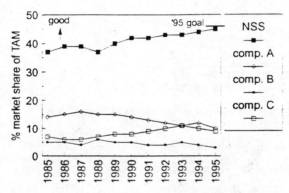

Figure 7.5.8 Gains and Losses in Market Share
NSS

Malcolm Baldrige
National
Quality
Award

1995
Colony Fasteners, Inc.
Evaluation Notes

SCORING SUMMARY
COLONY FASTENERS, INC.

Item	Scoring Range (%)
1.1	65-75
1.2	50-60
1.3	45-55
2.1	60-70
2.2	55-65
2.3	45-55
3.1	40-50
3.2	30-40
4.1	60-70
4.2	50-60
4.3	65-75
4.4	60-70
5.1	50-60
5.2	45-55
5.3	45-55
5.4	65-75
6.1	50-60
6.2	45-55
6.3	55-65
7.1	60-70
7.2	60-70
7.3	45-55
7.4	60-70
7.5	55-65

KEY BUSINESS FACTORS WORKSHEET

- **Applicant:** Colony Fasteners, Inc. (CFI) is a publicly owned firm founded in 1887 which designs and manufactures fasteners for use in a wide range of products and applications. Headquarters are in Philadelphia. Fasteners range from bolts and screws used in many applications to special fasteners designed for use in spacecraft and other unique applications.

- **Market Sectors:** There are four market sectors: CAS (consumer — $250M revenue), CAS (commercial & automotive — $400M), DAS (defense & aerospace — $200M), and nuclear & specialty — $50M.

- **Major Customers:** Major U.S. and Japanese automotive manufacturers, major airframe manufacturers, top defense contractors and their tiered sub-contractors.

- **Customer Requirements:** Primary customer requirements are delivery, price, quality, responsiveness, and ease of doing business.

- **Strategy:** Focuses on leadership in delivery (on time, defect free), high value, technology leadership, environment, and employee satisfaction. Special emphasis on reduction of variability.

- **Company Structure:** Manufacturing is organized by business sector and occurs in several locations throughout the world. Sales offices are also located worldwide, and most sales employees work out of small offices or their homes in order to be located with their customers.

- **Employees:** The employee base is approximately 10 thousand, of whom 56% are U.S. based. This % is projected to decline as a result of shifting to off shore labor. During the past decade the number of U.S. based employees has decreased from about 7 thousand to 5 thousand, while non-U.S. employees have increased from about 2 thousand to 5 thousand.

- **Teams:** Are a major mechanism to promote high performance. Profit sharing is split 50% for employees (shared equally), 50% corporation.

- **Locations:** 13 U.S. cities, 8 foreign countries.

- **Suppliers:** 420 in total and declining (although eligibility determination form indicates 788).

- **Regulatory Environment:** As a result of counterfeit bolts and fasteners, Congress passed the Fastener Quality Act of 1990, establishing regulations for the industry.

- **Competitive Environment:** Toughest in CAS, with off-shore competitive products at low prices.

1.1 SENIOR EXECUTIVE LEADERSHIP

PERCENT SCORE 65-75%

+/++	Area to Address	(+) Strengths
+	a	A company credo, originated by the founders, forms the basis for CFI's mission and values, and it is communicated to every part of the organization.
+	a	The senior executive team sets the standards of performance and behavior for the rest of the company.
+	a	Senior executives meet routinely (quarterly visits) with customers, suppliers and partners around the world.
++	a	The core values of the company are amplified and clarified for all employees by translation of them to explicit statements of values and the required behavior.
+	a	Key business strategies are consistent with and related to the core values.
+	a	All managers are regularly retrained in guidelines for measuring employee performance relative to the core values.
+	a	Senior executives are active leaders of processes and studies to improve both customer relationships and understanding of competitive and market environments.
+	a	Senior executives are intimately involved in measurement, assessment and review of all facets of CFI operations. This includes the allocation of company resources to stop declines in performance at any business unit.
+	b	Senior executives use employee feedback, operations reviews, surveys and customer feedback to monitor leadership effectiveness, and have made refinements such as simplification of the core value descriptions.
+	b	360° reviews of all senior managers are performed annually and include participation by members of the Board of Directors.

-/--	Area to Address	(-) Areas for Improvement
-	a	It is unclear what specific actions of the senior executive team have been and whether all senior executive team members are equally involved.
-	a	There is no evidence that values and expectations take into account all stakeholders; only shareholders, customers, and employees are cited.
-	a	It is not clear how customer-related performance is specifically reviewed.
-	a	The nature and depth of senior executive involvement in "Management by Planning" to set directions and performance goals is not defined.
-	b	The process for evaluating and improving leadership system effectiveness does not appear to be systematic or integrated.
-	b	It is unclear to what extent there have been cycles of improvement in the leadership system.

Site Visit Issues:

- Verify the extent of deployment of the Mission Credo, Core Values, and Behaviors. Understand how they drive processes and performance.
- Determine how visibly the senior executives are involved in leadership activities.
- Clarify to what extent cycles of improvement have taken place to improve Senior executive effectiveness.
- Verify the use of the evaluation tools such as "System Effectiveness Assessment."
- Examine the processes for reviewing overall company performance, and understand the role of Senior Executives in review and improvement.
- Review the employees and external surveys used to measure adherence to the values and to customer requirements.

1.2 LEADERSHIP SYSTEM AND ORGANIZATION   PERCENT SCORE 50-60%

+/++	Area to Address	(+) Strengths
+	a	There is a focus on core values which relate specifically to customer orientation, quality and results.
+	a	Goals are cascaded through the organization in a manner that enables each entity to contribute to an aggregated end result that meets or exceeds the overall company objective.
+	a	Organization and management of CFI by major customer sectors is used as a key to meeting unique customer needs.
++	b	There are multiple communication vehicles, both traditional and innovative, in use to insure values and expectations will be well deployed to the entire work force.
+	c	A comprehensive hierarchy of operation reviews is conducted at various levels and intervals.

-/--	Area to Address	(-) Areas for Improvement
--	a	How the leadership system focuses on customers and high performance objectives is not described.
-	b	There is no description of how the various communication activities or vehicles go beyond mere communications to strengthen the reinforcement of values, expectations and directions.
-	b	There is no evidence of the integration of various vehicles into a communications system.
-	c	There is no evidence presented on the content of operational reviews listed in Table 1.2.1.
-	c	There is no evidence of integration or linkage of various operational reviews or which operational reviews are conducted in each business sector.
-	c	There is no apparent participation in operational reviews by senior executive leadership.

- Review the cascading process of goals and how each level/entity establishes which portion of the overall goal is appropriate for it.
- Verify how the leadership system insures focus on high performance objectives and how customer needs are built into planning, execution and performance reviews.
- Verify participation of senior executives in different operational reviews conducted. Review the notes or documentation of those reviews.
- Review examples of all communication vehicles and understand how they reinforce values.
- Review the content of the operational reviews cited and understand how they are used to improve performance.

1.3 PUBLIC RESPONSIBILITY AND CORPORATE CITIZENSHIP PERCENT SCORE 45-55%

+/++	Area to Address	(+) Strengths
+	a	Formalized product and process risk assessments during design process as well as other environmental and regulatory assessments are integral to the new business acquisition and management process.
+	a	An annual environmental planning session in each sector evaluates short and long term impacts and the requirements of regulations.
+	a	Each manufacturing site has a committee to review the by-products of company processes and to look for ways to minimize impacts.
+	a	Significant training is conducted for all employees on ethical behavior and a formal Code of Conduct is reviewed in all performance reviews.
+	a	CFI has a goal of leading all competitors in complying with local regulations regarding the environment.
+	a	No inquiries, challenges or sanctions have been recorded due to the actions or conduct of any employee.
+	b	Employees presented over 235 quality-related speeches or papers in 1994.

-/--	Area to Address	(-) Areas for Improvement
-	a	How the company looks ahead to anticipate public concerns is not described.
-	a	The process by which various assessments are translated to operational requirements or targets is not explicit.
-	a	Although CFI is pictured as world leader in its industry, actions with regard to Fastener Quality Act appear reactive rather than proactive and only focus on compliance.
-	a	There is no evidence of a process or an attempt to connect public responsibility requirements with performance improvement objectives.

-	b	Description of corporate citizenship roles does not appear to be systematic or proactive in all areas.
-	b	It is not clear that community involvement is sustained across all locations.
-	b	There is no evidence of company-wide involvement in broad community service activities such as health and human services.

Site Visit Issues:

- Review samples of the 235 quality related speeches/papers given in 1994 for scope and substance.
- Review community involvement records and plans at all locations visited.
- Review local site committee records on by-product considerations.
- Examine content and methodology of risk assessment processes/approaches used.
- Investigate the linkage between regulatory/public responsibilities and performance improvement objectives.
- Verify the deployment and the level of understanding of the Code of Conduct at all employee levels.

2.1 MANAGEMENT OF INFORMATION AND DATA   PERCENT SCORE   60-70%

+/++	Area to Address	(+) Strengths
++	a	A very comprehensive set of data is collected and used to evaluate performance in many areas of quality and operational performance. The measures correspond to CFI's key values.
+	a	Most data are collected automatically with built in flags for significant variations from the norm.
+	a	90% of employees have a PC terminal at hand.
+	b	A semiannual, comprehensive review of the IS function is performed.
+	b	Customers are asked to comment on the utility of the data they receive.
+	b	Teams assess whether the recipients of the data are the right ones to make decisions based on these data.
+	b	CFI pays for phone lines into employees' homes to improve their access to company data. The company also contributes to the purchase of the computers for employees to use at home.
+	b	An E-mail address is available for comments about the data system.

-/--	Area to Address	(-) Areas for Improvement
-	a	It is unclear how well customer needs and requirements are reflected in the data collected.
-	a	The categories of data in Table 2.1.1 are not clearly linked to business drivers.

7

- a   There is little evidence that CFI's measures are integrated to identify interorganizational issues.
- b   Although there is evidence of improvements in the data collected, there is no evidence that there is an overall system for improving the data management system itself.

Site Visit Issues:

- Interview employees to determine their knowledge of what data are available and their satisfaction with data access and its support of their jobs.
- Determine the level of integration of the various data bases and the degree to which they are used identify cross cutting issues.
- Determine how many of the data are collected automatically and what controls are in effect to assure their accuracy and reliability.
- Understand the data presented in Table 2.1.1 and how they are specifically linked to business drivers.

2.2 COMPETITIVE COMPARISONS AND BENCHMARKING   PERCENT SCORE   55-65%

+/++	Area to Address	(+) Strengths
+	a	CFI has been benchmarking since 1989. They have developed the PTP process to institutionalize benchmarking.
+	a	CFI has well defined, effective criteria for identifying both benchmarking data needs and partners.
+	a	Benchmarking teams are responsible to incorporate changes in the processes at their parent location, document the results on a database, communicate the finding to other locations and assist other locations in implementing the changes as required.
+	a	Benchmarking data are used to establish stretch goals. Evidence and examples are presented on improvements that have resulted.
+	b	CFI has improved the selection of PTP partners.

-/--	Area to Address	(-) Areas for Improvement
-	a	It is unclear how superior process are identified in organizations that are outside of CFI's industrial community.
-	a	The description of stretch targets is primarily annecdotal. It does not describe how targets are set our how approaches are developed.
-	b	There is little information about how CFI assesses and improves the overall effectiveness of its benchmarking activities. The response is primarily anecdotal and describes examples of improvement, but not a systematic process.

Site Visit Issues:

- Review CFI's benchmarking activities to determine the impact on their performance and improvement plans and objectives.
- Examine CFI's benchmarking activities to determine if they have a well developed and deployed process.
- Determine if CFI has a methodology to evaluate and improve its benchmarking process.

2.3 ANALYSIS AND USE OF COMPANY-LEVEL DATA   PERCENT SCORE 45-55%

+/++	Area to Address	(+) Strengths
+	a	Market information is collected, analyzed and reviewed.
+	a	Open customer complaints are automatically flagged to anyone opening a customer file.
+	a	Comprehensive operational and performance data are collected, correlated and analyzed.
+	b	Trends and results from customer, product quality, and operational performance data are being used to set priorities and make decisions.

-/--	Area to Address	(-) Areas for Improvement
-	a	Little evidence is provided about how CFI uses data to better understand their customers.
-	a	There is no information on how CFI correlates the data from its various data bases to improve decision making.
-	b	Little information is provided about how CFI relates operational performance to changes in financial or market performance.

Site Visit Issues:

- Review the various customer data to determine the relationship to the customer's key values.
- Determine if CFI establishes correlations between operational performance improvement and financial performance.
- Verify the built-in analytical capabilities of the data systems and determine how data are used to drive decisions.
- Review the data flow of each of the systems, and understand how systems are linked into an overall network.

3.1 STRATEGY DEVELOPMENT

PERCENT SCORE 40-50%

+/++	Area to Address	(+) Strengths
+	a	The Management By Planning (MBP) process integrates inputs from many sources, including customers and suppliers.
+	a	Risks are explicitly recognized by quantifying various risk factors and then combining them to assign a risk factor to each of the different strategies under consideration.
+	b	The policy deployment process enables applicant to translate corporate objectives into objectives at each level in the company through a "catchball" process.
+	b	Quarterly meetings and many other mechanisms reinforce policy deployment.
+	c	Cycle time of the annual planning process was reduced from six to three months.

-/--	Area to Address	(-) Areas for Improvement
--	a	It is unclear how customer requirements and expectations are utilized as a primary element in the MBP process. Thus, it is unclear how Key Business Drivers are comprehended.
--	a	Projections of changes in customer requirements and of changes in competitive capabilities appear to be missing.
-	a	Resources are optimized within business units. It is unclear whether there is a mechanism to optimize resources among business units on a total company basis.
-	a	It is unclear how risks and uncertainties are integrated in order to develop preventive strategies to deal with them if and when they become real and known.
-	a	Discussion of company capabilities does not address HR, technology or R & D factors.
-	b,c	It is unclear whether the catchball process operates throughout all the elements of the planning cycle, or whether it occurs only once with a focus on objectives. As a result, both validation of process capability to achieve 100% of objectives and opportunity for employee involvement are unclear.
-	c	There is not a systematic approach for improving the effectiveness of the planning process.

Site Visit Issues:

• Clarify how customer requirements and expectations are utilized as a primary element in the MBP process.

• Determine whether and how projections of changes in customer requirements and of changes in competitive capabilities are included.

• Clarify whether there is a mechanism to optimize resources among business units on a total company basis.

• Clarify how risks and uncertainties are integrated in order to develop preventive strategies to deal with them if and when they become real and known.

• Clarify how process capability is validated for strategies.

• Determine how well objectives, strategies and goals are deployed and understood.

3.2 STRATEGY DEPLOYMENT

+/++	Area to Address	(+) Strengths
+	a	For each of the five corporate objectives, which are also identified as customer requirements, goals are set for each of the business sectors.
+	a	Alignment of goals with work units is achieved through the cascading process.
+	a	Productivity, cycle time reduction and waste reduction are included in objectives.
+	a	Alignment of goals with suppliers is achieved through the partnership process ("Pass Through Partnerships" or PTP). Through this approach, periodic plans are linked.
+	b	Strategic objectives have primary "owners" who are responsible for seeing that they are met.

-/--	Area to Address	(-) Areas for Improvement
--	a	It is unclear how line of sight to customer requirements is achieved for work units and suppliers. While there are specific, quantified objectives, it is unclear that achievement of these measures would result in achieving the intent of the corporate goals. Example: achieving a certain number of patents does not necessarily result in technology leadership.
--	b	Long term goals appear to be missing. Only 1995 goals are clearly identified (in Table 3.2.1)
-	b	It is unclear how the strategic objectives owners interact with work units and suppliers.
--	b	There are no comparisons of how CFI's value to customers (product and service quality) is projected to compare with that of competitors. Other benchmarks are also lacking.
-	a	Resources to support achievement of the strategy are missing, as is the process for determining the resources.
-	a	The foremost quality goal has no specific measurement and is not directly linked to corporate objectives (Ref. Table 3.2.1).
-	a	Productivity, waste and cycle time reduction are not addressed clearly.

Site Visit Issues:

• Clarify how line of sight to customer requirements is achieved for work units and suppliers.
• Determine whether there are long term goals.
• Clarify how the strategic objectives owners interact with work units and suppliers.
• Determine what resources are provided to support implementation of the strategies.

4.1 HUMAN RESOURCE PLANNING AND EVALUATION   PERCENT SCORE   60-70%

+/++	Area to Address	(+) Strengths
++	a	CFI views employees as a fundamental strength and has been implementing and continues to implement many activities to develop their skills.
+	a	A wide range of compensation and recognition techniques is available, including stock option programs, outstanding achievement awards and cash bonuses.
+	a	Employee recognition has shifted, starting 1985, from individuals to a strong team focus.
+	b	The HRET meets quarterly and is using a multi-variable correlation process to show the linkage of company results to HR initiatives. The data are correlated with the company goals and analyzed to establish factors most important for employee development.

-/--	Area to Address	(-) Areas for Improvement
-	a	The process that CFI uses to translate requirements into specific plans is implied to be corporation's MBP process, but the process is not clearly stated (ref. pp. 21 & 15).
-	a	Longer term plans for employee development and demographic changes are not clear. No specific mention is made of differences, if any, for their substantial overseas growth and domestic headcount reductions.
-	a	Despite the stated team emphasis, financial awards for individual performance outweigh those for team performance by 2.5 to 1.
-	a	It is not clear whether or how readily available employee data (absenteeism, employee turnover, accident rates, employee performance trends, etc.) are used in evaluating and improving human resource planning.
-	b	Specifically HOW the various types of HR information are used and linked to other information for company strategic and business planning is not clear.

Site Visit Issues:

- Verify the breadth of changes made and the systems developed to assure consistency across the entire company.
- Interview a sample of all types of employees to verify linkage between performance and the bonus systems. Look for the linkage as well as changes/improvements over time.
- Review HRET activities, process documentation and results obtained.
- Verify and clarify the financial awards given. Look for type of award (individual vs. team) as well as deployment across the entire company.
- Examine the Employee satisfaction results and turnover data. Verify how these results are included in the planning process.
- Examine the HR planning process for content, scope and deployment.

4.2 HIGH PERFORMANCE WORK SYSTEMS

PERCENT SCORE **50-60%**

+/++	Area to Address	(+) Strengths
+	a	CFI has a strong focus on 2-way communications throughout its business and has used teams, task forces, a decentralized suggestion program and self audit teams to create opportunities for self-directed involvement over a six year time.
+	a	A defined re-deployment process for displaced employees combined with strong relationships with colleges and universities has created a successful, flexible environment.
+	a	Teams and task forces can be long- or short-term and focused on a wide range of internally or externally motivated activities.
+	b	CFI's compensation and reward system has been improved over time and now includes trending of performance in its criteria.
+	b	The number of levels of employee performance evaluation was reduced from 5 to 3, reaffirming the efforts of the majority of the employees who fall into the middle category.

-/--	Area to Address	(-) Areas for Improvement
-	a	It is not clear how line workers are involved in or how job design is addressing simplification.
-	a	Although examples are provided, it is unclear whether there is a systematic process to create opportunities for initiative and self-directed responsibility. International deployment is not mentioned.
-	b	The process used to improve the compensation system's ability to reinforce effectiveness is not clear.
-	b	The linkage of the various recognition process with each other and with the company performance objectives is not clear.

Site Visit Issues:

• Verify CFI's re-deployment process and the breadth of its application.

• Verify the breadth and extent of communications and teams. Review a sample of the different vehicles used and clarify whether there is a communications systems in place and the breadth of its deployment.

• Examine the "trending" process for compensation and verify application and breadth of deployment.

• Clarify the system used to create initiative and self-directed responsibility. Especially examine evidence of deployment throughout all facilities — domestic and international.

4.3 EMPLOYEE EDUCATION, TRAINING, AND DEVELOPMENT   PERCENT SCORE 65-75%

+/++	Area to Address	(+) Strengths
+	a	CFI's training processes are driven by their various operations' business needs and the assessment of proficiency against the required skill level.
+	a	The identification of potential career paths and attendant training helps employees select appropriate training.
+	b	CFI has established relationships with 12 Universities and Colleges to help design and deliver appropriate training and provide options for employees seeking to expand their skills. Benchmarking techniques were used to develop the training processes.
++	b	A wide spread training system has been developed which utilizes many people throughout CFI to design and deliver appropriate training.
+	b	CFI has used and is expanding metrics to assess training effectiveness. The employee evaluation system includes acquisitions and use of skills and knowledge.
+	b	CFI spends almost 5% of its annual payroll for training.

-/--	Area to Address	(-) Areas for Improvement
-	a	It is not clear how education and training address objectives for high performance work units.
-	a	The alignment of education and training with key performance objectives is not clear.
-	b	The approach used to evaluate and improve the training programs is not clear.
-	b	It is not clear how many of the College/University partnerships are outside the U.S. — especially since almost 50% of CFI's employees are now based off-shore.

Site Visit Issues:

- Determine HOW CFI evaluates and improve their training processes. Verify the extent and type of benchmarking conducted both when creating and improving their systems.
- Determine how the assessment process enables employees to identify and address cross-functional skill gaps.
- Verify their systems to assess training effectiveness.
- Verify the content and scope of the many approaches they have described. Especially examine the College and University relationships outside the US.
- Verify whether the training needs assessment process includes company objectives, business unit needs and employee growth.
- Clarify how the value of spending 5% of annual payroll for training is determined.

14

4.4 EMPLOYEE WELL-BEING AND SATISFACTION

PERCENT SCORE   60-70%

+/++	Area to Address	(+) Strengths
+	a	CFI is conscious of the hazardous material they use and utilizes teams actively to reduce or eliminate usage. Benchmarking is used to determine possibilities.
+	a	The Safety Awareness Team conducts regular safety audits and action teams are assigned to eliminate the root causes.
+	b	CFI's EAP is very comprehensive and many recreational activities are supported by the company.
+	b	Domestic employees are allowed to take a 9 week sabbatical every 7 years and there is an equivalent plan for off-shore employees.

-/--	Area to Address	(-) Areas for Improvement
-	a	The safety audit system as described provides negative recognition for poor performance but no positive recognition for good performance.
-	b	Little information is provided about the variety of services provided in the different facilities. Compliance with the ADA is unclear.
-	c	It is not clear how employee satisfaction feedback, formal and informal, is used to drive satisfaction improvements.
-	c	It is not clear how employee satisfaction data obtained from various sources are compared and correlated for validation.

Site Visit Issues:

- Interview a sample of employee to verify that CFI is a "great place to work"
- Interview a sample of employees to verify their understanding of the availability of the support programs described in the application.
- Review linkage between the employee services and changes which have been identified and/or implemented. Determine what process is actually used an whether it has resulted in improved satisfaction of employees.
- Review the waste reduction and hazardous materials reduction goals, results and trends.
- Review the safety team's agendas, records and results. Clarify whether all types of employees are affected.
- Review the results of the Employee Satisfaction surveys, including differentiation of employee type as well as frequency and trends of results. Verify the system used to analyze results and drive improvements.

5.1 DESIGN AND INTRODUCTION OF PRODUCTS AND SERVICES Percent Score 50-60%

+/++	Area to Address	(+) Strengths
+	a	Internal and external customer satisfaction are considered as prime drivers for new or improved processes. Another driver is manufacturability.
+	a	The FSE provides important inputs regarding customer knowledge into the internal CFI design processes.
+	a	Figure 5.1.2 shows a five step flow in the product design cycle.
+	a	Suppliers are included in the early design phases, to insure that the basic raw materials they supply can be controlled for process consistency. The FDR provides data that show that the materials or services subjected to the specific processes meet the criteria, of a distribution of at least one-half the specification limit for the specific process step.
+	c	Within each department of each sector, processes are maintained by teams assigned the responsibility of designated processes. These teams continually review the status of processes to insure that the relationship between the element being acted on and the limits assigned is within at least a C_{pk} of 1.5.
+	c	Every quarter a review of the design process in each sector is accomplished. To insure continuous improvement, goals are set for improvement and they are reviewed for attainment at the next meeting.

-/--	Area to Address	(-) Areas for Improvement
--	a	The Application does not show a specific systematic process of how products, services, and production/delivery processes are designed. Figure 5.1.2. shows a design cycle, but it does not show the flow of a systematic process, including customer requirements, product and service design requirements, and how all requirements associated with products, services, and production/delivery processes are addressed early in the design cycle. Although each sector maintains its own design capability, none of the systematic sector processes are shown in the Application.
-	a	It is unclear specifically how product and service design requirements are translated into efficient or effective production/delivery processes.
-	a	A measurement plan approach is noted in the application, but specifics are not described.
-	a	It is not clear how Design for Manufacturability (DFM) is used in the design process.

Site Visit Issues:

- Understand the specific design process used, including the flow of information from the customers, how product and service design requirements are translated into effective and efficient production and delivery processes, and how all requirements are developed.
- Review the product design cycle shown in Figure 5.1.2. to understand the overall flow, timing and documents used.
- Review the involvement of suppliers early in the design phase.
- Understand the cycle for evaluating and improving processes.
- Review the DFM process.
- Understand whether a substantive measurement plan is used, and, if so, how.

5.2 PROCESS MANAGEMENT: PRODUCT AND SERVICE PRODUCTION AND DELIVERY PERCENT SCORE 45-55%

+/++	Area to Address	(+) Strengths
+	a	Figure 5.2.1 shows the key process flow chart for the processes which product products and services supplied to customers.
+	a	CFI has learned to balance off-shore manufacturing to stage products. They use warehouse sites as strategic locations close enough for major customers to meet just-in-time requirements. This has required a multi-layer distribution system.
++	a	During the design cycle, every process designed and proven before the design is released. The process certification demonstrates that the process has a capability of at least a C_{pk} of 1.5
+	b	The assigned process teams work to improve processes and reduce variability.
+	b	Benchmarking data are used for improving process characteristics in reducing cycle time.
+	b	Many of the improvements have been driven by customer contact, customer recommendations, and information from the customer base.

-/--	Area to Address	(-) Areas for Improvement
-	b	Although the process teams try to reduce variability, a systematic process being used by these teams is not described in the Application.
-	b	A systematic benchmarking process is not described in the Application, nor is how the company uses benchmarking data to systematically improve.
-	a	It is not clear which are key processes.

Site Visit Issues:

- Understand the use of alternative technology and its ability to improve processes.
- Understand the specific process improvement cycle, and how improvements are implemented and verified
- Walk through the flow of Figure 5.2.1 to understand the Key Process Flow Chart.
- Understand how key processes are determined.
- Understand the system for alternate technology infusion.

5.3 PROCESS MANAGEMENT: SUPPORT SERVICES

PERCENT SCORE **45-55%**

+/++	Area to Address	(+) Strengths
+	a	Each support service determines the key processes needed for support of its delivery products. These key processes flow from the strategic planning process.
+	a	Planning teams are formed during the data gathering phase for the strategic plan, and priorities are set.
+	a	Processes in the support functions are structured with specific limits for each step.
+	a	Table 5.3.1 shows the key company processes under 6 general areas.
+	c	Information from internal and external customer is used as input to evaluate processes.

-/--	Area to Address	(-) Areas for Improvement
-	a	Requirements determination appears to be driven by the team process of each individual team, and it is not systematic or repeatable within a division or across divisions.
-	b	Although Table 5.3.1 show the key processes, it does not describe those processes and their principal requirements.
-	b	The Measurement Plan is at a very high level and does not describe the specific systematic methodology for measurement.
-	b	The Measurement Plan does not specifically show how processes are maintained or the performance levels are maintained.
-	c	Improvements in cycle time are not specifically addressed in the Application.

Site Visit Issues:

- Understand how key requirements are determined for each support service and the flow of information from the requirements to evaluation and improvement cycles.
- Understand specifically how requirements are addressed early in the design process, and walk through examples of how early requirements are used for each of the major functional support service areas.
- Review the key company processes shown on Table 5.3.1 and understand the principal requirements.
- Understand **specifically** how key customer information is used from initiation (and whether a systematic process is used) through the usage and improvement cycle.

5.4 MANAGEMENT OF SUPPLIER PERFORMANCE

PERCENT SCORE 65-75%

+/++	Area to Address	(+) Strengths
+	a	The PTP process is used to establish special relationships with suppliers which includes sharing information including how to attain C_{pk}s of greater than 1.5, and how to meet requirements. Figure 5.4.1 shows the supplier certification process.
+	a	Currently 1/8 of the supplier base are PTP suppliers. This constitutes approximately 1/4 of the suppliers for raw material, products and materials integrated into salable products.
+	a	Certified suppliers receive special bar codes to attach to their products delivered, and they are connected with EDI. EDI contains product specifications and production requirements information as soon as CFI determines needs.
+	a	A series of meetings is held with suppliers (or printouts are mailed to suppliers) which reviews their performance.
+	a	A formal Supplier Rating System (SRS) is used, and information is provided to suppliers on a quarterly basis if they are not in the PTP Program information is presented more frequently if they are in the PTP Program.
+	b	A cost of Doing Business (CODB) factor has been established for all suppliers. this factor calculates the costs to CFI due to suppliers' failure to meet requirements, such as the cost to return lots which fail to meet specification. The CODB factor is used in subsequent procurements to give preference to high performing suppliers.
++	b	A Preferred Customer Certification Program (PCCP) has been initiated. This includes feedback from suppliers on the criteria for rating whether CFI is the customer of choice. Criteria include timeliness. quality, clarity of communication, and supplier satisfaction.

-/--	Area to Address	(-) Areas for Improvement
-	a	A reactive technique, inspection, is used for 3/4 of production materials and 7/8 of all suppliers.
-	b	One of the factors suppliers focus on is the C_{pk} of 1.5. This represents a defect level significantly above the Six Sigma level (C_{pk} of 2.0) which the company would like to achieve. It is unclear how the company can achieve an overall C_{pk} of 2.0 when suppliers only have to achieve 1.5.

- Understand the flow of Figure 5.4.1, the Supplier Certification Process. This should include reviewing documentation, and specific supplier certification examples.
- Understand how the principal quality requirements for suppliers of quality, delivery, and price are deployed in the organization. This should include priorities of the requirements, and specifically how they are used.
- Review performance feedback to suppliers including the PTP Program and the information on EDI and SRS.
- Understand the PCCP Program and review the flow of customer certification and how specifically, suppliers feedback information to CFI.
- Understand how six sigma CFI products are achieved when suppliers are only required to have a C_{pk} of 1.5.
- Compare the PTP to data presented in Item 6.3. Ensure the results are linked to the approach and deployment.

6.1 PRODUCT AND SERVICE QUALITY RESULTS   PERCENT SCORE 50-60%

+/++	Area to Address	(+) Strengths
++	a	A significant array of performance indicators was provided for most sectors of CFI. These data show sustained levels of improvement over ten years and relatively high levels of current achievement.
+	a	Responsiveness results are trending positively, as measured by calls resolved within 24 hours (Fig. 6.1.5), response time to problem calls (Fig. 7.2.2), time to resolve critical and urgent problems (Figs. 7.2.3 and 7.2.4), and problems escalated to manager (Fig. 7.2.5). Ease of doing business was best in industry in 1994 in CAS and NSS.
+	a	On-dock delivery performance has improved to 99% or better in all sectors shown.
+	a	Significant improvement has been realized in warranty costs.

-/--	Area to Address	(-) Areas for Improvement
--	a	No comparative data were provided for delivery, quality or responsiveness.
-	a	Price performance in 1994 was below industry best for CAS and NSS.
-	a	Ease of doing business was well below best competitor in 1994 for CPS.
-	a	Trend results over time are missing for price and ease of doing business.

Site Visit Issues:

- Determine if the measures provided are predictors of customer satisfaction.
- Examine price and quality metrics as viewed by CFI's customers.
- Find out if comparative data are available and how CFI performs relative to its competitors.
- Understand the percentage of critical processes which are able to achieve six sigma.

6.2 COMPANY OPERATIONAL AND FINANCIAL RESULTS   PERCENT SCORE   45-55%

+/++	Area to Address	(+) Strengths
++	a	A significant array of performance indicators was provided for many aspects of CFI. These data show sustained levels of improvement over ten years and relatively high levels of current achievement.
+	a	CFI has sustained positive trends in market share and revenue in all sectors.
+	a	Profit margins have improved in three of four sectors.

-/--	Area to Address	(-) Areas for Improvement
+	a	Few of the measures have comparative data supplied.
--	a	Although CFI's mission includes doing an outstanding job for shareholders there are no results reported that indicate return to shareholders.
-	a	Results measures for efficiency of use of financial assets on a total company basis (such as ROE) were not included.
--	a	Employee survey results show very low ratings in customer orientation which is a key corporate value.
-	a	Minimal comparative data were provided for functional and support areas. Where data were provided, CFI was considerably worse than best in class.

Site Visit Issues:

- Sample the remaining operational and financial indicators that were not included in the application.
- Ascertain why employee attitude survey results are so low especially in customer orientation reference (Figure 6.2.15).
- Explore the meaning of the training benchmarks provided in figure 6.2.18.
- Understand why CCS is not included in the charts reported in 6.2.
- Determine whether best in class trend data are available — so as to determine whether CFI is improving relative to benchmarks.

6.3 SUPPLIER PERFORMANCE RESULTS   PERCENT SCORE   55-65%

+/++	Area to Address	(+) Strengths
+	a	The number of certified suppliers has grown in all five sectors.
+	a	Many indicators were provided that demonstrate excellent supplier performance.
+	a	Very good progress has been made on SCAR's and DSCAR.

-/--	Area to Address	(-) Areas for Improvement
-	a	On time deliveries are only average.
-	a	CODB was cited in 5.4 as a key measure of supplier performance but no data were provided in item 6.3.
--	a	Relatively few measures have comparative data provided.

Site Visit Issues:

- Determine how the quality of products from certified suppliers are evaluated.
- Review the CODB data to determine if they are used to drive decision making.
- Understand the growth of supplier segmentation, as shown in table 6.3.1. This should include the reasons for growth in each of the sectors.
- Understand the relationship between SCAR's and DSCAR closures, as shown in figures 6.3.5 and 6.3.6 respectively.

7.1 CUSTOMER AND MARKET KNOWLEDGE

PERCENT SCORE 60-70%

+/++	Area to Address	(+) Strengths
+	a	A comprehensive closed-loop Customer Expectation Determination process is in place which gathers data and information from a variety of sources for analysis and use.
+	a	CFI is organized by market segment sectors. These sectors were established by using unique requirements.
+	a	Customer information is collected through surveys, customer focus groups, field service and sales representatives and from participation in professional societies. Information was compiled in a Market Data System (MDS). For professional societies, CFI is active in helping establish industry standards.
+	a	Data from the wide variety of sources are aggregated and compared to determine objectivity and validity. The resulting information is made available to all employees.
+	a	Customer focus groups are used to generate priorities for product features.
+	b	Sales representatives have received advanced training in customer listening to be attuned to emerging and future needs. This source of input is supplemented with engineering's keeping abreast of emerging technologies which may have potential for application to fasteners.
+	c	Continuous improvement cycles are built into the Expectation Determination process.
+	c	Non-respondents to customer surveys are contacted to develop a basis for improving survey instruments.

-/--	Area to Address	(-) Areas for Improvement
-	a	There is no evidence that data gathering and analysis of new customers for fasteners or new market segments are being addressed.
-	a	The description of how specifications are determined is generic, lacks accountabilities, and does not distinguish between sectors.
-	b	There is little evidence that long term requirements and needs of customers are being systematically addressed, such as fastener needs for composite material products.
-	b	There is no evidence that long-term environmental analyses are being conduct for trends which may affect CFI's product line. For example, the long-term stable availability of raw materials like titanium is not addressed.

Site Visit Issues:

- Verify the use of the Customer Expectation Determination Process including outputs of the MDS system.
- Verify how the information gathered on customers is correlated. Walk through the process used and documentation provided.
- Determine how CFI addresses new customers for fasteners or new market segments.
- Determine if long-term environmental analyses are being conducted.

7.2 CUSTOMER RELATIONSHIP MANAGEMENT

PERCENT SCORE **60-70%**

+/++	Area to Address	(+) Strengths
+	a	Several communications paths are provided to customers, including "800" numbers for both telephone and faxes, electronic mail, voice mail, and EDI communications media.
+	a	Managers' home phone numbers are provided to key customers for increased availability if problem escalation is required.
+	b	All complaints, formal and informal, are logged into the MDS system. Complaints are classified as critical or urgent by customers. Critical complaints are resolved within 2 hours and urgent within 24 hours. A review of complaints and complaint resolution occurs daily.
+	c	Customers who have had complaints are sampled for follow-up phone calls or visits on problem resolution satisfaction.
+	d	CFI's MDS database is designed around the ability to understand their customers and provides consistent timely information, which they use in a three step process to improve their customer relationship management.

-/--	Area to Address	(-) Areas for Improvement
-	b	There is little evidence of the existence of or use of a systematic process for elimination of the root causes of complaints which will ensure recovery of customer confidence. For example, changing a process and feeding that change information back to the customer.
-	c	There is no evidence that customers are proactively solicited for complaints or concerns to enable action to be taken before the complaints or concerns become critical
-	d	There is no evidence that processes are being evaluated and improved(such as the processes for aggregation and use of customer comments, complaints and other customer knowledge.
--	a-d	There is minimal differentiation of methods for managing customer relationships among the four sectors. These have widely differing structures, products, customers, competition, and requirements.

Site Visit Issues:

- Verify the customer comment and complain handling process, especially in sectors other than CAS.
- Determine how root causes of complaints are resolved.
- Determine if there is a metrology for determining customer concerns or complaints which haven't been actively voiced.
- Determine if the process for aggregation and use of customer comments and complaints and the customer knowledge accumulation process have been improved.
- Verify whether there is differentiation on methods for managing customer relationships among the four sectors.

7.3 CUSTOMER SATISFACTION DETERMINATION   PERCENT SCORE 45-55%

+/++	Area to Address	(+) Strengths
++	a	Two major third party survey types of customers and non-customers are conducted. The first is conducted twice per year and the second 12 times per year.
+	a	The results of the surveys and other customer information such as mail-back cards, are compared to validate the information received from customers regarding customer satisfaction.
+	a	The customer surveys are structured to determine repurchase intent as well as overall satisfaction.
+	b	In addition to use of surveys, CFI conducts analytical tests on competitors products purchased on the open markets, as well as using information from suppliers and field service engineers.
+	c	Focus groups are used to identify modifications in the Customer Satisfaction Determination process and to improve the surveys.

-/--	Area to Address	(-) Areas for Improvement
-	a	There is no evidence that cultural difference in the various market areas are being addressed in the survey methodology.
-	a	There is evidence of differentiation across sectors which would allow for varying classes of customer and industry requirements.
--	a	The process for aggregating the CFI and IFI results mixes data from 5 and 10 point scales respectively with no indication that the algorithm results in consistent data. Data from field reps are also combined, with no indication of relative weights and resulting objectivity or validity.
-	a	Although the surveys are structured to determine repurchase intent, no information was provided to show that the surveys capture the reasons why customers intend to repurchase.
-	c	There is little evidence that the rigor and effectiveness of the Customer Satisfaction Determination process are being evaluated and improved and that benchmarking has been conducted.
-	c	Measurement scales in use are not explicitly addressed regarding customer satisfaction determination.

Site Visit Issues:

- Verify how the information gathered from the surveys and other sources is used in determining customer satisfaction. Determine if they capture reasons why customers intend to repurchase.
- Determine what improvements have been made in the Customer Satisfaction Determination process through the use of focus groups.
- How are cultural difference in the various market areas addressed surveys?
- Determine whether there is methodological differentiation among the four sectors.
- Verify the algorithms used to enable them to combined the CFI and IFI survey results.

7.4 CUSTOMER SATISFACTION RESULTS

PERCENT SCORE 60-70%

+/++	Area to Address	(+) Strengths
+	a	The customer satisfaction rating has been steadily improving for the last 10 years.
+	a	Customer retention is at a sustained high level.
+	a	Customers indicate CFI products have a high value and they are highly satisfied with the products.
+	a	The number of patents issued annually has been consistently twice as high (or more) as the nearest competitor since 1988.
+	b	Trends in customer complaints have improved substantially in all four sectors.
+	b	Defect free deliveries have improved during the past three years in CPS and NSS.

-/--	Area to Address	(-) Areas for Improvement
--	a	The CAS sector customer satisfaction rating has been consistently below the competition since 1988 and the last three years CFI improvement rate has been less than the competition.
-	b	In 1994, on dock performance (defect free deliveries) declined in CAS and DAS.
-	a	It is unclear whether trends in customer value are increasing or decreasing.
-	a	Results for segments within the four sectors are not provided.

Site Visit Issues:

- Verify the results shown in Figure 7.4.1, 7.4.2, and 7.4.3 to understand if these show genuine improvement in Customer Satisfaction.
- Understand the aggregation leading to Figure 7.4.4.
- Verifying that the lowest curve (with diamonds) in Figure 7.4.2 represents CAS.

7.5 CUSTOMER SATISFACTION COMPARISON

PERCENT SCORE 55-65%

+/++	Area to Address	(+) Strengths
+	a	The CAS and NSS segments customer satisfaction exceeds the competition in three areas: delivery, responsiveness and ease of doing business.
+	a	The DAS sector is significantly better than the competition in responsiveness and somewhat better in price.
++	b	All market sectors show an appreciably higher market share than competitors with the share continuing to increase in all sectors.

-/--	Area to Address	(-) Areas for Improvement
-	a	The CPS segment lags behind the competition and best benchmark in all five areas of customer satisfaction measures: delivery, price, quality, responsiveness, and ease of doing business.
-	a	The CAS and NSS segments lag behind the competition in quality and price.
-	a	No comparisons of customer satisfaction were available for the CPS market segment.
-	a	All data on customer satisfaction compared to comparisons was for only 1 year; therefore the substainability of the results could not be ascertained.
-	a	Inconsistencies in the data in Figures 7.5.5 and 7.5.6 and Figure 6.2.6 prevent evaluation of these results

Site Visit Issues:

- Verify the data, and review source information.
- Determine if comparisons are available in the CPS sector.
- Determine if longer term data on customer satisfaction comparisons are available.
- Clarify the inconsistencies between Figures 7.5.5 and 7.5.6 and Figure 6.2.6.

SUMMARY

Colony Fasteners, Inc. (CFI) has made significant progress in establishing and improving processes and achieving results. Many of these results have sustained favorable trends over the past decade. Progress has been driven by an intense focus on reducing the variability of all processes in order to produce ever improving customer value and operational results. Throughout the company, people are engaged in process improvement activities which are driving continuous improvement. The results in operational parameters, including financial performance, are positive. Customer results are positive, particularly in market share gains where the improvement trend has been sustained for a decade.

There are two broad areas for improvement which cut across categories. The first area is well-linked deployment. Although the Senior Executive Leaders appear to be personally involved in the description of their activities in Category 1.0, it is unclear to what extent their involvement is genuinely deployed. Few Senior Executive Leadership activities are described in subsequent categories, and, if they are mentioned, no specifics are given. Thus, it is unclear how the Mission Statement is deployed through the organization to supportive values, goals, actions and rewards.

Throughout the application the examiners had difficulty with the clarity of definitions. For example, customer groups, market segments, key measures, categories of employees or criteria for data selection were not clearly defined or consistently used.

Throughout the application strong practices are documented. It is unclear, however, whether those practices are effectively integrated or part of a systematic, repeatable process. Additionally measurement plans are not clearly described.

There are other clear areas for improvement. One is the deployment of benchmarking. The benchmarking process is well articulated, but deployment to understand how the "Best in Class" companies achieve superior results is weak. Another area for improvement is recognition of the impact of significant employee reductions in the U.S.

In the beginning of the application five sectors are defined (Figure 0.2). Throughout the rest of the application, however, only four sectors are described. This leads the examiners to question why the Corporate Support Sector (CSS) is missing in the process and results categories, and whether approaches and processes are consistently deployed across all divisions.

In the reporting of results several questions arise. First, customers' quality requirements are not clearly described in the overview. This makes it difficult to determine whether the appropriate factors are reported in Item 6.1. Also, based on the data reported in Category 6.0, and the descriptions in previous categories, it is not clear that the results are achieved by the deployment of the approach.

The second broad area for improvement is the deployment of customer focus. Even though customer focus is expressed in CFI's credo, it is not well integrated into operations. Deployment is vague and lacks discipline. For example, business strategy elements are not well integrated with customer requirements, and a long term view is lacking. Quality values are not well articulated. And, the employee survey results indicate a low customer orientation.

The strong emphasis on C_{pk}'s does not include a clear process for connecting customer requirements with the setting of specification limits which are integral to the calculation and use of C_{pk}'s. Throughout the application CFI emphasizes the importance of six sigma. In several instances, however they are trying to achieve a C_{pk} of 1.5 which does not equal six sigma.

In summary, CFI has made clear improvements as a result of their process focus and intensity. With improved customer focus combined with other opportunities, they can continue to make significant progress in quality and operational results.

Malcolm Baldrige **National Quality Award**

CONTENTS

THE MALCOLM BALDRIGE NATIONAL QUALITY AWARD: A PUBLIC-PRIVATE PARTNERSHIP

Building active partnerships in the private sector, and between the private sector and government, is fundamental to the success of the Award in improving quality in the United States.

Support by the private sector for the Award Program in the form of funds, volunteer efforts, and participation in information transfer continues to grow.

To ensure the continued growth and success of these partnerships, each of the following organizations plays an important role:

The Foundation for the Malcolm Baldrige National Quality Award

The Foundation for the Malcolm Baldrige National Quality Award was created to foster the success of the Program. The Foundation's main objective is to raise funds to permanently endow the Award Program.

Prominent leaders from U.S. companies serve as Foundation Trustees to ensure that the Foundation's objectives are accomplished. Donor organizations vary in size and type, and are representative of many kinds of businesses and business groups.

National Institute of Standards and Technology (NIST)

Responsibility for the Award is assigned to the Department of Commerce. NIST, an agency of the Department's Technology Administration, manages the Award Program.

NIST's goals are to aid U.S. industry through research and services; to contribute to public health, safety, and the environment; and to support the U.S. scientific and engineering research communities. NIST conducts basic and applied research in the physical sciences and engineering and develops measurement techniques, test methods, and standards. Much of NIST's work relates directly to technology development and technology utilization.

American Society for Quality Control (ASQC)

ASQC assists in administering the Award Program under contract to NIST.

ASQC is dedicated to facilitating continuous improvement and increased customer satisfaction by identifying, communicating, and promoting the use of quality principles, concepts, and technologies. ASQC strives to be recognized throughout the world as the leading authority on, and champion for, quality. ASQC recognizes that continuous quality improvement will help the favorable repositioning of American goods and services in the international marketplace.

Board of Overseers

The Board of Overseers is the advisory organization on the Award to the Department of Commerce. The Board is appointed by the Secretary of Commerce and consists of distinguished leaders from all sectors of the U.S. economy.

The Board of Overseers evaluates all aspects of the Award Program, including the adequacy of the Criteria and processes for making Awards. An important part of the Board's responsibility is to assess how well the Award is serving the national interest. Accordingly, the Board makes recommendations to the Secretary of Commerce and to the Director of NIST regarding changes and improvements in the Award Program.

Board of Examiners

The Board of Examiners evaluates Award applications, prepares feedback reports, and makes Award recommendations to the Director of NIST. The Board consists of business and quality experts primarily from the private sector. Members are selected by NIST through a competitive application process. For 1995, the Board consists of about 270 members. Of these, 9 serve as Judges, and approximately 50 serve as Senior Examiners. The remainder serve as Examiners. All members of the Board take part in an Examiner preparation course.

In addition to their application review responsibilities, Board members contribute significantly to information transfer activities. Many of these activities involve the hundreds of professional, trade, community, and state organizations to which Board members belong.

Award Recipients' Responsibilities and Contributions

Award recipients are required to share information on their successful performance and quality strategies with other U.S. organizations. However, recipients are not required to share proprietary information, even if such information was part of their Award application. The principal mechanism for sharing information is the annual Quest for Excellence Conference, highlighted on page 50.

Award recipients in the first seven years of the Award have been very generous in their commitment to improving U.S. competitiveness, and manufacturing and service quality. They have shared information with hundreds of thousands of companies, educational institutions, government agencies, health care organizations, and others. This sharing far exceeds expectations and Program requirements. Award winners' efforts have encouraged many other organizations in all sectors of the U.S. economy to undertake their own performance improvement efforts.

INTRODUCTION

The Malcolm Baldrige National Quality Award is an annual Award to recognize U.S. companies for business excellence and quality achievement.

The Award promotes:
- awareness of quality as an increasingly important element in competitiveness,
- understanding of the requirements for performance excellence, and
- sharing of information on successful performance strategies and the benefits derived from implementation of these strategies.

Award Participation

The Award has three eligibility categories:
- Manufacturing companies
- Service companies
- Small businesses

Awards may be given in each category each year. Award recipients may publicize and advertise their Awards. In addition to publicizing the receipt of the Award, recipients are expected to share information about their successful performance strategies with other U.S. organizations.

Companies participating in the Award process are required to submit application packages that include completion of the Award Examination.

The Award Examination

The Award Examination is based upon performance excellence criteria created through a public-private partnership. In responding to these criteria, each applicant is expected to provide information and data on the company's improvement processes and results. Information and data submitted must be adequate to demonstrate that the applicant's approaches could be replicated or adapted by other companies.

The Award Examination is designed not only to serve as a reliable basis for making Awards but also to permit a diagnosis of each applicant's overall management system.

The Application Package

A complete Application Package consists of several components. Detailed information and the necessary forms are contained in the Application Forms and Instructions document. Ordering instructions for this document are given on page 49.

The objective of the Application Package is to provide sufficient information on management of products and services and results of improvement processes to permit a rigorous evaluation by the Board of Examiners. The Application Package consists of: an approved Eligibility Determination Form, with a listing of applicant company sites: a completed Application Form: a Business Overview, addressing the applicant's key business factors: the Application Report, responding to all Award Examination Criteria: and. Supplemental Sections, submitted by applicants whose applications include units that are in different businesses.

Application Review

Applications are reviewed and evaluated by members of the Board of Examiners in a four-stage process:

Stage 1 – independent review and evaluation by at least five members of the Board

Stage 2 – consensus review and evaluation for applications that score well in Stage 1

Stage 3 – site visits to applicants that score well in Stage 2

Stage 4 – Judges' review and recommendations

Board members are assigned to applications taking into account the nature of the applicants' businesses and the expertise of the Examiners. Assignments are made in accord with strict rules regarding conflict of interest.

Applications are reviewed without funding from the United States government. Review expenses are paid primarily through application fees; partial support for the reviews is provided by the Foundation for the Malcolm Baldrige National Quality Award.

Feedback to Applicants

Each applicant receives a feedback report at the conclusion of the review process. The feedback is based upon the applicant's responses to the Award Examination Criteria.

Purpose of This Booklet

This booklet contains the Award Examination Criteria, a description of the Criteria. scoring guidelines. and other information. In addition to serving as the basis for submitting an Award application. organizations of all kinds use the Criteria for self-assessment. planning. training. and other purposes.

If you plan to apply for the Award in 1995, you will also need the document entitled
1995 Application Forms and Instructions. Ordering instructions are given on page 49.

Eligibility Determination Forms due — March 3, 1995

Award Applications due — April 3, 1995

Award Criteria Purposes

The Malcolm Baldrige National Quality Award Criteria are the basis for making Awards and for giving feedback to applicants. In addition, the Criteria have three important roles in strengthening U.S. competitiveness:

- to help improve performance practices and capabilities;
- to facilitate communication and sharing of best practices information among and within organizations of all types based upon a common understanding of key performance requirements; and
- to serve as a working tool for managing performance, planning, training, and assessment.

Award Criteria Goals

The Criteria are designed to help companies enhance their competitiveness through focus on dual, results-oriented goals:

- delivery of ever-improving value to customers, resulting in marketplace success; and
- improvement of overall company performance and capabilities.

Core Values and Concepts

The Award Criteria are built upon a set of core values and concepts. These values and concepts are the foundation for integrating customer and company performance requirements.

These core values and concepts are:

Customer-Driven Quality

Quality is judged by customers. All product and service characteristics that contribute value to customers and lead to customer satisfaction and preference must be a key focus of a company's management system. Value, satisfaction, and preference may be influenced by many factors throughout the customer's overall purchase, ownership, and service experiences. These factors include the company's relationship with customers that helps build trust, confidence, and loyalty. This concept of quality includes not only the product and service characteristics that meet basic customer requirements, but it also includes those characteristics that enhance them and differentiate them from competing offerings. Such enhancement and differentiation may be based upon new offerings, combinations of product and service offerings, rapid response, or special relationships.

Customer-driven quality is thus a strategic concept. It is directed toward customer retention and market share gain. It demands constant sensitivity to emerging customer and market requirements, and measurement of the factors that drive customer satisfaction and retention. It also demands awareness of developments in technology and of competitors' offerings, and rapid and flexible response to customer and market requirements.

Success requires more than defect and error reduction, merely meeting specifications, and reducing complaints. Nevertheless, defect and error reduction and elimination of causes of dissatisfaction contribute significantly to the customers' view of quality and are thus also important parts of customer-driven quality. In addition, the company's success in recovering from defects and errors ("making things right for the customer") is crucial to building customer relationships and to customer retention.

Leadership

A company's senior leaders need to set directions and create a customer orientation, clear and visible values, and high expectations. Reinforcement of the values and expectations requires personal commitment and involvement. The leaders' basic values and commitment need to include areas of public responsibility and corporate citizenship. The leaders need to take part in the creation of strategies, systems, and methods for achieving excellence and building capabilities. The systems and methods need to guide all activities and decisions of the company. The senior leaders need to commit to the development of the entire work force and should encourage participation and creativity by all employees. Through their personal involvement in activities, such as planning, communications, review of company performance, and recognition of employees' achievements, the senior leaders serve as role models, reinforcing the values and encouraging leadership and initiative throughout the company.

Continuous Improvement and Learning

Achieving the highest levels of performance requires a well-executed approach to continuous improvement. The term "continuous improvement" refers to both incremental and "breakthrough" improvement. The approach to improvement needs to be "embedded" in the way the company functions. Embedded means: (1) improvement is part of the daily work of all work units; (2) improvement processes seek to eliminate problems at their source; and (3) improvement is driven by opportunities to do better, as well as by problems that must be corrected. Opportunities for improvement include: employee ideas; R&D; customer input; and benchmarking or other comparative performance information.

Improvements may be of several types: (1) enhancing value to customers through new and improved products and services; (2) reducing errors, defects, and waste; (3) improving responsiveness and cycle time performance; (4) improving productivity and effectiveness in the use of all resources; and (5) improving the company's performance and leadership position in fulfilling its public responsibilities and serving as a role model in corporate citizenship. Thus improvement is driven not only by the objective to provide better products and services, but also by the need to be responsive and efficient — both conferring additional marketplace advantages. To meet these objectives, continuous improvement must contain cycles of planning, execution, and evaluation. This requires a basis — preferably a quantitative basis — for assessing progress and for deriving information for future cycles of improvement. Such information should provide direct links between performance goals and internal operations.

Employee Participation and Development

A company's success in improving performance depends increasingly on the skills and motivation of its work force. Employee success depends increasingly on having meaningful opportunities to learn and to practice new skills. Companies need to invest in the development of the work force through ongoing education, training, and opportunities for continuing growth. Such opportunities might include classroom and on-the-job training, job rotation, and pay for demonstrated skills. Structured on-the-job training offers a cost effective way to train and to better link training to work processes. Work force education and training programs may need to utilize advanced technologies, such as electronic support systems and "information highways." Increasingly, training, development, and work organizations need to be tailored to a more diverse work force and to more flexible, high performance work practices.

Major challenges in the area of work force development include: (1) integration of human resource management — selection, performance, recognition, training, and career advancement; and (2) aligning human resource management with business plans and strategic change processes. Addressing these challenges requires acquisition and use of employee-related data on skills, satisfaction, motivation, safety, and well-being. Such data need to be tied to indicators of company or unit performance, such as customer satisfaction, customer retention, and productivity. Through this approach, human resource management may be better integrated and aligned with business directions, using continuous improvement processes to refine integration and alignment.

Fast Response

Success in competitive markets increasingly demands ever-shorter cycles for new or improved product and service introduction. Also, faster and more flexible response to customers is now a more critical requirement. Major improvement in response time often requires simplification of work organizations and work processes. To accomplish such improvement, the time performance of work processes should be among the key process measures. There are other important benefits derived from this focus: response time improvements often drive simultaneous improvements in organization, quality, and productivity. Hence it is beneficial to consider response time, quality, and productivity objectives together.

Design Quality and Prevention

Business management should place strong emphasis on design quality — problem and waste prevention achieved through building quality into products and services and into production and delivery processes. In general, costs of preventing problems at the design stage are much lower than costs of correcting problems which occur "downstream". Design quality includes the creation of fault-tolerant (robust) or failure-resistant processes and products.

A major issue in competition is the design-to-introduction ("product generation") cycle time. Meeting the demands of rapidly changing markets requires that companies carry out stage-to-stage coordination and integration ("concurrent engineering") of functions and activities from basic research to commercialization.

From the point of view of public responsibility, the design stage involves decisions regarding resource use and manufacturing processes. Such decisions affect process waste streams and the composition of municipal and industrial wastes. The growing demands for a cleaner environment mean that companies need to develop design strategies that include environmental factors.

Consistent with the theme of design quality and prevention, continuous improvement needs to emphasize interventions "upstream" — at early stages in processes. This approach yields the maximum overall benefits of improvements and corrections. Such upstream intervention also needs to take into account the company's suppliers.

Long-Range View of the Future

Pursuit of market leadership requires a strong future orientation and a willingness to make long-term commitments to all stakeholders — customers, employees, suppliers, stockholders, the public, and the community. Planning needs to anticipate many types of changes including those that may affect customers' expectations of products and services, technological developments, changing customer segments, evolving regulatory requirements, community/societal expectations, and thrusts by competitors. Plans, strategies, and resource allocations need to reflect these commitments and changes. A major part of the long-term commitment is developing employees and suppliers, fulfilling public responsibilities, and serving as a corporate citizenship role model.

Management by Fact

A modern business management system needs to be built upon a framework of measurement, information, data and analysis. Measurements must derive from the company's strategy and encompass all key processes and the outputs and results of those processes. Facts and data needed for performance improvement and assessment are of many types, including: customer, product and service performance, operations, market, competitive comparisons, supplier, employee-related, and cost and financial. Analysis refers to extracting larger meaning from data to support evaluation and decision making at various levels within the company. Such analysis may entail using data to reveal information — such as trends, projections, and cause and effect — that might not be evident without analysis. Facts, data, and analysis support a variety of company purposes, such as planning, reviewing company performance, improving operations, and comparing company performance with competitors' or with "best practices" benchmarks.

A major consideration in the use of data and analysis to improve performance involves the creation and use of performance measures or indicators. Performance measures or indicators are measurable characteristics of products, services, processes, and operations the company uses to track and improve performance. *The measures or indicators should be selected to best represent the factors that lead to improved customer, operational, and financial performance. A system of measures or indicators tied to customer and/or company performance requirements represents a clear and objective basis for aligning all activities with the company's goals.* Through the analysis of data from the tracking processes, the measures or indicators themselves may be evaluated and changed. For example, measures selected to track product and service quality may be judged by how well improvement in these measures correlates with improvement in customer satisfaction and customer retention.

Partnership Development
Companies should seek to build internal and external partnerships to better accomplish their overall goals.

Internal partnerships might include those that promote labor-management cooperation, such as agreements with unions. Agreements might entail employee development, cross-training, or new work organizations, such as high performance work teams. Internal partnerships might also involve creating network relationships among company units to improve flexibility and responsiveness.

External partnerships may be with customers, suppliers, and education organizations for a variety of purposes, including education and training. An increasingly important kind of external partnership is the strategic partnership or alliance. Such partnerships might offer a company entry into new markets or a basis for new products or services. A partnership might also permit the blending of a company's core competencies or leadership capabilities with complementary strengths and capabilities of partners, thereby enhancing overall capability, including speed and flexibility.

Partnerships should seek to develop longer-term objectives, thereby creating a basis for mutual investments. Partners should address the key requirements for success of the partnership, means of regular communication, approaches to evaluating progress, and means for adapting to changing conditions. In some cases, joint education and training initiatives could offer a cost-effective means to help ensure the success of an alliance.

Corporate Responsibility and Citizenship
A company's management should stress corporate responsibility and citizenship. Corporate responsibility refers to basic expectations of the company — business ethics and protection of public health, safety, and the environment. Health, safety and environmental considerations need to take into account the company's operations as well as the life cycles of products and services. Companies need to address factors such as resource conservation and waste reduction at their source. Planning related to public health, safety, and the environment should anticipate adverse impacts that may arise in facilities management, production, distribution, transportation, use and disposal of products. Plans should seek to prevent problems, to provide a forthright company response if problems occur, and to make available information needed to maintain public awareness, safety, and confidence. Inclusion of public responsibility areas within a performance system means meeting all local, state, and federal laws and regulatory requirements. It also means treating these and related requirements as areas for continuous improvement "beyond mere compliance." This requires that appropriate measures of progress be created and used in managing performance.

Corporate citizenship refers to leadership and support — within reasonable limits of a company's resources — of publicly important purposes, including the above-mentioned areas of corporate responsibility. Such purposes might include education improvement, improving health care value, environmental excellence, resource conservation, community services, improving industry and business practices, and sharing of nonproprietary quality-related information. Leadership as a corporate citizen entails influencing other organizations, private and public, to partner for these purposes. For example, individual companies could lead efforts to help define the obligations of their industry to its communities.

Results Orientation
A company's performance system needs to focus on results. Results ought to be guided by and balanced by the interests of all stakeholders — customers, employees, stockholders, suppliers and partners, the public, and the community. To meet the sometimes conflicting and changing aims that balance implies, company strategy needs to explicitly address all stakeholder requirements to ensure that actions and plans meet the differing needs and avoid adverse impact on the stakeholders. The use of a balanced composite of performance indicators offers an effective means to communicate requirements, to monitor actual performance, and to marshal support for improving results.

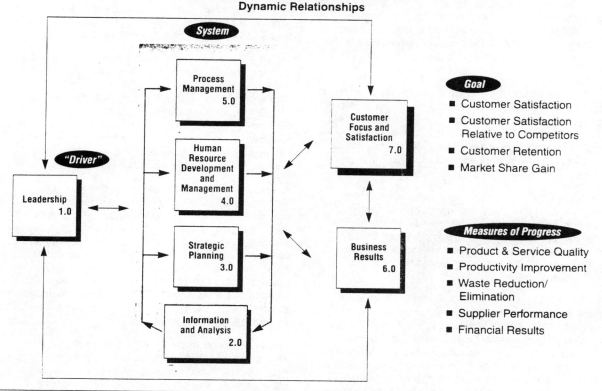

BALDRIGE AWARD CRITERIA FRAMEWORK
Dynamic Relationships

System

Process Management 5.0

Human Resource Development and Management 4.0

"Driver"

Leadership 1.0

Strategic Planning 3.0

Information and Analysis 2.0

Customer Focus and Satisfaction 7.0

Business Results 6.0

Goal
- Customer Satisfaction
- Customer Satisfaction Relative to Competitors
- Customer Retention
- Market Share Gain

Measures of Progress
- Product & Service Quality
- Productivity Improvement
- Waste Reduction/ Elimination
- Supplier Performance
- Financial Results

Award Criteria Framework

The core values and concepts are embodied in seven Categories, as follows:

1.0 Leadership
2.0 Information and Analysis
3.0 Strategic Planning
4.0 Human Resource Development and Management
5.0 Process Management
6.0 Business Results
7.0 Customer Focus and Satisfaction

The framework connecting and integrating the Categories is given in the figure above.

The framework has four basic elements:

Driver

Senior executive leadership sets directions, creates values, goals, and systems, and guides the pursuit of customer value and company performance improvement.

System

The system comprises the set of well-defined and well-designed processes for meeting the company's customer and performance requirements.

Measures of Progress

Measures of progress provide a results-oriented basis for channeling actions to delivering ever-improving customer value and company performance.

Goal

The basic aims of the system are the delivery of ever-improving value to customers and success in the marketplace.

The seven Criteria Categories shown in the figure are subdivided into Examination Items and Areas to Address:

Examination Items

There are 24 Examination Items, each focusing on a major requirement. Item titles and point values are given on page 20. The Item format is shown on page 43.

Areas to Address

Examination Items consist of sets of Areas to Address (Areas). Information is submitted by applicants in response to specific requirements of these Areas.

DESCRIPTION OF CATEGORIES, ITEMS, AND AREAS TO ADDRESS

Leadership

Leadership (Category 1.0) is the focal point within the Criteria for the company's leadership system, strategic directions, and expectations. The expectations include those relating to corporate responsibility and citizenship. The Category highlights the key roles of senior executives — those that cannot be delegated to others.

1.1 Senior Executive Leadership

This Item addresses how the company's senior executives set strategic directions and build and maintain a leadership system conducive to high performance, individual development, and organizational learning. Executive leadership needs to take into account all stakeholders — customers, employees, suppliers, partners, stockholders, the public, and the community.

Area 1.1a calls for information on the major aspects of leadership — creating values and expectations, setting directions, developing and maintaining an effective leadership system, and building company capabilities. Senior executives need to reflect these values, and the leadership system needs to include teamwork at the executive level.

Area 1.1b calls for information on how senior executives evaluate and improve the effectiveness of the company's organization and leadership system. This aspect of leadership is crucial, because of the fast pace of competition. A major target is to create organizations that are flexible and responsive — changing easily to adapt to new needs and opportunities. This Area recognizes that both factors — leadership and organization — are crucial to high performance. Through their roles in strategy development and review of company performance, the senior executives adapt leadership and organization to changing opportunities and requirements.

1.2 Leadership System and Organization

This Item addresses how the company's leadership system is translated into an effective overall organization and management system — focused on performance.

Area 1.2a calls for information on how the company's organization, management, and work processes support its customer and performance objectives. Functional and management barriers that could lead to losing sight of customers and cause decision paths to be ineffective and slow must be prevented. Performance measures provide an effective means to ensure alignment of company units.

Area 1.2b calls for information on how the company's values, expectations, and directions are "made real" throughout the company via effective communications.

Although senior executives' communications are necessary for effective overall communications, making values, expectations, and directions real demands constant reinforcement and "truth testing", as employees observe whether or not stated values and expectations are actually the basis for company actions and key decisions.

Area 1.2c calls for information on how company and work unit performance are reviewed. Important work process assessments should be included in these reviews. This information should address important aspects of reviews —types, frequency, content, uses and who conducts them. Frequency, content, uses and who conducts reviews could vary greatly, depending upon many factors. Most commonly, a review system, blending ongoing ("real time") and periodic reviews, is needed to meet differing requirements.

Reviews offer an effective means to communicate and reinforce what is really important, how performance is measured, and how well business objectives are being met. Important considerations in reviews are the content and organization of information to foster learning and to stimulate action. This means that reviews should include non-financial and financial information which together present a clear picture of status and trends relative to the company's key business drivers. Reviews also provide an effective means to assist units which may not be performing according to expectations.

1.3 Public Responsibility and Corporate Citizenship

This Item addresses how the company integrates its public responsibilities and corporate citizenship into its business planning and performance improvement practices.

Area 1.3a calls for information on three basic aspects of public responsibility: (1) making risk and legal requirements an integral part of performance improvement; (2) sensitivity in planning products, services, and operations to issues of societal concern whether or not these issues are currently embodied in law; and (3) making legal and ethical conduct visible in the company's values and performance improvement processes. Fulfilling public responsibilities means not only meeting all local, state, and federal laws and regulatory requirements, but also treating these and related requirements as areas for improvement "beyond mere compliance". This means that the company should maintain constant awareness of potential public impacts related to its products, services, and operations.

Area 1.3b calls for information on how the company leads as a corporate citizen in its key communities. The issues in this Area relate to the company as a member of different types of communities and being a positive influence upon other organizations. Opportunities for leadership and involvement include assistance by the company to strengthen community services, education, healthcare, the environment, and practices of trade and business associations. This includes community service by employees, encouraged, supported, and recognized by the company. For example, companies and their employees could help to influence the adoption of higher standards in education.

Information and Analysis

Information and Analysis (Category 2.0) is the focal point within the Criteria for all key information to drive the improvement of overall performance. In simplest terms, Category 2.0 is the "brain center" for the alignment of a company's information system with its strategic directions. The Category addresses the information and analysis requirements for performance improvement based upon the improvement of key processes.

2.1 Management of Information and Data
This Item addresses the company's selection and management of information and data to support overall business goals with primary emphasis on supporting process management and performance improvement.

Area 2.1a calls for information on how information and data needed to drive improvement of overall company performance are selected and managed. The Area has two parts. The first part addresses selection and emphasizes key business drivers — strategically important areas of performance. The second part addresses management of data and information, and emphasizes user needs — rapid access and update, and reliability.

Area 2.1b calls for information on how the company evaluates and improves its selection, analysis, and management of information and data. The Area emphasizes alignment with business priorities, support of process management, and feedback from information and data users. The evaluation might take into account factors such as paths of data use, extent and effectiveness of use, gaps, sharing, and organization of information and data.

Overall, Item 2.1 represents a key foundation for a performance-oriented company. This foundation should include non-financial and financial information and data.

Although the main focus of Item 2.1 is on information and data for the effective management of performance, information, data, and information technology often have strategic significance as well. For example, information technology could be used to build and disseminate unique knowledge about customers and markets and create the ability to operate more successfully in key markets. Also, information technology and the information and data made available through such technology could be of special advantage in business networks or alliances. Responses to Areas 2.1a

and 2.1b should take into account such strategic use of information and data. Accordingly, "users" should then be interpreted as business partners as well as company units.

2.2 Competitive Comparisons and Benchmarking
This Item addresses external drivers of improvement — data and information related to competitive position and to best practices. Such data may have both operational and strategic value.

Area 2.2a calls for information on how competitive comparisons and benchmarking information are selected and used to help drive improvement of overall company performance. The Area focuses on needs and priorities and criteria for selecting information and data. The Area also examines the use of data to develop an understanding of processes and process performance and to set stretch targets.

Area 2.2b calls for information on how the company evaluates and improves its processes for selecting and using competitive and benchmark information to drive performance improvement.

The major premises underlying this Item are: (1) companies need to "know where they stand" relative to competitors and to best practice performance for similar activities; (2) comparative and benchmarking information provides impetus for significant ("breakthrough") improvement and alerts companies to competitive threats and new practices; and (3) companies need to understand their own processes and the processes of others, before they compare performance levels.

Benchmarking information may also support business analysis and decisions relating to core competencies, alliances, and outsourcing.

2.3 Analysis and Use of Company-Level Data
This Item addresses company-level analysis — the principal basis for guiding a company's process management toward business results. Despite the importance of individual facts and data, they do not usually provide a sound basis for actions or priorities. Action depends upon understanding cause/effect connections among processes and between processes and business results. Process actions may have many resource implications; results may have many cost and revenue implications as well. Given that resources for improvement are limited, and cause/effect connections are often unclear, there is a critical need to provide a sound analytical basis for decisions. In the Criteria, this role is served by analyses of many types. Item 2.3 plays the key linkage role in an integrated data and analysis system that is built around financial and non-financial data.

Area 2.3a calls for information on how data and information from all parts of the company are aggregated and analyzed to support reviews, business decisions. and planning. The focus is on three key areas of performance: customers and markets; operational performance; and competitive performance. The analyses in this Area depend upon non-financial and financial data, connected to provide a basis for action.

Area 2.3b calls for analysis linking customer and market data, improvements in product and service quality, and improvements in operational performance to improvement in financial and/or market indicators. The purpose of this linkage is to guide the selection of improvement efforts, to achieve revenue growth, and to reduce operating costs.

Strategic Planning

Strategic Planning (Category 3.0) addresses strategic and business planning and deployment of plans, with a strong focus on customer and operational performance requirements. The Category stresses that customer-driven quality and operational performance excellence are key strategic business issues which need to be an integral part of company planning. Specifically:

- customer-driven quality is a strategic view of quality. The focus is on the drivers of customer satisfaction, customer retention, and market share — key factors in competitiveness and business success;

- operational performance improvement contributes to short-term and longer-term productivity growth and cost/price competitiveness. The focus on building operational capability — including speed, responsiveness, and flexibility — represents an investment in strengthening competitive fitness.

The Criteria also emphasize that continuous improvement must be an integral part of the daily activity of all work units. The special role of Category 3.0 is to provide an effective focus for daily work, aligning it with the company's strategic directions.

In particular, planning is needed to:

- understand the key customer and operational requirements as input to setting strategic directions. This will help ensure that ongoing process improvements will be aligned with the company's strategic directions.

- optimize the use of resources and ensure bridging between short-term and longer-term requirements which may entail capital expenditures, training, etc.

- ensure that deployment will be effective — that there are mechanisms to transmit requirements and achieve alignment on three basic levels: (1) company/executive level; (2) the key process level; and (3) the work-unit/individual-job level.

The Category requirements do not imply formalized plans, planning systems. departments, or specific planning cycles. Nor does the Category imply that all improvements could or should be planned in advance.

3.1 Strategy Development

This Item addresses how the company develops its view of the future, sets strategic directions. and translates these directions into actionable key business drivers. including customer satisfaction and market leadership requirements. The focus of the Item is on competitive leadership. Such leadership depends upon revenue growth as well as on operational effectiveness.

Area 3.1a calls for information on the key influences. challenges, and requirements that might affect the company's future opportunities and directions — taking as long a view as possible. The main purpose of the Area is to develop a thorough and realistic context for the development of customer- and market-focused strategy to guide ongoing decision making, resource allocation and companywide management.

Area 3.1b calls for information on how strategy and plans are translated into actionable key business drivers, which serve as the basis for operationalizing and deploying plan requirements, addressed in Item 3.2. This translation might include a determination of activities the company should perform itself and those for which it might utilize partners or seek partners.

Area 3.1c calls for information on how the company evaluates and improves its strategic planning and plan deployment processes. This might involve input from work units regarding key deployment factors — effective translation and communications of strategy and plans, adequacy of resources, and key new needs.

Item 3.1 plays a central directional role in the Criteria. It seeks to focus company leadership on developing a competitive strategy and on operationalizing this strategy. This requires the creation of a view of the future that takes into account not only the markets or segments to compete in but also how to compete. "How to compete" presents many options and requires good understanding of the company's and competitors' strengths and weaknesses. Operationalizing the strategy in the form of key business drivers is intended to highlight the importance of clear and measurable performance objectives. These objectives serve to guide the design and management of key processes. The objectives may also serve to align communications and compensation and recognition systems with performance objectives.

3.2 Strategy Deployment

This Item addresses how the company's key business drivers are deployed. Also addressed is a projection of key measures of the company's performance. The main intent of the Item is to focus on effective operationalizing of the key business drivers, including measures that permit the tracking of performance.

Area 3.2a calls for information on the company's key business drivers and how these drivers are translated into an action plan. This includes spelling out key performance requirements, alignment of work unit, supplier, and/or partner plans, how productivity, cycle time, and waste reduction are addressed, and the principal resources committed to the accomplishment of plans. Of central importance in this Area is how alignment and consistency are achieved — for example, via key processes and key measurements. The alignment and consistency are intended also to provide a basis for priorities for ongoing improvement activities — part of the daily work of all work units.

Area 3.2b calls for a projection of key measures and/or indicators of the company's quality and operational performance. It also calls for comparing projected performance versus competitors and key benchmarks. This projection/comparison is intended to encourage companies to improve their understanding of dynamic, competitive quality and operational performance factors, and to take into account their rates of improvement as a diagnostic management tool.

Human Resource Development and Management

Human Resource Development and Management (Category 4.0) is the focal point within the Criteria for all key human resource practices — those directed toward the creation of a high performance workplace. The Category addresses human resource development and management in an integrated way. This integration is concerned with how well the human resource practices tie into and are aligned with the company's strategic directions.

4.1 Human Resource Planning and Evaluation

This Item serves as the point of direct linkage between human resource planning and the company's strategic directions. The strategic directions should address the development of the entire work force and the needs of a high performance workplace. The Item addresses how the company aligns its human resource planning and practices with its business directions so that high performance workplace practices become part of a coordinated organizational strategy.

Area 4.1a calls for information on key human resource plans derived from company strategic and business planning. The Area calls for the primary thrusts, broadly defined, of the company's human resource plans — the ones needed to support its overall strategic directions. This is intended to provide a multiyear context and guide for human resource planning, management, and evaluation.

Area 4.1b calls for information on how the company evaluates and improves its overall human resource planning and management. This Area is the "brain center" for human resource processes and results, as it relies upon employee-related and company performance data and information, and ties the overall evaluation to company strategy and business results. However, the evaluation also must go beyond broad strategy to the essential details of human resource effectiveness. The evaluation needs to provide the company's senior executives with information on strengths and weaknesses in human resource practices and development that might bear upon the company's abilities to achieve its short-term and longer-term business objectives. For example, the evaluation should take into account the development and progression of all categories and types of employees, including new employees. The evaluation should also monitor the extent of deployment of education and training throughout the company, and how well education and training support company performance improvement. The overall evaluation needs to rely heavily upon the well-being and satisfaction factors addressed in Item 4.4.

4.2 High Performance Work Systems

This Item addresses how the company's job design, compensation, and recognition approaches enable and encourage all employees to contribute effectively, operating within high performance work units. The Item emphasizes that high performance requires effective work design and reinforcement.

Area 4.2a calls for information on job design and work organizations. The basic aims of such design and organizations should be to enable employees to exercise more discretion and decision making, leading to greater flexibility and more rapid response to the changing requirements of the marketplace. Effective job design and flexible work organizations are necessary but may not be sufficient to ensure high performance. Job and organization design needs to be backed by information systems, education, and appropriate training to ensure that information flow supports the job and work designs. Also important is effective communication across functions and work units to ensure focus on customer requirements.

Area 4.2b addresses the important alignment of incentives with work systems. The Area calls for information on employee compensation and recognition — how these reinforce high performance job design, work organizations, and teamwork. These are important considerations because there should be a consistency between the company's compensation and recognition system and its work structures and processes. Also, compensation and recognition may need to be based upon demonstrated skills and evaluation by peers in teams and networks.

4.3 Employee Education, Training, and Development
This Item addresses how the company develops the work force via education, training, and on-the-job reinforcement of knowledge and skills. Development is intended to meet the needs of a high performance workplace on an ongoing basis. This means that education and training need to be ongoing as well.

Area 4.3a calls for information on how the company's education and training serve as a key vehicle in building company capabilities and employee capabilities. The Area focuses on these two capabilities, treating them as investments the company makes in its long-term future and the long-term future of employees.

Area 4.3b calls for information on how education and training are designed, delivered, reinforced, and evaluated, with special emphasis upon on-the-job application of knowledge and skills. The Area emphasizes the importance of the involvement of employees and line managers in design of training, including clear identification of specific needs. This involves job analysis — understanding the types and levels of the skills required and the timeliness of training. The Area also emphasizes evaluation of education and training. Such evaluation could take into account line managers' evaluation, employee self-evaluation, and peer evaluation of value received through education and training relative to needs identified in design. Evaluation could also address the effectiveness of education and training delivery, impact on work unit performance, and costs of delivery alternatives.

4.4 Employee Well-Being and Satisfaction
This Item addresses the work environment, the work climate and how they are tailored to foster the well-being, satisfaction, and development of all employees.

Area 4.4a calls for information regarding a safe and healthful work environment to determine how the company includes such factors in its planning and improvement activities.

Area 4.4b calls for information on the company's approach to enhance employee well-being, satisfaction, and growth potential based upon a more holistic view of employees as key stakeholders. The Area emphasizes that the company needs to consider a variety of mechanisms to build well-being and satisfaction. Increasingly, these mechanisms relate to development, progression, employability, and external activities. This might include family or community service activities.

Area 4.4c calls for information on how the company determines employee satisfaction, well-being, and motivation. The Area recognizes that many factors might affect employee motivation. Although satisfaction with pay and promotion potential is important, these factors may not be adequate to assess the overall climate for motivation and high performance. For this reason, the company may need to consider a variety of factors in the work environment to determine the key factors in motivation. Factors inhibiting motivation need to be prioritized and addessed. Further understanding of these factors could be developed through exit interviews with departing employees.

Process Management

Process Management (Category 5.0) is the focal point within the Criteria for all key work processes. Built into the Category are the central requirements for efficient and effective process management — effective design, a prevention orientation, evaluation and continuous improvement, linkage to suppliers, and overall high performance.

5.1 Design and Introduction of Products and Services
This Item examines how the company designs and introduces products and services. A major focus of the Item is the rapid and effective integration of production and delivery early in the design phase. This integration is intended to minimize downstream problems for customers and/or eliminate the need for design changes that might be costly to the company.

Area 5.1a calls for information on the design of products, services, and their production/delivery processes. Three aspects of this design are examined: (1) the translation of customer requirements into the design requirements for products and services; (2) how the product and service design requirements are translated into efficient and effective production/delivery processes; and (3) how all requirements associated with products, services, and production/delivery processes are addressed early in the design process by all appropriate company units to ensure integration and coordination. Many businesses also need to consider requirements for suppliers and/or business partners at the design stage. Overall, effective design must take into account all stakeholders in the value chain.

It should be noted that although the main focus of Area 5.1a is on the design of products, services, and processes to meet customer requirements, effective design must also consider cycle time and productivity of production and delivery processes. This might entail detailed mapping of manufacturing or service processes to achieve efficiency as well as to meet customer requirements.

Area 5.1b calls for information on how product, service, and production/delivery process designs are reviewed and/or tested in detail prior to full-scale launch. Such review and/or testing is intended to ensure that all parts of the production/delivery system are capable of performing according to design. This stage could be a crucial one — with a positive or negative customer reaction and potentially high cost to the company if pre-launch changes are significant.

Area 5.1c calls for information on how designs and design processes are evaluated and improved to progressively improve quality and cycle time. This Area is intended to determine how companies extract lessons learned to build capabilities for future designs. Such evaluation might take into account delays and problems experienced during design, feedback from those involved, and post-launch problems that might have been averted through better design. The evaluation and improvement should strive for a continuous flow of work in the key design and delivery processes.

5.2 Process Management: Product and Service Production and Delivery

This Item addresses two different but related concerns — how the company maintains and how it improves key production and delivery processes.

Area 5.2a calls for information on the maintenance of process performance to ensure that processes perform according to their design. The information required includes a description of the key processes and their specific requirements, and how performance relative to these requirements is known and maintained. Specific reference is made to a measurement plan. Such a plan requires the identification of critical points in processes for measurement or observation. Implied in this plan is that measurements or observations be made at the earliest points in processes to minimize problems that may result from variations from expected (design) performance. When measurements or observations reveal such variations, a remedy — usually called corrective action — is required to restore the performance of the process to its design performance. Depending on the nature of the process, the correction could involve technical, human, or both factors. Proper correction involves correcting at the source (root cause) of the variation. In some cases, customers may directly witness or take part in the process, and contribute to or be a determinant of process performance. In such cases, variations among customers must be taken into account in evaluating how well the process is performing. This might entail specific or general contingencies depending on customer response. This is especially true of professional and personal services.

Area 5.2b calls for information on how processes are improved to achieve better performance. Better performance means not only better quality from the customers' perspective but also better operational performance — such as productivity — from the company's perspective. Area 5.2b anticipates that companies use a variety of process improvement approaches. Area 5.2b calls for information on how the company uses or considers four key approaches.

5.3 Process Management: Support Services

This Item addresses how the company designs, maintains, and improves its support service processes.

Area 5.3a calls for information on the design of key support service processes. Such design needs to be based upon the requirements of the company's customers and of other units ("internal customers") within the company — those within the company who use the output of the process. The requirements of effective design are as outlined in Item 5.1 — coordinated and integrated to ensure efficient and effective performance.

Area 5.3b calls for information on how the company maintains the performance of the key support service processes. This information includes a description of the key processes and their principal requirements and a description of the measurement plan and how it is used. The requirements of Area 5.3b are similar to those described above in Area 5.2a.

Area 5.3c calls for information on how the company evaluates and improves the performance of the key support service processes. The Area calls for information on how the company uses or considers four key approaches.

5.4 Management of Supplier Performance

This Item addresses how the company manages performance of external providers of goods and services. Such management might be built around longer-term partnering relationships, particularly with key suppliers.

Area 5.4a calls for basic information on the company's principal requirements for its key suppliers, expected performance and measures used to assess performance, how the company determines whether or not its requirements are being met, and how performance information is fed back to suppliers.

Area 5.4b calls for information on how the company evaluates and improves its supplier management. This includes three main elements: improving supplier abilities to meet requirements; improving its own supplier management processes; and reducing costs associated with the verification of supplier performance.

For many companies, suppliers are an increasingly important part of achieving not only high performance and lower-cost objectives, but also strategic objectives. For example, key suppliers might provide unique design, integration, and marketing capabilities. Exploiting these advantages requires joint planning and partner relationships. Such planning and relationship building might entail the use of longer-term planning horizons and customer-supplier teams.

Business Results

Business Results (Category 6.0) provides a results focus for all processes and process improvement activities. Through this focus, the Criteria's dual purpose — superior value of offerings as viewed by customers and the marketplace, and superior company performance reflected in productivity and effectiveness indicators — is maintained. Category 6.0 thus provides "real-time" information (measures of progress) for evaluation and improvement of processes, aligned with overall business strategy. Use of business results data and information is called for in Item 2.3.

6.1 Product and Service Quality Results

This Item addresses current levels and trends in product and service quality using key measures and/or indicators of such quality. The measures and/or indicators selected should relate to requirements that matter to the customer and to the marketplace. These features are derived from customer-related Items ("listening posts") which make up Category 7.0. If the features have been properly selected, improvements in them should show a strong positive correlation with customer and marketplace improvement indicators — captured in Items 7.4 and 7.5. The correlation between quality and customer indicators is a critical management tool — a device for focusing on key quality requirements. In addition, the correlation may reveal emerging or changing market segments, changing importance of requirements, or even potential obsolescence of products and/or services.

Area 6.1a calls for data on current levels and trends in product and service quality. The Area also calls for comparative information so that the results reported can be evaluated against competitors or other relevant markers of performance.

6.2 Company Operational and Financial Results

This Item addresses the operational and financial performance of the company. Paralleling Item 6.1, which focuses on requirements that matter to the customer, Item 6.2 focuses on factors that best reflect overall company operational performance. Such factors are of two types: (1) generic — common to all companies; and (2) business-specific. Generic factors include financial indicators, cycle time, and productivity, as reflected in use of labor, materials, energy, capital, and assets. Generic factors also include human resource indicators such as safety, absenteeism, and turnover. Productivity, cycle time, or other operational indicators should reflect **aggregate company performance**. Business- or company-specific effectiveness indicators vary greatly. Examples include rates of invention, environmental quality, export levels, new markets, percent of sales from recently introduced products or services, and shifts toward new segments.

Area 6.2a calls for data on current levels and trends in company operational and financial performance. The Area also calls for comparative information so that results reported can be evaluated against competitors or other relevant markers of performance.

6.3 Supplier Performance Results

This Item addresses current levels and trends in key measures and/or indicators of supplier performance. Suppliers are external providers of materials and services, "upstream" and/or "downstream" from the company. The focus should be on the most critical requirements from the point of view of the company — the buyer of the products and services. Data reported should reflect results by whatever means they occur — via improvements by suppliers within the supply base, through selection of better performing suppliers, or both.

Area 6.3a calls for data and current levels and trends in supplier performance. Measures and indicators of performance should relate to all key requirements — quality, delivery, and price. The Area also calls for comparative information so that results reported can be evaluated against competitors or other relevant markers of performance.

Customer Focus and Satisfaction

Customer Focus and Satisfaction (Category 7.0) is the focal point within the Criteria for understanding in detail the voices of customers and the marketplace. Much of the information needed for this understanding comes from measuring results and trends. Such results and trends provide hard information on customers' views and their marketplace behaviors. This provides a useful foundation for setting priorities and focusing improvement activities. The results and trends offer a means to determine whether or not priorities and improvement activities are appropriately directed.

7.1 Customer and Market Knowledge

This Item addresses how the company determines current and emerging customer requirements and expectations. The thrust of the Item is that many factors may affect customer preference and customer loyalty, making it necessary to listen and learn on a continuous basis.

Area 7.1a calls for information on the company's process for determining current and near-term requirements and expectations of customers. The information sought includes the completeness of the customer pool, including recognition of segments and customers of competitors. Other information sought relates to sensitivity to specific product and service requirements and their relative importance to customer groups. The Area is concerned with overall validity of determination methods. The validity should be backed by use of other data and information such as complaints and gains and losses of customers.

Area 7.1b calls for information on how the company addresses future requirements and expectations of customers — its key listening and learning strategies. Such strategies depend a great deal upon the nature of the company's products and services, the competitive environment, and relationships with customers. The listening and learning strategy selected should provide timely and useful information for decision making. The strategy should take into account the company's competitive strategy. For example, if the company customizes its products and services, the listening and learning strategy needs to be backed by a capable information system — one that rapidly accumulates information about customers, and makes this information available where needed throughout the company.

Area 7.1c calls for information on how the company evaluates and improves its processes for determining customer requirements and expectations. Such evaluation/improvement could entail a variety of approaches — formal and informal — that seek to stay in close touch with customers and with issues that bear upon customer loyalty and customer preference. The purpose of the evaluation called for in Area 7.1c is to find reliable and cost-effective means to understand customer requirements and expectations on a continuous basis.

7.2 Customer Relationship Management

Item 7.2 addresses how the company provides effective management of its responses and follow-ups with customers. Relationship management provides a potentially important means for companies to gain understanding about, and to manage, customer expectations. Also, frontline employees may provide vital information relating to building partnerships and other longer-term relationships with customers.

Area 7.2a calls for information on how the company provides easy access for customers specifically for purposes of seeking information or assistance and/or to comment and complain. This Area also calls for information on service standards and their use.

Area 7.2b focuses on the complaint management process. The principal issue addressed is prompt and effective resolution of complaints including recovery of customer confidence. However, the Area also addresses how the company learns from complaints and ensures that production/delivery process employees receive information needed to eliminate the causes of complaints.

Area 7.2c calls for information on how the company follows up with customers regarding products, services, and recent transactions to determine satisfaction, to resolve problems, and to gather information for improvement or for new services.

Area 7.2d calls for information on how the company evaluates and improves its customer response management. Such improvements may be of several types. Examples include improving service standards, such as complaint resolution time and resolution effectiveness, and improving the use of customer feedback to improve production/delivery processes, training, and hiring.

7.3 Customer Satisfaction Determination

This Item addresses how the company determines customer satisfaction and satisfaction relative to competitors.

Area 7.3a calls for information on how the company gathers information on customer satisfaction, including any important differences in approaches for different customer groups or segments. The Area highlights the importance of the measurement scale to focus on the factors that reflect customers' market behaviors — repurchase, new business, and positive referral.

Area 7.3b calls for information on how satisfaction relative to competitors is determined. Such information might be derived from company-based comparative studies or studies made by independent organizations. The purpose of this comparison is to develop information that can be used for improving performance relative to competitors and to better understand the factors that drive markets.

Area 7.3c calls for information on how the company evaluates and improves its processes and measurement scales for determining customer satisfaction and satisfaction relative to competitors. This evaluation/improvement process is expected to draw upon other indicators such as gains and losses of customers and customer dissatisfaction indicators such as complaints. The evaluation should also consider how well customer satisfaction information and data are used throughout the company. Such use is likely to be enhanced if data are presented in an actionable form meeting two key conditions: (1) survey responses tying directly to key business processes: and (2) survey responses translated into cost/revenue implications. .

7.4 Customer Satisfaction Results

This Item addresses two related but nevertheless different types of business results — customer satisfaction and customer dissatisfaction.

Area 7.4a calls for information on trends and current levels in key measures and/or indicators of customer satisfaction. The presentation of results could include information on customer retention and other appropriate evidence of current and recent past satisfaction with the company's products and/or services, such as customer awards.

Area 7.4b calls for trends in key measures and/or indicators of customer dissatisfaction. Such measures and/or indicators depend upon the nature of the products and/or services. Item 7.3, Note (3), lists a number of possible indicators of dissatisfaction. In addition, a company's survey methods might include a scale that uses ratings such as "very dissatisfied" or "somewhat dissatisfied."

The reason for including measures of both satisfaction and dissatisfaction is that they usually provide different information. That is. the factors in high levels of satisfaction may not be the same factors as those that relate to high levels of dissatisfaction. In addition. the effect of individual instances of dissatisfaction on overall satisfaction could vary widely depending upon the effectiveness of the company's resolution ("recovery") of a problem.

Although Item 7.4 is a results Item. it is anticipated that the results themselves are **input** drivers of improvement priorities — actions that affect customer retention and positive referral. That is. the main management approach involves viewing increasing satisfaction and decreasing dissatisfaction as a means. not an end. The end is retention and positive referral. Use of customer satisfaction data and information is called for in Item 2.3.

7.5 Customer Satisfaction Comparison

This Item addresses three related but nevertheless different customer-related results, important to managing in a competitive environment. These are: customer satisfaction relative to competitors; gains and losses of customers and customer accounts relative to competitors; and gains and losses in market share.

Area 7.5a calls for information on trends and current levels in key measures and/or indicators of customer satisfaction relative to competitors. The presentation of results could include information on gains and losses of customers and customer accounts relative to competitors.

Area 7.5b calls for trends in gaining or losing market share to competitors.

The reason for including the three measures is that they provide different information. Relative satisfaction and gains and losses of customers and customer accounts provide information on specific factors and the importance of these factors in customer decision making. Market share information provides a more aggregate view of markets that includes but goes beyond customer turnover.

Although Item 7.5 is a results Item. it is anticipated that the results themselves are drivers of improvement priorities and market understanding. reinforcing but going beyond the information presented in Item 7.5. Use of customer satisfaction comparison data and information is called for in Item 2.3.

KEY CHARACTERISTICS OF THE AWARD CRITERIA

1. **The Criteria are directed toward business results.**
   The Criteria focus principally on seven key areas of business performance, given below.

   > Business results are a composite of:
   > (1) customer satisfaction/retention
   > (2) **market share, new market development**
   > (3) product and service quality
   > (4) financial indicators, productivity, operational effectiveness, and responsiveness
   > (5) human resource performance/development
   > (6) supplier performance/development
   > (7) public responsibility/corporate citizenship

   Improvements in these seven results areas contribute to overall company performance, including financial performance. The results areas also recognize the importance of suppliers and community and national well-being.

   The use of a composite of indicators helps to ensure that strategies are balanced — that they do not trade off among important stakeholders or objectives. The composite of indicators also helps to ensure that company strategies bridge short-term and long-term goals.

2. **The Criteria are nonprescriptive.**
   The Criteria are a set of 24 basic, interrelated, results-oriented requirements. However, the Criteria imply wide latitude in how requirements are met. Accordingly, the Criteria do not prescribe:

   - specific tools, techniques, technologies, systems, or starting points;
   - that there should or should not be within a company a quality or a planning department; or
   - how the company itself should be organized.

   The Criteria do emphasize that these and other factors be regularly evaluated as part of the company's improvement processes. The factors listed are important and are very likely to change as needs and strategies evolve.

   The Criteria are nonprescriptive because:
   (1) The focus is on results, not on procedures, tools, or organizations. Companies are encouraged to develop and *demonstrate* creative, adaptive, and flexible approaches to meeting basic requirements. Nonprescriptive requirements are intended to foster incremental and major ("breakthrough") improvement.
   (2) Selection of tools, techniques, systems, and organizations usually depends upon many factors such as business size, business type, the company's stage of development, and employee capabilities.
   (3) Focus on common requirements within a company, rather than on specific procedures, fosters better understanding, communication, and sharing, while supporting creativity in approaches.

3. **The Criteria are comprehensive.**
   The Criteria address all internal and external requirements of the company, including those related to fulfilling its public responsibilities. Accordingly, all processes of all company work units are tied to these requirements. New or changing strategies may be readily adapted within the same set of Criteria requirements.

4. **The Criteria include interrelated (process→results) learning cycles.**
   There is dynamic linkage among the Criteria requirements. Learning (and action based upon that learning) takes place via feedback among the process and results elements.

   The learning cycles have four, clearly defined stages:
   (1) planning, including design of processes, selection of indicators, and deployment of requirements;
   (2) execution of plans;
   (3) assessment of progress, taking into account internal and external (results) indicators; and
   (4) revision of plans based upon assessment findings.

5. **The Criteria emphasize alignment.**
   The Criteria call for improvement (learning) cycles in all parts of the company. To ensure that these cycles carried out in different parts of the company support one another, overall aims need to be consistent or *aligned*. Alignment in the Criteria is achieved via connecting and reinforcing measures, derived from overall company requirements. These measures tie directly to customer value and to operational performance. The use of measures thus channels different activities in agreed-upon directions. Use of measures often avoids the need for detailed procedures or centralization of decision making or process management. Measures thus provide a communications tool and a basis for deploying consistent customer and operational performance requirements. Such alignment ensures consistency of purpose while at the same time supporting speed, innovation, and decentralized decision making.

6. **The Criteria are part of a diagnostic system.**
   The Criteria and the Scoring Guidelines make up a two-part diagnostic (assessment) system. The Criteria are a set of 24 basic, results-oriented requirements. The scoring guidelines spell out the assessment dimensions — Approach, Deployment, and Results — and the key factors used in assessment relative to each dimension. An assessment thus provides a profile of strengths and areas for improvement relative to the 24 requirements. In this way, the assessment directs attention to actions that contribute to the results composite described above.

Incremental and Breakthrough Improvement

Nonprescriptive, results-oriented Criteria and key measures and indicators focus on *what* needs to be improved. This approach helps to ensure that improvements throughout the organization contribute to the organization's overall objectives. In addition to fostering creativity in approach and organization, results-oriented Criteria and key measures and indicators encourage "breakthrough thinking" — openness to the possibility for major improvements as well as to incremental ones. However, if key measures and indicators are tied too directly to existing work organizations and processes, breakthrough changes may be discouraged. For this reason, analysis of processes and progress should focus on the selection of and the value of the measures and indicators themselves. This will help to ensure that measure and indicator selection does not stifle creativity that may lead to entirely new approaches.

Benchmarking may also serve a useful purpose in stimulating breakthrough thinking. Benchmarking may lead to significant improvements based on adoption or adaptation of current best practice. In addition, benchmarks help encourage creativity through exposure to alternative approaches and represent a clear challenge to "beat the best," thus stimulating the search for major improvements rather than only incremental refinements of existing approaches. As with key measures and indicators, benchmark selection is critical, and benchmarks should be reviewed periodically for appropriateness.

Business Strategy and Decisions

The focus on superior offerings and lower costs of operation means that the Criteria's principal route to improved financial performance is through requirements that seek to channel company activities toward producing superior overall value. Delivering superior value — an important part of business strategy — also supports other business strategies such as pricing. For example, superior value offers the possibility of price premiums or competing via lower prices. Pricing decisions may enhance market share and asset utilization, and thus may also contribute to improved financial performance.

Business strategy usually addresses factors in addition to quality and value. For example, strategy may address market niche, alliances, facilities location, diversification, acquisition, export development, research, technology leadership, and rapid product turnover. The Criteria support the development, deployment, and evaluation of business decisions and strategies, even though these involve many factors other than product and service quality. Examples of applications of the Criteria to business decisions and strategies include:

- management of the information used in business decisions and strategy — scope, validity, and analysis;

- requirements of niches, new businesses, and export target markets;

- use of benchmarking information in decisions relating to outsourcing, alliances, and acquisitions;

- analysis of factors — societal, regulatory, economic, competitive, and risk — that may bear upon the success or failure of strategy;

- development of scenarios built around possible outcomes of strategy or decisions, including risks and consequences of failures; and

- lessons learned from previous strategy developments — within the company or available through research.

Financial Performance

The Criteria address financial performance via three major avenues: (1) emphasis on requirements that lead to superior offerings and thus to better market performance, market share gain, and customer retention; (2) emphasis on improved productivity, asset utilization, and lower overall operating costs; and (3) support for business strategy development, business decisions, and innovation.

The Criteria and evaluation system take into account market share, customer retention, customer satisfaction, productivity, asset utilization, and numerous other factors that contribute to financial performance. The Criteria *do encourage* the use of financial information, including profit trends, in analyses and reporting of results derived from performance improvement. However, companies are encouraged to demonstrate the connection between operational performance improvement and financial performance.

Innovation and Creativity

Innovation and creativity are important aspects of delivering ever-improving value to customers and of maximizing productivity.

Examples of mechanisms used in the Criteria to encourage innovation and creativity include:

- Nonprescriptive criteria, supported by benchmarks and indicators, encourage creativity and breakthrough thinking as they channel activities toward purpose, not toward following procedures.
- Customer-driven quality places major emphasis on the "positive side of quality," which stresses enhancement, new services, and customer relationship management. Success with the positive side of quality depends heavily on creativity — usually more so than steps to reduce errors and defects which tend to rely more on well-defined techniques.
- Continuous improvement and cycles of learning are stressed as integral parts of the activities of all work units. This encourages analysis and problem solving everywhere within the company.
- Strong emphasis on cycle time reduction in all company operations encourages companies to analyze work paths, work organizations, and the value-added contributions of all process steps. This fosters change, innovation, and creative thinking in how work is organized and conducted.
- Focus on future requirements of customers, customer segments, and customers of competitors encourages companies to seek innovative and creative ways to serve needs.

Examples of specific process management mechanisms to improve new product and process innovation include:

- strong emphasis on cycle time in the design phase to encourage rapid introduction of new products and services derived from company research. Success requires stage-to-stage coordination of functions and activities ranging from basic research to commercialization.
- requirements for research and development units that address: climate for innovation, including research opportunities and career advancement; unit awareness of fundamental knowledge that bears upon success; unit awareness of national and world leadership centers in universities, government laboratories, and other companies; shortening the patenting cycle; effectiveness of services to research and development by other units including procurement, facilities management, and technical support; key determinants in project success and project cancellation; company communication links, including internal technology transfer; key technical and reporting requirements and communications; and key measures of success — such as problem-solving effectiveness, responsiveness, and value creation — for research and development units.

CHANGES FROM THE 1994 AWARD CRITERIA

The Criteria continue to evolve in four major ways: (1) toward comprehensive coverage of overall performance, including customer-driven quality performance; (2) toward better integration of overall performance, including employee performance, with business strategy; (3) toward further strengthening of the financial and business rationale for improvement priorities; and (4) toward increasing emphasis on results. The Criteria for 1995 are more future oriented, and more directed toward business strategy and competitiveness requirements. At the same time, the Criteria requirements are more focused and aligned, permitting a 40% reduction in the number of Areas to Address.

Key Themes Strengthened in the 1995 Criteria

- emphasis on key business drivers, derived from strategic and business planning, integrated into the Criteria framework. The key business drivers address business development and revenue growth, as well as cost reductions stemming from improved operational performance.
- emphasis on financial data in setting priorities for performance improvement
- emphasis on high performance and more flexible and responsive organizations and work systems as well as on the critical requirements, such as effective senior executive leadership, to build and sustain them
- emphasis on investment in developing work force capabilities as a key part of strengthening company competitive fitness
- emphasis on continuous learning as well as continuous improvement. The learning theme is particularly strong in four areas: strategy development; customer and market knowledge; employee development; and information and analysis systems.
- emphasis on business results, including financial results

Many changes have been made in the Criteria and in the Criteria booklet to strengthen key themes and to clarify, focus, and link requirements. Major changes are:

- The number of Examination Items has been reduced from 28 to 24.
- The number of Areas to Address has been reduced from 91 to 54. As a result of this reduction, the application page limit has been reduced from 85 to 70.
- The Description of the Award Criteria has been expanded to cover all Categories, Items, and Areas to Address.

Major changes, by Category, are:

Leadership

- Senior Executive Leadership (Item 1.1) is better focused on the efforts by senior executives in building the leadership system, setting strategic directions, and creating performance excellence goals.

- The title of Item 1.2 has been changed to Leadership System and Organization. The major thrust of this Item is toward flexible and responsive organizations and leadership systems — major themes of the 1995 Criteria.

Information and Analysis

- The title of Item 2.1 has been changed to Management of Information and Data. The scope of the Item is broader than Item 2.1 in the 1994 Criteria. The Item stresses alignment of information and data with user needs and with the key business drivers. A major thrust of the Item is that data and information need to support the more flexible and demanding needs and decision making of high performance work units.
- Item 2.2, Competitive Comparisons and Benchmarking, now focuses more on targeting benchmarking on company priorities and effective benchmarking practices rather than on scope.
- Item 2.3 emphasizes further the critical importance of company-level analysis in support of decision making and priorities. More examples of the use of cost and financial data are given. The Item is intended to serve as the key link between operational and customer-related performance and overall financial performance.

Strategic Planning

- The title of this Category has been broadened (from Strategic Quality Planning) to put major emphasis on business strategy as the most appropriate view-of-the-future context for managing performance. This change is intended to place more attention on the operational performance requirements derived from strategic initiatives. The Category stresses that customer-driven and operational performance excellence are key strategic business issues.
- The titles of the two Items in this Category have also been changed. They are now: Item 3.1, Strategy Development; and Item 3.2, Strategy Deployment.
- Strategy Development (3.1) plays a central directional role in the Criteria. The Item addresses how the company develops its view of the future taking into account the key factors in the environment — competitive, societal, and technological. The Item also addresses how strategy is developed and translated into actionable key business drivers which serve as the basis for **operationalizing** and deploying requirements.
- Strategy Deployment (3.2) addresses how the company's key business drivers are deployed. An important consideration in the Item is the establishment of measures that permit alignment of requirements throughout the company. The Item emphasizes that productivity and cycle time improvement should be included among the key requirements.

Human Resource Development and Management

- The title of Item 4.1 has been changed to Human Resource Planning and Evaluation to emphasize that this Item is the key link between company planning and overall human resource practices. **Evaluation** is crucial to maintaining the alignment between human resource management and company directions. This concern makes Item 4.1 the focal point for evaluating overall human resource systems in relation to business objectives, so that these systems become part of a coordinated strategy.

- A new Item, High Performance Work Systems, has been created to examine work and job design, and how promotion, compensation and recognition support such design. The Item stresses that full participation, high performance, and flexibility depend upon effective work and job designs. That is, participation and active contributions are design issues as well as motivational ones. The Item is thus concerned with the important alignment between incentives and work design. The new Item (4.2) replaces Items 4.2 and 4.4 from the 1994 Criteria.

- The title of Item 4.3 has been changed to Employee Education, Training, and Development to emphasize the larger, more continuing issue of **development**. Development is needed to support the more demanding high performance work and job systems. The Item is concerned with how education and training are designed, delivered, reinforced, and evaluated, with special emphasis upon on-the-job application of knowledge and skills. The focus is on both company performance and employee development. The scope of this Item is broader than the 1994 version, covering overall education, training, and development.

Process Management

- The title of this Category has been changed (from Management of Process Quality) to minimize confusion that sometimes results from multiple meanings of "quality". The Category addresses all key aspects of effective process management.

- The title of Item 5.3 has been changed to Process Management: Support Services. This change emphasizes that the processes to be described are those which support the key production and delivery processes, but which are not usually designed with them. For this reason, the Item addresses how the support processes are designed, as well as how they are maintained and improved.

- Item 5.5 (Quality Assessment) from the 1994 Criteria has been dropped. Item 1.2 deals with reviews of company performance. Process assessments and related review activities should now be described in Area 1.2c.

Business Results

- The title of the Category has been changed (from Quality and Operational Results) to reflect greater emphasis on business-oriented results to encourage companies to report data that demonstrate impact on customers, markets, and business and financial performance.

- The number of Items in this Category has been reduced from 4 to 3. This change is made by combining Items 6.2 and 6.3 from the 1994 Criteria.

- The new Item, Company Operational and Financial Results (6.2), examines overall company operational and financial improvements from all processes. Results indicators include generic and business-specific ones. The intent of the change is to focus better on company-level improvements and to eliminate reporting of results that might not actually reflect better overall company performance. This change is thus consistent with the more holistic approach to performance emphasized in the Criteria. Human resource results, such as safety, absenteeism, and satisfaction, are now reported in this Item because of their key contribution to operational performance. The point value of Item 6.2 has been increased greatly to emphasize the importance of operational and financial performance results and the use of these results in guiding performance improvement.

Customer Focus and Satisfaction

- The title of Item 7.1 has been changed to Customer and Market Knowledge. This Item now has a broader scope, a more analytical approach, and an ongoing learning requirement compared with the 1994 version. Particularly important in this Item are the company's key listening and learning strategies — those that provide key information about customers and markets on an ongoing basis.

- Item 7.2, Customer Relationship Management, has been narrowed in scope to better distinguish it from Items 5.2 and 5.3. It is now more nearly customer response management, including responses to complaints. Its title reflects the fact that the Areas addressed stress relationship building.

- Item 7.3 from the 1994 Criteria (Commitment to Customers) has been dropped. The Item dealt primarily with guarantees and warranties. Guarantees and warranties are product and service features and/or elements of company strategy. As such, they are addressed or implied in other Items. Their inclusion in the 1994 Criteria perhaps implied that guarantees and warranties are basic performance requirements. In many instances, guarantees and warranties may be useful marketing or management tools, but they are not necessarily basic requirements.

1.0 Leadership (90 pts.)

The *Leadership* Category examines senior executives' personal leadership and involvement in creating and sustaining a customer focus, clear values and expectations, and a leadership system that promotes performance excellence. Also examined is how the values and expectations are integrated into the company's management system, including how the company addresses its public responsibilities and corporate citizenship.

1.1 Senior Executive Leadership (45 pts.)

Describe senior executives' leadership and personal involvement in setting directions and in developing and maintaining a leadership system for performance excellence.

A   D   R

☑──☑   ☐

(See page 40 for a description of these symbols.)

AREAS TO ADDRESS

a. how senior executives provide effective leadership and direction in building and improving company competitiveness, performance, and capabilities. Describe executives' roles in: (1) creating and reinforcing values and expectations throughout the company's leadership system; (2) setting directions and performance excellence goals through strategic and business planning; and (3) reviewing overall company performance, including customer-related and operational performance.

b. how senior executives evaluate and improve the effectiveness of the company's leadership system and organization to pursue performance excellence goals.

Notes:

(1) "Senior executives" means the applicant's highest-ranking official and those reporting directly to that official.

(2) Values and expectations [1.1a(1)] should take into account all stakeholders – customers, employees, stockholders, suppliers and partners, the community, and the public.

(3) Activities of senior executives appropriate for inclusion in 1.1a might also include customer, employee, and supplier interactions, mentoring other executives, benchmarking, and employee recognition.

(4) Review of company performance is addressed in 1.2c. Responses to 1.1a(3) should reflect senior executives' personal leadership of and involvement in such reviews, and their use of the reviews to focus on key business objectives.

(5) Evaluation of the company's leadership system might include assessment of executives by peers, direct reports, or a board of directors. It might also include results of surveys of company employees.

1.2 Leadership System and Organization (25 pts.)

Describe how the company's customer focus and performance expectations are integrated into the company's leadership system and organization.

A   D   R

☑──☑   ☐

AREAS TO ADDRESS

a. how the company's leadership system, management, and organization focus on customers and high performance objectives.

b. how the company effectively communicates and reinforces its values, expectations, and directions throughout the entire work force.

c. how overall company and work unit performance are reviewed and how the reviews are used to improve performance. Describe the types, frequency, and content of reviews and who conducts them.

Note:

(1) Reviews described in 1.2c should utilize information from business and customer-related results Items — 6.1, 6.2, 6.3, 7.4, and 7.5 — and also may draw upon evaluations described in other Items and upon analysis (Item 2.3). The descriptions should address key measures and/or indicators used to track performance, including performance related to the company's public responsibilities. Reviews could also incorporate results of process assessments and address regulatory, contractual, or other requirements, including review of required documentation.

1.3 Public Responsibility and Corporate Citizenship (20 pts.)

Describe how the company includes its responsibilities to the public in its performance improvement practices. Describe also how the company leads and contributes as a corporate citizen in its key communities.

A   D   R

☑—☑   ☐

a. how the company integrates its public responsibilities into its performance improvement efforts. Describe: (1) the risks and regulatory and other legal requirements addressed in planning and in setting operational requirements and targets; (2) how the company looks ahead to anticipate public concerns and to assess possible impacts on society of its products. services. and operations: and (3) how the company promotes legal and ethical conduct in all that it does.

b. how the company leads as a corporate citizen in its key communities. Include a brief summary of the types of leadership and involvement the company emphasizes.

Notes:

(1) The public responsibility issues addressed in 1.3a relate to the company's impacts and possible impacts on society associated with its products. services, and company operations. They include environment. health, safety. and emergency preparedness as they relate to any aspect of risk or adverse effect, whether or not these are covered under law or regulation. Health and safety of employees are not included in Item 1.3. Employee health and safety are covered in Item 4.4.

(2) Major public responsibility or impact areas should be addressed in planning (Item 3.1) and in the appropriate process management Items of Category 5.0. Key results, such as environmental improvements, should be reported in Item 6.2.

(3) If the company has received sanctions under law. regulation. or contract during the past three years. briefly describe the incident(s) and its current status. If settlements have been negotiated in lieu of potential sanctions. give explanation. If no sanctions have been received. so indicate.

(4) The corporate citizenship issues appropriate for inclusion in 1.3b relate to efforts by the company to strengthen community services. education. health care. environment. and practices of trade or business associations. Such leadership and involvement depend upon the company's size and resources. However, smaller companies might take part in cooperative activities with other organizations.

2.0 Information and Analysis (75 pts.)

The *Information and Analysis* Category examines the management and effectiveness of the use of data and information to support customer-driven performance excellence and marketplace success.

2.1 Management of Information and Data

(20 pts.)

Describe the company's selection and management of information and data used for planning, management, and evaluation of overall performance.

A   D   R

☑——☑   ☐

AREAS TO ADDRESS

a. how information and data needed to drive improvement of overall company performance are selected and managed. Describe: (1) the main types of data and information and how each type is related to the key business drivers; and (2) how key requirements such as reliability, rapid access, and rapid update are derived from user needs.

b. how the company evaluates and improves the selection, analysis, and integration of information and data, aligning them with the company's business priorities. Describe how the evaluation considers: (1) scope of information and data; (2) use and analysis of information and data to support process management and performance improvement; and (3) feedback from users of information and data.

Notes:

(1) Reliability [2.1a(2)] includes software used in the information systems.

(2) User needs [2.1a(2)] should consider knowledge accumulation such as knowledge about specific customers or customer segments. User needs should also take into account changing patterns of communications associated with changes in process management and/or in job design.

(3) Scope of information and data [2.1b(1)] should focus primarily on key business drivers.

(4) Feedback from users [2.1b(3)] might entail formal or informal surveys, focus groups, teams, etc. However, evaluations should take into account patterns of communications and information use, as users themselves might not be utilizing well the information and data available. Even though the information and data system should be user friendly, the system should drive better practice. This might require training of users.

2.2 Competitive Comparisons and Benchmarking *(15 pts.)*

Describe the company's processes and uses of comparative information and data to support improvement of overall performance.

A   D   R

☑——☑   ☐

AREAS TO ADDRESS

a. how competitive comparisons and benchmarking information and data are selected and used to help drive improvement of overall company performance. Describe: (1) how needs and priorities are determined; (2) criteria for seeking appropriate information and data — from within and outside the company's industry; (3) how the information and data are used within the company to improve understanding of processes and process performance; and (4) how the information and data are used to set stretch targets and/or encourage breakthrough approaches.

b. how the company evaluates and improves its overall process for selecting and using competitive comparisons and benchmarking information and data to improve planning and overall company performance.

Notes:

(1) Benchmarking information and data refer to processes and results that represent best practices and performance.

(2) Needs and priorities [2.2a(1)] should show clear linkage to the company's key business drivers.

(3) Use of benchmarking information and data within the company [2.2a(3)] might include the expectation that company units maintain awareness of related best-in-class performance to help drive improvement. This could entail education and training efforts to build capabilities.

(4) Sources of competitive comparisons and benchmarking information might include: (a) information obtained from other organizations such as customers or suppliers through sharing; (b) information obtained from the open literature; (c) testing and evaluation by the company itself; and (d) testing and evaluation by independent organizations.

(5) The evaluation (2.2b) may address a variety of factors such as the effectiveness of use of the information, adequacy of information, training in acquisition and use of information, improvement potential in company operations, and estimated rates of improvement by other organizations.

2.3 Analysis and Use of Company-Level Data

(40 pts.)

Describe how data related to quality, customers and operational performance, together with relevant financial data, are analyzed to support company-level review, action, and planning.

A	D	R
☑	☑	☐

a. how information and data from all parts of the company are integrated and analyzed to support reviews. business decisions. and planning. Describe how analysis is used to gain understanding of: (1) customers and markets (2) operational performance and company capabilities; and (3) competitive performance.

b. how the company relates customer and market data. improvements in product service quality, and improvements in operational performance to changes in financial and/or market indicators of performance. Describe how this information is used to set priorities for improvement actions.

Notes:

(1) Item 2.3 focuses primarily on analysis for company-level purposes. such as reviews (1.2c) and strategic planning (Item 3.1). Data for such analysis come from all parts of the company and include results reported in Items 6.1, 6.2, 6.3, 7.4. and 7.5. Other Items call for analyses of specific sets of data for special purposes. For example, the Items of Category 4.0 require analysis to determine effectiveness of training and other human resource practices. Such special-purpose analyses should be part of the overall information base available for use in Item 2.3.

(2) Analysis includes trends, projections, cause-effect correlations. and the search for deeper understanding needed to set priorities to use resources more effectively to serve overall business objectives.

(3) Examples of analysis appropriate for inclusion in 2.3a(1) are:
- *how the company's product and service quality improvement correlates with key customer indicators such as customer satisfaction. customer retention. and market share; and*
- *cost/revenue implications of customer-related problems and problem resolution effectiveness.*

(4) Examples of analysis appropriate for inclusion in 2.3a(2) are:
- *trends in improvement in key operational indicators such as productivity, cycle time, waste reduction, new product introduction, and defect levels;*
- *financial benefits from improved employee safety, absenteeism. and turnover:*
- *benefits and costs associated with education and training:*
- *how the company's ability to identify and meet employee requirements correlates with employee retention. motivation. and productivity: and*
- *cost/revenue implications of employee-related problems and problem resolution effectiveness*

(5) Examples of analysis appropriate for inclusion in 2.3a(3) are:
- *performance trends relative to competitors on key quality attributes: and*
- *productivity and cost trends relative to competitors.*

(6) Examples of analysis appropriate for inclusion in 2.3b are:
- *relationships between product/service quality and operational performance indicators and overall company financial performance trends as reflected in indicators such as operating costs. revenues. asset utilization, and value added per employee;*
- *allocation of resources among alternative improvement projects based on cost/revenue implications and improvement potential:*
- *net earnings derived from quality/operational/human resource performance improvements;*
- *comparisons among business units showing how quality and operational performance improvement affect financial performance:*
- *contributions of improvement activities to cash flow and/or shareholder value:*
- *trends in quality versus market indicators;*
- *profit impacts of customer retention; and*
- *market share versus profits.*

3.0 Strategic Planning (55 pts.)

The **Strategic Planning** Category examines how the company sets strategic directions, and how it determines key plan requirements. Also examined is how the plan requirements are translated into an effective performance management system.

3.1 Strategy Development
(35 pts.)

Describe the company's strategic planning process for overall performance and competitive leadership for the short term and the longer term. Describe also how this process leads to the development of key business drivers to serve as the basis for deploying plan requirements throughout the company.

AREAS TO ADDRESS

a. how the company develops strategies and business plans to strengthen its customer-related, operational, and financial performance and its competitive position. Describe how strategy development considers: (1) customer requirements and expectations and their expected changes: (2) the competitive environment; (3) risks: financial, market, technological, and societal: (4) company capabilities—human resource, technology, research and development and business processes—to seek new market leadership opportunities and/or to prepare for key new requirements; and (5) supplier and/or partner capabilities.

b. how strategies and plans are translated into actionable key business drivers which serve as the basis for deploying plan requirements. addressed in Item 3.2.

c. how the company evaluates and improves its strategic planning and plan deployment processes.

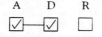

A   D   R

Notes:

(1) Item 3.1 addresses overall company strategy and business plans, not specific product and service designs.

(2) The sub-parts of 3.1a are intended to serve as an outline of key factors involved in developing a view of the future as a context for strategic planning. Strategy and planning refer to a future-oriented basis for major business decisions. resource allocations. and companywide management. "Strategy and planning," then, addresses both revenue growth thrusts as well as thrusts related to improving operational performance.

(3) Customer requirements and their expected changes [3.1a(1)] might include pricing factors. That is, market success may depend upon achieving cost levels dictated by anticipated price levels rather than setting prices to cover costs.

(4) The purposes of projecting the competitive environment [3.1a(2)] are to detect and reduce competitive threats, to improve reaction time. and to identify opportunities. If the company uses modeling. scenario, or other techniques to project the competitive environment. such techniques should be briefly outlined in 3.1a(2)

(5) Key business drivers are the areas of performance most critical to the company's success. They include customer-driven quality requirements and operational

requirements such as productivity, cycle time, deployment of new technology, strategic alliances, supplier development, employee productivity and development, and research and development. Deployment of plans should include how progress will be tracked such as through the use of key measures.

(6) Examples of strategy and business plans that might be the starting points for the development of key business drivers are:
* *new product/service lines;*
* *entry into new markets or segments;*
* *new manufacturing and/or service delivery approaches such as customization;*
* *new or modified competitive thrusts;*
* *launch of joint ventures and/or partnerships;*
* *new R&D thrusts; and*
* *new product and/or process technologies.*

(7) How the company evaluates and improves its strategic planning and plan deployment process might take into account the results of reviews (1.2c), input from work units. and projection information (3.2b). The evaluation might also take into account how well strategies and requirements are communicated and understood. and how well key measures are aligned.

3.2 Strategy Deployment
(20 pts.)

Summarize the company's key business drivers and how they are deployed. Show how the company's performance projects into the future relative to competitors and key benchmarks.

A   D   R

☑—☑ ☐

a. summary of the specific key business drivers derived from the company's strategic directions and how these drivers are translated into an action plan. Describe: (1) key performance requirements and associated operational performance measures and/or indicators and how they are deployed; (2) how the company aligns work unit and supplier and/or partner plans and targets; (3) how productivity and cycle time improvement and reduction in waste are included in plans and targets; and (4) the principal resources committed to the accomplishment of plans. Note any important distinctions between short-term plans and longer-term plans.

b. two-to-five year projection of key measures and/or indicators of the company's customer-related and operational performance. Describe how product and/or service quality and operational performance might be expected to compare with key competitors and key benchmarks over this time period. Briefly explain the comparisons, including any estimates or assumptions made regarding the projected product and/or service quality and operational performance of competitors or changes in key benchmarks.

Notes:

(1) The focus in Item 3.2 is on the translation of the company's strategic plans, resulting from the process described in Item 3.1, to requirements for work units, suppliers, and partners. The main intent of Item 3.2 is alignment of short- and long-term operations with strategic directions. Although the deployment of these plans will affect products and services, design of products and services is not the focus of Item 3.2. Such design is addressed in Item 5.1.

(2) Productivity and cycle time improvement and waste reduction [3.2a(3)] might address factors such as inventories, work-in-process, inspection, downtime, changeover time, set-up time, and other examples of utilization of resources — materials, equipment, energy, capital, and labor.

(3) Area 3.2b addresses projected progress in improving performance and in gaining advantage relative to competitors. This projection may draw upon analysis (Item 2.3) and data reported in results Items (Category 6.0 and Items 7.4 and 7.5). Such projections are intended to support reviews (1.2c), evaluation of planning (3.1c), and other Items. Another purpose is to take account of the fact that competitors and benchmarks may also be improving over the time period of the projection.

4.0 Human Resource Development and Management (140 pts.)

The *Human Resource Development and Management* Category examines how the work force is enabled to develop and utilize its full potential, aligned with the company's performance objectives. Also examined are the company's efforts to build and maintain an environment conducive to performance excellence, full participation, and personal and organizational growth.

4.1 Human Resource Planning and Evaluation *(20 pts.)*

Describe how the company's human resource planning and evaluation are aligned with its strategic and business plans and address the development and well-being of the entire work force.

A   D   R

AREAS TO ADDRESS

a. how the company translates overall requirements from strategic and business planning (Category 3.0) to specific human resource plans. Summarize key human resource plans in the following areas: (1) changes in work design to improve flexibility, innovation, and rapid response; (2) employee development, education, and training; (3) changes in compensation, recognition, and benefits; and (4) recruitment, including expected or planned changes in demographics of the work force. Distinguish between the short term and the longer term, as appropriate.

b. how the company evaluates and improves its human resource planning and practices and the alignment of the plans and practices with the company's strategic and business directions. Include how employee-related data and company performance data are analyzed and used: (1) to assess the development and well-being of all categories and types of employees; (2) to assess the linkage of the human resource practices to key business results; and (3) to ensure that reliable and complete human resource information is available for company strategic and business planning.

Notes:

(1) Human resource planning addresses all aspects of designing and managing human systems to meet the needs of both the company and the employees. This Item calls for information on human resource plans. This does not imply that such planning is separate from overall business planning. Examples of human resource plan elements or plan thrusts (4.1a) that might be part(s) of a comprehensive plan are:
* *redesign of work organizations and/or jobs to increase employee responsibility and decision making;*
* *initiatives to promote labor-management cooperation, such as partnerships with unions;*
* *creation or modification of compensation and recognition systems based on building shareholder value and/or customer satisfaction;*
* *creation or redesign of employee surveys to better assess the factors in the work climate that contribute to or inhibit high performance;*
* *prioritization of employee problems based upon potential impact on productivity;*
* *development of hiring criteria;*
* *creation of opportunities for employees to learn and use skills that go beyond current job assignments through redesign of processes or organizations;*
* *education and training initiatives, including those that involve developmental assignments;*
* *formation of partnerships with educational institutions to develop employees or to help ensure the future supply of well-prepared employees;*
* *establishment of partnerships with other companies and/or networks to share training and/or spread job opportunities;*
* *introduction of distance learning or other technology-based learning approaches; and*
* *integration of customer and employee surveys.*

(2) "Employee-related data" (4.1b) refers to data contained in personnel records as well as data described in Items 4.2, 4.3, and 4.4. This might include employee satisfaction data and data on turnover, absenteeism, safety, grievances, involvement, recognition, training, and information from exit interviews.

(3) "Categories of employees" [4.1b(1)] refers to the company's classification system used in its human resource practices and/or work assignments. It also includes factors such as union or bargaining unit membership. "Types of employees" takes into account other factors, such as work force diversity or demographic makeup. This includes gender, age, minorities, and the disabled.

(4) The evaluation in 4.1b might be supported by employee-related data such as satisfaction factors (Item 4.4), absenteeism, turnover, and accidents. It might also be supported by employee feedback and information from exit interviews. Evaluations might also be supported by comparative or benchmarking information.

Evaluation should take into account factors such as employee problem resolution effectiveness, and the extent of deployment of education and training throughout the company.

(5) Human resource information for company strategic and business planning might include an overall profile of strengths and weaknesses that could affect the company's abilities to fulfill plan requirements. This could result in the identification of specific needs requiring resources or new approaches.

4.2 High Performance Work Systems (45 pts.)

Describe how the company's work and job design and compensation and recognition approaches enable and encourage all employees to contribute effectively to achieving high performance objectives.

A   D   R
☑——☑   ☐

AREAS TO ADDRESS

a. how the company's work and job design promote high performance. Describe how work and job design: (1) create opportunities for initiative and self-directed responsibility; (2) foster flexibility and rapid response to changing requirements; and (3) ensure effective communications across functions or units that need to work together to meet customer and/or operational requirements.

b. how the company's compensation and recognition approaches for individuals and groups, including managers, reinforce the effectiveness of the work and job design.

Notes:

(1) Work and job design refers to how employees are organized and/or organize themselves in formal and informal, temporary or longer-term units. This may include work teams, problem-solving teams, functional units, departments, self-managed or managed by supervisors. In some cases, teams might involve individuals in different locations linked via computers or conferencing technology.

(2) Examples of approaches to create flexibility in work design to enhance performance might include simplification of job classifications, cross training, job rotation, work layout, and work locations. It might also entail use of technology and changed flow of information to support local decision making.

(3) Compensation and recognition refer to all aspects of pay and reward, including promotion and bonuses. The company might use a variety of reward and recognition approaches — monetary and non-monetary, formal and informal, and individual and group.

Compensation and recognition approaches could include profit sharing and compensation based on skill building, use of new skills, and demonstrations of self learning. The approaches could take into account the linkage to customer retention or other performance objectives.

Employee evaluations and reward and recognition approaches might include peer evaluations, including peers in teams and networks.

4.3 Employee Education, Training, and Development (50 pts.)

Describe how the company's education and training address company plans, including building company capabilities and contributing to employee motivation, progression, and development.

A   D   R
☑——☑   ☐

AREAS TO ADDRESS

a. how the company's education and training serve as a key vehicle in building company and employee capabilities. Describe how education and training address: (1) key performance objectives, including those related to enhancing high performance work units; and (2) progression and development of all employees.

b. how education and training are designed, delivered, reinforced, and evaluated. Include: (1) how employees and line managers contribute to or are involved in determining specific education and training needs and designing education and training; (2) how education and training are delivered, (3) how knowledge and skills are reinforced through on-the-job application; and (4) how education and training are evaluated and improved.

Notes:

(1) Education and training address the knowledge and skills employees need to meet their overall work objectives. Education and training might include leadership skills, communications, teamwork, problem solving, interpreting and using data, meeting customer requirements, process analysis, process simplification, waste reduction, cycle time reduction, error-proofing, priority setting based upon cost and benefit data, and other training that affects employee effectiveness, efficiency, and safety. This might include job enrichment and job rotation to enhance employees' career opportunities and employability. It might also include basic skills such as reading, writing, language, and arithmetic.

(2) Training for customer-contact (frontline) employees should address: (a) key knowledge and skills, including knowledge of products and services; (b) listening to customers; (c) soliciting comments from customers; (d) how to anticipate and handle problems or failures

("recovery"); (e) skills in customer retention; and (f) how to manage expectations.

(3) Determining specific education and training needs [4.3b(1)] might include use of company assessment or employee self-assessment to determine and/or compare skill levels for progression within the company or elsewhere. Needs determination should take into account job analysis — the types and levels of skills required — and the timeliness of training.

(4) Education and training delivery might occur inside or outside the company and involve on-the-job, classroom, or other types of delivery. This includes the use of developmental assignments within or outside the company.

(5) How education and training are evaluated [4.3b(4)] could address: effectiveness of delivery of education and training; impact on work unit performance; and cost effectiveness of education and training alternatives.

4.4 Employee Well-Being and Satisfaction *(25 pts.)*

Describe how the company maintains a work environment and a work climate conducive to the well-being and development of all employees.

A   D   R

AREAS TO ADDRESS

a. how the company maintains a safe and healthful work environment. Include: (1) how employee well-being factors such as health, safety, and ergonomics are included in improvement activities; and (2) principal improvement requirements, measures and/or indicators, and targets for each factor relevant and important to the work environment of the company's employees. Note any significant differences based upon differences in work environments among employees or employee groups.

b. what services, facilities, activities, and opportunities the company makes available to employees to support their overall well-being and satisfaction and/or to enhance their work experience and development potential.

c. how the company determines employee satisfaction, well-being, and motivation. Include a brief description of methods, frequency, the specific factors used in this determination, and how the information is used to improve satisfaction, well-being, and motivation. Note any important differences in methods or factors used for different categories or types of employees, as appropriate.

Notes:

(1) Examples of services, facilities, activities, and opportunities (4.4b) are: personal and career counseling; career development and employability services; recreational or cultural activities; non-work-related education; day care; special leave for family responsibilities and/or for community service; safety off the job; flexible work hours; and outplacement. These services also might include career enhancement activities such as skill assessment, helping employees develop learning objectives and plans, and employability assessment.

(2) Examples of specific factors which might affect satisfaction, well-being, and motivation are: effective employee problem or grievance resolution; safety; employee views of leadership and management; employee development and career opportunities; employee preparation for changes in technology or work organization; work environment; workload; cooperation and teamwork; recognition; benefits; communications; job security; compensation; equality of opportunity; and capability to provide required services to customers. An effective determination is one that provides the company with actionable information for use in improvement activities.

(3) Measures and/or indicators of satisfaction, well-being, and motivation (4.4c) might include safety, absenteeism, turnover, turnover rate for customer-contact employees, grievances, strikes, worker compensation, as well as results of surveys.

(4) How satisfaction, well-being, and motivation information is used might involve developing priorities for addressing employee problems based on impact on productivity.

(5) Trends in key measures and/or indicators of well-being and satisfaction should be reported in Item 6.2.

5.0 Process Management (140 pts.)

The *Process Management* Category examines the key aspects of process management, including customer-focused design, product and service delivery processes, support services and supply management involving all work units, including research and development. The Category examines how key processes are designed, effectively managed, and improved to achieve higher performance.

5.1 Design and Introduction of Products and Services
(40 pts.)

Describe how new and/or modified products and services are designed and introduced and how key production/delivery processes are designed to meet both key product and service quality requirements and company operational performance requirements.

AREAS TO ADDRESS

a. how products, services, and production/delivery processes are designed. Describe: (1) how customer requirements are translated into product and service design requirements; (2) how product and service design requirements are translated into efficient and effective production/delivery processes, including an appropriate measurement plan; and (3) how all requirements associated with products, services, and production/delivery processes are addressed early in design by all appropriate company units, suppliers, and partners to ensure integration, coordination, and capability.

b. how product, service, and production/delivery process designs are reviewed and/or tested in detail to ensure trouble-free launch.

c. how designs and design processes are evaluated and improved so that introductions of new or modified products and services progressively improve in quality and cycle time.

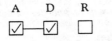

A   D   R

Notes:

(1) Design and introduction might address:
- *modifications and variants of existing products and services;*
- *new products and services emerging from research and development or other product/service concept development;*
- *new/modified facilities to meet operational performance and/or product and service requirements; and*
- *significant redesigns of processes to improve customer focus, productivity, or both.*

Design approaches could differ appreciably depending upon the nature of the products/services — entirely new, variants, major or minor process changes, etc. If many design projects are carried out in parallel, responses to Item 5.1 should reflect how coordination of resources among projects is carried out.

(2) Applicants' responses should reflect the key requirements for their products and services. Factors that might need to be considered in design include: health; safety; long-term performance; environment; measurement capability; process capability; manufacturability; maintainability; supplier capability; and documentation.

(3) Service and manufacturing businesses should interpret product and service design requirements to include all product- and service-related requirements at all stages of production, delivery, and use.

(4) A measurement plan [5.1a(2)] should spell out what is to be measured, how and when measurements are to be made, and performance levels or standards to ensure that the results of measurements provide information to guide, monitor, control, or improve the process. This may include service standards used in customer-contact processes. The term, "measurement plan," may also include decisions about key information to collect from customers and/or employees from service encounters, transactions, etc. The actual measurement plan should not be described in Item 5.1. Such information is requested in Item 5.2.

(5) "All appropriate company units" means those units and/or individuals who will take part in production/delivery and whose performance materially affects overall process outcome.

5.2 Process Management: Product and Service Production and Delivery *(40 pts.)*

Describe how the company's key product and service production/delivery processes are managed to ensure that design requirements are met and that both quality and operational performance are continuously improved.

A   D   R

☑——☑   ☐

AREAS TO ADDRESS

a. how the company maintains the performance of key production/delivery processes to ensure that such processes meet design requirements addressed in Item 5.1. Describe: (1) the key processes and their principal requirements; and (2) the measurement plan and how measurements and/or observations are used to maintain process performance.

b. how processes are evaluated and improved to achieve better operational performance, including cycle time. Describe how each of the following is used or considered: (1) process analysis and research; (2) benchmarking; (3) use of alternative technology; and (4) information from customers of the processes — within and outside the company.

Notes:

(1) Key production/delivery processes are those most directly involved in fulfilling the principal requirements of customers — those that define the products and services.

(2) Measurement plan [5.2a(2)] is defined in Item 5.1, Note (4). Companies with specialized measurement requirements should describe how they ensure measurement effectiveness. For physical, chemical, and engineering measurements, describe briefly how measurements are made traceable to national standards.

(3) The focus of 5.2a is on maintenance *of process performance using measurements and/or observations to decide whether or not corrective action is needed. The nature of the corrective action depends on the process characteristics and the type of variation observed. Responses should reflect the type of process and the type of variation observed. A description should be given of how basic (root) causes of variation are determined and how corrections are made at the earliest point(s) in processes. Such correction should then minimize the likelihood of recurrence of this type of variation anywhere in the company.*

(4) Process improvement methods (5.2b) might utilize financial data to evaluate alternatives and to set priorities.

(5) Process analysis and research [5.2b(1)] refers to a wide range of possible approaches to improving processes. Examples include process mapping, optimization experiments, basic and applied research, error proofing, and reviewing critical encounters between employees and customers from the point of view of customers and employees.

(6) Information from customers [5.2b(4)] might include information developed as described in Items 7.2, 7.3, and 2.3.

(7) Results of improvements in product and service delivery processes should be reported in Items 6.1 and 6.2, as appropriate.

5.3 Process Management: Support Services

(30 pts.)

Describe how the company's key support service processes are designed and managed so that current requirements are met and that operational performance is continuously improved.

A   D   R

☑—☑ ☐

a. how key support service processes are designed. Include: (1) how key requirements are determined or set: (2) how these requirements are translated into efficient and effective processes. including operational requirements and an **appropriate measurement plan; and (3) how all requirements are addressed** early in design by all appropriate company units to ensure integration. coordination. and capability.

b. how the company maintains the performance of key support service processes to ensure that such processes meet design requirements. Describe: (1) the key processes and their principal requirements: and (2) the measurement plan and how measurements are used to maintain process performance.

c. how processes are evaluated and improved to achieve better operational performance. including cycle time. Describe how each of the following is used or considered: (1) process analysis and research: (2) benchmarking: (3) use of alternative technology; and (4) information from customers of the processes — within and outside the company.

Notes:

(1) Support services are those which support the company's product and/or service delivery but which are not usually designed in detail with the products and services themselves because their requirements do not usually depend a great deal upon product and service characteristics. Support service design requirements usually depend significantly upon internal requirements. Support services might address finance and accounting, software services, sales, marketing, public relations, information services, supplies, personnel, legal services, plant and facilities management, research and development. and secretarial and other administrative services.

(2) The purpose of Item 5.3 is to permit applicants to highlight separately the improvement activities for processes that support the product and service design, production. and delivery processes addressed in Item 5.1 and 5.2. The support service processes included in Item 5.3 depend on the applicant's type of business and other factors. Thus, this selection should be made by the applicant. Together, Items 5.1, 5.2, 5.3, and 5.4 should cover all operations, processes, and activities of all work units.

(3) Process improvement methods (5.3c) might utilize financial data to evaluate alternatives and to set priorities.

(4) Process analysis and research [5.3c(1)] refers to a wide range of possible approaches to improving processes. See Item 5.2, Note (5).

(5) Information from customers [5.3c(4)] might include information developed as described in Items 7.2, 7.3, and 2.3. However, most of the information for improvement [5.3c(4)] is likely to come from "internal customers" — those within the company who use the support services.

(6) Results of improvements in support services should be reported in 6.2.

5.4 Management of Supplier Performance *(30 pts.)*

Describe how the company assures that materials, components, and services furnished by other businesses meet the company's performance requirements. Describe also the company's actions and plans to improve supplier relationships and performance.

A	D	R
☑	☑	☐

a. summary of the company's requirements and how they are communicated to suppliers. Include: (1) a brief summary of the principal requirements for key suppliers, the measures and/or indicators associated with these requirements, and the expected performance levels; (2) how the company determines whether or not its requirements are met by suppliers; and (3) how performance information is fed back to suppliers.

b. how the company evaluates and improves its management of supplier relationships and performance. Describe current actions and plans: (1) to improve suppliers' abilities to meet requirements; (2) to improve the company's own procurement processes, including feedback sought from suppliers and from other units within the company ("internal customers") and how such feedback is used; and (3) to minimize costs associated with inspection, test, audit, or other approaches used to verify supplier performance.

Notes:

(1) The term "supplier" refers to other-company providers of goods and services. The use of these goods and services may occur at any stage in the production, design, delivery, and use of the company's products and services. Thus, suppliers include businesses such as distributors, dealers, warranty repair services, transportation, contractors, and franchises as well as those that provide materials and components. If the applicant is a unit of a larger company, and other units of that company supply goods/services, this should be included as part of Item 5.4.

(2) Key suppliers [5.4a(1)] are those which provide the most important products and/or services, taking into account the criticality and volume of products and/or services involved.

(3) "Requirements" refers to the principal factors involved in the purchases: quality, delivery, and price.

(4) How requirements are communicated and how performance information is fed back might entail ongoing working relationships or partnerships with key suppliers. Such relationships and/or partnerships should be briefly described in responses.

(5) Determining how requirements are met [5.4a(2)] might include audits, process reviews, receiving inspection, certification, testing, and rating systems.

(6) Actions and plans (5.4b) might include one or more of the following: joint planning, rapid information and data exchanges, use of benchmarking and comparative information, customer-supplier teams, partnerships, training, long-term agreements, incentives, and recognition. They might also include changes in supplier selection, leading to a reduction in the number of suppliers.

(7) Efforts to minimize costs might be backed by analyses comparing suppliers based on overall cost, taking into account quality and delivery. Analyses might also address transaction costs associated with alternative approaches to supply management.

6.0 Business Results (250 pts.)

The *Business Results* Category examines the company's performance and improvement in key business areas — product and service quality, productivity and operational effectiveness, supply quality, and financial performance indicators linked to these areas. Also examined are performance levels relative to competitors.

6.1 Product and Service Quality Results (75 pts.)

Summarize results of improvement efforts using key measures and/or indicators of product and service quality.

A   D   R

☐—☐   ☑

Notes:

(1) Results reported in 6.1 should reflect performance relative to specific non-price product and service key quality requirements. Such key quality requirements should relate closely to customer satisfaction and customer retention. These requirements are those described in the Business Overview and addressed in Items 7.1 and 5.1.

(2) Data appropriate for inclusion are based upon:
* *internal (company) measurements;*
* *field performance;*
* *data collected by the company through follow ups (7.2c) or surveys of customers;*
* *data collected or generated by other organizations; and*
* *data collected by other organizations on behalf of the company.*

(3) Product and service quality measures and/or indicators may address requirements such as accuracy, timeliness, reliability, and behavior. Examples include defect levels, repeat services, meeting product or service delivery or response times, availability levels, and complaint levels.

(4) Comparative data might include industry best, best competitor, industry average, and appropriate benchmarks. Such data might be derived from independent surveys, studies, laboratory testing, or other sources.

6.2 Company Operational and Financial Results

(130 pts.)

Summarize results of improvement efforts using key measures and/or indicators of company operational and financial performance.

A   D   R

☐—☐   ☑

AREAS TO ADDRESS

a. current levels and trends in key measures and/or indicators of company operational and financial performance. Graphs and tables should include appropriate comparative data.

Notes:

(1) Key measures and/or indicators of company operational and financial performance should address the following areas:
- *productivity and other indicators of effective use of manpower, materials, energy, capital, and assets;*
- *cycle time and responsiveness;*
- *financial indicators such as cost reductions, asset utilization, and benefit/cost results from improvement efforts;*
- *human resource indicators such as safety, absenteeism, turnover, and satisfaction;*
- *public responsibilities such as environmental improvements; and*
- *company-specific indicators such as innovation rates and progress in shifting markets or segments.*

(2) The results reported in Item 6.2 derive primarily from activities described in Items 5.1, 5.2, and 5.3.

(3) Comparative data might include industry best, best competitor, industry average, and appropriate benchmarks. For human resource areas such as turnover or absenteeism, local or regional comparative information might also be appropriate.

6.3 Supplier Performance Results *(45 pts.)*

Summarize results of supplier performance improvement efforts using key measures and/or indicators of such performance.

A   D   R

☐—☐   ☑

AREAS TO ADDRESS

a. current levels and trends in key measures and/or indicators of supplier performance. Graphs and tables should include appropriate comparative data.

Notes:

(1) The results reported in Item 6.3 derive from activities described in Item 5.4. Results should be broken out by key supplies and/or key suppliers, as appropriate. Data should be presented using the measures and/or indicators described in 5.4a(1).

(2) If the company's supplier management efforts include factors such as building supplier partnerships or reducing the number of suppliers, data related to these efforts should be included in responses.

(3) Comparative data might be of several types: industry best, best competitor(s), industry average, and appropriate benchmarks.

7.0 Customer Focus and Satisfaction (250 pts.)

The *Customer Focus and Satisfaction* Category examines the company's systems for customer learning and for building and maintaining customer relationships. Also examined are levels and trends in key measures of business success — customer satisfaction and retention, market share, and satisfaction relative to competitors.

7.1 Customer and Market Knowledge (30 pts.)

Describe how the company determines near-term and longer-term requirements and expectations of customers and markets, and develops listening and learning strategies to understand and anticipate needs.

A D R

AREAS TO ADDRESS

a. how the company determines current and near-term requirements and expectations of customers. Include: (1) how customer groups and/or market segments are determined and/or selected, including how customers of competitors and other potential customers are considered; (2) how information is collected, including what information is sought, frequency and methods of collection, and how objectivity and validity are ensured; (3) how specific product and service features and the relative importance of these features to customer groups or segments are determined; and (4) how other key information and data such as complaints, gains and losses of customers, and product/service performance are used to support the determination.

b. how the company addresses future requirements and expectations of customers. Include an outline of key listening and learning strategies used.

c. how the company evaluates and improves its processes for determining customer requirements and expectations.

Notes:

(1) The distinction between near-term and future depends upon many marketplace factors. The applicant's response should reflect these factors for its market(s).

(2) The company's products and services might be sold to end users via other businesses such as retail stores or dealers. Thus, "customer groups" should take into account the requirements and expectations of both the end users and these other businesses.

(3) Product and service features refer to all important characteristics and to the performance of products and services that customers experience or perceive throughout their overall purchase and ownership. The focus should be primarily on factors that bear upon customer preference and repurchase loyalty — for example, those features that enhance or differentiate products and services from competing offerings.

(4) Some companies might use similar methods to determine customer requirements/expectations and customer satisfaction (Item 7.3). In such cases, cross-references should be included.

(5) Customer groups and market segments (7.1a) might take into account opportunities to select or <u>create</u> groups and segments based upon customer- and market-related information.

(6) Examples of listening and learning strategy elements (7.1b) are:
* *relationship strategies, including close integration with customers;*
* *rapid innovation and field trials to better link R&D to the market;*
* *close monitoring of technological, competitive, societal, environmental, economic, and demographic factors that may bear upon customer requirements, expectations, preferences, or alternatives;*
* *focus groups with demanding or leading-edge customers;*
* *training of frontline employees in customer listening;*
* *use of critical incidents to understand key service attributes from the point of view of customers and frontline employees;*
* *interviewing lost customers;*
* *won/lost analysis relative to competitors;*
* *post-transaction follow-up (see 7.2c); and*
* *analysis of major factors affecting key customers.*

(7) Examples of evaluation and factors appropriate for 7.1c are:
* *the adequacy and timeliness of the customer-related information;*
* *improvement of survey design;*
* *the best approaches for getting reliable and timely information — surveys, focus groups, customer-contact personnel, etc.;*
* *increasing and decreasing importance of product/service features among customer groups or segments; and*
* *the most effective listening/learning strategies.*

The evaluation might also be supported by company-level analysis addressed in Item 2.3.

7.2 Customer Relationship Management (30 pts.)

Describe how the company provides effective management of its responses and follow ups with customers to preserve and build relationships and to increase knowledge about specific customers and about general customer expectations.

A   D   R

☑—☑ ☐

AREAS TO ADDRESS

a. how the company provides information and easy access to enable customers to seek information and assistance. to comment. and to complain. Describe contact management performance measures and service standards and how these **requirements are set, deployed, and tracked.**

b. how the company ensures that formal and informal complaints and feedback received by all company units are resolved effectively and promptly. Briefly describe the complaint management process and how it ensures effective recovery of customer confidence. meeting customer requirements for resolution effectiveness, and elimination of the causes of complaints.

c. how the company follows up with customers on products. services. and recent transactions to determine satisfaction. to resolve problems. to seek feedback for improvement, and to build relationships.

d. how the company evaluates and improves its customer relationship management. Include: (1) how service standards. including those related to access and complaint management, are improved based upon customer information: (2) aggregation and use of customer comments and complaints throughout the company; and (3) how knowledge about customers is accumulated.

Notes:

(1) Customer relationship management refers to a process, not to a company unit. However, some companies may have units which address all or most of the requirements included in this Item. Also, some of these requirements may be included among the responsibilities of frontline employees in processes described in Items 5.2 and 5.3.

(2) Performance measures and service standards (7.2a) apply not only to employees providing the responses to customers but also to other units within the company which make effective responses possible. Deployment needs to take into account all key points in a response chain. Examples of measures and standards are: telephonic, percentage of resolutions achieved by frontline employees, number of transfers, and resolution response time.

(3) Responses to 7.2b and 7.2c might include company processes for addressing customer complaints or comments based upon expressed or implied guarantees and warranties.

(4) Elimination of the causes of complaints (7.2b) involves aggregation of complaint information from all sources for evaluation and use throughout the company. The complaint management process might include analysis and priority setting for improvement projects based upon potential cost impact of complaints, taking into account customer retention related to resolution effectiveness. Some of the analysis requirements of Item 7.2 relate to Item 2.3.

(5) Improvement of customer relationship management (7.2d) might require training. Training for customer-contact (frontline) employees should address: (a) key knowledge and skills. including knowledge of products and services: (b) listening to customers; (c) soliciting comments from customers; (d) how to anticipate and handle problems or failures ("recovery"); (e) skills in customer retention; and (f) how to manage expectations. Such training should be described in Item 4.3.

(6) Information on trends and levels in measures and/or indicators of complaint response time, effective resolution, and percent of complaints resolved on first contact should be reported in Item 6.1.

7.3 Customer Satisfaction Determination (30 pts.)

Describe how the company determines customer satisfaction, customer repurchase intentions, and customer satisfaction relative to competitors; describe how these determination processes are evaluated and improved.

A   D   R

☑—☑   ☐

AREAS TO ADDRESS

a. how the company determines customer satisfaction. Include: (1) a brief description of processes and measurement scales used: frequency of determination: and how objectivity and validity are ensured. Indicate significant differences. if any. in processes and measurement scales for different customer groups or segments; and (2) how customer satisfaction measurements capture key information that reflects customers' likely future market behavior, such as repurchase intentions and/or positive referrals.

b. how customer satisfaction relative to that for competitors is determined. Describe: (1) company-based comparative studies: and (2) comparative studies or evaluations made by independent organizations and/or customers. For (1) and (2), describe how objectivity and validity of studies or evaluations are ensured.

c. how the company evaluates and improves its overall processes and measurement scales for determining customer satisfaction and customer satisfaction relative to that for competitors. Include how other indicators (such as gains and losses of customers) and customer dissatisfaction indicators (such as complaints) are used in this improvement process. Describe also how the evaluation takes into account the effectiveness of the use of customer satisfaction information and data throughout the company.

Notes:

(1) Customer satisfaction measurement might include both a numerical rating scale and descriptors assigned to each unit in the scale. An effective (actionable) customer satisfaction measurement system is one that provides the company with reliable information about customer ratings of specific product and service features and the relationship between these ratings and the customer's likely future market behavior.

(2) The company's products and services might be sold to end users via other businesses such as retail stores or dealers. Thus. "customer groups" or segments should take into account these other businesses as well as the end users.

(3) Customer dissatisfaction indicators include complaints, claims, refunds, recalls, returns, repeat services, litigation, replacements, downgrades, repairs, warranty work, warranty costs, misshipments, and incomplete orders.

(4) Company-based or independent organization comparative studies (7.3b) might take into account one or more indicators of customer dissatisfaction as well as satisfaction. The extent and types of such studies may depend upon factors such as industry and company size.

(5) Evaluation (7.3c) might take into account how well the measurement scale relates to actual repurchase and/or customer retention. The evaluation might also address the effectiveness of pre-survey research used in design. and how actionable survey results are — how well survey responses link to key business processes and cost/revenue implications and thus provide a useful basis for improvement.

(6) Use of data from satisfaction measurement is called for in 5.2b(4) and 5.3c(4). Such data also provide key input to analysis (Item 2.3).

7.4 Customer Satisfaction Results *(100 pts.)*

Summarize the company's customer satisfaction and customer dissatisfaction results using key measures and/or indicators of these results.

A   D   R

☐——☐   ☑

AREAS TO ADDRESS

a. current levels and trends in key measures and/or indicators of customer satisfaction and customer retention. Results should be segmented by customer group, as appropriate.

b. current levels and trends in key measures and/or indicators of customer dissatisfaction. Address the most relevant and important indicators for the company's products/services.

Notes:

(1) Results reported in this Item derive from methods described in Items 7.3 and 7.2.

(2) Results data (7.4a) might be supported by customer feedback, customers' overall assessments of products/services, and customer awards.

(3) Indicators of customer dissatisfaction are given in Item 7.3, Note 3.

7.5 Customer Satisfaction Comparison *(60 pts.)*

Compare the company's customer satisfaction results with those of competitors.

A   D   R

☐——☐   ☑

AREAS TO ADDRESS

a. current levels and trends in key measures and/or indicators of customer satisfaction relative to competitors. Such indicators may include gains and losses of customers or customer accounts to competitors. Results may include objective information and/or data from independent organizations, including customers. Results should be segmented by customer group, as appropriate.

b. trends in gaining or losing market share to competitors.

Notes

(1) Results reported in Item 7.5 derive from methods described in Item 7.3.

(2) Competitors include domestic and international ones in the company's markets, both domestic and international.

(3) Objective information and/or data from independent organizations, including customers (7.5a), might include survey results, competitive awards, recognition, and ratings. Such surveys, competitive awards, recognition, and ratings by independent organizations and customers should reflect comparative satisfaction (and dissatisfaction), not comparative performance of products and services. Information on comparative performance of products and services should be included in 6.1.

SCORING SYSTEM: APPROACH, DEPLOYMENT, RESULTS

The system for scoring applicant responses to Examination Items (Items) and for developing feedback is based upon three evaluation dimensions: (1) Approach; (2) Deployment; and (3) Results. All Items require applicants to furnish information relating to these dimensions. Specific factors associated with the evaluation dimensions are described below. Scoring Guidelines are given on page 41.

Approach

"Approach" refers to how the applicant addresses the Item requirements — the method(s) used. The factors used to evaluate approaches include the following:

- appropriateness of the methods to the requirements
- effectiveness of use of methods. Degree to which the approach:
  - is systematic, integrated, and consistently applied
  - embodies evaluation/improvement cycles
  - is based upon data and information that are objective and reliable
- evidence of innovation. This includes significant and effective adaptations of approaches used in other applications or types of businesses.

Deployment

"Deployment" refers to the extent to which the applicant's approach is applied to all requirements of the Item. The factors used to evaluate deployment include the following:

- use of the approach in addressing business and Item requirements
- use of the approach by all appropriate work units

Results

"Results" refers to outcomes in achieving the purposes given in the Item. The factors used to evaluate results include the following:

- current performance levels
- performance levels relative to appropriate comparisons and/or benchmarks
- rate, breadth and importance of performance improvements
- demonstration of sustained improvement and/or sustained high-level performance

Item Classification and Scoring Dimensions

Award Examination Items are classified according to the kinds of information and/or data applicants are expected to furnish.

The two types of Items and their designations are:

	A	D	R
1. Approach/Deployment	☑	☑	☐

	A	D	R
2. Results	☐	☐	☑

Approach and Deployment are linked to emphasize that Items requesting information on Approach always require information to convey Deployment — consistent with the specific requirements of the Item. Although Approach and Deployment dimensions are linked, feedback to the applicant would reflect strengths and/or areas for improvement in either or both dimensions.

Results Items depend primarily on data demonstrating performance levels and trends. However, the evaluation factor, "breadth and importance of performance improvements", is concerned with how widespread and how significant an applicant's improvement results are. This is directly related to the Deployment dimension. That is, if improvement processes are widely deployed, there should be corresponding results. A score for a Results Item is thus a composite based upon overall performance, taking into account the breadth and importance of the performance improvements.

"Relevance and Importance" as a Scoring Factor

The three evaluation dimensions described above are all critical to the assessment and feedback processes. However, evaluations and feedback must also consider the relevance and importance to the applicant's business of improvements in Approach, Deployment, and Results. The areas of greatest relevance and importance are addressed in the Business Overview, and are a primary focus of Items such as 3.1, 5.1, 5.2, 6.1, and 7.1. Of particular importance are the key customer requirements and key business drivers.

Assignment of Scores to Examination Items

Baldrige Award Examiners observe the following guidelines in assignment of Item scores:

- All relevant Areas to Address should be included in the Item response.
- The Item responses and Examiner score should be consistent with the applicant's key business factors and key business drivers. Such factors are important in determining principal activities and results.
- In assigning a score to an Item, an Examiner first decides which scoring range best fits the overall Item response (e.g., 40% to 60%). Overall "best fit" does not require total agreement with each of the statements in that scoring range. Actual score within the range depends upon an Examiner's judgement of the Item response in relation to fit with the statements in the current range, and closeness to those in the next higher or next lower ranges.
- An Approach/Deployment Item score of 50% represents an approach that meets the basic objectives of the Item and that is deployed to the principal activities covered in the Item.
- A Results Item score of 50% represents clear indication of improvement trends and/or good levels of performance in the principal results areas covered in the Item.

SCORING GUIDELINES

SCORE	APPROACH/DEPLOYMENT
0%	▪ no systematic approach evident; anecdotal information
10% to 30%	▪ beginning of a systematic approach to the primary purposes of the Item ▪ early stages of a transition from reacting to problems to a general improvement orientation ▪ major gaps exist in deployment that would inhibit progress in achieving the primary purposes of the Item
40% to 60%	▪ a sound, systematic approach, responsive to the primary purposes of the Item ▪ a fact-based improvement process in place in key areas; more emphasis is placed on improvement than on reaction to problems ▪ no major gaps in deployment, though some areas or work units may be in very early stages of deployment
70% to 90%	▪ a sound, systematic approach, responsive to the overall purposes of the Item ▪ a fact-based improvement process is a key management tool; clear evidence of refinement and improved integration as a result of improvement cycles and analysis ▪ approach is well-deployed, with no major gaps; deployment may vary in some areas or work units
100%	▪ a sound, systematic approach, fully responsive to all the requirements of the Item ▪ a very strong, fact-based improvement process is a key management tool; strong refinement and integration — backed by excellent analysis ▪ approach is fully deployed without any significant weaknesses or gaps in any areas or work units

SCORE	RESULTS
0%	▪ no results or poor results in areas reported
10% to 30%	▪ early stages of developing trends; some improvements and/or early good performance levels in a few areas ▪ results not reported for many to most areas of importance to the applicant's key business requirements
40% to 60%	▪ improvement trends and/or good performance levels reported for many to most areas of importance to the applicant's key business requirements ▪ no pattern of adverse trends and/or poor performance levels in areas of importance to the applicant's key business requirements ▪ some trends and/or current performance levels — evaluated against relevant comparisons and/or benchmarks — show areas of strength and/or good to very good relative performance levels
70% to 90%	▪ current performance is good to excellent in most areas of importance to the applicant's key business requirements ▪ most improvement trends and/or performance levels are sustained ▪ many to most trends and/or current performance levels — evaluated against relevant comparisons and/or benchmarks — show areas of leadership and very good relative performance levels
100%	▪ current performance is excellent in most areas of importance to the applicant's key business requirements ▪ excellent improvement trends and/or sustained excellent performance levels in most areas ▪ strong evidence of industry and benchmark leadership demonstrated in many areas

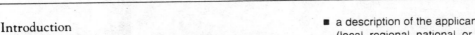

Introduction

This section provides guidelines and recommendations for writing the Business Overview and for responding to the requirements of the 24 Items of the Award Criteria. The section consists of six parts: (1) Description of the Business Overview; (2) Guidelines for Preparing the Business Overview; (3) Description of an Examination Item; (4) Guidelines for Responding to Examination Items; (5) Reporting Results and Trend Data; and (6) Reviewing the Overall Set of Item Responses.

(1) Description of the Business Overview

The Business Overview is an outline of the applicant's business, addressing what is most important to the business and the key factors that influence how the business operates.

The Award Examination is designed to permit evaluation of any kind of business. However, individual Items and Areas to Address may not be equally applicable or equally important to all businesses, even to businesses of comparable size in the same industry. The Business Overview is intended to "set the stage" for the Examiners' evaluation. It should help Examiners to understand what is relevant and important to the applicant's business.

> The Business Overview is used by the Examiners in all stages of the application review. For this reason, this Overview is a vital part of the overall application.

(2) Guidelines for Preparing the Business Overview

A Business Overview fully responsive to the Examiners' requirements should describe:

- the nature of the applicant's business: products and services
- principal customers (consumers, other businesses, government, etc.) and their special requirements. Special relationships with customers or key customer groups should be noted.

- a description of the applicant's major markets (local, regional, national, or international)
- key customer requirements (for example, on-time delivery or low defect levels) for products and services. Include all important requirements. Briefly note significant differences, if any, in requirements among customer groups or markets.
- the applicant's position (relative size, growth) in the industry and key factors in the competitive environment
- the applicant's employee base, including: number, type, educational level, bargaining units, etc.
- major equipment, facilities, and technologies used
- types and numbers of suppliers of goods and services. Indicate the importance to the applicant of suppliers, dealers, and other businesses, and any limitations or special relationships that may exist in dealing with such businesses.
- the regulatory environment within which the applicant operates relating to occupational health and safety, environmental, financial, products, etc.
- other factors important to the applicant. This might include: major new thrusts for the company such as entry into new markets or segments; new business alliances with suppliers, customers, or other partners; introduction of new technologies; major changes taking place in the industry; and changes in strategy.

Note: *Applicants are not required to reveal trade- or business-sensitive information such as trade secrets.*

If the applicant is a subsidiary or division of a company, a description of the organizational structure and key management links to the parent company should be presented. Also include percent of employees and relationships of products and services.

The Business Overview must be limited to four pages. These four pages are not counted in the overall page limit.

(3) Description of an Examination Item

Writing an application for the Award requires responses to the requirements given in the 24 Items. Each Item and its key components are presented in the same format as illustrated in the figure below.

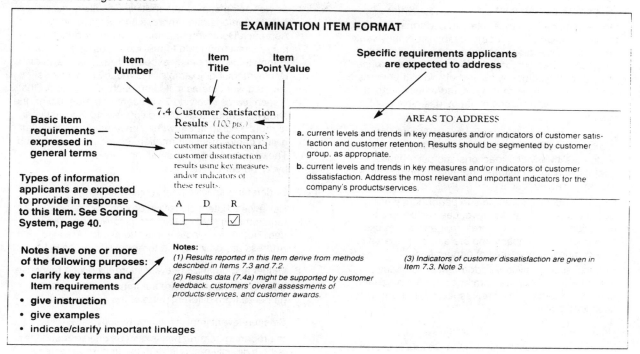

EXAMINATION ITEM FORMAT

Item Number — Item Title — Item Point Value — Specific requirements applicants are expected to address

Basic Item requirements — expressed in general terms

Types of information applicants are expected to provide in response to this Item. See Scoring System, page 40.

Notes have one or more of the following purposes:
- **clarify key terms and Item requirements**
- **give instruction**
- **give examples**
- **indicate/clarify important linkages**

7.4 Customer Satisfaction Results *(100 pts.)*
Summarize the company's customer satisfaction and customer dissatisfaction results using key measures and/or indicators of these results.

A   D   R
☐—☐ ☑

AREAS TO ADDRESS

a. current levels and trends in key measures and/or indicators of customer satisfaction and customer retention. Results should be segmented by customer group, as appropriate.

b. current levels and trends in key measures and/or indicators of customer dissatisfaction. Address the most relevant and important indicators for the company's products/services.

Notes:
(1) Results reported in this Item derive from methods described in Items 7.3 and 7.2.
(2) Results data (7.4a) might be supported by customer feedback, customers' overall assessments of products/services, and customer awards.
(3) Indicators of customer dissatisfaction are given in Item 7.3, Note 3.

(4) Guidelines for Responding to Examination Items

1. Read the entire Award Criteria booklet.

   The main sections of the booklet provide an overall orientation to the Criteria and how applicants' responses are evaluated.

2. Understand the meaning of "how".

   Items that request information on Approach include Areas to Address that begin with the word "how". Responses to such Areas should provide as complete a picture as possible to enable meaningful evaluation and feedback. Responses should outline key process details such as methods, measures, deployment, and evaluation factors. Information lacking sufficient detail to permit an evaluation and feedback, or merely providing an example, is referred to in the Criteria booklet as anecdotal information.

3. Understand the meaning of measures and/or indicators.

   Items calling for results require data using "key measures and/or indicators". Measures and indicators both involve measurement related to performance. When the performance can be measured directly, such as cycle time and on-time delivery, the term "measure" is used. When the overall performance may not be evaluated in terms of one type of measurement, and two or more measurements are used to provide ("indicate") a more complete picture, the term "indicator" is used. For example, innovation success is not easily described in terms of a single measurement. Patents and patent citations provide two measurements which are indicators of innovation success, but completing the picture requires other indicators, such as cycle time for bringing new products to market and market share gain from introduction of innovative products or services.

4. Understand the meaning of performance.

The word "performance" is used extensively throughout the Criteria booklet. Three types of performance are particularly important. These are: (1) operational performance; (2) customer-related performance; and (3) financial performance.

Operational performance refers to performance relative to measures and/or indicators used in company work processes. Operational performance assessments might be carried out for individual work units, groups of units, or the company as a whole. At higher levels of review, composite measures and/or indicators of operational performance might be desirable or necessary.

Customer-related performance refers to performance relative to measures and/or indicators that reflect customers' behaviors, reactions and perceptions. Examples include customer retention, complaints, and customer survey results.

Financial performance refers to performance using measures of costs and/or revenues, including asset utilization. Financial measures are generally tracked throughout the company and are also aggregated to give composite measures of performance.

Phrases such as overall performance, company performance, or high performance are more general and refer broadly to all three aspects of performance described above.

5. Understand the meaning of quality

The concept of quality used in the Criteria is customer-driven quality. It refers to all product and service characteristics that contribute value to customers and that influence satisfaction and preference. The Criteria place heavy emphasis upon developing a complete and reliable set of customer requirements. These customer requirements are then deployed throughout the company where they are translated into operational requirements for work units. This approach assumes that the operational requirements have associated key measures and/or indicators that create an internal basis for assessing performance relative to key external (customer) requirements and key external benchmarks.

6. Note the distinction between data and results.

There is a critical distinction between data and results — a distinction that is often misunderstood. Data are numerical information: results are the outcomes of activities. Data could be used as inputs to activities. as well as outcomes of activities. Results Items require data to demonstrate progress and achievement. Approach/Deployment Items. focused on processes. may benefit from data to provide a clearer and more complete picture of key aspects of Approach and/or Deployment. For example. a company may use self-directed work teams in its approach. It may report that 5 such teams involving 75 percent of the people on the shop floor undertook 11 projects during the past year to reduce scrap and rework. These data are input data giving deployment information related to the approach. These teams reducing scrap and rework by 17 percent would be a result.

7. Understand specific Item requirements.

Review each Item classification and the specific requirements given under Areas to Address and in Item Notes. Also, note that all Items and Areas to Address are described in this booklet (pages 6-14).

8. Gather and organize relevant information for a response.

Most of the Items require summaries of information gathered from different parts of the company.

9. Select relevant/important information.

In preparing Item responses. focus on information that is *both* directly responsive to the Item requirements and to key business requirements spelled out in the Business Overview. Information and data included should be relevant and important to both the Item and to the applicant's business.

10. Anticipate assessment and feedback.

A well-written response is one that lends itself to Examiner or other feedback. A response that facilitates assessment gives clear information on how (approach) and on the relevant use (deployment) of the approach. Anecdotal information or information lacking overall context should not be given as it is usually not possible to prepare meaningful feedback. Examples are. of course. helpful but examples often do not convey a picture of overall approach and deployment. If examples are used, make certain that they illustrate a more complete response already presented.

44

11. Make responses concise.

The application page limit (70 pages for all applicants) does not permit lengthy narrative or inclusion of information not directly responsive to Item requirements. For this reason, applicants are urged to make all responses concise and factual. Statements should be supported with data whenever appropriate.

12. Cross-reference when appropriate.

Although applicants should seek to make individual responses self-contained, there may be instances when responses to different Items are mutually reinforcing. In such cases it is appropriate to reference responses to other Items, rather than to repeat information presented elsewhere. In doing so, applicants should make the reference specific by using Item and Area designators (for example, "see 2.3a").

13. Review each response.

Each response should be reviewed to make certain that it addresses the Item requirements and is consistent with the applicant's key business requirements spelled out in the Business Overview. It is also important to ensure that a response is consistent with information reported in Items that are closely linked.

(5) Reporting Results and Trend Data

1. Results Items require data to demonstrate progress (trend data), achievement (performance levels), and breadth of deployment. Evaluation of achievement is usually based upon two factors: (1) that the performance level has been sustained or is the current result of a favorable trend; and (2) that the performance level can be compared with that of other appropriate organizations.

2. Applicants are required to report trend data to show progress and to show that improvements or outstanding performance levels are sustained. No minimum period of time is specified for trend data. Time periods may span five years or more for some results. Trends may be much shorter in areas where improvement efforts are new. In cases where the trend line is short, the Examiners' evaluation will place more emphasis on demonstrated levels of performance.

3. The spacing between data points on a trend line (annual, monthly, etc.) should reflect a natural measurement/use scheme for such results. That is, how the data are used in process management should determine the spacing between data points. For example, measurement frequency should support timely improvement and correction.

4. In reporting trend data, applicants should be aware that breadth of results is a major factor in the Examiners' evaluation. For this reason, it is important to report data reflecting wide deployment of improvement activities. Use of graphs and tables offers a good means to present many results compactly.

5. Graphs and tables should be integrated into the body of the text, wherever possible.

The following graph illustrates data an applicant might present as part of a response to Item 6.1, Product and Service Quality Results. The applicant has indicated, in the Business Overview and in Item 7.1, on-time delivery as a key customer requirement.

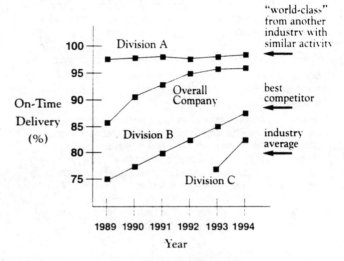

Using the graph, the following characteristics of clear and effective data presentation are illustrated:

- the trend lines report data for a key business requirement
- both axes and units of measure are clearly labeled
- results are presented for several years
- meaningful comparisons are clearly shown
- the company shows, using a single graph, that its three divisions separately track on-time delivery

To help interpret the Scoring Guidelines (page 41), the following comments on the graphed results would be appropriate:

- the current overall company performance level is excellent. This conclusion is supported by the comparison with competitors and with a "world class" level.
- the company exhibits an overall excellent improvement record
- Division A is the current performance leader — showing sustained high performance and a slightly positive trend. Division B shows rapid improvement. Its current performance is near that of the best industry competitor but trails the "world class" level.
- Division C — a new division — shows rapid progress. Its current performance is not yet at the level of the best industry competitor.

(6) Reviewing the Overall Set of Item Responses

It is helpful to review, as a whole, the complete set of 24 Item responses. There are four main considerations in this review:

1. emphasis on the applicant's most important business requirements. This emphasis should be clear throughout the set of responses and consistent with the Business Overview. For example, the key customer requirements described in the Business Overview should be clearly evident in all relevant Items, such as 3.1, 5.1, 5.2, 6.1, and 7.1. It is particularly important to report results related directly to key customer requirements and to key company performance requirements.

2. balance in the use of page limits. Ample page space should be given to results Items which are weighed heavily in the Examiners' evaluation. Items and Areas that address factors particularly important to the applicant's business should receive relatively more emphasis.

3. overall consistency. Responses should be checked to ensure that responses to related Items are consistent, and that there is appropriate cross-referencing to minimize duplication of information.

4. final check on deployment information. The overall application should convey widespread and consistent implementation, not merely an outline of approaches. The final review allows an assessment of how well the application as a whole covers all key company requirements, responsibilities, and processes.

Basic Eligibility

Public Law 100-107 establishes the three eligibility categories of the Award: Manufacturing, Service, and Small Business. Any for-profit business located in the United States or its territories may apply for the Award. Eligibility for the Award is intended to be as open as possible to all U.S. companies. Minor eligibility restrictions and conditions ensure fairness and consistency in definition. For example, publicly or privately owned, domestic or foreign-owned, joint ventures, incorporated firms, sole proprietorships, partnerships, and holding companies may apply. Not eligible are: local, state, and national government agencies; not-for-profit organizations; trade associations; and professional societies.

Award Eligibility Categories

1. Manufacturing

Companies or subsidiaries (defined below) that produce and sell manufactured products or manufacturing processes, and those companies that produce agricultural, mining, or construction products.

2. Service

Companies or subsidiaries that sell services.

- Proper classification of companies that perform both manufacturing and service is determined by the larger percentage of sales.

3. Small Business

Complete businesses with not more than 500 full-time employees. Business activities may include manufacturing and/or service. A small business must be able to document that it functions independently of any other businesses which are equity owners. For example, a small business owned by a holding company would be eligible if it can document its independent operation and that other units of the holding company are in different businesses.

If there are equity owners with some management control, at least 50% of the small business' customer base (dollar volume for products and services) must be from other than the equity owners, or other businesses owned by the equity owners.

Subsidiaries

For purposes of the Malcolm Baldrige National Quality Award application, a subsidiary will be taken to mean an actual subsidiary, business unit, division, or like organization. In the Manufacturing and Service categories, subsidiary units of a company may be eligible for the Award. Small businesses must apply as a whole; subsidiary units of small businesses are not eligible.

The following application conditions apply for subsidiary units:

- The unit must have existed one year or more prior to the Award application date (April 3. 1995).

- The unit must have clear definition of organization as reflected in corporate literature, e.g., organization charts, administrative manuals, and annual reports. That is, the unit must function as a business entity, not as a collection of activities aggregated for purposes of writing an Award application.

- The unit must have more than 500 full-time employees. OR

  The unit must have 25% of all employees in the worldwide operations of the parent company. ("Parent company" refers to the company that owns or controls subsidiary units through the ownership of voting stock.)

- The entire unit must be included in the application: no parts of the unit may be excluded.

Restrictions on Eligibility

The intent of Public Law 100-107 is to create an Award process incorporating rigorous and objective evaluation of the applicant's management of its products, services, and operations. *Award recipients are to serve as appropriate models for other U.S. companies.* Customer satisfaction is to play a major role in the Examination. Site visits are required to verify descriptions given in written applications.

The nature of some companies' activities is such that the central purposes and requirements of Public Law 100-107 cannot be fulfilled through their participation in the Award Program; companies or subsidiaries whose businesses cannot fulfill these purposes are not eligible. Specifically, four restrictions apply:

1. A company or its subsidiary is eligible only if the practices associated with all major business functions of the applicant are inspectable in the United States or its territories. One or both of the following conditions must apply:

   - more than 50% of the applicant unit's employees must be located in the U.S. or its territories. OR

     more than 50% of the applicant unit's physical assets must be located in the U.S. or its territories

Note: *The functions/activities of foreign sites must be included in the Application Report in the appropriate Examination Items.*

2. At least 50% of a subsidiary unit's customer base (dollar volume for products and services) must be free of direct financial and line organization control by the parent company. For example, a subsidiary unit is not eligible if its parent company or other subsidiary of the parent company is the customer for more than one-half of its total products and services.

3. Individual units or partial aggregations of units of "chain" organizations (such as hotels, retail stores, banks, or restaurants) are not eligible.

   For purposes of this application, a chain organization is defined as an organization where each unit (e.g., subsidiary or franchise) performs a similar function or manufactures a similar product. Accordingly, a potential applicant is not eligible if the parent company or another unit of the parent company provides similar products or services for substantially the same customer base. Similarly, an individual unit is not eligible if customers would be unable to distinguish easily which unit of the company provides the products or services to them.

4. Company units performing any of the business support functions of the company are not eligible. Examples of business support functions include: Sales/Marketing/ Distribution, Customer Service, Finance and Accounting, Human Resources, Environmental-Health-Safety of Employees, Purchasing, Legal Services, and Research and Development.

Multiple-Application Restrictions

1. A subsidiary and its parent company may not both apply for Awards in the same year.

2. Only one subsidiary unit of a company may apply for an Award in the same year in the same Award category.

Future Eligibility Restrictions

1. If a company receives an Award, the company and all its subsidiary units are ineligible to apply for an Award for a period of five years.

2. If a subsidiary unit receives an Award, it is ineligible to apply for an Award for a period of five years.

3. If a subsidiary unit consisting of more than one-half of the total sales of a company receives an Award, neither that company nor any of its other subsidiary units is eligible to apply for another Award for a period of five years.

Eligibility Determination

In order to ensure that Award recipients meet all reasonable requirements and expectations in representing the Award throughout the U.S., potential applicants must have their eligibility approved prior to applying for the Award.

Determination takes into account the following factors:

- small business status
- subsidiary unit status and subsidiary functions performed
- customer base
- sales to a parent company or another unit or units of the parent company
- status as a company operating in the U.S. and/or its territories
- relationship of products and services to those of the parent company or other units of the parent company
- number and type of support services provided by the parent company or other units of the parent company

Potential applicants for the 1995 Award are encouraged to submit their Eligibility Determination Forms as early as possible and no later than March 3, 1995. This form is contained in the 1995 Application Forms and Instructions booklet. For information on how to obtain a copy of this booklet, see page 49.

HOW TO ORDER COPIES OF 1995 AWARD MATERIALS

Note: The **1995 Award Criteria** and the **1995 Application Forms and Instructions** are two separate documents.

Individual Orders

Individual copies of either document can be obtained free of charge from:

> Malcolm Baldrige National Quality Award
> National Institute of Standards and Technology
> Route 270 and Quince Orchard Road
> Administration Building. Room A537
> Gaithersburg, MD 20899-0001
> Telephone: 301-975-2036
> Telefax: 301-948-3716

Bulk Orders

Multiple copies of the **1995 Award Criteria** may be ordered in packets of 10:

American Society for Quality Control
Customer Service Department
P.O. Box 3066
Milwaukee, WI 53201-3066
Toll free: 800-248-1946
Telefax: 414-272-1734

Order Item Number T999

Cost: $29.95 per packet of 10 plus postage and handling

Postage and handling charges are:

Order Amount	U.S.	Canada
0 – $34.99	$ 4.00	$ 9.00
$35.00 – 99.99	6.25	11.25
Over $100.00	12.50*	17.50

For orders shipped outside of the continental United States. there is a fee of 25 percent of order value to cover postage and handling. This fee does not apply to Canada.

Payment

Payment options include check. money order, purchase order. VISA, MasterCard, or American Express.

Payment must accompany all mail orders.

Payment must be made in U.S. currency. Checks and money orders must be drawn on U.S. institutions.

Make checks payable to ASQC.

Shipment

Orders delivered within the continental United States and Canada will be shipped UPS or first class mail.

If actual shipping charges exceed $12.50, ASQC will invoice the customer for additional expense.

FEES FOR THE 1995 AWARD CYCLE

Eligibility Determination Fees

The eligibility determination fee is $50 for all potential applicants. This fee is nonrefundable.

Application Fees

- Manufacturing Company Category—$4000
- Service Company Category—$4000
- Small Business Category—$1200
- Supplemental Sections—$1500

These fees cover all expenses associated with distribution of applications, review of applications, and development of feedback reports. A brief description of companies required to submit Supplemental Sections is given on page 1. Detailed information is given in the **1995 Application Forms and Instructions** document.

Site Visit Review Fees

Site visit review fees will be set when the visits are scheduled. Fees depend upon the number of sites to be visited, the number of Examiners assigned, and the duration of the visit. Site visit review fees for applicants in the Small Business category will be charged at one-half of the rate for companies in the Manufacturing and Service categories.

These fees cover all expenses and travel costs associated with site visit participation and development of site visit reports. Site visit review fees are paid only by those applicants reaching the site visit stage.

Eligibility Determination Forms due — March 3, 1995
Award Applications due — April 3, 1995

HOW TO ORDER AWARD EDUCATIONAL MATERIALS

Each year, the Award Program develops materials for use in training members of the Board of Examiners, and for sharing information on the successful quality strategies of the Award winners. The listed materials and information may be obtained from the American Society for Quality Control (toll free: 800-248-1946). Prices and/or availability dates for all materials are given below.

Case Studies

The case studies are used to prepare Examiners for the interpretation of the Award Criteria and the Scoring System. The case studies, when used with the Award Criteria, illustrate the Award application and review process. The case studies are sample applications written for fictitious companies applying for the Baldrige Award. The case studies can provide valuable insights into the Award Criteria and Scoring System for companies interested in making application, as well as for self-assessment, planning, training, and other uses.

Great Northern Case Study Packet

Based on the 1994 Examiner Preparation Course

Item Number T551: $ 49.95

The Great Northern Case Study Packet is also available on diskette.

Item Number T516: $500.00

Varifilm Case Study Packet

Based on the 1993 Examiner Preparation Course

Item Number T515: $ 49.95

Award Winners Videos

The Award winners videos are a valuable resource for gaining a better understanding of excellence in quality management and quality achievement. The videos provide background information on the Award Program, highlights from the annual Award ceremony, and interviews with representatives from the winning companies.

1994 – *Available February 1995.*
1993 – Item Number TA515: $20.00
1992 – Item Number TA512:   20.00
1991 – Item Number TA996:   15.00
1990 – Item Number T992:   15.00
1989 – Item Number T502:   10.00
1988 – Item Number T993:   10.00

1992 Expanded Video

An expanded, 55-minute video, entitled "Quality Leadership: A Culture For Continuous Improvement", is available. The video highlights each 1992 Award Winner — AT&T Network Systems Group, Transmission Systems Business Unit; Texas Instruments, Defense Systems and Electronics Group; AT&T Universal Card Services; The Ritz-Carlton Hotel Company; and the Granite Rock Company.

Item Number TA914: $249.95

1991 Expanded Video

An expanded, 46-minute video, featuring the three 1991 Award winners — Solectron Corporation, Zytec Corporation, and Marlow Industries, shows the viewer the ingredients for successful implementation of a quality system within their organization.

Item Number TA910: $195.00

QUEST FOR EXCELLENCE VII CONFERENCE

The Annual Quest for Excellence Conference provides a unique opportunity to hear firsthand the Award-winning strategies of the past year's winners. Presentations are made by the CEOs and other key individuals who are transforming their organizations. The annual Quest for Excellence Conference is the principal forum for Award winners to present their overall strategies in detail.

The two and one-half day Quest for Excellence VII Conference will provide ample opportunities to explore the Award Criteria in depth, network with executive-level individuals from around the country, and view displays of each of the Award-winning organizations.

The Conference dates are February 5-8, 1995. The Conference will be held at the Washington Hilton and Towers, in Washington, D.C. For further information, contact the Association for Quality and Participation (AQP). (Toll-free: 800-733-3310 or FAX: 513-381-0070)

THE MALCOLM BALDRIGE NATIONAL QUALITY IMPROVEMENT ACT OF 1987 – PUBLIC LAW 100-107

*The Malcolm Baldrige National Quality Award was created by Public Law 100-107, signed into law on **August 20, 1987**. The Award Program, responsive to the purposes of Public Law 100-107, led to the creation of a new public-private partnership. Principal support for the program comes from the Foundation for the Malcolm Baldrige National Quality Award, established in 1988.*

The Award is named for Malcolm Baldrige, who served as Secretary of Commerce from 1981 until his tragic death in a rodeo accident in 1987. His managerial excellence contributed to long-term improvement in efficiency and effectiveness of government.

The Findings and Purposes Section of Public Law 100-107 states that:

" 1. the leadership of the United States in product and process quality has been challenged strongly (and sometimes successfully) by foreign competition, and **our Nation's productivity growth has improved less than our competitors'** over the last two decades.

2. American business and industry are beginning to understand that poor quality costs companies as much as 20 percent of sales revenues nationally and that improved quality of goods and services goes hand in hand with improved productivity, lower costs, and increased profitability.

3. strategic planning for quality and quality improvement programs, through a commitment to excellence in manufacturing and services, are becoming more and more essential to the well-being of our Nation's economy and our ability to compete effectively in the global marketplace.

4. improved management understanding of the factory floor, worker involvement in quality, and greater emphasis on statistical process control can lead to dramatic improvements in the cost and quality of manufactured products.

5. the concept of quality improvement is directly applicable to small companies as well as large, to service industries as well as manufacturing, and to the public sector as well as private enterprise.

6. in order to be successful, quality improvement programs must be **management-led and customer-oriented**, and this may require fundamental changes in the way **companies and agencies do business.**

7. several major industrial nations have successfully coupled rigorous private-sector quality audits with national awards giving special recognition to those enterprises the audits identify as the very best; and

8. a national quality award program of this kind in the United States would help improve quality and productivity by:

   A. helping to stimulate American companies to improve quality and productivity for the pride of recognition while obtaining a competitive edge through increased profits;

   B. recognizing the achievements of those companies that improve the quality of their goods and services and providing an example to others;

   C. establishing guidelines and criteria that can be used by business, industrial, governmental, and other organizations in evaluating their own quality improvement efforts; and

   D. providing specific guidance for other American organizations that wish to learn how to manage for high quality by making available detailed information on how winning organizations were able to change their cultures and achieve eminence. "